THE NEW GROVE®

ORGAN

THE NEW GROVE®

DICTIONARY OF MUSICAL INSTRUMENTS

Editor: Stanley Sadie

The Grove Musical Instruments Series

ORGAN

PIANO

in preparation

BRASS

EARLY KEYBOARD INSTRUMENTS

VIOLIN FAMILY

WOODWIND

THE NEW GROVE®

ORGAN

Peter Williams   Barbara Owen

W. W. NORTON & COMPANY

NEW YORK   **LONDON**

Copyright © 1980, 1984 and 1988 Macmillan Press Ltd, London

Copyright © 1980, 1984 and 1988 Peter Williams, James McKinnon, Reginald
Foort, Susi Jeans, Lyndesay G. Langwill

Copyright © 1984, 1988 Barbara Owen, Durward R. Center
Copyright © 1988 Barbara Owen

Parts of this material first published in
The New Grove® Dictionary of Musical Instruments,
edited by Stanley Sadie, 1984

and

The New Grove Dictionary of Music and Musicians®,
edited by Stanley Sadie, 1980

The New Grove and *The New Grove Dictionary of Music and Musicians*
are registered trademarks of Macmillan Publishers Limited, London

First published in UK in paperback with additions 1988 by
PAPERMAC
a division of Macmillan Publishers Limited
London and Basingstoke

First published in UK in hardback with additions 1988 by
MACMILLAN LONDON LIMITED
4 Little Essex Street London WC2R 3LF
and Basingstoke

British Library Cataloguing in Publication Data
Owen, Barbara
    Organ.—(The new Grove musical
    instruments series)
    1. Organ—History
    I. Title   II. Williams, Peter, *1937 May 14–*
    III. The new Grove dictionary of musical
    instruments
    786.6′2   ML550

ISBN 0–333–44445–0   (hardback)
ISBN 0–333–44446–9   (paperback)

First American edition in book form with additions 1988 by
W. W. NORTON & COMPANY
500 Fifth Avenue, New York NY 10110

FPT   ISBN 0-393-02555-1 (hardback)
FPT   ISBN 0-393-30516-3 (paperback)

Printed in Hong Kong
1 2 3 4 5 6 7 8 9 0

Contents

List of illustrations

Illustration acknowledgments

We are grateful to the following for permission to reproduce illustrative material: Museum of Classical Archaeology, Tripoli (fig.1); Musée National, Carthage (fig.2); Oxford University Press: after J. Perrot, *The Organ from its Invention in the Hellenistic Period to the End of the 13th Century* (Eng. trans., 1971) (figs.3, 4, 5); Faculty of Music, University of Edinburgh: after S. Newman and P. Williams, *The Russell Collection of Early Keyboard Instruments* (Edinburgh, 1968) (fig.6); Fonds Mercator SA, Antwerp: after D. A. Flentrop, from F. Peeters and M. A. Vente, *The Organ and its Music in the Netherlands* (Eng. trans., 1971) (figs.7, 8, 12, 13a); Macdonald & Co., London: after W. L. Sumner, *The Organ: Its Evolution, Principles of Construction and Use* (4/1973) (figs.9a, 14a, 15); Paul G. Bunjes, Melrose Park, Illinois: after P. G. Bunjes, *The Praetorius Organ* (1966) (figs.9b, 18, 20a); after G. A. Audsley, *The Art of Organ-building* (repr. 1965) (figs.11, 19, 20b, 21); George Allen & Unwin Ltd, London, and Oxford University Press Inc., New York: after P. G. Andersen, *Organ Building and Design* (1969) (fig.14b); Staatliches Konservatoramt für das Saarland, Saarbrücken (fig.23); Jean Perrot, Sainte-Geneviève (figs.24, 25, 26; fig.25 from L. Nagy, *Az Aquincumi orgona/Die Orgel von Aquincum*, 1933); Bibliotheek der Rijksuniversiteit, Utrecht (fig.27); Bibliothèque Municipale, Dijon (fig.28); British Library, London (figs.29, 59); Orgelbau Th. Kuhn AG, Männedorf/photo Maurice Wenger, Sion (fig.30); Antikvarisk-Topografiska Arkivet, Stockholm/photo Nils Lagergren (fig.31); photo ACL, Brussels (fig.33); Giraudon, Paris (fig.34); photo Gino Barsotti, Florence (fig.35); Hofkirche, Innsbruck (fig.36); photo Viktor Rihsé, Stade (fig.38); National Monuments Record, London (fig.41); Russell Collection of Harpsichords and Clavichords, University of Edinburgh (fig.42); Carlós de Azeredo, Lisbon (fig.43); photo MAS, Barcelona (figs.44, 45); Bavaria-Verlag, Gauting bei München (fig.46); Rijksdienst voor de Monumentenzorg, Zeist (fig.47); Kerkelijk Bureau der Hervormde Gemeente, Haarlem (fig.48); Bildarchiv Foto Marburg/photo Lala Aufsberg (fig.49); photo J. L. Coignet, Châteauneuf, Val-de-Bargis (fig.50); UNM Photo, Albuquerque (fig.52); South Bank Centre, London (fig.53); N. P. Mander Ltd, London/photo Sydney W. Newbery (fig.54); photo Heinrich Weber, Hanover (fig.55); John Brombaugh & Associates, Inc., Eugene, Oregon (fig.56); Jürgen Ahrend, Leer (fig.57); C. B. Fisk Inc., Gloucester, Massachusetts/photo Robert Cornell (fig.58); The Earl of Wemyss and March/photo Edinburgh University Press (fig.62); Mansell Collection, London (fig.64); Archiv für Kunst und Geschichte, Berlin (cover)

Abbreviations

AcM	Acta Musicologica	JAMS	Journal of the American Musicological Society
AMf	Archiv für Musikforschung	JBIOS	Journal of the British Institute of Organ Studies
AMw	Archiv für Musikwissenschaft	MT	The Musical Times
AMZ	Allgemeine musikalische Zeitung	PBC	Publicaciones del departamento de música de la Biblioteca de Catalunya
AnM	Anuario musical		
c	circa [about]		
CHM	Collectanea historiae musicae (in series Bibliotheca historiae musicae cultores) (Florence, 1953–)	PMA	Proceedings of the Musical Association
		RdM	Revue de musicologie
		ReM	La revue musicale
Cz.	Czech.	RIM	Rivista italiana di musicologia
EMDC	Encyclopédie de la musique et dictionnaire du Conservatoire	RMARC	R[oyal] M[usical] A[ssociation] Research Chronicle
fl	floruit [he/she flourished]	S	San, Santa, Santo, São [Saint]
Grove 1(–5)	G. Grove, ed.: A Dictionary of Music and Musicians, 2nd–5th edns. as Grove's Dictionary of Music and Musicians	Ss	Santissima, Santissimo
		STMF	Svensk tidskrift för musikforskning
		viz	videlicet [namely]
		ZI	Zeitschrift für Instrumentenbau
JAMIS	Journal of the American Musical Instrument Society		

Preface

This volume is one of a series of short studies derived from *The New Grove Dictionary of Musical Instruments* (London, 1984). Some of the material was originally written for *The New Grove Dictionary of Music and Musicians* (London, 1980), in the mid-1970s. For the present reprint, all the articles have been reread and modified, mostly by their original authors, and corrections and changes have been made in the light of recent work.

The main part of the text for this volume is written by Peter Williams and based on his article 'Organ' published in *The New Grove Dictionary of Musical Instruments*. It is however supplemented by material drawn from other articles in that dictionary, many by Dr Williams himself, but also by Barbara Owen, who has contributed updating material to virtually all sections of the book and gave particular assistance over the Glossary of Terms and the Bibliography. She also supplied the 'Reed organ' article on which Chapter 9 is based. James McKinnon contributed material used in Chapter 2 (1) and Chapter 3; Reginald Foort wrote Chapter 5 (5); and sections (1), (2) and (4) of Chapter 8 were provided respectively by Susi Jeans, the late Lyndsey G. Langwill and Durward R. Center. Appendix 4 is based on material on individual organ builders as published in *The New Grove Dictionary of Musical Instruments*. I should like to express particular gratitude to Barbara Owen for her generous help and advice over the shaping and editorial preparation of the present volume.

S.S

CHAPTER ONE

Origin and Construction

The organ is, together with the clock, the most complex of all mechanical instruments developed before the Industrial Revolution. Among musical instruments its history is the most involved and wide-ranging, and its extant repertory the oldest and largest. The organ belongs to the family of winds. It consists of one or more scale-like rows of pipes; a wind-raising device, from which air under pressure is directed towards the pipes, thus causing them to sound; a set of valves, which controls the flow of air; and a keyboard, by means of which the valves are operated. Despite its essentially indirect and therefore relatively inflexible production of sound, no other instrument has inspired such avowed respect as the organ, 'that great triumph of human skill ... the most perfect musical instrument' (*Grove 1*), 'in my eyes and ears ... the king of instruments' (Mozart, letter to his father, 17–18 October 1777).

1. THE TERM

Plato (*Laws*) and Aristotle (*Politics*) both used the term 'organon' to denote a tool or instrument in a general sense; something with which to do a job of work (*ergon*, from root *uerĝ-*; cf *Werk*, 'work'). Plato (*Republic*) and later authors also used it to denote any kind or all kinds of musical instrument or contrivance. No Greek author used it to mean 'pipe organ', and even in the term 'hydraulic organ' (1st century AD) used by Hero of Alexandria 'organ' has the sense of tool, so that the whole term properly indicates 'an aulos-like device or instrument, operated by water'. (In this context, moreover, 'aulos' may indicate not the musical wind instrument of that name but 'pipe', 'conduit' etc; i.e. 'hydraulic' refers to the water and air conduits.) Classical and patristic Latin show a fairly clear evolution of the terms 'organum', 'organa', 'organis' from a general to a specific sense, and a musical

1. Hydraulis with tuba and two cornua, at a gladiator contest: Roman mosaic (1st century AD) from a villa at Dar Buk Ammera, near Zliten, Libya

connection is often clear from the context, more consistently so than in Greek. 9th- and 10th-century Arabic had its own versions of the Greek, for example *hedhrula* ('hydraulis') and *urghanon* ('organon'). The use of 'organum' to denote a kind of polyphony is of course post-classical.

In his commentary on Psalm cl St Augustine correctly explained the Vulgate word 'organum' as derived from 'a Greek term', and thought it unlikely to be correct in this psalm. He defined it as follows (the English translation is by John of Trevisa, 1398): 'Organum is a generall name of all Instrumentes of Musyk: and is nethelesse specyally apropryte to the Instrument that is made of many pipes; and blowen wyth belowes'. In one sentence St Augustine used the singular *organum* and the plural *organa* for the same object, thus foreshadowing late medieval usage of the plural in English and in Old High German (Notker Labeo's *diu organâ* and *orglun*) and present-day usage in Slav (*varhany*, *orgány*: plural). The English derivatives of 'organ' ('organic', 'organize') are mostly post-medieval terms, and are sometimes found first in the musical sense (i.e. 'organic': 'like organs'), sometimes first in the non-musical sense: 'organize', 'to give an orderly structure to', appears in the 17th century, while 'organize', 'to supply one or more sets of organ pipes to a harpsichord or piano', appears in the 18th century, probably from French usage. The plural 'organs' denoting a single object (e.g. *orgues/ogres*, *Orgenen/Orgeln* in 12th-century French and German verse) belongs to the musical use of the term. In some languages, notably French, the singular *orgue* seems much the later term, but documents are inconsistent (e.g. 'money paied to the organe maker for the orgonis', 14th century). A 'pair of organs' was a phrase used in 17th-century England generally to denote an organ of two manuals, or more exactly of two cases (Great and Choir organ; by 1613 the new two-manual organ of Worcester Cathedral was called 'Double Organ', and it is this kind of instrument that was normally meant both in 17th-century contracts (e.g. those of Durham, Wells and Canterbury, all 1662) and in the voluntaries for Double organ popular from around 1640. The agreement from Canterbury is explicit: 'A Double Organ, vizt a great Organ and a Chaire Organ'. During the 16th century, particularly in documents prepared by non-musicians, a 'pair of organs or virginals' may perhaps have indicated an instrument with longer than average compass, but more probably meant merely an 'instrument of many pipes or strings' (cf a 'pair of stairs' in 15th-century French and English). Biblical use of 'organ' in English translations is unreliable. Septuagint Greek uses *organon* most often in its general sense of 'tool'; Old Testament Hebrew uses *ûgab* on four occasions, apparently to indicate some kind of wind instrument, perhaps a vertical flute; Vulgate Latin uses *organum* indiscriminately for both.

'Organ', 'orgue' and 'organo' are also used in the sense of *Werk* to denote individual manual or pedal departments of the whole instrument. Before about 1675 such terms applied only to departments built into separate organ cases; in England, Echoes and Swells were not usually called 'Swell Organ' before about 1800, although by about 1850 all departments of an organ were referred to in this manner.

2. Terracotta lamp in the form of a hydraulis (? 2nd century AD) found at Carthage

ORIGIN AND CONSTRUCTION

2. CONSTRUCTION

There are three main parts to an organ: the wind-raising device, the chest with its pipes, and the mechanism admitting wind to the pipes (consisting of the keyboard and valves). These three parts are common to any pipe organ; it is in their precise nature that essential differences lie – from the small hydraulic organ of the 3rd century BC to the monster electric organ of the 1920s. At different points in history builders have tended to develop different parts of the instrument, while at other times (*c*1400 and *c*1850) all parts saw intense development.

(i) The hydraulis

Approximately 40 representations of the hydraulis survive, in rough outline, in mosaics (see figs. 1 and 23), vases, coins and sculptures. The instrument's height from its base to the top of its pipes was about 165 cm to 185 cm. The base itself, often octagonal, was about 30 cm high and 90 cm in diameter; on this was a brass cistern which appears to have been covered with decorated wood. The cistern might be cylindrical, octagonal or rectangular and was from 60 cm to 90 cm in height with a diameter somewhat less than that of the pedestal; usually it was flanked by a pair of cylindrical pumps. Resting on it was the rectangular wind chest, approximating the base in size. Finally there were the pipes, whose overall height represented from a third to half the total height of the instrument. The number of pipes appearing in a rank ranged from four or five to 18, approximately eight being the average. There were no more than four ranks. Normally only the front of the instrument was shown, with the organist looking out over the pipes. On the exceptional three-dimensional views such as that on the Carthaginian lamp, he is seen seated at a keyboard which extends from the wind-chest (see fig. 2).

A description of the precise functioning of the hydraulis (see fig. 3*a*, p. 6) is given by Hero of Alexandria (possibly 1st century AD) in his *Pneumatica*. Vitruvius, writing in the early 1st century AD, described the chest as having four, six or eight channels, each running beneath a separate rank of pipes, and being opened or closed by a stopcock fitted with an iron handle. This stop action is very simple in conception: it is nothing more than a division of the wind-chest into separate compartments. However, it creates serious practical difficulties, particularly for the slider, which is subject to an increase in both friction and the leakage of air. Modern experiments, particularly those of Jean Perrot, indicate that the difficulties become insuperable with more than four

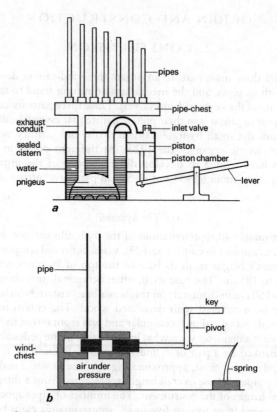

pipes

pipe-chest

exhaust
conduit

inlet valve

sealed
cistern

piston

piston chamber

water

pnigeus

lever

a

pipe

key

pivot

wind-
chest

air under
pressure

spring

b

*3. (a) Blowing mechanism of the hydraulis as described by
Hero of Alexandria; (b) playing action of the hydraulis*

ranks, a conclusion confirmed by ancient iconographic and archaeological evidence. Vitruvius, using the terms tetrachordal,
hexachordal and octochordal, was evident6ly indulging in a kind of
theoretical symmetry.

Vitruvius and Hero were technical writers who limited their
descriptions to the mechanical aspects of the instrument; they thus
force speculation on the most basic musical considerations. Two in
particular demand attention: timbre and pitch.

The central question concerning timbre is whether the hydraulis
had not only flue pipes but also reeds (as several organologists have
maintained). On the positive side is the name of the instrument, from
the two Greek words 'hydōr' ('water') and 'aulos' ('pipe'). There are
also literary references to the instrument's widely differing tone

quality, at one time sweet and at another thunderous. Organologists have tended to associate the latter quality with reed pipes.

On the other hand, surviving representations do not at all suggest reed pipes. The absence of anything resembling the bulbous *holmos* of the aulos which houses the reeds is particularly noteworthy. Also very much to the point is Walcker-Mayer's reconstruction of the Aquincum organ's pipes with the same kinds of metal as were used in the original pipes. The organ has four ranks, all of flue pipes, of which three are stopped and one open. He found both open and stopped to be entirely unlike any modern pipes in timbre, the open being particularly harsh and shrill and the stopped only somewhat less harsh, with a kind of throaty rattle. In summary, the case for reed pipes has yet to be proven, and it is seriously anachronistic to assume that the variety of tone suggested by the literary sources takes the form of a contrast between, for example, a sweet flue Gedackt and a thunderous reed Cornopean.

The question of pitch and its corollary, tonality, is even more difficult than that of timbre. Archaeological remains might be expected to lead to firm conclusions. Nevertheless the two modern scholars, Walcker-Mayer and Perrot, who have studied the pipes of the Aquincum organ (see fig. 25, p. 48), differ radically, the former maintaining that the instrument was diatonic, the latter that it was chromatic.

The study of pictorial evidence is similarly inconclusive. The method normally employed is to measure the longest pipe and the shortest, thus determining the instrument's range, and then after counting the number of pipes to fill in the intermediate pitches and establish the tonality. Behind this method lies the fallacious assumption that each representation was a precisely scaled depiction of a particular instrument rather than a conventional schematization. Possibly the most serious specific problem is created by the angle of the slanting line described by the tops of the pipes. It is always a straight line; if the artists had been attempting realistic depictions, the line, while not describing the parabolic curve of the equal-tempered scale, would necessarily have described something other than a straight line. Moreover, it requires only a minor variation in the angle, in the length of the pipes or in the number of pipes to change the presumed tonality from one genus to another. This is particularly true if the organologist grants himself the liberty of deciding whether conjunct or disjunct tetrachords are involved.

Possibly the least valuable evidence for determining pitch is that of the theoretical sources: a wide gap separates the theory of late antiquity (with its mathematical bias) from musical practice. But even ignoring

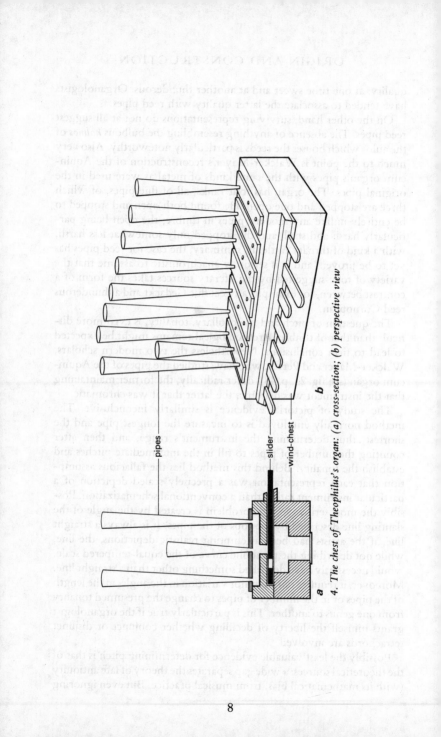

4. The chest of Theophilus's organ: (a) cross-section; (b) perspective view

pipes

slider

wind-chest

a

b

this gap and taking the sources literally, as several historians of the organ have done, leads to unsatisfactory conclusions. The conventional starting point is the assertion of the Bellermann Anonymous that the hydraulis plays in no tropes but the Hyperlydian, Hyperastian, Lydian, Phrygian, Hypolydian and Hypophrygian. Theorists such as Alypius indicate that the precise meaning of these tropes results in a hydraulis capable of playing more than 30 notes. In attempting to reconcile this with the relatively simple instrument of pictorial evidence organologists have tended to opt for either of two unsatisfactory alternatives. According to one of them, each organ was tuned in only one trope; thus there were Hyperlydian organs, Hyperastian organs, etc. According to the other, each rank represented a different trope; in this case an instrument must have been confined to four of the six desired tropes, resulting in an uneconomical duplication of pitch and the preclusion of the mixture or register principle.

It seems, in summary, that the state of the evidence allows only the most general conclusions. Pictorial evidence indicates a relatively high tessitura for the pipes and a relatively small compass for each rank; literary sources indicate substantial versatility in dynamics if not timbre. A similar situation of uncertainty, therefore, prevails as with other ancient instruments, the one difference being the remarkably precise knowledge gained from Vitruvius and Hero of the hydraulis's mechanical functioning.

It is not certain whether the hydraulis could play polyphonic music; on the negative side is the generally non-polyphonic character of Greco-Roman music, but on the positive side is the instrument's technical capacity. All literary, pictorial and archaeological evidence indicates that the keys were depressed by the fingers, and with relative facility, thus creating obvious polyphonic possibilities for the two hands of the organist. Yet to what extent such possibilities were exploited or in what musical direction they tended (for example, drones, parallelisms) is not known.

(ii) A medieval chest

Figure 4 shows how in Theophilus's organ (11th century) the wind, raised by two or more bellows operated by the blowers' body-weight, is admitted to the several ranks of pipes when a perforated hand-slider is pulled out until its hole is aligned with the vertical channel between the wind-chest and the pipe-foot; to obtain a 'clean' sound, the slider must be operated as quickly as possible. To stop the sound, the slider is pushed back. The whole chest could be made of wood or moulded metal.

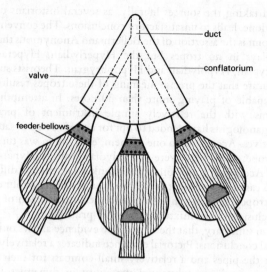

5. Bellows of Theophilus's organ

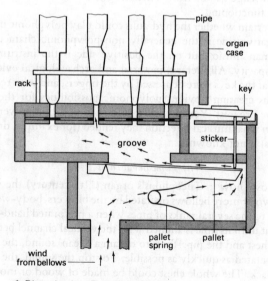

6. Pin action in a Renaissance chamber organ

Other medieval chests differed significantly. According to the description in the Berne Codex (11th century), the wind did not pass to the two ranks of pipes from one duct; rather each pipe had its own duct from the wind-chamber below. Thus the hand-slider required as many holes to be aligned as there were ranks. Also the 'key' was (like Hero's) a pivoted square which, when depressed, would push the slider into sounding position, while a spring pulled it back afterwards to its blocking position. Early medieval positives and portatives probably worked by one or other of such systems, which do not of themselves presuppose any particular size.

(iii) A medieval bellows

In fig. 5, also derived from Theophilus's organ, air is fed in turn by three 'feeder-bellows' through channels meeting inside the *conflatorium* to make one central duct (the inner construction is shown with dotted lines); before the channels meet, the wind passes through a copper valve which flaps open as the bellows send out air and flaps closed as soon as they are emptied. The collected wind is then directed along a trunk curving up to the pipe-chest. There may be more than one *conflatorium*, and the bellows can be in pairs or larger sets.

(iv) A chamber organ action

In the 'pin action' portrayed in fig. 6, wind accumulated in the lower chamber or pallet box is admitted to each upper chamber or groove when the corresponding key depresses the hinged pallet. The new, crucial device in this system is the pallet and its groove, both of unknown origin. The effectiveness and versatility of the resulting chest construction promoted the development of the Renaissance organ. In theory and (many organists believe) in practice, the grooved or 'barred' chest facilitates tonal blend between the several pipes belonging to each key. Later medieval positives probably had a similar action, in most cases to fewer (and often sliderless) ranks of pipes; later medieval portatives also probably worked from a similar (though simpler and more compact) pin action, whatever the shape and size of the keys.

(v) Details of medieval and Renaissance chests

Figure 7a (p. 12) shows a medieval block-chest: the opened pallet admits wind to all the pipes on one groove (i.e. all those belonging to one key) and the player is unable to separate the ranks of pipes. To obtain variety of sound some organs had grooves divided into two parts, each with its own pallet; each resulting 'half-chest' could have its wind

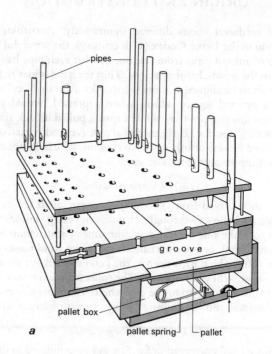

pipes

groove

pallet box

pallet spring — pallet

a

blocked off with a valve somewhere between bellows and pallet box, though in practice the front half-chest (whose pipes were those of the case front or Open and perhaps Stopped Diapasons) played all the time. Each key in such a double chest operated two pallets and two pallet-springs. The reliability and wind-saving virtues of this system gave it some popularity in the Netherlands during the 15th century.

In the slider-chest (possibly late 15th century) shown in fig. 7*b*, the opened pallet admits wind to each single or multi-rank 'stop' by means of a perforated slip of wood ('slider') running longitudinally in the board between the pipe-foot and the groove on the upper level of the chest. The slider can be aligned either to allow wind to pass through ('stop drawn') or to prevent it passing through ('stop pushed in'). By means of rods, trundles and levers, the sliders can also be operated by a 'stop-knob' near the player (below and in front of the chest itself). Sliders were known first in small organs, perhaps from about 1400, but were not much used in larger ones (or the larger departments of two-manual organs) until the 16th century.

Figure 7*c* shows a spring-chest (early 16th century) in which the

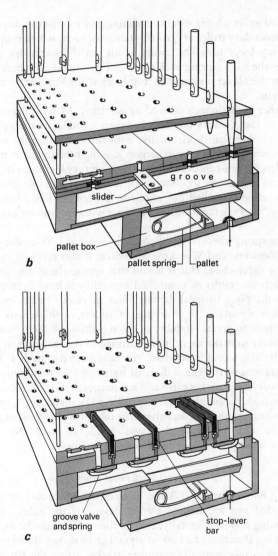

b

groove

slider

pallet box

pallet spring — pallet

c

groove valve
and spring

stop-lever
bar

7. Medieval and Renaissance chests: (a) medieval block-
chest; (b) ?late 15th-century slider-chest; (c) early 16th-
century spring-chest

ORGAN

opened pallet admits wind to each single or multi-rank stop by means
of a secondary pallet or 'groove-valve' for each, which is operated by
the stop-lever bar. The spring acting on the secondary pallet also
causes the bar to spring back to the 'off' position unless prevented (i.e.
unless the player notches the stop-lever at the keyboard into the 'on'
position).

Other spring-chests differed significantly. Many Italian ones from
the late 15th century onwards had their secondary pallets placed vertically rather than horizontally, with the result that the bar moved
horizontally. Because brass springs lose their flexibility in time, some
builders in 16th-century Italy and 17th-century Germany designed the
chest so that all the secondary pallets belonging to one groove could
on occasion be pulled out in one strip (looking like a long, narrow
drawer) and the faulty spring replaced without dismantling the pallet
box.

The spring-chest is troublesome to make, as 17th-century theorists
like Mersenne and Werckmeister noted; it also takes up more room
than a slider-chest. But it is said that spring-chests last longer, and
(though no results of controlled experiments have been published)
cause the pipes to speak better. Since there can be no loss of wind
through shrinking or warping of sliders, spring-chests probably
contribute to greater stability of tuning, although their complexity is
also likely to make them more sensitive to the extremes of humidity
and dryness found in modern, centrally heated churches. While the
spaciousness of the chests dictated by the spatial requirements of the
'groove-valves' makes pipes and action more accessible for tuning and
repair, it also causes the main key pallets to be made larger, making the
touch heavier and less sensitive than that of slider-chest organs. This
may be why the spring-chest was abandoned in the North, where
higher wind pressures complicated this situation.

(vi) Mechanical action

In Fig. 8b (see pp. 16–17) the mechanisms illustrated in fig. 8a are
expanded and augmented by the device of the roller, which, by
displacing leverage laterally, enables the width of the keyboard to be
much less than that of a rank of pipes. Fig. 8b shows all the mechanical
devices in a theoretically complete 'tracker action mechanism'.

(vii) Key mechanism of a single-manual organ

The principle illustrated in fig. 9 (p. 18) is one of the commonest
associated with the organ from the 17th century onwards. Even older

14

(used from at least the 15th century) is the so-called 'suspended' action, found in early organs such as that in Oosthuizen (*c*1530) and used by the French into the early 19th century, although superseded by the later version in England and Germany. In a suspended action (Fr. *traction suspendue*) the fulcrum of the key is at the far end, the tracker being attached to the middle of the key and thence to a rollerboard and to the chest (fig. 10, p. 19). As there is no transfer of motion in this type of action, it tends to be lighter and more sensitive, even in fairly large organs such as the Clicquot organ at Poitiers Cathedral (1787–90). In later periods subsidiary chests might be added (e.g. a *Brustwerk* above the music desk, a Pedal section behind the main chest); the case might lose its simple shallow design and altar-like facial curves; the action might have splayed trackers or backfalls instead of a rollerboard, etc (see also Chapter Seven, §2, below).

(viii) Wedge-bellows

The late medieval *Spanbalg* ('Span' denoting a 'board') was a wedge-bellows constructed of hinged wooden boards, ribs and strips of leather. It could be single (see fig. 12*a*, p. 21) or multifold (fig. 12*b*). Both kinds could be small and simple, worked directly by hand or by the body-weight of the bellows blower; larger versions with operating levers are depicted here. The multifold design shows the principle of alternation between two bellows, the use of a lead or stone weight to increase the weight of the upper board whose fall expels air under pressure from the cocked bellows, and the wind canal going directly from bellows to pipes, without collection or stabilization other than that resulting from the cushioning of air in the wind-trunk.

Wind pressure has varied over the centuries, one purpose of the hydraulis system being to supply air on a higher and steadier pressure than ordinary forge-bellows. Such *Spanbälge* as these were made to supply an average pressure of 75–100 mm; i.e. the wind was sufficient to displace by 75–100 mm the level of water in an open glass U-tube.

Two other types of feeder-bellows were of particular significance, though neither necessarily supposed a reservoir between bellows and chest. The square, lantern-shaped bellows (Fr. *soufflets à lanterne*) were known by at least about 1625; the top was raised by a pulley and the inflated bellows slowly collapsed, expelling wind through the trunk below. The box-bellows (Ger. *Kastenbalg*) worked on the principle of a pulley-raised box falling slowly within a second, slightly larger open-topped box and expelling wind through a trunk below; such bellows, which did not have perishable leather hinges, were known from the 17th century though perfected only by about 1825.

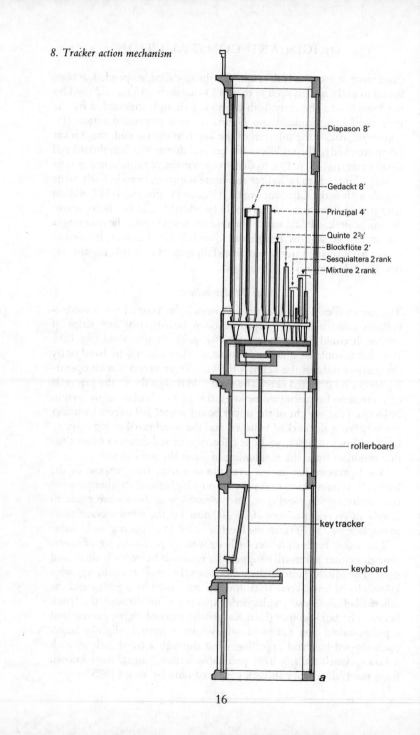

Diapason 8'

Gedackt 8'

Prinzipal 4'

Quinte 2⅔'
Blockflöte 2'
Sesquialtera 2 rank
Mixture 2 rank

rollerboard

key tracker

keyboard

a

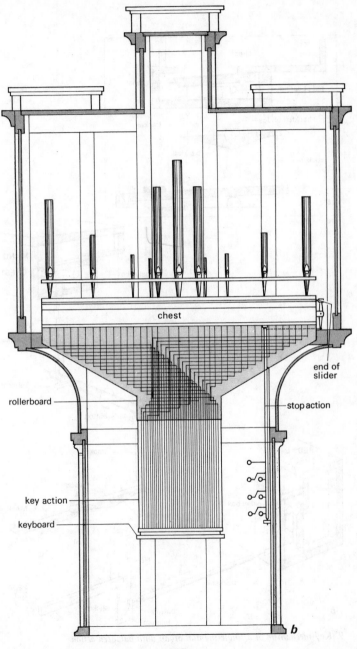

chest

end of
slider

rollerboard

stop action

key action

keyboard

b

17

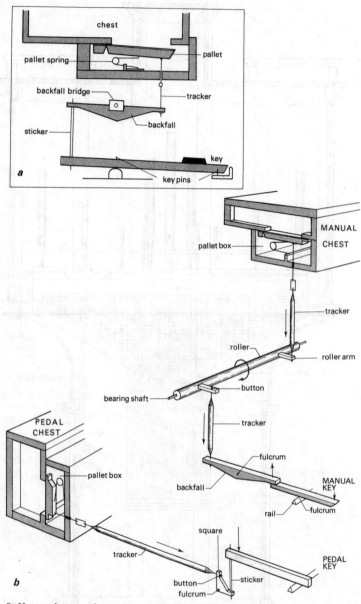

chest

pallet spring — pallet

backfall bridge

tracker

backfall

sticker

key

key pins

a

MANUAL
CHEST

pallet box

tracker

roller

roller arm

bearing shaft — button

tracker

PEDAL
CHEST

pallet box

fulcrum

backfall

MANUAL
KEY

rail

fulcrum

tracker

square

PEDAL
KEY

button

sticker

fulcrum

b

9. *Key-mechanism of a single-manual organ with balanced action*

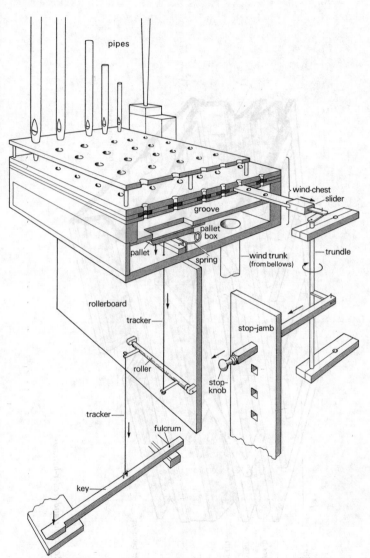

10. Key- and stop-mechanism of a single-manual organ with suspended action

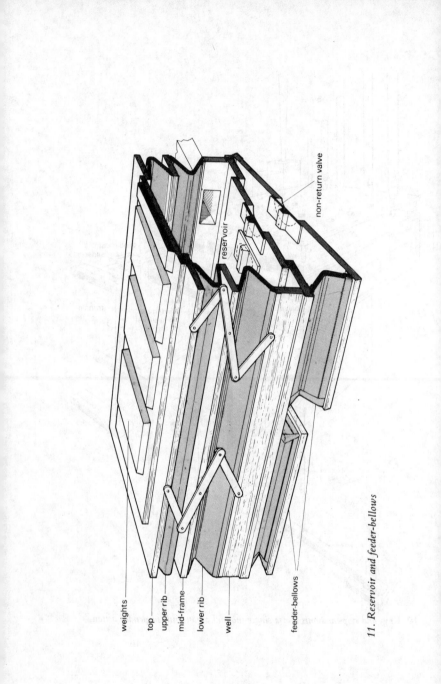

non-return valve

weights
top
upper rib
mid-frame
lower rib
well
feeder-bellows

reservoir

11. *Reservoir and feeder-bellows*

20

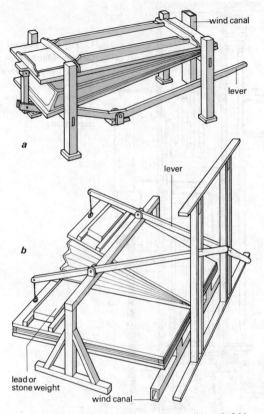

12. Spanbalg (wedge-bellows); (a) single; (b) multifold

All of these types of bellows sucked in air through apertures opened by an intake valve which closed as soon as the full bellows began to expel wind; all had a further valve in the trunk which allowed wind to pass along from the bellows but checked it from rushing back when the bellows were reinflated.

(ix) Reservoir and feeder-bellows

Feeder-bellows (cocked and compressed in *Spanbalg* fashion) expel air under pressure to a receiver or reservoir, shown in the top of fig. 11, which then delivers the wind to the trunks at a constant pressure. The reservoir or main bellows has 'inverted ribs' (lower ribs closing inwards and upper ribs closing outwards) for stability of exhaust pressure. In England this system dates from about 1762; the inverted

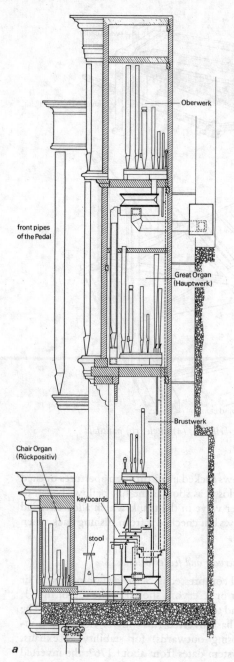

13. (a) Four-manual German-Dutch organ in cross-section; (b) Tremblant doux, and (c) Tremblant fort shown in 'on' position (arrows show movement of stop action)

Oberwerk

front pipes of the Pedal

Great Organ (Hauptwerk)

Brustwerk

Chair Organ (Rückpositiv)

keyboards

stool

a

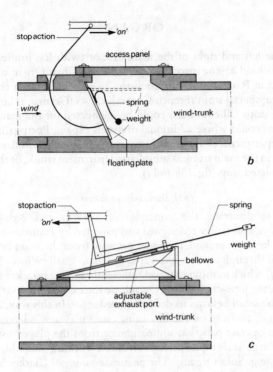

b

c

rib construction was not adopted in the USA until the mid-19th century and was seldom used on the Continent. Some reservoirs were merely a second diagonal single-fold bellows into which the first sent wind (Snetzler, *c*1740), but by 1825 or so, horizontal bellows of the type shown were usual. During the 19th century, various means were employed to supply energy sufficient to raise the feeder-bellows, for example by mains water under pressure actuating cylinders moving the feeder-arms, or electric motors driving the feeders. Later, devices delivering wind directly to the reservoirs were used, notably the electric rotating-fan motor (from about 1890); most organs old and new are now fed with wind by this method. Moreover, within the airtight chamber of the blower more than one fan can rotate along the same spindle, each successive fan increasing the pressure as it receives and passes on the wind. The wind can be tapped off at any stage and conducted to the appropriate reservoir at the pressure required.

(x) A North European organ

Figure 13*a* shows a four-manual instrument in cross-section; only a selection of pipe-ranks is indicated. In this design, the pedal-chests may be to the left and right of the main case or (with less immediacy of sound) behind it. The space between stool and Chair Organ was often enlarged in Roman Catholic countries to accommodate a choir and orchestra; special stops (French Cornet), chests (German echo chests), and toy stops (all countries) could be conducted off the main wind-trunks, as could whole additional divisions (Spain, Portugal); one or more departments could be enclosed in a Swell box; Tremulants could be fixed in the main trunk, a subsidiary department trunk, or the trunk of an isolated stop (fig. 13*b* and *c*).

(xi) Barker-lever action

Figure 14*a* illustrates the principles of a 19th- and 20th-century mechanism constantly redesigned and patented by countless builders. When a key is depressed, air under pressure from the main bellows is admitted through a pallet-like valve to inflate small bellows (one for each key) which in moving travel sufficiently to pull a tracker connected with the pipe-chest pallet. On release the exhaust valve at the top allows the small bellows to deflate immediately. In this way, average light finger pressure on the key brings into play a wind-power sufficient to operate pallets at some distance from the player, especially those of large-scale pipes, perhaps on chests working under high wind pressure (e.g. Solo Organs). The pneumatic unit, or 'Barker lever', is placed near the keyboard, at a point where the tracker rises vertically from the keys. Perhaps one of its most important applications is to intermanual couplers, allowing additional manuals to be coupled to the main manual without increasing key resistance.

(xii) Cone-chest (Kegellade)

The cone-chest, or ventil-chest with cone-shaped valves, is found particularly in 19th-century German organs (fig. 14*b* shows a mid-century example) and was one of several chests developed between 1775 and 1875 in the interests of mechanical reliability. Though bulky, the cone-chest avoided the faults to which a working slider-chest was subject; it also required less refined and skilled construction. In the cone-chest all the pipes belonging to a rank are mounted on one channel running the length of the chest; to the whole of this channel wind is admitted when the stop-knob is drawn. There are no lateral channels or grooves in such 'barless chests'. Each key activates a series of cone-shaped valves, one for each stop; thus although only one stop may be required by the organist, all the other valves move. The valves need not be cone-shaped; they may even be replaced by little discs operated by small bellows-like pneumatic motors ('bellows-chest').

24

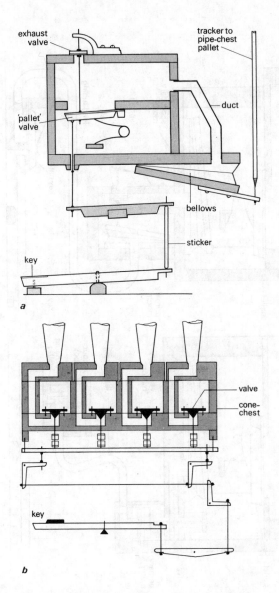

14. (a) Barker-lever action; (b) mid-19th-century cone-chest

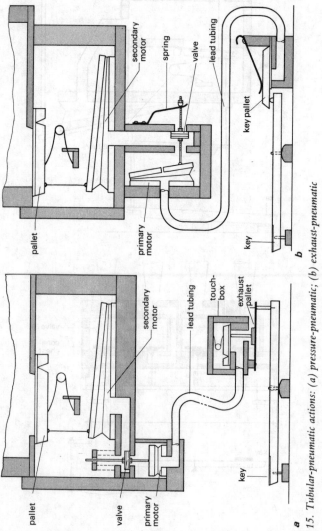

15. *Tubular-pneumatic actions: (a) pressure-pneumatic; (b) exhaust-pneumatic*

26

The membrane-chest, associated with simple pneumatic or electric actions, also has longitudinal channels and is thus another 'barless or stop-channel chest' (*Registerkanzellenlade*). It works on an abundance of wind and may be explained without a diagram; air pressure from below the channel pushes a membrane up against the mouth of a conduit leading to each pipe-foot, thus preventing wind held inside the channel from reaching the mouth of the conduit and hence the pipe; the depressed key releases the pressure from below the channel, so that the membrane is pushed down from the end of the conduit by the wind destined for the pipe-foot itself. German and American builders of the later 19th century devoted much energy and ingenuity to devising such ventil wind-chests, often in clear rivalry to each other.

(xiii) Tubular-pneumatic action

When a key is depressed, air under pressure in the touch-box above the key is admitted along the lead tubing to the pneumatic motor operating the pipe-chest pallet. To compensate for loss of force in the wind as it passes along the tubing, a secondary or 'relay' pneumatic motor may be built in, adjacent to the pallet box. Such a system works by air under pressure near the key being admitted towards the mechanism operating the pallet, hence the name 'pressure-pneumatic action'. 'Exhaust-pneumatic action' is that in which the air under pressure is contained near the pipe-chest pallet, pushing it closed when at rest; a valve near the key allows this wind to escape along the lead tubing away from the pallet, thus pulling it open. Pressure-pneumatic action never became popular in France, and in England many builders preferred exhaust-pneumatic, believing it to be more prompt, more silent and more durable (see fig. 15a and b).

(xiv) An electric action

In the 'electro-pneumatic action' shown in fig. 16 (p. 28), an electromagnet is activated when the key is depressed and its circuit completed. The armature acts as a valve, rising to the magnet and thus allowing the wind to escape from a pneumatic relay (previously filled with wind from the pallet box) which in turn collapses, opening the port below the main pneumatic motor and thus allowing its wind to escape. On collapsing, the pneumatic motor pulls down the pallet. On the release of the key, the circuit is broken, the magnet drops the armature-valve and wind is restored to the small pneumatic motor, while the external spring closes the port under the main pneumatic motor which inflates and pushes up the pallet.

A 'direct electric action' is one in which a magnet operates the pallet

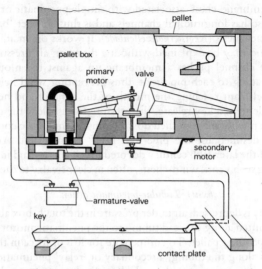

pallet

pallet box

primary
motor

valve

secondary
motor

armature-valve

key

contact plate

16. Electro-pneumatic action

itself, pulling it open; such pallets need to be small, however, and the consumption of electric current is high. The system is suitable chiefly for individual pipes (e.g. those of the unit-chest organ discussed below in Chapter Six, §4) and has never been highly favoured for important organs outside the USA. The electric magnet, generally quicker than the electric motor, may be applied to other moving parts of the organ, particularly the stop-action (sliders etc) and couplers. Electric actions allow the keyboards to be placed as far from the pipes as required; unfortunately they also deprive the organist of control over pipe-speech, and in practice they satisfy only those builders whose tonal ideals, like their instruments, are virtually outside the realm of true organs.

CHAPTER TWO

Pipework

There are several classes of organ pipes, the two oldest and most integral to the development of the organ, being flue pipes and reed pipes. More common by far, though not necessarily more varied, are flue pipes. Both types operate on the coupled-air system of sound production common to flutes, recorders, oboes, clarinets etc.

1. FLUE PIPES

Air under pressure from the chest passes through the foot-hole (bore) at the base of the pipe-foot (fig. 17, p. 30) and so through the flue or windway, to issue in a flat sheet of wind striking the edge of the upper lip; the refracted wind causes eddies to form at the mouth, first on one side of the upper lip, then on the other. The pipe's natural frequency is coupled to the note of the 'edge tones' produced at the upper lip and gives to the eddies a rate of production that becomes the frequency of the note produced. Thus the effective length of the pipe is the principal factor in the pitch of the note.

Pitch and timbre are affected by several other factors, few of which, however, are variable outside narrow limits. A narrow pipe, to produce a certain pitch, must be longer than a wide one; a conical one must likewise be longer if it narrows towards the top, but shorter if it tapers outwards. Such variations in shape, however, are generally more important for their effect on a pipe's timbre than on its pitch. A cylindrical pipe stopped at the end will sound approximately an octave lower than if it were open; for a conical pipe the difference is not quite so great. A half-stopped cylindrical pipe (i.e. with its cap pierced and usually a tube passing through the hole) speaks somewhat higher than a stopped pipe.

The narrower the mouth or the smaller the flue, then the smaller the volume of air (at any given pressure) striking the upper lip and the

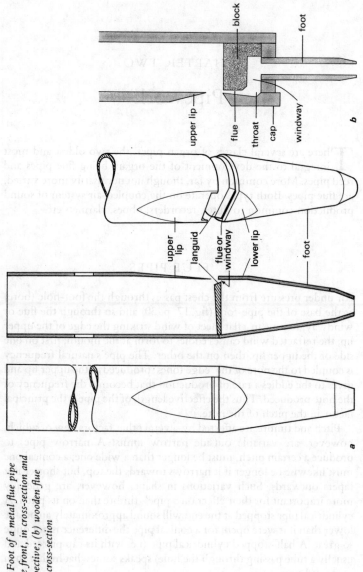

17. (a) Foot of a metal flue pipe from the front, in cross-section and in perspective; (b) wooden flue pipe in cross-section

upper lip

languid

flue or windway

lower lip

foot

upper lip

flue

throat

cap

windway

block

foot

a

b

30

softer the sound; the higher the mouth in relation to its width (i.e. the greater the 'cut up'), then the rounder, duller or more flute-like the tone; the narrower the pipe as a whole, the richer the harmonic spectrum and the more string-like the tone. It has been said that the harder the metal, the richer the harmonic spectrum; or the more lead contained in the pipe-alloy, the 'duller' the sound. But recent work (Backus and Hundley, 1966) has established from theoretical and experimental evidence that 'the steady tone of a pipe does not depend on the material of the pipewall. The belief that the use of tin in constructing pipes gives a better tone appears to be a myth unsupported by the evidence'. Experienced voicers, however, will aver that the composition of pipe metal does affect tone quality, and that it is impossible to match exactly the tone quality of two otherwise identical pipes made of very different alloys. More to the point, perhaps, is that tin-lead alloys are easy to work and shape, thus allowing the builder a high degree of adjustment at the parts of the pipe crucial to voicing processes (see also Chapter Three, §7).

Most of these factors can be used only to a certain degree: a point is soon reached when a pipe will not speak at all, even when other factors are altered, e.g. increasing or decreasing the wind pressure. Consequently the various interrelated factors require pragmatic expertise in their manipulation.

In addition to its more general usage, the term 'scale' refers to a pipe's diameter in relation to a norm ('wide' or 'narrow' scale), and the relationship or ratio between one pipe's diameter and that of its octave below in the same rank (3:5 etc). One well-known norm is the *Normprinzipal* suggested at the German Organ Reform conferences in the 1920s; this norm is 'one pipe larger' than that promulgated by J. G. Töpfer about 1845 (thus the diameter of Töpfer's *C* pipe is that of the *Normprinzipal C♯*). G. A. Sorge had been the first to use logarithms to find constant scalings for organ pipes (*c* 1760), calculating pipe diameter, pipe length, mouth width and mouth height by this method. Other 17th- and 18th-century theorists (such as Mersenne and Bédos de Celles) suggested scaling-figures by means of tables culled from practical experience and from the empiricism of organ builders themselves. Only two generations after Sorge did Töpfer develop the idea of arithmetical calculation for pipes (with immense influence on builders of his time): he calculated the cross-sectional area of a pipe an octave higher than the given pipe by applying the ratio $1 : \sqrt{8}$. Thus a pipe with half the diameter of a given pipe is not an octave (12 pipes) above but 16 or 17 pipes above. Such a factor as $1 : \sqrt{8}$ was itself reasonable, and many older builders had worked

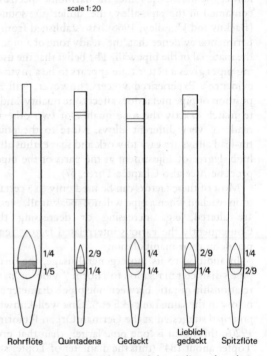

scale 1: 20

Rohrflöte 1/4 1/5

Quintadena 2/9 1/4

Gedackt 1/4 1/4

Lieblich gedackt 2/9 1/4

Spitzflöte 1/4 2/9

18. Various flue-pipe shapes scaled to indicate the relative sizes of different pipes all producing the same C

more or less to it, though empirically and not rigidly; indeed, Töpfer's formula can be deplored for the encouragement it gave to 19th-century 'organ-factory builders' who applied a constant scale irrespective of the acoustics of the church or indeed any other variable of importance to organ tone.

Figure 18 shows some flue-pipe shapes and is scaled to indicate the relative sizes of different types all producing the same C. (The *Normprinzipal* diameter of the C pipe at a pitch standard of $a' = 435$ is

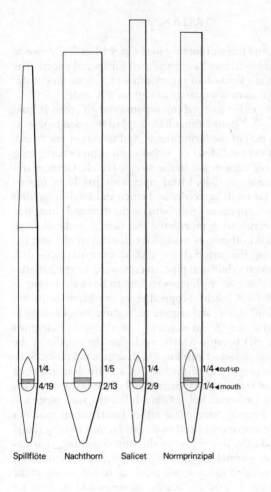

Spillflöte	Nachthorn	Salicet	Normprinzipal
1/4	1/5	1/4	1/4 ◀cut-up
4/19	2/13	2/9	1/4 ◀mouth

155·5 mm; at a pitch standard of $a' = 440$, the diameter for C would be reduced to 154·17 mm – a fine point of difference since variations in temperature will change the pitch this much). Most historic types of English Open Diapason, French Montre and Venetian Principale have been wider in scale than the *Normprinzipal*, and for many builders it remains merely one of the possible norms. It must also be remembered that the diagram does not refer to factors other than scaling, such as wind pressure. Mouth widths are usually expressed as proportions of the circumference, and those ordinarily used range from 2 : 7 down to 1 : 6, though further extremes have been used for special effects. The cut-up is expressed as a fraction of the mouth width, 'quarter cut-up' indicating that the mouth is a quarter as high as it is wide.

Wooden pipes are either stopped (most commonly 8′, then 16′ and 4′) or open (16′, 8′, 4′, 2′); sometimes half-stopped wooden pipes (i.e. with a pierced stopper) of the Rohrflöte or Spillflöte type are found, especially in small organs. Metal or wood conical pipes narrowing towards the top have been found in the largest Dutch, German and Spanish organs since about 1540. Metal pipes with 'pavilions' (inverted conical caps) were made especially by French and English builders for about a century from about 1840, both on the flute and string side of tone-colour. Overblowing pipes have also been popular in large organs and in special instruments made for colourful secular use; the most common during the period c1600–1800 was the narrow-scaled, narrow-mouthed open cylindrical pipe, overblowing to the 2nd partial or 'at the octave' above. Such pipes require to be twice as long as the pitch length (8′ for 4′ pitch). Stopped pipes overblow to the 3rd partial or 'at the 12th' above, and require to be three times as long as the normal stopped length (6′ for 4′ pitch). Overblowing flute pipes (Flûte harmonique etc) became widely used after the middle of the 19th century, having been developed to a high degree in France. Such pipes are of double length but of the scale of a normal-length open flute, and are pierced at the node (approximately halfway up from the mouth) with one or two small holes. Given full wind, such pipes will overblow, giving a strong, sweet and rather fundamental tone not unlike that of the modern orchestral flute, but are not usually found below $1\frac{3}{5}′$ $e′$ in pitch, the lower part of the stop consisting of wide-scaled open pipes of normal length. Alternatively, to prevent overblowing in narrow-scaled string-toned pipes, or to aid tuning at the mouth of stopped pipes, 'ears' or 'beards' are often added: these are short metal plates or rods of metal soldered or held to the sides of (and sometimes below) the mouth, protruding from it and helping to direct the vortices of wind on to the edge of the upper lip.

2. REED PIPES

Air under pressure from the chest passes through the bore into the boot and so through the opening in the shallot (fig. 19); in so doing the wind sets the thin, flexible brass reed-tongue into vibration; this in turn sets

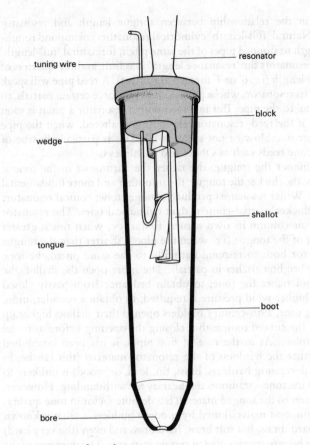

tuning wire

resonator

block

wedge

shallot

tongue

boot

bore

19. Foot of a reed pipe

the air column in the pipe or resonator into vibration, producing a coupled system. The frequency of the note produced is determined by the length of the air column in the resonator and by the length, mass and stiffness of the reed-tongue.

The pitch and tone of the pipe are affected by many factors; if all the factors are constant, then the longer the reed-tongue, the lower the pitch. To produce a required pitch in reed pipes with either cylindrical or conical resonators, the resonator must be shorter the longer the tongue. But in practice this property is used within only a small margin, as the tone is more immediately and strikingly affected by a change in the relationship between tongue length and resonator length. Natural 'full-length' cylindrical resonators correspond roughly in length to stopped pipes of the same pitch; for natural 'full-length' conical resonators the 'resonance length' is as little as three-quarters of the pitch length (i.e. 6' or 7' for an 8' Trumpet). A reed pipe will speak without its resonator, whose purpose is to reinforce certain partials, to 'give tone' to the pipe. But in a reed with a resonator a point is soon reached, if the reed–resonator relationship is altered, when the pipe will either overblow or not speak at all. This is particularly true of double-cone reeds such as Oboes and Schalmeys.

The thinner the tongue, the richer the harmonics in the tone it produces; the thicker the tongue, the smoother and more fundamental the tone. Wider resonators produce stronger tone; conical resonators have a 'thicker' partial-content than cylindrical ones. The resonator gives its air column its own natural frequency; when this is greater than that of the tongue (i.e. when the pipe is shorter than the tongue requires for both to respond naturally to the same pitch) the tone becomes brighter, richer in partials. The more open the shallot, the louder and richer the tone; to obtain brilliance from partly closed shallots, higher wind pressure is required; to obtain a rounder, more horn-like tone, 19th-century builders opened their shallots higher up the reed, the curved tongue thus closing the opening before its travel was complete. As in the case of flue pipes, it has been established recently that the hardness of the resonator material (this can be, in order of decreasing hardness, brass, tin, lead, or wood) is unlikely to influence the tone – tradition and hearsay notwithstanding. However, the hardness of the tongue material is a definite factor in tone quality. The commonest material used by modern builders is what is known as 'half-hard' brass, but soft brass, hard brass and even (the very hard) phosphor bronze are also used in certain instances. The thickness of the tongue likewise has an effect on tone.

Reeds with very short resonators (whatever their shape), and usually small scale, are called regal stops and were known from at least about 1475. In practice, most regals are either predominantly conical in shape or predominantly cylindrical; they also exhibit an inconstant scale (i.e. relative to the reed-tongues, the resonators in the treble are progressively longer than in the bass). Reed stops with resonators of twice or even four times natural length were sometimes made in the later 19th century, especially by French and English builders, and became equivalent to overblowing flue pipes, although such over-length resonators are generally used above the pitch of 2' *c'*. 19th-century builders, particularly in those two countries, very often placed their reeds on higher wind pressure than the flue stops (18 cm upwards); the desire to supply 'carrying power' by such means, particularly in the treble, had grown in France from about the second third of the 18th century onwards.

Figure 20 (pp. 38–9) shows models of some of the more popular reeds of the early 17th century (Praetorius, 2/1619; fig. 20*a*) and the late 19th (Audsley, 1905; fig. 20*b*). A great deal depends on the use of various shapes and proportions of shallots or 'reeds', and these, like the tube, block and boot, may be made of wood (though this is more often a feature of low-pitched pedal reeds than a general alternative).

3. FREE REEDS

Free reeds were developed in Europe (probably after the Asian *sheng*) towards the end of the 18th century in several areas around the Baltic, and offered the first radically different type of organ pipe since flues and reeds had been perfected. Instead of a shallot with an orifice against which the tongue beats when wind excites it, a thick, oblong plate of brass is perforated with a narrow opening through which vibrates the close-fitting brass tongue (see fig. 21, p. 40). It swings freely, hence 'free reed'. The boot needs to be larger than that of a corresponding reed stop to allow copious winding. When made by German builders about 1825 and French builders about 1850, free reeds had resonators of various types and tone-colour, thus being legitimate ranks of organ pipes. Some stops, however, such as the Physharmonika had instead of individual pipe-resonators one resonating chamber common to all notes of the rank, thus taking less room on the chest and less time at the factory. It was such pipeless free reeds that led to the various kinds of harmonium, or reed organ, of the 19th century (see Chapter Nine). Free reeds could be mass-produced more easily than the so-called beating-reed stops, although in itself the workmanship was not inferior. The best builders by no means regarded them as easy alternatives to beating reeds.

Though less incisive in articulation and weaker in volume than the beating reed, the free reed had a quality highly favoured by its period: it could be made 'expressive'. On admitting more wind to a free reed, the amplitude, but not the frequency, of the swinging tongue is increased; it can thus produce a louder tone without rising in pitch, like a more or less excited tuning-fork but unlike a beating reed. When the free reed was a separate stop in a large organ, however, this property

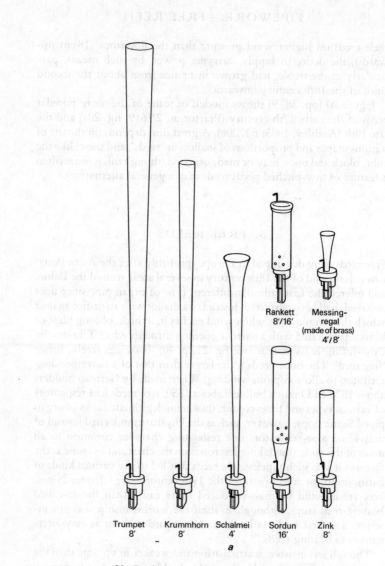

Rankett
8'/16'

Messing-
regal
(made of brass)
4'/8'

Trumpet
8'

Krummhorn
8'

Schalmei
4'

Sordun
16'

Zink
8'

a

20. Reed pipes: (a) after Praetorius, 2/1619; (b) after
Audsley, 1905

38

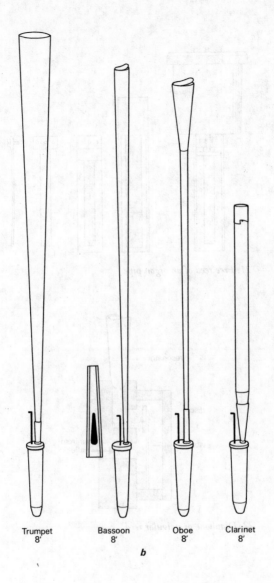

Trumpet Bassoon Oboe Clarinet
8'   8'   8'   8'

b

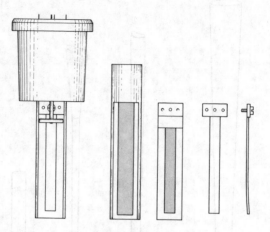

21. *Free reed of an organ pipe*

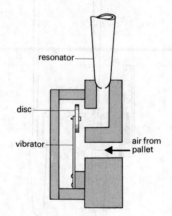

resonator

disc

vibrator

air from
pallet

22. *Diaphone or valvular reed*

could not easily be exploited. Rarely outside the period 1810–1910, and then most often only in parts of northern France, central Germany and northern Italy, did the free reed and its meagre tone achieve much popularity.

4. DIAPHONES (VALVULAR REEDS)

In 1894 Robert Hope-Jones took out a patent for a 'pipe', making use of the age-old observation that any device allowing puffs of compressed air to be projected into a tube or resonating box (i.e. into a chamber holding a column of non-pressurized air) will create a sound if the frequency becomes audible (fig. 22). On activation from the keyboard, air under pressure is admitted through the bore and sets the thin 'vibrator' into motion, whereupon the pallet-like disc attached to its free end admits a rapid and regular succession of puffs of air into the resonator (i.e. the pipe standing above). As with the free reed, the tone increases in volume but not in frequency as the wind pressure is increased; but as is not the case with the free reed, greater wind pressure can make for much power. The tone itself is always 'unblending' and useful only in organs (chiefly cinema organs) conceived on ideals current in a few areas of Europe and the USA between 1900 and 1940.

CHAPTER THREE

The Classical and Medieval Organ

Since the 3rd century BC it has been possible to regard the organ as an instrument composed of four elements: (i) a wind-raising device operated by lever, pulley or other mechanism, directing air under pressure to (ii) a 'chest' in which the wind is stored until admitted by (iii) a mechanism operated by some kind of keyboard to (iv) one or more ranks, or rows of pipes. The absence of any one of these elements prevents an instrument from being properly considered an organ, however well it is fashioned. But other instruments could well have presented models or given ideas to early organ makers, particularly those in east Mediterranean countries. It is unlikely that at any single period the hydraulic organ was so firmly established that builders were indifferent to the influence of such wind instruments as the syrinx (a form of the panpipes in ancient Greece), the *magrephah* (an ancient Jewish instrument) and the bagpipe.

The most comprehensive recent surveys of archaeological and documentary evidence relating to classical and medieval organs are the books of Jean Perrot (1965) and K.-J. Sachs (1970 and 1980).

1. GREEK AND ROMAN ANTIQUITY

No evidence, literary, iconographical, archaeological or even mythological, suggests that the pipe organ existed before the Hellenistic period or originated in any other than the Hellenistic sphere of influence. Ancient Greek writers on music, for example Athenaeus, Pseudo-Plutarch and Pseudo-Aristotle, very often named the inventors of musical instruments; these inventors, however, are generally mythical figures or men who long postdate the instrument's first appearance. The inventor of the hydraulis is a significant exception. All the evidence suggests that the instrument was invented by Ctesibius, a famous Alexandrian engineer who lived in the 3rd century

BC and who was less remarkable for his theoretical ability than for his highly ingenious solutions to practical problems. He was the first to use air pressure to operate mechanical devices, in particular the pump with plunger and valve, the water clock, the pneumatic catapult and the hydraulis. He described his work in the *Commentaries*, a book frequently cited in classical times (for example by Vitruvius and Pliny the Elder) but not now extant.

The invention of the hydraulis was first attributed to Ctesibius by Philo of Byzantium, an engineer of the late 3rd century BC, who if not actually his pupil was much under his influence. He described the hydraulis as a 'syrinx played by the hands'. Vitruvius, the famous technical writer of the 1st century AD, also attributed the hydraulis to Ctesibius and gave one of the two extant descriptions of the instrument. The other is by Hero of Alexandria, a mathematician and engineer of the later 1st century AD; although Hero did not explicitly mention Ctesibius, he is generally believed by both ancient and modern authors to have been dependent upon him when he described pneumatic devices.

Taking into account these facts and the absence of any references to the hydraulis predating Ctesibius, there is strong evidence for supposing him to be the instrument's originator. Moreover, it is particularly plausible that the hydraulis should have been the invention of a single individual and should have originated in Alexandria at that time. It was not, as Curt Sachs has suggested, simply the union of a panpipe with a new wind mechanism, since it also included a highly sophisticated wind-chest and keyboard. It did not, then, have the elemental evolutionary origin of most ancient musical instruments. It is a complex machine involving more new elements than old, and therefore precisely the kind of invention one might expect from the 3rd-century Alexandria of Euclid, Eratosthenes, Archimedes and Ctesibius. Accordingly it was first looked upon more as a mechanical marvel than a musical instrument. That Ctesibius was also said by Vitruvius to have invented a water clock offers an interesting parallel to the makers of organs and clocks in the medieval cathedrals of western Europe: such makers were, in effect, specialists in complex machinery.

Although the hydraulis was at first viewed as a marvel of mechanical ingenuity, its musical potential was realized in a relatively short time. The claim of Athenaeus that Ctesibius's wife Thais was the first organist has an apocryphal air about it, but there is no reason to doubt a Delphic inscription which describes the success of the hydraulis player Antipatros in the *agones* of 90 BC.

Texts mentioning the hydraulis, particularly at Rome, multiplied

23. Hydraulis and cornu players: from a Roman mosaic (AD 230–240) at Nennig bei Trier

during the following centuries. Suetonius wrote of Nero's infatuation with the instrument; the *Aetna* poem placed it in the theatre and Petronius referred to its accompanying of chariot fights in the arena.

There are approximately 50 known literary references to the instrument and rather fewer pictorial representations of it. The impression they create is of an instrument in fairly general usage, if not so common as the smaller and presumably less expensive kithara and tibia. Both at Rome and in the provinces it was found in the homes of the wealthy, the theatre and the arena, this last setting being the most characteristic, particularly in pictures, where it is shown sometimes alone but more often playing with brass instruments like the cornu and the Roman tuba; see figs. 1 and 23.

Another type of hydraulis, replacing Ctesibius's hydraulic pump with bellows, was at first less prominent than the hydraulis proper. Bellows had been in use long before the invention of the hydraulis, but were not practical for musical purposes because they could supply only intermittent air pressure. However, it seems to have been simple to adapt Ctesibius's principles by replacing the cistern with a flexible leather reservoir, weighted on top, fitted with valves to prevent the escape of air and fed by one or more bellows. This device had the advantages of being lighter, cheaper and less likely to corrode.

The principle of the water-pump is shown in fig. 3. But forge bellows were known much earlier, and their power potential had already been described in the *Iliad*. Bellows could have provided wind either directly to a regulator-chest under a row of pipes, or indirectly via the cistern of a water organ. But there is no evidence that either of these was done before the 2nd century AD, and it is possible that the organ was indeed born as a kind of engineering model, demonstrating the efficiency of Ctesibius's wind-raising and wind-stabilizing equipment. Hero's account gives no details of the pipes (whether flue or reed, open or stopped) or what the material, size, compass, tuning, pitch or voicing was. Certainly the term 'hydraulic' does not of itself imply an *aulos*-like sound (see Chapter One). The attributions of tonal power to the larger outdoor organs of the late Roman Empire can be interpreted in several ways; they might, for instance, refer to the putative high Mixture of the *magrephah*.

Vitruvius's musical interests are more obvious than Hero's. The ranks of his organ were made to play separately (though for what reason is not known) by means of a specially constructed chest in which a channel ran lengthways under each row of pipes, wind being admitted to the channel through a valve operated by an iron handle. The keys are returned to position by an iron spring, unlike Hero's piece of horn. As the key was set immediately under its pipes, either the close-set pipes or (more likely) the keys may have been unequally spaced; in either event organ playing would be rather awkward.

The oldest reference to organ playing is a century and a half after Ctesibius: the 'Delphic inscription' (90 BC), full of implication about the organ's fame. Cicero, Lucretius, Petronius and other authors wrote of its powers, presumably not all from hearsay, and at least one emperor (Nero) let himself be known as an inordinate organ player. By the 2nd century AD the Roman organ was heard in some of the more important theatres, games, amphitheatres, circuses, banquets and perhaps processions; a 3rd-century source (a Greek inscription at Rhodes) even suggests that it was played in Dionysian festivals. But the cylinder-pump water organ had so many disadvantages – requiring precision engineering and good metal, yet difficult to maintain, move and keep from corrosion – that it is easy to imagine bellows being applied over the years. Eventually, they replaced both pump and cistern, but it is not known when, where or how. Sources of the 2nd century (Julius Pollux) and 4th century (Porfyrius Optatianus) may refer to bellows replacing either pump or cistern. Even in the later Roman Empire, however, organs were to be heard, and such poets as Claudian (c400) show organ playing to have been a major contribution to the celebrations attending accessions to a consulate, weddings and banquets during a period when 'the singer has thrust out the philosopher' (Ammianus Marcellinus, c350). Inscriptions found in several provinces far from Rome (Arles, Colchester, Budapest, Asia Minor) make it clear that organ playing was well known in gladiator contests (see fig. 1).

The few 5th- and 6th-century references include one or two by early Church Fathers, particularly those on the south and east coasts of the Mediterranean. But whether it was from personal experience that such writers as Boethius wrote of hydraulic organs, or Cassiodorus of a bellows-organ with wooden keys, is not certain; nor has 20th-century research shown what music the organ played, much less whether it played polyphony. Much can be tentatively conjectured from the iconographical evidence. The Nennig mosaic, for example (fig. 23), shows an organ rather over two metres high and one metre wide, with its player poised during a gladiator fight to play at a suitable moment – perhaps as a death signal, or to rouse the spectators, or to 'illustrate' the action. The player is seated or standing in an elevated position, watching the combat over his 27 or 28 pipes. These pipes decrease in length very little over the compass, but it is not known whether this is due to an enharmonic tuning or to pictorial licence. A modern reconstruction of a hydraulis such as classical authors have described is shown in fig. 24.

Parts of two Roman organs are said still to exist: fragments from Pompeii (now in the Museo Nazionale, Naples) and major remnants of a small organ found in Aquincum, Hungary (now in the Aquincum Museum, Budapest; fig. 25, p. 48). But the Pompeii fragments, which seem to belong to two different instruments, are not certainly parts of an organ, although their pipes are cast, like those of an organ. The Aquincum organ is more complete, and was so 'reconstructed' in 1959 that its parts are not now open to more enlightened interpretation. Its dedicatory plaque has the date 228. It has four rows of 13 bronze flue pipes, one row open and three stopped with oak stoppers; all pipes are cast. The wind-chest was made of wood, lined inside and out with thin bronze sheets. The whole organ is very small, about 60 cm high, 38 cm wide and 25 cm deep. Inside the chest below each row of pipes runs a channel to which wind is admitted by slotted metal sliders pierced with one central hole; the wooden keys operate further sliders and are pressed down by the player. The pipes show a complex structure at the mouth, whereby the airstream is directed by the shape of the pipe-foot itself on to the upper lip; the open and stopped pipes differ in detail but not in principle.

Two crucial questions remain about the Aquincum organ. First, how did the organ receive its wind? No trace of this part of the mechanism exists, and until recently it was not known whether the organ was a small Vitruvian hydraulis (as the inscription 'hydra' on it suggests) or a cisternless bellows-organ of the later medieval type, with wood and leather bellows of a kind liable to perish easily or be later misunderstood by inexperienced archaeologists. It has recently been shown, however, that the organ was not bellows-blown but was a hydraulis. Second, were the four ranks designed to be played

24. Full-size reconstruction by Jean Perrot of the hydraulis described in Greek and Latin sources

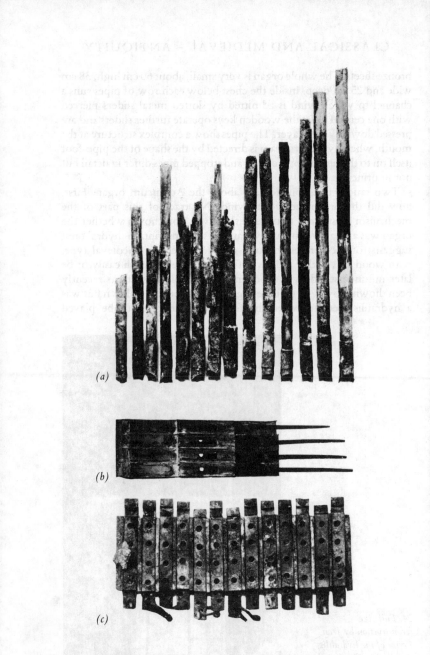

25. *Remains of a Roman organ (AD 228) found at Aquincum:*
(a) pipes; (b) sliders; (c) sliders in position

together at choice or do the non-proportional variations in length between one rank and another – which can be modified by the stoppers or, in the case of the open pipes, by bronze tuning-slides – indicate that each rank played 13 notes of one particular mode? The latter has been plausibly suggested by Walcker-Mayer (1970), who gave the open rank a Pythagorean diatonic scale and the three stopped ranks sections of the Hyperiastian, Lydian and Phrygian *tonoi*. The little organ would then have been able to make a single-rank, portative-like contribution of treble flute sounds to music in four different *tonoi*, the makeup and character of which exercised theorists over many centuries (see also Chapter Seven, §4). Some late sources suggest that different wind and string instruments had different *tonoi*. While iconographic remains are usually untrustworthy or vague (certainly it is over-optimistic to see the 'Carthage terracotta' shown in fig. 2 as representing a three-rank, quarter-tone organ), it is possible that rows of pipes were tuned, if not 'microtonally' (too modern a concept), at least so that several modal scales were possible.

Reconstructions of the hydraulis suggest that it might have had a wind pressure anywhere between 7·5 cm and 30 cm; also unknown is whether the pipework was always flue and, if so, whether the diameters were constant. While written sources give no firm evidence, iconography seems to suggest that: the pipes were usually flue; their diameter was constant; the tuning (in the more complete examples) was not diatonic, chromatic or enharmonic but multiple, providing a choice of modes for rather less than an octave; and multi-rank chests may have provided different timbres with or without octave- and 5th-sounding ranks. But none of these conclusions is reliable. The Aquincum organ supports the case for flue pipes, contradicts the suggestion that the diameter was constant, and leaves the tuning and timbre uncertain.

2. THE BYZANTINE ORGAN

By the end of the 5th century the new Roman Empire of the East, with its base at Constantinople, had achieved a character of its own, intellectually conservative and favouring a world of abstract thought far removed from the practical technology of ancient Alexandria and Rome. Although the old Greek treatises were preserved in Byzantine copies and hence known to the Arabs, engineering projects like organ making remained undeveloped for a millennium. But by the 8th century western Europe itself no longer knew such masterpieces of Roman engineering as the Vitruvian hydraulis. All the sources suggest that the European 9th- and 10th-century 'organ revival' came about because the instrument was reintroduced from Byzantium.

Despite some hints in the sources, the organ was certainly not used in the Byzantine Church itself (and indeed is still not). But at least two facts seem to be clear: that most references relate to bellows-organs, and that the instrument continued to be part of the secular, courtly pomp in the capital city. In the first connection, a 10th-century Arabic source suggests that three (or two) bellows fed air into a large reservoir below the pipe-chest; in the second, it was no doubt because of their use at banquets, chariot races, weddings, processions and the like that organs were decked out in gold and costly decoration. Both the 'blue' and 'green' factions at court had an organ, but the instrument otherwise naturally remained a rarity. At his palace the emperor had both automata (the famous 'golden tree' with moving, whistling birds activated by wind under water pressure; see fig. 26) and true organs, in which at least one emperor (Theophilus, 9th century) took an interest. Nothing is known of the pipework, sound, compass, precise function or repertory of the organ in the Great Reception Room, or indeed anywhere else, though one 9th-century source does refer to '60 copper pipes' in what appears to have been a large table-organ.

Organs became objects of visual and aural show, eliciting wonder and respect as diplomatic gifts or signs of royal power. In 757 a famous diplomatic instrument was sent to Pepin, King of the Franks at Compiègne; many sources of the period lay great store by this gift to Pepin. Later a monk of St Gall (possibly Notker Balbulus) reported that the 'King of Constantinople' also sent an organ to Charlemagne in 812, with bronze pipes, 'bellows of bull leather' and three sound-effects (rumbling thunder, trembling lyre, tinkling *cymbala*) possibly indicating *pleno*, flutes and little bells; but the source is doubtful, the language hyperbolic (or possibly psalmodic) and the whole reference perhaps merely a gloss on the Pepin episode. In any case such instruments were not church organs but extravagant gifts, like the 13th-century organ of 90 pipes sent from one Arab court to the Emperor of China.

An event of evident importance in the 9th-century chronicles was the arrival at Aachen in 826 of Georgius, a Venetian priest who undertook to construct a hydraulis. According to a poem glorifying Charlemagne's son Louis, Georgius's organ was a kind of royal or national symbol of power: 'The organ, not seen in France before, a subject of pride for the Greeks, the only reason the people of Constantinople felt themselves your master: even the organ is now represented

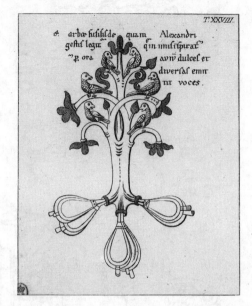

26. *Byzantine 'golden tree', with whistling birds activated by wind kept under water pressure: drawing after a 12th-century MS from St Blasien, published by Martin Gerbert in his 'De cantu' (1774)*

in Aachen'. Its intricate technology must have been the justification for such respect. The Aachen organ was used for occasions of pomp, not for chapel services; the Utrecht Psalter (compiled in France, perhaps near Rheims) depicts, with little understanding, a hydraulis taking part in an ensemble illustrating Psalm cxlix (see fig. 27, p. 52); this too has little to do with church services.

3. THE ORGAN OF THE ARABS

The high level of Arabic and Islamic culture from the 8th century to the 10th gave theorists and craftsmen the opportunity to work on bellows-organs; theorists in particular knew of such 'instruments' but seem rarely, if ever, to have seen one. A famous source, the Epistle to (or from) Muristus, describes two organs, one of which is a kind of siren or signal-organ; the sources containing Muristus's writings are also interesting in that two of them (in Beirut and in the British Museum, London) show particularly clearly how a diagrammatic plan can become, under the scribe's hand, an unintelligible pattern of abstract design.

27. *Hydraulis (centre) with horns, cymbals, lyres, a psaltery and lute: drawing illustrating Psalm cxlix from the Utrecht Psalter (9th or 10th century, possibly after a model from 5th- or 6th-century Alexandria or Byzantium)*

Nothing is known of Muristus, and the graphic similarity of his name in Arabic to Qatasibiyus (Ctesibius) was pointed out in 1931 by Farmer; Muristus appears to have been a Greek (or Byzantine), and in any case derived his instruments directly from Ctesibius's *Commentaries*. But neither of them is a true organ. The first contains a chest of 12 pipes fed with wind from the lungs of four men blowing gently through tubes into a regulator; the weight of the pipes compresses the wind; the pipes themselves appear to be reeds, all of the same length but of varying diameter and requiring different volumes of wind; the wind is admitted to each pipe through a valve, presumably one worked by some kind of key. This seems to be the instrument of 'formidable power' referred to in the 'Letter to Dardanus' once attributed to St Jerome. The second or 'Great organ' is a signal-organ perhaps not unlike the (smaller) *magrephah* and containing a siren pipe or pipes blown at great pressure, used in battle by the Greeks, according to Muristus, or for similar purposes by other Middle Eastern peoples. The siren worked on the same principle as the hydraulis, four pumps or cylindrical bellows providing wind pressurized by water in a cistern.

There is no evidence that the organ became known again in western Europe through the cultural activities of the Arab caliphate of Córdoba in Spain. But the possibility that this might have been the case adds further importance to any work undertaken on this period in Iberian musical history, for links may perhaps be discovered between Spanish–Arab instrument making and 9th-century Benedictine musical life. In the eastern caliphates organs seem to have developed into mere ingenious automata; but even in that state the Eastern organ seems not to have survived the fall of Constantinople in 1453.

4. EARLY CHURCH ORGANS

The famous gift to King Pepin in 757 was a Byzantine organ, called 'organum' in the chronicles and still perhaps regarded as an 'engineering contrivance' rather than a musical instrument. The supposed gift to Charlemagne in 812 was also Byzantine. The fanciful clock given to the emperor in 807 by an envoy of the Persian king was Arabic; the priest Georgius, sent to Aachen in 826, was Venetian, but possibly trained in Byzantium. Several Western writers from the 8th century to the 13th knew of the Greek–Roman organ but in most cases from vague written sources from which even the more astute authors got the impression that the pipes were made to sound by water – an idea sustained by the Jesuit amateur physicists of a later century. The well-known picture in the Utrecht Psalter (see fig. 27) of a hydraulic organ with two players and four alternating pump blowers is also based on a misunderstanding of the Mediterranean water organ. Many of the early church writers refer to organs in such hyperbolic or apparently unreal terms that their sources of 'information' must have been in most cases literary. It is even possible that such references to organs with 100 pipes, like that of St Aldhelm, were mistaken allusions to the *hydra*, the 100-headed monster whose name is the same as a documented abbreviation for the hydraulis. All ecclesiastical references to organs before the 10th century are to be treated with caution, and even scepticism.

All these organs were secular. One of the great unsolved puzzles of music history is how and why the organ came to be almost exclusively a church instrument in western Europe from about 900 to about 1200. The early church was subject to two particular influences against any instrument in church, and especially in the liturgy: the liturgy's origins in the Jewish synagogue, and Patristic resistance to anything of profane or luxurious association. By the 9th century, however, the intellectual and liturgical style of the church had changed. Like sung organum, the instrument owed a great deal to Benedictine cultural centres, not only in their literacy and scholarship but also in the opportunities which their large churches gave to the advancement of music. The monastic revival in the late 10th century must itself have been a factor in the appearance of organs, which had become ingenious objects for the use of the clergy, not the people. The organ was never officially approved or even acknowledged in any known papal or pontifical document despite the traditional legend that Pope Vitalian (657–72) introduced it. Nor, for one reason or another, are any of the references to organs placed or used in church before the 9th century at all reliable.

Organs, like tower bells later, were one of the irrelevances complained of by the new reformed order of the Cistercians, judging by remarks made by St Aelred, abbot of Rievaulx in 1166; his reference to the sound of the bellows, the tinkling of bells and the harmony of organ pipes is highly reminiscent of older reports. St Aelred also referred to the crowd of people watching this display as if in a theatre, 'not a place of worship', which suggests that organs were placed inside buildings, perhaps for example a large Benedictine church. But all this does not necessarily indicate that an organ was used during the service, nor even before or after the service. Perhaps it was rather an object of curiosity, like a cathedral almanac clock. Other 12th-century sources imply more clearly that an organ was used in some way during the services, perhaps for signalling purposes, like bells at the Elevation.

Whether organs were used liturgically is not clear from the many 9th- and 10th-century references to them. The notice describing the consecration in 972 of the Benedictine abbey of Bages, Spain, for example, makes it clear that an organ played near the entrance, 'praising and blessing the Lord'; but to surmise more is conjecture. Much the same could be said for the archiepiscopal coronation at Cologne Cathedral in 950. Pope John VIII (872–82) wrote of an organ required 'for the purpose of teaching the science of music', for which it remained useful to scribes writing about and teaching musical proportions, for example at Benedictine centres such as Fleury and St Gall. The practical function of organs set up by, or in memory of, great abbots or landowners is unknown; reference to organs used on feast days (e.g. in the Life of St Oswald, 925–92) suggests if anything that they were extra-liturgical, a kind of church carnival object. The Benedictine abbot Gerbert (Archbishop of Rheims, 991–5) was said by William of Malmesbury to have had a hydraulic organ put into the cathedral: an object of mechanical ingenuity, once again coupled with a clock in the written account. Gerbert may have learnt the principles of the water organ from the Arabs in Córdoba, where he lived for a time, since Benedictine manuscripts of the period do not suggest any practical familiarity with the writings of Hero or Vitruvius. Nothing is known of other 10th-century organs, such as that set up in Halberstadt Cathedral under its Benedictine bishop Hildeward; nor are contemporary references such as those of Notker Balbulus (d 912) helpful towards an understanding of the nature and purpose of organs. So many of these writers, often interpreted literally, were merely indulging in metaphor.

One detail of the Bages consecration of 972 was that the organ music 'could be heard from afar', which may or may not imply that the organ was outside the church. But a large number of references, second-hand or glossed though many must be, suggest that the organ was a loud instrument by standards of the day. Is it possible to see the famous late 10th-century organ in one of the adjacent cathedrals of Winchester as a signal organ, used on feast days to summon the congregation or overawe them (perhaps before or after services)? This does not preclude its having keys and some musical potential; 'signal-organ' describes its tone, something obviously more sophisticated than Muristus's war-siren. If the Winchester organ was placed near the west or south door (stone screens were not known until the next century,

28. Organ with sliders and a conflatorium: drawing from the Harding Bible (French, 11th or 12th century)

and at Winchester only the nave may have been capacious enough) its use could hardly have been liturgical. Nor is it easy to see how an organ could have been liturgical in a much partitioned church of the type known to the later Cistercians.

The Winchester organ was built by about 990, some decades after the Benedictines were fully established there and later than modern commentators have said. Details of it appear in a fanciful verse letter written shortly afterwards by the monk Wulfstan. Much quoted, much translated and much misunderstood, the poem speaks of 26 bellows and 400 pipes in ten ranks, with the 40 notes arranged as two sets of 20 keys played by 'two brethren of concordant spirit'. Each key was a perforated slider pushed in and probably pulled out – hence the need for two or more players. Clearly some kind of organ did exist; but there are good reasons for distrusting Wulfstan's account: despite the fanciful references by St Aldhelm to what appear to be 100- and 1000-pipe organs, there are no other firm details extant of such large organs, at Winchester or anywhere else; the numbers given for bellows, blowers (70), pipes, ranks and keys are not plausible, whatever the diameter of the pipes and however the wind was raised (even the number of players smacks of literary tradition or at least of the poorly drawn hydraulis in the Utrecht Psalter, perhaps known to Wulfstan personally); the general style and character of Wulfstan's poem are those of an impressionable layman not concerned with technical accuracy (for further details see McKinnon, 1974).

Theophilus's organ (see fig. 4) could be placed within the wall, presumably at gallery level, with only its chest and pipes visible from the church and these indeed covered by a cloth 'tent' when not in use. Later 13th-century screen organs would have been equally well placed, in some cases better placed, when they came to serve as *alternatim* instruments in the liturgy. Many details of Theophilus's organ are unclear, not least its function in the church. Theophilus was a monk, probably German, working in the first half of the 11th century on a large encyclopedia describing techniques used in making church objects – glass blowing, painting, gilding, metal forging, bell casting, organ-making. The sources of his treatise leave its authenticity uncertain, the last part of it probably being a later compilation. A second 11th-century treatise is the anonymous Berne Codex, a manuscript possibly originating at the Benedictine abbey of Fleury; a third is a note by Aribo on pipe making. These three sources are rather more practical than many later medieval manuscripts (see §5 below).

Theophilus first advised his reader or builder to equip himself with a treatise on pipe measurement ('lectio mensurae'); this 'lectio' would presumably contain a table of concrete values or actual pipe-scales, rather than mere Pythagorean ratios. The pipe copper was to be beaten very thin and shaped on a gently conical mandrel (i.e. the foot and the resonator would be of one conical piece), a statement not easily credible. Information in the Berne Codex seems to suggest the familiar pipe-foot. Theophilus's pipes are equal in diameter, which may not be unreasonable in an organ of less than two octaves. The Berne Codex gives 'almost 4″' as the longest pipe but does not indicate the length of the foot unit. It is not certain that actual pipes could be made to the given scales since no allowance is made for end correction, and the compass and arrangement correspond rather to the 'theoretical' texts then in circulation. The pipes are soldered, and their mouths probably resemble the pressed-in apertures familiar from late Roman iconography. Theophilus also referred to voicing of the pipes carried out at the mouth, whereby the tone could be made 'more round' ('grossam') or 'thinner' ('graciliorem'). No chest is known to have had sliders or separate stops, and the organ supplied a strong sound rather than the Vitruvian-Aquincum variety of softer organ-colour.

In his section on forging Theophilus described bellows, and from other sources of the period it seems that such bellows were large, capacious, and planned to compensate for leaks between feeder and pipe. The feeders direct wind into a *conflatorium* or receiver, shown in some 11th- or 12th-century miniatures such as the Harding Bible (see fig. 28) and Cambridge Psalter. In the Berne Codex the valve preventing the return of wind when the bellows are refilled is placed in the collector, while Theophilus's valve is in the head of each bellows. The main duct can be curved or straight (possibly not mitred) and is usually shown as generously proportioned. The keys of the Berne Codex organ closely resemble Hero's, consisting of a 'square' depressed at one end, pushing in a perforated slider (to which it is attached) at the other, and pulled back by a horn-spring to which it is tied. By the 13th century, according to a miniature in the Belvoir Castle Psalter (see fig. 29), organists were using their fingers separately (and rather elegantly) to depress the keys, which in this miniature were broader and more substantial than some reproductions of it suggest.

5. MEDIEVAL ORGAN THEORISTS

In the absence of any known organ remains between the 3rd-century organ of Aquincum and the positives of Sweden believed to date from the late 14th century (see §6 below), historians must turn to the body of 'medieval organ pipe theory', readings of which have led to some misleading ideas about medieval organs. The many sources have been seen as 'treatises on organ building' (Frotscher, Mahrenholz, Fellerer) or 'treatises on pipe measurement' (Perrot, 1965); but after 1966 researches into the now completely collated texts (see K.-J. Sachs, 1970) have led to a new assessment of their purposes.

The texts, in some cases only a few sentences in clerical Latin, fall into three main categories. The largest group (about 30 texts in 155 sources from the 10th century onwards) are those concerned with the length of organ pipes calculated by ratios from an 'initial' pipe, itself of no specified length; most of the length measurements take account of end correction which, in the case of a row of pipes of the same width and mouth shape, is constant. A smaller group of texts (11, in 11

29. *King David playing a positive organ (apparently depressing the keys with separate fingers), with a symphonia (hurdy-gurdy) and cymbalum: miniature from the Rutland (Belvoir) Psalter (English, c1270)*

sources) is concerned with the width or diameter of organ pipes, ignoring end correction in calculating the length; some of these discuss the relationship of mouth width, cut-up and foot-hole to the pipe diameter; none dates from before the 14th century. Neither of these two groups covers the whole subject, since in fact variable pipe-widths and quasi-Pythagorean demonstration of end correction are mutually exclusive. The third group of texts (three only, all 11th-century) deals with technical pipe making. These texts are Theophilus's *De diversis artibus* (bk 3, pp.81ff), *Cuprum purissimum* (the Berne Codex), and the section 'Sicut fistulae' on pipe making from Aribo's *Musica*. Some aspects of the organs described in this last group of sources have received attention in §4 above.

The 'pipe-length treatises' rarely offer concrete usable measurements, nor do they outline any pattern of values in which practical experience may have had a hand. Instead, the scalings concern proportional value corresponding to the Pythagorean ratios known from monochord theory. On the one hand, it is obviously possible to make an organ without determining the acoustical phenomenon of pipes; on the other, no careful measuring of pipes leads to usable pitches without proper tuning. Many treatises so resemble the numerous scaling texts for the monochord and *cymbala* that the significance of their pipe-scalings should not be interpreted in isolation; for pipes, strings and bells might have been cited primarily as examples of Pythagorean ratios according to which a pipe approximately half as long as another will sound the octave above, one approximately two-thirds as long as the 5th above and so on. Comprehensive instruction treatises covering such matters include the works of Notker Labeo, Aribo, Engelbert of Admont, Jerome of Moravia, Walter Odington and Georgius Anselmi; an important branch in the tradition was the widely known *Scolia enchiriadis* of the late 9th century. In no way were such sources recipes for making instruments; rather, they outlined the kind of number theory which theorists since Boethius had applied to music.

Both Theophilus and the writer of the Berne Codex were dependent on ancient accounts, namely those of Vitruvius and Hero. Aribo's account probably refers back to a manuscript tradition around the uncertain figure of Wilhelm of Hirsau, who seems indeed to have been concerned with actual pipe measurement. Most of the copies of a text ascribed to him are provided with drawings showing the scale of the first pipe (not unlike the measure line in Schlick's *Spiegel*, 1511). But in other writers, end correction, the very factor 'disturbing' the neat theory of Pythagorean ratios, was itself determined proportionally, calculated as a fraction of the diameter. For such calculation the diameter was assumed to be constant; hence the frequently repeated conclusion that the medieval organ builder made a rank of pipes all to the same diameter. Optimistically interpreted iconography has been seen to support this idea. But it should be remembered that the general medieval approach to making things (i.e. before print technology brought craftsmen gradually to depend on visual models) weighs against the practical significance of written-down treatises. Only two of the texts cover organ building as such, and they are partly derived or even (in the case of Theophilus) the result of a compilation. Moreover, practical details such as the remark in the Berne Codex that pipes follow the modern diatonic genus ('si . . . sit diatonicum genus quo maxime decurrent moderne cantilene') do not necessarily indicate an actual organ used in liturgical music. The Sélestat manuscript (11th century) and the Berne Codex describe pipe-chests of seven notes, and the former seems to make it clear that its three ranks are unison, octave, unison; at the same time, an 11th- or 12th-century miniature, in the Harding Bible, shows a keyboard of C, D, E, F, G, A, B♭, B♮, a set of keys showing one each of the known notes (see fig. 28). But it is not known whether these treatises and miniatures reflect more than certain literate, second-hand and even non-empirical traditions passed on, perhaps indirectly, to their scribal 'authors'.

6. THE CHURCH ORGAN 1100–1450

Rarely in music history is conjecture taken more confidently as fact than in this area. Despite bold and apparently plausible modern assertions that playing in 4ths and 5ths was known by 9th-century clerical organists, that *alternatim* chants were known in the Mass during the 11th century, and that large organs played the *puncti organici* (and even the quicker upper parts or *voces organales*) in the Ile-de-France organa of the 13th century, there is no irrefutable evidence to support them. It may be reasonable to assume that in the larger Benedictine abbeys (St Gall, Metz, Benevento) polyphony, organ playing and troping of plainchant were all linked; but it is not known during which century the more cosmopolitan of the abbeys may have begun to use the organ more integrally during Mass than they were ever to use their other expensive mechanical equipment such as bells or clocks. Nor are technical matters concerning the structure of organs any more certain. There is no evidence that, between the 10th and 12th centuries, octave- and 5th-speaking ranks were used in abundance, or that reed and stopped pipes were also known, as more than one modern writer has claimed. Much later still, basic assumptions are unreliable. Iconography by no means establishes that organists had to use all of each hand to thump the keys, at this or any point in organ history. Nor are archives less equivocal; church accounts do not prove that the 'little organs' sometimes mentioned from about 1390 onwards were second manuals of large organs or that, if so, such manuals were placed together or had the same pitch. Possibly the second keyboard, up until at least the time of the Innsbruck Hofkirche organ (1550; the oldest extant two-manual organ), should be seen rather as an extension to the compass of the first. Organ research from about 1960 has been directed towards a circumspect interpretation of the evidence, and a new period of doubt about the evolution of the organ is inevitable.

Certainly the period 1100–1450 was one of great activity. During the 11th century more organs are known to have been in monastic churches throughout western Europe; they were played at ceremonies (probably outside the liturgy) and succumbed to the fires that frequently swept medieval cathedrals (Canterbury 1114, Freising 1158, Merseburg, 1199) – which suggests perhaps that they were fixed in place. Some literary sources imply that the organ was played during Mass, for instance the *Roman de brut* (*c*1155, Normandy):

Quant li messe fu commensie ...
Mout oissiés orgues sonner
Et clercs chanter et orguener

– but such references are vague and merely image-evoking; poets' sources were usually other poets. More authentic sources of the 9th and 10th centuries suggest, however, that sequences as well as the *Te Deum* were the most open to polyphonic vocal treatment, just as later they were the movements most closely associated with the organ. A small portative and psaltery are shown in a 12th-century miniature but no ecclesiastical function is implied, any more than for the portatives illustrating psalms in earlier psalters (e.g. the organa hanging on willow trees at Psalm cxxxvii in the Stuttgart Psalter, 10th century). But by the 13th century all instruments other than the organ were excluded from various churches in Spain, Italy and France. The phrase 'great organs' is found in church documents (e.g. Erfurt Peterskirche, 1291) and by 1296 one French bishop referred to the organ sounding five times in connection with the Sanctus – perhaps as a signal rather than for music as such. There is no evidence that it played the tenor in Sanctus movements or in any motet following at that point during Mass. But by the end of the 13th century secular cathedrals from

Exeter to Prague, Barcelona to Lübeck, were as likely to have organs as the larger abbey churches. Whether erected on screens (as in England) or hanging on an upper wall of nave or quire, the organs were usually located near the *cantores*, i.e. no longer near the west or south entrances nor specifically near the main altar. It is not known, however, when large organs were fixed in Theophilus's manner, and illustrations for psalm texts usually show much smaller organs in ensemble. The phenomenon of the smaller fixed organ attached to, associated with, and in some cases paid for by specially bequeathed chapels belongs to the 15th rather than the 13th century.

The large organ seems to have been an exclusively ecclesiastical instrument from the 9th-century Western Church to 17th-century Italy. Probably by the late 13th century the cathedral or abbey organ was occasionally used in *alternatim* music with the *cantores*, though presumably not with the congregation itself. Jovannes de Florentia referred (*c*1350) to rendition 'partim organo partim modulatis per concentum vocibus'. Early 15th-century keyboard repertory extant in the Faenza Codex (Biblioteca Comunale, Faenza, 117) complements such explicit references as the mid-15th-century Castilian rubric 'los organos tañían un verso et los clerigos cantavan otre'. 14th-century documents usually suggest that whatever the organ played, it did so on traditional church or local feast days, for example at Halberstadt Cathedral on Christmas Day, for Easter Week, Sunday after Easter, *Kreuzerfindung*, Reliques of St Stephen, Ascension, SS Peter and Paul, Dispersal of the Apostles, Mary Magdalene, SS Stephen and Sixtus, Assumption, Patron, Nativity of Mary, St Michael, St Gall, All Saints and 12 other feast days including Trinity and Annunciation. For three centuries organs were used only on feast days. But by the end of the 13th century some churches had decreed against other instruments (Milan, 1287); by the 14th, *alternatim* performances took place, especially in the Office; by the early 15th, many areas, such as the Upper Rhineland, north-central Germany, some English and Italian cities, and the stretch from Rouen to Utrecht had organs in most of their larger churches, and the future of the instrument was completely assured.

It is impossible to trace this history step by step, despite a certain amount of archival, musical and iconographical evidence. But certain general points can be made about the 14th and early 15th centuries. Organs became known in cathedrals less as an exception and more as a norm; by 1425 the large positive (with front pipes arranged from left to right) was usually distinct from the fixed church organ (with front pipes in mitre form with a set of larger pipes to each side, thus requiring a rollerboard). All the evidence suggests that only open metal flue pipes were known, though some commentators have seen such references as 'plom ... per las horguenas' (Eglise des Cordeliers, Avignon, 1372) as evidence that lead pipes were used for distinctive tone-colour. Larger organs in certain areas (Normandy and later the Netherlands) occasionally had Trompes during the period 1390–1450 (i.e. a set of ten or so large open metal Bourdon pipes, possibly played by a separate manual or pedal keyboard and placed to one side, or both sides, of the main organ). Presumably they also had a *Blockwerk* although apart from the number of pipes in a few famous examples (e.g. 2000 at Amiens in 1429) little is known in this regard before 1450. Presumably their compass, whether from (apparent) *B* or any other note, was roughly equivalent to that of men's voices, the total perhaps being divided up and distributed over more than one keyboard. However, so many unknowns of paramount importance are raised by such summaries that describing the church organ before its clearly defined types of 1450 is mostly a matter of citing facts about individual instruments.

The organ at Sion, Switzerland, is usually dated about 1380 (although recent research suggests that a date in the early 15th century is more plausible) and has been much rebuilt. Despite opinions expressed on its tone, and although some of the original pipework seems to be incorporated in the present organ, nothing is certain of its original sound, disposition, compass, pitch, voicing, pressure, bellows, position, purpose or provenance. Nevertheless, its case (fig. 30) shows interesting elements: it has the typical shape for such instruments, with central mitre lines (like Arnaut de Zwolle's organ at Salins); the castellated 'towers' to left and right overhang the sides; and the wings (painted and perhaps made about 1434–7) enclose the pipes completely. At Bartenstein in East Prussia parts of the organ dated about 1395 existed before World War II. The organ had a large chest for 27 keys (possibly $FGA-a'$) with three divisions for large chorus of nine (bass) to 21 (treble) ranks, case-pipes of 16', and Principals 8' + 4'. An ingenious reconstruction of the chest was sketched by Karl Bormann in 1966 but little is certain, particularly of the stop-mechanism whereby wind was admitted to chorus and principals at will; perhaps the device was made not in 1395 but one or two centuries later. The organ at Norrlanda (c1380), now pipeless and in the Musikmuseet, Stockholm, is a large positive with a putative *Blockwerk* of three to six ranks. A set of 12 rollers conveys not only both pedal and manual key-travel to the larger pipes held in small side towers but also the action of certain pairs of keys ($C\sharp/c\sharp$, $D\sharp/d\sharp$, $F\sharp/f\sharp$, $G\sharp/g\sharp$) to a single pallet.

30. Organ (c1380, pedal pipes 1718), perhaps from Abondance Abbey (Savoy), now on the west wall of the Cathedral of Notre Dame de Valère, Sion

31. Positive organ (c1380, now pipeless) from Norrlanda

This is so sophisticated an arrangement, not least in its resulting chromatic keyboard of nearly two octaves (*C–a* or *c–a'*; fig. 31), that doubts must also arise about the age of the organ – which is in any case constructed out of panels from some older choir stalls.

Extant 12th- and 13th-century church accounts merely record the presence of an organ; about many areas of Europe, curiously little is known. Only during the 15th century were the great Gothic churches of some areas constructed (e.g. in the Netherlands), but many were immediately provided with an organ as part of the regular furniture. The first real details of church organs occur in such documents as builders' contracts from about 1390 onwards, when for reference purposes the anonymous scribe would distinguish the 'opus maius' from the 'parvum opus organum' (Utrecht Cathedral, perhaps suggesting an organ with *Rückpositiv*, but more likely simply referring to the presence of two organs of different sizes in the building) or the 'principaulx' pipes from the Bourdons (Rouen Cathedral, suggesting Trompes and other major Fourniture ranks), or even by 1420 'cinch tirants' (Aragonese royal chapel, suggesting separate stops in a large positive). Otherwise it was enough for an organ to be entrusted to the craftsman concerned, who had merely to see that it was 'decent, good and to the honour' of the church (S Giovanni Evangelista, Venice, 1430).

Henri Arnaut de Zwolle, writing in the 1440s, described several organs he knew, including those at Salins (*c*1400, *Blockwerk* of 6–15 ranks) and Dijon (*c*1350, 8–24 ranks); an account of his treatise is given below (Chapter Four, §1). The most famous 14th-century organ is that of Halberstadt Cathedral (*c*1361, rebuilt 1495), described in some detail by Praetorius (2/1619). The four keyboards were as follows: I, called *Diskant* by Praetorius, playing the plenum (case pipes + Hintersatz Mixture), *B–c'* (14 keys); II, also called *Diskant*, playing case pipes (Prinzipal) only, same compass; III, called *Bassklavier*, *B–a* (12 keys, long protruding levers perhaps worked by the knee, playing the 12 large bass pipes); IV, pedal keyboard, same compass as III, used with (perhaps pulling down the keys of) the top manual. The largest rank of pipes was at the equivalent of 32' pitch, the total number about 1192, from 16 ranks at pedal *B* to 56 at top manual *a'*. (These pitch names are by Praetorius; it should be remembered that in this or any other account of a keyboard instrument before about 1500, to express the compass of pitches in terms of *c–a* or *b–c'* etc is anachronistic and hence misleading.)

Praetorius by no means understood the historical nature of such old organs, nor is it clear from his report what in the organ dated from

32. *Positive organ: engraving of an organist and his wife by Israel van Meckenem (d1503)*

1361, what from 1495. But it is probable from his account that the *Blockwerk* had multiple ranks of octaves and 5ths such that the manual disposition was approximately as follows:

B–e 16.16.8.8.8.5⅓.5⅓.5⅓.5⅓.4.4.4.4.4.2⅔.2⅔.2⅔.2⅔.2⅔.2⅔.2.2.2.2.2.2.2.1.1.1.
1.1.1

f–c' 16.16.8.8.8.8.5⅓.5⅓.5⅓.5⅓.5⅓.4.4.4.4.4.4.2⅔.2⅔.2⅔.2⅔.2⅔.2⅔.2⅔.2.2.2.
2.2.2.2.2.1.1.1.1.1.1.1.1.1.1

d–a 16.16.8.8.8.8.8.5⅓.5⅓.5⅓.5⅓.5⅓.5⅓.4.4.4.4.4.4.4.4.2⅔.2⅔.2⅔.2⅔.2⅔.2⅔.
2⅔.2⅔.2.2.2.2.2.2.2.2.2.2.2.2.1.1.1.1.1.1.1.1.1.1.1.1.1

From the details given, the pitch level seems to have been $a' = c505$. Praetorius also described the sound of this *Blockwerk*; 20 bellows supplied the wind, all presumably needing to be operated for the plenum, though his drawing shows only two men.

Praetorius gave other details about organs he described as old, and his suggestions could be the starting-point for organ historians. For example, he guessed that semitones appeared in keyboard compass from about 1200 and pedals from about 1220, that by 1450 only open pipes were known, but that spring–chests had been built by about 1400 and separate stops by about 1250. The first date is late by two centuries if it is a question of B♭ only, perhaps a reasonable guess if intended to refer to the first *ficta* semitone (i.e. other than B♭), but early by at least one century if all five semitones were meant. The date for pedals must be about a century too early. The date for open pipes is probably correct, and that for spring–chests could be correct but is probably a little early. The date for separate stops seems early by at least two centuries if it refers to a full-sized church *Orgelwerk*. Other details given by Praetorius are more certain, for example that some keys were as broad as about 60 mm, that some keyboards had a compass of B–f' or c–a' (diatonic only) and the curious-seeming statement that some early pedals played only the bass notes. Obvious though the last may appear, the large Bourdons or 'teneurs' (Notre Dame, Rouen, 1382) may in fact often have been operated by a keyboard played in the hands or even by the knees. The term 'teneur' is evocative, but what it signifies is uncertain: perhaps the keys played the long notes of a vocal composition or an *Intavolierung*; perhaps 'teneurs' meant merely large pipes as distinct from small ('menus' at Rouen, 1382, 'Diskant' in Praetorius). Certainly the playing of a cantus firmus *en taille* on the pedals is a later speciality of the 16th century. But whatever 'teneurs' was meant to imply, builders of the period knew well how to fashion pipes of various sizes and scale, according to Praetorius.

At the end of the 14th century, then, a large organ in the area lying

33. Portative organ with chromatic keys: detail from 'The Mystic Marriage of St Catherine' by Hans Memling (c1435–94), in the Hôpital St Jean, Bruges

within Rouen, Utrecht, Magdeburg and Orvieto might be presumed to have had a *Blockwerk* of anything up to 80 or more ranks with open cylindrical pipes of metal, played by a broad-keyed manual of 16 to 22 notes, possibly with a further keyboard playing Trompes with or without their own chorus mixture, and exceptionally with a second smaller organ in some way connected with the first. Smaller but independent organs may have had, by custom, a longer compass, smaller keys, and a *Blockwerk*, of fewer ranks. Not enough is yet known for generalizations to be made about the organ of about 1390 outside the region specified above.

7. THE PORTATIVE AND POSITIVE

Although the positive and portative form virtually separate subjects, they offer a useful gloss on organ history at this point because each demonstrates a striking uniformity unknown to the larger fixed organ, and each demonstrates the limitations of iconographical evidence. Portative, strictly the same as *organetto*, *organino*, is the name given in the 14th and 15th centuries to the little organ of treble flue pipes carried (Lat. *portare*) by a strap over the player's shoulder, played by the right hand (fingering 2-3-2-3 is implied in many paintings), its bellows blown by the left hand. It contained one, two or more octaves of pipes in single or multiple ranks, sometimes with one or two larger pipes like the Bourdons of larger positive organs. The keys are earlier shaped like buttons or typewriter keys. The sound no doubt was like a set of flutes played by a keyboard. Some composers, such as Landini and Dufay, are represented playing small organs, and the instrument was useful in the many 15th-century Italian paintings (especially Venetian ones) of angel choirs at the Virgin's Coronation etc. French sources give the impression of not knowing the term (a bill from St-Maclou, Rouen, in 1519, refers to 'portaige d'une petites orgues'), while *portiff* was used in Germany (Frankfurt, 1434) and also *organi portatili* in Italy. (Barcotto, *Regola ... ogni sorte d'istromenti*, MS, Civico Museo Bibliografico Musicale, Bologna, *c*1650) and England (Roger North, MS, British Library, London, Add. 32506 and 32531–7, *c*1715). Since in England 'positive organ' is a term very rarely used, such references as 'portatives' (poem of Gawin Douglas), 'payre of portatives' (1522 will), 'portatyffes' (St Andrew, Canterbury, *c*1520) are as likely to mean a small, movable organ as a portative proper, especially since some such organs evidently contained a regal stop (1536 contract).

Often, as in Henry VIII's inventory of 1547, such a 'payre of portatives' in a privy chamber is contrasted with the larger 'organes' in the
chapel.

Positives were blown by a pair of larger bellows operated by a
second person (see fig. 32), and were played by both of the organist's
hands on a more or less chromatic keyboard exceeding two octaves
(usually beginning at *B*) and composed of short finger-keys; two rows
of pipes would form one complete rank, often with Bourdon pipes
pitched in the bass, perhaps an octave below. Some portatives also had
(shorter) Bourdon pipes. In all known cases the pipes were open and
of metal; the scaling is progressive and the diameters diminish, at least
in the better depictions; cut-ups often appear low and the scale narrow;
unless chords of more than two notes were played, the wind supplied
by the hand bellows must have been quite adequate, though presumably low in pressure.

That paintings always leave problems of interpretation may be
demonstrated by one of the best known of all organ paintings, the Van
Eyck altarpiece at Ghent (1432). Despite the beauty and apparent
precision of the picture, the pertinent section of which is reproduced
in fig. 34, there are several puzzles. The front pipes, though painted
well, are not placed naturally; the tips of the feet rest right at the front
of the chest top-board, while each pipe body, whatever its diameter,
passes behind the supporting brace, itself, however, of constant thickness. The feet of the inner row of pipes are placed almost without
depth of perspective, all exactly in the middle of those of the first row
– despite the latter's perspective. Unless the keyboard ran no higher
than appears (blocked by the player's hand and arm) the two rows of
pipes must produce only one rank; yet if the keyboard continued up
symmetrically (as far to the right as the bass goes to the left) the organ
would have at least 35 keys, implying a unique pipework of two
non-chromatic ranks. The line made by the pipe-tops corresponds
neither quite to a diatonic nor to a chromatic tuning, and the pipes in
the bass are unnaturally narrow in scale. Apart from these problems of
depiction, the painting gives no information at all on certain points,
such as the purpose of the latch-key on the lower left: if it is for a
Tremulant, one might expect other evidence of the period for such
stops; if it is a stop mechanism operating a valve to the rear chest, one
must assume that there are other pipes not seen but making up the
second rank; if it is a key to operate Bourdon or drone pipes, the pipes
should be in evidence. Such questions can be answered plausibly
enough, but only by means of simple conjecture, for comparisons
with other instruments are too distant to be useful.

34. *Angel musicians with positive organ, harp and fiddle: panel from a polyptych, 'The Adoration of the Lamb' (1432), by Jan Van Eyck, in the cathedral of St Bavon, Ghent*

CHAPTER FOUR

1450–1800

While much research remains to be done for the beginning of this period, especially on developments in German organs of the area lying within Mainz, Nuremberg, Innsbruck and Basle, a provisional historical sketch can be derived from Henri Arnaut's treatise and from certain documents concerning organs about 1450 that contain details necessary to those drawing up church contracts (such was the growing complexity and variety of the organ).

1. THE TREATISE OF HENRI ARNAUT DE ZWOLLE

Although concerned primarily with small organs, Arnaut's treatise (Bibliothèque Nationale, Paris, lat.7295; ed. and facs. in Le Cerf and Labande, 1932) throws much light on the potential which organs were seen to have by 1450. The treatise was written in Dijon between 1436 and 1454, partly by Arnaut, a Dutch polymath at the Burgundian court of Philip the Good, and partly by two other authors or scribes. It reflects a lively cultural exchange between Burgundy, Paris and the Low Countries, which, however, is sometimes over-estimated in the absence of primary source material for other major 'organ schools' of the period. Arnaut's remarks are more practical than those of any treatise since the 11th century. His description of an organ pipe is empirical and systematic; details suggest a widely tapered scale, i.e. with some ten semitones narrower than *Normalmensur* at bass B but some seven semitones wider than *Normalmensur* at a hypothetical treble b''. The mouth width is about a quarter of the circumference ($\frac{2}{7}$ for bigger-toned pipes), the cut-up a quarter of the mouth width; the foot-hole diameter of a quarter of the pipe width was large, though easily reducible. From the measurements it is unclear whether Arnaut was working from two pitches of $a' = c395$ and $a' = c435$ or from a mean *tonus cori* of $a' = c415$. Two portative or positive chests ('ciste portivorum') are drawn and described. In one, a single rank of pipes for the compass $b-g'''$ a''' is arranged 'ad modum mitre episcopalis' (i.e. as a mitre, tallest pipes in the middle); in the other, a rank for the compass $b-f'''$ is arranged in the more usual chromatic manner, tallest to left, shortest to right ('ciste communis' or 'the usual chest'). Arnaut also drew the front of a standard larger organ of the Sion type, probably the instrument at Salins (Salin, formerly in Burgundy), whose 4' *Blockwerk* he later specified as B (6 ranks)–f''' (21 ranks).

On f.127 of Arnaut's manuscript occurs the first incontrovertible reference in organ building to reed stops. On a page of scarcely 20 words (and ten figures) apropos the 'diapason ... calamorum dei custodientium' ('scales ... of the pipes in the church of the Dei custodientes') occurs the phrase 'l'anche de F', which apparently refers to the reed and block of a reed pipe. Arnaut seems to be saying that a rank of such pipes from B to b' needs eight different sizes of block. Why he gave no other details is unknown.

Of the organ of about 1350 in Notre Dame, Dijon, Arnaut noted that the pipes $(B-a'')$ are already old and corroded ('antiqui et pulverosi'); the pipe mouths were generally about half an octave too narrow, in his opinion. The Fourniture is mentioned, apparently the only separable part of the plenum. The total number of pipes in the organ was 768; the leather bellows (possibly $c1350$ or $c1440$) had three folds and measured $c160$ cm by $c70$ cm. Arnaut also gave in tabular form the disposition of four different *Blockwerke*, one of F (8 ranks)–e''' (21 ranks), two of $B'-f''$ (6–21, 6–15 ranks) and one of B' (10 ranks)–$a'b'$ (26 ranks). The first has three categories (Principal, Cymbale, Fourniture), suggesting 'stops' made to play separately by two manuals or perhaps by some mechanical device (possibly a divided chest operated by a *Sperrventil*). The Principal 8' has at the top four ranks and the Fourniture 14 (making 8.8.8. $5\frac{1}{3}$. $5\frac{1}{3}$.4.4.4.4.4.4.4.4.4); the Cymbale is nothing less than a three-rank *Terzzimbel*, indeed the first documented mixture containing a Tierce rank. The Cymbale repeats, 29.31.33 at B, 8.10.15 at e'''.

One of the other three organs was apparently that at Salins, which had a long-compass 4' *Blockwerk* of:

$B'-E$	8.8.15.15.19.22
$F-Bb$	8.8.15.15.19.19.22.22
$B-e$	8.8.12.12.15.15.19.19.22.22
$f-bb$	8.8.12.12.15.15.19.19.19.22.22.22
$b-e'$	8.8.8.12.12.15.15.15.19.19.19.22.22.22
$f'-bb'$	8.8.8.12.12.15.15.15.19.19.19.22.22.22.22
$b'-f''$	8.8.8.12.12.15.15.15.19.19.19.22.22.22

Even more important, perhaps, is that Arnaut's Fourniture is not an accumulative *Blockwerk* but a Mixture that breaks back in the upper octaves.

Arnaut referred also to the 12 'fistulas tenoris' at St Cyr (probably Nevers Cathedral), i.e. 12 Trompes or bass pipes, half as long again as the lowest ranks of the chorus. These pipes had no Fourniture ranks of their own, and were thus presumably played from a separate keyboard. At the church of the Cordeliers (possibly Dijon), the ten 'sub-dupla tenoris' pipes had a separate keyboard which could couple with that of the chorus, thus affording three effects: the usual chorus, the chorus + *tenor* or Bourdon pipes, and the *tenor* pipes played by the left hand while the right hand played the chorus or *discantus*. It is unclear whether 'double Principal' ('duplicia principalia') meant that the 8' Diapason had two open pipes or one open and one stopped; nor is it clear from later accounts (e.g. the contract at All Hallows, Barking, 1519) what exactly 'double principals' meant, despite assertions made by some modern writers. The 'simplicia principalia' of the Dijon court chapel organ was described by Arnaut as 'in duo divisa', which may mean either one halved rank (with treble and bass stops) or the usual paired Principals separated off, perhaps by a slider. Two quints and an octave gave the organ a total of 'quinque registra' ('five registers'), possibly with five push-pull slider-ends.

Further light is thrown on Chair organs ('tergali positivo'). Arnaut described one with 195 pipes, *FG–f'''* at 4' pitch and a four- to seven-rank *Blockwerk* of octave ranks only. The front pipes were of tin and the others of lead, the measurements of neither the mouths nor the foot-holes were systematic or regular in the organ he was referring to, and he was puzzled as to why it nevertheless sounded well.

Though never completed, Arnaut's draft treatise stands as something unique in organ building, not least in its description of certain *Blockwerk* and *plein jeu* choruses, which produce the most characteristic of all organ sounds. During the whole of the next century no source was to describe in such detail how an organ builder could plan his chorus. Contemporary documents, like modern histories, prefer to dwell on the new colour stops and other, essentially secondary, effects.

2. DEVELOPMENTS 1450–1500

Not only do Arnaut's remarks give a partial picture of the organ at this period, but contracts and other documents from other areas of Europe give corroborating details. Thus the organ at St Sebald, Nuremberg (by H. Traxdorf, 1439–41), had Principal, Fourniture and Cymbale, perhaps of the type described by Arnaut. Such a division of the chorus became a kind of norm, not only at Nuremberg but also at St Florian, Koblenz (1467), St George, Hagenau (1491), Weimar (1492), St Peter, Basle (1496), Louvain (1522) and in organs farther west. Yet it seems that the instrument of 1474–83 in S Petronio, Bologna, already had a large-scale, 50-note complement of nine single-rank stops (smaller in all respects than the organ as it now is), thus presenting a quite different tradition of organ building.

Clearly the crucial questions are: how were stops separated, giving the organ different colours and effects, and why did builders of some areas give an organ several manuals while those in others concentrated on one manual? As to the second question, it can only be conjectured that southern builders learnt earlier than northern ones – perhaps their materials made it more feasible – how variety could be given by one keyboard with separate ranks and a long, versatile compass (e.g. the 53 or 54 notes at S Martino, Lucca, in 1473); and that northern builders, requiring only a few different effects (Diapasons alone, or the plenum) found that two or even three shorter or unequal keyboards with one or two registrations each were more useful and probably more powerful. Division of an organ into several chests was practical from the point of view of wind supply. As to the first question of how stops were separated, the situation is clearer. Several documents from the middle of the 15th century onwards refer to the varieties of sound achieved by a particular organ: Arnaut used 'registra'; references in church archives include, 'registros' (Treviso, 1436), 'tirans' (Aragon, 1420; Barcelona, 1480), 'division de veus' (St Mathieu, Perpignan, 1516), 'dreen gelueden' ('three sounds', Grote Kerk, Zwolle, 1447) and even 'a la moderna cum registri sei' ('with six stops in the modern manner', Cattaro, 1488). How were these varieties achieved? 'Registers' and 'tirants' (even five 'registres sive tirans' at Avignon in 1539) certainly suggest slider-chests (see fig. 7b). After all, the Roman organ of Aquincum had latitudinal sliders, and its keys admitted wind to the pipes by these means. Longitudinal sliders running the whole length of a rank of pipes were different only in application, not in principle. However, when and where stop-sliders were first made is not known; no doubt they first appeared on small organs. A further system, the spring-chest (see fig. 7c), was introduced in the Netherlands about 1520 to give greater reliability in larger organs, but was already known in Italy during the previous century: Orvieto Cathedral is said to have had an organ in 1480 with two spring-stops and two slider-stops. The most common 15th-century arrangement, particularly in the area from Rouen to Zwolle, was the 'double chest', useful especially for Chair organs. In such a chest the channels were divided into two parts, front (case pipes) and back (Mixture or Hintersatz), each with its wind box, the back one of which was provided with a shut-off valve allowing the Mixture to be taken off. Evidence for such chests is fairly clear from several Dutch contracts of the period (Zwolle, 1447; The Hague, 1487).

Much less clear is the origin of stopped pipes, although it is usual to suppose that the 'double Principal' of late 15th-century organs implied an inner rank of stopped pipes sounding with the open case pipes. 'Coppel' was a name used at first probably for case pipes (Limburg, 1471), later for stopped Diapason pipes (Bienne, Switzerland, 1517). Much the same may be said about the term 'Flotwerck' (Bassevelde, 1481). The 'lead pipes' for inner ranks referred to in contracts of many languages and areas have also often been assumed to be stopped pipes, but the documentary evidence is unclear. The Quintadena is a stopped rank referred to and often called *Schallpfeifen* early in the next century; it is possible that the emphasis on new organ colours at this later period was responsible for stopped pipes in general. Thus the stopped Holpyp is authenticated from about 1500, but hardly before. Schlick (1511) was still ambiguous about stopped pipes; even Flute stops at that period (e.g. St Michel, Bordeaux, 1510) were open, as indeed they remained in Italian organs of a later century.

To sum up, in 1500 the average organ in northern Italy or southern France could be expected to have a chorus of ten or so separate stops, probably achieved with a spring-chest if the organ were somewhat large, with sliders if smaller; the upper ranks may have been duplicated here and there. Spain, at least in cities influenced by Flemish or 'German' builders (Barcelona, Valencia), followed more the transalpine organ. The bigger instruments of the Netherlands and Rhineland had two or even three manual departments, in most cases each with its own keyboard but all at the same (or octave) pitch. The English organ, judging by the All Hallows document of 1519 (see §9 below), was of the smaller Flemish kind, though it is possible that at least in secular or aristocratic circles Italian organs may have been known.

Some examples of organ schemes at their best before the turn of the century are shown in Tables 1–3. That such schemes were distinctly regional can be seen in a 1000-pipe instrument built by the German Bernhard Dilmano at Milan in 1464–6, probably a large northern organ of Principal, Mixture, Zimbel etc. The instrument was updated in 1487 but still had only eight separate stop-levers in 1508. However,

TABLE 1

Netherlands (Oude Kerk, Delft)
Adriaan Pieterszoon, 1458 (rebuild)

Grote werk: Blockwerk of 38 keys (*FG A–g″ a″*), 16′, ranks from about 6 to 32 (total *c*750 pipes)

Rugpositief: Double chest of 28 keys (*f–g″ a″*), with two 'sounds', *een doef* (2-rank Principal 4′ or 8′) and *positief* (Mixture)

TABLE 2

Rhineland (St George, Hagenau)
F. Krebs, 1491

Manual
  'driifach fleiten' (3-rank Principal 8′, 8′, ?4′)
  'das werk' (Mixture)
  'ein zymmet' (Zimbel)

Postif
  'zwifach' (2-rank Principal or perhaps 'chest with two stops')

Pedal
  'fleiten' (Principal)
  'klein tenor' (? Principal octave above)
  'zymmet' (Zymbel)

TABLE 3

Italy (S. Giustina, Padua)
Leonhard of Salzburg, 1493

One manual of 38 keys (*FG A–g″ a″*)

Tenori	8	Decimanona	$1\frac{1}{3}$
Ottava	4	Vigesimaseconda	1
Decimaquinta	2	Flauto	8

it is not known how many ranks of a native Italian organ of 1475 would be separate (as in later Italian organs). As to the sound of such organs, only conjectures can be made, even when much of the original material still exists, as it does at S Petronio, Bologna. Although some contracts make it clear that specific sweetness or strength of tone was often required, much – perhaps too much – can be read into the use of words like 'lieblich' or 'süss' in early documentation.

ORGAN

3. ARNOLT SCHLICK'S 'SPIEGEL DER ORGELMACHER'

Against the background of the special effects demanded of new organs and promised to their clients by the builders, for example the Schwiegel, Waldhorn, Quintadena (Scheelpipen), Trumpets, Shawms, Zinks, Rauschpipe, Drums and 'other unusual stops' promised by Hans Suys at Antwerp Cathedral in 1509, Arnolt Schlick wrote a splendid, forthright little book on organs, publishing it in 1511 under imperial auspices and indeed apparently intending it as a kind of standard code of practice for organ builders in Maximilian's empire. Schlick lived in the central Palatinate court town of Heidelberg, and no doubt his influence was wide. The organ described in his *Spiegel* contained about 15 stops, 'not too many of the same type', as shown in Table 4. Schlick said that in addition, the *Hauptwerk* might contain a Krummhorn ('Kromphörner') and the pedal a Klein octaff and Zymmel, but that the latter two do not belong there. All stops should be playable separately so that the pedal if required could take the

TABLE 4

Organ described by A. Schlick (1511)

Hauptwerk
    'die Principaln' (2- or more rank Principal)
    'ein Oktaff einer langen mess' ('long Octave', or *doppel* if a large organ was required)
    'Gemsserhörner ... kurtz weit moss' ('wide Gemshorn', an octave above the Principals)
    'ein Zymmel' (Zimbel)
    'Hindersatz' (large chorus mixture)
    'die rauss Pfeifen' (Rauschpfeife imitating a shawm, ? i.e. a reed stop)
    'hültze Glechter' (an unusual stop 'whose sound resembles that of small boys hitting a pot with a spoon', ? i.e. Quintadena)
    'der Zinck' (Zink or Cornett, either a reed or a Tierce-holding flue Mixture)
    'Schwiegeln' (Flageolet, ? of 2')
    'Register ... gleich ein Positiff ein Regall oder ein Superregal' (another stop ... 'like a Positive, Regal or Octave-regal', ? i.e. a Regal stop)

Rückpositiv
    'die Principaln' (Principal, 'either of wood or of tin voiced like wood')
    'Gemsslein' (small Gemshorn)
    'Hindersetzlein' (small Mixture)
    'guts rheins Zymmelein' ('good clean Zimbel', ? i.e. without Tierce)

Pedal
    'Principaln ym Pedal' (Principal, ? transmitted from the *Hauptwerk*)
    'Octaff'
    'Hindersats' (Octave and Mixture, ? also transmitted)
    'Trommetten oder Busaun' (Trompete or Posaune)

cantus firmus. The Hintersatz should not contain the very low ranks of the 'large Mixture' (possibly, that is, old *Blockwerk*), nor the 'low-pitched 3rds and 5ths' sometimes met with. There is little point in making separate $5\frac{1}{3}'$ stops, while the addition of various little chests such as *Brustwerke* merely increases cost and produces 'much sauce for little fish'. Reeds are not unreliable if properly made, and Schlick thought a competent organist could soon learn how to make the necessary minor adjustments to them. Stop-levers (preferably not push-pull) should be conveniently placed, not too long or too heavy to work from the keyboards.

Thus Schlick knew an organ of Principals, Mixtures and reeds; two manuals and pedal; probably a manual coupler; different open metal scalings (circumference to length 1 : 5, 1 : 6 or 1 : 7); and conical metal pipes, but not, evidently, stopped pipes or wooden ones. He recommended a compass of $F-a''$ and a pitch level about a tone lower than that of today (his $a' = 374$–92, depending on the diameter of the pipe). The pipe metal was pure (or mostly pure) tin and the Principal was doubled (two open metal ranks of different scale). While recommending an irregular tuning with an A♭ that could also serve (if ornamented) as G♯ in a cadence on A, Schlick recognized that some preferred a regular mean-tone temperament (with major 3rds slightly larger than pure).

Some of Schlick's general attitudes to organs are informative. He felt that eight or nine stops in the Great were all that were needed; they should be clearly different in tone; and the second manual was to be regarded as a kind of small positive, in no sense a match for the Great. The organ (or a quire organ version of it) was used in connection with the liturgy, he observed; the priest at the altar was given notes for most Mass movements from the Gloria onwards. And since the organ had a particular part to play in such music as sequences, it was placed near the choir for convenience. The pedal may have been transmitted from the Great; certainly it should have stops of the same pitch as the main manual. The pedal must have separable stops like the Great; it should not be made up only of suboctave stops, as it then inverts the harmony. (This must presumably be a double reference to organs with extra large pedal pipes always sounded by the pedal keyboard, and to the practice, then probably rather new, of using the pedals to play inner tenor or cantus firmus lines.) Reed stops can be made well (some are mentioned that sounded new though nine years old). As to Mixtures, neither those consisting of 5ths and octaves nor those of 3rds and 5ths should contain low ranks. The full chorus should be able to play chords, i.e. the 5th ranks in Mixtures should not produce too dissonant a sound when the 5th C–G or the 3rd C–E is played; at the same time, the precise number of ranks in a Mixture depends on the size of the church. Manual keys should not be too long or short, too wide or narrow, nor spaced too far or too near; the given measurements suggest relatively stubby keys with an octave span about the same as on modern instruments.

Some of Schlick's own music in *Tablatur etlicher Lobgesang* (1512) is contrapuntal in a way that closely anticipates later organ chorales which use the theme imitatively in three or four parts; in such pieces the pedal took the tune when it appeared in the bass. Schlick also knew pedal playing in two, three and even four parts, as well as pedal runs; for none of these functions would the old Trompes have been useful. The inner-voice cantus firmus technique, however, apparently requiring pedals for music from the Buxheim Organbook onwards, should not necessarily be taken at face value: such organ 'scores' must often have been open to various interpretations or playing methods.

The largest chapters of the *Spiegel* are concerned with tuning (Schlick proposed an irregular temperament that varied slightly from the mean-tone system), the making of chests, and the bellows. Schlick's advice is always very practical; for example, the wind must be generous (presumably for homophonic textures on full organ), the organ constantly played (even during Advent and Lent), and only the best and most experienced builders trusted. The little book thus surveys the whole field of organ activity – building, playing, composing – and even the long chapters on chests and tuning are full of good, pithy advice. For its size and single purpose, the *Spiegel* has never been bettered.

4. THE NEW POTENTIAL OF THE 16TH CENTURY

Soon after 1500 organs could produce a greater variety of colour and tonal effects than ever before because they had separate stops or several keyboards, or both. Many new stops (above all Flutes and reeds) were invented, and one or two extant documents of the period indicate how they were used. About 1510 in both the Rhineland (Worms) and southern France (Bordeaux), such documents contained advice (perhaps from the builder) about registration (see Appendix One, §1). Plena were mentioned, of course, but more interesting in view of Baroque registration were the two- and three-stop combinations; the list in Table 5 can be inferred from the Bordeaux 'instruction pour le jeu d'orgue'. The Bordeaux organ was an Italianate instrument of nine separate single-rank stops, and within a small spectrum such ranks would yield many combinations. More instructive still are the German registrations (St Andreas, Worms; see Table 6), since they concern an organ with pedal and multi-rank stops. Schlick too wanted stops drawn in different combinations, and registrations changed.

TABLE 5

16 + 8	16 + 8 + 4 + 1⅓
16 + 1⅓	8 + 4 + 2⅔ + 2 + 1⅓ + 1
16 + 8 + 4	etc

TABLE 6

Germany (St Andreas, Worms)
c1510

Principals 4′ or 2′ alone
Hohlflöte 8′ + Principal 4′ or Hohlflöte 4′
Principals 4′ + 2′
Principal 4′ + Hohlflöte 4′
Hohlflöten 8′ + 4′ + Quinte 1½′
Regal 8′ + Hohlflöte 8′ + Quinte 1½′ make an imitation Zink
Regal 8′ + Hohlflöte 8′ make an imitation Krummhorn
Zimbel best with the two Hohlflöten
Manual and Pedal mixtures only in the plenum
Drum stop bad outside the key of C
Tremulant not to be used with the Regal
Posaune not to be used alone 'on account of the force of the wind'

Particularly important in the documents concerning such new organs as that of Daniel van der Distelen for one of the guild-chapels in Antwerp Cathedral (1505) was the implied distribution of sounds into distinct groups: Principals, Flutes, Reeds and Mixtures. From then on, such families were to be paramount. Mutations, whether scaled as Principals or Flutes, belonged to more southern organs at that period; but at Antwerp there were at least four reeds, all for specific colour imitations (Cornett, Bagpipe-Regal, Trumpet and Krummhorn/ Dulzian). Such imitations became so important during the 16th century that both reed pipes and compound flue stops were used to give the desired effects; often it is not clear from a document which of the two a certain Zink, Cornet, Nachthorn or Rauschpipe was. Trumpets and Krummhorns, however, were always imitated by reed stops. It is also unclear from the documents of about 1510 whether the many kinds of Flute mentioned were open or stopped. In most cases it could well be that they were open and that stopped pipes were reserved for special colour stops like the Quintadena or perhaps for the inseparable second ranks backing the Open Diapasons of the case front. In 1518 Sager promised in his contract for St Mary Magdalene, Basle, that 'the stopped pipes shall be bold and sweet [*tapferer und liblich*] so that they are not too puerile [*nit zu kindlich*] but audible throughout the church'.

During the period from 1500 to 1550 Flemish, north German, north French and Spanish organs had much in common. The Netherlanders in particular developed a mature organ of archaic features, described in Vente's *Die Brabanter Orgel* (1958). In 1510, however, the organ of the Upper Rhineland may have been the most advanced in Europe, having (in addition to Principal and Mixture stops) wide Flutes, narrow stopped pipes, several reeds and smaller *Brustwerk* chests as at Bozen (1495). As so often, very little real connection between this type of organ and the music supposedly written for it can be demonstrated; it is even difficult to understand the relation between Schlick's own music and the organ he prescribed. The connections seen by many modern writers between a south German organ of about 1520 and the group of south German tablature sources of the same period are only speculative. In fact there was in about 1510 so much international activity between builders that national types are difficult to distinguish.

The early 16th-century organ was full of colour: manual reeds, regals in the Positive departments (*Rückpositiv*, *Brustwerk*), pedal reeds; Gedackt, Quintadena, Rohrflöte stops (Alkmaar, St Laurents, small organ, 1511); Gemshorn and Hohlflöte; Sifflöte, Schwegel $1\frac{1}{3}'$ and other Flute mutations. The last are very significant, often uncertain in documents but usually associated with some special colour effect and even special etymology ('Nasard', 'Larigot'). Tremulants, toy stops and moving statuary, were known by the end of the 15th century. The structural developments were very important, particularly the Netherlands builders' division of the Great organ into two departments (each often with its own manual): Principal chorus and trumpets on the *Hauptwerk*, or main manual, and Flutes, Gedackts and mutations on the *Oberwerk*, or upper chest. This separation ensured good wind supply, greater freedom of registration, safer chest construction and better acoustical dispersal from shallower cases. The *Oberwerk* was to influence, even create, the special potential in the next century of the north German *Werkprinzip* organ, in which each 'department', or *Werk* (i.e. a keyboard with its chest or chests) had a separate structure. Some examples typifying the schemes of about 1550 at their best, organs to which the previous developments were leading, are given in Tables 7–10.

In the Iberian Peninsula, organs were generally built by Italians (e.g. Évora Cathedral, 1562) or Netherlanders (El Escorial, *c*1580); there were scarcely distinct Iberian characteristics. Yet Évora had more Mixtures than an Italian organ, and El Escorial had its secondary manual in the form of an internal *Positive* rather than a Dutch-Flemish *Rückpositiv*. In England organs appear to have remained single-manual instruments until the late 16th or early 17th century, although some of

TABLE 7

The Netherlands (Oude Kerk, Amsterdam)
Hendrik and Herman Niehoff, with Hans Suys 'von Köln', 1539–42

Das Prinzipal (Hauptwerk)		Oberwerk	
Probably *FG A–g″a″*		*C–a″* (? no *g♯″*)	
Prinzipal	16	Two chests	
Oktave	8 + 4	Prinzipal	8
Mixtur		Holpijp	8
Scharf		Offenflöte	4
		Quintadena	8 or 4
Rückpositiv		Gemshorn	2
F–a″ (? no *g♯″*)		Sifflöte	1 or 1⅓
Two chests		Terzzimbel (?)	
Prinzipal	8	Trompete	8
Oktave	4	Zinck	(? 8 treble)
Mixtur			
Scharf			
(these four to make the Prinzipal)		*Pedal*	
Quintadena	8	*F–d′* could be coupled to	
Holpijp	4	*F′* of the *Hauptwerk*	
Krummhorn (?)	8	*C–d′* for own stops	
Regal	8	Nachthorn	2
Baarpijp (regal)	8	Trompete	8
Schalmei	4		

Pedal stops placed on *Hauptwerk* chest
Keyboards not aligned: *Oberwerk* above *Rückpositiv*, *Hauptwerk* probably a 4th to the left or 5th to the right
Six bellows (probably single-fold)
Wind pressure: *c*90 mm
Couplers: ? *Rückpositiv* to *Hauptwerk*; *Rückpositiv* to *Oberwerk*
Tremulant (? in the main trunk)
All chests probably spring-chests
Alterations in 1544: *Hauptwerk* made 'stronger'; *Oberwerk* Quintadena replaced by a Nasard; *Rückpositiv* Krummhorn replaced by Sifflöte 1⅓
Holpijp stops were probably Chimney Flutes

ORGAN

TABLE 8

Central Europe (Hofkirche, Innsbruck)
G. Ebert, 1555–61

(Hauptwerk)		*Rückpositiv*	
CDEFGA–g″a″		FGA–g″a″	
Prinzipal	8	Prinzipal	4
Gedackt	8	Gedackt	4
Oktave	4	Mixtur	
Quinte	2⅔	Hörnlein	
Superoktave	2	Zimbel	
Hörnlein	II	Tremulant	
Hintersatz	X		
Zimbel	II		
Trompete	8		
Regal			

Pedal
(activating second row of pallets in *Hauptwerk* chest; ? 16th century)

Seven or eight bellows in original organ
Pitch: $a' = 445$
Rückpositiv chest under organ stool
Suspended action (keys hanging from trackers)
Tremulant undulations decrease as larger pipes played (*tremblant doux*)
Rückpositiv rollerboard original (*Hauptwerk* new)

TABLE 9

Italy (S Giuseppe, Brescia)
Graziadio Antegnati, 1581

One manual (C′D′F′G′A′–g″a″, 53 notes)

Principale	8 (halved) (16′ from C)
Ottava	4 (8′ from C)
Quintadecima	2 (etc)
Decimanona	1⅓
Vigesimaseconda	1
Vigesimasesta	⅔
Vigesimanona	½
Trigesimaterza	⅓
Trigesimasesta	¼
Flauto in ottava	4
Flauto in duodecima	2⅔
Flauto in quintadecima	2
Fiffaro	8 (treble)

Pedal pulldowns, original compass uncertain
Originally spring-chest
Wind pressure: *c*42 mm
Pitch: about one semitone above $a' = 440$

these, particularly in large monastic foundations, may have reached a fairly good size before the Reformation. While early 17th-century English organs had the Italianate characteristic of single, individually available ranks at unison and quint pitches, early 16th-century organs were more Flemish in style and appear to have had the partially divided *blockwerk* scheme of north-west continental organs of about 1500. Wooden pipes, and even organs with wooden pipes only, were known in the 16th century, but there is no evidence of reed pipes having been incorporated into large church organs until the late 17th century, although small regals containing both reed (short-length) and flue pipes were much in evidence and are described in some detail in an inventory of Henry VIII's household furnishings (see §5 below). Early in the 16th century the English organ acquired a slightly larger key compass than the organs of northern Europe, an advantage it held into the 18th century. The double organ with Great and Chair (*Rückpositiv*) division appeared very early in the 17th century, and inspired the writing of a type of voluntary in which solo passages were played by the left hand on the Great against an accompaniment on the Chair, both hands usually going to the Great in the final section.

As the 16th-century Italian organs in Innsbruck and Brescia still exist, various subjective descriptions of their tone have been made. At Brescia (see Table 9) the average to narrow scalings (apparently untransposed) and the low pressure give a mild tone, round, rich and singing. Low pressure may also explain the absence of reed stops in such organs, or vice versa. The downward compass of Italian organs varied with the size of the church: the larger the church, the lower the compass. The top note was almost always a'', the bottom c, G or F (positives), C, G', F', or even C' (full-sized organs). The organ at S Petronio, Bologna, went to A' or G' at 16' pitch (i.e. into the 32' octave). When pedal-boards were added later to such organs, they were thought of as mechanical conveniences for pulling down the bass keys. As for the pipework, only open metal pipes were included. The ranks of the separated high stops break back no higher than the pipe sounding $c\sharp''''''$; i.e. the top treble of the compass has an accumulation of ranks usually no higher than Principale 2', resulting in a kind of circumscribed *Blockwerk*. The lower ranks are often divided between b and c'. Musically, such organs had a distinct function and character. Costanzo Antegnati's rules for registration (1608) show timbre, musical style and liturgical function to have been effectively combined; for example, the ripieno or tutti for sustained music of the *durezze e ligature* styles was applied to such pieces as toccatas at the end of the 'Deo gratias'. Flute stops of all pitches were 'da concerto' (i.e. 'for solo

ORGAN

TABLE 10

France (St Gervais and St Protais, Gisors)
N. Barbier, 1580

Grand orgue		Positif	
Montre (tin)★	16	Bourdon (lowest octave of wood)	8
Montre (lead)★	8	?Prestant (lead)	4
Bourdon (lead)★	8	?Doublette (lead)	2
Prestant (tin)★	4	Petite Quinte (tin)	$1\frac{1}{3}$
Flûte (lead)★	4	Cymbale (tin)	II
Nasard (lead)★	II	Cromorne	8
Doublette (tin)★	2		
Sifflet (lead)			
Fourniture (tin)★	IV	Pédale	
Cymbale (tin)★	III	Jeu de pédale (wood)	8
Quinte-flûte (lead)	?$1\frac{1}{3}$	Sacquebouttes (tin)★★	8 (from F')
Cornet (from c')	V		
Trompette	8		
Clairon	4		
Voix humaine			

Compass $C–c'''$ (48 notes)
Positif inside main case (the 4′ rank may have been a stopped 4′ Bourdon)
Tremulant (? in main trunk)
Coupler: Positif to Grand orgue
Pedal reed on two chests either side of the Grande orgue
Grand orgue spring-chest
Four bellows (5′ × 2′, Flemish foot)
Grand orgue Quinte-flûte à biberon, i.e. Chimney Flute with domed cap
1618: Chair organ added by C. Carlier
Principals and reeds, tin bodies with lead feet

★servant pour le Plein jeu
★★possibly 16′

use'), not for accompanying motets or filling out the ripieno. The undulating Fiffaro was drawn with the Principale alone and played slow music 'as smoothly and legato as possible', often with melodic snatches in the right hand (cf Frescobaldi's toccatas). Some useful combinations were those shown in Table 11. At the same time, as Diruta showed, some keys (i.e. ecclesiastical tones) were associated with particular moods and hence particular registrations. He recommended 16′ with Flauto 8′ for the mournfulness of E minor (Phrygian); but for D minor (Dorian, full and grave) he added as alternative suggestions 16.8 and 16.16. For F major (Lydian, moderately gay) he recommended 8.4 with Flauto 4; but for G major (Mixolydian, mild and lively), 8.4.2. Equally important is that three is the largest number of stops drawn in many such lists of registrations, apart from the various big ripieni used only once or twice in a service. It is never certain how far or wide such rules apply, but much Italian music of about 1620 can be seen in terms of the older Antegnati organ, more modest though the organs of Rome, Naples and elsewhere seem to have been. The greatest developments in Italian organ building between 1475 and 1575 were rather in the design of the cases (Gothic to Renaissance; see fig. 35, p. 90) than in the technical or musical sphere, where there is an unusual conformity.

The Innsbruck organ (see Table 8 and fig. 36, p. 91) is very strong in tone, neither manual proving useful for accompanying a choir. The cases are shallow (*Rückpositiv* less than 50 cm), the chests spacious, the organs contained in resonant wooden boxes. Since all the Chair organ stops have close equivalents in the Great organ, yet at only 4′ pitch (as so often during the 16th century and late 15th), the two manuals can be regarded partly as extensions of each other in different directions. Indeed, the Innsbruck organ puts in a new light the perennial question of the purpose of second manuals (a question rarely admitting of any obvious answer, despite common assumptions). The stopped pipes at Innsbruck are very strong in tone, with a big mouth and a tone-colour ranging from wide, vague flute sound in the bass to strong, breathy treble colour. The two Hörnli stops are very keen, repeating Terzzimbeln. Throughout the organ there is a distinct change of tone from bass to treble, enabling the *Hauptwerk* bass keys to produce a different quality of sound from right-hand solo lines in the treble.

The Amsterdam organ (see Table 7) was that known to Sweelinck and shows the 'Brabant organ' at its most characteristic: big Principal chorus, large flute stops on an *Oberwerk* chest, smaller stops but yet greater variety in the Chair organ, and the pedals playing the *Hauptwerk* chorus for plenum registrations, and also a pair of high-pitched, strong-toned solo stops for (presumably) cantus firmus music. The

TABLE 11

Ottava 8′ + Flauto 8′, good for quick passages and canzonas
Principale + Flauto in duodecima, good for quick passages and canzonas
Principale + Flauto in quintadecima, good for quick passages
Pedal pipes, good for occasional long note in a toccata

Ripieno: $16.8.4.2\frac{2}{3}.2.1\frac{1}{3}.1.\frac{2}{3}$

Mezzo ripieno: $8.4.1.\frac{2}{3}$ with Flauto in ottava
               or 8.4 with Flauto in ottava
               or 8.4 with Flauto in duodecima
Use half-stops 'per far dialoghi'

35. *Ss Annunziata, Florence, showing the southern organ of a pair built in 1523 and facing each other across the east end of the nave*

36. Organ by Jörg Ebert (1551–61) in the Hofkirche, Innsbruck: the Annunciation scene on the shutters was typical of 16th-century Venetian organs, while the flat Rückpositiv, designed as a small version of the main case, was unfamiliar outside southern Germany

sheer variety in the manuals alone would have encouraged variations on psalm tunes and folk melodies over the next century or so, even had there been no tradition of weekday organ recitals occasioned by the prohibition of the use of the organ in the Reformed liturgy until early in the 17th century. From surviving examples of Niehoff pipework, it seems that the inner parts were of thick, hammered lead of good quality; the Principals were narrow in the bass, round in the treble; and the whole had a mild-voiced, singing quality quite different from the Baroque organ. Flutes were wide to very wide; reeds penetrating, particularly in the bass. The spring-chests were considered an advance on the slider-chests already known for smaller organs (Alkmaar small organ, extant slider-chest of 1511) and for the Chair organs of larger instruments; and in some areas (north Italy, Westphalia) spring-chests of different types remained popular for well-spaced, large-scaled organs. The Amsterdam organ was evidently of a very high class, and its concept and musical repertory were known in Brabant, the Netherlands, Cologne, Würzburg, Lüneburg and much farther east. Some examples had big pedals, resulting during the period 1575–1600 in an

37. *Regal: woodcut from Praetorius's 'Syntagma musicum' (2/1619)*

organ type known from Groningen to Danzig, Frederiksborg to Prague, and passed on by a group of composers directly or indirectly under Sweelinck's influence.

The musical position of the organ at Gisors (see Table 10) is less certain, as indeed is that of all French organs before about 1660. The French organ of 1520–75 often had a wide array of colour, whether of the Bordeaux–Italian type in the south, or the southern Flemish variety of reeds and compound stops in the north. Reeds of 16', 8' and 4' could be expected in a larger organ of about 1575; so could one or more Quint mutations; 8', 4' and possibly 16' ranks of stopped (often wooden) pipes; a few 'obsolescent' stops like the 1' Principal; and even a mounted Cornet, often called 'Flemish horn' (see Appendix Two, 'Cornet'). In many respects the Gisors organ was Flemish: the *Positiv* construction (in French instruments the Chair organ had become temporarily uncommon), the spring-chests, the *CD–c'''* compass, the Quint flutes of 1⅓', the 8' pedal stops, and the *grand ravalement* for the pedal reed. In sound, no doubt the instrument was nearer to the Netherlands organs of Niehoff than to the late classical French organs of F.-H. Clicquot.

5. THE REGAL

The regal is a kind of small organ in which the sound is produced by one or more sets of beating reeds provided with fractional-length resonators of wood, metal, or even varnished paper, and in many cases no resonator at all. It usually has direct-pin action. With this action the key depresses a short rod below the finger-end, which in turn presses down and opens the pallet; the bellows are usually placed on the same level as the keyboard, at the other side of the row of reeds or, in larger instruments, in a detachable stand below. Thus the whole instrument at its simplest has a depth of several centimetres (for this reason the larger regals are placed on a table when they are played) and a horizontal section that is either rectangular (in which case the keyboard is on one of the shorter sides) or square (see fig. 37).

The term regal is also applied to a group of organ stops in a larger flue-pipe organ, built on the same principles as reed stops (but lacking their longer resonators) and around 1600 often provided with a prefixed name describing their sound or construction (*Apfelregal, Rackettregal* etc). (See Appendix Two.)

ORGAN

(i) History

The terminology, etymology and origin of the regal are equally uncertain, and likely to remain so. As with 'virginals' and *orgues* the
plural is the more traditional form of the name. English versions given
in such sources as church contracts are 'regalles' (1537), 'regalls' (1538),
'reygaals', 'regols' (1554, 1556) and 'regal' (1676); French stop names
include 'ung jeulx de regalles' (Bordeaux, 1531), 'régalle pour servir de
voix humaine' (St Gervais et St Protais, Gisors, 1580) and 'regales ou
voix humaine' (Mersenne, *Harmonie universelle*, 1636–7); German instrument names were *Regale* (Virdung, *Musica getutscht*, 1511), *Regahll*
(Praetorius, *Syntagma musicum*, ii, 2/1619), *Rigal, Rygal* (16th century).
However, the first post-classical reference to organ reeds, Arnaut de
Zwolle's manuscript of about 1450 (Bibliothèque Nationale, Paris, lat.
7295), uses instead *l'anche*; the word regal does not appear in England
until at least around 1500; and some later Italian sources call the regal
organi di pivette (1565). For the more general name 'regal' many explanations have been offered. Praetorius said some people thought the
instrument so named because it could serve as a royal gift; more recent
authors have related it to *rega* (a 'row' of reeds, cf *Reihe*), to *rigole* (late
French term for the reed-pipe shallot), to *rigols/régale* (for Grassineau
a kind of xylophone or row of wooden strips, hence *régale à bois*), to
rigabello (obscure term in one 16th-century source), to *regula* ('regulating' the pitch of the singers, cf *regolo*).

Already by 1511 (Schlick, *Spiegel der Orgelmacher*; and Virdung)
there was a clear distinction in central Europe between reed stops with
long resonators, organ stops of the *regall oder super regall* kind (8' and
4', Schlick), and the independent keyboard instrument called regal or
Regal. But it is noticeable that the Flemish and Netherlands organ
builders who were most inventive in creating reed and regal stops
around 1510 found more picturesque names than simply 'regal' – e.g.
the *moesele* ('bagpipes'), *queenkens* ('old woman's voice') and *hom-
melkens* (possibly a Zink stop) at Notre Dame in Antwerp (1505). Such
names as Vox humana arose as descriptive adjectives for the organ stop
regal (or *reael* at St Sulpitius, Diest, 1530), as seen in the phrase above
from the Gisors stop-list. As far as the organ stop is concerned, both the
name 'regal' and its sound are neutral until for the one a prefix and for
the other an adequate coupled-system resonator are supplied, as they
both were during the 16th century.

As instruments, regals also underwent certain development. In England from about 1540 a 'payre of Regalls' was a standard term, while
'Double Regals' almost certainly indicated a compass below *G*; the
two phrases are very likely related. In various royal inventories (e.g.

Henry VIII's of 1547) it is clear that makers had begun to add other, presumably small-scaled flue stops to the regal rank or ranks, such as 'one Stoppe of pipes of woode' and 'a Cimball' (high metal Mixture); a set of spinet or virginal strings (8' or 4') might also be added, the whole making an instrument still easy to carry. The regal illustrated by Praetorius may be considered the standard simple type, but clearly the small boxed section holding the reeds would be enlarged if fuller resonators were added. Several German engravings of the 16th century show such resonators as already very fanciful in shape though still rather drastically mitred in scale, i.e. the bass pipes were very short in relation to the treble; also, the resonator, whatever its shape, was basically a half-stopped pipe. The completely open, inverted conical resonator (often of a hard metal such as copper) was a recognized type of regal, the so-called *Trichterregal*; but most ingenuity was to be found in the little cylindrical or square-section stopped or half-stopped regal, right through from 1500 to 1750, and across Europe from Seville to Königsberg. Praetorius noted that Austrian builders were distinguished regal makers, and mentioned others in Augsburg, Nuremberg and Regensburg, as well as an unnamed maker who, to Praetorius's scepticism, claimed to be able to make a regal that would stay in tune.

It was a Nuremberg maker, G. Voll, who was said to have made the first 'Bible regal' towards the end of the 16th century, that is a regal whose pair of bellows are shaped like two halves of a book, the whole folding up to resemble a large closed bible. However, such inventors were seldom isolated. Praetorius also credited another Nuremberg maker in the late 15th century with inventing a stop that was 'said to sound like a Schalmey' (a regal or reed stop, or a flue Rauschpfeife) but which in fact must have been known by many makers before 1500.

(ii) Usage

In large organs regal ranks served to give varieties of tone-colour, especially in the manual and pedal *Brustwerk* departments. The latter were in many instances before about 1650 nothing more than a kind of regal instrument incorporated in a church organ. The regal instrument in its own right was used in many ways. By 1713 Mattheson (*Das neu-eröffnete Orchestre*) thought it 'extremely disgusting' as a sound ('höchst eckelhafft') and recommended the use of other keyboard instruments for continuo in church; but his remarks make it clear that it was still in use in Hamburg churches. Earlier it had been useful to the writers of *intermedii* in Florence (c1589) and the music at English guild feasts (Parish Clerks, 1522), pageant plays (Coventry, 1550s) and drama (mourning song in Edwards's *Damon & Pythias*, 1565). It was used in early opera and its later imitations (Monteverdi's *Orfeo*, 1607, to accompany Charon; Cesti's *Il pomo d'oro*, 1666–7, for the infernal scene) when expense was not spared, in princely chapels with *cori spezzati* groups of instruments for motets (Praetorius, Schütz) or Passions (Selle, *Johannespassion*, 1643), where organ might be used for the chorus, regal for the soloists, or organ for accompanying brass instruments, harpsichord for strings, regal for cornets and oboes, etc.

The regal was probably used in Germany longer than anywhere else, and Praetorius (2/1619, pp.72ff) showed that it was used there for continuo (for which it was better than a harpsichord because more sustained in tone, and could play loud or soft depending on whether the cover above the reeds was open or not), in princely convivial assembly, in large and small churches ('almost better than a positive organ') and portable enough to be taken from one to the other (hence requiring care if taken from a cold church to a warm dining-room).

In England 'tuner of the regalls' was one of the titles in the court appointments until at least 1767, but it is doubtful if it kept its literal meaning beyond the Restoration. To James Talbot (Christ Church, Oxford, MS Music 1187, *c*1695) the name was puzzling. He applied it both to full-length reed stops in general and to a little 4′ Vox humana stop, but not to a self-contained keyboard instrument. Many of the major theorists around 1700 (North, Muffat, Saint-Lambert) and even a century earlier (Banchieri, Agazzari) mentioned it as a continuo instrument rarely if at all. Praetorius seems to have preferred the soft sound of the stopped, sweet Dolcian-like regal (*regale dolce* in Munich *intermedii*, 1568); and it is certainly the coarser sound of regals with short, open copper-alloy resonators that helped to make the instrument lose its popularity, even in central and north Germany.

6. STRUCTURAL DEVELOPMENTS ABOUT 1600

From the many enormous and apparently amorphous organ specifications given by Praetorius it could be reasonably thought that many central German builders of the late 16th century did not have clear control of the organs that their technology enabled them to build. The number of stops and stop types listed by Praetorius is evidence of his attempt to give order to a somewhat embarrassing luxury of choice. The number of 4′ solo Flutes alone, for instance – narrow, wide, open, stopped, chimney, spindle, narrow-stopped, narrow-conical and overblowing–narrow-stopped – contrasts strongly with the systematized French classical organ of average size, where there was probably only one plain Stopped Diapason 4', and that with a very specific function. Some of the biggest organs, such as those in Prague and Danzig, are scarcely credible: Prague Týn Church appears to have had a four-manual, 70-stop organ built between 1556 and 1588, but it is likely that it was a conglomerate instrument, finished in part, no doubt, but never all playable or ready at once.

More important was the potential opened up by new mechanical skill in disposing multiple chests – giving the Pedal, for example, a pair of back or side chests for the large pipes, using front chests for middle Principals and a *Brustwerk* chest or two for smaller-scaled solo stops. Each pedal key then connected with two or even three pallets. The first such 'multiple action' may have been built earlier in the century in the central Netherlands (Antwerp Cathedral, 1505; St Zwysen, Diest, 1523), but the evidence is inconclusive. Certainly by the end of the century extravagant court chapel organs were built with some of the richest mechanical layouts ever known before pneumatic action, allowing an immense array of stop combinations. If the simple organ of 1563 for the Dresden court chapel allowed 77 manual combinations with its 13 stops and Tremulant, as stated in a contemporary document, then hundreds were no doubt possible on the famous Groningen court chapel organ of 1592–6 (see Table 12, p. 98). Whether there was enough fish for all this sauce might have been doubted by Schlick.

Clearly the Groningen organ offered many colourful effects, particularly those of two or three stops only; indeed, the number of stops normally drawn at once by organists of that time cannot be assumed from modern practices. With the exception of three Principal choruses of four or five stops, the registrations at Dresden (referred to above) were all of three stops or less. Quite apart from what this fact might imply about the state of contemporary wind-raising techniques, it suggests that organs of the period were geared towards subtle colour and musical variety, at least in smaller churches or those with good vocal or instrumental traditions. As to the 'multiple chests' themselves, a very plausible attempt to describe their complex action, double pallets, transmission and extension system has been made by Bunjes (1966). The most useful arrangement was the most traditional and long-lived, namely the multiple pedal division in which the biggest bass pipes would take one or two chests, and the cantus firmus and other high stops another chest. Wind could be prevented by a *Sperrventil* from entering any chest not immediately needed; and a low

ORGAN

TABLE 12

Groningen court chapel organ
Details from M. Praetorius: *Syntagma musicum*, ii (Wolfenbüttel, 1618, 2/1619/R1958 and 1980), 188f
Case extant (since 1770 in Halberstadt Martinskirche)
David Beck, 1592–6

Im Oberwerck Manual

Principal	8
Zimbeldoppelt	
Gross Querflöit	8
Mixtur	(?)8
Nachthorn	4
Holflöiten	8
Klein Querflöite	4
Quinta	$5\frac{1}{3}$
Octava	4
Grobgedact	8
Gemsshorn	8
Gross Quintadehna	16

Im Pedal auff der Oberlade
(Pedal stops on upper chest)

Untersatz	16
Octaven Bass	8
Quintadeen Bass	16
Klein Octaven Bass	4
Klein Quintadeen Bass	4
Rauschquinten Bass	
Holflöiten Bass	2
Holquinten Bass	
Nachthorn Bass	4
Mixtur	

Fornen in der Brust zum Manual
(*Brustwerk* keyboard)

Klein Gedact	2
Klein Octava	1
Klein Mixtur	2
Zimbeldoppelt	
Rancket	8
Regal	8
Zimbel Regal	2

Im Rückpositiff

Principal	4
Gemmsshorn	4
Quintadehn	8
Spitzflöite	2
Gedact	4
Octava	2
Quinta	$1\frac{1}{3}$
Subflöite	1
Mixtur	(?)4
Zimbel	$2\frac{2}{3}$
Sordunen	16
Trommet	8
Krumbhorn	8
Klein Regal	4

In den beyden Seit Thörmen zum Pedal
(Pedal stops in the large side towers)

Gross Principal Bass	16
Gross Gemsshorn Bass	16
Gross Querflöiten Bass	8
Gemsshorn Bass	8
Kleingedact Bass	4
Quintflöiten Bass	$5\frac{1}{3}$
Sordunen Bass	16
Posaunen Bass	16
Trommeten Bass	8
Schallmeyen Bass	4

In der Brust auff beyden Seiten zum Pedal
(Pedal stops on small *Brustwerk* side chests)

Quintflöiten Bass	$10\frac{2}{3}$ (sic)
Bawrflöiten Bass	4
Zimbel Bass	$2\frac{2}{3}$
Rancket Bass	8
Krumbhorn Bass	8
Klein Regal Bass	4

pressure could be the better sustained if no chest were above a certain size.

A circumspect reading of Praetorius reveals three main types of complex layout, two of them multiple-action: (i) the double action enabling two or more chests to be played by one keyboard (e.g. *Brustwerk* and *Oberwerk* from *Oberwerk* keys only); (ii) the transmission chest (with two pallets), enabling one or more ranks of pipes to be played by two keyboards (usually the bigger stops of the *Oberwerk* played by pedal keys); (iii) octave and even quint transmission or 'extension', i.e. a chest construction enabling a rank of pipes to be played at unison, quint or octave pitches. The third was very rare, but important in view of later developments. Since couplers were also much to the fore in organs using complex action, and since the *Sperrventil* increased the registration possibilities (by making drawn stops inoperative until required), it can be seen that an important musical aim was maximum variety for a given number of ranks. But such aids had the potentially bad effect of overemphasizing the main *Oberwerk* chest to the detriment of true secondary manuals, weakening the independence of the pedal, and encouraging the cultivation of intricate workmanship as an end in itself. But the Chair organ remained an independent department in the major organs, and as such helped to provide the right conditions for most idiomatic organ music of 17th-century Germany, as it also did in France, the Netherlands, Scandinavia and England.

7. THE *WERKPRINZIP* ORGAN

The Chair organ was indeed the manual that supplied the true balanced chorus to the Great; but in areas or periods in which second manuals were required for simple echo effects or soft background colours (Spain and Italy during the whole period, France during the 16th century, England after 1700) or in smaller churches where expense had to be avoided, the Chair organ was dispensed with and smaller chests were incorporated in the main case.

The visual characteristics of the *Werkprinzip* organ (the term is a modern one, coined by the 20th-century reformers) – the single main case, the Chair organ, the separate pedal towers – were all known by the end of the 14th century. But by the time of Praetorius, owing to the range of available organ colour and the widespread mechanical skill in making good actions, builders were able to develop a type of

99

instrument using such features put to new, unified purpose. Scheidt's remarks in his *Tabulatura nova* (1624) imply a sophisticated and codified practice for organs and their music, and show the instrument to have developed well along the lines laid down by Schlick and beyond recognition of those laid down by Arnaut. Indeed, it is a mistake to relate the *Werkprinzip* Chair organ and (even more so) its pedal towers to the organ of Arnaut's period. It is often very uncertain whether in about 1450 the Chair organ of a large instrument had the same pitch as the Great or its keys aligned with it; nor was two-manual playing necessarily known outside Schlick's area and period. Similarly, although side towers or Trompes held bass pipes, they were not necessarily played by pedal keys; in any case, a vital function of *Werkprinzip* pedal towers is that they contain cantus firmus solo stops near to the Protestant congregation situated in or below the gallery. No doubt the larger instruments of about 1550 might have had pedal towers combining both characteristics; but the *Werkprinzip* organ flourished many hundreds of kilometres north-east of the areas knowing the old Trompes.

One of the attractions of the *Werkprinzip* was that an organ could be altered and its potential enlarged simply by adding a new department to the old. While the famous Totentanz organ of Lübeck (destroyed in 1942) is much less understood than modern references to it suggest, it is certain that its four departments expressed the ideals of four quite different periods: the Great organ, the late 15th century; the Chair organ, the mid-16th century; the *Brustwerk*, the early 17th; and the completed pedal organ, the mid-18th. Many famous organs of this type in northern Europe (e.g. Jakobikirche, Lübeck; Johanniskirche, Lüneburg) are in fact composite instruments (quite apart from modern rebuilds), accumulations of *Werke* constantly altered in compass, specification, tuning and no doubt voicing by builder after builder. The big organs of the Neihoffs, the Scherers, and the Compenius and Fritzsche families were like living organisms; except for the large chamber organ in the chapel of Frederiksborg Castle, Denmark, none remains in anything like its original state.

Organ historians are often tempted to trace the organ's evolution in terms of the best-known builders. Frequently, however, contributions are attributed to a builder on the basis of mere conjecture or even fable. Probably not a single item in the list of innovations commonly attributed to Gottfried Fritzsche, for instance, is specifically his: inclusion of a fourth manual; more systematic use of 32′ and 16′ reeds to written *C*; introduction to north Germany of rare stops, both flue (Viol, Schwiegel, imitative flutes) and reed (Sordun, Ranket); contrast

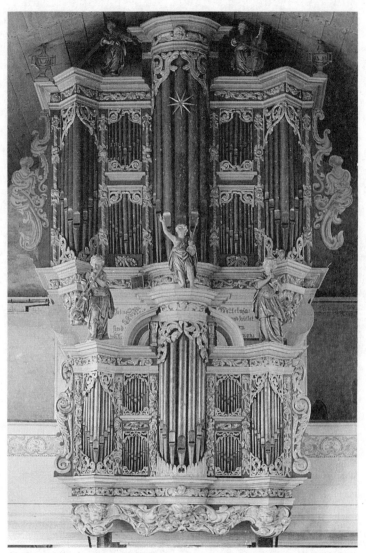

38. Organ by Arp Schnitger (1695), originally in the Johanniskirche, Hamburg, now in the west-end gallery of the village church at Cappel

ORGAN

TABLE 13

Nikolaikirche, Hamburg
Arp Schnitger, 1682–7

Hauptwerk

Prinzipal	16 (case)
Quintadena	16
Rohrflöte	16
Oktave	8
Spitzflöte	8
Salizional	8
Quinte (? open)	$5\frac{1}{3}$
Oktave	4
Oktave	2
Flachflöte	2
Rauschpfeife	III
Mixtur	VI–X
Scharf	III
Trompete	16

Rückpositiv

Bourdon	16
Prinzipal	8 (case)
Gedackt	8
Quintatön	8
Oktave	4
Blockflöte	4
Querflöte	2
Sifflöte	$1\frac{1}{3}$
Sesquialtera	II
Scharf	VI–IX
Dulzian	16
Trichterregal	8
Schalmei	4

Compass: ? *CD–d'–c'''*
Three Tremulants

Ventil to each chest
Wind pressure: *c*71 mm

Pitch: about $\frac{3}{4}$ tone above *a'* = 440
Couplers unknown

Oberwerk

Weitpfeife	8
Hohlflöte	8
Rohrflöte	8
Quintatön	8
Oktave	4
Spitzflöte	4
Nasat	$2\frac{2}{3}$
Gemshorn	2
Scharf	VI–IX
Zimbel	III
Trompete	8
Krummhorn	8
Vox humana	8
Trompete	4

Brustwerk

Blockflöte	8
Prinzipal	4
Rohrflöte	4
Quinte	$2\frac{2}{3}$
Waldflöte	2
Nasat	$1\frac{1}{3}$
Terzian	II
Scharf	IV–VI
Dulzian	16
Bärpfeife	8

Pedal

Prinzipal	32 (case)
Oktave	16
Sub-Bass	16
Oktave	8
Quinte	$5\frac{1}{3}$
Oktave	4
Nachthorn	4
Rauschpfeife	III
Mixtur	X
Posaune	32
Posaune	16
Dulzian	16
Trompete	8
Krummhorn	8
Trompete	4
Cornett	2

between narrow 'male' and wide 'female' stops (e.g. Nasat $2\frac{2}{3}'$ and Quinte $2\frac{2}{3}'$ on the same manual); reduction of the big Brabant Scharf Mixture to a high repeating two-rank Zimbel; greater use of tin in the pipe metal, and also of wooden pipes (reeds, flues, stopped, open); and systematic adherence to C compass, often with split keys (D♯/E♭ etc). But they certainly belong to his period. Such a list, taken with the provincialisms running through Praetorius's *Syntagma musicum* (2/1619), does lead to a distinct kind of organ. The chief musical characteristics of the *Werkprinzip* thus emerging in a purer form in the North were: the contrast between a full, round *Hauptwerk* and a thin, piercing, more variable *Rückpositiv*; the versatile pedal; and the clarity of the whole in average parish churches of little reverberation. In most cases it was the *Rückpositiv* that was understood to be the 'solo manual'. The idiom was clearly defined for organists, who seem to have been in little need of registration hints either from composers or from builders. (Balanced contrast could easily be achieved between two manuals if the same number of stops was drawn in each.) Explicit and firm registration rules have been formulated only in areas and at periods in which organs were more uniform (e.g. in northern Italy $c1600$, France $c1700$ and England $c1750$).

The Hamburg *Werkprinzip* organ reached maturity and indeed satiation in the work of Arp Schnitger, famous in his day far and wide, the possessor of many privileges, and, with Gottfried Silbermann, the inspiration for the German Organ Reform (*Orgelbewegung*) of the 1920s. Despite work in progress, surprisingly little is certain about Schnitger – how responsible he was for his instruments (his workshop was large and active), what his scaling policy was (scales vary hugely, depending on the church, the pitch, the value of the old pipework he re-used etc), what his pitch and temperament were, why he usually changed small multifold bellows to large single-fold bellows in his rebuilds, why he dropped the *Rückpositiv* in his late work around Berlin, and who designed his cases (see fig. 38). Research has established that his wind pressures varied between 94 mm or higher (the large organs in Hamburg) and 67 mm, an average being about 85 mm (Nikolaikirche, Flensburg). Table 13 gives the stop-list of his first four-manual organ (destroyed in 1842). Such very large organs give a kind of highest common factor of instruments known to such composers as Buxtehude, Lübeck and Bruhns and on which toccatas and chorales of the older composers (Scheidemann, Weckmann, Tunder and others) were still played. In some areas of the Netherlands, north Germany and Scandinavia, such an organ remained the model

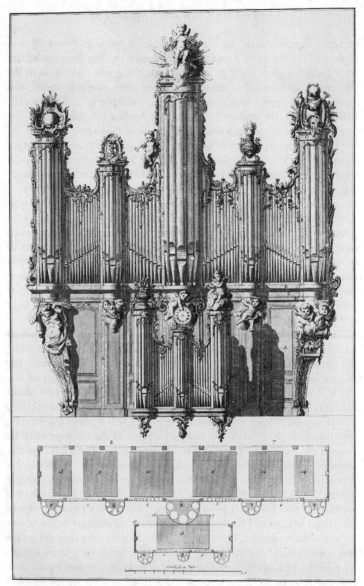

39. Design for a grand organ case: engraving from 'L'art du facteur d'orgues' (1766–78) by Bédos de Celles

until 1850 or so, and the *Werkprinzip* can be recognized behind later organs very different in sound and appearance from the Hamburg Nikolaikirche.

8. THE FRENCH CLASSICAL ORGAN

In northern Italy the 'classical Brescian organ' of the late 16th century remained a norm to which the occasional 17th-century two-manual organ was an exception (and one probably built by a foreign builder); it was only in the mid-17th century that the French organ achieved its classical form, intimately bound up with music of a distinct and well-characterized idiom. The very number of *livres d'orgue* published suggests a remarkably unified 'organ school'. Every stop in a French organ of about 1700 came to have an appointed purpose, and the *livres* from Nivers (1665) to Marchand (*c*1715) and beyond give the impression that late 17th-century Paris had shaken off outside influences past and present.

But Flemish influence had originally been paramount in northern France as Italian had been in parts of southern France. Titelouze's plenum was much the same as that of a Netherlands composer. Even the Cornet was Netherlands, from the time of the organ in Antwerp (1565) onwards. Yet while many details in Mersenne's *Harmonie universelle* may point to northern influences like that of Praetorius, important moves towards the organ of the *livres d'orgue* were made at this period, above all in Paris. Narrow- and wide-scaled Tierces soon became common (narrow at St Nicolas-des-Champs, 1618; wide at St Jacques-de-la-Boucherie, 1631) and with them a general change towards mutation colour (e.g. more $1\frac{3}{5}'$ ranks, fewer 1'). Mersenne knew Tierces as ranks used both in the *plein jeu* and for solo combinations. More important still were the new short-compass keyboards of solo or quasi-solo character: the 25-note Cornet manual (i.e. a *Récit*) at St Séverin, Paris (1610), set a new fashion, though intended at first only as a little keyboard giving the raised Cornet chest a second row of keys. Were the little extra chest to be placed below the *Grand orgue* it would be called *Echo* and probably have a shorter keyboard and more ranks. By 1660 a large organ could be expected to have four manuals (two plus two halves) supplying classical Great–Chair organ contrast and also right-hand solo manuals for music influenced by the monodic *récit dramatique* of the *ballet de cour*.

The organ played by Nicolas Lebègue (see Table 14), one of the organists to Louis XIV, shows the French scheme of the period at its best. Rarely can an organ have been so closely related to the music of its period as such an instrument to the works of Lebègue, Raison, de Grigny, Couperin and others. Standardization was one of the chief aims. To obtain the *plein jeu* for those movements in the Mass that required it (such as the Kyrie), for example, the organist drew the Principals 16', 8', 4', 2', then added the Fourniture, whose composition was almost certainly something like:

C–e	15.19.22.26.29
f–e'	8.12.15.19.22
f'–c'''	1.5.8.12.15

and then finally the Cymbale:

C–B	29.33.36
c–e	26.29.33
f–b	22.26.29
c'–e'	19.22.26
f'–b'	15.19.22
c''–e''	12.15.19
f''–c'''	8.12.15

which, if it was a large four-rank Cymbale, included the 26th as well. Such schemes were formulated by Bédos de Celles at the end of the great period but can be taken as typical; thus, for instance, his specification of 1766 (for the case design, see fig. 39) is almost indistinguishable from that of the 1674 organ at Le Petit Andely. Important points about the French chorus, which also influenced Gottfried Silbermann in Saxony, are that the Cymbale broke back more often than the Fourniture but generally duplicated the Fourniture in the treble; no rank is higher than 2' at c''' (i.e. 28 mm long); and ranks were not duplicated in either Mixture. The *plein jeu* was rarely brilliant, never shrill; it was rather a further 'colour' of the organ.

Pitch, at least from about 1680, was a semitone below $a' = 440$. Pipe metal was hammered, including the lead pipes for flute stops. The keyboards were always pivoted at the end, and the mechanism suspended from the chests above, trackers passing straight to the pallet box ranged vertically above the keys (fig. 40, p. 108). The *Positif* stickers connect with a lever which raises the pallet placed above the channel-end. Such systems were simple, logical and very easy for the player.

To obtain the *grand jeu*, which was used for certain interludes in the Mass such as the exuberant finales to the Kyrie, Gloria, Agnus Dei and offertory, the organist drew a varying combination of reeds, Cornet, Prestant 4' and Tierces. The reeds supplied volume and brilliance; the

TABLE 14

St Louis-des-Invalides, Paris
Alexandre Thierry, 1679–87

Grande orgue CD–c'''		Positif CD–c'''	
Montre	16	Montre	8
Bourdon	16	Bourdon	8
Montre	8	Prestant	4
Bourdon	8	Flûte	4
Prestant	4	Nasard	$2\frac{2}{3}$
Flûte	4	Doublette	2
Grosse Tierce	$3\frac{1}{3}$	Tierce	$1\frac{3}{5}$
Nasard	$2\frac{2}{3}$	Larigot	$1\frac{1}{3}$
Doublette	2	Fourniture	III
Quarte de Nasard	2	Cymbale	II
Tierce	$1\frac{3}{5}$	Cromorne	8
Fourniture	V	Voix humaine	8
Cymbale	IV		
Cornet	V	Pédale	
Trompette	8	A'–f (20 notes)	
Clairon	4	Flûte	8
Voix humaine	8	Trompette	8
Echo c–c'''		Récit c'–c'''	
Bourdon	8	Cornet	V
Flûte	4	Trompette	8
Nasard	$2\frac{2}{3}$		
Quarte	2	Tremulants	
Tierce	$1\frac{3}{5}$	Coupler: *Positif* to *Grande orgue*	
Cymbale	II		
Cromorne	8		

Cornet boosted the thin reed trebles; the Tierces encouraged the overtone level that gave prominence; and the Prestants strengthened the basic tone without taking too much wind or adding obtrusive 8′ flue sound. Fugues were often played on such registrations, and other fugal colours, such as Tierce combinations with Tremulant, give an impression quite different from that of Italian or German fugues of the period 1650–1750. On larger organs, a pair of Trompettes on the *Grand orgue* after about 1750 gave a timbre peculiar to the bass depth and brilliance of French reeds. Late in the period a Trompette was also put on the *Positif*, and after Notre Dame, Paris (organ by Thierry, 1733), Bombarde manuals were also occasionally included – keyboards coupled to the *Grand orgue* and playing the large-scaled Bombarde 16′, perhaps with other large reeds. The chief purpose of this was

40. Cross-section through an 18th-century French organ, showing among other details the multifold bellows, narrow wind-trunk, trackers and rollerboard, pallets from the Grand orgue, side-chest for pedals, and Positif (behind the player): engraving from 'L'art du facteur d'orgues' (1766–78) by Bédos de Celles

to give the ranks their own chest and wind supply, which was often experimentally high by the end of the classical period. Similarly, it was the treble 'boosting' supplied by the Cornet that led eventually to higher pressures and double-length harmonic resonators during the next century. The reed basses, however, remained the chief glory, encouraging composers to write special 'basse de trompette' music from about 1650 onwards. 'De grosse taille' ('of large scale') is a phrase often applied in 17th-century contracts to the Trompette.

Even in *plein jeu* registrations, the French organ was not overdrawn. Only a handful of stops was involved in any of the characteristic French registrations, and all the codified ingenuity – native to the organ of this country, as to so much else – was geared towards clearly marked colours. Thus the texture of a piece marked 'Tierce en taille', one of the most beautiful effects known to organists, would consist of the following elements: (i) left hand on *Positif*, Bourdon 8′ + Prestant 4′ + Doublette 2′ + Nasard + Tierce (perhaps + Larigot), playing a free melody in the middle of the texture, gambalike; (ii) right hand on *Grand orgue*, Bourdons 16′ + 8′ + 4′ ('jeux doux'), playing accompaniment above or around the melody; and (iii) pedal playing the bass line on a Flûte 8′ (or perhaps coupled to *Grand orgue* Bourdon 16′). There was some variety in such registrations: Bédos de Celles, for instance, did not like 16′ manual stops in accompaniments. On the other hand, the Tierces were so characteristic of French organs that many combinations were possible: a right-hand Cornet line on the *Grand orgue*, for instance, could be accompanied in dialogue by a left hand *Jeu de tierce* registration on the *Positif*. From D'Anglebert (1689) onwards, Quatuors and Trios had been played using three different colours including pedal; indeed, the chief purpose of the pedal was 'pour pouvoir jouer les trios' (according to Joyeuse's contract at Auch in 1688) and to play 8′ and 16′ cantus firmus in pieces built on a plainsong. The biggest drain on wind supply and narrow channels must have been the slower, sustained music written for *concert de flûtes* and *fonds d'orgue* registrations, comprising all available Montres, Prestants, open Flûtes and Bourdons. Such sounds became fashionable about 1750; but whatever the combination, no organist in the provinces need have been in doubt about how the Parisian composers expected their pieces to sound.

The splendid French organ at the eve of the Revolution (1789) may well have been far superior to the music written for it, as were the Dutch organ of 1700 and the English organ of 1850; but it is the very decadence of the music that best draws out the extravagant contrasts, brilliant reeds, round flutes, echoes, big choruses and immense colour potential available on such extant late instruments as those at St Maximin-en-Var (J.-E. Isnard, 1773) and Poitiers Cathedral (F.-H. Clicquot, 1787–90). The French organ received a serious setback when the Revolution disrupted life in the cities. It was ripe for development at the very moment when Clicquot's sons became soldiers; but not until St Denis in 1841 did Poitiers have a worthy successor.

9. THE ENGLISH ORGAN

Rimbault thought that the John Roose at work on the organ of York Minster in 1457 was the 'first English organ builder of whom we have any authentic account'. But Roose was possibly not English, for a builder of the name lived in Utrecht during the 16th century and built the organ in the Wasserkirche, Münster, in 1572. The name appears to be High or Low Dutch and pinpoints the likely influences on English organs at the beginning of the period. The Flemish organ taken to Louth in about 1500 is a rare example of such explicit influence, but the unique document concerning the organ at All Hallows, Barking, in 1519 (quoted by Rimbault in 1865 and copied unverified ever since) also seems to suggest a Flemish organ:

> the pryncipale to conteyn the length of v foote, so folowing wt Bassys called Diapason to the same, conteyning length of x foot or more: And to be dowble pryncipalls thoroweout the seid instrument.

This probably means:

> the Chorus [a kind of divided *Blockwerk*, like the Dutch *Principael*] to have several ranks from 5′ C upwards [compass *CDEFGA–g″a″*, perhaps at low pitch, the scribe's foot-stand being now unknown], those inside the organ being of [almost] as good metal as those in the casefront; with a suboctave of wooden pipes [or, with a set of incorporated bass pipes].

It is interesting that Arnaut too wrote of 'double Principals', a phrase in other organ documents of about 1500 taken to mean a pair of open and stopped Diapason ranks; his use of the term 'diapason' was more in the common tradition of Greek terminology but possibly suggested to English builders a useful term for the basic rank 'running through all' the compass. The 1519 'Bassys' may have been Trompes–like bass pipes. Either way, the English terms 'Diapason' and 'stop' were already in use.

It is not known if any English organs before 1600 had separate quint ranks, but the inventories of Henry VIII's instruments mention more than one Cymbale stop of two ranks, presumably including a quint. Whether they were English-built instruments is also unknown, however. By 1550 extreme miserliness already characterized the commissions given for English organs (as it continued to do for the next three centuries), and an English organ of 1600 would most likely have had no more than one keyboard of half a dozen ranks (of large-Positive proportions). It is thus possible that Italian rather than Dutch influences are reflected in the English organ between about 1525 and about 1600. But no known documents give any definite detail of a single organ before 1606 (accounts of King's College, Cambridge), and it is therefore very tempting to make much of the 'small regals' mentioned at St Martin-in-the-Fields in 1561, the putative stop-list of the clock-organ sent to the Sultan of Turkey in 1599, the compass of '27 plain keys' at Coventry in 1526, the 'cimbale' and regals mentioned in the inventories of Henry VIII's instruments (1547), or the French–Flemish elements in extant early 17th-century cases at Tewkesbury, Gloucester (Chaire) and Framlingham.

For Worcester Cathedral in 1613 Thomas Dallam made what was or became a standard English Double organ (see Table 15). At York in 1632 a similar instrument by Dallam had a compass of 51 notes, three bellows and 'drawinge stoppes' (a term analogous to the French *tirants* and lending credence to the supposition, drawn from earlier references, that stops in the previous century were commonly controlled by levers rather than draw-knobs). It is not known whether the 51 notes gave a compass of $CD-d'''e'''$ or $G'A'Bb'B'CDE-c'''$ (or some similar long compass), though the latter is the more likely. Though small, this

TABLE 15

Worcester Cathedral
Thomas Dallam, 1613

Great organ		*Chair organ*	
Open Diapason	8	Diapason of wood (probably	8
Open Diapason	8	stopped)	
Principal	4	Principal	4
Principal	4	Flute of wood	4
Small Principal	2	Small Principal	2
Small Principal	2	Two & Twentieth	1
Recorder (stopped) (perhaps 8)	?4		

Pitch: Open Diapason *C* to be 'of 10 foot long' (i.e. probably sounding Ab at $a' = 440$; but foot-standard uncertain)

Pitch names of stops not specified

type of organ led to a genre of organ music (the double voluntary) and gave good service to choirs placed below (near the screen over which the Chair organ hung); it was quite independent of organs abroad. The nomenclature (Fifteenth, Two & Twentieth etc) and compass, however, were distinctly Italianate. Likewise the use of wooden pipes, sometimes to the exclusion of metal ones (just as in the Italian 'organi de legno' and small quire organs of central Europe). The relationship of the two manuals was also comparable to that found in the occasional two-manual Italian organ (e.g. S Maria in Aracoeli, Rome, 1585–7) and in no way resembled that of the Netherlands or German *Hauptwerk* and *Rückpositiv*.

Larger secular organs like those at Chirk Castle (1631) and Adlington Hall (possibly, but also possibly a post-Restoration organ incorporating older parts) as early as about 1650, would have second manuals contained within the main case and even held on the same chest. More important is the tonal scheme that emerged. Mutations began to appear, and the Adlington Hall Great organ has what seems to be an original specification of $8.8.4.2\frac{2}{3}.2.2.1\frac{3}{5}.1\frac{1}{3}.1.8.8$. All its ranks were single, as at Great Packington 80 years later; it is still far from the scheme prepared by Robert Dallam in 1654 for a Great organ at the Priory of Lesneven, Brittany: $8.V.8.4.4.2\frac{2}{3}.2.2.1\frac{3}{5}.1\frac{1}{3}.1.III.II.8.8.8.4$, which is pure French of the period, complete with Cornet V, two Mixtures, reeds, regals and mutations. By then, Dallam was at work in France, and the Civil War (1642–9) and subsequent Restoration (1660) were to give a change of direction to the English organ.

Though exaggerated by English 18th-century historians, the French influences on the English organ, through Renatus Harris, were very important. Harris was the son of Thomas Dallam's daughter and Thomas Harris (Harrison). In 1686 he replanned (in the new style) his father's organ of 1638 at Magdalen College, Oxford, doing away with the paired ranks of stops which, he pointed out, were difficult to keep in tune and gave little return in increased sound. Therefore the 1638 Great organ of $8.8.4.4.2.2.1.1$ (all open) would be better replanned (1686) as Open 8.Stopped $8.4.2\frac{2}{3}.2.1\frac{3}{5}.II–III$. Soon after 1661 Robert Dallam had put in a scheme for New College, Oxford, that was of particular importance as an indication of new tastes: it was a complete French organ of two manuals and 24 stops, showing a Fourniture breaking back once each octave and a Simbale breaking back twice each octave (see §8 above). But other English builders continued the styles of 1640 after 1660, and the picture is much less clear and detailed than is suggested by most modern writers. It does indeed seem that it was Harris and 'Father' Smith (who built several organs in Hoorn,

Netherlands, had previously worked in Bremen and was probably a north German by birth) who gave impetus to the new directions.

Smith's Chapel Royal organ in Whitehall, described in Table 16, was made between 1662 and 1672. Any north European influences that

TABLE 16

Chapel Royal, Whitehall
'Father' Smith, 1662–72

Great organ $G'A'-c'''$		*Choir organ* $G'A'-c'''$	
Open Diapason	8	Stopped Diapason	8
Stopped Diapason	8	Principal	4
Principal	4	Flute (wood, from $c\sharp'$)	
Block Flute (metal, from $c\sharp'$)		Vox humana	8
Twelfth	$2\frac{2}{3}$	Cremona	8
Fifteenth	2		
Sesquialtera	III	*Echo*	
Cornet (from $c\sharp'$)	III	$ga-c'''$	
Trumpet	8	Open Diapason	8
		Principal	4
		Cornet	II
		Trumpet	8

Account in Leffler's MS (*c*1810), where it is noted that 'the Echo is placed immediately over the Keys – behind the Music Desk – and not as usual enclosed in a box'
Pitch length of the flute stops uncertain (? both 4')
Cornet II '12th & Tierce' = Sesquialtera 12.17
Great organ listed with a wooden Flute; perhaps this should be a 2' Flute for the Choir organ
Compass as given by Leffler
? Tremulant

were felt through Smith's work seem to have been dominated by Harris's French innovations, although Smith obtained the two best-known commissions (the Temple Church, 1683–7, and St Paul's Cathedral, 1694–9). But terminology itself is a poor guide; the Great organ Sesquialtera, for example, may have been originally called something else, a Tierce Mixture of the later Harris type, an English Bass Cornet, or a Dutch or German Mixture of octaves and quints. Certainly the Echo Cornet was, despite its name, a Dutch Sesquialtera; and the first known Mixture by a completely native builder (Thamar for Winchester Cathedral, 1665) was called 'Fourniture'. The picture is therefore confusing, although it is very significant that the first English treatise to deal with the organ (by James Talbot, MS, Christ Church, Oxford, Music 1187, *c*1695) was French-influenced, by Mersenne's writings and Harris's organs.

41. Organn by Richard Bridge (1730) in Christ Church, Spital-
fields, London

Yet curiously little is clear about the Smith–Harris organs; it is not known whether the Choir organ chests were placed in the upper or lower part of the organ; whether the Whitehall Echo was a kind of *Brustwerk*; whether they were French in conception; whether the early Sesquialteras had a Tierce rank; whether the Trumpets were French or Netherlands; or whether the Diapason scalings, voicing, key-action, chest construction, metals and wind pressure were traditional English or French. The absence of real technical information and of properly assembled documents dealing with the English organ at two of its most crucial periods, 1660–90 and 1820–50, means that no adequate history of the English organ can yet be written. The three or four original attempts made since 1850 have necessarily been selective and conjectural.

Some general points are fairly certain, however. Harris was probably born and brought up in Brittany, and Smith was almost certainly of continental birth and lineage; both at any rate had considerable European training. By at least the 1680s even Smith was making French-influenced organs, despite the Holflute, Spitts flute, Cimball, Quinta Dena and Gedackt at the Temple and St Paul's; old-English–Italian influences were still strong enough for builders to dispense with pedals (though perhaps not always pulldowns which, like Tremulants and Couplers, were often not specified in contracts); builders kept to a longer compass than in France and the Netherlands (*F′* at the Temple, *C′* intended at St Paul's); and the largest organ had fewer than 30 stops. Indeed, although Harris enlarged the organ of Salisbury Cathedral by adding a French battery of Mixtures and mutations (on the Great organ a Tierce, Cornet V, Fourniture III, and Cymbale II; on the Positif a Larigot) and noted that the Tierce 'is a Stop of much variety', the instrument was nevertheless still not able to produce the full Parisian effect of *Tierce en taille*; neither were comparable organs in Brittany and Flanders. Much evidence, particularly the extant examples from organs of the later Harris school (*c*1720–50), suggests that the reeds which now could be expected in an average-sized English organ were of French quality, but there seems to have been an opinion among some musicians that both reeds and Mixtures were unnecessary. Of reeds, Roger North wrote in about 1720: 'the basses will always snore, and that defect cannot be conquered, so that in Organs they are rather an incumbrance than useful'; and of Mixtures and mutations, J. Blewitt wrote in about 1790 that they are 'put in by Organ-Builders, merely to make a show of Stops to draw, at a small expense . . . they only encumber an organ'. As for pedals, Harris himself recommended them in his 1712 scheme for St Paul's on the two grounds that the organist would then 'be able to do as much as if he had four hands . . . and therefore Pedals are used in all the great Organs beyond the seas', but no English pedal pipes are known for certain to have existed before the 'six large Trumpet Pipes down to 16 foot tone to be used with a pedal or without' at St Paul's in 1720–21; and then it is clear that they could be played from the Great organ. (The first separate pedal pipes seem to be those of St Catherine-by-the-Tower, 1778.) From 1712, what occupied much more attention was the expressive use made of the box enclosing the little Echo chests in a three- or (as at St Magnus, London Bridge, 1712) four-manual organ. Abraham Jordan, the builder at St Magnus, claimed this Swell organ as an original invention, though similar devices had been applied to solo stops in Spanish organs over the previous half-century or so, and Harris claimed to have tried it out in the Salisbury organ. By 1730 every average new organ had a Swell; by 1825 it was ousting the Choir organ as the chief second manual.

In view of these appallingly limited views on what organs were for, it is surprising that the Harris school was allowed to build an organ so effective as that at St Mary Redcliffe, Bristol, seems to have been (see Table 17). Its pedal pulldowns seem (from the circular published by Harris & Byfield) to have been able to draw the octave above on the Great, i.e. both from 16' (or C') and from 8' (or C); the builders also betrayed an attitude of the period in adding that although pedals had been supplied 'not withstanding the Touch is as good as need be desired'. Clearly the Harris school was competent on the technical side, for in 1725 at St Dionis Backchurch, London, it had even attempted regulation of the wind by fitting springs to the four bellows.

The strength of British insular traditions is also clear in the work of John Snetzler, a German Swiss who worked with the Egedacher firm of Passau and, like many other keyboard makers, went to London early in the 1740s. Certain of Snetzler's techniques, particularly the voicing and actions, may derive from the Egedachers, but again despite the popular accounts remarkably little of importance is known about Snetzler, or even why so many extant chamber organs are ascribed to him. Nevertheless, the English nature of his specifications is clear from written evidence, and only his earliest major organs like that at King's Lynn (1754) show obvious foreign influence (e.g. the manual 16' Bourdon). There is evidence that Snetzler attempted to introduce other up-to-date central European colour stops, such as Viola da Gamba, Salicional, overblowing German Flute, or over-blowing Dulciana; but only the easiest of these, the narrow-scaled, open cylindrical Dulciana, caught the taste of English organists. Such

TABLE 17

St Mary Redcliffe, Bristol
Harris & Byfield, 1726

Great organ			Chair organ		
$C'-d'''$ (63 notes)			$G'-d'''$ (56 notes)		
Open Diapason	8		Stopped Diapason	8	
Open Diapason	8		Principal	4	
Stopped Diapason	8		Flute almain	4	(? or 8', half-
Principal	4				compass)
Twelfth ($G'-d'''$ only)	$2\frac{2}{3}$		Flute	2	(? or 4')
			Sesquialtera	III	
Fifteenth ($G'-d'''$ only)	2		Bassoon	8	
Tierce ($G'-d'''$ only)	$1\frac{3}{5}$		*Swell*		
			$G'-d'''$ (44 notes)		
Sesquialtera	V		Open Diapason	8	
Cornet (from c')	V		Stopped Diapason	8	
Trumpet	8		Principal	4	
Clarion	4		Flute	4	
			Sesquialtera	III	
Pedal			Trumpet	8	
1 octave pulldown			Hautboy	8	
			Cremona	8	
			French Horn ·	8	

Four bellows
Couplers: Great organ to Pedal; Great organ octave to Pedal

Dulcianas soon became necessary on all organs containing more than four stops. Its held-in tone seems indeed to have coloured English organ building in general; at least Snetzler's contemporary Samuel Green was recognized in the best circles of his day as the builder of large organs little superior in tone to chamber organs. That he might lead fashion by enclosing whole organs in Venetian swells such as used by some English harpsichord makers is further condemnation of his ideas.

Snetzler's organ of 1757 in the Savoy Chapel had several foreign features: manual coupler (rare), Tremulant (fairly rare), pedal pulldowns (rare in organs of this size). But these devices remained without much influence. The German Chapel in the Savoy, however, was interesting in one respect: it was a foreign church and as such points to an interesting factor in English organ building over the whole period 1750–1875, namely the 'advanced' ideas put into practice in organs built not for Anglican or established churches but for the chapels of embassies, and later for Methodist churches and those of other evangelical movements. From 1800 to 1875 it was the concert hall and eventually (after about 1835) the town hall that commissioned organs incorporating the most advanced techniques of building or the most cosmopolitan German-inspired stop lists. Such influences were already fairly strong in the late 18th century, partly through the émigré builders like Snetzler, partly through travellers like Burney, partly through touring virtuosos like Abbé Vogler, and not least through the inactivity in the established church itself. The virtues (such as they were) of English organ music in the form of solo-stop voluntaries by John Stanley and his contemporaries were also fast disappearing by 1790. Both the instrument and its repertory were ripe for German and other continental influences early in the next century.

10. THE CHAMBER ORGAN

The term 'Chamber organ' is generally used to denote an organ intended for domestic use. Such instruments, developed from the 16th-century positive, were popular in the 17th, 18th and early 19th centuries in England and were also found throughout the Continent, particularly in Switzerland and the Netherlands, as well as in the USA during the 18th and early 19th centuries.

The typical chamber organ is housed in a compact furniture-quality cabinet, often of hardwood and sometimes elaborately ornamented, of a size suitable to the scale of domestic rooms. It commonly has one manual and no pedals (although an additional manual and/or pedals are sometimes found on later specimens), and is blown by the player's foot. The commonest blowing arrangement consists of a single wedge-shaped feeder below a weighted reservoir, which may be either wedge-shaped or horizontal. Occasionally one finds a two-feeder system, sometimes referred to as 'cuckoo feeders', but still activated by a single pedal, attached to a rocking bar. Double blowing pedals of the reed organ type are occasionally encountered in late continental examples.

Chamber organ action, particularly in earlier examples and in some of Snetzler's smaller instruments, is usually of the 'pin' type (see fig. 6), in which a sticker below the key pushes down directly on the pallet, although many larger and later examples have a more complex action similar to the normal tracker action of a larger organ. The stop action is often of the trundle type, with drawknobs, and one finds many ingenious variations of this made for space-saving reasons, especially

42. *Chamber organ
(English, 17th-century)
possibly made by 'Father'
Smith*

in late Dutch and American examples. In very early (17th-century) instruments, stop control may be by levers.

Chamber organs were often made to resemble other pieces of furniture (fig. 42); that described by Mace (*Musick's Monument*, 1676) was in the form of a large table, around which singers and instrumentalists might sit to perform ensemble music. In the 18th century, chamber organs in the form of bureaux and desks were popular, and Snetzler is known to have made several of these. A desk organ by Adcock & Pether (*c*1760) is in the collection of Colonial Williamsburg, Virginia, and an unusual Avery organ (*c*1800), resembling a sideboard, is in the County Museum, Truro, Cornwall. Dutch chamber organs also sometimes took this form, and a good example is found in the collection of D. A. Flentrop, Zaandam, the Netherlands. The Smithsonian Institution, Washington, DC, owns a bureau organ (*c*1815) by the Boston builder Ebenezer Goodrich.

Stop-lists of chamber organs varied, but a typical early disposition is that of the fine instrument of the Smith school (*c*1670), now in the possession of N. P. Mander, London: Stopt Diapason (8'); Principal (4'); Fifteenth (2'); Mixture (12th–17th, apparently not original). The compass is 49 notes, *C–c'''*. The case is of oak, with speaking front pipes, and doors. Organs of this size often had only dummy front pipes, or a front of carving or cloth. A slightly larger, but also typical, scheme is that of the organ by Snetzler (1761) now in the Smithsonian Institution: Stopt Diapason (8'); Open Diapason (8', treble, from *c'*); Flute (4'); Fifteenth (2'); Sesquialtera (II, 19th–22nd, bottom two octaves); Cornet (II, 12th–17th, from *c'*). Most of the 18th- and 19th-century chamber organs had divided stops and some were entirely divided. Many also had a machine stop to silence all stops above 8' (sometimes 8' and 4') pitch. These two features made the chamber organ surprisingly flexible, permitting both right-hand and left-hand solos as well as echo effects. Some late chamber organs also had swell mechanisms of various sorts, including a simple raised lid over the case, or compact sliding shutters.

11. THE SPANISH BAROQUE ORGAN

The organ of the Iberian peninsula has many special characteristics. Yet Baroque organs of Spain and Portugal differ in detail from area to area, and while the visual parts of such instruments were indigenous and individual, their musical characteristics are founded more securely in common European traditions. In 1500 Spanish organs stood at much the same point as those of northern France, the Netherlands and northern Germany. The influences were Dutch rather than Italian – a Pedro Flamench ('Peter the Fleming') was at work in Barcelona in 1540 – and even the term 'Fleutes' for Principals (a later term was Flautado) was Netherlands. Principals and Mixtures (Mixtura, Forniment, Simbalet) were the stop changes or *mutaciones* available on the new big organs of 1550, although positives were already showing an array of slider-stops, including regals, reeds and wooden flutes. Evidently Dutch builders brought Chimney Flutes and Quintadenas with them, and by the 1550s new large organs of splendid proportions could be expected to have large-scaled reed stops. Often these reeds had colourful names: Trompetas naturals a la tudesca ('German or Dutch trumpet stops with natural-length resonators'), Claríns de mar ('trumpets of the sea', as used for naval signals) or Claríns de galera, molt sonoroses ('gallery trumpets, very sonorous') at Lérida in 1554.

43. Organ with reeds en chamade in the convent of S Maria, Arouca, Portugal

Although none of these was horizontal, the terms are evocative and probably played their part in the evolution of the remarkable Iberian reed stops.

Just as Flemish singers were called to Philip II's court chapel in Madrid, so Flemish organ builders were commissioned (notably the Brebos family), putting into practice their up-to-date ideas at El Escorial. The Brebos organ had a large *Hoofdwerk* of two chests and big flue and reed choruses, as well as flute mutations; the pedal was similarly a large modern department. But the only other manual was a *Brustwerk* (though one of 12 stops), and indeed Chair organs were never to become important in Spanish organ building. Barcelona seems to have been a centre for German builders, but registrations left at S Juan de las Abadesas, Barcelona, in 1613 show the stops to have been used in a traditional or old-fashioned way, and during the 17th century emphasis shifted south and west.

Nobody knows when the first reeds were placed *en chamade*. The term is French and refers to trumpet calls when parleys are summoned (Lat. *clamare*); but placing regals and (a little later) reeds horizontally in the case front was convenient for sound (penetrating in big churches where the organ did not face the congregation), accessibility (for quick tuning), reliability (gathering little dust), economy (replacing cathedral trumpeters) and appearance (see fig. 43). They may date from about 1620, perhaps at first in the South. But the documents rarely specify whether reeds were horizontal or not, just as documents before the end of the 18th century rarely specify whether or not 'Eco' chests or interior Trumpets and Cornets were placed in a Swell box. The fine organ at Alcalá de Henares, for instance, had some specially described reed stops which may well have been horizontal (Juan de Echevarría, *c*1680): Trompetas reales, 'of which there can be three kinds'; Dulzainas; Orlos, resembling 'the guitar and harpsichord' (*zitara y clavicordio*); Trompeta mayor; 'a stop found in few other organs'; Bajoncillos, 'also newly invented'; Voz humanas; and Angeles o Serafines, angel statues blowing trumpets. By 1750 a large organ would have a huge battery of reeds, vertical and horizontal, many kinds of chorus, large Swell departments and even a pedal rank or two. The well-known organ of Granada (fig. 44) can be taken as an example and its stop-list is given in Table 18 (p. 124). No large Spanish organ can be called fully 'typical'. As in Italy during the next century, the larger the organ, the greater the variety of solo stops; the large organ of Toledo (1796), however, shows no advance on the concept of smaller organs built nearly a century earlier.

The only known registration guide of the Spanish Baroque organ,

44. Organ (1745–7) in Granada Cathedral, showing the rear façade of the Epistle
organ, with tiers of dummy pipes or flats, and a single rank of reeds en chamade (8′
treble, 4′ bass); note the low cut-up of the mouths of the large pipes to right and left

ORGAN

TABLE 18

Granada Cathedral
Organ on Epistle side, case dated 1747

Organo grande

(left-hand stops)		(right-hand stops)	
Flautado	16	Flautado	16
Flautado	8	Flautado	8
Flautado	8	Flautado	8
Flautado violón	8	Flautado violón	8
'Quintatön'	8	'Quintatön'	8
Octava	4	Flauta traversa	8
Lleno		Octavo	4
Nasardos	IV	Lleno	
Bombardos	16	Corneta	V
Trompeta	8	Bombardos	16
Trompeta★	8	Trompeta	8
Orlos★	8	Trompeta★	8
Viola★ (regal)	8 (wood)	Orlos★	8
Clarin★	4	Oboe★	8
Clarin★	4	Regalia★	8
Clarin de atras★	4	Clarin de atras★	8 (? 16)
(facing side-aisle)		Clarin★	4
Violeta★ (regal)	2	Trompeta magna★	16

Cadireta (Chair organ)

(left-hand stops)		(right-hand stops)	
Flautado violón	8	Flautado violón	8
Octava	4	Octava	4
Tapadillo	4	Tapadillo	4
Nasardo	2⅔	Flauta	4
Nasardo	2	Lleno	III
Nasardo	1⅓	Corneta	III
Lleno	III	Trompeta magna	8
Trompeta recordata	8	(full-length)	
(short)		Viejos	8
		Clarin (en chamade)	8

Organo expresivo (Swell)

Flautado violón	8	*Pedal*	
Flauta armonica	8	Flautado	16
Trompeta	8	Flautado	8
Oboe	8		
Voz humana	8		

Compass: now $C'-b-c'''$, complete
Some Swell stops and stop names of doubtful origin
★ = horizontal

made at Segovia Cathedral in about 1770, suggests the few staple requirements organists made of these extravagant creations. They comprise French *dialogues* (two-part pieces with mutation stops or reeds in each hand), regal solos (e.g. Dulzaina in either hand), half-stops for each hand on the same manual, echo effects and manual contrasts for two- or three-part music, flutes contrasted with reeds (? in homophonic music), inner vertical reeds with outer horizontal trumpets, cornets and reeds 8', 4' or 8', 2' combined. Because of the halved stops ('medio registro'), the right hand could produce a line lower than that of the left hand, or one very much higher. The 'Swell' is also mentioned, not for swelling but to soften the effect of certain registrations. Pedals are ignored.

Over the whole period, the bellows of the Iberian organ were usually multifold and generally operated by hand. Wind pressure was low (about 50–60mm), though up to 90mm on larger instruments. The chests were always slider-chests, usually divided into bass and treble (i.e. not C and C♯ chests as elsewhere). The division was between *b* and *c'* in Catalonia, between *c'* and *c♯'* elsewhere. As in French organs, the pallets are ranged vertically above the keys and the action is of the suspended type. The chest layout is often very complicated, each group of stops set on quasi-separate chests at different heights, easy to tune and reach, and often some way removed from the pallet. Neither bellows nor trunks and channels allow the families of stops to be combined, but the rigidity of registration enabled builders to include helpful accessories like 'shifting movements' to aid stop-changes. Subsidiary chests like Echo organs are placed on the floor of the main case ('cadireta interior') and operated by a sticker action; if there is a Chair organ, the pallets are below and directly in line with the lower keyboard, and the channels pass below the close-spaced organist's seat. A middle manual may operate pallets of a pair of chests placed in the rear case front of the organ, facing the side aisle. There are no manual couplers. Pedal keys are short, sometimes mushroom-shaped, usually encompassing only a few notes; there may be a rank of eight to ten wooden pipes but most pedals are pulldowns, presumably for *points d'orgue* and cadences. The hinged lid of the Swell box – known for Cornet chests by about 1675 but including reeds by about 1710 – was raised by a pulley and rope operated by a pedal-lever that needed to be kept down if the lid was to remain open.

The scaling of the Principal is often narrow, the tone restrained; Flutes are gentle, and the Cornets expansive but thinner than the French. The quiet Flutes contrast greatly with the reeds, which were designed to fill the spaces of a large Spanish church outside the

45. Organ (1443) in Saragossa Cathedral; the reeds en chamade were added possibly in the 18th century

126

immediate intimacy of the quire or *coro* over which the organ looms. Horizontal reeds and regals encouraged solo music, and Correa de Arauxo's 1626 publication (*Libro de tientos y discursos de música practica, y theorica de organo intitulado Facultad organíca*) shows a matured technique of left- or right-hand solos, a technique not very different in effect from other 17th-century dialogue music such as the English double voluntary. The reeds also played chords, not only for the celebrated *batallas* (battle-pieces) but also for imposing intradas on feast days.

At Saragossa (extant case dated 1443; see fig. 45) Spanish *coro* organs were already placed between pillars. It was probably this position that encouraged large flat façades bearing little resemblance to the inner construction of the organ itself, indeed often giving it the appearance of having more chest levels than it has. Certainly the amount of empty space within a Spanish organ absorbs strong partials in the plenum and helps to produce the mild quality of the flue choruses.

12. THE 18TH-CENTURY ITALIAN ORGAN

The essentials of the Brescian classical organ were established by 1575 at the latest: large, shallow cases (somewhat altar-like in shape, open-spaced above the pipes), with one chest at the level of the case pipes (spring-chest, mortised with well-spaced channels often of equal size), and multifold bellows and low wind pressure. The compass would rise to *a″* or *c‴*, with all but case pipes of leaded metal (thick-walled, Principals relatively narrow in the bass, Flutes wider with smaller mouths) and completely separate ranks (the upper of which break back an octave at regular intervals). The tuning would be some form of mean-tone temperament, but the general pitch level would vary from organ to organ ('come si vuole', as Antegnati remarked), sometimes with an octave or so of pedal pulldowns (short keys sloping up like a reading-desk or 'pedali a leggio'), and occasionally after about 1600 with wooden Pedal Principals. Registration was standar-dized, and each combination suggested to the player a certain modal style to be played at a certain moment of the Mass (e.g. 'Voce umana' for the Elevation) and vice versa.

Italian builders and organists remained faithful to these ideas, modi-fying them gradually but leaving them recognizable even in the large organs of 1850. Yet it could be that historians have overemphasized the Brescian organ, for each city or region had its own version of the

ORGAN

TABLE 19

S Maria Assunta, Candide
Gaetano Callido, 1797–9 (opus 367)

Organo grande $F'-f'''$		Organo piccolo $F'-f'''$	
Principale	8 (halved)	Principale	8 (halved)
Ottava	4	Ottava	4 (halved)
Decimaquinta	2	Decimaquinta	2
Decimanona	$1\frac{1}{3}$	Decimanona	$1\frac{1}{3}$
Vigesimaseconda	1	Vigesimaseconda	1
Vigesimasesta	$\frac{2}{3}$	Voce umana	8 (treble)
Vigesimanona	$\frac{1}{3}$	Flauto	4
Trigesimaterza	$\frac{1}{3}$ (to f only)	Flauto	$2\frac{2}{3}$
Trigesimasesta	$\frac{1}{4}$ (to f only)	Flauto	$1\frac{3}{5}$ (treble)
Voce umana	8 (treble)	Tromboncini	8 (halved)
Flauto in ottava	4 (halved)	Violoncello	8 (halved)
Flauto in duo- decima	$2\frac{2}{3}$ (halved)	*Pedal*	
Cornetto	$1\frac{3}{5}$ (treble)	$CDEFGA-b\flat$	
Violetta	4 (treble)	Contrabassi	16
Tromboncini	8 (halved)	Ottava	8
		Ottava	4
Tamburo (drum stop)		Tromboni (reed)	?8

Halved stops divided at $a \,/\, b\flat$
Second manual chest to left of keyboards

---

general plan. Certainly a Flemish builder Vincenzo Fulgenzi had already introduced stopped pipes (Flute $2\frac{2}{3}'$), Chimney Flute (2′), conical flute ($1\frac{2}{3}$), reeds (Tromboni 8′) and regals (Voce umana 4′) at Orvieto Cathedral by 1600, as well as a Tremulant and an aviary of toy stops. Less than a century later, another German (the Silesian Johann Caspar, or Eugen Casparini) was introducing Mixtures and even Cornets in organs of the Tyrol, as well as confirming the trend towards the German–French $C–c'''$ compass. But indirect Italian influences appear to have been strong elsewhere early in the 17th century, notably Provence, possibly England (college chapels) and Jesuit Poland (conventual churches). Two-manual organs remained the exception, and the one made by the Dalmatian builder Petar Nakić (Pietro Nacchini) for S Antonio, Padua, in 1743–9 presented a character little different from that of S Maria in Aracoeli, Rome, in 1587: I Ripieno, Voce umana, two flutes, Tierce, regal; II Ripieno, Voce umana, one flute, Tierce, regal; Pedal 16′. As builders began collecting the upper Ripieno ranks on to one slider, a Mixture resulted that was not so different from a French *Fourniture cymbalisée*. A particular taste grew during the 18th century for Tierce or (as they were called) Cornetto ranks, but these had already been included in some two-manual registrations written down in Rome in 1666. Moreover, during the 18th century large, experimental organs were built on special commission, spreading new ideas from Bergamo to Sicily. But although rivalry with the fine organs 'at Marseilles, Trent and Hamburg' may have been the motive behind the five-manual organ at S Stefano dei Cavalieri, Pisa (Azzolino Bernardino della Ciaia, 1733–7), and elsewhere, the result was peculiarly unlike any of them. The 1730s may have seen a parting of the ways when builders throughout Europe were developing techniques beyond musical requirements; but the five-manual, three-console, 55-stop organ at Catania, Sicily (Duomo del Piano, 1755), though admired and even copied in the next century, was little more than an accumulation of several classical Italian organs, collected together. The effect of Spanish rule on the Kingdom of Naples has yet to be explored from the point of view of organ building, but it seems doubtful whether Spanish influences ever went further east than the Balearics.

A characteristic and influential organ of the later 18th century was the Venetian, brought to fruition by Nacchini and his pupil and successor Gaetano Callido. The Callido firm built hundreds of single-manual organs and many with two manuals (the pipes of the second being enclosed in a Swell box from about 1785), summing up many of the 17th- and 18th-century trends, discarding the more extravagant elements, giving their organs a velvety tone far removed from Antegnati; indeed in their wide-scaled Principals they influenced many a so-called *Italienisch Prinzipal* in modern German organs. The stop-list of an instrument by Callido is given in Table 19; for ease of tuning, the regal stops were placed in front, standing vertically before the Principale. Registrations provided by Callido elsewhere show orchestral imitations to have been important to organists of the period; there is no subtle play of two manuals, and in general Swell shutters seem to have been used either quite open or quite closed, rather than expressively.

13. THE ORGAN OF J. S. BACH

In many ways the organs of Bach's main area of activity, Thuringia, Weimar and Leipzig, showed the same kind of influences as his music: a basic German traditionalism tempered with French colour and

129

Italian fluency. Neither the organ nor the music was as local in origin or as independent of other regional ideas as was usually the case elsewhere, even in the mid-18th century. Bach himself is known to have been intimately acquainted with organ music of many countries and periods, as were such contemporaries as J. G. Walther; later colleagues, however, seem in some respects to have had less wide knowledge. C. P. E. Bach's remark that his father registered stops 'in his own manner', 'astounding' other organists, might conceivably refer to either a French or a 17th-century north German approach to stop-combinations, neither of which may have been familiar to players of the younger generation, who thought that 'the art died with him'. On the other hand, J. S. Bach is said to have complained that Gottfried Silbermann's Mixtures were 'over-weak', with 'not enough sharp penetration', as if he did not appreciate that Silbermann's French *plein jeu* was different in function from a north German *organo pleno*, being one of the many colours rather than a total chorus. Moreover, the period in which Bach worked was one of a changing aesthetic for organs, when the large west-end organ became increasingly associated with congregational hymn singing, requiring big chests, large bellows capacity, many 8' stops, a powerful 16' pedal tone and a range of sound characterized more by extremes of loud and soft than by a full array of equal, piquant colours.

Apart from the qualities of his music, then, the position of Bach in organ history is important, and can serve to show some of the currents affecting the flow of German organ music. In the course of two centuries, the area between Hanover and Breslau produced great builders (the Fritzsche and Compenius families, Casparini, Silbermann, Joachim Wagner, Engler, Hildebrandt and Schulze) and some even more influential theorists (Praetorius, Werckmeister, Adlung, Agricola, Knecht, Seidel and Töpfer). Its composers included many who travelled to hear and see great organ traditions elsewhere (for example Bach, who went to Lübeck to hear Buxtehude and to Hamburg to prove his ability on a Schnitger organ) or who settled down in another part of Germany and formed schools of keyboard playing around them (Froberger, Pachelbel, C. P. E. Bach). Many details of the stop-lists of J. S. Bach's organs at Arnstadt (1703–7), Mühlhausen (1707–8) and Weimar (1708–17) will forever remain unclear, as will larger matters of registration and tonal effect; but the Arnstadt organ (see Table 20) can be taken as typical, one known by the Pachelbel school as well as Bach's family. The particular kind of second manual on this instrument, the pedal department, and the range of 8' manual colours had long been traditional in this part of Germany, and in style

TABLE 20

Bonifaciuskirche, Arnstadt
J. F. Wender, 1703

Hauptwerk (*Oberwerk*)		*Brustwerk*	
Quintadena★	?16	Stillgedackt	8
Prinzipal	8	Hohlflöte★★ (*g–d'''*)	8
Viola da gamba	8	Prinzipal	4
Gemshorn★	8	Nachthorn	4
Grobgedackt	8	Quinte	2⅔
Quinte★ (open)	5⅓	Spitzflöte	2
Oktave	4	Sesquialtera	?II
Oktave	2	Mixtur	IV
Mixtur	IV		
Zimbel	III	*Pedal*	
Trompete	8	Sub-Bass	16
		Violon Bass	16
		Prinzipal Bass	8
		Posaune	16

Compass: *CDE–d'–d'''*
Couplers: *Hauptwerk* to Pedal: (? *Brustwerk* to Pedal, *Brustwerk* to *Hauptwerk*); (? *Hauptwerk* to Pedal coupler stop later addition)
Two tuned Zimbelsterne (*Glockenaccord*, ?1703)
Tremulant (*Hauptwerk*)

★pitch length uncertain
★★compass and manual uncertain

the Weimar court chapel organ followed much the same patterns.

Larger church organs began to allow for new attitudes towards the plenum. When Bach lived in Lüneburg in 1700 or visited Lübeck in 1706 organists there would not have 'mixed the families' of organ stops by drawing more than one rank of any given pitch even on the larger organs. The *Werkprinzip* organist played in a more discreet, regulated manner. As Werckmeister had written in 1698, organists should not draw two stops of the same pitch because wind supply and tuning problems would prevent them from being fully in tune together, but by 1721, shortly after Bach's visit to Hamburg, Mattheson was suggesting an *organo pleno* of all stops except reeds – Principals, Bourdons, Salicionals, Flutes, Quintatöne, Octaves, Fifths, Mixtures, Tierce, Sesquialteras etc. The significance of any remark made by Mattheson, or its precise meaning, is often a matter of conjecture, but a little later Adlung and Agricola both seem to have supported the idea of mixed stops. Adlung thought that good modern bellows ought to allow an organist to draw Manual Prinzipal 8′ + Gedackt 8′ + Gemshorn 8′ + Rohrflöte 8′ with Pedal Contrabass 32′

ORGAN

TABLE 21

Freiberg Cathedral
Gottfried Silbermann, 1710–14

Hauptwerk		Oberwerk	
Bourdon (lead)	16	Quintadena (tin)	16
Prinzipal (tin)	8	Prinzipal (tin)	8
Rohrflöte (lead)	8	Gedackt (lead)	8
Viola da gamba	8	Quintadena (tin)	8
(tin)		Oktave (tin)	4
Oktave (tin)	4	Spitzflöte (tin)	4
Quinte (tin)	$2\frac{2}{3}$	Superoktave (tin)	2
Superoktave (tin)	2	Flachflöte (tin)	
Tierce (lead)	$1\frac{3}{5}$	Mixtur (tin)	III
Mixtur (tin)	IV	Zimbel (tin)	II
Zimbel (tin)	III	Cornet (lead)	V
Cornet (lead)	V	(boxed)	
(mounted)		Krummhorn (tin)	8
Trompete	8	Vox humana (tin)	8
Clarin	4		

		Pedal	
Brustwerk		Untersatz (same	32 (stopped wood)
Gedackt (lead)	8	slider as	
Prinzipal (tin)	4	Oktave)	
Rohrflöte (lead)	4	Prinzipal	16
Nasat (lead)	$2\frac{2}{3}$	Oktave (same	16 (wood)
Oktave (tin)	2	slider as	
Tierce (lead)	$1\frac{3}{5}$	Untersatz)	
Quinte (tin)	$1\frac{1}{3}$	Sub-Bass	16 (stopped wood)
Sifflöte (tin)	1	Oktave (tin)	8
Mixtur	III	Oktave (tin)	4
		Mixtur (tin)	VI
		Posaune (lead)	16
		Trompete (lead)	8
		Clarin (lead)	4

Lead = metal with high lead content (Gedackts, wooden pipes in bass)
Tremulant *fort* to three manuals together
Tremulant *doux* for Vox humana
Sperrventile to each department
Couplers: *Oberwerk* to *Hauptwerk*; *Brustwerk* to *Hauptwerk*; (original *Hauptwerk* to
    Pedal uncertain)
Pitch: about $\frac{7}{8}$ tone higher than $a' = 440$
Wind pressure: $c85$ mm (manual), $c94$ mm (pedal)
Compass: $CD-c'-c'''$
Zimbel ranks duplicate smaller pipes of mixtures
Cornets: 1.8.12.15.17

+ Posaune 32′ + Sub-Bass 16′ + Violon 16′ + Posaune 16′ + Oktave 8′ + Gedackt 8′; and composers such as Gronau drew Prinzipal 8′ + Flute 8′ + Oktave 4′ + Flute 4′ + Salicet 4′ + Trompete 8′ + Oboe 8′ to bring out the melody of an organ chorale. Thus, during Bach's lifetime, ideas about what constituted Full organ were in the process of changing, as were ideas about the number and kind of solo stops.

In Lüneburg, Lübeck and Hamburg Bach would have heard organs with *Rückpositiven*, but after about 1710 Chair organs were rare in new instruments of his own area; some cities had not known them since about 1650. The *Rückpositiv* at Mühlhausen already had a stop list (8.8.4.4.2.2.1⅓.?.II.III) quite different from the bright, colourful manual of Netherlands and French organs, and, where gallery space was sufficient, builders preferred to hold such second-manual chests within the Great case, usually above the Great. The resulting 'Oberwerk' was thus different in origin from the Niehoff–Schnitger *Oberwerk*. At the same time French influences appeared; pedals became increasingly less able to provide solo colour for cantus firmus music, itself a dying genre; and organs took on a stereotyped character that varied only if the builder was sensitive to different voicing and scalings demanded by different church acoustics.

The privileged organ builder to the court of Saxony was Gottfried Silbermann, a native of Saxony who had learnt in France and Alsace and returned to make the friendship of such composers as Kuhnau and Bach. Silbermann's early and recently restored organ in Freiberg Cathedral (1710–14) already demonstrated many of these developments (see fig. 46, p. 134 and Table 21). Here was not a mass of clumsy auxiliary stops, but a unique blend of Saxon and Parisian elements, full of well-thought-out balance between the three manuals, and implying a mode of registration needing to be learnt carefully by the organist. Silbermann's voicing is strong, particularly of the Principals; his smaller village organs have great power and energy. Wind pressure (as in Joachim Wagner's organs) was about 94 mm (manuals) and about 104 mm (pedals) in later organs, about 10 mm higher than that of good large organs of about 1700.

There is little direct connection between any of Bach's organ music and such instruments as that at Freiberg; but were the Trio Sonatas, for instance, known to the organist of such a church, he may well have drawn for lively movements the combination of stops noted by the local priest as having been recommended at Silbermann's Fraureuth organ (1739–42) for *jeu de tierce en dialogue* (called *Tertien-Zug zweystimmig*): right hand Prinzipal 8′ + Rohrflöte 8′ + Oktave 4′ +

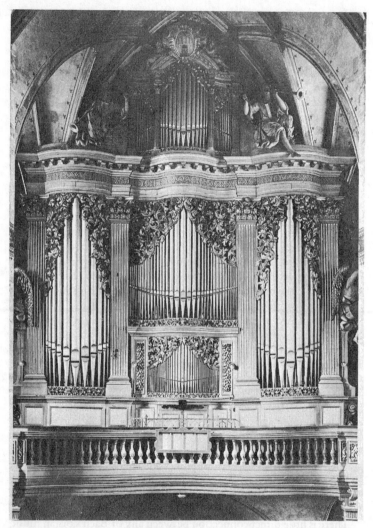

46. Organ by Gottfried Silbermann (1710–14; case by E. Lindner) in Freiberg Cathedral

Quinte $2\frac{2}{3}'$ + Prinzipal 2' + Tierce $1\frac{3}{5}'$; left hand Gedackt 8' + Rohr-flöte 4' + Nasard $2\frac{2}{3}'$ + Oktave 2' + Quinte $1\frac{1}{3}'$ + Sifflöte 1'; and Pedal Sub-Bass 16' + Posaune 16'. Given a free choice, as he may have been in the design for Hildebrandt's large organ at St Wenzel, Naumburg (1743–6), Bach might well have chosen to combine the features of several organ types: three manuals including Chair organ, 53 stops including Cornet and solo pedal stops, and each manual designed as an entity with its own auxiliary stops (Viola, Fugara, Unda maris, Weitpfeife, Spillflöte etc). As in all organs frequently played by Bach, that of Naumburg had several string-toned stops, either narrow and cylindrical, or conical. Tierce ranks, alone or as constituents of the Sesquialtera–Cornet, were indispensable for solo melodic lines in an organ chorale. Manual reeds were never numerous (even at Naumburg, they accounted for fewer than 10% of the manual stops) and were, except Vox humana and Krummhorn, for chorus purposes. The Mixtures at Naumburg were more in the bright German tradition than Silbermann's *pleins jeux*, and the pedal reeds (32', 16', 8', 4') no doubt had little of Silbermann's élan. A contemporary critic of one of Hildebrandt's organs in Dresden thought its tone dull and heavy, owing to increased wind pressure, higher cut-ups, and new voicing methods in general which spoilt the Praetorian 'Lieblichkeit der Harmonie'. But such factors were characteristic of the new mode of the 1730s and 1740s in general.

In view of the cross-currents in German organ design from 1700 to 1750, it is not surprising that Bach should have left only a few registrations, and those only of a general nature. The published Schübler preludes (*c*1746) make it clear whether the pedal is a 16' quasi-continuo bass line or a 4' cantus firmus melody line, but they do not specify colour. The manual Prinzipal 8' and pedal Trompete 8' registered in the autograph manuscript of the *Orgelbüchlein* prelude BWV600 are there as much to indicate that the canonic voices are to sound an octave apart as to suggest actual stops to be drawn. For a concerto or a prelude and fugue it is rarely clear on whose authority the manuals (and particularly the manual changes) have been specified in the manuscript copies. The subject is thus open to many solutions and suggestions. But on no single organ that Bach is known to have played would all his organ music have sounded at its best or been given a registration suitable to its carefully conceived style and genre.

ORGAN

14. SPLENDOURS OF NORTHERN EUROPE, 1650 – 1800

Between 1725 and 1750 a large number of important organs were built: the great organs of Haarlem, Gouda, Weingarten, Herzogenburg, Naumburg, Dresden, Breslau, Potsdam, Uppsala, Catania, Pisa, Tours, Paris (Notre Dame), Granada and Braga. All these and many other organs of their type were designed both to fill their churches with big sound and to tickle the ear with delicate effects. Neither purpose was known to the 16th-century builder. The very tendency to build organs exclusively at the west end of the church pinpoints this move towards extremes of sound, for apart from the large conventual churches and larger French parish churches, the new west-end organ was the only instrument in the building, especially in Protestant countries, where the need for a smaller auxiliary organ in the liturgy had largely disappeared. The generation of builders who produced the even bigger, later organs of the 18th century (Toledo, St Maximin, Hamburg Michaeliskirche, Rostock Marienkirche, Arnhem, Nijmegen, Amorbach, St Florian and Oliwa) or theorists who planned yet bigger ones (Vogt, 1719, and Bédos de Celles, 1766–78) were seeking mostly to exploit the same extremes.

Earlier, however, characteristic national developments had frequently resulted in organs which, though conceived within classical limits and not, as it were, stepping outside idiomatic, traditional usage, nonetheless had greater potential than their composers seem to have been aware of. Thus the problem with organs of 1650 to 1750 is to know for certain what they were meant to play and how they were meant to sound, whereas the problem with organs of 1750 to 1850 is that the music for which they were built, often with great ingenuity and unsurpassed technical skill, may be difficult to admire.

Two good examples of the northern organ in about 1650 are at Klosterneuburg and Alkmaar; both retain many features of their originals in spite of extensive rebuilding. Much is still unknown, however, of the detail of the originals, and it is necessary to rely on the stop-lists (see Table 22, pp. 138–9). At Klosterneuburg neither the *Brustwerk* nor even the *Rückpositiv* competes with the main chest (*Hauptwerk* and Pedal), either in sound or appearance. The *Hauptwerk* dominates the ensemble, in the true 16th-century tradition of central Europe; perhaps it, not the pedal, was originally meant to take the 16′ pipes in the case. The instrument should be seen not so much as a three-manual organ but as a group of three independent organs: *Hauptwerk* for postludes etc, *Rückpositiv* for interludes and major accompaniments, *Brustwerk* for continuo. It is uncertain whether the organ originally had manual reeds, other than the Regal; but mutations are also few, and colours were obtained by a variety of 8' and 4' ranks. 8' colour stops were becoming very popular throughout the area lying within Vienna, Ulm and Prague, and on paper the main chests of such organs often appear misleadingly large. 14 out of 28 stops at the Prague Týn Church (J. H. Mundt, 1671-3) were on the *Hauptwerk*, 16.8.8.8.8.8.4.4.2⅔.2.1⅓.1.VI.IV, but four of the 8' stops were colour changes, not chorus ranks. Salicional 8', Viola 8' and similar stops were characteristic of late 17th-century Habsburg Europe; Salicet 4', Fugara 4' and Dulciana 4' were common by the early 18th century; and reeds, except a pedal rank or two, gradually disappeared. Theorists like the Cistercian writer Vogt (1719) emphasized 8' colour stops; and for such registration rules as those given by J. B. Samber (1704), the conical Viola 8' was useful in many varied combinations: continuo playing, Viola 8'; fantasias, Viola 8' + Flöte 4'; fugues, Viola 8' + Mixtur III; versets, Viola 8' + Zimbel II.

Soon after the organ at Klosterneuburg, organ cases in the area became divided into a kind of Habsburg equivalent of the *Werkprinzip* design, with one case for the *Hauptwerk*, one for the Pedal and one for an Echo chest (Waldhausen, 1677). Such division led over the years to a rigorously applied design followed by most Austrian organs of the mid-18th century, with a half-case to one side of the west-end gallery (*Hauptwerk*), a second half-case to the other (Pedal) and a *Rückpositiv* in front, the total gallery being spacious enough to accommodate a considerable choir and orchestra for the Mass on feast days. By 1740 or so, the keyboards would be placed (in the form of a 'detached console') in a commanding position on the gallery floor, and the various parts of the case strewn around the west-end windows. In theory such an arrangement would encourage idiomatic, two-chorus organ music of the north German type, but in practice it did not.

Little is known about the music played on the great series of Netherlands organs built between the death of Sweelinck (1621) and the vogue for Bach's music two centuries later. But the array of mutations and flute and reed colours on the St Laurents instrument at Alkmaar would have made possible an immense variety in the settings of, and variations on, psalm tunes. In the 1685 rebuild the *Hauptwerk* chest had to be lowered (see fig. 47, p. 140), perhaps because by then the organist wished to be able to accompany the congregation during hymns (but such accompaniment was then still new). It is clear how the Alkmaar organ developed from the Brabant organ of Niehoff with its limited pedal, big *Hauptwerk* chorus, 8' *Rückpositiv* used for solo effects, and a quasi-*Oberwerk* (here placed below the main chest, however) with stops found on the main manual of other European organs. According to John Evelyn's diary, such Netherlands organs were used 'only for show and to recreate the people before and after their Devotions, while the Burgomasters were walking and conferring about their affairs'. By association, then, the organs were secular, often indeed owned by the town council, who saw such magnificent creations as objects of rivalry. Hence the building of the organ at St Bavo, Haarlem, by Christian Müller (1735–8) is to be seen as a sign of competition with Zwolle (Grote Kerk; new organ by Schnitger's sons, 1718–21), Alkmaar (rebuilt 1723–6), Amsterdam (Oude Kerk; Christian Vater, 1724–6), Gouda (St Jan; Jean Moreau, 1733–6) and elsewhere. Moreau was from the South; but Müller, Vater and F. C. Schnitger were German, and from then on the Netherlands organ was dominated by

---

TABLE 22

Augustinerchorherrenstift, Klosterneuburg
J. Scherer, c1550, J. G. Freundt, 1636–42

Hauptwerk
CDEFGA–c'''

Prinzipal	8		
Prinzipalflöte	8 (wide)		
Coppel	8 (wide)		
Quintadena	8		
Oktave	4		
Offenflöte	4 (wide)		
Dulcian (Tolkaan)	4		
Oktavcoppel	4 (wide)		
Quinte	2⅔		
Superoktave	2		
Mixtur	XII–XIV (4')		
Zimbel	II(½')		
Posaune (1950)	16		
Posaune (1950)	8		

Rückpositiv

Nachthorngedackt	8 (wide)
Prinzipal	4
Spitzflöte	4
Kleincoppel	4
Oktave	2
Superoktave	1
Zimbel	II
Krummhorn	8

Brustwerk

Coppel	4
Prinzipal	2
Spitzflöte	2
Regal	8

Pedal

Portunprinzipal	16 (case)
Sub-Bass	16
Oktave	8
Choralflöte (open)	8 (wide)
Superoktave	4
Mixtur	VI–VIII (4')
Rauschwerk	III (2')
Posaune	16
Posaune	8

All metal pipes
Pedal and *Hauptwerk* ranks all
  placed on the same chest
Some stop names conjectural
Coupler: *Rückpositiv* to
  Hauptwerk
Wind pressure 55–65 mm

German builders who imported new ideas (big pedals from Hamburg, heavy voicing from Westphalia), added them to Netherlands features, and produced large, powerful instruments, but unfortunately often without either German brilliance (which Marcussen mistakenly tried to 'correct' at Haarlem in 1961 with new pedal Mixtures and a new Great Mixture which unsuccessfully attempts to convert the 16′ chorus to an 8′ chorus) or French éclat (thin reed trebles and a Cornet designed to outline the psalm-tune melody rather than to function in a *grand jeu*). Although such tonal matters are subjective, the cases themselves can be more clearly seen to have lost their native Netherlands characteristics, particularly the well-featured, classical, almost clock-like designs of the 17th century, and to have begun to sprawl. It is true that at Haarlem, Müller and his architect kept the traditional vertical emphasis and other essential details in the arrangement of

St Laurents (Groote Kerk), Alkmaar
L. Eckmans, Galtus & Germer Hagerbeer, 1639–45

Hauptwerk (manual III)		*Unterwerk* (II)	
$F'–d'''$ (short, for first 2 stops)		$C–d'''$ (short)	
$C–d'''$ (short)		Bourdon	16
Praestant	16	Praestant	8
Praestant	8	Holpijp	8
Oktave	4	Oktave	4
Grosser Scharf		Quintadena	8
Kleiner Scharf		Offenflöte	4
Terzian		Echo Holpijp	4
Trompete	8	Superoktave	2
		Tierce	$1\frac{3}{5}$ (?1685)
Rückpositiv (I)		Nasard	$1\frac{1}{3}$
$C–d'''$ (short)		Gemshorn	$1\frac{1}{3}$
Praestant	8	Sifflöte	1
Quintadena	8	Sesquialtera	II
Oktave	4	Trompete	8
Flöte	4	Vox humana	4
Superoktave	2		
Tierce	$1\frac{3}{5}$ (?1685)	*Pedal*	
Nasard	$1\frac{1}{3}$	$F'–f'$ (at present) coupled to	
Quintanus	$1\frac{1}{3}$	*Hauptwerk*	
Sifflöte	1	$C–f'$ (at present) for pedal	
Mixtur	III–IV	stops	
Scharf	IV	Prinzipal	8
Sesquialtera (treble)	(?1685)	Oktave	4
Trompete	8	Trompete	8
		Couplers etc unknown	
		Rebuilt 1685 (J. Duyschot),	
		1723–6 (F. C. Schnitger)	

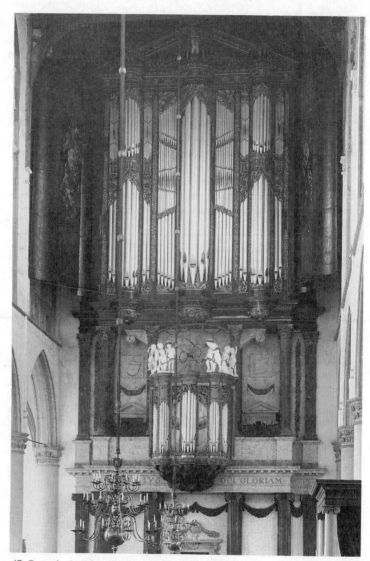

47. Organ by L. Eckmans, Galtus & Germer Hagerbeer (1639–45; case by Jacob van
Campen) in the Groote Kerk, Alkmaar

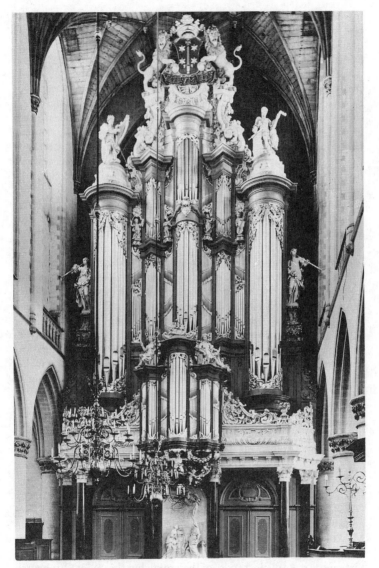

48. *Organ by Christian Müller (1735–8; case probably by J. van Logteren) in the Groote Kerk, Haarlem*

towers and flats; but even there the classical pediment surmounting the best old Netherlands cases gave way to an unstructural, Baroque coat-of-arms (see fig. 48).

Although the condition of the organs at Weingarten and Haarlem is not anything like as authentic as their fame leads admirers to assume, they do serve on paper (see Table 23, pp. 144–5) as useful examples of their 'schools', being at once both traditional and exceptional, both formative and unapproachably 'ideal'. The details of the Weingarten organ – the bells, the cherrywood stops, the ivory pipes, the doubled ranks, the undulating colours, the big Mixtures, the complex action – require a book to themselves, and it could be that a first-rate restoration of the instrument would fill out its tone. Nevertheless, the principles behind its dispensing of organ colours can be seen, and Gabler's little quire organ in the same church contained an even clearer indication of his passion for 8′ and 4′ colour stops. Some writers have described the west-end organ as a 'Rococo–Gothic conception', but it is more like a southern European grotto organ. Three echo divisions (*Oberwerk, Unterwerk, Kronpositiv*) are bound to lead to a mocking of true organ tone, however logical an extension it may have been of current ideas in south Germany as a whole. Only the two *Rückpositiven* offer well-balanced effects in the idiomatic north-German manner; yet to an 18th-century organist visiting Weingarten after Salzburg Cathedral (organ by J. C. Egedacher, 1703–6), such *Rückpositiven* must have seemed conservative and slightly puzzling. The original mechanical action must have been very troublesome to make, since even in this sprawling and unique case (see fig. 49) only eight of all the case pipes do not speak; clearly the detached console was the only practical arrangement. The influence of the whole instrument was wide and long-lasting; theory books (e.g. Hawkins, 1776; Bédos de Celles, 1766–78) gave it notoriety, and it held a significant position between the colourful Renaissance organ of south Germany and the large factory organs of the 1830s.

Swabia also saw a remarkably good compromise organ during the 1760s: the larger instrument at Ottobeuren, built by K. J. Riepp (1761–8), incorporated French elements (learnt by its builder in Burgundy) and German ones (learnt in the vicinity of Lake Constance). Most major organs in both parish and conventual churches in Switzerland, Württemberg, and Bavaria had such a mingling of organ cultures as to create distinct styles of their own; but the one at Ottobeuren was a simple amalgam. All the classical French registrations were possible on it, but so were German pedal music and hymn variations, from the evidence of its stop list.

49. Organ by Joseph Gabler (1737–50) in the west end of the church of Weingarten Abbey, showing the two Rückpositiven (manual and pedal)

Such composite schemes were curiously rare in the 18th century. It was more characteristic of organ building in general that even adjacent areas (e.g. Carinthia and Veneto, or Saxony and Bohemia) had totally different organs, as if builders of one area or religious denomination were thoroughly opposed to the ideals of their neighbours. Some of the major religious orders, particularly the Cistercian and Augustinian, had something of an international style crossing political frontiers, but even this kind of uniformity was not conspicuous. It was regional style that carried the day, giving the organ at Klosterneuburg,

ORGAN

TABLE 23

Benediktinerabtei, Weingarten
Joseph Gabler, 1737–50

Hauptwerk

Prinzipal	16
Prinzipal (narrow)	8
Rohrflöte (narrow)	8
Oktave★	4
Superoktave★	2
Hohlflöte★	2
Piffaro	V–VII
Sesquialtera	IX–VIII
Mixtur	XXI–XX
Zimbel	XII
Trompete	8

Oberwerk

Bourdon (part wood)★	16
Prinzipal	8
Coppel	8
Violoncello★	8
Salizional	8
Hohlflöte (wood)	8
Unda maris (wood)	8
Mixtur	IX–XII
Kronpositiv (high chest played	
from *Oberwerk* keys)	
Oktave douce (bass)	4
(treble)	8
Viola douce★	8
Nasat	$2\frac{2}{3}$
Zimbel	II

Unterwerk

Bourdon (wood)	16
Prinzipal (part wood)	8
Quintatön	8
Flöte (wood, conical)	8
Viola douce	8
Oktave (conical)	4
Hohlflöte★	4
Piffaro douce	II
Superoktave (conical)	
Mixtur	V–VI
Cornet (narrow)	VI–V
Hautboy	8
Tremulant	

Rückpositiv (south case, manual keys)

Prinzipal doux	8
Flûte douce	8
Quintatön	8
Violoncello	8
Rohrflöte	4
Querflöte (wood)	4
Flauto traverso★	4
Flageolet	2
Piffaro	VI–V
Cornet (narrow)	XI–VIII
Vox humana	8
Hautboy	4
Carillon (32 bells, f–c''')	

Pedal

(a) main case

Contrabass (open)★	32
Sub-Bass	32
Oktave (wood)	16
Violon★	16
Mixtur	V–VI
Bombarde	16
Posaune (wood)	16
Carillon (20 bells at 2′)	

(b) north *Rückpositiv* case

Quintatön	16
Superoktave	8
Flûte douce	8
Violoncello	28
Hohlflöte	4
Cornet	XI–X
Sesquialtera	VII–VI
Trompete	8
Fagott	8

La Force, pedal 'stop', playing 48 pipes
  of C major triad (4′)
Compass: C–g–c'', complete
Stops marked ★ have doubled ranks for
  all or part of the compass
Wind pressure now 70mm
Modern pitch

St Baaf, Haarlem
Christian Müller, 1735–8

Hauptwerk

Praestant	16
Bourdon	16
Oktave (doubled rank from *g*)	8
Rohrflöte	8
Viola de gamba★	8
Rohrquinte	$5\frac{1}{3}$
Oktave	4
Gemshorn	4
Quintpraestant	$2\frac{2}{3}$
Waldflöte	2
Terzian	II
Mixtur	IV–X
Trompete	16
Trompete	8
Hautboy	8
Trompete	4

Rückpositiv

Praestant (doubled rank from *g*)	8
Quintadena★	8
Holpijp	8
Oktave	4
Flûte douce	4
Spitzflöte	$2\frac{2}{3}$
Superoktave	2
Sesquialtera	II–IV
(doubled rank from *c'*)	
Cornet (from *c'*)	V
Mixtur	VI–VIII
Zimbel★	III
Fagott	16
Trompete	8
Trichterregal★	8

★replaced in 1961

Oberwerk

Quintadena	16
Praestant (doubled rank from *g*)	8
Quintadena	8
Baarpijp (conical)	8
Oktave	4
Flachflöte	4
Nasard	$2\frac{2}{3}$
Nachthorn	2
Flageolet	$1\frac{1}{3}$
Sesquialtera	II
Mixtur★	IV–VI
Zimbel★	III
Schalmei	8
Dulzian	8
Vox humana	8

Pedal

Praestant	32
Praestant	16
Sub-Bass	16
Rohrquinte	$10\frac{2}{3}$
Oktave	8
Holpijp	8
Quintpraestant	$5\frac{1}{3}$
Oktave	4
Holpijp	2
Rauschquinte	III
Posaune	32
Posaune	16
Trompete	8
Trompete	4
Zink	2

Two Tremulants
Couplers: *Oberwerk* to *Hauptwerk*:
  Ruckpositiv to *Hauptwerk*; (Pedal
  couplers 1961)
Wind pressure *c*75 mm
Pitch: $a' = c\,440$
All pipes of metal
Compass: *C–d'–d'''*, complete (contract
  gave *c'''*; pedal now to *f'*)

ORGAN

TABLE 24

Michaeliskirche, Hamburg
J. G. Hildebrandt, 1762–7

Hauptwerk			*Oberwerk*	
Prinzipal (tin)	16		Bourdon (metal)	16
Quintadena (metal)	16		Prinzipal★	8
Oktave★ (tin)	8		Spitzflöte (metal)	8
Gedackt (metal)	8		Quintatön (metal)	8
Gemshorn (tin)	8		Unda maris (tin)	8 (treble)
Viola da gamba (tin)	8		Oktave (tin)	4
Quinte (tin)	$5\frac{1}{3}$		Spitzflöte (metal)	4
Oktave (tin)	4		Quinte (tin)	$2\frac{2}{3}$
Gemshorn (metal)	4		Oktave (tin)	2
Nasat (metal)	$2\frac{2}{3}$		Rauschpfeife (tin)	II
Oktave (tin)	2		Zimbel (tin)	V
Sesquialtera (tin)	II		Echo Cornet (tin)	V (treble)
Mixtur (tin)	VIII		Trompete★ (tin)	8
Scharf (tin)	V		Vox humana (tin)	8
Cornet (tin)	V (treble)			
Trompete (tin)	16			
Trompete (tin)	8		*Pedal*	
			Prinzipal (tin)	32
			Sub-Bass (stopped)	32
			Prinzipal (tin)	16
Brustwerk			Sub-Bass (stopped)	16
Rohrflöte (metal)	16		Rohrquinte (metal)	$10\frac{2}{3}$
Prinzipal★ (tin)	8		Oktave (tin)	8
Flauto traverso	8		Quinte (tin)	$5\frac{1}{3}$
(metal)			Oktave (tin)	4
Gedackt (metal)	8		Mixtur (tin)	X
Rohrflöte (metal)	8		Posaune (tin)	32
Oktave (tin)	4		Posaune (tin)	16
Rohrflöte (metal)	4		Fagott (tin)	16
Nasat (metal)	$2\frac{2}{3}$		Trompete (tin)	8
Oktave (tin)	2		Trompete (tin)	4
Tierce (tin)	$1\frac{2}{3}$			
Quinte (tin)	$1\frac{1}{3}$			
Sifflöte (tin)	1			
Rauschpfeife (tin)	II–III			
Zimbel (tin)	V			
Chalumeau (tin)	8			

Compass: $C-d'-f'''$, complete
Zimbelstern
Tremulant (*Hauptwerk*), i.e. *tremblant fort*
Schwebung (*Oberwerk*), i.e., *tremblant doux*
Couplers: *Hauptwerk* to Pedal; (? *Oberwerk* to *Hauptwerk*)
Swell for three stops (? last three of *Oberwerk*)
Stops marked ★ have doubled ranks for part of the compass

for example, great influence over the one built nearby a century later by a foreign builder well versed in other organ types (Augustinerstift, Herzogenburg; J. Henke, 1747–52). It may well have been such provincialism, however, that helped to produce the good, conservative designs (Amorbach; Rot an der Rot), the late flowers of Baroque organ art that were able to resist the emaciating extremes of fashion.

The large organs of the late 18th century were individually distinctive, keeping regional characteristics despite the availability to organists of many printed sources of music from other countries. The Michaeliskirche in Hamburg had a 70-stop, three-manual organ by J. G. Hildebrandt (son of Silbermann's pupil Zacharias Hildebrandt); although he took with him many Saxon colours (Cornet, Unda maris, Chalumeau etc) and followed contemporary ideas common to many regions (no *Rückpositiv*, thickening Quints etc), the instrument remained a Hamburg organ, more complete and comprehensive than an organ could have been anywhere else. The massive case (for which Burney did not care) has an unmistakable 19th-century look about it; the stop-list (Table 24) is typical of a large organ, but many writers who heard the instrument commented on its 'noble power', described by Burney as 'more striking by its force and the richness of the harmony than by a clear and distinct melody'. Yet the organ was no mere sacrifice to fashion, which was then rather geared to imitations of orchestral families, of wind concertos, and the like. Theorists like Hess and Knecht encouraged particular imitations of string stops and in general helped to deceive organists into thinking they could duplicate orchestral effects. So did Abbé Georg Joseph Vogler (1749–1814), who typifies the less reputable side of late 18th-century organ playing, and whose bizarre organ-concert programmes sometimes proved irresistible to popular audiences in large cities from London to Vienna. Vogler's simplification system, however, in which bulky reeds were replaced with free reeds, and costly Mixtures and 32' stops with low Mutations, has received more attention than it merits historically, for the development of the organ would have been little different without him. More important was the impasse brought about at the end of the century by the technical perfection of the late Baroque organ. Quite apart from the Napoleonic holocaust, the organ historian must feel that the multiplied colour stops of St Florian and Oliwa monastic churches (1770s), the reeds of St Maximin, Poitiers and Toledo, and the choruses of Hamburg and Rostock parish churches, all pushed the classical organ as far as it would go. A total rethinking was necessary early in the next century.

ORGAN

15. ORGANS IN THE AMERICAS

The Spanish conqueror Cortez arrived in Central America in 1519; Franciscan and Dominican missionaries arrived soon after, and by 1530 a small organ was recorded in use at the newly founded Mexico City Cathedral. By the end of the 16th century music had been published in Mexico, and the use of organs and other instruments in churches was fairly widespread. During the 17th century the use of organs spread to Peru and other areas south of Mexico, as well as to northern missions; in 1630 17 small organs are recorded in what is now the state of New Mexico. Organs were both imported from Spain and built by immigrant builders and by Indians taught by them, and surviving cases indicate that some were fairly large, although more were of positive size.

In 1667 the new cathedral of Mexico City was dedicated, and a large Spanish organ was ordered in 1693 and first used in 1695. A number of other large cathedral organs followed, in places such as Puebla and Guadalajara, and a second organ for Mexico City Cathedral, facing the first, was completed by José Nassarre in 1735. Meanwhile organs had been introduced by the French colonists in Canada as early as 1657 (Quebec City), and between 1698 and 1705 a two-manual organ was imported for the church of Notre Dame in Montreal.

In the English colonies on the eastern seaboard of America, the first recorded use of an organ in church was at a Lutheran ordination in Philadelphia in 1703. This was a small positive borrowed from some German settlers who had arrived in 1694. In 1713 a four-stop chamber organ, possibly the work of Smith, was placed in King's Chapel, Boston. Previously in a residence, it is known to have existed as early as 1708 and it may have been imported before 1700.

Although English organs began to be imported in increasing numbers during the remainder of the 18th century, with significant examples of the work of Jordan, Bridge, England and Snetzler reaching American shores, the first to build organs in the colonies was J. G. Klemm, a Saxon who emigrated in 1733. While most of Klemm's instruments were small, he built one with three manuals for Trinity Church, New York, in 1741. His work was carried on by David Tannenberg, who built over 40 organs between 1758 and 1804, mostly for a small area of Pennsylvania. Tannenberg's work reflects the influence of the Silbermann school, presumably transmitted through Klemm, and he was familiar with the writings of Sorge.

Because of Puritan (Calvinist) objections to the use of instruments in worship, nearly all colonial organs until the end of the 18th century were located in Anglican, Lutheran or Moravian churches, and chamber organs were as popular as in England. The first organ builder in Boston was a multi-faceted craftsman, Thomas Johnston, but it was not until the first decades of the 19th century that one could pursue the trade of organ building full-time in the English colonies. English organs by builders such as Gray and Elliot were occasionally imported as late as the 1830s, but by this time, although the Pennsylvania German school had virtually died out, a vigorous native school, encouraged by an increasing demand for church organs, was established in Boston and New York. The founder of the Boston group was William Goodrich, self-taught and exceptionally gifted, in whose workshop were trained Thomas Appleton, George Stevens, and Elias and George G. Hook, who were to make Boston a major centre of organ building by the middle of the 19th century. Thomas Hall was the first New York builder of importance, but he was eclipsed by his pupil Henry Erben, who in turn trained many later builders, such as Richard M. Ferris.

The work of the early 19th-century builders was rooted in the English tradition, both visually and tonally, although it had many unique characteristics of its own. Stop-lists reflected English conventions, voicing was mild but lively and casework was often exceptionally handsome. The long (G or sometimes even F) compass was used until the middle of the century, as were various forms of mean-tone tuning. Pipe metal was usually about 25% tin, zinc for basses not coming into use until almost 1850, and stopped diapasons were almost invariably of wood, along with 4′ Flute stops. Casework was of either mahogany veneer or pine, the latter always painted, sometimes to resemble hardwood. Few of the larger organs of this period remain intact, but in 1982 a fine 1830 Appleton organ was acquired by the Metropolitan Museum in New York.

CHAPTER FIVE

Developments 1800–1930

1. GENERAL INFLUENCES ABOUT 1800

A total rethinking did not manifest itself until well into the 19th century. In some countries, notably Italy, England, the Netherlands and Scandinavia, there was little perceptible change in direction until the second third of the century; one of the chief differences between an average organ of 1790 and 1840 in these areas was that the latter was bigger, and the builder had probably explored further the simple colour stops, Swell boxes and pedal departments. But colour stops were by nature foreign to Scandinavian organs, pedals to English and Swell boxes to Dutch. In other countries, notably France, Spain, Austria, central and southern Germany and their neighbours (Bohemia, Poland etc), events outside music not only caused organ building to receive less attention and money from churches but gave to the revival of organs in the 1830s an impetus towards new techniques.

In Austria the reforms of church music undertaken by Joseph II during the 1780s encouraged simple organs in parish churches – instruments contrasting hugely with the large monastic creations of St Florian (1770) and Heiligenkreuz (1802). In countries occupied by the French in the wake of the Revolution, such as the Netherlands, Spain, south Germany, Austria, Prussia, Poland and Moravia, services were often suspended. Only here and there were organs destroyed; more physical damage was done in France itself, where it was followed by a scarcity of funds and then, after 1815, an equally harmful overreaction: from 1792 a church may have been closed to Christian use but its organ was just as useful for 'awakening and inspiring a holy love of the Fatherland', as the new département administrators knew. But in Germany and Austria it was the dissolution of the monasteries (particularly after 1803) that changed organ tradition. In Spain and Portugal the organ suffered an eclipse, only partial in some areas but severely evident in others, taken in the wake of Wellington's and

Napoleon's armies and by the reappropriation (*desamortización*) of church funds in 1830. Farther north, Denmark kept its organ traditions largely undisturbed, but Sweden produced some advanced ideas in the 1820s, not least as a result of cultural ties with Saxony and central Germany.

Some of the important influences on organs and their music at the end of the 18th century were more directly musical. One was the theory of difference tones, quite familiar to theorists since Tartini. Vogler's ideas were based in part on the observation that the exploitation of harmonics might enable builders to dispense with large pipes, the combination of 16′, 10$\frac{2}{3}$′ and 6$\frac{2}{3}$′, for instance, producing a 32′ effect. But the idea is too naive for serious consideration, and Vogler must have had other assets to justify the respect with which he was held in Sweden and Salzburg. 10$\frac{2}{3}$′ ranks had been known in Silesia and Bohemia during the late 17th century, and a flat 7th appeared in one Berlin organ of 1776.

A second major influence, or a symptom of the new emphases, was the idea propounded by J. H. Knecht (1795) and others that the organ was a kind of one-man orchestra, its three manuals having an orchestral spectrum of strings, brass and woodwind. To this end, Vogler's specially made organ, the Orchestrion, was hawked all over Europe during the 1790s. There was of course nothing new either in stops imitating string instruments or in regarding the organ as a 'compendium of all instruments whatsoever' (Mersenne, 1636–7); nor were organ transcriptions new, being as old as written-down organ music itself. But by 1800 the orchestra itself was heavier, more stratified and conventionalized than it was in 1600, and imitations of it would therefore be farther removed from the organ's own nature.

A third factor was the general assumption that the hundreds of new parish church organs of average size required in about 1820 were to be built chiefly for the sake of accompanying the congregation, for which 8′ stops were the most useful. This was partly because mutations were less carefully made in a period of quickly built organs, partly because intelligent theorists like J. Wilke despised Voglerian claims about harmonic stops, and partly because Mixtures were difficult to justify in theory. Some of the ill-repute of Mixtures in the period must have been due to their all too common Tierce rank (particularly ill-suited to equal temperament, which was coming into use in this period in all countries save England and the USA, where it was not accepted until the 1850s), and such compromise all-purpose Mixtures as those of Snetzler and countless other builders throughout Europe were neither good chorus Mixtures nor good solo Cornets. Such an organ as that at

Karlskrona, Sweden (P. Z. Strand, 1827), must have got its characteristic 'decadent' specification, whatever its voicing, in reaction to
poorly made mutations and Mixtures too often met with at the time:

I	16.16.8.8.8.4.4.2.8
II	8.8.8.4.4.8
Pedal	16.8.8.4.16

A further influence on the design of organs soon after 1820 was the
international scope of the repertory available to an average organist. In
England, for example, such firms as Boosey imported an immense
amount of German organ music of all kinds during the first few decades
of the century. These imports reached their culmination in the international Bach revival. Bach sonatas and other major works ('Grand
Preludes and Fugues') were available from 1800 and shortly after; for his
sake alone, countless old English and French organs, and some Italian
and Spanish, were being altered by 1840: pedals added, short manuals
completed, second choruses added. The result, however, was not that
national organ types lost their identity but that they kept it in a less overt
and certainly less charming manner, so that the Bach revival rarely led in
any country to well-balanced classical organs of the Silbermann type.
No doubt this situation was in part due to the 'organ ethos' of the period:
a general anti-Baroque view of organs as sombre, solemn, ecclesiastical
and ecclesiological objects whose music (as can be seen from Vincent
Novello's travel diaries) was expected to be more 'elevated' than the
galanteries of the previous generation. But it prompted organists of different national schools to suppose that their organ alone was the best for
Bach; countless English organists, for example, have resisted the idea
that Bach did not write for the Swell pedal.

Apart from the details produced by such factors, several general
observations can be made. There were strangely few magnificent
organs built anywhere between 1800 and 1825, and the new big instruments of 1825–50 show a bigger break with the past than those of any
other period in organ history. Casework as well underwent extreme
changes in design and ornamental detail. While it is probably true that
in 1830 churches spent less on their organs than they did in 1730, the
later organs were in fact larger. In proportion to material bulk a
Walcker organ must have cost only a fifth of the price of a Silbermann.
The sounds the new organs were expected to produce accorded with
the sobriety and gloom of the post-Revolution church, although the
organist had a more variegated repertory to choose from than at any
previous period. Few great organ builders stand out between 1800 and
1825, and major practical and theoretical developments were left to

the next generation. Some areas, however, kept their traditions: the *Brustwerk* of 1898 at St Anders, Copenhagen, must be regarded as a survival rather than a revival.

In the USA, particularly in Boston and New York, a native school of builders was rapidly developing in the early 19th century to meet the needs of the many new churches in the expanding cities and prospering rural areas. These builders, notably Goodrich and Appleton in Boston, and Erben and Hall in New York, worked in the refined style inherited from 18th-century England and may be said to have brought it to its final fruition. By the 1850s the effect of continental developments, both tonal and mechanical, was being felt, and large factories (such as that of E. & G. G. Hook in Boston) were replacing the small workshops.

2. 19TH-CENTURY TECHNICAL ADVANCES

Audsley's monument to the Romantic organ, *The Art of Organ-building* (1905), shows that the organ builder of about 1900 had a vast array of pipework to choose from; he also had many types of chest, action, bellows, gadgets and case designs at his disposal. On the whole Audsley was describing a high-quality instrument, but the profusion of elements he described affected the smallest and cheapest builder. Similarly, the organist's repertory was in theory immense. It was towards these two positions of technical and musical profusion, of embarrassing choice for both builder and player, that the organ gradually moved during the 19th century.

Although the period is now poorly documented and ill-understood in detail, the general outlines are clear. Different areas of Europe exercised major influence at different periods, and often an individual builder advanced concepts or techniques without which the overall development would have been different. Publicity for a new idea became increasingly easy (particularly from such concourses as the Great Exhibition in London, 1851); builders travelled far (like Cavaillé-Coll and Canada's Casavant brothers) to view developments, published papers or became associated with well-known theorists, and took commissions much farther from home than they had been used to doing (early examples were central German builders at work in the Netherlands and Scandinavia about 1760). New and rare stops were introduced into such foreign organs, perhaps sometimes for ostentation (e.g. Schulze's three-sided and wooden cylindrical pipes at

Doncaster, 1862). An advanced organ of 1825 anywhere in Europe would at any rate have features gathered from various sources: from changing taste (several string stops), theory book notions of harmonics, quick factory methods, foreign influences (e.g. English Swells) and new visual ideas. 40 years later the amalgam was yet richer, and huge organs produced in the factories of Walcker, Sauer, Willis and Cavaillé-Coll were taken all over the world.

Thus the developments about 1825 in central Germany had an influence throughout Europe, not least because English and French organs of the period were particularly susceptible to new ideas. The theorists Wolfram (1815), Seidel (1843) and above all Töpfer (1833, 1855) were better known in Hamburg, Paris and London than Praetorius had been and had even crossed the ocean to America. Töpfer's new scientific description of the techniques of building (with tables and technical details for pipe-scales, wind-chambers, pallets, bellows, action etc) were immensely useful to every new builder. His ratio for pipe-scales (the so-called Normal Scale or Diapason Norm) was a theoretical model, not honed to the particular conditions of any church or local tradition; but it was adopted by builders of cheaper, commercial organs, and indeed forms part of the definition of the 'cheap, commercial organ'. J. F. Schulze also found it useful, and in itself it is not far removed from what had been customary in central Germany.

Töpfer's calculation was that the area of the cross-section of a Principal pipe was $\sqrt{8}$ times the area of the cross-section of a pipe an octave higher. Scaling therefore halved at the 17th inclusive pipe (i.e. eight whole tones above). So it had for many an organ before Töpfer. (But he seems to have thought that if pipes retained their proportions the ratio would be $\sqrt{16}:1$, while constant diameter would be $\sqrt{1}:1$ and a mean thus $\sqrt{8}:1$.) Such a simple constant was convenient at the workbench. So were Töpfer's other formulae for calculating the wind consumption and the height of the pipe mouth. Meanwhile the improved bellows and reservoirs of his period not only allowed copious wind and constant pressure but encouraged builders to experiment with higher pressure for the pipes or with pipes scaled to either extreme. Organists now demanded to be able to play with heavier registrations; these were at least as important as constant scalings, and Töpfer has perhaps been unjustly maligned for his $\sqrt{8}:1$ formula.

Many of the experiments were short-lived. Free reeds were popular in central Germany from about 1780 to 1850 but not often elsewhere, although Gray and Davison used 32′ free reeds at the Crystal Palace (1857) and Leeds Town Hall (1859), and 8′ free reeds were sporadically used as a novelty stop in large American organs as late as the 1870s. New materials, such as the cast-iron case and zinc pipes at Hohenofen (1818), became associated with poorer instruments once the novelty had worn off. Double pedal-boards and solo manuals were reserved for the largest instruments, though octave couplers and detached consoles never lost popularity once they had gained it soon after 1830. In England, Swell boxes were constantly 'improved', most often with a view to reducing the closed box to a true *pp* (Hodges of Bristol, 1824). In Germany, J. Wilke wrote major articles during the 1820s in the *Allgemeine musikalische Zeitung* listing devices for producing Swell effects such as triple touch, operating couplers or bringing on more stops as the key was depressed; increased wind admitted to the free reed stops (Grenié, Paris); lowered wind pressure brought about by a net curtain in the wind-trunk (Vogler); 'roof swells', devices for raising the lid of Swell boxes; and 'Door swells' or 'jalousie swells', the English systems of (horizontal) Venetian shutters, perhaps encasing a complete organ. For most of the century, the Swell box mechanism remained simple, as indeed the idea itself is extremely primitive: horizontal shutters were controlled by a wooden or metal foot-lever hanging to the right of the pedal keys, which had to be notched into position if the box was to remain open. With such pedals, constant see-sawing and swelling of sound were not very practical. Only occasionally were other systems tried, such as Bryceson's hydraulic system of about 1865 in which water was communicated along a lead pipe from the pedal to the Swell mechanism.

The resulting organ of about 1840 was usually a compromise between old and new. At Halberstadt Cathedral, for example, J. F. Schulze built a four-manual organ in which three manuals and pedal were of the large, standard classical type familiar in the later 18th century, and couplers and accessories were conventional, even to a Zimbelstern; but the fourth manual, its purpose very unclassical, played new stops in a high echo chest:

Lieblich Gedackt	16 (wood)
Lieblich Gedackt	8 (wood)
Terpodion	8 (tin)
Flauto traverso	8 (turned wood)
Harmonika	8 (wood)
Prinzipal	4
Flauto traverso	4 (turned wood)
Physharmonika	8 (zinc) (free reed)

Such echo organs were a luxury, like apse organs in a few English cathedrals a century later. More popular in the advanced organ of 1850 were the Solo organ, an extravagant manual (usually the fourth, sometimes the third) devoted to solo stops, and the full Swell organ with its characteristic 16′ reed and bright Mixture (Henry Willis, 1855). In Germany, Swells of the distant *Echowerk* type remained popular and still colour German organ design.

It was E. F. Walcker who is said to have invented (or improved) the cone-chest (*Kegellade*, see fig. 14*b*), which he patented in 1842. Cavaillé-Coll, Willis and other great builders rejected it, as did American builders after a brief experimental attempt by the avant-garde Boston builder Simmons in his organ for Harvard University (1859). In America, cone-chests were briefly attempted a decade later (again unsuccessfully, due to the adverse effects of the climate) by the immigrant Moritz Baumgarten, who had trained with Walcker. But Walcker's output was immense, and certainly the boom in north European organ building meant that the more systematic a builder's concepts (and hence his workshop), the bigger part he could play in providing organs for the hundreds of new parish churches of that period. Metal-planing machines, for example, were drawn by Töpfer and manufactured by Walcker; such machine tools provided pipe metal of great precision and uniformity, obviating all capricious and 'imperfect' elements in pipe manufacture. The Walcker firm moved to Ludwigsburg in 1820 and was able from there to command a vast area of central Europe. Its organ for the Paulskirche, Frankfurt (1827–33), was highly influential, with its 74 stops on three manuals and two pedal-boards; but it too was a compromise. The 14-stop Swell was a large Echo organ, with free reeds and Dulcianas; the action was mechanical, the chests slider-chests, the couplers standard. However, the Swell mechanism was balanced; and once the free reeds were replaced by long-resonator reed stops, the specification became standard. Indeed, the whole Walcker style had great influence, from the Rhine to the Black Sea. But in 1849 (Ulm Minster) and 1863 (Music Hall, Boston, USA), Walcker monster organs still had not outgrown compromise; more thoroughly modern designs were achieved by builders less set in their ways, such as A. W. Gottschalg, whose large organ for Cologne Cathedral was influenced by Cavaillé-Coll. The influence of the Walcker instrument in Boston on American organ building, already well established in its own conventions, has been much overrated. The cone-chest had already been tried and rejected, Americans continued to develop their own scaling and voicing systems (although influenced by Töpfer and other theorists and by general European trends). The Barker machine was already in widespread use and the only real novelty, the free reed stops, enjoyed but limited vogue. The importation of the Walcker organ was, in truth, an aberration, for in the period in which it was built the major American builders, such as Hook & Hastings and Roosevelt, could and did produce large, well-engineered and tonally sophisticated Romantic organs for large churches, cathedrals and concert halls.

In France much important work was done during the 1820s and 1830s before Cavaillé-Coll began to dominate the scene. The Englishman John Abbey went to France (at the instigation of Erard) to work in the Restoration period, taking with him the improved English bellows-with-magazine, Venetian Swell and refined voicing, and rebuilding organs from Rheims to Caen. His Swell at Amiens in 1833, for example, was a typical English Echo organ of 1750: 8.8.4.V.8.8. Farther east, Daublaine & Callinet came under the Walcker influence with their free reeds, double pedal-boards and general specifications in a few large organs, but essentially Callinet and his fellow Alsatian Stiehr remained conservative. Their small and average-sized church organs retained the basic classical physical and tonal layout in the mid-19th century, but with some suppression of upperwork and introduction of Gambas and Harmonic Flutes, and with the use of free reeds with resonators. By 1841 Cavaillé-Coll was making over-blowing stops, both flue and reed. His new scheme that year for the organ of St Denis is discussed in §3 below.

High pressure was applied to reeds in England by the late 1830s, the first well-known example being Hill's Tuba mirabilis at Birmingham Town Hall (1840). But although by 1855 Hopkins could write that 'stops of this kind are now made by nearly all the English organ-builders', no real technical details are known of these early stops. On the analogy of wood and brass wind instrument playing in general, treble pipes in the reed ranks were also put on higher pressure from the organ of St Denis onwards. This of itself was a major advance, as can be readily seen by comparing a Trumpet at St Sulpice with one at Haarlem. For centuries French builders had appreciated that reed trebles needed 'boosting' if the splendid bass was not to peter out above g' or so: hence one of the functions of the mounted Cornet. Cavaillé-Coll's overblowing double-length flue and reed pipes were thus new not in principle but in character. A Flûte harmonique or Trompette harmonique is so made for bigger, rounder tone and, unlike the narrow-scaled overblowing flutes of the 17th century, always requires strong, copious wind. The formation of nodes in over-blowing flue pipes is helped by a small hole piercing the pipe rather less than halfway along from the mouth, the exact position affecting the overtone content of the pipe. In reeds, the hole is not necessary. The

50. *Organ by Ducroquet (1854; case after plans by Baltard) at St Eustache, Paris*

blow-air-into-pipe), established by small holes piercing the pipe, either
just halfway along from the mouth (under-expression, affecting the
overtone structure of the pipe, in effect, the hole overcrown) of the

tone of neither flue nor reed harmonic pipes blends idiomatically with the Principal chorus; 17th-century builders therefore reserved such flutes for solo colour, but the larger 19th-century organs contained small choruses of harmonic stops. Reed and flue harmonic stops show the desire felt in the 1840s for smooth reeds that stay in tune, and precisely voiced flue stops with no subsidiary 'chiff'. Full- or double-length resonators gave smoothness to the reeds, while in flue pipes the chiff was eliminated by mouth paraphernalia of nicked languids, 'ears and beard' and rollerbeards aiding prompt, smooth speech.

Further technical advances made between 1825 and 1845 concern the action. Many 19th-century builders were ingenious with mechanisms composed of wooden levers, rods, battens etc for such accessories as double Venetian swells (H. Willis, Gloucester Cathedral, 1847), stop-combinations (Ladegast, Sauer, Roosevelt), crescendo pedals (Haas) and various couplers. Improved bellows-with-reservoir, greater application of two or even more wind pressures in an organ, improved slider-chests (and eventually cone-chests) were all at the skilled builder's disposal by 1845 at the latest. So was the 'Barker lever' or mechanical-pneumatic action (see fig. 14a). By 1833, Booth in England and Hamilton in Scotland had constructed such actions. C. S. Barker worked on power pneumatics and compressed air, offering an apparatus to York Minster (1833), Birmingham Town Hall (1834-5) and, in France, to Cavaillé-Coll (1837). The pneumatic principle could also be applied to sliders and to such accessories as 'thumb-pistons' (H. Willis, 1851). Barker's French patent was taken out in 1839 (his own notes, quoted by Hopkins and others, sketched the development as he saw it), and he applied his action to the organ under construction at St Denis by Cavaillé-Coll, whose high-pressure stops were indeed said to have been unplayable without this key-action. It was probably also in France that the first fully pneumatic action was made, in which all the tracker's backfalls, squares, rollers etc were replaced by one pneumatic tube from key to pallet. The system is accredited to P.-A. Moitessier (1845), and was later modified with a partly mechanical action and adopted by such major builders as Willis (St Paul's Cathedral, 1872). Although Walcker applied this so-called tubular pneumatic action to his cone-chests in 1889, on the whole the action gained only a minor success outside England (and, to some extent, the USA) because the action was sluggish when the keys were too far removed from the chests. As for the chests themselves, English, American and French builders preferred improved slider-chests to barless chests, often modifying the larger pallets with secondary mechanism allowing them to be opened without undue key-pressure (Willis patent dated 1861, etc).

Audsley was witness to much American activity in designing 'pneumatic chests' in the late 19th century. Around the turn of the century, American builders such as Steere and Estey developed a reliable tubular-pneumatic action using ventil-chests which they employed quite extensively, as did Möller and some of the midwestern builders, but other builders, such as Hook & Hastings, Hutchings and, in Canada, Casavant, went almost directly from Barker-machine mechanical to electro-pneumatic actions.

Electric organs were devised during the same period in England (Wilkinson 1826, Gauntlett 1852, Goundry 1863) and France (Du Moncel, Barker, Stein & fils). Electro-pneumatic action (see fig. 16) overcomes the difficulty of directly opening a pallet by electro-magnets in that the magnet opens instead the smaller valve of a pneumatic motor which then opens the pallet. One such system is usually accredited to Péschard (c1860), who took out a joint patent with Barker in 1868, and who in turn licensed Bryceson to build such an action in the Theatre Royal, Drury Lane (1868). According to Hopkins, an electrification of the organ at Gloucester Cathedral for the Three Choirs Festival of 1868 allowed the keyboards to be placed nearer the conductor, far from the pipes, an obvious and updated version of the 'long movements' of the tracker-action organ used in the 1784 Commemoration of Handel in Westminster Abbey. A decade or more before the end of the century Walcker in Germany, Merklin in France, Roosevelt in the USA, and Willis in England were all producing reliable electric actions and could thus build detached consoles some way away from the organs high up at the west end or in a triforium gallery of the quire. The stop mechanism could also be operated electrically (Bryceson patent, 1868). Particularly in the USA, where church or cathedral organs were less bound by tradition than in England, many electric actions were patented and improved during the 1890s, becoming a norm shortly after 1900, some 25 years before the Willis firm, for example, turned exclusively to electro-pneumatic action. During the 20th century, particularly before the Organ Revival made itself felt, most important organ builders throughout the world devised one or other type of electro-pneumatic action (see Whitworth, 1930, 3/1948). Clearly, electric systems could serve the accessories such as stop-combinations ('free combinations', 'adjustable combinations') whereby a button or switch of some kind could bring on preselected stops, or Swell pedals operating variously worked shutters around part or all of the pipework. Most of the ingenuity exercised on such accessories belongs to the early 20th century rather than the 19th.

3. SOME INFLUENTIAL ORGANS

Reference has already been made to Walcker's organ for the Pauls-kirche, Frankfurt, and Schulze's for Halberstadt Cathedral. Walcker's habitual scheme brought his instruments close to such later 18th-century organs as that at St Michael, Hamburg, with a large, heavy Great organ (often 32′) and a pedal booming and powerful yet removed from true chorus purposes. Other German firms such as Schulze and Ladegast seem often to have made a brighter sound, with large-scale Mixtures and a tonal chorus brash yet recognizably in a tradition. Schulze's influence in England was great, as his large Diapasons caught the taste of the time and indeed governed it for some decades after the Great Exhibition of 1851. Even his little colour stop, the narrow-scaled Lieblich Gedackt, became standard in English organs for the next 100 years. Such builders had a high standard of workmanship and the mass of 'good solid pipework' of foundational pitches in an influential organ like Sauer's for the Thomaskirche, Leipzig, was seen as a great advance on the little Baroque ranks of a Silbermann or Schnitger. The craftsmanship and materials in a major Cavaillé-Coll organ are immensely impressive, as are the spaciousness and complicated actions (allowing pipes 'room to speak') and the careful planning of several chest levels. The drawings of the various elevations, tiers and cross-sections of the St Sulpice organ, for example, are witness to one of the great engineering masterpieces of the 19th century.

Although the St Denis organ has a well-known position in organ history, few technical details have been published and only its restoration will make its real character clearer. The casework had already been designed when several builders tendered for the work, and Cavaillé-Coll's two plans of 1833 and 1841 show the great changes in organ building during that crucial decade. Flutes and mutations were reduced, overblowing stops were introduced, string stops gave a new stridency, Barker's action allowed new arrangements of the chests, and the wind supply was increased and improved. Despite its ancestry in Bédos de Celles' scheme for a large 32′ organ, the instrument at St Denis (see Table 25, p. 162) was a great step along the 19th-century path. The Bombarde and Pedal departments became an ideal for hundreds of French or French-inspired organs over the next century or so; the scaling throughout became wider than classical French scaling, and the voicing, as well as the wind pressure, stronger. It is not always clear how Cavaillé-Coll intended his organs to be registered, but since such stops as the Flûte harmonique are simply new versions

ORGAN

TABLE 25

St Denis Abbey (now St Denis Cathedral), Paris
Aristide Cavaillé-Coll, 1833–41

Grand orgue (II)			*Positif* (I)	
Montre	32		Bourdon	16
Montre	16		Bourdon	8
Bourdon	16		Salicional	8
Montre	8		Flûte (open)★	8
Bourdon	8		Prestant	4
Viole	8		Flûte octaviante★	4
Flûte traversière★	8		Nasard ou quinte	2⅔
Flûte octaviante★	4		Doublette	2
Prestant	4		Flageolet★	2
Nasard ou quinte	2⅔		Tierce	1⅗
Doublette	2		Fourniture	IV
Grosse Fourniture	IV		Cymbale	IV
Petite Fourniture	IV		Trompette★	8
Grosse Cymbale	IV		Cor d'harmonie	8 (bass)
Petite Cymbale	IV		Hautbois	8 (treble)
Cornet (mounted)	V		Cromorne	8
I Trompette★	8		Tremblant	
II Trompette★	8			
Basson	8 (bass)			
Cor anglais	8 (treble)			
Clairon octaviant★	4			

Récit (IV)			*Bombarde* (III)	
			Grand Cornet	VII
Bourdon	8		Bourdon	16
Flûte★	8		Bourdon	8
Flûte★	4		Flûte	8
Quinte	2⅔		Prestant	4
Octavin★	2		Nasard ou quinte	2⅔
Trompette★	8		Doublette	2
Voix humaine★	8		Bombarde	16
Clairon★	4		I Trompette★	8
			II Trompette★	8
			I Clairon★	4
			II Clairon★	4

Pédal

Flûte ouverte	32	Compass: $C–f–f'''$ (pedal reeds $F'–f$)
Flûte ouverte	16	Harmonic and reed stops on heavier wind
Flûte ouverte	8	Combination pedals (swell, couplers IV/II,
Gros Nasard ou quinte	5⅓	III/II, II/II, I/II, high-pressure basses,
		high-pressure trebles, sub-octave coupler
Flûte ouverte	4	to all manuals, pedal couplers to all
Basse-contre	16 (24)	manuals)
Bombarde	16 (24)	*Grand orgue* did not play until II/II pedal
Basson	8 (12)	operated
I Trompette	8 (12)	Stops marked ★ are double-length harmon-
II Trompette	8 (12)	ic stops
I Clairon	4 (6)	
II Clairon	4 (6)	

of the auxiliary 8′ ranks drawn in old *fonds d'orgue* combinations, it is likely that he expected them to be used in choruses as well as solos. Much the same could be said for the string stops (complete with tuning-slots at the top of the pipe) and the thick, stopped Bourdons. Nicking of languids was generally severe, at least in later organs of this builder; this, added to the slots cut into even the smallest Mixture pipes, aided smooth, constant tone. Conical and narrow-scaled stopped pipes were not conspicuous, and Cavaillé-Coll's spectrum of pipe forms was not particularly great. The foundation stops (*jeux de fonds*) of one manual were placed on one wind-chest, the reeds and (sometimes) flute mutations (*jeux de combinaison*) were placed on another. Each chest could have its own wind pressure and each could be controlled by a valve that admitted wind only when required, thus allowing a registration to be 'prepared'. The *Grand orgue* was never underbuilt in relation to the Swell, as it often was in England. Feeder and reservoir bellows were generous, and the pneumatic action somewhat cumbersome in the space it took. As with Schulze organs, soundboards were ample in size for the boldly treated pipework. But neither electric actions nor general crescendo gadgets were found on Cavaillé-Coll's organs.

In Italy, Serassi, like his French and English colleagues, 'extended' local traditions and made many quite large organs of a curious Venetian compromise. The main manual would control 20 or more stops, including 16′ or even 32′ Principale and flutes and violas of 8′ and 4′; most chorus stops were divided; the highest ranks were collected into Mixtures; and solo and chorus reeds were strong in tone. One or two subsidiary manuals, of six to ten halved stops often in a Swell box, provided echo effects but no true chorus. The compass was long (frequently from *C*′); the pedal organ had six to eight bass stops; and there were many accessories, both sounding (bells, thunder, drum) and mechanical (composition pedals, couplers, including octave and suboctave).

In Spain, organ building came to something of a standstill, while the farther cities of eastern Europe were completely conquered by the central German and Bohemian organ building, organ repertory and organ players, as once they might have been by the Austrian. The outposts of German organ art in east Prussia and Silesia had long known large instruments (both Protestant and Roman Catholic) and the new techniques led to wide dissemination of ideas. Occasionally a builder would try something new, such as Buchholz's solo organ, 16.8.8.8.8.8.4, in Kronstadt Cathedral (1839); but on the whole builders were more anxious to improve action, accessories, bellows and chests of the more conventional organs.

ORGAN

In many ways the country best able to develop its organ was England, where a new awareness of foreign designs and repertory coincided with favourable economic conditions. While much work remains to be done on the position of the organ in France and Italy during the period 1830–50, the general picture of the English organ is clear enough. During the 1820s, the Choir organ was superseded by the Swell; pedals came to be regarded as normal (though only with a rank or two of large-scaled wooden pipes); the compass generally remained no lower than G'; and organists did as well as they could with the newly favoured music of J. S. Bach – *Das wohltemperirte Clavier* being as much played as the true organ music. Much of the newness of the British organ before Henry Willis's influential instrument for the 1851 Exhibition has been accredited to the friendship between H. J. Gauntlett, the composer and organist, and William Hill, organ builder and former partner in the firm of Elliot. About 1833 Gauntlett visited Haarlem, apparently on the advice of Samuel Wesley (who presumably knew of it from Burney's account in his *Travels*), and there are various hints throughout Gauntlett's career as *Orgelsachverständiger* ('expert adviser on organs') that such instruments were in his mind. His personal library too shows him to have been a good example of the outward-looking early Victorian musician. Of the dozen or so organs built by Hill under Gauntlett's influence, certainly the one at Great George Street Chapel, Liverpool (1841), was the most indicative of things to come. Like Hopkins, Gauntlett knew enough German organ music to see the C compass as most useful for manuals, while S. S. Wesley favoured G' compass even on the new Willis masterpiece of St George's Hall, Liverpool. Much the same reason lay behind Gauntlett's scheme for the pedal departments of larger organs, for example the one at Christ Church, Newgate Street (1838); such a scheme (see Table 26) presupposed 'continental scaling' and not the large open-wood pedal scales described by Hopkins as over twice too large.

Cavaillé-Coll visited Hill's workshops in 1844, as he did others at that period, and the influence they had on each other deserves closer study. The French, German and Italian stop names of many Hill–Gauntlett organs suggest at least paper knowledge of and interest in foreign organs; as late as 1871, Willis's new organ for the Albert Hall can be related closely to Cavaillé-Coll's for St Sulpice. Hill's Liverpool organ was a compromise between traditional English and new continental styles, with a 16-stop Swell (including 16′ reed), a small Choir organ of flutes, a high-pressure Tuba played from the Swell, six couplers, five composition pedals, and a complete compass of $C–d'f'''$

Hill also designed a new kind of pallet that slid open and admitted high-pressure wind without increasing the touch-resistance. Neither he nor Gauntlett felt obliged to give up the long-established tradition of combining many international features: their organ at St Olave, Southwark (1846), for instance, was almost Serassian in its big Great and its solo Swell. It was left to Willis's organ for St George's Hall, Liverpool (1855), to establish fully the 'first modern British organ' (see Table 27), which remained an ideal throughout the British Empire at its apogee. Less opulent instruments by Willis and the builders he influenced would merely have had fewer choices of 8′ and 4′ colour. Large though such organs were, their priority was not music and its needs; rather they encouraged even further the age-old regard for large organs *per se*, useful for transcriptions of orchestral and vocal music but nonetheless basically engineering projects with fashionable paraphernalia – in this case, inclined stop-jambs, pneumatic thumb-pistons, concave and radiating pedal-board (perfected by Willis soon after 1851), Barker levers to each department, varied wind pressures,

TABLE 26

Open Diapason	16
Open Diapason	16
Montre	16
Bourdon	16
Principal	8
Fifteenth	4
Tierce Mixture	V
Larigot Mixture	V
Contra Posaune	16
Posaune	8

TABLE 27

St George's Hall, Liverpool
Reconstructed 1867, under supervision of W. T. Best

Choir organ: 16.8.8.8.8.8.8.4.4.4.2⅔.2.2.IV.8.8.8.4
Great organ: 16.8.8.8.8.8.8.5⅓.4.4.4.4.3⅕.2⅔.2.2.II.V.IV.16.8.8.8.4.4
Swell organ: 16.8.8.8.8.8.4.4.4.2⅗.2.2.2.II.V.16.16.8.8.8.8.8.8.4.4
Solo organ: 16.8.8.4.2.16.8.8.8.8.4.8.8.8.4 (last four on heavy wind, 380 mm to 500 mm)
Pedal: 32.32.16.16.16.16.8.8.5⅓.4.V.IV.32.16.16.8.4
Compass: *G′–a′′′*; pedal *C–f′*
Ten couplers (including Suboctave Swell to Great, Superoctave Swell to Great)
42 pneumatic pistons
Two bellows blown by a steam engine (8 horsepower)
Wind pressure: from 90 mm to 510 mm
Pneumatic lever (doubled for pedals)

ORGAN

new wind-raising devices, pneumatic couplers and a Swell pedal. The
Swell alone was a good example of the general attitude. Of the 'double
Venetian front' at Gloucester Cathedral (1847), Willis himself observed that 'the pianissimo was simply astounding' but gave no reason
why he thought this a desirable aim.

The old-fashioned unequal temperament at Liverpool, applied on
the advice of S. S. Wesley, was changed in 1867 (though the old G'
compass was not changed to C until 1898). The wind pressure of the
solo reeds was raised to 48·5 cm in the bass and 62 cm in the treble.
Along with greater power went the demand for apparatus to control
it. In 1857 Willis had patented a crescendo pedal – a foot-lever rotating
a cylinder that activated pneumatic motors at the ends of the sliders.
There were many other devices. In later organs, Willis took his
schemes to a logical end by ousting the Choir organ for a Solo organ
in certain three-manual instruments (e.g. Sheldonian Theatre, Oxford, 1877); already at Gloucester (1847) the Swell had been made
nearly three times as large as the Choir. Thus the fitful English secondary chorus, first documented in the early 17th-century Chair organs,
became 'obsolete'.

It is clear from the lists of specifications given by Hopkins and
Rimbault, as it is in earlier lists by Seidel, Hamilton and others, that
each major firm about 1850 had its hallmarks. Each introduced into
many organs a characteristic stop (e.g. Hill's Octave Clarion 2′) or
principle of construction or occasional foible (e.g. Cavaillé-Coll's
Septième ranks); each had its own patented action, chest and wind-
raising device; and each had a known attitude towards some major
development like harmonic reeds, exploiting them or rejecting them
as the case may be. Major German organs built about 1860 were in
general either less inventive or more traditional than in England and
France, and this difference was reflected in those organs of the USA
and the British Empire that followed the foreign models favoured by
their respective builders. St George's Hall, Liverpool, had the ideal
town-hall organ, a distinct type anticipated by such concert organs as
Elliot's in the Hanover Square Rooms, London (1804, 12 stops). It was
the secular organ (Exeter Hall, London, and Birmingham Town Hall,
both 1849) that first saw the application of the pneumatic lever to key
action, and one of Hill's secular organs in London (The Panopticon,
1853) that first had pneumatically operated sliders, as well as higher
pressure for treble pipes and a reversible crescendo pedal pushing out
the organ stops one by one. The Solo organ or fourth manual, whether
enclosed (Leeds, 1859) or not, also had its origins in the town-hall
organ. The emphasis behind such contemporary designs as, say,

Willis's organ for St Paul's Cathedral and Hill's for Melbourne Town Hall, Australia, reflects their ecclesiastical and secular natures: one would expect the latter to have bigger Solo manuals, smaller Choir manuals, perhaps a bigger compass, and certainly a larger array of unusual tone-effects.

It was the crescendo and diminuendo of a British town-hall organ (Glasgow; T. C. Lewis, 1877) that led Hans von Bülow to write to the local newspaper and claim never to have 'met with an organ so good in Germany'. Indeed, by comparison the German organ may well have seemed a dreary instrument, with little ability to blend or offer the organist much delight in its tone, touch or musical potential. It can hardly be assumed, however, that the tone of new German organs did not occasionally delight; organists may well have liked the sounds produced by Schulze's highly differentiated voicing in a small two-manual like that at Etzelbach (1869). Such an organ (see Table 28) was utterly typical in its day, though in some ways Schulze was old-fashioned (e.g. with his diagonal bellows at Doncaster, 1862).

TABLE 28

Manual I		Manual II	
Bordun	16	Lieblich Gedackt	8
Prinzipal	8	Salizional	8
Hohlflöte	8	Dolce	8
Gamba	8	Gedacktflöte	4
Oktave	4		
Mixture	III	*Pedal*	
		Sub-Bass	16
		Violonbass	16
Couplers: Manual I to II; Manual I to Pedal		Gedacktbass	8

Much German music of the late 19th century was written for a large, somewhat sombre-voiced instrument which depended for effect more on weight and extremes of loudness and softness than on the sort of colour provided by, for instance, Cavaillé-Coll's Bombarde manual or Willis's Swell. Indeed, the very size and gravity of such instruments is their chief musical attribute, and Liszt, Reubke, Reger and others capitalized impressively on these qualities. Specifications were often much more classical in appearance than their voicing and general tone justify. Extremes of timbre in the form of harmonic reed choruses were not much favoured, and it is not always easy to see exactly why a German organ, even in its various neo-classical guises, needed a third or fourth manual. The large instrument in Magdeburg Cathedral (see

ORGAN

TABLE 29

Magdeburg Cathedral
Reubke, 1856–61

I: 16.16.8.8.8.5⅓.4.4.4.2⅔.2.IV.IV.IV.16.8
II: 16.8.8.8.8.8.4.4.2.II.V.III.8
III: 16.8.8.8.8.8.4.4.4.2⅔.2.V.16
IV: 16.8.8.8.8.8.4.4.4.2⅔.2.IV.8.8
V: 8.8.8.4.2⅔.2.II–III (Echo played from III)
Pedal I: 32.32.16.16.16.10⅔.8.8.8.5⅓.4.2.V.IV.32.16.8.4
Pedal II: 16.8.8.5⅓.4.2.16

Table 29), built by the firm of Reubke, expresses the potential sought by such composers as its scion Julius Reubke (1834–58), Walcker's organ of 1886 for St Stephen's Cathedral, Vienna, was even less systematic, with an ordinary Pedal but a huge Great organ manual of 35 stops strewn over the west end, and two further manuals; only one stop was in a Swell box. Similarly, not until 1857 at Ulm did Walcker use the Barker lever and not until 1890 a fully pneumatic action. A lack of inventiveness was also evident in the stop-lists themselves: Sauer's two organs in Leipzig, both with about 60 stops (the Petrikirche, 1885, and the Thomaskirche, 1889), had almost identical specifications, both full of heavy 8′ stops. Such were the instruments played by Reger and Straube, and for which registrations were fairly standardized. Thus 8′ ranks were mixed freely, according to choice, but a 4′ stop aided their blend, particularly a wide 4′ above a narrow 8′. An organ that cannot provide an accompaniment of Gedackt 8′ + Voix céleste 8′ + Spitzflöte 4′ voiced on late 19th-century principles cannot provide the sounds intended by Reger.

For such music it is also vital to be able to change stops quickly. Accessories became a priority, and by 1900 a German organ of 12 speaking stops could have as many as 12 'aids'. This was in addition to the Swell, which by then usually took the form of a cylinder rolled by the foot (*Walze*) and operating horizontal shutters. Other aids were the manual coupler, pedal coupler, octave and suboctave couplers, several pre-set combinations (labelled *p*, *mf*, *pp* etc), one or more free combinations (set as required), General Crescendo (likewise operated by a foot cylinder or *Rollschweller*) and so on. But it is a mistake to assume that such composers as Reger necessarily required a General Crescendo or fixed combinations. The free combination, which requires good precision work on the builder's part, is more useful, whether mechanical or pneumatic. Thus a large proportion of any organ's cost in about 1900 must have been allocated to the accessories, particularly in the untraditional and large organs of the USA (Roosevelt) and Canada (Casavant Frères). Similarly, the high-pressure reeds and large-mouth flues (called Seraphon) made by Weigle between 1890 and 1940 needed careful engineering, 'hard' though the tone undeniably sounded even at the time (as is shown by Schweitzer's opinion of the Stuttgart Liederhalle organ built in 1894–5).

Although all 19th-century organs may now deserve the status of historical monuments, little musical sense can be made of such mature Romantic organs as Weigle's at Lauterbach (1906), of which the stop-list is given in Table 30. Such organs were not so much 'Romantic' as perversions of a legitimate ideal current from Gabler to Walcker; it is hard to see them being fashionable again. Yet even Weigle's Stuttgart organ was criticized by Audsley in 1905 for making 'absolutely no attempt to place at the disposal of the *virtuoso* the ready means of producing complicated orchestral effects or of massing special tone-colours'. Why Audsley and his contemporaries found such aims important is puzzling.

As an example of a true Romantic organ close to the music of a lively, century-long tradition, Ladegast's organ for Merseburg Cathedral (built 1859–62 in a classical case by Thayssner), for which

TABLE 30

Lauterbach Weigle, 1906			
Manual I		*Manual II*	
Bourdon	16	Geigenprinzipal★	8
Prinzipal	8	Flöte★	8
Gedackt★	8	Viola	8
Flûte octaviante	8	Quintatön	8
Gamba★	8	Salizional	8
Dulziana	8	Aeoline	8
Oktave	4	Voix céleste	8
Rohrflöte	4	Fugara	4
Oktave	2	Traversflöte	4
Mixtur	IV–V	Kornett	III–IV
Trompete	8	Oboe (flue)	8
Tuba mirabilis	8		
		Stops marked ★ were Seraphon stops	
Pedal			
Kontrabass	16		
Violonbass	16		
Sub-Bass	16		
Quintatön	16		
Violoncello	8		
Posaune	16		

Liszt wrote his Prelude and Fugue on B–A–C–H, would serve, although it is of interest that this large organ possesses no enclosed divisions, nor playing aids beyond a few couplers and Sperrventils; so would Cavaillé-Coll's for Ste Clotilde, Paris, where César Franck was organist from 1859 to 1890:

Grand orgue 16.16.8.8.8.8.4.4.2⅔.2.V.16.8.4
Positif 16.8.8.8.8.8.4.4.2⅔.2.8.8.4
Récit 8.8.8.8.4.2.8.8.8.4
Pédale 32.16.8.4.16.16.8.4

The superiority of Cavaillé-Coll's voicing, particularly of the reeds, would have given Franck a more musical instrument than Weigle's at Lauterbach. The several 8′ stops are there for variety, and registrations followed traditional ideas of *plein jeu, grand jeu, fonds d'orgue* etc, for which the *pédales de combinaison* were essential. In general the principles behind the specification at Ste Clotilde were quite different from those of Weigle, though it cannot be assumed that the French repertory from Franck to Messiaen necessarily requires the edgy tone and reed brilliance of French organs. Certainly, however, French builders remained faithful to slider-chests both in practice and theory (cf J. Guédon: *Nouveau manuel*, 1903).

As an example of *fin de siècle* development beyond the demands of organ music, the Great organ manual of Walcker's Paulskirche organ, Frankfurt (1827), can be compared with its rebuild by the same firm 72 years later. The stop-list alone makes clear the change of taste and the manner in which the over-confident revision destroyed the early 19th-century monument:

(1827) 32.16.16.16.8.8.8.8.5⅓.4.4.4.3⅕.2⅔.2.2.1⅗.2.2.1⅗.1.   Cornet.V.IV.16.8
       mechanical action, slider-chest

(1899) 16.16.8.8.8.8.8.8.8.8.4.4.4.2.2.Cornet.VI.16.8.8.4 pneumatic action,
       cone-chest

From the mid-19th century organs in the USA broke from the older English pattern with increasing use of European innovations (often demanded by organists who had studied in Europe). Gambas and Harmonic Flutes (the latter usually at 4′ pitch) assumed a permanent place in the stop-lists of even small organs, and solo divisions and high-pressure or harmonic-length reeds appeared in larger ones. The Barker machine was commonly used in large organs, and early experiments (Roosevelt, 1869) were made with electric actions. Immigrant builders, mainly from Germany, began to do significant work in the mid-west (Pfeffer, Kilgen, Koehnken, etc) but appear not to have had significant influence on the large eastern builders. Little distinction was made between church and secular organs: Hook's large organs in Mechanics Hall, Worcester, Mass. (1864; recently restored) and Immaculate Conception Church, Boston (1863; under threat as from 1987), were very similar in size, stop-list, and voicing, and were indeed expected to play much the same repertory.

4. ELECTRICITY AND THE ORGAN

Apart from electronic 'organs', the instruments of Robert Hope-Jones and his lesser imitators are considered the worst in organ design. Unfortunately not a single Hope-Jones organ survives in authentic form, so severe has been the rejection and so untrustworthy the working parts of his instruments. In specification they extend the principles behind such organs as that at Lauterbach by omitting all ranks above a wide flute 2′, resulting in such schemes as the following for the Great organ manual at Worcester Cathedral (1896): 16.8.8.8.8.8.8.4.4.2.16.8 plus ten couplers to Great and seven composition keys. The tone was characterized by a corresponding smoothing out of acoustic 'interest' and a princely indifference to traditional chorus-blending. Ignored by French and German organ historians, Hope-Jones built few instruments himself and had only limited business success in Britain and the USA; but his influence was great and typifies the trend against which the Organ Revival reacted.

During the 25 years from 1889 to 1914 Hope-Jones made two major contributions: to key-action (electric, with stop-switches for registration, 'double touch' for keys and accessories), and to pipework and specification (large harmonic Trombas, very narrow Trumpets, heavy-pressure Diapasons with leathered lips to reduce brightness, very narrow string stops and wide-scaled Clarabellas). His diaphone pipe of 1893 was itself a new departure (see fig. 22), many examples of which can still be heard in the English-speaking world. Though no doubt more effective as a foghorn (an earlier version was accepted as such by the Canadian government, and diaphones were used as lighthouse fog-signals as late as the 1960s by the US Coast Guard), the diaphone is a good guide to the tone required by some musicians about 1900. Hope-Jones's actions were too finely designed for organs (they were more effective in telephone exchanges), but the period was one of experiment in electrical technology and his contributions are important. So many devices or facilities, such as those enabling the organist to 'prepare' stops which remained silent until required, or to open Swell shutters one by one, were made much easier with electricity; so was 'borrowing' stops, still disapproved of by Audsley in 1905 but in principle leading to 'unit-chests', 'extension organs' and other systems using one rank of pipes for several purposes. Hope-Jones thus typifies a movement that led to such extraordinary achievements for their time as the stadium organ in Chicago (Bartola, 1929), where 44 ranks of pipes and various percussion effects produced an organ of six manuals (hanging in lofts above an auditorium of 25,000 seats) controlled by a movable console of 884 stop-knobs and accessories, and blown by pressures of 40 to 140 cm, the latter for the diaphones. The extension organ of 1938 in the Civic Hall, Wolverhampton, was more modest and typical (see Table 31).

Electricity has been used to replace key-pallet action (see fig. 16), operate stop-mechanisms and accessories (couplers, combinations, tremulant, Swell shutters etc), drive a motor for raising the wind and replace older chest types. The design of circuits requires great skill and was perfected only during the 20th century. Certain sophisticated

TABLE 31

Civic Hall, Wolverhampton
John Compton Organ Co., 1938

Chamber I	Pitch	Pipes	Pedal	Choir	Great
Sub-Bass	32	62	32.16.8.4		
Contrabass	16	56	16.8.4		
Bombarde	16	56	16.8.4		
Contra Salicional	16	109	16.8	16.8.4.2⅔.2.1⅓.1	
Gemshorn	8	61		8	
Vox angelica	4	49		8 (from c)	
Lieblich Gedackt	16	97	16	16.8.4.2	
Claribel Flute	8	61		8	
Flauto traverso	4	61		4	
Nazard	2⅔	61		2⅔	
Tierce	1⅗	61		1⅗	
Double Open Diapason	16	97	16.10⅔.5⅓	8	16.8.4.2
First Diapason	8	61			8
Second Diapason	8	61			8
Stopped Diapason	8	61			8
Octave	4	61			4
Twelfth	2⅔	61			2⅔
Superoctave	2	61			2
Furniture IV	1⅓	244			IV
Harmonics V	6⅔	364	V at 16', V at 8'		V
Contra Posaune	16	85	16.8	8	16.4
Tromba	8	61			8
Horn	8	61		8	8

gadgets like Willis's 'infinite speed and gradation Swell' (where the amount by which the pedal is pushed forward is a measure of the speed at which the shutters open) date from the 1930s. In 1905 Audsley was still justifying the 'incomplete' nature of his discussion of electro-pneumatic actions by 'the tentative state of that branch of organ construction at this time'. By then, however, knowledge of such actions was advanced enough for E. M. Skinner's system to be applied at St Bartholomew, New York, to a console playing two organs, one at each end of the church. Skinner was perhaps America's most innovatory designer of actions; his 'pitman-chest', still widely used in the USA, was first developed during his employment with Hutchings in the 1890s and was a radical departure from other systems then in use which were, with the exception of Austin's equally original 'Universal Air Chest', largely electrified adaptations of the older slider-, ventil- and cone-chests.

Perhaps the most radical application of electricity to organ building was that enabling any key to be connected to any pipe; each pipe can

Chamber II				Swell	Solo
Contra Viola	16	85	16	16.8.4	
Geigen	8	61		8	
Voix célestes	4	49		8 (from c)	
Rohrflute	8	61		8	
Geigen Octave	4	61		4	
Fifteenth	2	61		2	
Mixture IV	1⅓	244		IV	
Double Trumpet	16	85	16	16.4	8
Trumpet	8	61		8	
Hautboy	8	61		8	
Violoncello	8	61			8
Viole céleste	8	61			8
Harmonic Flute	8	61			8
Harmonic Flute	4	61			4
Clarinet	8	61			8
Orchestral Oboe	8	61		Choir	8
Tuba	8	73		8	8.4

Contained in two Swell boxes in the roof of the hall, without case or case front, the sound escaping between plaster roof-sections
50 ranks of pipes
Electric action for keys, stops and accessories
26 double-touch pistons to manuals and pedal
20 toe-pistons
11 other pistons, 3 Tremulants and 2 'Sustainers' (Choir, Solo)
15 couplers
Electronic section for Solo Organ (flute and reed effects, chimes)

be given its own little chest or 'unit' to stand on, and such unit-chests can be used for one or more ranks of an organ. A 2' pipe could be c' of a nominal 8' rank, c of a 4' rank, F of a $2\frac{2}{3}'$ rank etc, and the row of pipes 'extended' to allow complete compass at all levels. The principle of 'extension' was known to Praetorius for a little table positive, and Marcussen applied it to six of his *Hauptwerk* stops at Siseby in 1819; an 'extension organ' is merely one taking the idea of such 'duplexed ranks' to a logical conclusion. Clearly electric actions made such systems much easier, either by unit-chests or by electric couplers. That the idea is basically inimical to true organ tone, since no consistently scaled rank will serve two purposes, did not escape the attention of the better builders. At Wolverhampton, for example, the principle is applied very discreetly. But extended ranks cannot provide as much power and variety as their stop-knobs promise, and builders therefore compensated by coarsening yet further the tonal quality of the pipes concerned: the pressure was raised, languids sharp-angled, upper lips 'leathered' (i.e. thin leather was glued round the edge of the lip), scaling enlarged or narrowed excessively, perhaps with a double languid (drawing in air from outside) or double mouth (two sides of a square pipe provided with a mouth), reed-tongues 'weighted' to encourage stronger foundational tone, cheaper metal used, and often (in the pedals) a diaphone-type resorted to (with cylindrical resonator-tubes of large diameter). Many of the orchestral colours imitated by builders and recommended by influential writers were themselves ephemeral (e.g. the euphonium). New chests, particularly the pitman-chest (as designed by E. M. Skinner) were devised in which the key and drawstop had equal access to the pallet valve below the pipe, only sounding it when both were activated.

Builders of the period 1840–1940 often disagreed with one another's taste in details. Hope-Jones's diaphones were not made by most builders or Cavaillé-Coll's slotted pipes by others, or English leathered Diapasons outside a certain period, or the unit-chest by most builders of church organs. The origin of many voicing techniques, such as weighting reed-tongues with brass or lead, is obscure; so many had their origins in much earlier periods that only the extremes of various kinds (high pressure, diaphone pipes, electro-pneumatic action etc) can be dated from the 19th century. It was these extremes that led to the cinema organ about 1925. A large-looking Wurlitzer organ of this highly idiosyncratic period contained only a few ranks of pipes voiced to either extreme and 'extended' to provide many stops available at every pitch on every manual: a *reductio ad absurdum* of the principle of 'floating' chests. With its percussion traps and effects, its high-pressure pipework enclosed in one or two grille-fronted chambers, its movable console operating electric actions and sound-modifiers, the cinema organ can be seen not only following on from the 'serious' organs of Hope-Jones, Pendlebury, Franklin Lloyd and others, but as an updated version of Vogler's orchestrion. Again it was not the church organ but the secular that demonstrated an idea taken to its logical end.

5. THE CINEMA ORGAN

The cinema organ was designed to take the place of instrumental players in early 20th-century cinemas and theatres. It was developed in the USA by the Wurlitzer Company in conjunction with Robert Hope-Jones and manufactured from 1910. Wurlitzer set out to build an organ with two manuals and pedals which would provide the perfect accompaniment to silent films (early models were known as 'Wurlitzer Hope-Jones Unit Orchestras'). In the USA the term 'theatre organ' is preferred.

The unification principle was adopted throughout: all stops (16', 4', 2' etc) were 'borrowed' by a complicated system of relays from the basic 8' ranks designed to imitate orchestral instruments; most of the stops in the various pitches were duplexed from manual to manual. Many of the strange new voices invented by Hope-Jones were incorporated, including the Quintadena, Kinura, Krumet etc, and above all the Tibia clausa, which became the fundamental sound of the theatre organ; it was evolved from the stopped-flute family by voicing very large-scale wood pipes on high wind pressure with throbbing tremulants. The expressive resources were further enhanced by enclosing the entire organ in Swell boxes, evolving an ultra-rapid electro-pneumatic action, and adding Second Touch for playing counter-melodies with the left hand. The result was an amazing instrument with a warm, novel sound, ill-suited to the music of Bach but ideal for its intended purpose.

Every possible pitched percussion instrument was imitated – xylophone, harp, chimes, glockenspiel, vibraphone – while non-pitched percussion instruments, such as drums, cymbals, castanets and triangle, were included with a dozen or more 'traps' (sound-effects), for example steamer whistle, telephone bell, surf, horses' hooves, birds, police siren etc, to form what became known as the 'toy counter'. Stop-keys were used instead of drawknobs and the 'horseshoe' console was adopted (see fig. 51), partly for appearance, partly for ease of playing. The stop-keys were coloured for easy distinction: white for flue pipes, red for imitations of reeds, amber for imitations of strings, black for couplers. The president of the Royal College of Organists was heard to remark that the instrument looked more like an ice-cream stall than an organ. In most theatres the console was installed on a lift to bring the organist up into full view while he played his solo and down again for accompanying the films. Wurlitzer built 2000 cinema organs, far more than any of its competitors. Perhaps the best-known of Wurlitzer's instruments was also its largest: that at Radio City Music Hall in New York. In due course more than 60 firms produced similar instruments, including Robert Morton, Möller and Compton.

With the great advantage over an orchestra in being able to extemporize, organists could provide individualized accompaniment to any film, especially a comedy, and audiences often found as much to laugh at in the musical comments of an accomplished player as in the film. The theatre organ's heyday in the USA was the late 1920s, when many organists had become so famous that theatre-goers went to hear them irrespective of the rest of the programme. But immediately films began projecting their own hitherto missing sounds, theatre organs faded out.

In Britain, however, most of the organists were retained, at first in case the 'talkies' broke down (which they frequently did), but later because theatre owners discovered that 10 or 15 minutes of organ playing, with the organist spotlit at the top of the lift, was a welcome contrast to the mechanically reproduced film music. Theatre organ music attained its greatest popularity in Britain through the medium of radio; about 1936 the BBC installed its own four-manual Compton organ, which was as popular as any other radio entertainment. Ultimately, however, the genre foundered in the wake of television. As theatres began to be pulled down or rebuilt and the organs were in danger of destruction, societies were formed in the USA and Britain to reinstall instruments in auditoriums, restaurants and homes, or, where possible, to preserve them *in situ* in restored cinemas.

6. THE NATURE OF ORGANS ABOUT 1900

To most musicians outside the organ world, and to an increasing number within it, the mature post-Romantic organ of about 1900 produces an unsatisfactory sound even when playing music written at the time. Whether the builder at the turn of the century was more indifferent to the musical purposes of organs, or whether the music itself was less suited to the organ idiom than had been the case about 1700 is impossible to say. It is assumed too readily that the Romantic organ was in this respect different from and inferior to its predecessor. But in its ingenious mechanism and sophisticated technology, the organ of 1900 had much in common with the Greek hydraulis: technical ingenuity merely outstripped musical application or at least pushed it into second place.

The real difference between an average organ of 1900 and one of 1700 is at once more elusive and more obvious: it sounds different. Builder and player had consciously rejected the sound of old organs, but the reason for it has to be defined and refined by each interpreter of organ history. It was not the desire for intense tone as such; 16th-century voicing must often have been taken 'to the limit', though naturally on lower pressure. It was not the newly invented pipe forms themselves; every period invented colourful stops that were by nature

51. Cinema organ by the Wurlitzer Company, Chicago

peripheral to the basic Diapason chorus, though less numerous. It was not pneumatic and electric actions which, though invariable and therefore requiring less 'lively' voicing, were invented only for practical convenience. It was not the imitation of orchestral sound as such, despite the orchestra's increased intensity. It was not the sombre setting in the 19th-century church that forced organ builders to avoid Baroque brilliance (nor in any case were church organs as 'advanced' as secular ones). It was not that organists became more out of touch with general musical taste; on the contrary, a parish church organist of 1900 knew much more of the contemporary situation in orchestral music than did one of 1700. It was not that organ building became merely a technical end in itself; the moving statuary of a late medieval organ bewitched the impressionable observer even more than Willis's Tubas. Nor is it easy to define the interaction of organs and music. On one hand an organ may appear to be ahead of its music: it was the 'orchestral counterpoint' of Cavaillé-Coll's organs (melody–accompaniment–bass) that suggested the texture of so much of Franck's music, not vice versa. On the other hand, the music often seems ahead of the organ: Liszt's Prelude and Fugue on B–A–C–H was written for the classical organ of Merseburg which, as can still be heard, aimed at a contrapuntal clarity quite different from the atmospherics demanded by Liszt.

It is difficult to be certain of basic facts. Fewer scaling figures have been published of the organs by Cavaillé-Coll, for example, than of those by Clicquot or Silbermann, while virtually no such details of English organs are known outside a few builders' workshops. The sheer size, number and variety of the period's large organs overwhelm the historian, as they did contemporary writers. Some of the qualities admired during their day, such as reliability, were traditional; but others, particularly the appearance of solid workmanship, may have had a bad influence. For instance, small pipes in mutations and Mixtures were often said by theorists of about 1820 to be old builders' means of deceiving clients. The sound produced by the new arrays of $8'$ foundational stops need not have been 'solid' and indeed was too frequently either aggressive or puny; the *Hauptwerk* built by Gabler for the quire organ of Weingarten Abbey in 1739 had a specification as much dominated by $8'$ stops as any of 1900: 8.8.8.8.8.8.8.4.4.2.XII, but (quite apart from the Mixture) the sound is unlikely to have been anything like Hope-Jones's in Worcester Cathedral. The first might be considered to lead directly to the second, but it was more the indefinable factors, the 'spirit of the times', that were manifest in the tone itself.

Characteristics tend to run together in organ building: electric action (slow, remote, invariable) from a detached console (gadget-ridden, distracting) to chests of pipes crude in tone (planned, manufactured, spaced and voiced untraditionally) and placed behind a pseudo-front (not an integrated resonating case), the whole catering for music written either for another kind of instrument (voices, orchestra) or for another culture. It is hardly surprising that in sum the organist's art became a kind of guesswork, isolated, insular and often chauvinistic.

CHAPTER SIX

Organ Revival

'Organ Revival' is a term used increasingly often as an English equivalent to *Orgelbewegung* (coined about 1930 as a simplified form of Gurlitt's phrase *Orgel-Erneuerungsbewegung* of 1926). The movement is concerned with 'reviving' some of the 'historic principles' of the organ, because it was thought in German musicological circles of the 1920s that the 'true purpose and nature' of the organ had 'declined' and required 'regeneration'. Although such words are still much used in Germany, it is probably fair to say that most of the best results have been achieved by organ builders of other countries, notably the Netherlands, Denmark and Switzerland.

During the 1920s, not least in the light of current political movements, many aspects of German cultural life were re-examined, and before 1933 there were more or less formulated movements in folk music, youth music, church music, and the music of particular composers (e.g. the *Schützbewegung*). These movements had certain aims or assumptions in common:

(i) Their followers reacted to a previous period. The *Orgelbewegung* was a protest against the thick, loud sonorities of the orchestral organ, the factory organ, the 'expressive' or symphonic organ, the organ as an engineered machine rather than an apparatus or 'tool of music'. As such, reacting against late 19th-century organ ideals is equivalent to reacting against late 19th-century music, and insufficient explanation has been given for why an organ of Sauer is less worthy of revival than, say, Wagner's *Parsifal*.

(ii) They assumed that criteria could be determined. In 1906 Schweitzer's test for an organ, 'the best and sole' standard, was its fitness for playing J. S. Bach's music. Unfortunately, that ideal in the 1820s had already deflected the French and English organs from the better features of their native paths; and it is not *per se* a reliable criterion, since not only do opinions differ as to the 'nature of Bach's organ' but the composer himself played organs of quite opposing aims. The 'Bach organ' was more a generic term merely signifying instruments built and voiced 'in the Baroque manner'. Schweitzer's rallying-cry was perhaps not to be taken too literally, though several builders in Alsace and south Germany met under its banner and adopted stop-lists (if nothing else) conducive to Bach registration. The resulting 'Alsatian Organ Reform' has been seen as the precursor of the Organ Revival.

(iii) They attempted in general to lead to standardization. Schweitzer's views expressed at the Vienna Congress of the International Musical Society in 1909 and at the 3rd Organ Conference at Freiberg in 1927 aimed at a general return to old ideals. Although in 1909 it may have been reasonable to equate *tonschön* with *alt*, a blanket equation of the two leads to over-uniformity and a kind of lazy norm often to be heard as simple anonymity in the tone of hundreds of neo-Baroque organs built in Germany since the mid-1930s.

1. EARLY INDICATIONS

Schweitzer's book *J. S. Bach, le musicien-poète* (1905) and the pamphlet *Deutsche und französische Orgelbaukunst* (1906) were highly formative, and still govern German attitudes to the 20th-century organ. A precursor in the workings of the Alsatian Organ Reform has been seen in Emil Rupp, for whom Walcker built a 'reformed organ' at St Paul, Strasbourg, in 1907. But equally indicative of the inevitable change in direction were works of more general musical scholarship. For example, Guilmant's series of old French organ music (begun in 1901 under the title 'Archives des maîtres de l'orgue') was much in advance of Karl Straube's 'editions' of old German composers (1904). Also important was the pioneering work in the interpretation of old music published by Arnold Dolmetsch and others. Dolmetsch no doubt owed much to a favourable musical climate in England where Charles Salaman, Carl Engel and A. J. Hipkins had already reintroduced the harpsichord to public music-making. But as in France and Germany, renewed interest in harpsichords did not necessarily lead to enlightenment with regard to organs. Nevertheless what Dolmetsch wrote in 1915 reflected his views over the past decades and summed up the situation admirably for anyone wishing to heed them:

> Church organs had that power based on sweetness which constitutes majesty. The change came on, and for the sake of louder tone, pressure of wind was doubled and trebled. The same pressure acting on the valves which let the wind into the pipes made them too heavy for the fingers to move through the keys.

A machine was then invented which did the work at second hand [and] the music of the organ dragged on after the player's fingers as best it could. Personal touch, which did so much for phrasing and expression, was destroyed.

Then fashion decreed that the organ should be an imitation of the orchestra. ... The organist, if he is clever, can give a chromolithograph of the *Meistersinger* Prelude; but he has not the right tone with which to play a chorale, if his organ is up-to-date. Modern compositions are intended for this machine, and all is well with them; but it is a revelation to hear Handel's or Bach's music on a well-preserved old organ.

There is nothing here about 'the Baroque organ', and the term was only later taken over from art historians to evoke an organ type more imaginary than real.

In England practice did not reflect enlightened theory. The ideas of organ advisers like Thomas Casson (1842–1910) and George Dixon (1870–1950) kept early 20th-century organs from being any worse; but they were still only insular compromises. As with so many English writers of the period 1875–1975, their emphasis on stop lists and imaginary 'ideal organs' was not basic enough to lead to radical rethinking. Factions in organ building are common, and in France any modern organ has one of two totally opposed characters depending on what the builder and his adviser favour. But in England, almost all organists have still only a compromise instrument of mixed and dubious lineage going back to William Hill and taking in a few non-establishment influences from Hope-Jones on one hand and D. A. Flentrop on the other. *Grove 5* ('Organ') gives the specifications of several such organs, often built well and at great expense. Until the 1930s the situation in the USA was much the same as in England, although Willis's influence on Ernest Skinner prompted him to reintroduce the Great principal chorus in some of his organs in the 1920s. The increasing interest in Bach's music (as shown in the popularity of Lynnwood Farnam's recitals of the complete organ works of Bach in 1929) was an early sign of coming change.

2. GERMAN DEVELOPMENTS IN THE 1920s

A practical step was taken in 1921 when Oscar Walcker, with the collaboration of Wilibald Gurlitt, designed and built the Freiburg Praetorius-Orgel, inaugurated by Karl Straube. This was the first attempt at reconstructing the tonal character of a so-called Baroque organ according to some of the details given by Praetorius in his *De organographia* (*Syntagma musicum*, ii). Compromises were evident:

suitable casework was not made, the stop list was modified, the pipes were placed not on a slider-chest but a 'stop-channel chest', and the action was electro-pneumatic. But the organ was very significant, not least in the publicity it gained during the organ conference held at Freiburg in 1926 before 600 members. After the instrument was destroyed in 1944, a second, less compromising one was made in 1954–5. The change in approach indicates clearly how German organ thinking had developed over 30 or so years: Gurlitt was still the adviser, but the organ was built by Walcker-Mayer with the collaboration of acoustic and technical experts (Lottermoser, E. K. Rössler) and closely modelled on the first specification in Praetorius's *De organographia*, with data taken from extant pipework by Praetorius's friend Esaias Compenius, and with mean-tone tuning, a slider-chest, mechanical action and a thorough *Werkprinzip* structure; the stop-list is given in Table 32. Were a third Praetorius organ to be built, one could expect that all compromises away from his specification would be dropped and an early 17th-century casework incorporated, being an integral part of the total sound-production. In 1969 Walcker-Mayer showed the firm's continuing activity in experimental old organs by producing a further reconstruction-copy of the Roman organ of Aquincum.

Although both Schweitzer's and Gurlitt's views were directed

TABLE 32

Freiburg University, 'Praetorius' organ II
W. Walcker-Mayer, 1954–5

Oberwerk		*Rückpositiv*	
Principal	8	Principal	4
Gedackt	8	Quintadena	8
Oktave	4	Hohlflöte	4
Gemshorn	4	Nachthorn (wood)	4
Gedackt (wood)	4	Blockflöte	2
Nasat	$2\frac{2}{3}$	Oktave	2
Scharfquinta	4 (?$1\frac{1}{3}$)	Quinta	$1\frac{1}{3}$
Superoktave	2	Zimbel	
Mixtur III	2	Schalmei	8
Brustpositiv		*Pedal*	
Krummhorn (wood)	8	Untersatz (open wood)	16
Quintetz	$1\frac{1}{3}$ (?4)	Posaune (Sordun)	16
Zimbel	II	Dolcan	8
Sifflöte	1	Bauerflötlein	1
		Singend Cornet	2

Zimbelstern
Tremulants *(Oberwerk, Rückpositiv)*
Couplers: *Rückpositiv* to *Oberwerk*; *Oberwerk* to *Pedal*; *Rückpositiv* to *Pedal*

towards certain music – that of J. S. Bach on the one hand and that of
Scheidt and Schütz on the other – results were only gradually seen in
organ building. After Rupp and Walcker visited Mutin, Cavaillé-
Coll's successor, one or two organs were built with the express purpose of combining the musical potential of the German and French
organs. One such instrument was at St Reinold, Dortmund,
inaugurated in 1909 by Schweitzer and attracting the attention of
Reger, for whom a festival was held at Dortmund in 1910. The dual
polyphonic–homophonic nature of Reger's mature style would in
theory gain much from the character of an Alsatian Reform organ.
The eclecticism aimed at in such organs was elusive and may well be
illusory; but it led to giant organs such as that at Passau Cathedral
(Steinmeyer, 1930; 208 stops) in which one section serves as a 'German
Romantic organ', another has a 'French character' (reeds, Cornet) and
yet another provides a 'Baroque department'. While in north Germany such firms as Ott and Kemper remained closer to orderly
tradition, the influence of Steinmeyer was wide, and only gradually
has eclecticism begun to lose its lustre.

Yet returning to full *Werkprinzip* design was also only gradual. Like
the 1921 Praetorius-Orgel, the influential organ of St Mary, Göttingen (Furtwängler & Hammer, 1925), was a compromise with
pneumatic action, but in its specification and scalings, prepared by
Christhard Mahrenholz, it pointed the way to future development:

Hauptwerk   16.8.8.8.4.4.2.V.V.8
Rückpositiv 8.8.8.4.4.2.2.III.II.16.8
Oberwerk   8.8.8.4.4.2$\frac{2}{3}$.2.1.III.16.8.4
Pedal   16.16.10$\frac{2}{3}$.8.8.8.4.2.IV.32.16.2.16.8.4

The 'Hindemith organ' – that thought ideal for the performance of his
sonatas – was itself a mean between extremes: but important work was
begun on technical aspects of organ building, and a climate of opinion
was being created with regard to acoustics (*Akustische Zeitschrift*, 1936;
AMf, 1939), slider-chests and their influence on tone (H. H. Jahnn: *Der
Einfluss der Schleiflade*, 1931), pallets (*ZI*, 1933), casework (W. Supper:
Architekt und Orgelbau, 1934) and scaling (Mahrenholz, 1938). In Italy
questions concerning old organs had been discussed for many years
(e.g. *Musica sacra*, 1901–3), and even large electric organs like that in
the Pontificio Istituto di Musica Sacra (Rome, 1933) had never shaken
off traditional features. But in France technical achievement lagged
behind historical research: the documents and archives published by
Raugel and Dufourcq led to the discovery of many old organs, as a
result of which almost all were rebuilt over the next few decades, and
many altered beyond recognition.

3. OLD ORGANS

The position of surviving old organs in the Organ Reform was a difficult one. Important though the Schnitger organ in Hamburg's Jakobikirche or the Lübeck Totentanzorgel were to a writer like H. H. Jahnn (*Kongressbericht: Leipzig 1925*), or the Silbermann in Freiberg to E. Flade (*3. Tagung für deutsche Orgelkunst: Freiberg in Sachsen 1927*), in practice they were, obviously, not suitable for all the organ repertory. They would not allow, for instance, the gradual crescendo demanded by Reger and obtained on one manual by piling up three or four 8′ stops before the first 4′ was added. Oversimplified claims were often made – for instance, that 'stop-channel chests' are by nature 'bad'. It is probably true that, compass apart, an organ of 1700 is more versatile than one of 1900; but no valid doctrine can be formed on the basis of such a generalization.

Nevertheless, the beauty of the Freiberg Cathedral organ was not questioned, and publication in facsimile of treatises by Werckmeister, Praetorius, Bédos de Celles, Mattheson, Adlung and Schlick heightened interest in the few extant remains of organs they described. One result, however, was that much-altered instruments were over-respected, and an organ like that at Amorbach (1774–82) or the Totentanzorgel gave, over the years, many misleading impressions. In this respect, progress since the 1920s has been slow, however well the music itself has been understood. Enlightened opinion may no longer claim that 'it is the large Schnitger organ that best corresponds to the demands made by J. S. Bach's music' (Klotz, 1934), but it is still almost impossible to be sure what kind of sound Schnitger was aiming at.

As examples of ill-conceived restorations, many organs in England, Ireland, France, Spain and Germany could be described, and as much damage has been done during the last 30 years as at any other period. The organ of Herzogenburg Abbey, Austria, can serve as an example. By 1964 most of its original character had either survived or was fairly easily ascertainable; but the 'restoration' of that year resulted in major changes based upon unauthentic concepts. The main chests were enlarged to give a modern compass of $C–f′–g′′′$, thus discarding the original short octaves, the incomplete (but characteristic) pedals and most of the original chests; the action was discarded and newly made; manual and pedal Mixtures were changed in content; new ranks and stops of a kind unsuitable to an Austrian organ of 1749 were made; the instrument was revoiced throughout; and the original detached console was discarded and replaced by a new oak console. This organ would need a radical rebuild if it were ever again to give an organist a true impression of the instruments known to Mozart.

By 1971, however, certain builders were attempting closer authenticity in their restorations, as is shown in a second Austrian organ, that of the Hofkirche, Innsbruck (see Table 8, p. 86, and fig. 36, p. 91). Here the original wind-trunk was preserved, the wind pressure ascertained and voicing recovered; the original short $C-a''$ compass was restored (though the keys perhaps date from the 18th century); the original pitch level ($a' = 445$), case, chests etc were restored; and the instrument was tuned in an unequal temperament. Were the modern bellows to supply wind with fluctuations characteristic of the period, the organ would represent well the contemporary ideals of restoration.

Almost wholly overlooked until the 1960s, however, were many noteworthy 19th-century organs in all countries. After World War II large numbers of these continued to be ruthlessly rebuilt or electrified, or, ironically, tonally ruined in attempts to make them conform to neo-Baroque ideals.

4. SCANDINAVIAN AND DUTCH ORGANS

An especially more radical 'rethinking' of the organ appears to have been achieved in Scandinavia, but it is more likely that national organ types had been less extremely developed there during the crucial period 1870–1910. It is less a question of revival than of survival of old organ design. On the whole the Swedish organ had become more 'decadent' than the Danish, but interest in, for instance, mutations survived here and there. Naturally, German stop-channel chests were found in Scandinavia, and Theodor Frobenius, a German-born builder who settled in Copenhagen, made the first Danish electric action. But the ideas aired by the Alsatian Organ Reform soon became respected in Denmark.

Simpler than the organ at St Mary, Göttingen, yet put in a very imposing case by builders alert to correct acoustical placing, was the quire organ of the extraordinary Grundtvigskirke, Copenhagen (1940), built by Marcussen. In 1922 the head of this firm was Sybrand Zachariassen, who was joined a little later by P.-G. Andersen; by the late 1930s the firm was producing almost nothing but mechanical action and doing good formative work in restoration (Sorø Cathedral, 1942). The Grundtvigskirke organ (1940) was quite uneclectic (see Table 33).

TABLE 33

Grundtvigskirke, Copenhagen
Marcussen, 1940

Hoofdwerk		Rugwerk		Pedal	
Principal★	8	Principal★	4	Sub-bass	16
Nachthorn	8	Gedakt	8	Bordun (transmitted)	8
Octav	4	Rørfløtje	4	Octav (transmitted)	4
Quint	2⅔	Quintatøn	2	Dulcian	16
Octav	2	Scharf	II		
Mixtur	IV	Krumhorn	8		

The *Hoofdwerk* and Pedal pipes are on the same chest
★ = case pipes

TABLE 34

Schoondijke
Flentrop, 1951

One manual, $C-e'''$

Prestant	4
Holpijp	8 (halved)
Quintadeen	8
Spitsfluit	4 (halved)
Octaaf	2
Scherp	IV
Sesquialter	II (treble)
Ranket	16 (halved)

Doetinchem
Flentrop, 1952

Hoofdwerk		Rugwerk	
Prestant	8	Prestant	4
Quintadeen	16	Holpijp	8
Roerfluit	8	Quintadeen	8
Octaaf	4	Roerfluit	4
Ged. Fluit	4	Octaaf	2
Nasard	2⅔	Quint	1⅓
Octaaf	2	Scherp (1′)	IV
Mixtur (1⅓′)	V–VI	Sesquialter	II (treble)
Trompet	8	Dulciaan	8

Borstwerk		Pedaal	
Prestant	2	Prestant	16
Fluit (wood)	8	Octaaf	16
Fluit	4	Octaaf	4
Gemshoorn	2	Nachthoorn	2
Octaaf	1	Mixtur (2′)	IV
Cymbel (1⅓′)II		Bazuin	16
Regaal	4	Schalmei	4

Couplers: *Rugwerk* to *Hoofdwerk*; *Borstwerk* to *Hoofdwerk*; *Hoofdwerk* to *Pedaal*;
Rugwerk to *Pedaal*

Also in 1940 a *Rückpositiv* was added by Frobenius to the early 16th-century *Hauptwerk* from St Petri, Malmö, now in Malmö Museum, showing that builders were aware of the practical convenience of *Werkprinzip* elements. By 1944 the new organ of Jaegersborg, near Copenhagen, had three uncompromising *Werkprinzip* manuals complete with a Trumpet *en chamade*, so made for power rather than for imitations of Spanish tone. (This has remained true of *Orgelbewegung* reeds *en chamade*.) Important too were the smaller organs made by the new builders after the war. Flentrop's eight-stop organ at Schoondijke (1951) was in its way even more influential than his perfect *Werkprinzip* organ at Doetinchem (1952), which soon became a model for the design of *Hauptwerk* + *Rückpositiv* + Pedal towers. (The stop-lists of both are given in Table 34.)

Open-toe voicing, mechanical action and encased departments were by now standard among the younger builders. Such instruments went far beyond the theories of the *Orgelbewegung*, and it is a mistake to regard them as mere 17th- or 18th-century pastiche. Frequently they serve as practical demonstrations of intricate theory and knowledge. Frobenius's paper on end correction, for example (Copenhagen, 1947), is the most important work by an organ builder in this field since Cavaillé-Coll.

5. THE ORGAN REVIVAL IN THE USA

The main builders of the early revival in the USA were Holtkamp of Cleveland and G. D. Harrison, an Englishman working for the Skinner Organ Co. In 1933 Holtkamp had contracted for a *Rückpositiv* in the large organ of the Cleveland Museum of Art, but the slider-chest had a multiple-valve system doomed to be dropped in the purer atmosphere after the war. Harrison's influence on tone was more important than his structural reforms, for he had applied low pressure to a fairly large organ contracted for at Groton School in 1935. This organ, like the slightly smaller but more coherent instrument built a year earlier for the Church of the Advent in Boston, was one of the first attempts in the USA at a large, classically designed instrument, although its voicing hardly follows classical principles and its general effect lacks articulation. More successful and certainly more influential, was the small, unencased, two-manual organ built in 1937 for the Germanic (now Busch-Reisinger) Museum at Harvard University, which was heard by a vast audience through the broadcasts and

52. Organ by the Holtkamp Organ Co. (inaugurated 1967) at the University of New Mexico, Albuquerque

recordings of E. Power Biggs, an early champion of the Reform movement. These and other isolated instruments of the period testify to a growing interest in historic European principles among some American organists and builders, Cavaillé–Coll and Silbermann being especially admired. Such organs, for all their drawbacks of voicing and electric action, possessed greater clarity than had been heard from American organs for some decades, and they made their point musically. Partly due to Holtkamp's efforts, most of these organs were free-standing rather than in the all-too-common chambers, but the musical importance of casework was as yet unrealized, and only low wind pressures and gentle voicing curbed a tendency of 'pipes-in-the-open' to sound raw and unblending.

But soon after World War II growing awareness changed the main-stream. Academic and musicological writers leant heavily on 17th-century German literature and indeed tried to create a more rational language of organ terms (Bunjes, 1966), while organists and organ students became much influenced by the various restored organs of West Germany. The relative inaccessibility of East German organs, notably those of Silbermann, has affected American–European organ design. European builders exported small but important organs to the USA (Rieger about 1952, Flentrop in 1954) and Beckerath con-solidated the trend by taking a 44-stop four-manual organ to Cleveland in 1957. Large firms like Schlicker were bound to be in-fluenced by such instruments, and while Beckerath went on to build several equally important organs in Canada, other builders like Char-les Fisk of Methuen (later Gloucester), who very early showed an inclination toward French classical elements as opposed to the more popular German Baroque, and Casavant Frères of Quebec soon produced their own versions of the new styles. Fisk's large two-manual organ in Mt Calvary Church, Baltimore (1961) was remark-able for its early use of classical *Werkprinzip* casework, suspended action and an uncompromisingly classical tonal scheme scaled and voiced on the principles of Andreas Silbermann. Casavant's organ of 1963 in Acadia University (see Table 35) is a typical small organ of the kind inspired by such builders as Beckerath. From the point of view of the Organ Revival, such instruments were far in advance of the huge unencased organs made by the larger firms (e.g. Möller's paired organs in the shrine of the Immaculate Conception, Washington, DC, 1970), although it is fair to point out that inventive and contemporary visual effects can often be achieved with unencased chests.

Many North American builders are willing to consult advisers who have practical or theoretical knowledge of historic organ types of Europe; at its best the collaboration is highly successful. Flentrop's organ of 1958 for the Busch-Reisinger Museum at Harvard reflects a further element: the strength of taste developed by players (in this instance E. Power Biggs) experienced in European organs. In North America, Flentrop, Metzler, Ahrend and Brunzema and others have gone on to build important instruments of great beauty, and recently other influences have become evident, such as the French elements in the stop-list and voicing at St Thomas, New York (G. F. Adams,

ORGAN REVIVAL – ENGLAND, FRANCE, ITALY

TABLE 35

Acadia University
Casavant Frères, 1963

Hauptwerk		Brustwerk		Pedal	
Quintaden	16	Gedackt	8	Sub-bass	16
Prinzipal	8	Spitzflöte	4	Prinzipal	8
Rohrflöte	8	Prinzipal	2	Choralbass	4
Oktav	4	Quinte	1⅓	Mixtur (2')	IV
Waldflöte	4	Sesquialtera	II	Fagott	16
Flachflöte	2	Zimbel (¼')	II		
Mixtur (1')	IV	Holzregal	8		
Trompete	8				

Couplers: *Hauptwerk* to Pedal; *Brustwerk* to Pedal; *Brustwerk* to *Hauptwerk*

Mechanical action

1969), or the Italian elements in the large electric organ of the First Congregational Church, Los Angeles (Schlicker, 1969). It is true that neither instrument demonstrates a thorough understanding of its quasi-models, but such attempts are important stepping-stones towards stricter historical copies – a trend also followed by American harpsichord makers over recent years and one leading to less compromising organs (see §8 below). The specific influence of the German-orientated *Orgelbewegung* may well be waning in the USA and Canada; like the new organ terminology sometimes attempted, it was too artificial a graft to bear much fruit.

6. ENGLAND, FRANCE AND ITALY

It seems to be true that the Organ Revival in England 'really took root only with the opening of the organ for the Royal Festival Hall, London in 1954' (Clutton and Niland, 1963; see fig. 53, p. 192). Despite careful planning by the adviser (Ralph Downes) and meticulous workmanship by the builders (Harrison & Harrison), the composite nature of the organ made it little more than a quickly dated compromise. Its 103 stops give the impression of immense adaptability, and the German flutes, Anglo-German chorus and French reeds allow many types of organ music to be given reasonable performance; but the very size (quite apart from the semi-unencased construction and the electropneumatic action) make true sympathy with most musical styles impossible. Although much admired by players in both England

53. Organ by Harrison &
Harrison (inaugurated
1954) in the Royal
Festival Hall, London

and the USA, the instrument has had curiously few successors; new designs have not appeared, despite an awareness of continental organs (e.g. the Organ Club's visit to Frobenius in 1958) and the obvious qualities of tracker action (St Vedast, London, rebuilt by Noel Mander, using an 18th-century case, and much antique pipework). J. W. Walker's organ of 1959 in the Italian Church, London, showed a rather confused scheme, but it helped to open the path to 'Baroque' influences:

Great organ	16.8.8.4.4.2$\frac{2}{3}$.2.II.IV.8
Choir organ	8.4.4.2.2.1$\frac{1}{3}$.II.III.8
Swell organ	8.8.8.8.4.4.2$\frac{2}{3}$.2.IV.16.8.8.
Pedal	32.16.16.16.8.8.8.5$\frac{1}{3}$.4.4.IV.16.16.8.4

The French organ has developed on rather similar lines, 'neo-classical' indicating a Frenchified composite organ designed with both de Grigny and Bach, both Franck and Messiaen in mind. Most major French churches have such organs, many made by Gonzalez with the advice of Norbert Dufourcq, a collaboration which also unfortunately engineered the rebuilding of many intact classical and Romantic organs in a hybrid quasi-Germanic mould, with the stated aim of making them more fit for the playing of Bach. Closer imitations of old French styles have been attempted more recently, for example the partial copy of a Bédos de Celles organ (complete with low pitch) by J.-G. Koenig at Sarre-Union (1968). In particular, the importance of the traditional French classic form of 'suspended' action has been recognized, and such actions, notable for their sensitivity, have since successfully been made by American, Dutch and German builders as well as the French. In both England and France, 'restoration' of old organs has been almost universally disastrous. French builders and advisers have not by any means abandoned the ideals which caused the 1693/1832 pedal department (Flutes 8′ and 4′ (C–e), Trompette 8′ and Clairon 4′ (ravalement F′–e)) at Auch Cathedral to be altered in 1959 (Principal 16′, Sub-Bass 16′, Bourdon 8′, Flûte 8′, Flûte 4′, Bombarde 16′, Trompette 8′, Clairon 4′). Few builders in England or France have shown enlightened attitudes towards the subtler historical problems of pitch and voicing, although in France the journal *Connaissance de l'orgue* has helped propagate better ideas, as have the *Organ Yearbook* in England and the Organ Historical Society in the USA.

In Italy the late 1960s saw a movement towards a kind of modified *Werkprinzip* organ but with characteristic Italian choruses and even at times Italian reeds. The organ at S Maria Assunta (B. Formentelli, 1967–8) has a *grand'organo* of 8.4.2.1$\frac{1}{3}$.1.$\frac{2}{3}$.$\frac{1}{2}$.$\frac{1}{3}$ + $\frac{1}{4}$.8.4.2$\frac{2}{3}$.2.1$\frac{3}{5}$.8.4, the last of them reeds. Large three-manual organs such as that at the Chiesa dei

54. Console of the organ in St Paul's Cathedral, London, rebuilt 1972–7 by N. P. Mander

Servi, Bologna (Tamburini), united an Italian chorus, German mutations, Spanish Trumpet, Italian compass, mechanical action and general *Werkprinzip* relationships between the manuals. Smaller organs too have attempted comprehensiveness; the instrument at S Severino, Bologna (G. Zanin & Figlio, 1968), has the following scheme:

Grand'organo	8.4.2.1⅓.1.IV.8.2.II.8.8.
Positivo	8.4.2.1⅓.1.8.2⅔.8
Pedale	16.8.8.4.16

7. SOME GERMAN DEVELOPMENTS SINCE WORLD WAR II

An important factor in postwar Germany was the prominence and high standard of many new and small firms, while the older and larger ones faded into the background. The appointment of organ advisers for each of the districts of Germany encouraged smaller builders as it also encouraged local variety and enterprise. From the early 1950s Beckerath of Hamburg and the two Schuke firms of Berlin (East and West) produced organs of strong character, often influenced by old instruments they had rebuilt (Schnitger organs rebuilt by Beckerath, Joachim Wagner organs by Alexander Schuke); as noted above, Beckerath also took instruments to the USA and, in 1970, a smaller example to Britain (Clare College, Cambridge). Ahrend and his former partner Brunzema (pupils of Paul Ott) continued the trend towards strong-toned organs, omitting mutations and relying on highly coloured flue and reed stops (usually made of hammered metal); old instruments restored by the firm (e.g. at Westerhusen) have a natural, unforced but startlingly powerful, breathy tone. The organ at Westerhusen, like Metzler's restoration at Nieuw Scheemda, Führer's at Hohenkirchen and Ahrend's in Stade, is a revelation of the musical colour open to a 17th-century organist of Friesland and Groningen. The stop-lists seem nondescript; an example by Ahrend & Brunzema (Bremen-Oberneuland, 1966) is:

Hauptwerk	16.8.8.4.4.2. Mixtur. 8
Rückpositiv	8.4.4.2.1⅓.II.Scharf. 8
Pedal	16.8.4.16.8.2

But the sound is far from nondescript, and the idiosyncratic tone of such instruments is well removed from the neo-Baroque anonymity typical of so many organs of the 1950s.

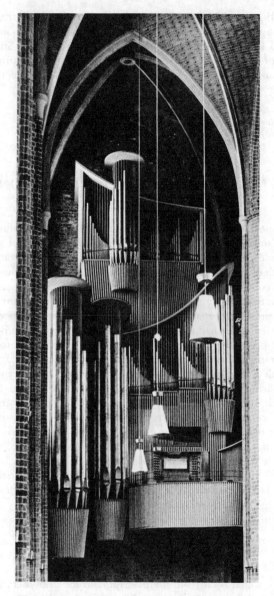

55. Organ by Rudolph von Beckerath (1954) in the Markt-kirche, Hanover

Before 1973 German builders rarely developed good designs for organ cases, relying on simple geometric shapes that are pleasing but repetitive and often careless. Some imagination has been shown·here and there in designing a sinuous front with 'modern' motifs (Markt-kirche, Hanover; by Beckerath, 1954; see fig. 55) and the square or rectangular box sometimes conforms with its surroundings (Gedächt-niskirche, Berlin; by Schuke, 1962). Non-German builders more often tend to look at old models, as witness the influence of the Perpignan organ on that at Linz Cathedral (Marcussen–Andersen, 1968). Swells, either as enclosed *Oberwerk* or enclosed *Brustwerk*, are still popular in Germany, and it is often not possible to see them as anything more than ambiguous in nature and limited in conviction. On the other hand, standard German practice in making mechanical action has done little but good, and German builders are correct to point out that 'Recent organ music (such as Ligeti's *Volumina*) with its note-clusters, requires mechanical action. ... The cluster technique shows complex flutter beats; the foreign nature of untempered, non-harmonic sound-elements can be produced only by mechanical action and its associated voicing' (*ISO Information*, no.8, 1972, p.45).

8. THE PRESENT SITUATION

While it must be assumed that compromise organs and eclectic organs will continue to be built over the next few decades, in three respects knowledge has increased beyond the level anticipated by the Organ Reformers of 1920. These are: understanding the true nature of each particular organ type; deducing the requirements of each particular organ type; deducing the requirements of each particular composer; and restoring old organs without compromise. Naturally, the three trends are closely related but only in the widest sense are they historic-ally committed: they do not favour any one period and they recognize that even the eclectic organ is a historical phenomenon. At the same time it is possible to imagine organs of a new type, wild developments beyond the dreams of Hope-Jones in which new pipe forms or electronic sound-producers are operated by whatever means contem-porary technology suggests, 'organs' for which some schools of com-position have already found appropriate musical language.

The lines of development in Europe are evident in the work of a few builders whose specialized and conscientious restoration of old organs (of whatever period) is matched by a pronounced notion, in their new organs, of what constitutes tonal beauty. A good example is Metzler & Söhne of Dietikon, Switzerland. They have restored several Baroque Swiss organs to their intended tone, in some cases surprisingly strong; meanwhile a certain line of development can be discerned in their new organs. The one at Grossmünster, Zurich (1959), has a *Werkprinzip* case of modern geometric design and a huge stop-list composite in its make-up (Swell, reeds *en chamade*, harmonic Trumpet, Septime etc) though without a full palette of string and Romantic flute stops. At Frauenfeld (1969) they made fewer compromises: the third manual is a truer *Brustwerk*, the stop-list is thoroughly classical and the large, shallow, solid oak case is more truly fitting in its context. The importance of this case to the sound cannot be overemphasized; the whole organ shows (in the words of the builder) 'a logical arrangement deplored by adversaries as being merely historical yet [which] is modern in design and technologically advanced'. Such builders have a wide spectrum of historic colour at their disposal, including rarer stops like Dolkan, Suavial, doubled case-pipes (joined at the feet) and French reeds. The enthusiasm aroused by Metzler's organ in St Pierre, Geneva (1965), assures the firm of a place in organ history, not least for its attempt to pay tribute to classical French colours.

The tendency towards strict and specific stylistic imitation is becoming increasingly marked. A builder may introduce 'flexible' wind supply to a restored organ (Évora Cathedral, 1562; restored by Flentrop, 1969), imitating the wind and voicing conditions of the original instrument; or a completely new organ in old style may be built, attempting to imitate the qualities of sound due to the old manner of wind supply, voicing, scaling, pipe material, chests, mechanism, casework and stop-lists of the model copied. Such an instrument was completed in 1972 at the Ashland Avenue Baptist Church, Toledo, Ohio (John Brombaugh & Co.; fig. 56), its 19 stops following models by the 16th-century Netherlands master Heinrich Niehoff. Whether the original compass, pitch-level, key-shapes and other factors crucial to the musical repertory of a particular old organ are also copied must depend on the purpose of the modern counterpart. An exhibition or museum organ may be built to suit the purist; a church is usually assumed to be subject to what are called 'liturgical demands' – Swell boxes for Anglican chant, a large compass for modern organ music, standard pitch for accompaniment etc. It is probable that the gap between the two kinds of organ, secular and ecclesiastical, will grow, and the secular will remain the more advanced, even though this may mean strict fidelity to what had been thought to be obsolete ideals. One particular avenue opened to

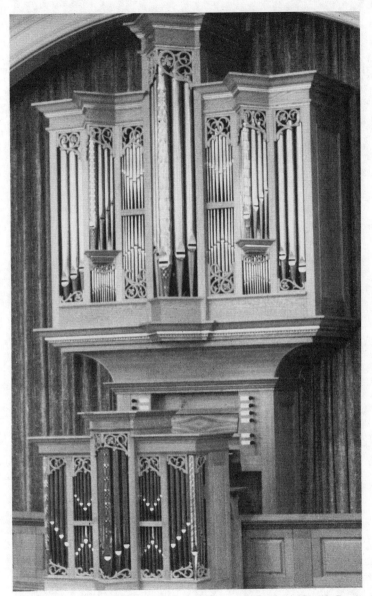

56. *Organ by John Brombaugh & Co. (1972) in the Ashland Avenue Baptist Church, Toledo, Ohio*

57. Organ by Jürgen Ahrend (1981) in the Church of the Augustins, Toulouse

exploration in the late 1970s has to do with temperament. Interest in pre-19th-century music and its authentic performance has sparked a growing interest in various historical unequal temperaments. Werckmeister and Kirnberger tunings are gaining acceptance in church organs and are extensively used by some builders along with their own 'shop' temperaments; builders such as Fisk, Noack, Brombaugh, Taylor, Mander, Ahrend, Garnier, Führer, Flentrop, Riel, Koenig and Kern are now routinely tuning even large instruments in unequal temperaments. A four-manual Flentrop at Duke University, Durham, North Carolina (1976), is tuned in Chaumont, and Fisk's large four-manual at House of Hope Church in St Paul, Minnesota (1978), is tuned to a special shop temperament. Split-key, mean-tone instruments have been built by Brombaugh (Oberlin College, Ohio, 1981) and Fisk (Wellesley College, Massachusetts, 1981; see fig. 58, p. 217).

Metzler's church organ at Frauenfeld has an unequal temperament, and its low pressure (manuals 75 mm, pedal 85 mm) combines with the voicing techniques to suggest, in the words of the builders, 'a choir's breathing. The over-perfected and explosive speech of the neo-Baroque organ of the fifties has completely disappeared. One can once again experience with this instrument that an organ is a large wind instrument'.

CHAPTER SEVEN

Recent Research and Areas for Study

Although those periods in the history of the organ or those aspects of its construction that are still imperfectly understood may appear to be matters for the scholar or theorist, in practice all such knowledge affects at least the better informed organ builders and players of today. For them, to understand the function and functioning of an organ or organ type of the past is a living part of their thought and work today. This is a distinctly new phenomenon in the history of all instrument making and reflects a fuller and more complete understanding of the past than was previously possible or even thought desirable. Conversely, it has only gradually become clear how inadequate are certain older ideas on the history of organs because those engaged today in the practical issues of performance and construction have found them to be so. Thus in the following outline of the areas still imperfectly understood there are many practical lessons for performer and builder.

1. WORD ORIGIN

Though it might be thought a rarefied aspect of organ study, the understanding of how words were used at particular moments in the history of the instrument is often important for an understanding in general of how the instrument evolved. For example, it has become clear that at a crucial point in the development of Western music, during and around the 9th century, 'organum' in original sources can mean not an instrument at all but an 'organ of learning', such as a book; there are other examples of this ambiguous usage, such as 'psalterium' (a psalter or a psaltery) and even, later on, 'manual' (a handbook or a keyboard). Thus every single reference in Christian sources to organs before the church contracts of the high Middle Ages needs to be scanned anew and tested against this possibility. Later terms are of course less open to such ambiguity, but a wider reading outside musical sources can shed new light on difficult words. One example can be found in 16th-century Portugal, where church accounts speak of choir stalls as the 'cadeira'; this suggests that the 'cadeireta' or 'Chair organ' is so called not because it is behind the organist's chair but because it was part of (hanging over or built into the superstructure of) the choir stalls. Perhaps then one is also to infer that at first it was seen not as a 'second manual' to the large organ but as a more or less independent (if small) instrument: the large organ for special occasions (i.e. a kind of signal-organ), the small for the choir work (i.e. a musical participant). Some such situation was the case in Durham Cathedral where, according to a report made in 1672, there was or had been in the previous century a large organ called the Cryers (possibly *Schreier* – a *Blockwerk*?) used on special occasions and placed on the north of the quire, and an organ of wooden pipes 'over the quire door'.

Another example of the need to be alerted to word-implications is the use in 18th-century Germany of the word 'Brustwerk': some references (e.g. Walther's *Lexicon* of 1732, under 'Brust') say it can be placed above the Great, still (in a sense) 'within the breast' of the organ but obviously bigger, more diffuse and no longer geared towards bass continuo work at the level of the gallery floor near the singers. In such cases, 'Brustwerk' means the same as 'Oberwerk'. The early term *Positiv im Stuhl* likewise has been re-examined in the light of the use of the word 'Stuhl' to refer to the lower part of the organ case. Thus a *Positiv im Stuhl* may not be a Chair organ, as previously supposed, but an internal division in the lower part of the case, similar to the Iberian *cadereta interior*.

2. CONSTRUCTION

The work of the better builders of today, prompted in particular by the increasing number of players aware of the characteristics of touch and the nature of historic organ types, has become more and more directed towards the simplest kind of keyboard mechanism, the 'suspended action'. This is the system shown in fig. 10. Here the keys hang from their trackers, and their 'feel' is an incomparable combination of the light and the crisp. Not only the *Haupt* or *Brustwerk* manuals can be so made, but such builders as Joachim Wagner, working in Prussia during the Bach period, designed a suspended action for both his *Haupt* and *Oberwerk* manuals that could serve as a model for any builder today who wished to take the 'tracker revival' one step further. Indeed, many contemporary builders are now using this type of action, sometimes in fairly large organs (House of Hope Church, St Paul, Minn., Fisk, 1979; Duke University, Flentrop, 1976; Holy Cross College, Worcester, Mass., Taylor & Boody, 1985; Mill Hill School, London, Mander, 1985).

A similar point can be made about the two kinds of Tremulant, known now from their codification in French sources as Tremblant fort and Tremblant doux but at one time more widespread than those terms suggest. The Tremblant doux, or internal tremulant, achieves its effect by disturbing the flow of wind in the wind-trunk by means of a floating plate which, when released by the stop action, oscillates up and down with the aid of a weighted spring. The Tremblant fort, as its name implies, gives a stronger undulation to the wind flow by the oscillation of a small bellows which emits small puffs of air through a small exhaust port. When not in use, the plate of the Tremblant doux is pushed up against the side of the wind-trunk, and the bellows of the Tremblant fort is fixed in a closed position (see fig. 13b and c). Not only modern 'copies' (Basle, Leonhardskirche, T. Kuhn, 1969; Montreal, McGill University, H. Wolff, 1981) but new instruments are likely to have both types of Tremulant. From an understanding of historical tastes, witnessed by both written sources and a few extant examples, has come an awareness that most Tremulants of the last 200 years beat too fast for earlier music, and that organ Tremulant effects were attempted by composers in certain 'affecting' music (e.g. Scheidt, Kuhnau, J. S. Bach's *Erbarm dich mein* BWV721).

A further kind of historic awareness, though of a different ethos, is the respect paid to the experiments of the great 19th-century engineer-builders, in particular the sensitive and durable electric actions (such as Willis's for Canterbury Cathedral in 1886) and the ingenious systems of the innovators. Though apparently irrelevant to the revival of early music as now understood, the achievements of the inventive years around 1900 earn their own respect. Of the many publications from that period, one example – the report of Robert Hope-Jones's organ in the McEwan Hall, University of Edinburgh – can be taken to show the obvious awe and delight in such skill (quoted from T. Elliston: *Organs and Tuning*, 3/1898):

> It may be interesting to learn ... that the action of all the key-boards together requires no more electricity than is needed for the common household electric bells, and this current is supplied by a few dry cells. This may be more easily comprehended when it is understood that all the current is required to do is to energise a very small electro-magnet, which has to attract a minute armature (in

shape of a circular metal disc as light as a pin) away from the valve-seat on which it rests. This disc only moves one-sixty-fourth part of an inch, but in so doing it opens up a way of escape for compressed air, which immediately causes the sudden collapse of a small motor, and at the same moment pulls down the pallet and allows the wind to rush into the pipe.

3. PIPEWORK

Amongst the many areas of constant experimentation and discovery for an organ builder are the ways in which a pipe behaves, particularly in two respects: its winding (what kind of wind it receives and the way it treats it or is treated by it) and its material (the nature of its metal or wood, whether or not the metal is hammered or beaten, how hard the wood is). In the absence of data provided by controlled experiments, builders and those attempting to understand the art can only agree with Bédos de Celles (*L'art du facteur d'orgues*, 1766–78, Pt ii) on the need to hammer pipe metal (especially that for the case-pipes), on the desirability of hardening with alloys the metal used for pipe-feet but not for the pipe-bodies; and on the visual effect of lacquering the pipes. How far the current trends amongst thinking organ builders for varnishing all pipes and 'thus improving their tone' (as distinct from their looks) can actually be supported by proper evidence has not yet been tested, but if it were a valid point it is strange that Bédos of all people did not say so. Either way, the wider use of Bédos' treatise in recent English, German and French editions continues to keep alive the basic issues. Recent research by Herman Greunke (1984) and other Americans, as well as the increasing number of articles on pipe metal casting and composition in *ISO-Information* by Continental builders, testifies to the interest of the organ industry in these matters, particularly in their application to historic pipework. Builders are studying more closely such matters as languid angles and thicknesses, the treatment of upper and lower lips (scribing, flatting, and the central German practice of making the upper lip slightly overhang the lower lip), and the importance of the *Gegenphase* as an alternative to nicking in the suppression of undesirable 'sizzle' in flue pipes. Builders in all countries are producing reeds based on the study of historic examples, from colourful Renaissance regals to French classical (Cliquot) Trumpets and Cromornes and foundational north German Baroque Trumpets and Trombones with leathered shallots; in large organs an increasingly eclectic choice of reed colours can be found.

ORGAN

Much work still needs to be done on the way pipes are actually made to speak by wind passing through them – work done not so much from the point of view of the physicist as by the builder; Charles Fisk's essay (in Pape, 1978) deserves follow-up studies by those properly qualified, especially in its suggestion that organ counterpoint, in its mixing of sustained and moving lines, is by nature an essay 'in the handling of organ wind – when to disturb the wind deliberately [by moving from one note to another, causing movement of the pallet and thus changes in the status of the wind] and when not'. That in the earliest periods of organ history the method and quality of wind supply were a preoccupation of the more literate and scientifically trained minds is clear from Greek, Latin and Arab authors, all of whom described the making of organs entirely in terms of their wind-raising and its application; pipe-making and practical tuning were not subjects for philosophers, but wind-raising was.

4. THE CLASSICAL AND MEDIEVAL ORGAN

Werner Walcker-Mayer's suggestion that the four ranks of the Roman organ of Aquincum were made according to four particular modes or *tonoi* (see Chapter Three, §1) has not been proved or disproved during the last decade or so, but it has been material to the continual attempt to understand the evolution of the octave-scale and the keyboard.

1 (open):	*g*	*a*	*b♭*	*c′*	*d′*	*e♭′*	*e′*	*f′*	*g′*	*a′*	*b♭′*	*c″*	*d″*
2 (stopped):	*e*	*f♯*	*g*	*a*	*b*	*c′*	*c♯′*	*d′*	*e′*	*f♯′*	*g′*	*a′*	*b′*
3 (stopped):	*d*	*e*	*f*	*g*	*a*	*b♭*	*b*	*c′*	*d′*	*e′*	*f′*	*g′*	*a′*
4 (stopped):	*c*	*d*	*e♭*	*f*	*g*	*a♭*	*a*	*b♭*	*c′*	*d′*	*e♭′*	*f′*	*g′*

Thus, if the Aquincum organ did have the above notes supplied by its four registers (as suggested by Walcker-Mayer), it did not support J. P. Kirnberger's observation that in the strict modal system the pitch of notes differed depending on their position: a Pythagorean E calculated as a 3rd from C would not be the same note calculated as a 2nd from D; and C–D, D–E would be two different kinds of 2nd (*Die Kunst des reinen Satzes in der Musik*, i, 1771, pp.4ff). Whether Kirnberger was right to claim that the different 'moods' attributed by ancient writers to the different modes came from this difference in tuning is likewise uncertain (ii, 1776, pp.49–50), but he was probably right to claim that the 'moods' were as much a question of the kind of music sung as of the nature of the modes themselves; of course, the two ideas are not contradictory.

If the four registers of the Aquincum organ produced different C's etc depending on modal context, the medieval keyboard scales appear even more of a compromise than they must have done to the generations of theorists from the later 15th century onwards who discussed organ tuning and temperaments, precisely perhaps because the 'rise of the triad', as it is usually called (e.g. Lindley, 1980), required new thinking about the major 3rd. Also, perhaps the well-known medieval compass from B arose because in theory its first four notes (B–C–D–E) would correspond to the Greek diatonic tetrachord (semitone–tone–tone); so would E–F–G–A, and the note between the two (B♭) would be the first semitone to be added (not necessarily higher than the others in the actual keyboard: see fig. 28), and would be desirable as the octave-scale produced notes sung in the common repertory. But if each key played only one tone, without the variability at each step that strict modal accuracy would have required and which the Aquincum organ may have provided, the medieval keyboard was from the start so inaccurate that it could well have forced music into adopting simpler scale-types, i.e. the medieval modes. 'Music' in this sense has to be understood as literate music of the Western kind, distinct from music of other cultures and from the vocal 'folk music' of Western culture. This whole area – the evolution of the keyboard, the relationship of fixed and non-variable tones to the development of modes and thus diatonic scales, and the effect of these developments on the tuning of the 12 notes of the octave – has often received attention in the past but deserves a total rethinking in the coming years, now that sources are so much better understood.

It has also been recently shown, very convincingly, that the Aquincum organ was a water organ or hydraulis, rather than a bellows-blown organ (E. L. Szonntagh, *Scientific Honeyweller*, ii, 1981, pp.54–60), but in the case of the oldest Christian drawing of an organ (the Utrecht Psalter; see fig. 27) the doubts have always been about other details: the presence of two players, what they are doing with their hands, why there are only twice four pipes and what the significance is of the apparent pipe-lengths (ratio of 1 : 2 : 3 : 4). One recent examination (Hardouin, 1966) has suggested that the instrument looks like a siren organ of the kind described by Muristus (see Chapter Three, §3), even as far as the pipe-proportions are concerned; the four sounds might even correspond to those of the four bells used for signalling in the liturgy (*quadrillon = carillon*). However, as with so much medieval 'evidence', there may well be other elements in the representation disguising, even destroying, the technical information we are hoping to see there. For example, if a vertical line is drawn down from the central figure at the top (a central figure of some importance, of course), each half of the drawing closely mirrors the other, including the angels, the winds, the two ranks of instrumentalists, the hydraulis-pumpers, the organists and (though not in mirror image) the pipes. Nevertheless, whether or not the sets of four pipes symbolize the four winds (i.e. artefacts activated by wind), it cannot be assumed, as it often is, that the organist's hands as drawn are placed without any knowledge or understanding: the mechanism of Arab 'organs' took the form of some kind of lever somewhere near the foot of the pipe. Of course, whether or not the drawing reflects Byzantine influence, it could certainly be the product of someone who had never seen any such instrument and was relying on written sources (a verbal description, diagram etc).

That the Utrecht Psalter drawing might have represented some kind of signal-organ raises the question of how organs came to be used in the Western church and what they were used for. Recent work (Williams: 'How did the Organ become a Church Instrument?', 1980) suggests that truly musical use of organs is unlikely to date back earlier than the 12th century, especially the *alternatim* use with the choir. Even then, it was a question of special occasions in the most important monastic or secular churches. The earliest appearance of the organ in church, perhaps in the 9th century and certainly in the 10th and 11th centuries, probably related more to noise than to music, i.e. it was used for signalling purposes (perhaps as a kind of bell-substitute), not for music in the liturgy. In Constantinople, the *organon* was used on particular days during processions and receptions in the area around the emperor's palace – when the people cried 'Agios' ('Holy') in the courtyard outside to mark the close when the celebrant signalled, after the people had acclaimed the emperor, after a processional song and in the hall as the emperor was enthroned. Not only a Carolingian king but a powerful Benedictine abbot or bishop may well have received the same kind of treatment in his palace or cathedral. This is almost certainly the origin of organs in the service of the only provincial Christian church to have had them, i.e. Charlemagne's western European church under allegiance to Rome.

Two further ancient and famous organs known about from written sources continue to attract attention: those of Winchester and Grado. After attempts to reduce the exaggerated language of the 10th-century poem describing the first and to place it as a signal-organ in the westwork of the Saxon Cathedral of Winchester, a recent interpretation has seen it as an organ of 40 (not 400) pipes, ten keys playing four pipes each (1.8.12.15, perhaps like the Utrecht Psalter organ) and twice 13 bellows (Hardouin, 1981). But much still remains to be conjectured about the early organ – why it was an attribute only of the western European church (Carolingian-Benedictine), what ranks it had, how the keyboard evolved, where the organ was placed in church, whether it played any bigger part in the abbey than, for example, the clock, and what it had to do with early polyphony. At least one important experiment was made during the 1980s: in the Netherlands, Louis Huivenaar and Jan de Briujn reconstructed conical pipes of the kind described by Theophilus (see Chapter Three, §5) and placed them on a chest made, after imaginative reconstruction-work, according to Zarlino's description of the chest from Grado, Venice, believed to date from the 11th century (*Sopplimenti musicali*, iii, 1558, pp.290–91). Though a crude block made presumably from a rough copy by some-body unacquainted with organs, Zarlino's drawing does show some salient points: there were 15 notes (probably push-pull sliders activated by spade-shaped 'keys' not entirely unlike those in fig. 28), two ranks of pipes (Zarlino himself said that there was no way of telling whether they were of metal or wood, at unison or octave pitch), and, at the rear of the chest, round sockets into which the bellows had fitted (perhaps a pair, or three as in Virdung: see Meyer, ed. and trans., p.32), 'such as one sees them placed in modern regals'. Huivenaar and Briujn's ex-periments suggest that the conical pipes had a very strong and complex overtone content, producing a quite extraordinary vocal quality, sus-taining the pitch and serving for playing a chant-melody with a con-stancy totally unavailable on any other instrument of the time, much less the human voice. A not dissimilar breathy, ringing quality of tone can still be heard in the three very old ranks of the famous organ at Sion, Switzerland (see Chapter Three, §6).

5. THE ORGAN 1450–1800

Recent work has been directed towards the historical position of Henry Arnaut's manuscript treatise (Sachs, 1980), towards an under-standing of the 15th-century keyboard (Meeùs, 1971; Lindley, 1980; de Graaf, 1982) and, in one very notable case, towards a circumspect restoration of an extant old organ (S Petronio, Bologna, reopened 1982). For its theoretical discussion of pipe-scales, Arnaut's treatise now seems more indebted to earlier writings than was previously thought; on its more practical side, it is clear on the one hand that the two forms of pipe-mouth were accurate enough for them still to be found in the 17th century, on the other that the celebrated reference to reed stops cannot be dated to the 15th century with total certainty. Also uncertain in date, though confidently ascribed to 1380 in the century after A. G. Hill so dated it in his book of drawings (1883–91), is the extant Gothic case in Salamanca, now thought by de Graaf (1982) to belong to about 1500. Its compass seems to have been C/E-c''' (45 keys), not as a unicum but as one of the then long compasses known to Italian and Spanish builders who built according to the space or money available. It had a half-stop (from f), a pitch probably about a major 3rd above $a' = 440$, a pipe-rack above rather than below the mouths and at least one kind of *subsemitonium* (divided sharp, as in some Italian long-compass organs of the 15th century).

More certain is the Bologna organ. It had ten stops of 51 notes ($F'G'A'$-a'', ranks at 16[=24]. 8.4.2$\frac{2}{3}$.2.1$\frac{1}{3}$.1.$\frac{2}{3}$.$\frac{1}{2}$.Flute 4), a pedal probably of 17 notes (corresponding to the three larger pipe-flats in the façade) and a pitch of $a' = c521$. As for the early 16th-century organ in general, facsimile editions with translations of Schlick and Virdung make more accessible the salient characteristics, particularly those of the all-important Rhineland organ of $c1500$ which Schlick described with a forthrightness still worth heeding – for instance, when he described the essential uselessness of split sharps as a method of dealing with temperament problems. It is also clear that the thick slider positioned above the slider-chest and directing the wind through curling ducts between pallet and pipe (described by Schlick as the 'four-finger-thick slider') is not only to be seen as yet another attempt by late medieval builders to make firmly constructed, fault-free chests (see Chapter One, §2(v)) but must also have resulted in a controlled wind-attack for the speech of each pipe.

The speech of pipes, their winding and their tuning become more and more the concern of both historically minded players and carefully reasoning builder-restorers. Much closer attention is being paid by many builders to specific historic voicing techniques and pipe construction techniques, such as languid angles steeper than 45°, blunted languid edges, the importance of correct cut-ups, the use of more open windways and, in the case of late 18th-century and early 19th-century organs, wind control at the toe-hole.

The newly restored Gothic organ of Lübeck (the small organ in the Jakobikirche), though now predominantly in the form given it by Friedrich Stellwagen in 1636, has a partly extant Principal chorus of the late 15th century, built up of pipes of 97% (or more) of lead. The characteristics of Stellwagen's flues and reeds raise all the questions of how such pipes spoke and what kind of sound they were meant to produce – in particular, what kind of vocal quality they were imitating, as all organs must. The evolution of singing tone in 16th-century Europe is itself a major question for historians – though one would not think so from reading standard histories of music – and for the moment one can suggest only generalities: for example, just as voices were beginning to produce the smooth characteristics of 'bel canto' (was the production of sweet, lyrical tone still one of the 'new' elements in Caccini's *Le nuove musiche* of 1601?), so organs were expected to smooth out some of the rougher characteristics of earlier tone. Thus, somewhere during the 16th century (perhaps in Hamburg, about 1550), builders began to make reed-shallots in such a way as to thicken the tone, i.e. thin out the overtone content: shapes were changed (narrowed), and edges were leaded and even leathered (so that the tongue came into contact with lead or leather, not brass). It seems as if those countries where church music progressed in purer form by remaining more exclusively vocal and polyphonic (Italy, Spain, England) preferred to do without reeds. During the 1980s there have been spectacular restorations of the north European organs with massive choruses and quieter colour-stops (Hagerbeer's organ in the Nieuwe Kerk, Amsterdam; Schnitger's in the Maartenskerk, Groningen); but from the point of view of music's evolution as a whole there is no doubt that more thought must be given to the singing, vocal traditions of Italian organs.

In general terms, it cannot be doubted that over the centuries the changing ideas of what constituted 'good singing' were reflected in contemporary organ building, not only in tone but in tuning. A crucial characteristic of the north European organ during the 17th century must be the mean-tone tunings long preferred by builders but constantly modified by composers whose assumptions – like that of other craftsmen in the western European traditions – had been that their duty was to develop and to achieve new things in new ways. It is certainly no coincidence that the most startling things done in harmony in the period around 1600 were in those areas in which solo or choral singing, and vocal counterpoint, were paramount (Italy and England). In France, the organ by 1675 had developed voicing and colouring which (whether or not they can be likened to the newly standardized French nasal vowel-sounds) were essentially unsuitable for vocal music but which could serve very well as interludes to it, consciously different from it in tone and thus making excellent *alternatim* idioms for the Mass and Offices. For the Parisian, the organ was no longer seen as a voice-substitute; the Principals became rounder and the reeds yet more *éclatant*, and the liturgists found it necessary to specify certain sounds at certain moments lest the wide-ranging palette of colours become chaotic or anarchic (for a discussion of liturgical use see Van Wye, 1980). For the German organ, a useful starting-point in coming years for those anxious to understand the general lines of development for organ tone might well be to assume that the Reformation brought with it a change of emphasis away from properly trained singers towards the fuller and coarser sound of congregations, and thus away from discreet vocal tone in organs towards the leaded reeds and thicker *organo pleno* of a later age.

In J. S. Bach's Thuringia and Saxony, the organ's primary purpose in most churches – to accompany or at least to introduce the chorales for the congregation, perhaps from time to time performing 'recital music' – may well have made it seem best to builders to remove the (by then) heavy pedal to the back of the organ, to deepen the casework generally, to remove the immediacy of pipe-sounds and to add string stops. The effect was gradually to 'round out' the tone both in its colours and in its acoustical properties (the two have tended to go together in organ history) – and this on behalf of the congregation who were positioned in several galleries around the flat-ceilinged churches. In the case of the 'Italian Baroque organ', a well-restored instrument such as that of Gaetano Callido in Calceranica (near Trent) is witness to a vocal ideal still by no means spent at the end of the 18th century: both Principale 8′ and Voce umana speak with an age-old breathy tone that has a variable edge to it (variable because of its sensitivity to keyboard-touch). This is perennially useful for Italian vocal (but not German instrumental) counterpoint. The very excellence of workmanship in a Callido organ, including that of the screw-adjusted regals, shows that the Italian efforts up to 1800 and beyond were always geared to this vocal quality, eschewing the hard plena, the reeds, the auxiliary chests, the versatile pedals and all the other clever gadgets of the organ north of the Alps. The recent research by Umberto Pineschi into the important Tuscan school of building has added much to knowledge of the Italian organ of the 17th to 19th centuries; and the state-sponsored organ restoration workshop in Florence, superintended by P. P. Donati, is ensuring that significant examples of the Italian organ heritage will now be properly preserved and available for study.

In the case of the English organ, the tastes and priorities of the old builders are only gradually becoming clearer, and no documentary history of the English organ has yet been made. A new transcription of the All Hallows, Barking, document of 1519 (see Chapter Four, §9, and Blewitt and Thompson, 1977) has not clarified the issues except to establish how uncertain the scribe was of the technical details he was being asked to write down. His specification for the inner pipes, that they 'shalle be as fyne metalle and stuff as the utter partes that ys to say of pure Tyne', has muddled the information he was given: one can guess that the case-pipes were to be of tin, the inner of metal (stuff, *étoffe*) but in their way as good in quality as the case-pipes. This suggests that the vocal quality of the organ's basic sound, i.e. the case-principals or Diapasons, was richer than it would be if they were made of the lead then becoming popular in northern Europe (cf Lübeck above) but less so in Italy. The scribe's following phrase, 'of pure Tyne wythe as fewe stoppes as may be conuenient', might be seen as meaning not 'with as few separated ranks and stop-knobs as con- venient' (whatever that could mean) but 'with as few stopped pipes as its position on the screen makes desirable' (i.e. for the sight-lines not to be harmed by pipes protruding from the top). Much recent research on the English organ of the 16th and 17th centuries has been aimed at providing a more accurate definition of its sound, uses and con- struction. Reinterpretation of documents has been helped by the archaeological study of remaining evidence (Dean Bargrave's organ, Canterbury, 1626; St Nicholas, Stanford on Avon, c1635, etc).

Putting English organs more in their general European background can certainly lead to interesting possibilities in some instances, as in the idea, for example, that the larger pipes at All Hallows, Barking, like some at Coventry and later in Exeter Cathedral, were rather in the manner of the continental Trompes (see Chapter Three, §6, and Owen, 1980) – though the modest size of at least the All Hallows and Coventry organs would make it impossible for such bass pipes to serve as they did at Rouen, Haarlem etc. As for the organ of the Restoration period, it is clear that Smith's and Harris's organs had much the same purpose as those in Thuringia and Saxony summarized above, though parsimony made pedals so rare as to be virtually unknown. Also, the Breton influences on Harris, and through him on Smith, resulted in an array of Frenchified colours more suitable for French Mass-interludes of the kind familiar in several areas removed from Paris (e.g. Walloon Flanders, now in Belgium). As the Breton influences on the Dallams and on Harris gradually become clearer (see Bicknell, 1981), so do the Frisian on Smith (Rowntree, 1978; Thistlethwaite, 1978); it is not quite accurate to refer to 'French' or 'Dutch' in these contexts. From the stop-lists alone one might think that the English organ tone was, at any rate before the Smith–Harris generation, closely related to the

Italian organ in its two vocal ideals, i.e. for the main manual to sing as a voice and for the subsidiary manual to accompany the voice:

> Dallam Organ at Durham Cathedral (?1620 before ?1661)
> *Great* 8.8.4.4.2⅔.2.1. 'Furnetura'
> *Choir* 8.4.2.1.Flute

In coming years, comparisons with the other organ cultures of Europe may well shed further light on the aims of the several historic English organ types. A good example is the fact that Joachim Hess, in his Dutch treatise of 1774, was surprised by the effect of a Swell on an English organ imported to Curaçao in 1770. It seems astonishing that he needed news from across the Atlantic to tell him that Swell boxes produced a realistic crescendo – until one appreciates that only the closed-toe English voicing (in its keeping the wind back from the languid and lip) made such Swells useful in the way they would not be with more forthright voicing. Unless he travelled away from northern Europe, an author had no conception of such organ tone (Hess, 1774, p.99), and to this day northern builders seem not to have grasped the fact that a true Swell needs very particular voicing methods.

6. SOME DEVELOPMENTS 1800–1930

That at least at times the Dutch builders kept to older notions well into the 19th century is clear from recently published gazetteers (*Langs Nederlandse orgels*, 1977–9). *Rückpositiv* departments were added to new organs soon after they were made (at Genemuiden in 1824–9, at Oldemarkt in 1828–49), even sometimes only as case-fronts (at Enschede in 1892). In comparison, France in the 1840s was full of experimentation, not only in the celebrated work of Cavaillé-Coll at St Denis (Hardouin, 1979–80) but in the new actions and construction of countless builders, such as the *orgue à piston* (a 'barless chest') announced in 1845 by Claude Frères and reported on by Guédon in 1903. Guédon's book describes many a device of the period (such as Moitessier's pneumatic action of 1845: see Chapter Five, §2) and served as a kind of French equivalent to Audsley's treatise (1905). Less clear are the reasons for the recent marked increase in interest (particularly in Germany and those parts of the organ world concerned with French organ music since around 1850) shown in the works and theories of Aristide Cavaillé-Coll (Douglass, 1980; Huybens, 1979; Sabatier,

1979; Salies, 1979). The amount of detail released by such studies probably amounts to more than that for any other organ builder who ever lived, and the admiration frequently expressed for the few relatively untouched Cavaillé-Coll organs (e.g. St Sernin, Toulouse, 1887) suggests that especially for those players in the USA and Germany who went through the less pleasant phases of the *Orgelbewegung* (see Chapter Six), the warm Romantic tone and sheer craftsmanship of such organs serve as a fine antidote. This is so perhaps precisely because Cavaillé-Coll organs have an orchestral palette, pneumatic actions and a voicing style totally opposed to the vocal/mean-tone immediacy of organ tone about 1600. One might think such French organs have a very circumscribed musical quality and usefulness. But that orchestral palette is richer and better-blending than much of the neo-Baroque tone of 1950; and those actions are not more unpleasant than the actions (often of metal, with many squares etc) made in the same period. One author (Sabatier, 1979) asks whether the recent admiration for Cavaillé-Coll does not 'invite one to pursue one's own ideal for the exploitation of resources offered by modern technology and further creation of a new instrument in the dimension of our time'. But it could be thought that there lurk here too many begged questions concerning an instrument that is by nature a 15th-century achievement, if not invention.

In the interests of a nostalgic searching for heavier organ tone than Baroque revivals have provided, a certain interest in Robert Hope-Jones is also being revived in English-speaking circles (e.g. essays in *The Organ*, 1981, 1982). That his actions often failed is accounted for by a too low amperage, not unexpected in days before the universal availability of electricity; their principles of construction are now much admired for the degree of technological inventiveness they exhibit. Besides, as Fanselau has shown (1973), understanding the Hope-Jones organ is still important for grasping the aims of a major school of composition and one that is by no means extinct. The claims made for Hope-Jones's organ in Edinburgh were quoted above (§2) and, as a reaction to the propaganda for the (often poor) tracker actions over the last quarter-century, the revived interest in them is understandable. Similarly, that the extension organ born of Hope-Jones's work is not entirely without virtues (i.e. organ-building logic) is now often pointed out; the sheer workmanship is admired (as indeed it is admirable) and the stop-lists themselves, such as that for the Civic Hall, Wolverhampton (see Chapter Five, §4) are often claimed to leave unencumbered a full Diapason chorus irrespective of the auxiliary ranks that are so extended. It can be assumed, however, that even in the interests of 'giving each period its own praise', the organ world is not yet ready for a Hope-Jones copy or for a revival of the Wolverhampton voicing.

In the USA there has been a revival of interest in the work of Ernest M. Skinner, whose imitative stops and 'symphonic' tonal designs provide a more refined alternative to the excesses of Hope-Jones and whose instruments are an ideal vehicle for transcribed music (Lemare, etc) which is also experiencing a revival. This recent interest in early 20th-century organs has led, in several instances, to the retention of an older organ when a new one of a different style has been installed – for example, at Stanford University, where a large Baroque-inspired Fisk organ (1984) shares the gallery with a sizable Romantic instrument (1901) by the Californian builder Murray M. Harris.

7. THE ORGAN REVIVAL

The over-simplification of the issues involved in organ building put about by the Organ Revival, especially its German form the *Orgelbewegung*, have become increasingly clear to both good builders and careful scholars. The history of the Revival itself can also now be seen as more complex than those many German authors who were chiefly indebted to other German authors have interpreted it. For example, an enlightened Swiss attitude was already clear from Jacques Handschin's paper ('Die Orgelbewegung in der Schweiz') given at the *Freiberger Tagung* of 1927 and from Kuhn's *Rückpositiv* at Berne Münster in 1930 (a more French than German department in this instance). The revised edition of P. H. Kriek's *Organum novum* (1981) has traced in more detail the priorities of the Dutch builders during the 20th century. In Germany itself there were some marked contradictions between one kind of activity and another, between the advanced (i.e. historically aware) ideas and the conventional. At one of the worst periods, a *Werkprinzip* organ could receive sympathetic consideration (e.g. the pedal-towers added at Stendal Marienkirche between 1940 and 1944) or a church could find itself guided by its repertory towards old ideas (e.g. the little choir organ built for the Thomaskirche, Leipzig, in 1932 with pipes made to some kind of Schnitger scale). On the other hand, while in 1932–3 the Hildebrandt organ at St Wenzel, Naumburg (see Chapter Four, §13), was remade according to its stop-list of 1746, it was given at the same time a new electric console in a different gallery! Historicism took the form of so electrifying the pallets that the old

58. Organ by C. B. Fisk (1981) at Wellesley College, Massachusetts

trackers and old keyboards were left.

These and similar incidents become clearer as more and more archival and other material is published; although there is still no full history of the German organ or separation of the main issues appearing in the many gazetteer-like books, journals and articles in German, the organ student is in a better position as each year passes. Such organs as Charles Fisk's Fritzsche-influenced instrument in Wellesley College, Massachusetts (1981), with its traditional wedge-shaped bellows worked by the blower's body-weight and old elements such as its case, keys, voicing and split-sharp tuning, raise and interpret these issues as perhaps no other endeavour can.

Research into the north German and French classical organ continues to occupy many of the smaller American firms, but there is increasing interest in the Italian Renaissance organ, the central German 'Bach' organ, the 18th-century English organ, and the 19th-century work of Cavaillé-Coll, Merklin and Willis, as well as

American builders such as Tannenberg, Appleton and Hook. Mechanical matters such as the Barker machine and alternative wind-raising devices are also being investigated. Organs embodying the results of recent research in these areas include those at Holy Cross College (Taylor & Boody, 1985), Mount Holyoke College (Fisk, 1984), Southern Missionary College (Brombaugh, 1986), Emory University (Taylor & Boody, 1985), St Mark's Church, Grand Rapids, Michigan (Bedient, 1986), St James's Church, Woodstock, Vermont (Moore, 1987) and Trinity Church, Portland, Oregon (Rosales, 1987). It is probably no accident that organs such as these are generally found in or near institutions of learning.

In England, increasing attention is being given to the country's own heritage, resulting in interpretations of historic relics (Martin Renshaw's 'Dean Bargrave' organ), sympathetic rebuildings of badly mutilated 18th-century organs (St James, Clerkenwell, London, Mander, 1983), as well as new organs by several builders based on Restoration and 18th-century tonal principles. At the other end of the spectrum, Victorian organs, including some notable town hall organs (Birmingham, 1835, Hill; West Bromwich, 1878, Forster & Andrews), are being sympathetically rebuilt or restored.

The Organ Revival (if that is indeed still a valid term) must thus be seen as a constantly evolving phenomenon whose only real common denominator is the continuing quest for understanding of the relationship between an instrument and its literature. While hardly unique to any one instrument, this quest always has been and probably always will be made difficult by the long history and complex variety in respect to which the organ stands virtually alone.

CHAPTER EIGHT

Special Types

1. WATER ORGAN

The water organ, or hydraulic organ, is a kind of automatic organ without bellows. It is blown and sounded by air compressed directly by water that is activated by natural forces (e.g. by a waterfall or solar heat). Water organs play without human intervention once they are set in action. Ancient and modern writers have frequently confused them with the Greco-Roman hydraulis, a type of pneumatic organ in which air was supplied by hand-operated air pumps and water was used in a device to steady the wind-pressure (see Chapter One, §2(i)).

Water organs were described in the texts of Ctesibius (300–270 BC), Philo of Byzantium (3rd century BC) and Hero of Alexandria (AD c62). Like the water clocks of Plato's time, they were not regarded as playthings but might have had a particular significance in Greek philosophy, which made use of models and simulacra of this type. Hydraulically blown organ pipes were used for the imitation of bird-song, as well as to simulate the awe-inspiring sound emitted by Memnon's statue at Thebes. For the latter, solar heat was used to syphon water from one closed tank into another and so to produce compressed air for sounding the pipes.

Arab and Byzantine engineers developed, among other specimens, an automatic water organ (described in a 9th-century treatise by the Banū Mūsā; see Farmer, 1931) and the musical tree at the palace of Khalif al-Muqtadir (ruled 908–32). By the end of the 13th century hydraulic automata had reached Italy, where craftsmen soon learned to copy them, and the rest of western Europe. During the Renaissance water organs again acquired magical and metaphysical connotations among followers of the hermetic and esoteric sciences. The organs were put into ornate cases and placed in the gardens, grottoes and conservatories of royal palaces and the mansions of rich patricians, where they delighted onlookers not only with music but also with displays of dancing figurines, wing-flapping birds and hammering cyclopes, all operated by movements attached to the musical cylinder (see fig. 59). Another type of water organ, not provided with a case and played out of view, was used to simulate musical instruments 'played' by hydraulically operated statues in mythological scenes such as 'Orpheus playing the viol', 'The contest between Apollo and Marsyas' and 'Apollo and the nine Muses'. Or the statue of a nymph in a grotto might appear to play, on a water organ, music which was echoed by another nymph playing on a smaller, distant water organ.

The most famous water organ of the 16th century was at the Villa d'Este in Tivoli (see fig. 60, p. 222). Built about 1550, it stood about six metres high under an arch, and was fed by a magnificent waterfall; it was described by Mario Cartaro in 1575 as playing 'madrigals and many other things'. Other famous examples of the period were at Pratolino, near Florence, and in the pope's gardens at the Quirinale, Rome. In the early 17th century water organs were built in England; Cornelius Drebbel built one for King James I (see Harstoffer, 1651), and Salomon de Caus built several at Richmond while in the service of Prince Henry. After the marriage of Princess Elizabeth to the Elector Palatine Prince Friedrich V, de Caus laid out for them the gardens at Heidelberg Castle which became famous for their beautiful and intricate waterworks. The brothers Francini constructed waterworks and organs, at St-Germain-en-Laye and Versailles, which reached new heights of splendour and extravagance.

By the end of the 17th century, however, interest in water organs had waned. As their upkeep was costly they were left to decay and were soon forgotten; not one has survived (the so-called water organ at Hellbrunn, Salzburg, is a pneumatic organ driven by hydraulically operated bellows). Their mechanism was subsequently misunderstood until the Dutch engineer Van Dijk pointed out in 1954 that the method of air supply to the water organ was the same as that used in forges and smelting works in the 16th and 17th centuries. The most important factor is that the water sucks in air as in a simple laboratory filter pump. This can be done in several ways. In fig. 61 (p. 223) air is drawn through a small pipe placed in a larger vertical pipe, which takes water from a stream or pond. Both water and air arrive together in the *camera aeolis* (wind chamber), which is situated a considerable distance below ground. Here water and air separate and the compressed air is driven into a wind-trunk on top of the *camera aeolis*, to blow the organ pipes. The two sieve plates or 'diaphragms' with little holes in them were intended to prevent the water spray from getting into the organ pipes. The water, having been separated from the air,

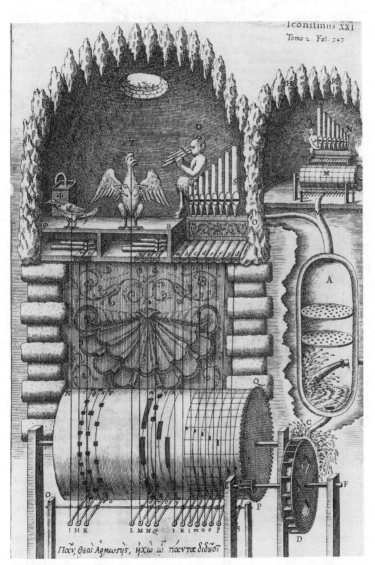

Iconifmus XXI

Tomo 2. Fol. 343

Παν, θεος Αρμωσης, ήχω ώ παντα διδθσι

59. *Water organ in the grotto of Villa Aldobrandini, Tivoli: engraving from Kircher's 'Musurgia universalis' (1650)*

60. *Water organ (c1550) built in the gardens of the Villa d'Este, Tivoli: from an engraving in G. G. Rossi's 'Le Fontane di Roma', pt.iv (c1675)*

leaves the *camera aeolis* at the same rate as it enters it and is used to drive a water wheel, which in turn drives the musical cylinder and the movements attached. To start the organ, the tap above the entry pipe has to be turned on and, given a continuous flow of water, the organ plays until the tap is closed again. Many water organs had simple wind-pressure regulating devices. A working model of a water organ, built of easily available materials by the harpsichord maker Christopher Stevens, is in the possession of Susi Jeans in Dorking.

Among Renaissance writers on the water organ, Salomon de Caus was particularly informative. His book of 1615 includes a short treatise on making water organs, advice on tuning and registration, and many fine engravings showing the instruments, their mechanisms and scenes in which they were used. It also includes an example of suitable music for water organ, the madrigal *Chi farà fed' al cielo* by Alessandro Striggio, arranged by Peter Philips.

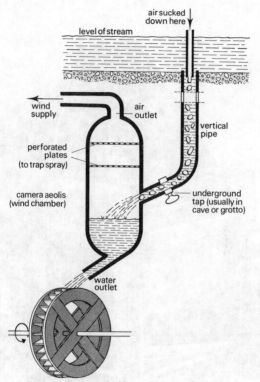

61. Diagram showing the blowing system of a water organ

2. CLAVIORGAN

Claviorgan is the English equivalent to the quasi-Latin *claviorganum*, denoting a keyboard instrument in which strings and pipes 'sound together to produce a pleasing sound' (Praetorius, *Syntagma musicum*, 2/1619). In early sources, late 15th-century Spanish and 16th-century Italian collections, for example, it cannot be assumed that *clabiórgano* etc denotes a composite keyboard instrument of this kind; often the word may have been used for (secular) organs in general, perhaps to distinguish them from portatives or regals. The English term seems to have appeared only at the end of the 19th century (when it was used

62. Claviorgan by Jacob Kirckman and John Snetzler, 1745–51

by such authors as Carl Engel and Alfred Hipkins) but it may have been used earlier. The adjective 'organisé' was used in France at least by the middle of the 16th century and copied by English lexicographers (e.g. Randle Cotgrave, *Dictionarie of the French and English Tongues*, 1611).

The true claviorgan remained on the fringe of music-making for at least three centuries; its history is thus neither continuous nor connected but comprises a series of important types. In the 16th century spinets or virginals 'with pipes undernethe' are known to have existed from documentary evidence (e.g. at least five are listed in the inventories of Henry VIII, 1547) and from surviving examples (e.g. the spinet-regal-organ formerly in Schloss Ambras); double- or triple-strung, full-size harpsichords with positive organs incorporated are to be found in Germany (a Dresden inventory, 1593), Italy (Banchieri, *L'organo suonarino*, 1605), England (one made by Theewes, 1579) and elsewhere. Many examples must have been little more than toys (e.g. the mechanical claviorgan patented in Venice, 1575). In the 17th century there was immense variety, from the clavichord-organ combinations known from theorists (Barcotto, *Regola . . . ogni sorte d'istromenti*, MS, Civico Museo Bibliografico Musicale, Bologna, *c*1650) and extant examples (V. Zeiss of Linz, 1639) to the organ-spinet-harpsichord-Geigenwerk made in Rome by M. Todino in about 1670. The acoustic and mechanical theorists (Kircher, Schott etc) were attracted to the more doubtful aspects of these composite instruments. From about 1580 to about 1780, many large organs are known to have had a row or two of harpsichord strings, especially those in German court churches, but also in various other places from Sicily to Coventry. Particularly in England, chest-like or even harpsichord-shaped chamber organs were made during the 18th century specifically to carry a harpsichord on top, whose keys depressed the organ pallets below through simple stickers; this is known both from theoretical sources (e.g. Burney: 'Schudi', 'Snetzler' in *Rees's Cyclopaedia*, 1819, and the varied and detailed drawings given by Bédos de Celles in 1778) and from extant examples (e.g. the Earl of Wemyss's Kirckman-Snetzler claviorgan of 1745–51, shown in fig. 62). Even in many quite late sources it is not clear what exactly 'claviorgano' denoted (e.g. Cristofori's accounts, Florence, 1693). Late in the 18th century many pianos, particularly large, square ones, were made with several ranks of flute and chorus organ pipes, often by the best makers in London (e.g. Broadwood) and, to a lesser extent, Paris (Taskin). By about 1840 harmonium-pianos played only a minor role amongst the vast array of composite, hybrid and other fanciful, constantly patented inventions.

3. BARREL ORGAN

The barrel organ is a mechanical organ in which a wooden cylinder (or barrel), placed horizontally and armed on its outside circumference with brass staples or pins, slowly revolves; in doing so the pins raise trigger-shaped keys which correspond with a simple mechanism communicating with pallets that on being opened allow wind to enter the required pipes. The wind is provided by bellows which are worked by the same rotary motion of a handle that turns the barrel. The mechanism of the barrel organ is illustrated in fig. 63.

The barrel organ has a long history. What appears to have been a form of the instrument was described by Ctesibius of Alexandria. According to H. G. Farmer, an Arabic manuscript attributed to 'Muristus' (c9th century – the name may be a corrupt form of Ctesibius) also described an automatic hydraulis. Archimedes (d 212 BC) was credited by Tertullian (De anima, xiv) with having invented an automatic hydraulic organ of a different type from those later called hydraulic in Europe. A similar device is described by Apollonius of Perga (fl 3rd century BC). Both instruments employed two compensating cisterns which filled alternately through valves. The 9th-century Arabic text by the Banū Mūsā ('Brothers Moses', i.e. Muhammad, Ahamad and Hasan of Baghdad) deals in detail with an improvement on the hydraulic organs described by Archimedes and Apollonius.

In 1597 the Levant Co., with the approval of Queen Elizabeth I, decided to send an elaborate mechanical organ as a gift to the Sultan of Turkey, and Thomas Dallam was entrusted partly with assembling it, partly with making it, and also delivering and erecting it in the Sultan's palace. Dallam's diary, reproduced by Mayes (1956), gives full details of the organ and of his voyage, but is rather less specific on the details of the instrument.

In 1615 Salomon de Caus described and illustrated a barrel organ in which the barrel was divided into bars and each bar into eight beats for the quavers. The whole drum was pierced with holes at the intersecting points, the pins being movable so that they could be reset to produce another tune. De Caus did not claim the invention as his own but merely the adaptation of hydraulic power to revolve the drum. The organ was bellows-blown. He admitted that he derived inspiration from the writings of Vitruvius (1st century AD) and Heron (3rd century AD).

Robert Fludd's treatise Utriusque cosmi (Oppenheim, 1617–24) depicts, very inaccurately, a barrel organ activated by hydraulic air compression. Almost equally inaccurate is the drawing of an automatic organ, similarly activated, by Athanasius Kircher (1601–80). Similar drawings and descriptions were given at this period by Caspar Schott (1608–66).

An 'organo portatile' depicted by Filippo Bonanni in his Gabinetto armonico (1722) is a small barrel organ shown resting on the player's left hip, supported by a sling over the right shoulder; the player turns the handle with his right hand. An ingenious machine, invented in 1752 by J. F. Unger (1716–81) and a Berlin mechanic, Hohlfeld, was

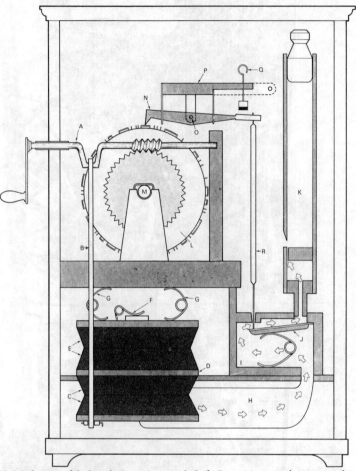

63. *Mechanism of the barrel organ: A: crank shaft; B: reciprocator between crank shaft and bellows; C: bellows (or feeders); D: fixed board of bellows assembly; E: air reservoir fed by bellows; F: spring-loaded valve; G: spring; H: windway connecting reservoir with wind-chest; I: wind-chest; J: pallet (open) controlling passage of air to pipe; K: pipe (wood stopped diapason shown); L: barrel, with wire bridges and pins; M: axis of barrel; N: key, controlling the pallet; O: key pivot; P: key frame; Q: device to take up slack movement; R: rod (or sticker) connecting key and pallet*

*64. Barrel organ
(technically a barrel
piano) in a London street,
c1905*

intended to improve the technique of pinning the barrels. Concurrently with this, Creed, an Englishman, constructed a melograph which would 'write fantasies or other pieces of music'. Illustrations of the construction of the barrel organ in the 18th century were given by Marie Dominique Joseph Engramelle (1727–1805), whose studded barrels of mechanical instruments have become an important source for the study of late Baroque performing practice in France, and in particular of the rhythmic convention of *notes inégales*, according to which certain divisions of the beat moved alternately in long and short values, even if they were written equally, and by Bédos de Celles. The latter account is of special importance as it describes the method of pinning the barrels to give a particular tune.

There can be few musical instruments whose nature and construction have given rise to such confusion in terminology. Today even the average musician will immediately associate the barrel organ with the small street organ or barrel piano (see fig. 64) formerly played mainly by Italian mendicants, often accompanied by a monkey. These musicians were recalled to Italy after 1922 by Mussolini, who considered their presence abroad derogatory to the Italian nation. The instruments, however, were made in England and families noted for their products were active around Saffron Hill in Clerkenwell – for example Rissone, Chiappa, Pesaresi, Pasquale, Rossi, Spinelli and Tomaso. The last-named survived until 1944 though latterly he ceased to be a maker and hired out his stock to London 'grinders'. In 1900 there were still two barrel piano factories in Manchester, Simon Robino and Wright & Holmes Brothers. All are gone now, but Canon A. O. Wintle of Lawshall, near Bury St Edmunds, taught himself the craft in 1907 during his curacy at St Mary's, Crumpsall, Manchester. He founded a village industry at Lawshall Rectory (the East Anglian Automatic Piano Co.), teaching and employing six to eight villagers during the agricultural depression between the wars. Carts, covers, barrel organ and barrel piano frames and cylinders were made and the barrels were 'marked' for pinning. The industry was brought to an end with Canon Wintle's death in 1959.

A much more sophisticated form of the barrel organ made its appearance in England in the middle of the 18th century when it replaced the small church bands which normally played in the west gallery, with the choir around the instrumentalists. The introduction of a barrel organ to an English church dates from around 1700. It has been said without substantiation that in that year one was installed in the church of King Charles the Martyr, Peak Forest, Derbyshire, and was still there in 1870. It has been repeatedly asserted that early in the

18th century a certain Wright of London built a barrel organ for
Fulham Church, but the date is not known exactly and the statement
cannot be confirmed. The main period of the church barrel organ,
however, may be regarded as from around 1760 to around 1840;
during that time hundreds of them were made by over 130 makers,
principally in London. Among the earliest was E. Rostrand of Orange
Court, Leicester Fields, London, who made 'all sorts of Chamber-
Organs to play with fingers or barrels' (see below). A small chamber
barrel organ of his from Stanton Harcourt, Oxfordshire (now in the
Pitt Rivers Museum, Oxford), has four stops, and two barrels of eight
tunes. The instrument is dated 1764 and is still in working order. The
chief makers were G. Astor, T. C. Bates, Bevington & Sons, J. C.
Bishop, H. Bryceson, B. Flight (& Kelly), Gray & Davison, G. M.
Holdich, H. Holland, J. Langshaw, J. Robson & Son, and J. W.
Walker & Sons, all of London; Forster & Andrews of Hull; and J. R.
Rust of Chelmsford.

Certain other makers specialized in chamber barrel organs, i.e. those
for use in the home; the barrels in these cases were pinned with secular
tunes. The titles of some 1300 such tunes have been recorded by
Langwill and Boston. John Langshaw (1718–98) was employed
around 1761, under the direction of Handel's amanuensis John Christopher Smith, in setting music on 36 of the 60 barrels of a very large
organ built by Snetzler and others for Luton Park, seat of the Earl of
Bute. Unfortunately, this organ was later destroyed by fire. Chamber
barrel organs were often enclosed in very handsome cases which
reflect the high standard of cabinet making of the period.

Church barrel organs, too, were set in elegant cases but varied
greatly in size. Some were placed in a gallery or loft as at Brightling,
Sussex; Hampton Gay, Oxfordshire; Wood Rising, Norfolk;
Raithby, Lincolnshire; Avington, Hampshire; Sutton, Bedfordshire;
and Muchelney, Somerset. Others, usually of small dimensions, were
on the floor of the church. In some instances, the bellows were
operated conjointly with the barrel by the crank handle. In others, a
pedal for the bellows was operated by the left foot independently of
the crank handle.

An ingenious device was introduced in about 1800 to enable a barrel
mechanism to be applied to a normal manual organ. This was termed
a 'dumb organist' and consisted of an oblong box containing a barrel,
pinned with eight or ten hymns or psalm tunes. The box had no base
so as to allow rods, operated by the barrel pins, to depress the
appropriate keys on the manual. A number of dumb organists survive,
and one can appreciate their value in tiny rural churches where the

services of an organist were unobtainable. A further development was the incorporation of barrel mechanism in existing manual organs. These instruments were termed 'barrel & finger organs' and several survive. This normally necessitated additional pipes, as few church barrel organs were built with a chromatic range. To save pipes and consequent space, as well as expense, tunes were frequently pinned in only two or three keys, G and D being usual. An indication of the end of the barrel organ period may be gained from the last advertisement of Bates & Son, who in 1864 were selling off secular organs from £2 2s., and church organs at £10.

Canon Boston made a special study of church barrel organ tunes recorded on the tune lists invariably pasted on the organ cases. Knowledge of the dates of the organ helps to date the tunes and to indicate their comparative popularity. In smaller organs, barrels had to be changed by withdrawing one and sliding another in its place. Larger organs, on the other hand, were sometimes fitted with a revolving frame on which three barrels were mounted, each barrel having ten tunes. Forster & Andrews of Hull advertised a barrel organ with three barrels in a frame in 1845, and in the following year offered to install improved instruments with three, four or five barrels in a frame. A large barrel organ with a revolving frame for four barrels was built for Northallerton Church by Bishop in 1819. Such a device is to be seen at Wissington, Suffolk; Mattishall Burgh, Norfolk; Staunton in the Vale, Nottinghamshire; and Raithby, Lincolnshire.

Handel wrote music specially for the Earl of Bute's barrel organ. Burney commented on the very general use of barrel organs and added 'the recent improvements of some English Artists have rendered the barrel capable of an effect equal to the fingers of the first-rate performers'. Ord-Hume, one of the expert authorities on barrel organs and musical automata of all kinds, declared that 'the mechanism of the barrel organ is one of simplicity and extreme effectiveness. That some instruments are still in playing order after 150 years, with little or no attention, is evidence of the practical design and durability of the basic organ component assemblies'.

4. FAIRGROUND ORGAN

The fairground organ (known as 'band organ' in the USA) is a mechanical organ used to provide music for carousels, and in amusement parks, circuses, and skating rinks. It produced loud music that could be heard above the noise of the crowd, and consisted of several ranks of organ pipes, with accompaniment generally provided by a built-in bass drum, snare drum, and cymbal. The fairground organ was usually built in an elaborately carved, colourfully painted case that sometimes incorporated moving figures in its façade. All but the very largest instruments were designed to be portable.

The earliest fairground organs, developed during the 18th century, were essentially barrel organs (see §3 above): they had a wooden cylinder or barrel covered with metal pins that formed a musical program. By 1880 these organs were being produced in large sizes: they had more than 100 keys, several hundred pipes, and a variety of percussion effects. These large instruments were powered by steam or water engines and later by electric motors. Important builders of barrel-operated fairground organs included Wilhelm Bruder of Waldkirch, Limonaire of Paris, and Eugene DeKleist of North Tonawanda, New York. In 1892 the firm of Gavioli in Paris developed a new system for playing fairground organs that used perforated cardboard sheets; these were hinged together to form a continuous strip that when folded up resembled a book. As the cardboard strip passed through the keyframe, the music was 'read' by a row of small metal keys extending through the perforations; other keys operated percussion effects and turned ranks of pipes on and off. There was no limit to the length of a musical selection that could be played by a book-operated fairground organ, which was not the case with a barrel-operated instrument; the new system was also cheaper and more responsive. As a result the manufacture of barrel-operated fairground organs declined after 1900, and the 'book-music' system came to be used widely by such European builders as Bruder, Limonaire, Charles Marenghi of Paris and A. Ruth of Waldkirch.

Shortly after 1900 the Rudolph Wurlitzer Manufacturing Co. of North Tonawanda and Bruder in Germany began to manufacture fairground organs using the paper-roll system, in which a perforated roll of paper passed across a tracker bar (a brass bar with a row of holes along it). When a hole in the tracker bar was uncovered by a perforation passing over it, air was sucked into the hole, triggering a pneumatic mechanism that actuated the proper note or function. Most fairground organs made in the USA used paper rolls, and read them with vacuum, or negative, pressure; European organs used positive pressure. Paper rolls could accommodate a large number of selections, which ranged from classical pieces to popular songs of the day.

The pipework used in fairground organs consisted of both flue and reed pipes voiced on 20 to 30 cm of pressure (as measured by tubes filled with water). Flue pipes were the fairground organ's equivalent of flutes, piccolos, violins and cellos; reed pipes imitated trumpets, clarinets, baritones and trombones. Pipes were usually made of wood, but in earlier organs the reed pipes had polished brass resonators arranged symmetrically, for the sake of appearance, in the façade. The pipework was divided into bass, accompaniment, melody and countermelody sections. On a small organ a typical distribution might be 5, 9, 14 and 13; on a large instrument 21, 16, 21 and 38. Only in very large organs were these sections chromatic. Some notes of the scale were omitted in smaller organs to keep the size of the instrument to a minimum; this precluded the correct performance of many pieces and led to the practice of making transpositions and arrangements.

Of similar design to the fairground organ was the European dance organ, designed to provide music with a strongly accentuated rhythm and a variety of percussion effects. Since these instruments were for indoor use, they were voiced more softly and on lower wind pressure than the fairground organ; they used either books or rolls and were produced in immense sizes. The Dutch street organ, or *pierement*, a smaller but similar type of instrument, also used book music, but was turned by hand, although many are now operated by petrol engines. It had a selection of mildly voiced pipes which gave it a particularly sweet and lyrical tone.

The economic conditions of the 1930s caused the failure of most fairground organ companies, though a small number of craftsmen still build instruments and restore original organs. The London firm Page & Howard, which specializes in instruments based on Gavioli models, has recently exported organs to the USA, indicating a revival of interest in an area where fairground organs had virtually become extinct.

CHAPTER NINE

Reed Organ and Harmonium

'R eed organ' is a generic term applied to keyboard instruments
whose sound is produced by freely vibrating reed tongues
(usually without individual resonators) and activated by air under
either pressure (fig. 65a, p. 236) or suction (fig. 65b). Common names
for such instruments include harmonium (often used in Europe),
melodeon, vocalion, seraphine, *orgue expressif* and cabinet organ; the
term 'American organ' is generally applied in Europe to suction instruments to distinguish them from pressure ones. Particularly during
the 19th century, an increasing number of patents were taken out for
various types of reed organ under such names as Aeolina, Euphonion,
Mélodiflute, Organochordium and Physharmonika. Other members
of the reed organ family include such portable instruments as the
accordion and concertina. Reed organs range in size from compact,
single-manual instruments with one set of reeds, powered by one or
two foot treadles, to large, two-manual and pedal instruments (or,
rarely, three-manual ones) having several sets of reeds of differing
colours and pitches, and powered by a separate blowing lever or an
electric motor, as in pipe organs. The commonest types had two to
five sets of reeds, one manual and such accessories as octave couplers
and a tremulant. Such instruments vied with the piano for popularity
as domestic instruments for much of the 19th century (hence the use
of such terms as 'cottage' organ and 'parlour' organ) and were used
extensively in small churches and chapels as an inexpensive substitute
for the pipe organ.

1. HISTORY

The principle of producing musical sound from freely vibrating reeds
(as opposed to reeds vibrating against a fixed surface, as in the reed
stops of pipe organs) dates from prehistoric times; the earliest instru-

ments using this principle were hollow straws with a flap cut in the side. A much more sophisticated version of the principle is applied to the *sheng*, an Asian mouth organ, in which several reed-driven pipes of varying lengths are controlled by one player. Such instruments were first documented around 1100 BC.

A free-reed instrument based on the regal and called 'organino' is said to have been made by the Italian instrument maker Filippo Testa in 1700, but no example of it remains. Testa's instrument ushered in a century of experimentation with free-reed keyboard instruments. An instrument of this type is said to have been used in the mid-18th century by the St Petersburg musician Johann Wilde, prompting Christian Gottlieb Kratzenstein, a physicist from Copenhagen, and, later, his compatriot the organ builder Kirschnigk to experiment with free-reed keyboard instruments. Between 1782 and 1789 Kirschnigk built a kind of claviorgan called the Organochordium, in which free reeds were combined with a pianoforte. Kirschnigk's work came to the attention of the Abbé Vogler (1749–1814), who, intrigued by the expressive possibilities of the free reed, commissioned the Swedish organ builder Rackwitz, a former associate of Kirschnigk, to make a set of free-reed pipes (probably with resonators) for a portable organ which he called the orchestrion (not to be confused with the self-playing instrument of the same name popular in the late 19th century); this embodied the principles of Vogler's simplification system (see Appendix Three, 'Simplification system') and had four manuals, pedals and 63 stops, all fitted into a case 9′ square. The orchestrion is said to have inspired Johann Nepomuk Maelzel of Vienna to include one or more free-reed stops with the flue pipes, beating reeds and percussion of his complex barrel organ which he called the panharmonicon, a *tour de force* of musical instrument technology that according to various accounts was capable of imitating the sounds of the horn, clarinet, trumpet, oboe, bassoon, German flute, flageolet, drum, cymbal and triangle. The sounds of the panharmonicon were actually produced by various flue, reed and free-reed organ pipes, as well as air-driven percussion devices. It was for this instrument that Beethoven's 'Battle Symphony' (*Wellingtons Sieg*, 1813), later transcribed for orchestra, was originally written.

It was not until the early 19th century, however, that free-reed instruments recognizable as true reed organs were made. As is often the case, these began to appear independently in various countries. In Germany Bernard Eschenbach (1769–1852) of Königshofen, with his cousin the organ builder Johann Caspar Schlimbach, built his Aeoline (c1810), a keyboard instrument with reeds fashioned in the manner of

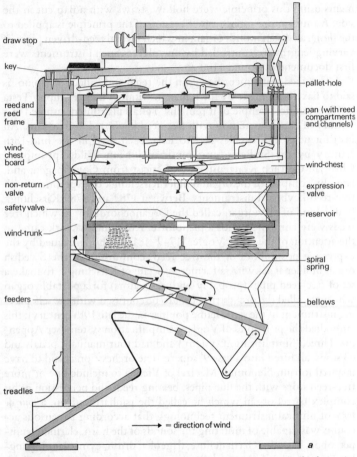

draw stop

key

reed and
reed
frame

wind-
chest
board

non-return
valve

safety valve

wind-trunk

feeders

treadles

pallet-hole

pan (with reed
compartments
and channels)

wind-chest

expression
valve

reservoir

spiral
spring

bellows

→ = direction of wind

a

65. Mechanisms of (a) the compression reed organ (with expression); (b) the suction reed organ (without expression)

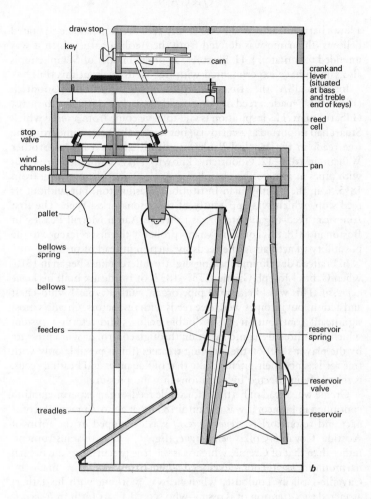

draw stop

key

cam

crank and lever (situated at bass and treble end of keys)

reed cell

stop valve

wind channels

pan

pallet

bellows spring

bellows

feeders

reservoir spring

reservoir valve

treadles

reservoir

b

a Jew's harp and activated by air under pressure from a knee-operated bellows (the name was derived from the Aeolian harp, which it was intended to imitate). J. H. Förstner, an organ builder of Mannheim, is also said to have experimented with free reeds at about this time.

In the USA the Boston organ builder Ebenezer Goodrich (1782–1841) made a reed organ, possibly as early as 1809, for the artist Gilbert Stuart. His inspiration is said to have come from a *sheng* which Stuart had imported as a curiosity, but it may also have come from the free reeds in the Maelzel Panharmonicon exhibited by his brother William in 1811–12. Goodrich is known to have combined free reeds with pipes in some of his chamber organs. One of these, dating from 1815, is in the Smithsonian Institution, Washington, but without its reed stop, which was apparently of the resonatorless type. The first American reed-organ patent was issued to Aaron Merrill Peasley of Boston in 1818; this contains what is probably the first reference to the possibility of activating the reeds by suction instead of pressure.

In France a development along slightly different lines began in 1810, when Gabriel-Joseph Grenié (1757–1837) of Bordeaux built his *orgue expressif*. This was like a small pipe organ, with a typical wind-chest and action, but its pipes were free reeds with resonators. Grenié's most significant contribution was a double bellows and reservoir system which permitted dynamic variation through control of wind pressure by the player's feet on the blowing treadles (this is possible only with free reeds, since their pitch, unlike that of flue pipes and beating reeds, is relatively unaffected by variations in wind pressure).

Grenié was ahead of his time, for while reed-organ experimentation continued in France, it was not until 1830 that a more practical, compact and resonatorless *orgue expressif* was developed in the form of Aristide Cavaillé-Coll's *poïkilorgue* (fig. 66). It is this instrument, rather than that of Grenié, which was the true precursor of the French harmonium as it later developed. The first *poïkilorgue* (made by Cavaillé-Coll in Toulouse, when he was working with his father) attracted the attention of Rossini, who scored a part for it in *Robert le diable* and was responsible for the young instrument maker going to Paris in 1833. The *poïkilorgue* was small and portable, having originally only one set of reeds and a variant of Grenié's blowing system. In his early years in Paris, Cavaillé-Coll built several other *poïkilorgues*. One was exhibited in Paris in 1834, and others were sold for use as choir organs in churches as late as 1841 and 1842. Shortly afterwards, in order to devote himself wholly to pipe organs, he turned over the instrument to Alphonse Mustel.

The first significant developments in England are noted in 1828 and

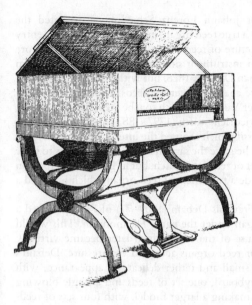

1829, when Charles Wheatstone (1802–75) patented reed organs
under the names Aeolina and Symphonium. Around 1830 John Green
of London built an instrument which he called the Royal Seraphine.
In Green's *Concise Instructions for Performance on the Royal Seraphine or
Organ* (London, 1833) the instrument is sufficiently described to identify it as a true reed organ of the pressure type. Its original features
included a crude swell, achieved by raising the top panel of the case
with a pedal, and a means of colouring the tone quality by placing
strips of differing materials over the reeds. No reed-organ industry
comparable to that of France, Germany or the USA ever developed in
England, but reed organs were made there throughout the 19th century and in the early 20th W. Dawes of London patented a 'melody
attachment' in 1864 and later a 'pedal bass'. Some sources attribute the
invention of the 'double touch' (later employed by Mustel) to the
English inventor Augustus L. Tamplin.

Much experimental activity was also going on in Germany and
Austria in the first half of the 19th century. In 1821 Anton Haeckl of
Vienna made a compact instrument of four octaves with the reeds
directly beneath the keyboard; he named this Physharmonika, a term
which would later be applied to free-reed stops in pipe organs. The

Stuttgart piano maker Johann Lorenz Schiedmayer patented the Euphonion, apparently a true reed organ, in 1816, but that firm's entry into the actual manufacture of reed organs did not occur until more than 30 years later. An instrument similar to Haeckl's was made in Paris by Johann Christian Dietz in 1828, but with an improvement in the form of a resonance chamber over the reeds. A patent was taken out by the organ builder Voit of Durlach for the Aeolodikon in 1820, and a few years later Friedrich Sturm (1797–1883) of Suhl in Thuringia built an *orgue expressif* which aroused the interest of the composer Spontini, and to which he gave the same name. Sturm appears to have been the first to add a set of reeds at 4′ pitch, but in 1838 J. B. Napoléon Fourneaux of Paris made a two-manual reed organ which included a set at 16′ pitch.

In 1840 Alexandre François Debain (1809–77) of Paris patented a single-bellows reed organ under the name Harmonium. This would appear to be the first use of the term which later became virtually universal in Europe for reed organs activated by pressure. Debain's first instruments were small and rather delicate in appearance, with only a three-octave keyboard, one set of reeds and a single blowing pedal. By 1842 he was making a larger model, with four sets of reeds divided between bass and treble and a sub-octave coupler. While Debain attempted to retain sole use of the name 'harmonium', it was soon used to refer to the instruments of two serious competitors whose work was ultimately to eclipse Debain's (because of Debain, they at first used the term *orgue expressif* in their advertising). These were Jacob Alexandre (1804–76), who had been making free reed instruments since 1829, and Victor Mustel (1815–90), to whom Cavaillé-Coll had turned over the rights to the *poïkilorgue* in the 1840s. The name was later widely used in England and on the Continent to refer to all reed organs, regardless of size or construction. Louis-Pierre-Alexandre Martin, a member of the Alexandre family firm, invented a percussion device acting directly on the reed tongues in 1841 and later a sustaining device called *prolongement*, both of which were later widely used by European harmonium makers. Mustel's firm, too, made some significant improvements, including the *double expression, forte expressif* and *harpe éolienne*, all first introduced in 1854 (see fig. 67), and Victor's son Charles invented a muting device called Métaphone in 1878. Mustel and Alexandre may be regarded as jointly responsible for bringing the harmonium to a high level of sophistication.

Despite all of the early experimentation in Germany, the first firm to undertake the mass production of reed organs in that country was founded by Julius and Paul Schiedmayer, sons of the piano maker.

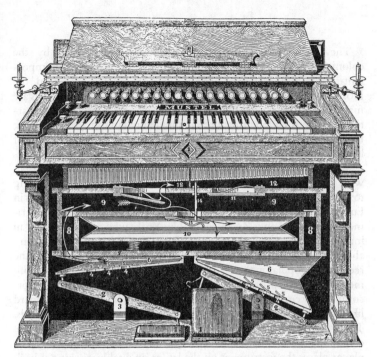

67. Mustel's harmonium (19th century), with front removed to show mechanism; white arrows indicate the direction of wind flow from feeders to reeds

Trained in the workshops of Alexandre and Debain, they returned to Stuttgart in 1853 to begin the manufacture of a modified version of the French harmonium, patented in 1851. They too made significant contributions to the development and popularity of the instrument; towards the end of the century they produced some instruments of considerable size, used not only in churches but for concerts. In 1881 a Russian musician named Hlavatch was giving recitals on a 24-stop Schiedmayer 'Concert Harmonium' in St Petersburg, and a Herr Poenitz gave several concerts on Schiedmayer instruments in Berlin in the 1890s. Music played in such concerts consisted of both original works and transcriptions. As in America and elsewhere, some piano makers, including Hildebrand of Halle, added harmoniums to their wares, as did such organ builders as Steinmeyer of Oettingen. In 1913 no fewer than 55 firms are listed as making reed organs within the boundaries of Germany, but of these Schiedmayer unquestionably had the largest output.

241

The harmonium was widely disseminated, especially by the colonial powers, in Africa and India, where it came to play an important role in local traditions. Though upright models are found, the most common is a small, portable instrument set in a box; models are made in various sizes with a range of stops and couplers. The harmonium has for a long time been manufactured in India and Pakistan; Palitana, in Gujarat, is regarded as a centre for the manufacture of harmonium reeds.

While European builders were perfecting the pressure reed organ with its expressive possibilities, American makers, early turning towards the suction type, followed a largely independent course. As in Europe, progress during the early 19th century was slow and experimental. In 1832 Lewis Zwahlen of New York, who may have been an immigrant, was issued a patent for a 'Seraphina or harmonicon organ', about which nothing further is known. An American variant of the reed organ popular in the early and mid-19th century was the 'rocking melodeon' or 'lap organ', a miniature portable instrument of short compass (three octaves or less), originally played by a button keyboard like an accordion, although later examples have normal keyboards. The wind is supplied by a double-wedge bellows underneath the case containing the keyboard and reeds, with an internal return spring. The player places the instrument on the lap or on a table, rocking it back and forth with the heels of the hands or elbow to activate the bellows while playing. The inventor of this instrument appears to have been James A. Bazin, an immigrant from the Isle of Jersey who settled in Canton, Massachusetts, in 1778. His design was later adopted by the New Hampshire instrument maker Abraham Prescott, who in 1836 began manufacturing a three-octave lap organ with a normal keyboard in Concord, an early centre of reed-organ manufacture.

After 1840 the making of reed organs accelerated in the eastern USA, as they became more popular as domestic instruments. 39 patents for reed organs and reed-organ improvements were issued by the US Patent Office between 1840 and 1858. The most significant of these was that granted in 1846 to Jeremiah Carhart of Buffalo, New York, for the exhaust (or suction) bellows. Such bellows had been attempted before, in both Europe and America, but because a fire a decade earlier had destroyed many patent records, it was at first thought that Carhart was the first to patent the idea. It was immediately licensed to George A. Prince, then Carhart's employer, and later to others, but during the ensuing years Carhart was frequently embroiled in litigation over the use of the exhaust bellows. In the 1850s one such lawsuit unearthed evidence, including Peasley's mention of a suction bellows in his 1818 patent, which caused Carhart's patent to be declared void, and henceforth the suction system was almost universally employed in America. Its advantage over the pressure system was stability, although at the sacrifice of the expressive properties so valued by the French.

The second half of the 19th century could well be called the era of the reed organ in America. At least 247 companies, many of them small, have been recorded as having made these instruments. Prescott, Prince and Carhart, as well as Carpenter of Brattleboro and Shoninger of New Haven, were pioneers; but after the middle of the century several firms began to eclipse them. Led by the firm of Estey, they also included Riley Burditt (later Burdett) of Brattleboro, Chicago and Erie; Daniel F. Beatty of New Jersey; Wilcox & White of Meriden, Connecticut; the Fort Wayne Organ Co., founded by I. T. Packard; Story & Clark of Chicago; Cornish & Co. of Washington, New Jersey; and S. D. & H. W. Smith of Boston, makers of the 'Smith American Organ'. But the two firms which vied with Estey for volume and popularity were those of W. W. Kimball of Chicago, which by the end of its reed-organ production in 1922 had manufactured 403,390 instruments, and Mason & Hamlin of Boston (formed in 1854). This firm was responsible for a number of improvements that were adopted by the entire trade, including the double bellows and knee swell.

Something of a latecomer was the vocalion, a pressure-type instrument developed by an Englishman, James Baillie-Hamilton, who began manufacture in Worcester, Massachusetts, in 1886. This instrument was unique in its use of unusually wide reed tongues, which gave it a smoother, more organ-like tone so that it became popular for use in churches. Vocalions ranged in size from foot-operated instruments having one manual to instruments with two (or occasionally three) manuals and pedal. Hamilton sold his interest in the vocalion to the New York Church Organ Co. in 1890. Vocalions were later made by Mason & Risch of Worcester and as late as 1910 were still being made by the Aeolian firm.

The instruments made by these American firms in the first half of the 19th century had a single manual and usually only one set of reeds. They were most commonly called melodeons, but the term 'seraphine' was also used, and occasionally other names were applied to instruments of this class, such as the Aeolodeon patented by Rufus Nutting in 1848, said to be more pleasing and less nasal in quality than other melodeons. These early reed organs had the appearance of a square piano, sometimes with 'lyre' legs. The number of stops increased in the 1850s and 1860s; instruments of two manuals were made, and the 'square piano' and 'lyre leg' styles gave way to the more continental-looking, boxy 'flat-top' model, with its two large treadles. The more familiar 'gingerbread' type of parlour organ, often sporting ornamental lamp stands, bric-a-brac shelves and mirrors, began to appear in the 1870s and 1880s (fig. 68). By this time reed organs were being made in all possible sizes, from Mason & Hamlin's portable 'Baby' organ, introduced in 1882, to large church instruments such as Estey's Phonorium of the 1890s, with two manuals and pedals, which had a façade of dummy organ pipes.

It is interesting to contrast the use of the reed organ in various countries. The French *orgue expressif* reached a high degree of mechanical and musical sophistication in the late 19th century and was treated with respect by serious composers and musicians. Because pedalling had to be carefully coordinated with playing, it was not an easy instrument to master, and for the novice it was necessary to provide a mechanism allowing it to be winded from a fixed-pressure reservoir as well as directly from the blowing treadles. Harmonium playing was taught in conservatories, and the instrument developed a considerable literature. The Germans made suction as well as pressure instruments, a good proportion of which were fixed-pressure instruments intended for supporting congregational singing in village churches. French harmoniums were used in churches as well, but usually as supplementary choir organs for liturgical use. The British also used reed organs in homes and small chapels; but domestic production was never on a par with other countries, and instruments were imported from the USA, Germany and France. By 1877 sufficient French harmoniums were in use in England to prompt the organist John Hiles to publish an instruction manual for their proper use.

American reed organs, made with few exceptions on the exhaust principle, were of simpler construction and less musical sophistication. As early as 1856 Carhart patented a machine to mass-produce reed cells, and it was not long before large factories were being established to mass-produce low-cost reed organs; Estey even surrounded theirs with a 'mill village' of workers' houses. Because of its simple construction, low price and ability to stay in tune, the reed organ superseded the chamber organ and actually exceeded the piano in use as a domestic instrument for more than half a century. The smaller, lighter versions were the first keyboard instruments taken to the West by the pioneers. As small new churches sprang up, their first instrument was usually a reed organ, and larger churches with pipe organs in their main

68. Reed organ by Story & Clark, Chicago, 1895

auditoriums used reed organs in Sunday schools and chapels. It was a popular instrument with such travelling evangelists as Moody and Sankey, and was taken abroad by missionaries. This resulted in its introduction to Japan, one of the few countries where reed organs are still manufactured, and India, where its integration resulted in the small, portable harmoniums still made there. At the height of their popularity American reed organs could be found throughout the world; in Europe they were even copied by such builders as Mannborg of Saxony and others in Scandinavia.

Interest in the reed organ began to wane in the first decades of the 20th century. Mass-production techniques had been applied to piano making, lowering the cost of pianos and increasing their availability and desirability as domestic instruments. Pioneer churches were prospering and buying pipe organs, and attempts to introduce reed organs for use in theatres met with little success. Around 1911 Story & Clark, Shoninger and many others sold their reed-organ interests and concentrated on pianos. Estey and Kimball diversified, adding pianos and pipe organs while slowly phasing out reed organs; Estey continued to make them until after World War II, their output including a government-issue folding 'chaplain's organ' and an amplified electrified reed organ. Mason & Hamlin sold their reed-organ interests outright to the Aeolian Co., which shortly afterwards began marketing the Orchestrelle, a large player reed organ in an elaborate case, which enjoyed a brief vogue. The idea of a self-playing reed organ was not new, however. Before the turn of the century small, table-top 'roller organs' with such names as 'Mechanical Orguinette' and 'Chautauqua Organ' were popular. Operation was by a hand crank which operated both the small bellows and the pinned wooden player roll. In Europe Schiedmayer continued to make both pressure and suction reed organs into the 20th century, but Alexandre ceased business and Mustel increased production of the celesta, which they had invented. Before the mid-20th century electronic instruments, some of the earliest of which were simply amplified reed organs (Everett Orgatron, etc), had taken over the domestic market, and the reed organ became a collector's item.

From the 1970s the reed organ was the subject of renewed interest as an antiquarian instrument; several businesses specializing in their restoration and sale were established, and in 1981 the Reed Organ Society was formed, which publishes the quarterly journal *ROS Bulletin*. Private reed organ museums have been established at Victoria Hall, Saltaire, West Yorkshire, and in Palmer, Mass.

2. CONSTRUCTION

The sound-producing element in all reed organs is the free reed: a unit, usually entirely of brass, in which a thin tongue vibrates freely in an aperture when excited by air under suction or pressure. Length of the reed tongue determines pitch, and timbre is determined by several factors, chiefly the reed tongue's width and thickness, although a slight twisting of the tongue also has an effect on tone quality. Reeds are tuned by scraping or filing either on the end (to sharpen) or at the base (to flatten); to prevent possible damage to the tongue, this is usually done with a thin piece of brass (reed slip) placed between the tongue and its mounting. Reeds are removed from their cells with a special tool called a reed hook, which fits a notch cut into one end of the unit.

In the pressure type of reed organ (fig. 65a), wind is supplied by two feeder-bellows, which fill a spring-loaded reservoir above. Wind then flows from this reservoir into the valve-box of a wind-chest not unlike that of a pipe organ. Stop-valves admit air into channels above, one for each set of reeds. When a key is depressed, opening a valve above all reeds of that note, air will exhaust through the reeds from any channel which has been pressurized by drawing a stop-knob, thus causing the reeds to sound.

In the *orgue expressif*, a stop-knob labelled 'E' or Expression allows a mode of operation in which the reservoir is bypassed, opening a set of valves which feed air to the reed chest directly from the feeder bellows. Because the pressure in the feeders can be increased or decreased by the action of the player's feet on the treadles, a wide and controllable dynamic range can be achieved. This requires skill on the part of the player in order to keep the wind supply smooth.

In the suction type of reed organ (fig. 65b), foot treadles (one in early organs; two in most later ones) operate suction bellows which exhaust a spring-loaded vacuum reservoir of wedge shape. Use of the exhaust system simplifies the construction of the wind-chest (or 'pan'), which consists simply of a shallow box with a single note-valve for each note in the top board, depressed by a sticker pushed down by the key. The reed units are above the valves, each in its own 'cell' routed into a covering board. The stop action opens or closes the apertures of a given set of cells, so that when a key depresses its valve, only those reeds sound whose cells are open, allowing air to be drawn down through them by the vacuum. In two-manual organs the chest for the upper manual is usually in an upside-down position, so that the key-stickers are pushed up from the key tails, rather than down from the key fronts. When there is a pedal keyboard, its chest is usually located in the bottom or at the back of the case.

The pitch of reed organ stops parallels that of pipe organs, with 8' pitch the basic or normal level, but with the possibility of additional stops of 16', 4' and, occasionally, 32' and 2' pitch. In most single-manual reed organs, both American and European, the stops are divided usually at *c'*, requiring a 'treble' and a 'bass' knob to activate the entire stop. Swell or Forte mechanisms are also usually divided to enhance possibilities for playing and accompanying solos on a single manual, and in some French harmoniums it is also possible to apply varying pressures to the treble and bass, providing further flexibility and shading possibilities. In American reed organs the knee-operated swell is used for shading.

French reed organs were fairly standardized in specification, although varying in size. The standardization of stop-names and their location on the stop-jamb above the keyboard made it possible for composers and publishers of harmonium music to indicate registrations in a kind of shorthand (in parentheses in Table 36) which could be applied to instruments of most major makers.

A typical medium-sized instrument was Mustel's Model 2-A, with speaking stops as shown in Table 36. It also had the following accessory stops: Prolongement ('Pr'), a device operated by a small lever near

TABLE 36

Bass	Treble
(1) Cor anglais 8'	(1) Flûte 8'
(2) Bourdon 16'	(2) Clarinette 16'
(3) Clairon 4'	(3) Fifre 4'
(4) Basson 8'	(4) Hautbois 8'
(5) Harpe éolienne 2'	(5) Musette 16'
	(6) Voix céleste 16'
	(7) Baryton 32'

the player's left heel which causes any note depressed in the lowest octave to be held until the next note is played (in some larger models it acts on the entire keyboard); Métaphone ('Met'), a kind of mute which, by almost completely closing the reed cell apertures, softens and subdues a normally bright reed tone; and Forte expressif ('O'), a simple swell-shutter device above the reeds (called Forte in other makes), but in Mustel's instrument operated by a pneumatic one which responds to changes in wind pressure when the Expression knob ('E' or 'Ex'; see above) is drawn. In addition (lp) provides stop (l) with a percussion effect caused by actually striking the reed tongues with small hammers. The Harpe éolienne and Voix céleste both consist of two sets of reeds, one tuned slightly sharp to produce a gentle, undulating effect.

Debain, Alexandre and others made models of similar resources, though without some of Mustel's patents; thus Alexandre's Forte ('O') was a simple shutter which was either open or closed, with no gradations. Many instruments also had Grand jeu ('G'), a pleno stop which brought on all stops except the undulating ones. The basic style was copied in other countries, and a Viennese version (c1875) by Peter Titz uses French stop nomenclature and the usual shorthand symbols, including Sourdine ('S'), a mute for the Cor anglais, and Tremblant ('T'), a stop not as common on European reed organs as it later was on American ones. Like Mustel and some others, Titz divided his keyboards between e' and f' rather than between b and c'. In the hands of a knowledgeable player organs such as these are capable of a wide range of effects both subtle and dramatic.

American reed organs also achieved a certain amount of standardization, although on a less official level than in Europe, and without the registration symbols. A typical parlour organ would have two to four sets of reeds divided at c'. A Smith American Organ of the 1870s, a fairly typical example, has the resources shown in Table 37. The two reed sets were a Diapason 8' and a Principal 4', the other two stops on each side being softer versions produced by closing a muting shutter over the reed cell unit. The only accessory is a pair of knee-levers which allow these shutters to be opened or closed independently, and with gradation.

TABLE 37

Bass	Treble
Diapason (8')	Diapason forte (8')
Diapason dolce	Dulciana
Principal (4')	Principal forte (4')
Principal dolce	Flute
Octave coupler	Octave coupler

A slightly larger instrument was Estey's Model 38, with three full sets of reeds plus a 12-note Sub-Bass extension (for specification, see Table 38). This instrument also has a Forte knob which opens the shutters (or mutes) and a Tremolo. This latter, sometimes also called Vox humana, was a simple device consisting of a suction-activated

TABLE 38

Bass	Treble
Diapason (8′)	Diapason (8′)
Dulciana	Dulciana
Vox jubilante (8′)	Vox jubilante (8′)
Flute (4′)	Flute (4′)
Sub-bass (16′)	Treble coupler
Bass coupler	

rotating dowel fitted with two vanes of metal, pasteboard or thin wood, and placed near enough to the reed cell openings to produce an undulation. The Vox jubilante is a loud stop, analogous to the Diapason, and in some organs had two sets of reeds; the Dulciana is a muted Diapason, although in larger organs there is occasionally an independent set of reeds with this name. Despite many patents taken out by Americans on reed organs, these usually concerned improvements in construction or production methods rather than tonal innovations. American instruments generally lack some of the more esoteric mechanical devices found in European ones, but they include such oddities as reed organs combined with sewing machines, writing desks and pianos; chime or bell stops of steel bars (perhaps inspired by Mustel's *Orgue-celesta*); and a pure example of Yankee ingenuity in Kimball's 'safety pedal', which folded up in such a way as to prevent mice from entering the cabinet.

By the late 19th century reed organs ranged in size from Mason & Hamlin's 39-note 'Baby' organ, patented in 1882 and popular with Sunday schools, to Lyon & Healy's 'Peloubet Church Organ' (1892) of three manuals, 36 stops and 1948 reeds. The home models, which evolved into masterpieces of Victorian 'gingerbread' design, represented the bulk of every manufacturer's production. These typically had one keyboard, two to five sets of reeds and the usual accessories of tremulant and knee swell. Towards the end of the century several firms produced reed organs of two manuals and pedal, designed to be blown by a second person, for use in churches and for practice.

The larger the instrument, the more it attempted to emulate a pipe organ. A fairly typical example is the Schiedmayer two-manual and pedal suction model of about 1900 (see Table 39), which was quite capable of supporting the singing of a congregation of 100 or more with all Forte stops and couplers drawn. In addition, there is a *Manual Koppel* operated by both a knob and a foot lever, and a *Volles Werk* foot lever which brings on all but the Dolce stops, which are only

TABLE 39

Manual I (lower)	Manual II (upper)
Bourdon 16′	Salicional 8′
Principal 8′	Aeolsharfe 8′
Principal Dolce 8′	Flöte 4′
Gamba 8′	Forte II Manual
Viola 4′	
Viola Dolce 4′	Pedal
Forte I Manual	One set of reeds, permanently
Oktav Koppel	on Pedal Forte

mutes, and the Aeolsharfe, which is an undulating stop with two sets of reeds.

Many American makers built instruments similar to this example, Estey going so far as to make a 'Student organ' model around 1920, in which the cumbersome reed box under the lower manual was eliminated to make the key-desk proportions as close to those of a pipe organ as possible. Alexandre and some of the Americans even made a few instruments (not totally successful because of tuning problems) combining pipes and reeds, and Alexandre also made a powerful instrument expressly for church use enclosed in an organ-type swell-box. Some of the larger vocalions were, internally, hardly distinguishable from a small tracker-action pipe organ. In the 20th century Estey and others made a small number of reed organs operated by electric action, on the principle of a unit organ, and the Everett piano firm for a short time made a reed organ with electronic amplification, the Orgatron, which was the first electronic organ to be manufactured on a large scale. These instruments failed to compete successfully with fully electronic instruments, although some of the older mechanical-action reed organs of this type (two manuals and pedal) remain in use as church and practice organs.

3. REPERTORY

During the late 19th century in Europe the reed organ was regarded as a serious instrument for serious musicians, and harmonium courses were taught at the Paris Conservatoire, at one time by César Franck. Numerous harmonium tutors were published, and such composers as Franck, Louis and René Vierne, Guilmant, Dubois, Lemmens, Loret, Merkel, Lefébure-Wély, Leybach, Karg-Elert and Reger wrote original works for harmonium. Catalogues of the period are also filled with transcriptions for harmonium from operas, oratorios and orchestral, piano and organ works. In America the literature tended to be simpler, although reputable composers including Buck, Zundel, Clarke and Bird wrote tutors and original compositions, as did Pearce and Rimbault in England. American reed organ books in general, however, are aimed at the amateur performer. Secular music, particularly operatic transcriptions, folksongs, popular songs, marches and dances, makes up the bulk of such collections, as well as a few hymns and voluntaries for church use.

In Europe there was less emphasis on the 'home amateur'. Franck's two volumes entitled *L'organiste* (published 1896–1900) and Louis Vierne's *24 pièces en style Libre* (1913) are examples of serious harmonium music that is still performed, although usually on the pipe organ. Karg-Elert wrote a harmonium tutor and a number of useful church pieces. The reed organ was used extensively for ensemble music on the Continent, especially with violin, cello, flute and piano (Franck even arranged some of his own organ works for harmonium and piano), and one catalogue of around 1900 lists music 'for three or four hands'. Reed organs were also used extensively in salon orchestras as a substitute for brass and woodwind instruments. Many transcriptions, ranging from Strauss waltzes to Mozart overtures, were made for these ensembles, including some transcribed by Schoenberg.

The harmonium was also extensively used to accompany voices; Rossini and others scored for it in some of their operatic and church music. Perhaps one of the last instances of such use is in the original score of Weill's *Die Dreigroschenoper* (1928). In America, perhaps because of the virtual absence of a serious literature and limited expressive properties, the reed organ was unable to compete with the piano or organ as a concert instrument, although it was widely used to accompany voices, and sometimes used for this purpose in small concert halls possessing no pipe organ. After 1900 no American composers took any interest in the reed organ with the exception of Arthur Bird (1856–1923), commissioned to write some harmonium pieces by a German firm, and possibly Ives, who may have intended accompaniments to such songs as *Serenity* (1919) for reed organ.

In the later 20th century research into the literature and the desire for authenticity in performance have resulted in the occasional appearance of reed organs in concerts and on recordings. They are also being restored for use in chapels and small churches at the request of musicians who prefer them to electronic substitutes, and because they are more durable.

APPENDIX ONE

Registration

The selection of different pitches and tone-colours available on an instrument is known as its registration. The musical forces of the organ are available selectively by means of separate stops, or registers, which together provide the entire tonal capacity of the instrument. Each of the registers controls the 'on' or 'off' position for a series of pipes, grouped so that one or more pipes will respond to each key on a manual or pedal keyboard. The term 'organ registration' takes in the large body of advice about what is appropriate when combining organ stops, as well as the aggregate tonal effect of any combination drawn for a particular musical need. There is a rich store of information about registration for the organ that can be classified generally into two categories; practical advice, often supplied by organ builders, which consists of lists of combinations capable of being turned to good use; and instruction from composers or theoreticians about combinations appropriate for performing a particular musical composition.

1. GENERAL HISTORY

The history of organ registration is inextricably bound up with changing styles in organ building. Its origins lie in the transition between the stopless organ (*Blockwerk*) and instruments equipped with selective registers. In the *Blockwerk* of the early 15th century, the plenum, a mighty mixture of pipes sounding fundamentals and harmonics, was the only registration, and such an organ was indivisible. The introduction of the *fluitwerk-sterkwerk* option, the second manual division (*Positif-de-dos*, or *Rückpositiv*) and Trompes (Bordunen) made some variety in registration possible; but still there was no selectivity in the modern sense within the sections of the instrument. In Italy towards the end of the 15th century there were one-manual organs whose plena had been parcelled out to separate stops, each controlling a rank of pipes. As this new fashion spread northwards through France and Germany, organists were confronted for the first time with the necessity of choosing and blending their registrations, and builders often supplied them with advice about the most attractive combinations available. The earliest known organ music and the earliest instructions for registration date from the 15th century.

But until the first decade of the 17th century there was no apparent attempt to identify any registration with a certain musical texture.

Mersenne, in his *Harmonie universelle* (1636–7), opened his section on organ registration by summing up possible combinations of stops for an instrument of 22 registers. Taken in pairs, he said, the individual sounds of the instrument may be varied in 231 ways; taken in threes, 1540 ways; and taken in fives, 26,334 ways. But 'among the many possible combinations there are several which are disagreeable'. This statement suggests that a player of good taste should refer to Mersenne's advice to find the most agreeable registrations, and eventually learn enough about the tonal design of the organ 'to invent several others by experimenting at the keyboard'.

Mersenne's lists of 'agreeable' registrations summed up more than a century of innovatory development for the French organ, a period from which considerable information about habits of registration has survived. A typical organ contract of the 16th century, or a list of registrations made out to assist the player, first described the plenum (called *plein jeu* or *fourniture*). The plenum was the ancient *Blockwerk* split into three or more registers controlling doubled or tripled ranks of 16′, 8′ and 4′, with two mixtures, called Fourniture and Cymbale. These mixtures held diverse ranks of many pitches contributing to the plenum. They were not useful by themselves, but neither was the plenum complete without them. Alongside the plenum, additional registrations developed for newly invented stops – flutes, reeds, bells, birdcalls, drums – bearing the names of their most distinctive components, such as Nasard, Doublette and Cromorne. Names of familiar sounds were applied to certain registrations, such as *petit carillon*, 'parrot', 'canaries' and the 'voice of pilgrims of St Jacques'.

Major developments in organ building during the 16th century and the early 17th led to sharp stylistic delineations along national lines. Mersenne's 'agreeable' registrations would not have suited the tastes of Italian or German musicians of his time, whose instruments were designed according to different tonal concepts. Yet organ builders and theorists supplied the broadest range of advice available for playing early organ music. Schlick, in his *Spiegel der Orgelmacher und Organisten* (1511), mentioned that preludes should be played on the plenum, and the cantus firmus could be brought into prominence on the *Hauptwerk*. Numerous characteristic sonorities were discovered and recorded, such as the Krumhorn and Zimbel, which appeared in the Netherlands as early as 1505.

2. EARLY SPANISH ORGANS

Two post-Cabezón documents deal fully with possibilities for one- and two-manual organs contemporary with Francisco Correa de Arauxo. They are the *Documents per a la historia*, which relate to the organ in S Juan de las Abadesas, Barcelona (1613), and *Archivo musical* (document 1404 at the cathedral of

APPENDIX ONE

Lérida) for a 25-stop, two-manual organ built in 1624–5. The latter is most remarkable for its systematic coverage of 117 registrations. One-manual combinations were classified under the following headings: plenum, Flautados, Nasardos and Misturas. Two-manual registrations, usually using the *cadira* (*Rückpositiv*) for melodic purposes, were grouped as: *unisonus*; 'other combinations' to be used with or without Tremulant; Flageolets; Gaytilles; Cornetillas; Regalies; and ways of using the 'medio registro partido' (half-registers split between bass and treble). Although Correa's tientos seem to have been written mostly for a one-manual organ with split stops (divided at *c'*), the Lérida manuscript shows richer possibilities for contemporary adaptation to an instrument with a *cadireta*.

The introduction of the famous horizontal trumpets of Spanish organs (Clarines, or Trompettes *en chamade*) in the 17th century further heightened the contrasts between those instruments and organs in the other European countries. As early as 1706 directions for using horizontal trumpets were given in the titles of pieces in the *Flores de música ... por Fray Antonio Martin y Coll, organista de San Diego de Alcalá*: 'Cancion de clarín, con eco, a discreción', 'Entrada de clarines' and 'Registro de clarines, mano derecha'.

A late 18th-century Spanish source shows the influence of Bédos de Celles, the third volume of whose *L'art du facteur d'orgues* (1770) gave valuable advice on registration. A series of letters to a friend by Don Fernando Antonio of Madrid, dealing with the construction and maintenance of organs, was published in 1790. Despite his feeling that organists should know how to find suitable registrations for their own playing, Don Fernando was persuaded to add a section on registration. It is, in effect, a Spanish adaptation of Bédos' instructions.

3. EARLY ITALIAN ORGANS

The Italians, the first to use spring- and slider-chests that made registration possible on the organ, called attention to the correlation between certain registrations and suitable musical textures. Diruta, in his *Seconda parte del transilvano* (1609), assigned moods to the 12 modes, and recommended a registration for each. Banchieri, in *L'organo suonarino* (1605), not only noted registrations but even included changes between sections of two compositions, the 'Battaglia' and the 'Dialogo'. But the most significant contribution came from the builder Costanzo Antegnati, in *L'arte organica* (1608), written in the form of a dialogue between father and son. Antegnati explained his 12-stop organ at Brescia Cathedral, and gave instructions on how to play it during the Mass. The stops all spoke from one manual keyboard, typical for Italian organs of the period, with a coupled pedal which controlled the bass section of a Principal stop (see no.2 below):

1. The complete Principale (24')
2. The split Principale (24'), divided at *d*, the bass played by the pedals.

3. Ottava (12')
4. Quintadecima
5. Decimanona
6. Vigesimaseconda
7. Vigesimasesta
8. Vigesimanona
9. Trigesimaterza
10. Another Vigesimaseconda, to play in concert with the Ottava, and Flauto in ottava and Decimanona, which gives the effect of cornets.
11. Flauto in quintadecima
12. Flauto in ottava

Registrations and important comments were as follows:

1. *Ripieno*, for intonation, introits or preludes; 1.3.4.5.6.7.8.9
2. *Mezzo ripieno*: 1.3.8.9.12
3. 1.3.12
4. 1.12
5. 3.5.6.12 for the concerto style. These four stops resemble a consort of cornets.
6. 3.12. These two are excellent for playing diminutions and for canzonas 'alla francese'.
7. 3.12 + Tremolo; for the same sorts of pieces, but not for diminutions.
8. 1 alone. 'I usually play this at the Elevation of the Mass'.
9. 1.2 in unison may be played together.
10. 12 alone
11. 12 + 2. When played in the treble, this makes a kind of accompanied harmony of two stops; then going down to the bass one hears the flute alone . . . thus one comes to make a dialogue with the help of the Contrabasse of the Pedal.
12. 11.1 should be played in diminutions; 3 may be added.

Antegnati continued with stop-lists and comments about registration for the nine-stop organ at the Church of S Faustino and the Braces, Brescia, S Grata, Bergamo, the Carmine Church, Brescia, and S Marco, Milan. Additional advice about registration is summarized as follows:

a The *ripieno* should be used at the *Deo gratias*, with toccatas, using pedals.
b For accompanying motets in concertato style: the Principale and Flauto in ottava. For motets with few singers: Principale alone, also with Tremolo, but in that event without diminutions.
c The Tremolo can be used with the Ottava and Flauto in ottava, or Flauto in Ottava alone, but then slowly and without diminutions.
d The Fiffaro should be played only with the Principale, slowly and legato.
e For canzonas 'alla francese', a good effect for flourishes is achieved with the Principale, Flauto in duodecima, Ottava and Flauto in ottava, without Tremolo.
f Finally Antegnati discussed the advantages of split stops for dialogues between the bass and treble ranges.

Italian organ music was seldom annotated with the composer's instructions for registration. Rare examples are found in the organ part for Monteverdi's *Vespro della Beata Vergine* (1610; see the *Magnificat* settings for six and seven voices); in the titles of organ sonatas (1742–7) by Padre Martini; in Zipoli's *Pastorale* (1716); and in the organ sonatas (1785; others in the Conservatoire

APPENDIX ONE

National de Musique, Paris, and the Biblioteca Nazionale Marciana, Venice) of Gaetano Valeri, the registrations for which were indicated for an organ by Callido. A number of organ builders' registration-lists appeared from the mid-17th century until the end of the 19th. These often introduced the innovations of foreign builders, such as Willem Hermans (Como, 1650; Rome, 1666) and Eugen Casparini (Trent, 1687). Although the classic Italian ripieno usually survived intact, there were registers and devices unfamiliar to most Italian organists, such as the Tierce, the mounted Cornetto, the Sesquialtera or the Tromboni, and such toy stops as the Rusignoli, Grillo and Cuccù. The second manual division was meant to function as an echo (*organo piccolo*). In the late 18th century the Swell was introduced as an enclosed *organo piccolo*, without powerful reed stops at first. New mechanical devices included the *tiratutti* and the *terza mano* (octave coupler).

4. NORTH-WESTERN EUROPE

The impetus for the development of what are now known as the classical French, the Dutch and the north-west European styles of organ building came from the internationally active group of 16th-century Flemish builders. Virtually all the sources dealing with registration in northern countries before the publication of the second volume of Praetorius's *Syntagma musicum* (1618) apply to the Flemish style before sharp outlines of national development had been manifested. Sweelinck played on an organ of this type built by Heinrich Niehoff, of 's Hertogenbosch. No comparable advice for registration exists for the magnificent organs built by the Scherer family, of Hamburg, and their successors in north-west Germany, but contractual documents and the surviving instruments may serve to complement the music composed for them. In the Lüneburg tablatures (Augustiner-Chorherrenstift, Klosterneuburg), for instance, there are references to manual changes, to the *Rückpositiv* for florid melodic passages, or to the *Hauptwerk* as an echo. There were also instructions for registration in the preface to Praetorius's *Musae Sioniae* (1610). Some doubt arises about the authenticity of certain hints found in the organ works of Buxtehude, but Georg Friedrich Kauffmann, in his *Harmonische Seelenlust* (1733–6), left careful recommendations for specific stops for each piece. There is no evidence of a comprehensive record of the vast possibilities for registration on the greatest instruments built in the 17th century, such as those in the Catharinenkirche, Hamburg, where Heinrich Scheidemann was organist from 1625 to 1663, or the Jacobikirche, where his pupil, Matthias Weckmann, played from 1655 to 1674.

A valuable indication of registration in a related tradition comes from Samuel Scheidt, who played a Compenius organ in Halle, and published the following instructions in his *Tabulatura nova* (1624):

To Organists
Every organist who has an organ with two manuals and pedal can play these

ORGAN

Magnificat settings and hymns, as well as some of the psalms found in parts i and ii; the chorale melody might be played with a penetrating stop on the *Rückpositiv* (in order to bring it more clearly into relief), particularly when it appears in the soprano or tenor. When it is a bicinium and the chorale is in the soprano, the chorale is played on the upper manual or *Werck* with the right hand, and the second part with the left hand on the *Rückpositiv*. If the chorale is in the soprano of a four-part verse, it is then played on the *Rückpositiv* with the right hand, the alto and tenor with the left hand on the upper manual or *Werck*, and the bass on the pedal. If the chorale is in the tenor, the chorale is played with the left hand on the *Rückpositiv* and the other parts with the right hand on the upper manual or *Werck*, the bass on the pedal.

In a four-part verse the alto may also be played specifically on the *Rückpositiv*, but the soprano must be played with the right hand on the upper keyboard, with both the tenor and bass voices together on the pedal; it must be specially composed, however, so that the tenor is no higher than C [*c'*], since one seldom finds D [*d'*] in the pedals, and also so that these parts are not spaced too widely apart, only an octave, 5th, or 3rd, since one cannot span a larger distance well with the feet.

But ... [it is] most beautiful and far more comfortable to play the alto on the pedal. But the advantage of this way depends upon the stops and particular voices in the organ, which must have been disposed knowledgeably in terms of 4' and 8' pitch levels. The *Positiv* must always be based on 8' pitch; and the Pedal on 4' pitch. Soprano, alto and tenor should be played on the *Rückpositiv* on a 8' stop. The alto will be played on the pedal with a 4' stop. Voices of a sharp 4' tone in the Pedal: 4' Oktave and Zimmel, 4' Gedackt and Zimmel, Cornett (bass) 4', and so on. When such 4' stops are drawn the alto sounds in the correct pitch relationship. ...

Certain registers or stop divisions to draw when one will play a chorale on two manuals and hear it clearly:

On the Hauptwerk

Gross Gedackt 8' }
Klein Gedackt 4' } drawn together

or

Prinzipal 8' alone and other stops according to preference.

Sharp stops on the *Rückpositiv* to hear the chorale clearly: Quintadena or Gedackt 8' and the Klein Gedackt or Prinzipal 4', with the Mixtur or Zimmel or Superoktave; these stops together or others according to preference.

To hear the chorale clearly on the Pedal: Untersatz 16', Posaune 8' or 16', Dulzian 8' or 16', Shalmei, Trompete, Bauerflöte, Cornett, and others which are found often enough in small and large organs.

The foregoing I would nevertheless prescribe only to those who do not yet know the style and who would like to do it properly. Other distinguished persons and sensible organists, however, will be left to direct such things after their own inclination.

Mattheus Hertel (*Kurtzer unterricht ... Orgelwerkes*, 1666) refers to and enlarges upon Scheidt's registrations. Hertel wrote that the Tremulant, which was to be used for doleful melodies, also 'can be used for preludes, and also even for fugues'.

APPENDIX ONE

In later theoretical works (Werckmeister, 2/1698; Niedt, ed. Mattheson, 1717; Adlung, 1768; Marpurg, 1760) it can be seen that strict rules about the combination of stops of the same pitch were gradually being relaxed. The most important of these limitations to registration had been the exclusion of flute stops from the plenum. Adlung made the point that 'good' wind systems would not cause fluttering when two 8′ stops were drawn together. Registration-lists by M. Heinrich Rothe for the Silbermann organ in Fraureuth (1739–42) and by J. G. Schenke (instructions dated 1780) for Silbermann's organ at Grosshartmannsdorf (1738–41) reveal the growing taste for combinations of fundamental-sounding stops, such as Principals, Flutes and Gambas, at least in south and central Germany.

Towards the end of the century additional information was supplied by Daniel Türk (*Von den wichtigsten Pflichten eines Organisten*, 1787) and J. H. Knecht (*Vollständige Orgelschule*, 1795), in which early attempts at crescendo registration are documented. The 'tutti' concept, employing all the stops and couplers, was firmly entrenched by this time, and eventually replaced the traditional orientation of the organ's tonal design around the plenum.

The classical purity of national styles of organ building was breaking down by the late 17th century, as is shown by the work of several builders who moved from their home countries: Casparini (German) and Hermans (Dutch), who worked in Italy; Riepp (French), working in southern Germany; and the brothers Andreas and Gottfried Silbermann, who moved from Saxony to France (Gottfried Silbermann later returned to Germany with first-hand practical experience of the classical French tradition). Registration-lists survive for organs made by these builders: for Casparini's organ at S Maria Magiore, Trent (1687); Hermans's organ at S Apollinare, Rome (1666); and for Silbermann's instruments at Fraureuth (1739–42) and Grosshartmannsdorf (1738–41). Riepp himself wrote four lists for organs in Salem, including a 'gourmet' rendition of the classical French tradition, and hints for registrations for particular audiences, such as 'a king', 'an officer', 'a child' or 'an ignoramus' (see Meyer, 1938, pp.167ff). Certain excessive treatments in the construction of organs must have had their effect at least on local habits of registration. For example, Riepp's Trinity organ at Ottobeuren (1757–66) had eight Tremulants, two for each of four manual divisions.

Bach's directions for registration of his organ compositions are comparatively sparse. Names of stops are given in the Concerto in D minor after Vivaldi (BWV 596) and the chorale preludes on *Gott, durch deine Güte* (BWV 600) and *Ein' feste Burg* (BWV 720). Pitch levels are indicated in four of the six 'Schübler' chorale preludes (BWV 645–7, 650). *Forte and piano, Rückpositiv* and *Oberwerk*, and *organo pleno* are indicated in several large chorale works and preludes and fugues. It is said that Walther wrote in the names of stops Bach had used for playing his chorale prelude on *Ein' feste Burg* – Fagotto and Sesquialtera. But more interesting speculation arises from the notes in the first movement of the Concerto in D minor. Here the instructions call for separate Oktave 4′ on *Oberwerk* and *Brustpositiv* with Prinzipal 8′ for the Pedal, changing in the course of the movement to Sub-Bass 32′ in the Pedal and Prinzipal

8' and Oktave 4' for the *Oberwerk*. The 4' opening pitches reflect Vivaldi's original score, but did Bach mean to add 16' and 32' in the Pedal? The sparse information coming directly from Bach's hand, as indicated above, is best translated into practical use in the light of C. P. E. Bach's statement to Forkel:

> No-one understood registration as well as [J. S. Bach]. Organ builders were terrified when he sat down to play their organs and drew the stops in his own manner, for they thought that the effect would not be as good as he was planning; then they heard an effect that astounded them.

5. CLASSICAL FRENCH ORGANS

The ultimate refinement in registration for composed music is an achievement of the French, who since the mid-17th century have maintained a precise relationship between the indigenous character of specific registrations and musical textures to which they best respond. While the Germans have left performers more or less free to choose their own registrations, subject basically to the instrument's natural restrictions, the French have wedded timbre and articulation with the musical score to an exemplary degree. Lebègue (*Premier livre d'orgue*, 1676) enjoined his contemporaries to play according to the exact directions for registration: 'There are several pieces in this book that are not useful to organists whose instruments lack the stops necessary for their execution'. Even the more flexible approach of André Raison (*Livre d'orgue*, 1688) provided free choice in registration only within the limitations of the design of organs generally in favour in his own time: 'As I vary the choice of stops and manuals a great deal, it is not necessary to play all my pieces exactly as marked'. The classical French repertory was forgotten during the 19th century because French organs no longer made the sorts of sounds that could articulate that repertory.

Among many excellent sources of information on the classical French tradition of organ registration, Gaspard Corrette's preface to his *Messe du 8e ton* (1703) provides the best available clarification of the important relationships between registration, musical texture and style of performance. The registrations he specified for particular pieces are as follows:

> For the Plein Jeu, couple the manuals. On the *Grand jeu* [sic], the Bourdon 16', Bourdon, Montre, Prestant, Doublette, Fourniture and Cymballe. On the *Positif*, the Bourdon, Montre, Prestant, Doublette, Fourniture and Cymballe.
>
> For the Fugue, couple the manuals. On the *Grand jeu*, the Bourdon, Prestant and Trompette. On the *Positif*, the Bourdon, Prestant or Montre and the Cromhorne.
>
> For the Trio à deux dessus, the manuals are uncoupled; the right hand playing on the *Positif*, and the left on the *Grand jeu*. On the *Grand jeu*, the Bourdon, Prestant, Montre, Tierce, Grosse Tierce, Nazar and Quarte de nazar. On the *Positif*, the Bourdon, Prestant or Montre, Cromhorne and Tremblant doux.

The Duo is played with the manuals uncoupled, the right hand on the *Positif*, and the left on the *Grand jeu*. On the *Grand jeu*, the Bourdon 16′, Bourdon, Prestant, Tierce, Grosse Tierce, Nazar and Quarte de nazar. On the *Positif*, the Bourdon, Prestant or Montre, Tierce and Nazar.

The Récit de Nazar is played on the *Positif*, with the accompaniment on the *Grand jeu*. On the *Grand jeu*, the Bourdon and Montre 4′. On the *Positif*, the Bourdon, Prestant or Montre and the Nazar.

The Dessus de Petite Tierce is played on the *Positif*, with the accompaniment on the *Grand jeu*. On the *Grand jeu* the Bourdon and Prestant. On the *Positif*, the Bourdon, Prestant or Montre, Tierce and Nazar.

For the Basse de Trompette, the manuals are uncoupled. On the *Grand jeu*, the Bourdon, Prestant and Trompette. On the *Positif*, the Bourdon and Prestant or Montre.

For the Basse de Cromhorne, the manuals are uncoupled. On the *Grand jeu*, the Montre and Bourdon. On the *Positif*, the Prestant or Montre, Nazar, Tierce, Doublette, Larigot and the Cromhorne – not the Bourdon.

For the Cromhorne en Taille, on the *Grand jeu*, the Montre, Bourdon, and the Pedalle de flûte. On the *Positif*, the Bourdon, Prestant or Montre and the Cromhorne.

For the Tierce en Taille, on the *Grand jeu*, the Bourdon 16′, Montre, Prestant and the pedalle de flûte. On the *Positif*, the Bourdon, Prestant or Montre, Nazar, Tierce, Doublette and Larigot.

For the Fond d'orgue, the manuals are coupled. On the *Grand jeu*, the Bourdon 16′, Bourdon, Prestant and Montre. On the *Positif*, the Bourdon and the Prestant or Montre

For the Concert de Flûte, the manuals are coupled. On the *Grand jeu*, the Bourdon and Flûte. On the *Positif*, the Bourdon, Flûte and the Tremblant doux.

For the Dialogue de Voix Humaine, the manuals are not coupled. On the *Grand jeu*, the Bourdon and Flûte. On the *Positif*, the Bourdon, Flûte, the Voix humaine and the Tremblant doux.

For the Dialogue à deux Choeurs, the manuals are coupled. On the *Grand jeu*, the Bourdon, Prestant, Trompette, Clairon and Cornet. On the *Positif*, the Bourdon, Prestant or Montre and the Cromhorne.

For the Dialogue à trois Choeurs, the manuals are coupled. On the *Grand jeu*, the Bourdon, Prestant, Trompette, Clairon, Cornet, Nazar, Quarte de nazar and Tierce. On the *Positif*, the Bourdon, Prestant or Montre, Cromhorne, Tierce and Nazar. The third *choeur* is played on the *Clavier d'écho*, and the Tremblant à vent perdu is used.

6. ENGLISH ORGANS

Among the few indications of registration practice before the Commonwealth are those suggested by the double voluntaries of Orlando Gibbons and John Lugge. The texture of the music indicates contrasting full Great and Chaire divisions, and manual changes are clearly marked. The choruses of such organs contained principals of pitches up to 1′ and 1⅓′, but no mixtures or reeds. After the Restoration, French (and to some extent, Dutch) registration practices strongly influenced English organ building and playing. Some of the earliest registration indications are those of Christopher Gibbons, some of whose double voluntaries call for solos on the Cornet, Trumpet and Sesquialtera. John Blow's early 18th-century manuscripts also contain some registrations, including 'Cornett' solos, 'the two diapasons' (i.e. open and stopt at 8' together) and solo 4' flute. Thomas Mace (*Musick's Monument*, 1676) commented on the use of reeds in a chamber organ, noting that the 'Hooboy stop ... (together with the Regal) makes the Voice Humane'.

In the 18th century English registration practices became as rigidly codified as the French ones; these usages continued well into the 19th century and are documented as late as 1855, in Hopkins's and Rimbault's *The Organ*. They are also found in numerous early 19th-century North American sources. By the mid-18th century such composers as John Stanley gave registration indications in their published voluntaries as a matter of routine, and by the late 18th century there were rules for registration in the prefaces to voluntary collections and treatises. Jonas Blewitt (*A Complete Treatise on the Organ*, 1795) gave registration hints for particular types of music: the Open Diapason may be used alone for 'slow fugues', but the Stopt Diapason must be added for livelier movements; the Diapasons may be alternated with the Swell; the Flute or Flageolet 'requires airy music'; the Trumpet music is 'martial and grand'; the Cremona or Vox Humane are suited to Adagio movements; and the Twelfth and Fifteenth are never to be used without the 8' and 4' foundations. John Marsh (preface to his *18 Voluntaries*, 1791) warned that the Cornet should be used only for solos, never with full organ, and prescribed five different kinds of full organ:

1. Great up to sesquialtera
2. The furniture added to the sesquialtera
3. The trumpet added instead of the furniture
4. The trumpet and furniture both added
5. The clarion added to the whole

As English organs usually did not contain manual 16' stops until the second quarter of the 19th century, it follows that all the above combinations are based on the 8' open diapason. Solo and echo effects are frequently found in 18th-century English music, and are in fact so much part of this literature that most chamber organs of the period contain divided stops or half-stops as well as a machine stop, in order to facilitate the playing of such music on a single manual.

7. REGISTRATION IN THE 19TH CENTURY

Technological advances during the 19th century, including the introduction of machine tools, transformed the craft of organ building into an industrial pursuit. To assure their commercial success and artistic recognition organ

builders competed for prominence by displaying their latest mechanical innovations in the great industrial exhibitions in London and Paris, and by
courting favourable comment from the press. Soon the ancient concepts that
had previously limited the musical resources of the organ were abandoned.
Vastly expanded tonal capacity resulted from the application of pneumatic,
and later electrical, devices to relieve the key-action; stable and practically
limitless wind supplies were provided by more and more men at the bellows,
by steam engines and eventually by electrical blowers which fed into large
reservoirs. Because of these 'advances' and the musical demands of the new
Romantic aesthetic, organists were quite content gradually to relinquish the
time-worn architectural concepts that had previously governed registration.
The *plein jeu* was forsaken in favour of the reed-dominated tutti. Mutations
were replaced by wind-hungry ranks at the fundamental pitches: open flutes,
harmonic stops and broad strings. Wind pressures rose continually, but no one
dreamt that in the America of the 1920s organs would be built demanding
wind more than ten times as strong as the 19th-century maximum.

To respond to the call for a smooth crescendo from the whisper of soft stops
speaking behind closed Venetian shutters to the immense roar of the tutti,
pneumatic motors were installed to provide the player with pre-set combinations (St Sulpice, Paris, 1863). A single player could move skilfully about,
using all the sounds of a mammoth organ with great ease and speed. Registration, by ventil pedals in France, by *Rollschweller* in Germany, and by electrically operated combinations in England and the USA, was gradually reduced
from an art to a formula.

The essential ingredients for the registration of 19th and early 20th-century
organ music were the building blocks of the tutti, beginning with enclosed 8'
stops, which were then combined with unenclosed 8' flue stops in the manuals
and 16' and 8' stops of the pedal always coupled together. Steps along the way
provided for the addition of foundation stops (16', 8' and 4' on all keyboards),
followed by reeds and mixtures. The Swell shades were fully opened before
the final introduction of the most powerful unenclosed sounds. The *Rollschweller*, or crescendo pedal, did this job efficiently by the gradual 'blind'
addition or subtraction of registers in a predetermined order.

The music of Mendelssohn and Rheinberger was written with post-classical
registration in mind, while Reger demanded the continuous dynamic alterations inherent in the system described above. Mendelssohn, in the preface to
his Six Sonatas (1845), explains his dynamic markings in terms of registration:
'By *fortissimo* I mean all the power of the organ, and by *pianissimo* generally a
soft 8' stop; by *forte*, all the fundamental stops with a few reed stops; by *piano*,
a combination of several 8' stops, etc'. Franck, Widor and their successors
wrote specifically for Cavaillé-Coll's system of stop-controls, which consisted
mainly of mechanical devices for the introduction or blocking-off of wind
from sections of the chests (*fonds* and *anches*). Sub-octave coupling was important for the *grand choeur*.

ORGAN

8. AUTHENTICITY

Each new generation has felt a persistent urge to impose new fashions over established tastes. Only since the mid-20th century has there been a perceptible desire to preserve intact or to respect the musical traditions of the past; nor did earlier players scrutinize the evidence relating to those traditions. Whatever was resurrected came dressed in the current fashion. For example, in the 19th century it was not considered inappropriate to adapt the rediscovered works of J. S. Bach to registrations considered suitable for Romantic music. Schweitzer, perhaps the world's best-known Bach lover, wrote: 'What a joy it is ... to play Bach on the beautiful Walcker organs built between about 1870 and 1875', and 'how happy Bach would have been could he have had a finer *piano* on his third manual by the Venetian shutter swell!'. Widor, Schweitzer's teacher and collaborator, maintained: 'The organ of Aristide Cavaillé-Coll remains the true organ, the organ of J. S. Bach'. Yet Widor protested at the Americanization of French organs, calling on the Académie des Beaux-Arts to preserve the French (i.e. Romantic) organ heritage, and Schweitzer was influential in helping to preserve the old Dutch and German instruments before the dawn of the classical revival.

The least satisfactory approach to authenticity in registration lies in the notion that it can be achieved by applying information from simple lists of stops to any instrument equipped with stops bearing those names. Equally fallacious is the notion that an all-purpose organ can be devised, suited to the registration needs of the entire literature. Recently, organ building has tended to rely increasingly on inspiration derived from a single historical tradition, rather than a fusion of various stylistic patterns. This approach provides a new hope for authenticity in the registration of early organ music.

APPENDIX TWO

Organ Stops

Just as the term 'stop' is of uncertain origin and meaning, so the many stop names have a complex history and usage. Thus, for example, the Spitzflöte may be said to be 'a stop consisting of open metal pipes made of an alloy with high or fairly high tin content and shaped conically, so that the pipe is tapered from the mouth upwards, giving a tone rather flute-like in character but richer in formants, and serving as a solo or chorus colour halfway between the flute and the diapason ranks'. But all stop names leave many factors unclear, and 'Spitzflöte' cannot be thought of as indicating more than an approximate sound or pipe construction in organs of certain kinds, since (*a*) the name signifies different sounds (timbre, volume) in different organs, from one builder, area or period to another, such details as mouth size, wind pressure, scaling and metal alloy being varied; (*b*) the name would arise at first only in a large organ of *c*1580 when a builder wished to distinguish in his contract between one open metal stop and another; (*c*) the name would be used only in northern Europe, but the pipe form elsewhere; (*d*) although some builders elsewhere had an equivalent in their own language for the name (Flauto a cuspido, Flûte à fuseau etc), few used it, preferring either to leave such ranks without names that indicated pipe construction or to give them a more fanciful name indicating tone-colour – especially in the 19th century; (*e*) conical pipes might be used for a rank (or part of a rank) already given another name indicating some other factor in its nature or function (e.g. 'Nasard'); (*f*) occasionally, especially during the 19th century, a builder might use the name for a rank imitating the tone-quality it is associated with though constructed differently, perhaps of wooden pipes or open, cylindrical, metal pipes. (See also Appendix One, §1.)

The evolution of stop names naturally reflects the evolution of the organ as a complex instrument. During the 15th century in northern France, the Netherlands and the Rhineland, such terms as 'Principal' were used to indicate the basic sound of the organ, the *pleno* chorus; and the case pipes (Prestant, Montre, Doif etc) were increasingly specified in sources, they being the first ranks to be separated off from the chorus in a big church organ. In most cases large secular organs, which had a longer tradition for separate and sometimes highly colourful ranks, have no associated verbal descriptions that specify names. By 1500 builders were making many kinds of ranks and almost without exception giving them the names of instruments or sounds which the ranks were thought to imitate (Trumpet, Horn, Nine-holed Flute), sometimes picturesquely so (Old Women's Voice, Nightingale), even when we now scarcely recognize them as orchestral instruments (Gemshorn, Swiss flute etc). It is quite misleading to assume that the 19th-century liking for orchestral effects was in itself a sign of decadence in organ building. The exceptions to these instrumental names were important, since they usually indicated the construction of pipes concerned and were thus intrinsic to the organ as an independent instrument (Gedackt, Hohlflöte, Spitzflöte etc). It is particularly difficult to understand the origin of the names of some stops, including those that appear to be words taken from other contexts – musical (Diapason, Regal), architectural (Trompes), theoretical (Sesquialtera) or even onomatopoeic (Bourdon). In some cases, notably those of Trompes and Bourdons, it is not clear whether the use of the term in the organ context precedes any other. By the end of the 16th century names in all countries and languages had become regular and reliable as indications of a stop's purpose, if not always of its tone; whether such names remained in the builder's contracts or were actually written on stop labels at the organ is less clear. Labels were hardly necessary, for instance, on Italian and English organs, and remained uncommon on chamber organs until the late 18th century.

The great organ theorists and those giving lists of specifications, such as Praetorius, Mattheson, Bédos de Celles and Hopkins, gave a somewhat misleading impression of the uniformity and reliability of stop names. Readers of Praetorius, for instance, are led to believe not only that the names of the many Regal stops were neatly codified but also that such stops were more important – i.e. common over a wider area and for a longer time – than was indeed the case. Certainly written reports must always have increased the interest of organists and builders in new or foreign stops, particularly perhaps in those cases where writers expressed doubt as to the success of a certain builder in imitating such sounds as the human voice, sea waves, orchestral horn and so on. Remarkably few stops in name, sound or construction originated during the 18th century, and many of those so popular in the 19th (overblowing stops, string-scale flues) originated in the early 17th. The cheap workmanship of so many 19th-century organs meant an abuse of many stop names, but the mid-20th-century revival has led to a return to traditional practices.

The definitions or descriptions that follow have been compiled with certain points in mind: (a) transliterations of stop names (e.g. Kwinta for Quinte) are not given, nor nordic variants of German names (e.g. Spetsfloït for Spitzflöte) unless they indicate a different kind of stop (e.g. Baarpijp and Bärpfeife); (b) a short phrase indicates the family of stops which a name indicates (flue or reed; open, closed or semi-closed; metal or wood); two stops of the same name can have a different combination of such factors, as they can also serve quite different purposes from organ to organ (chorus/solo; Principal/Flute/mutation); (c) examples are taken from typical instruments, and no attempt has been made to list every maker's fanciful name or wayward invention; (d) examples may refer to a stop whose pipes are constructed in the manner normally associated with the name even when the builder's own term is unknown;

(*e*) only few names are included of those families of stops invented at different periods for purposes of little relevance to idiomatic organ music, particularly Renaissance and Baroque toy stops (birds, tinkling bells etc), late 18th-century free reeds of the harmonium type, late 19th-century high-pressure flue or valvular reed stops; (*f*) stop types with names in several languages (e.g. Querflöte, Flauto traverso) are entered under the most commonly used name unless a difference in construction is implied (e.g. Nachthorn, Cor de nuit). For further details see Williams (1966).

Cross-references within this appendix are indicated in the form, for example: See FAGOTTO; cross-references to another appendix are indicated thus: See Appendix Three, 'Quint'.

Aeolina. (1) A narrow, metal flue stop of soft tone first found in Germany *c*1820.

(2) A free reed of gentle tone, invented *c*1815 (possibly by Eschenbach) and popular in central Germany (Schulze etc).

(3) Free reeds with derived names: 'Claveoline' 8′ or 16′, sometimes with wooden resonators (by Beyer, *c*1820), 'Aeolodicon' 16′ (Walcker, *c*1840).

Baarpijp (Dutch). (1) Barem was a soft Gedackt stop during Praetorius's period (*c*1620).

(2) 'Baarpyp' at Haarlem (1735–8) and in other Dutch organs of that period was a soft stop of tapered pipes. In earlier sources (from the late 16th century), often the same as Quintadena. The name may come from *baar* (Middle Dutch: 'bright') or *barem* ('to scream') or from the German *Baar* ('pole' or 'rod'). *See also* BÄRPFEIFE.

Bajete, Bajón (Sp.). Late 17th-century Spanish reeds: a 4′ Bajete was gentle in tone, often a bass-half stop only, sometimes *en chamade*; Bajón was an 8′ Bassoon stop (the 4′ version called 'Bajoncillo'), stronger in tone, usually with flaring metal resonators. 'Bajoncillo y Clarín' was a single 4′ rank in two halves.

Bärpfeife (?Ger., ?Dutch). A reed stop of the mid-16th century (name first used by Niehoff, possibly 1540), the predecessor of Regal stops with fanciful resonators, strong in tone, 'Schreyer' (Praetorius, 2/1619) and 'Kryther' (St Eusebius, Arnhem, 1506) seem to be alternative names. The term has nothing to do with growling bears, however coarse the tone.

Bassflute. A 19th-century 8′ pedal stop, usually of stopped wood (like the 16′ Bourdon), sometimes open; 'Flötenbass' is an older German equivalent, of various constructions.

Basson (Fr.). *See* FAGOTTO.

Bassoon. (1) An English reed stop of quiet tone, once found frequently from *c*1680 onwards (R. Harris), particularly on the Chair organ; most examples probably had small-scaled flaring resonators.

(2) An English 19th-century reed stop, usually called Fagotto, of the same construction but at 16′ pitch on the Swell organ.

(3) A French 18th- and 19th-century reed stop, serving as the bass half to a treble Hautbois.

(4) On 19th-century English and American organs, the separately drawing bass octave of an Oboe or Hautboy.

Bauernflöte (Ger.: 'peasant's fife'). A penetrating 2' or 1' flue stop, of open wide scale, sometimes stopped or as a Chimney Flute, found especially in the Brabant organ of *c*1550, the Fritzsche-Compenius organ of *c*1620 and organs of Saxony *c*1690; popular as a 1' solo pedal stop for cantus firmus music.

Bazuin, Buzain (Dutch). *See* POSAUNE.

Bell-diapason (Fr. *flûte à pavillon*). French stop from the 1840s, containing cylindrical pipes with a flaring cone soldered at the top; a loud Flute.

Bell Gamba. A tapered flue stop of 16' or 8' pitch with a short, conical section at the top of the pipes, found on 19th-century continental and American organs.

Bifara, Biffaro. (1) A double Flute whose pipes have two mouths at different heights, producing a soft tremulant sound; it was popular in south Germany and Austria from *c*1660.

(2) In Walcker's organs (*c*1830) a double rank of 8' stopped and 4' open, producing a soft, string-like tone.

Blockflöte (Ger.). A wide, conical metal flue stop imitating the recorder; it can be open, closed or overblowing (*c*1620), sometimes made of oak (late 17th-century Friesland and England), usually at 4' pitch.

Blockwerk (Ger.; Dutch *blokwerk*). Not strictly a stop name, it denotes the undivided chest of the medieval organ based on a 'double Principal' without other 'stops' separated off. (See Appendix Three, 'Blockwerk'.)

Bocktremulant (Ger.). *See* TREMULANT.

Bombardon (Fr. *bombarde*; Ger. *Bomhard, Pommer*). (1) In France, the basic manual or pedal 16' reed, from at least 1587 (Arras), of great importance to the French classical organ, with strong tone, metal or wood resonators and sometimes its own keyboard (Notre Dame, Paris, 1733).

(2) 'Pombarda', according to Praetorius, was a 16' or 8' reed of strong tone and two-thirds length resonators.

(3) 'Bombarda' signified long pedal reeds on the enlarged Italian organ of *c*1820 (Serassi).

(4) 'Bombardon' was the name given to a rather mild-toned English Bombarde of *c*1850.

Bourdon (Fr.). (1) The earliest 'Barduni' were low-compass bass pipes played not by manual keys but 'latched' on (Arnaut de Zwolle, *c*1450) (*See* TROMPES).

(2) Occasionally, 'Perduyn' or 'Pardoenen' indicated case-front pipes (*c*1550), more often inside pipes an octave below the case pipes.

(3) The most important use of the term was for the stopped pipes an octave below the main Diapason rank in the French organ. The scaling was narrow – stopped wood for lower octaves, stopped or Rohrflöte metal for the upper

– and the musical application larger than for any other stop.

(4) A medium- to large-scale 16′ pedal stop of stopped wood, often found in English and American organs from *c*1820 onwards.

Campanello (It.). (1) *See* CARILLON.

(2) A high, repeating, wide-scaled mutation, giving a bell-like effect (England, Germany, *c*1850).

Carillon. Various stops achieving bell-like effects. (1) Real bells of 4′ or 2′ pitch, played by hands or feet, on many organs, especially in central and south Germany, from 1737–50 onwards; there were trackers to small striking hammers.

(2) A common Italian stop of the same type, popular in the early 19th century.

(3) An important Dutch Tierce Mixture found *c*1750–1850 as a kind of Echo Cornet.

Celeste. *See* UNDA MARIS and VOIX CÉLESTE.

Celestina.(1) A soft 4′ open wood Flute, sometimes found in English organs *c*1860.

(2) In 19th-century American organs, often a soft 4′ string.

Cembalo (It., Cz.). *See* ZIMBEL.

Chalumeau (Fr.). (1) The same as Schalmei in some German sources of the 18th century.

(2) A small-scaled, flaring reed stop in central Germany *c*1750, sometimes cylindrical.

Cheio (Port.). A chorus Mixture of the same type as the Compuestas de Lleno (Sp.).

Chimney Flute. *See* ROHRFLÖTE.

Chirimía (Sp.). A kind of 4′ or 2′ Schalmei, imitating the shawm in 17th- and 18th-century organs, sometimes *en chamade*.

Choralbass, Choralflöte (Ger.) An open metal or wood 4′ Flute found on the pedals of 17th- and 18th-century German organs for playing cantus firmus melodies; in some cases an open manual 8′ Flute.

Cimbala (Sp.). *See* ZIMBEL.

Clairon (Fr.). *See* CLARION.

Clarabella. The early 19th-century English and American name for an open wood Flute of pretty tone (used by Bishop, *c*1825), often in the treble only, originally replacing an 18th-century mounted Cornet and useful for solos.

Claribel Flute. A mid-19th-century name for a fairly strong Great organ 4′ Flute (Willis, *c*1860), sometimes harmonic for the top octave.

Clarín (Sp.). Spanish Trumpets of various kinds, originating mostly in the later 17th century. (1) An 8′ Clarín was a standard Trumpet, vertical inside the organ or horizontal at the case front. 'Real' Trumpets (Clarines, Trompetas) were usually vertical (not horizontal), the name indicating 'real' in the sense of 'full-length' resonators'; but by c1750 'trompeta real' often meant 'royal trumpet'.

(2) 'Clarín de eco' was a smaller-scaled Trumpet in an Echo or Swell box.

(3) 'Clarín fuerte [suave]': a strong [soft] Trumpet. Both the strong and soft stops had flaring tin resonators.

(4) Clarines usually indicates a 2' reed of soft Trumpet tone, sometimes a bass-half stop only.

(5) 'Clarín de batalla', 'Clarín de compaña': military-like Trumpet stops *en chamade*.

(6) 'Clarín de mar': Trumpet stops *en chamade*, such as were used for naval signals.

Clarinet. A reed stop of many different types and purposes. (1) Clarinette (little Clarín) was a Spanish Regal, sometimes *en chamade*, found in the heyday of Iberian organs (c1750).

(2) Clarinetto: an Italian Regal (18th century); or a German pedal Clarin 2' stop (c1830) or 4' stop (c.1775).

(3) Clarinetto was occasionally a clarinet-imitating reed stop (c1790, south Germany). As 'Clarinet', 'Clarionet' or 'Cremona' it is frequently found in English and American Choir organs from the early 19th century onwards; its cylindrical resonators show its ancestry in the Cromorne [Krummhorn].

Clarino (It.). *See* CLARION.

Clarion (Ger.; Fr. *clairon*; It. *clarino*). Reed stops. (1) A 4' Clairon is the main French chorus Trumpet, supplementary to the Trompette 8', common on the main manual from at least c1580, and as such found elsewhere both in Frenchified organs (England, Alsace) and those quite independent (central Germany).

(2) Clarino: a rare Italian Trumpet, of metal or wood; Trombetta and Clarone were other Italian terms used here and there from around 1600.

(3) *See* CLARÍN.

Claron (Sp.). A Nasardos or Tierce Mixture.

Compensationsmixtur. *See* MIXTURE.

Compuestas (Sp.). A mixture or Lleno, like the Fourniture but more varied in content.

Contra (Lat.). Used with the meaning 'an octave below': found especially in the Latinized stop-lists of c1800. (1) Contrebasses were 19th-century French strong-toned pedal stops imitating the double bass (Cavaillé-Coll).

(2) Contrabass more generally indicates a (pedal) stop an octave below the open Principal.

(3) Contras are Spanish pedal ranks of open or stopped pipes, often without their own stop-knob; thus Contras en Bombardas denotes the 16' pedal Bombarde.

Coppel, Koppel (Ger.; Lat. *copula*). (1) A coupler.

(2) A stopped 16', 8' or 4' rank in Habsburg Europe, sometimes called 'Koppelflöte'. In many organs the equivalent of the Gedackt, and made of metal or wood.

(3) Coppel elsewhere sometimes indicates a Gemshorn, Spillflöte or even Principal (*c*1540), probably so called because it was coupled to or drawn with Principals, Flutes or reeds.

Cor anglais (Fr.; It. *corno inglese*). 19th-century reeds with narrow resonators shaped like the orchestral instrument (*c*1850); in Italy the stop is older (used by Serassi, *c*1820) and of coarser tone, and has wide, cylindrical resonators.

Cor de nuit (Fr.). An open or stopped flue rank of wide scale, at 8', 4' or 2', found in French organs *c*1850 and in those in England and the USA which they influenced.

Cornamusa (It.). A Regal toy stop once common (*c*1600) and producing the drone sound of two held reed pipes, thus leaving the hands free to play 'zampogna' or 'musette' music.

Cornet (Fr.; It. *cornetto, corneta*; Sp. *corneta*). Various stops imitating the cornett, a wooden, valveless trumpet used from the late 15th century to the late 17th. (1) A very important French solo Mixture stop, one to three examples of which were found on every classical organ from 1650 to 1850; it was treble only, from *c'*, with five wide-scaled ranks (1.8.12.15.17) often placed on their own small chests ('mounted Cornet') from *c*1640. Examples during the second half of the 16th century were often given a distinguishing name, such as 'Cornetz à boucquin', 'Nachthorn', 'Cornet d'Allemagne' or stop 'imitating the zink'. The term is not to be confused with the organ stop Cornett, though sources are often unclear on this point.

(2) Cornetto and Corneta were Italian Flute mutation ranks from *c*1680 – primo might be the Tierce, secondo the Nasard, terzo the Quarte de nasard etc.

(3) Spanish Cornet stops ('Corneta clara', 'reale', 'tolosana', i.e. 'from Toulouse') were also common but not so stereotyped in pipe content.

(4) Cornets often had fewer ranks in the 19th century (two-rank Cornettin in Sweden), or were built up of Geigen pipes (France) and Dulciana pipes ('Dulciana Cornet' in England).

Cornett, Kornett (Ger.). A reed stop imitating the Zink or cornett (*See* CORNET), usually in the pedals, of 4' or 2' pitch, and found throughout central and northern Germany from 1600 to 1800. Praetorius noted that the flaring resonators are only just longer than those of the 'Trichterregal'. 'Singende Kornette' were so called partly because of the smooth tone, partly because such stops were used for melodic cantus firmus lines.

Corno (It.). A name found fairly frequently for various stops. (1) Italian Cornetto, a reed stop in old sources.

(2) Corno dolce is either a soft reed stop (built by Serassi, *c*1810) probably developed from Venetian Regals, or a wide Flute stop in Italy (*c*1750–1900), sometimes in the form of an inverted cone.

(3) Corno di bassetto, like the Corno inglese, is an imitative reed stop of the 19th century with cylindrical resonators (used by Willis).

Cornopean. An English reed stop (Hill, Willis) imitating the *cornet à pistons*, of rather thin tone, 8′ pitch and chiefly of use on the mid-19th-century Swell organ.

Cromorne (Fr.; Ger. *Krummhorn*). Reed stops imitating the crumhorn; later versions of the name (Cormorne, Cremona) are corrupt. (1) German Krummhorn stops were of varied construction (Praetorius, 2/1619): they had metal or wood resonators and were open or stopped, short or half-length, cylindrical or double-cone-shaped etc.

(2) French Cromornes appeared somewhat later, i.e. late in the 16th century, becoming the standard *Positiv* reed in the classical organ; they usually had narrow, cylindrical, half-length metal resonators. The tone was modified as builders in *c*1800 began to make it resemble the clarinet.

(3) English Cremona stops date from *c*1680 and presumably copied French models, keeping the same design until they began to disappear in *c*1900.

Cymbale (Fr.). *See* ZIMBEL.

Decem, Decima (It.: 'tenth'). A mutation rank sounding the 10th or 17th; largely a theorist's term (Samber, 1704–7; Adlung, 1768).

Diapason (?Gk.). (1) Octave stops, sounding an octave above the case pipes, according to theorists (Werckmeister, 1705; Hess, 1774); found in organs with Grecized stop names *c*1790.

(2) In England, the term may have denoted Trompes in *c*1500, but by 1613 it had its present meaning of Open Diapason (main Principal rank, usually 8′) and Stopped Diapason (Gedackt). As a term, 'Diapason' may be derived from the Dutch Doif (*c*1450) only later, having taken a quasi-Greek form that is scarcely relevant; as a registration direction 'Diapasons' is an indication to use the Stopped Diapason, whose mild but harmonically rich tone has a strong emphasis on the quint, to colour the Open Diapason. English builders seem to have prided themselves on their Diapason tone, Renatus Harris's examples (*c*1690) being already richer than those of his French models; as such, it helped to hinder the development of the English organ, its very name giving the stop a mystique absent from more traditional terms like Montre and Principal.

Diaphone. One of Hope-Jones's valvular reeds, useful in cinemas. (See Chapter Two, §4, and fig. 22.)

Diez (Sp.: 'ten'). Hence 'Diez y novena' is the 19th or Larigot $1\frac{1}{3}$′ (sometimes chorus Quint).

Doef, Doif, Doff, Doof (Dutch). Terms denoting the Principal stop in those early sources that used the word 'Prinzipal' to mean 'plenum' or main chorus from *c*1450, e.g. 'le prestant ou doeuf' at Namur, 1598. Spellings are sometimes confusing, e.g. Praetorius's 'Doiflöte' is a Doppelflöte, not a Doef.

Dolcan (Ger.). *See* TOLKAAN.

Dolce (It.; Fr. *douce*). The verbal coincidence of Dolce, Dolcan, Dulciana and Dulzian has led to much confusion; probably all terms derive from Dulcis, a stop with 'sweet' tone. Dolce or Flauto dolce was common for any soft stop from *c*1600 to 1800, whether of wood or metal, and whether narrow and cylindrical or conical. Adlung gave other spellings and versions: Dulzfloit, Dolzflöte, Dulceflöt, Süssflöte.

Doppelflöte (Ger.). *See* BIFARA. From *c*1600 to *c*1900 makers experimented with pipes with two mouths either for soft, undulating effects or for greater volume (*c*1830). Late 19th-century German and American examples are of stopped wooden pipes with a powerful fundamental tone; the stoppers are occasionally bored.

Double. A prefix indicating pitch an octave lower than usual (Double Trumpet, Double Diapason).

Doublette (Fr.). The 2′ Principal rank of the French classical organ. The name was often used in the larger organs of the more cosmopolitan English builders of *c*1860, under the influence of Cavaillé-Coll's large 2′ ranks.

Douce (Fr.). *See* DOLCE.

Dulcian, Dulciana. Gentle flue stops of various form, found in the non-Latin countries of Europe from at least *c*1640, and in name deriving presumably from *dulcis* ('sweet'). Early examples in Austria and hence, through Snetzler, in England, were as likely to have been small-scaled Dolcan stops in the form of an inverted cone as the narrow, small-mouthed, miniature Diapason ranks familiar in most 19th-century organs, either as single ranks or in Mixtures. The earlier examples, especially *c*1725, seem mostly to have been at 4′, not 8′; by 1820, 16′ stops were also common in larger English organs, particularly on the Choir manual.

Dulzian (Ger.; Cz. *dulceon* Dutch *dulciaan*; Sp. *dulcayna*;). A reed stop of fairly gentle tone, with cylindrical resonators incorporating a conical foot, of 16′ (pedal, manual) or 8′ (secondary manuals), found in the Netherlands and north Germany. Early forms of the name were Touzyn, Toussein, Douseynen (*c*1510), showing a different origin from Dolcan–Tolkaan, despite Praetorius's confusion. Some Dulzians had fanciful resonators, some were similar to Cromornes. Iberian Dulcaynas were short, conical reeds (*c*1740), often *en chamade* below the Trompetas, closer as an imitation of the *dolzaina*, a medieval reed instrument, than the northern types.

Echo. (1) A small-scaled Cornet in many 18th-century German organs.

(2) A prefix indicating a soft colour-stop (Echo Flute, Echo Gamba etc) in 18th- and 19th-century organs throughout northern Europe.

English Horn. An imitative, double-belled reed stop, developed in the 1920s by the American builder Skinner; it is smoother in tone than the older Cor Anglais, and different in construction.

Erzähler (Ger.: 'narrator'). A narrow, tapered flue stop of soft tone, developed by Skinner in the early 20th century and still popular with American organ builders; it is often accompanied by a Celeste rank.

Espigueta (Sp.). *See* ROHRFLÖTE.

Euphone. One of the free reeds invented *c*1820 and found on French and Italian organs, often with no resonators.

Faberton (?Ger.). Probably a corruption of 'faburden', but apparently a stop producing a high, tinkling, bell-like tone, perhaps a Mixture (c1490), high Principal rank (c1550) or high, wide mutation stop (c1700).

Fagotto (Fr. *basson*; Dutch, Ger. *Fagott*). (1) The German 16' or 8' Fagotto was a fairly soft-toned reed with long, narrow resonators, from c1575 onwards; it could be open, stopped (Niedt, 1721) or fanciful in shape (Praetorius, 2/1619).

(2) 'Basson' by Bédos de Celles' period (c1775) was a French reed with short, conical pipes, sometimes capped with a double cone.

(3) In Italy, a rare wooden Regal (c1675); in Spain, a short reed with half-length resonators sometimes *en chamade*; in England, the name occurs only in the bigger organs c1860 for a narrow, conical 16' Swell reed.

Feldpfeife, Feldtrompete (Ger.). 'Feld' here means 'field' in the military sense. (1) A narrow, open flue stop of assertive Flute tone, usually at 2' or 1', found occasionally in 17th-century German organs.

(2) The German imitative trumpet, not *en chamade* as in Spain but often held in the case vertically; others were interior trumpets, all of a thin, strong tone.

Fernflöte (Ger.: 'far-away flute'). Found in a few English and American Echo organs, in imitation of the *Kronwerk* flutes of south Germany c1750 or (more directly) their successors in the large organs of c1840.

Fiffaro (It.). *See* BIFARA and PIFFARO.

Fifteenth. The Principal 2' rank on English organs (any manual), so called from at least c1610, although early contracts qualify it as 'small principal'. (See also Appendix Three, 'Superoctave'.)

Flachflöte (Ger.). Probably a corruption of 'flageolet–flute' rather than 'flat-flute' (i.e. one made of wide, shallow, wooden pipes). The name was used for several pipe forms. (1) 8', 4', or 2' conical pipes (Praetorius, 2/1619), perhaps like a Spillflöte (Zang, 1829), with strong, round tone.

(2) French Flageolets of the early 17th century were usually 1' or 1⅓' ranks of open, cylindrical pipes (*see* LARIGOT).

Flageolet (Fr.). *See* FLACHFLÖTE. Also a name very common in 19th-century England (used by Willis) for a round, wide, rather discreet rank of metal 2' pipes.

Flautado (Sp.). The Principal or Diapason pipes, 32', 16' or 8' (52, 26 and 13 *palmos*), in the organs of Spain, Roussillon etc from c1475. The name probably originated in Flauto etc but later became more specific: 'Flautado de violon', the Spanish Gedackt rank (usually of wood) in the 17th and 18th centuries; 'Flautadito', the 4' Principal or Octave stop.

Flautino (It.). 19th-century name in Germany, England etc for a soft 2' or 4' open Flute.

Flauto (It.; Eng. *flute*; Fr. *flûte*; Ger. *Flöte*). Originally the generic term for organ pipes other than the Mixtures when the *Blockwerk* was divided into 'stops'; later a word applied throughout Europe either to stopped pipes of 8' or 4' (as in 18th-century England) or to colour-stops with prefixes denoting shape (Spitzflöte etc) sound (Sifflöte etc) or function (Flûte majeur etc). Thus 'driifach fleiten' at Hagenau in 1491 indicated the three-rank Principal (8' 8' 4'); 'verdeckt floutwerk' indicated the Gedackts at the Stiftskirche, Einsiedeln, in 1558; 'flauto coperto' indicated a stopped Flute rank (a Nasard $2\frac{2}{3}'$) at Orvieto Cathedral in 1591; and 'flauto reale' an open Flute rank in Venetian organs c1800. Other terms would indicate department ('flûte de pédale' was the 8' or 4' stopped wooden rank in the French classical organ, but often also an 8' open metal stop of principal quality), construction ('flûte à fusée' was a Spitzflöte at Bordeaux, 1627), imitation ('flûte à neuf trous' the 16th-century French Recorder stop), compass ('dessus de flûte' a treble, open, imitative Flute stop of French organs c1740) etc. In addition, there were many attempts at imitating the recorder or transverse flute, usually specified in the name, e.g. 'Flauto allemano' or 'travesiera' in Spain, 'Querflöte' or 'flauto traverso' in Germany, 'flûte d'amour' in exceptional organs anywhere; on the other hand 'Flet' was the usual Habsburg name for stopped ranks of ordinary 4' or 8' Gedackt type. Some of the flute imitations were highly ingenious, involving overblowing (central Germany, c1610; France and England, c1850), fanciful construction or exotic woods (south Germany, c1725; southern Italy, c1725; Netherlands, c1775,), and in some cases conduits leading the air under pressure to strike a flute-like lip in the pipe mouth (Westphalia and Spain, c1775, and some 19th-century orchestrions).

Flute. *See* FLAUTO.

Flûte à cheminée (Fr.). *See* ROHRFLÖTE.

Flûte à pavillon (Fr.). Used c1850 for a large-scaled, metal 8' flue stop, whose cylindrical pipes are capped by inverted conical *pavillons*; common in large organs c1875–1925.

Flûte d'amour (Fr.). A mild 4' Flute of wood, sometimes stopped, often found in American organs from the late 19th century onwards.

Flûte harmonique (Fr.). The term was first used by Cavaillé-Coll, and hence his disciples in England and the USA, to describe the large-scaled, open, metal Flute rank incorporating the 17th-century technique of over-blowing, aided by each pipe having a small hole bored halfway along the pipe cylinder. The resulting 1st harmonic tone is strong.

Fourniture (Fr.). French classical Mixture 'furnishing' the *pleno* with the ranks separated off from the Montres in early 16th-century organs; *see* MIXTURE. In the stereotyped 18th-century organ, the Fourniture broke only once in each octave, the Cymbale twice. The term was also to be found in England in the organs of the French-influenced Renatus Harris (c1680 onwards), where, however, they frequently contained a Tierce rank, particularly by c1740.

French Horn. An imitative reed stop, made in England and the USA *c*1875–1950, often of high-pressure reeds with thick tongues; also occasionally found in 18th-century England, where the pipes probably took the form of a large-scaled, wide-flaring Hautbois.

Fugara. A term derived from Slav words for a shepherd's pipe (e.g. Polish *fujara*) and denoting a soft, rather slow-speaking string-toned stop of 8' or 4'; first known in 17th-century Silesia, soon after in Bohemia, Austria, Switzerland, Swabia etc. The pipes were usually long, narrow, metal and cylindrical, but slightly tapered forms were also known – both types reminiscent of the German Viola da gamba stop.

Gaitas (Sp.). A regal with short resonators, imitating the bagpipe with its thin, nasal but quiet tone, known in Spain from *c*1600.

Gamba. *See* VIOLA DA GAMBA and GEIGEN.

Gedackt (Ger.). A rank of 'stopped' pipes, more specifically the Stopped Diapason of German organs, in Austria called Coppel, in France Bourdon etc. In England the term was first used *c*1850 in connection with the narrow-scaled Lieblich Gedackt.

Geigen (Ger.). A 'string-toned' or narrow-scaled stop, usually of open metal pipes, found in central Germany *c*1620 and becoming indispensable in all national types of 19th-century organ. 'String-toned' is only a comparative or analogous term.

Gemshorn (Ger.). A sharply tapering, wide, metal Flute stop, with a tone between those of flute and string (more towards the flute) and known from at least 1500 in the Rhinelands, where it imitated the gemshorn, a medieval recorder made from the horn of the chamois. The shape and tone were more widely known than the name, and many mutation stops in France and Spain have pipes of this kind. 19th-century organs have narrower, more string-toned Gemshorn stops than the classic ranks of 16', 8', 4', 2', $5\frac{1}{3}'$, $2\frac{2}{3}'$ and $1\frac{1}{3}'$ noted by Praetorius.

Glockenspiel (Ger.). Usually a row of steel, copper or bronze bars hit by hammers activated by pedals or the keys of a secondary manual; in organs of 1720 (Swabia, Silesia, Saxony) of soprano or bass compass only, in organs of 1920 often complete. *See* CARILLON. Some Glockenspiels were called 'Stahlspiel' ('steel instrument').

Gravissima (Lat.). A 64' 'Acoustic Bass' stop whose tone was produced by a 32' pipe sounding with a softer pipe of $21\frac{1}{3}'$; made by several 19th-century builders (Schulze, Willis, Walcker).

Gross. A prefix generally indicating a stop of large scale (Grossflöte, Gross Gamba), but also applied to a mutation stop pitched an octave lower than usual (Gross Tierce).

Haemiol, Hemiol. A term derived from Slav words for 'delicate' (e.g. Czech *jemny*) and used in central Europe during the 17th and 18th centuries for a soft, narrow-scaled, small-mouthed flue stop.

Harfe, Harfa, Harp etc. A Regal toy stop found on some 16th-century organs, probably giving a kind of bagpipe drone effect. Some complete Regal ranks of 16' and 8' were also so called, in central Germany (Harfenregal) *c*1620, in Spain *c*1750.

Harmonia, Harmonika. Although these terms occasionally appear in early contracts, they were chiefly used by certain 19th-century builders for soft stops of various kinds: Harmonia aetheria, a soft Echo Mixture as in Schulze's instruments; Harmonika, a soft open flue stop of indeterminate tone (Walcker) or a free reed stop (*c*1830).

Harmonic (Fr. *harmonique*). A prefix (suffix) generally used to denote pipes of double length (Harmonic Flute, Trompette harmonique).

Hautbois, Hautboy, Oboe. Like Cornet, Hautbois has indicated stops of several kinds over the centuries, all presumably imitating the instrument which itself changed and inspired builders in various ways. (1) In early 16th-century French organs, Hautbois was probably a registration (i.e. Flutes and mutations), not a stop; by *c*1600 the stop called Hautboy-Cornet was probably a strong-toned reed stop.

(2) The French classical Hautbois originated as a soft *récit* Trompette, with small-scalled, flaring, metal resonators; called 'French Schalmei' by Mattheson, and found on most French organs and those they influenced elsewhere, notably in England (Harris).

(3) In Germany, stops of this name had various constructions, from fanciful Regals to small-scaled Schalmeien, none very important.

(4) 19th-century attempts to imitate the tone varied from free reeds (*c*1840, France, central Germany) to the ubiquitous, ultimately French-inspired English Swell Oboe.

Hintersatz (Ger.). The ranks of pipes 'placed behind' the case pipes in the late medieval organ, thus the Mixture of the *Blockwerk* remaining when the Prestants were separated off. Schlick (1511) assumed that it would contain at least 16–18 ranks. To some extent, the name remained as an occasional alternative to 'Mixtur'.

Hohlflöte, Hohlpfeife (Ger.; Dutch *holpijp*). (1) Rather wide, open, cylindrical metal pipes between Principal and Nachthorn in scale, found in organs of central and north Germany from *c*1500. The name is probably derived not from *hohl* ('hollow') but from *Holunder* ('elder tree', *see* SALICET). Many German contracts of the 18th century confuse *Hol, Hohl* and *Holz* (wood) as stop-name prefixes, and the popular 19-century stop can usually be assumed to be of wooden pipes.

(2) During the 16th century, the name in its various forms often indicated a stopped rank of wide scale (Rhineland, south Germany). In the Netherlands it might be a Gedackt, Rohrflöte or even Quintatön, many 18th-century examples being simple stopped Flutes.

Horn, Hörnli (Ger.). (1) Several kinds of imitative reed stop (*see* FRENCH HORN).

(2) Suffix for a group of stop names (Gemshorn, Nachthorn), like the

ORGAN

related term 'Cornet' popular with 16th-century builders expanding organ colours.

(3) More specifically, the Hörnli was a 16th-century stop found in the upper and lower Rhineland, composed of the same ranks as stops elsewhere called Cornet and Sesquialtera, i.e. a solo (or solo and chorus) Tierce Mixture.

(4) Horn Diapason was a late 19th-century stop whose Diapason-scaled pipes had a vertical slot cut at the top and back, the tone apparently hardened in the process.

Jubal, Tubal. A rare, open Flute found in some German organs *c*1690–1740 to imitate the imagined sounds produced by Jubal, the 'Inventor of Music'.

Jula, Iula. A rare stop name with different meanings in different German organs: a Quint (J. Samber, 1707), a Spitzflöte (Zang, 1829), a soft, narrow mutation (Praetorius).

Kalkant (Ger.). An accessory stop-lever found in Germany over the centuries, which when pulled caused a bell to ring and communicated with the bellows-blower.

Keraulophon. A quasi-Greek term invented by Gray in *c*1820 to denote a stop type long known by other builders, i.e. a quiet, reedy-toned 8′ Flute stop. The pipes usually have a hole near the top.

Kinura. A keen-toned reed stop with very narrow, cylindrical resonators, often used in cinema organs.

Koppel (Ger.). *See* COPPEL.

Kornett (Ger.). *See* CORNETT.

Krummhorn. *See* CROMORNE.

Kuckuck (Ger.). *See* VOGELGESANG.

Kützialflöte (Ger.). An open Flute of 4′, 2′ or sometimes 1′ pitch, occasionally found on German organs from Praetorius onwards, evidently imitating a Slav instrument (*cewzial*: 'flute').

Larigot (Fr.). A term probably derived from 'l'arigot' ('flageolet' – cf *haricot*) and used in the 16th century (and hence the later French classical organ in general) to denote the $1\frac{1}{3}$′ wide mutation rank found in large and small organs and used for both chorus and solo registrations. Outside France, other terms like Superquinte, Quintanus and Flageolet were used.

Lieblich Gedackt (Ger.). (1) The 'pleasant stopped rank' known from at least Praetorius onwards to refer to the Stopped Diapason used for continuo playing or for soft (often echo) effects.

(2) More specifically, the pretty-toned Gedackt made popular by the influential 19th-century builders (Walcker, Schulze), of metal or wood, with a high cut-up and characteristic tone.

Lleno. *See* COMPUESTAS; see also Appendix Three, 'Organo Pleno'.

Major, Minor. Terms denoting the size (rather than function) of a stop. Flöte major [minor] were common in 18th-century Habsburg Europe for 8′ and 4′

APPENDIX TWO

Gedackts; 'Majorbass' was fairly common in Germany between 1650 and 1900 for the 16' or 32' open or stopped pedal rank.

Melodia. A medium- to wide-scaled, open, wood Flute stop of 8' pitch; the pipes usually have reversed mouths and sometimes sunken blocks. It was widely used in England and the USA from the middle of the 19th century.

Mixture (Fr. *fourniture*; Ger. *Mixtur*). Names for the collected ranks of the *Blockwerk* when the Principals and Flutes had been separated off, the contents, planning, voicing, making and scaling of which distinguish national organ schools as much as any other stop. 'Mixture' was normally used to denote the Principal-scaled chorus Mixture as distinct from the high Zimbeln or the solo Cornets. The 'true Mixture' is often said to contain Octave and Quint ranks only, but Tierces have been found in many national types of Mixture (17th-century Spain, 18th-century England), some of which were highly influential during the 19th century. Early names for the stop, which was presumably activated by levers, were 'Position', 'Locatio' and 'Starkwerk', all known before 1520; late types from around 1820 were the 'Compensationsmixtur', which decreased in number of ranks, strength and volume as it ascended, and the 'Progressio harmonica', which increased as it ascended.

Montre (Fr.). The case pipes of the French organ, corresponding to the English Open Diapason, the German Prestant and the Italian Principale. Early alternative names included 'le principal de devant' and 'devanture en monstre' (Rheims Cathedral, 1570). The tone of the classical French Montre was somewhat more foundational or fluty than the various English Open Diapason types.

Nachthorn (Ger.). A term probably derived from *Nachhorn* or *Nachsatz*, i.e. a rank of pipes distinguished from the *Hintersatz*, and having nothing to do with the Cor de nuit in origin. (1) Nachthornen were frequently the same as Cornets in the 16th century, more particularly in northern France and the Netherlands; cf the Spanish term Nasardos.

(2) By Praetorius's time, the name denoted a rank of very wide-scaled 4' or 2' pipes, stopped like the Quintatön and more horn-like than the Hohlflöte, owing to its Quint partial. The familiar 17th-century Nachthorn useful in the north German repertory was a very wide, metal, open Flute, used for cantus firmus in manual or pedal.

Nachtigall (Ger.) *See* VOGELGESANG.

Nasard (?Fr.; Ger. *Nasat*). Terms probably derived from *Nachsatz*, i.e. the rank or ranks between the Principals and the *Hintersatz* of a separated *Blockwerk*. Early usages of the name refer to a registration or effect rather than a single rank of pipes (*c*1530, France), and *nazard* meant the rank helping to produce the characteristic sound, i.e. 2⅔' or 1⅓' Flutes. The form could be open or stopped, Chimney Flute or tapered. The French classical Nasard was usually a stopped rank of 2⅔', often a Rohrflöte for some or all its compass, that on the *Grand orgue* usually different in type from that of the *Positiv* manual. In Germany, there was frequently no distinction drawn in stop-lists between

Quinte and Nasard, nor were the differences in form, volume, tone and function between the two so clear-cut as in France.

Nasardos (Sp.). A term probably derived from 16th-century French and Flemish usage to denote either the single mutation ranks (Octave, Quint or Tierce) making up the Corneta or, more importantly, the chorus/solo Mixture; a kind of bass version of the treble Corneta, found over the centuries on most Iberian organs.

Nason (?Eng.). A stopped Flute introduced to England at the end of the 17th ntury by Smith and copied by many builders for two centuries. Very often of oak, with a characteristic sweet tone, the Nason is only a Gedacktflöte and the origins of its name are unclear.

Night Horn. *See* NACHTHORN.

Nineteenth. The English term is meant to indicate the Principal-scaled $1\frac{1}{3}'$ rank, something more like the Italian Decimanona than the classical French Larigot.

Octave (Fr. *prestant*; Ger. *Oktave*; It. *ottava*; Sp. *octava*). (1) The 4' Principal of an organ based on an 8' Open Diapason, the 8' of one based on a 16' Diapason etc. In England 'Octave 4'' implies a strong Principal 4' rank, such special meaning originating *c*1850.

(2) A prefix indicating pitch an octave higher than usual (Octave Flute).

Octavin (Fr.; It. *ottavina*). Open metal Flutes made by Venetian builders *c*1790 and Cavaillé-Coll *c*1860.

Open Diapason. *See* DIAPASON and PRINCIPAL.

Ophicleide. Strong reed stop supposedly imitating the ophicleide (a brass instrument belonging to the keyed bugle family) and popular as a pedal rank in Willis organs.

Orchestral. A prefix denoting a stop of particularly imitative tone (Orchestral Oboe, Orchestral Flute), found in many early 20th-century organs.

Orlos (Sp.). An 8' Regal with short, cylindrical resonators, sometimes *en chamade* and common in Iberian organs by *c*1730.

Pauke, Trommel (Ger.; It. *timballo*; Sp. *tambor*). Drum stops were popular in the larger organs of all European countries until the early 19th century, and the percussion varieties in theatre organs *c*1920 were only revivals. Sometimes real timpani were provided, tunable and played by *putti* activated by pedal levers (Berlin, *c*1730), but more usually the many drum-effects were produced by two or more large-scaled wooden pipes out of tune with each other. Frequently the quasi-pitches produced were A and D, allowing realistic 'trumpet-and-drums' music: 'with trumpet, shawm or fife' according to the Trier Cathedral contract of 1537 (P. Briesger).

Physharmonika. A free-reed stop with resonators introduced to Germany in the mid-19th century by builders such as Walcker and Ladegast and widely used for a time in large organs. It was also briefly popular in England and the USA.

Piccolo. A 19th-century 2' or 1' Flute stop made by English builders to a design labelled Octavin, Flöte, Flageolet etc by other builders; pipes are sometimes of harmonic (double) length.

Pifano (Sp.). Open or stopped Flute 4' or 2'; the name was used over the centuries and was probably a corruption of Pfeife etc.

Piffaro, Fiffaro (It.). Although in other musical contexts Fiffaro often denoted a reed instrument, organ stops of this name fall into two different classes. (1) An open Flute found in Rhineland organs of the 16th century, high-pitched and later overblowing or double-mouthed, producing a tone imitative of the cross-blown fife.

(2) An important Italian stop of the 16th century onwards; it had treble compass Principal-scaled pipes mistuned with the Principale 8' and thus producing an undulating effect (Schwebung), more singing and less reedy than 19th-century *céleste* stops. It was sometimes called Voce umana.

Pommer (Ger.). *See* BOMBARDON.

Portunal (flöte) (Ger.). A term, probably a corruption of Bourdon, denoting in 17th- and 18th-century German organs a rank of 8' or 4' open, wood or metal pipes (sometimes in the form of an inverted cone), producing a modified Open Flute colour.

Posaune (Ger.; Dutch *bazuin, buzain*). A common name for 16' or 32' pedal reed stops of varied construction in certain areas and periods. Resonators two-thirds long were generally considered desirable, but they could be of wood or metal. The 'stille Posaune' seems, from Praetorius, to have been a stopped reed, but many builders used 'Posaune' in general for their big reed other than the Bombarde, from at least *c*1580 onwards.

Praestant (Lat.; Fr., Ger. *Prestant*). Pipes 'standing in the front' of the organ case. (1) In the Netherlands, since 'Principal' denoted the main chorus as a whole in *c*1525, 'Praestant' was used to refer to the case pipes or Open Diapason itself. German builders *c*1550–1800 used Praestant and Principal as synonyms, depending on local custom.

(2) In France, 'Prestant' soon came to denote the 4' Principal rank distinct from the Montre 8', as 'Principal' in England has always indicated the 4' Principal rank distinct from the Open Diapason 8'; both French and English usage were established by 1600.

Principal (Ger. *Prinzipal*). *See* PRAESTANT. The term first arose soon after 1500 in the Netherlands (and hence probably in England) to denote not a single rank of pipes but the Diapason chorus as a whole, i.e. the undivided Mixture or *pleno*; in English and American organs from the 18th century onwards, however, it usually denotes a 4' stop. By Praetorius's time the 'stop formerly called Praestant or Doeff' was called Prinzipal in Germany. In the 20th century Prinzipal has become useful as a term denoting the relatively colourless German basic 8′ rank as opposed to the various English Diapason tones.

Quartane. *See* RAUSCHPFEIFE.

Quarte de nasard (Fr.). The stop a 4th above the Nasard on the French classical organ, i.e. a 2′ Flute mutation rank rather than the chorus Doublette. Usually open, the bass octave was sometimes a Chimney Flute.

Querflöte (Ger.). The transverse flute has been imitated in various ways. The organ stop so called is properly an open, cylindrical, metal or wood stop, usually 4′, overblowing to the 1st or 2nd overtone because of the narrow scale and small mouth; a small hole halfway along the pipe facilitates the overblowing (cf Cavaillé-Coll's Flûte harmonique). Such overblowing Schweizerpfeifen seem to have been known in late 15th-century south Germany. The effect is gentle. Construction can vary: stopped and wide-scaled (Praetorius, 2/1619); long, narrow pipes overblowing at the 12th (built by Compenius, Fritzsche); conical (Snetzler); 'blown from the side' (Wagner); simple, stopped 2′ Flutes (*c*1600); fanciful, large-scaled pipes (*c*1840), perhaps of turned hardwood (*c*1730).

Quint. Like Nineteenth, Fifteenth etc, Quint has usually since about 1550 indicated chorus ranks (not Flute mutations) sounding $10\frac{2}{3}$′, $5\frac{1}{3}$′, $2\frac{2}{3}$′ and $1\frac{1}{3}$′. (See also Appendix Three, 'Quint'.)

Quintadecima (It.). The Fifteenth or 2′ Principal chorus rank, sometimes perhaps doubled or paired in Italian organs before *c*1500.

Quintadena, Quintatön (Ger.). An important stop of narrow-scaled, stopped, metal pipes, preferably of a high tin content, blown on generous wind and producing a quiet tone with a marked 5th (i.e. 2nd overtone) in it; the pipes are near overblowing. Like other basic organ-pipe shapes, it was known by 1500 and more commonly used throughout Europe than the name itself. The origin of the term is uncertain, all the variants (e.g. Quintade, Quintaden, Quintiten) suggesting the '5th-tone' nature of the sound. Schällenpfeifen ('bell-pipes', referring to the tone) was an early 16th-century alternative name; a Gedacktpommer was a strong-voiced 4′ Quintatön in the 17th century. Many types of Stopped Diapason before *c*1775 have much of the tonal quality of a Quintadena.

Rankett, Rackett (Ger.). A 16′ Regal with short resonators and gentle tone, found fairly often from the end of the 16th century in northern Europe, particularly in small organs and the secondary manuals of large ones. Shape and materials varied, but the pipes were always short. Such Regals were entirely out of fashion from 1710 to 1930.

Rauschpfeife, Rauschquint, Rauschwerk (Ger.). Words of doubtful origin – probably unconnected with *rauschen* ('to murmur') – properly denoting three distinct kinds of chorus Mixture in the various German organ types from *c*1575. (1) Rauschpfeife of two ranks (15.19 or 2′ + $1\frac{1}{3}$′); other additional ranks would be the 12th and 22nd.

(2) Rauschquinte of two ranks (12.15 or $2\frac{2}{3}$′ + 2′), otherwise called Quar-

tane. Neither term was used reliably by builders until recently.

(3) Rauschwerk is frequently used to replace one or other term; but for early sources (e.g. A. Schlick, 1511), 'Rauschwerk' was a term denoting either a semi-Flute solo compound stop imitating a reed instrument, or a reed stop itself, probably of more refined tone than the Trompete. 'Rauschende Zimbel' (Russzimbel etc) was an early term for, it seems, high Mixtures, perhaps with Tierce ranks.

Recorder. In England, the term appears in a few 17th-century contracts to refer to a flute stop, probably of 4′ pitch ('unison to the Principall': York Minster, 1632). It could be a stopped metal rank (Worcester Cathedral, 1613) or of wood (St John's College, Cambridge, 1635), and both forms are encountered up to the beginning of the 18th century.

Regal. A term of uncertain origin (see Chapter Four, §5) denoting a family of organ stops probably descending from the late medieval instrument; the small or very small resonators made such ranks useful in the subsidiary chests of larger organs. Early 16th-century names were frequently specific, at other times more cumbersome, such as 'Regal to make the human voice' (Vox humana). Fanciful names and pipe forms were found chiefly in northern Germany from c1575 to c1700 and should not be overestimated: Apfelregal (short resonators with a little perforated ball at the end), Geigenregal (delicate 4′ Regal, treble sounding as a violin when drawn with a Quintatön, according to Praetorius), Harfenregal, Jungfernregal (thin tone 'like a girl's voice'), Knopfregal and Kopfregal ('knob-' and 'head-shaped Regal'), Messingregal (short brass pipes), Singendregal ('singing Regal' of light tone, useful for cantus firmus melodies), Trichterregal (important type with 'funnel-shaped' or conical resonators like small trumpets). In other countries, Regal usually had freer names, e.g. Orlos, Tromboncini, Vox humana.

Resultant. A pedal stop, usually of 32′ pitch, made up of 16′ and $10\frac{2}{3}$′ ranks of pipes sounding simultaneously.

Ripieno (It.). (1) The full chorus, i.e. either a registration of drawn stops or the *Blockwerk* itself.

(2) The classical Italian chorus Mixture, known when single ranks became less the norm on the Italian organ than they had once been (c1800).

Rohrflöte (Ger.; Eng. *Chimney Flute*; Fr. *flûte à cheminée*; It. *Flauto a camino*; Sp. *Espigueta*). The name of an important pipe form known throughout Europe but so called only north of a line from Breslau to Antwerp. The pipes are 'half-stopped', the metal canisters or stoppers pierced to allow a narrow tube to pass through. The length and width of the tube have varied from builder to builder, some tubes held entirely within the pipe and not protruding. The resultant tone is very charming, the stopped Flute sound modified by several faint overtones. 19th-century Chimney Flutes are basically the same in construction, but the name was often given to plain Flute stops. The pipe form probably originated in the Rhineland at the end of the 15th century; some early Netherlands examples were called 'Hohlflöte' in the sources. Praetorius noted that such stops could be at 16′, 8′, 4′, 2′ and even 1′; Adlung (1768) added

ORGAN

the mutations: $10\frac{2}{3}'$, $5\frac{1}{3}'$, $2\frac{2}{3}'$ and $1\frac{1}{3}'$. In France and Spain certain pipes (e.g. the lower octaves) in a Flute rank might be Chimney Flutes, as could a complete rank in Cornets; Mersenne (1636–7) noted that the length of tube affected the sound. Some early 20th-century builders, especially in the USA, made use of internal, inverted chimneys, thought to be more stable.

Rosignolo [rusignolo] (It.). *See* VOGELSANG.

Rossignol (Fr.). *See* VOGELGESANG.

Sackbut. A term occasionally used *c*1550 or *c*1850 (both periods notable for ingenious inventors) for big reed stops, bigger than Posaunen.

Salicet, Salicional. A term derived from the Latin *salix* ('willow tree') during the later 16th century to denote a rank of open, cylindrical pipes of narrow (sometimes conical) scale giving a fairly delicate, almost string-like tone by way of auxiliary 8' or 4' colour extra to the Flutes and Principals. The most common pitch may have been 4', as it was for the early Dulciana. The stop was a speciality of Habsburg Europe until itinerant builders took it elsewhere (e.g. Snetzler to England, where it became very popular in the 19th century at both 8' and 4' (Salicet) pitches). The small mouths made side ears advisable. In central Germany *c*1725, 'Sollicinal' was a two-rank Sesquialtera.

Schalmei (Ger.). (1) From *c*1550, a reed stop with narrow, flaring resonators giving it a tone closer to a smooth trumpet than a real shawm. The tone must have varied over the centuries, but the stop seems to have been particularly associated with cantus firmus playing. It was rare from 1750 to 1930.

(2) In some central European sources of *c*1775, the Schalmei seems to have been an auxiliary 8' flue stop.

Scharf (Ger.; Dutch *scherp*). Narrow-scaled chorus Mixture of 'sharp' penetrating tones, found throughout northern Europe from *c*1500 onwards. (1) Early Dutch and German Scharf Mixtures were high-pitched like the Zimbel, and properly distinct from the Terzzimbel.

(2) The basic Mixture of subsidiary manuals was often called Scharf whether or not it was Zimbel-like. Those of the mid-19th century frequently contained a high Tierce rank.

Schnarrwerk (Ger.). 17th-century term for the 'rattling stops' or Regals.

Schwebung (Ger.). *See* TREMULANT and PIFFARO.

Schwegel, Schweigel (Ger.). A term derived from the High German *suegela* ('flute') to denote a delicate Flute stop of fairly narrow scale, common in south and central Germany from 1550 to 1850, chiefly on subsidiary manuals. Some 'Schwegli' were $1\frac{1}{3}'$, others 4', 2' and even 8' (the last especially *c*1750); some open, wide pipes, others conical, yet others in the form of a double cone or overblowing. 19th-century Schwegels are usually bland, wide, high Flutes.

Schweizerpfeife (Ger.). To play a flute 'in the Swiss manner' in early 16th-century sources meant to play it cross-blown, like a fife. (1) Organ imitations of the period took various forms (*see* QUERFLÖTE and FLAUTO).

(2) In the 18th century, the name often denoted an 8' or 4' rank, in the form

of an inverted cone or narrow and cylindrical, either way resembling the so-called Viola da gamba in tone.

Sedecima (?It.). A term found in Habsburg Europe of the 17th and 18th centuries to denote a $1\frac{1}{3}'$ Sifflöte.

Septième (Fr.). Cavaillé-Coll's name (hence that used by English builders) for the 'Seventh' or $4\frac{4}{7}'$, $2\frac{2}{7}'$ and $1\frac{1}{7}'$ mutation series, first known as an idea in Prussia c1780 but coming into prominence as an extra colour in a large organ of c1860, and as a sharply colourful rank in the *Oberwerk* of a neo-Baroque organ of c1950, particularly in Germany.

Seraphon. Weigle's name for a group of high-pressure flue and reed stops popular in Germany during the early 20th century.

Sesquialtera. A term perhaps derived from the Latin sesquialtera ('one and a half') and used to denote a two-rank solo/chorus mutation stop containing the 12th and 17th $(2\frac{2}{3}' + 1\frac{3}{5}')$, written carelessly as 'Quinte $3'$ + Terz $2' = 3{:}2 = 1\frac{1}{2}'$. Other forms of the name suggest clever etymologies: 'Sexquialter' (England, late 18th century), apparently referring to the 6th contained between the $2\frac{2}{3}'$ and $1\frac{3}{5}'$ pipe, 'Sex quintaltra' and 'Sexquintalter' (ditto), 'Flautt in 6ta' (Italy, late 17th century) etc. F. Hocque's phrase 'Sesquialtera called by some Vox humana or Nasard', for what was in fact a Cornet stop (Trier Cathedral, 1590), shows the interdependence of names at that period. (1) The classic two-rank Sesquialtera was a flute-like, semi-Cornet solo stop, often treble only, found in north-west German organs of c1630–1790.

(2) The English Sesquialtera was, during the late 17th century, a bass complement to the treble Cornet stop; during the 18th century a complete chorus Mixture including a narrow-scaled Tierce rank; and during the 19th century often the only Mixture (still with a Tierce) in the whole organ.

Seventeenth. *See* TIERCE.

Sifflöte (Ger.). A term probably derived from *siffler*, 'to whistle', although many German spellings suggest a wider derivation: cyvelet (Amsterdam, Oude Kerk, 1539 – cf zuffolo: 'shepherd's fife'), Sufflet (Dresden, 1563), Schufflet (Münster, 1579), Suff Flöte (by Christoph Donati, 1683), Suiflöt/Duiflot and Subflöte (Praetorius, 2/1619). (1) A high-pitched Flute stop, narrow, wide or conical; good examples have a characteristic sibilant tone.

(2) Throughout its period of popularity, the stop could be either $1'$ or $1\frac{1}{3}'$, some builders (e.g. G. Silbermann) preferring the first, others (e.g. Schnitger) the second. Much the same was true of the Sedecima, the Sifflöte of Habsburg countries.

Sordun. A very short, stopped Regal imitating a woodwind instrument, soft (cf sordino) and somewhat thin in tone, popular during the 17th century in north central Germany.

Soubasse (Fr.). *See* SUB-BASS.

Sperrventil (Ger.). The 'blocking valve' for preventing wind from reaching a chest, saving it for other chests or keeping it from sounding a ciphering note.

Such valves were the first means of dividing the *Blockwerk* in some instances; they remained a common accessory in northern Europe until *c*1850. During the 19th century the valve's potential as a registration aid was exploited by such builders as Cavaillé-Coll, who (like certain 17th-century builders) made several chests for each department or manual, each of which could have prepared stops that would sound only when the valve was activated.

Spillflöte (Ger.). Probably a corruption of 'spindle-flute', a rank of open, wide, cylindrical pipes which suddenly taper towards the top. The pipe form could be used for an 8', 4' or 2' stop (north Germany, 17th century) or for part of a mutation rank (various countries) of discreet tone.

Spitzflöte (Ger.). The 'pointed flute' stop whose pipe form – gently tapering or conical from mouth to top – was more common than the occurrences of its name suggest, especially outside Germany, the Netherlands and Scandinavia. The taper is more pronounced than that of the Gemshorn, and the tone is that of a reedy or breathy flute, good for blending either at 8' pitch or as a mutation. Such pipe forms are known from the late 15th century (8' at Lübeck Totentanzorgel, 1492) and frequently had a part in a French mutation rank, a Spanish Corneta or an Italian Flauto; the name itself appears to be late 16th-century. 19th-century examples in Germany and England tend to be too string-like in tone.

Stentorphone. One of Weigle's late 19th-century open flue stops of very loud, nondescript tone, popular in larger German and American organs *c*1890–1920.

Stopped Diapason. *See* DIAPASON and GEDACKT.

Suavial, Suabe Flöte (?Ger.). A term probably derived from *suavis* ('sweet'; not from Swabia, 'schwäbisch') and used to denote a narrow-scaled 8' or 4' metal stop popular in southern Germany, Switzerland and the Habsburg countries from *c*1710 to the early 19th century. Burney described one in Frankfurt as 'meant for that sweet stop in Mr. Snetzler's organs which he calls the Dulciana'.

Sub-Bass (Ger.; Fr. *soubasse*). An unspecific term that usually denoted a stopped wooden rank of 16' pedal pipes of average scale. During the 19th century some German and French builders used it for the 32' Bourdon rank.

Superoctave. *See* FIFTEENTH; see also Appendix Three, 'Superoctave'.

Tambor. *See* PAUKE.

Tapada, Tapadillo (Sp.; It. *tappato*). Prefix denoting 'stopped' pipes. Tapadillo was the Spanish Flute 4' of the 17th and 18th centuries, usually stopped but on occasion open, and either conical or a Rohrflöte.

Tenori (It.). An occasional 16th-century name for the Principal 8'.

Tenoroon (?Eng.). The name applied in some early 19th-century sources to describe a flue or reed stop of short compass, often going no lower than Tenor C in the bass.

Terpodion. A quasi-Greek name for delicate stops of 'delightful' tone in early 19th-century German organs. (1) A free reed (c1830).

(2) A small-scaled, open, metal flue (used by Schulze).

Tertian, Terzian (Ger.). Properly a two-rank solo and chorus Tierce Mixture, found more especially in northern Europe during the 17th and 18th centuries and consisting of the ranks 17.19 ($1\frac{3}{5}' + 1\frac{1}{3}'$) as opposed to the 12.17 of the Sesquialtera. Theorists have pointed out that it could contain 15.17 ranks (Werckmeister, 1705) or 10.12 (Adlung, 1768), and many examples did break back an octave around c'. As with all mutations, the scaling was somewhat wider than that of the Principal.

Terza mano (It.). The 'third hand' or octave coupler found on late 18th-century and 19th-century Italian organs, feasible in view of the often long compass of the main manuals.

Terzzimbel. *See* ZIMBEL.

Theorbe (Ger.; Sp. *tiorba*). (1) German reed stop of the 17th and 18th centuries, rare but of a distinct type, i.e. a gentle 16' tone imitating, in some way, the theorbo.

(2) More familiar Spanish reed with short resonators, often *en chamade* c1750.

Tibia (Lat.). General name for 'pipe', used in the Latinate contracts of the late 18th century and by the technician-inventors of the late 19th century. Thus Tibia angusta is a narrow Flute, Tibia clausa a Gedackt, 'cuspida' a Spitzflöte, 'sylvestris' a Waldflöte etc.

Tierce (Fr.; Ger. *Terz, Tertia*). The $1\frac{3}{5}'$ Flute mutation rank, more particularly of the French classical organ. Such third-sounding ranks were contained in Arnaut de Zwolle's Cymbale of c1450, but evidently their scaling widened over the centuries, achieving a characteristic horn tone by 1750. Some Parisian organs c1630 had two such ranks, one wide, the other narrow and thus used in one or other *pleno*. The Double Tierce $3\frac{1}{5}'$ (Grosse Tierce) was first known c1660 and contributed to the array of melodic colours in French organ music. Outside France the stop was found as a single mutation rank only in organ types influenced by the French, e.g. those of the Rhineland and Saxony. Besides French terms, 18th-century names were Ditonus, Decima, Sixtil (all in various northern European countries) and Corneta (Italy).

Tiratutti (It.). A mechanical device known in Italian organs from c1700 whereby the organist could 'draw all the pleno ranks' at once.

Tolkaan (Dutch; Ger. *Dolcan*). A term of uncertain origin denoting a rank of open, inverted, conical, metal or wood pipes, often confused with Dulzian, Dulciana etc. As in other instances, the pipe form was known in more versions and over greater areas than the name itself. The Tolkaan was a speciality of large Netherlands and Hanseatic organs of c1580 as was the Trichterflöte ('funnel-shaped flute') early in the next century. The pipe form was also found in the case of Spanish flutes, Austrian Dulcianas, Neapolitan Voci umani (all of c1750) and many soft or fairly soft colour-stops in German organs c1825.

Tremulant (Fr. *tremblant*; It. *tremolo*; Sp. *temblor*). An important accessory stop contained in most larger European organs from c1500 to the present day, although not always specified in the contract. Two chief types were known to 17th- and 18th-century builders, the French usually incorporating an example of each. (1) Tremblant fort (Bocktremulant) was also called 'Tremblant à vent perdu', i.e. a sprung valve, balanced and adjustable, which would allow wind to escape intermittently from the trunk, the remaining wind admitted in uneven pulses to the pipe chests.

(2) Tremblant doux did not allow wind to escape but acted as a sprung gate in the trunk, momentarily blocking the flow when activated. It was especially suitable for a single chest or even an isolated stop, serving as a Schwebung, e.g. for the Vox humana. It is clear from some musical imitations of the Tremulant c1600 that the pulse or rate of trembling then normal was slower than the various familiar 19th-century Tremulants.

Trichterregal. *See* REGAL.

Trombone. *See* POSAUNE.

Tromboni, Tromboncini (It.). (1) A 'small-large trumpet' reed stop introduced now and then into Italy by various Flemish and German builders.

(2) Tromboni were long and strong-toned 16′ or 8′ reed stops on many national types of organ c1820.

(3) Tromboncini were an important type of Regal on Venetian organs of the late 18th century, with very small-scale, square-sectioned metal resonators standing in front of the case pipes.

Trommel (Ger.). *See* PAUKE.

Trommet, Trompete, Trompette, Trumpet, etc (Ger.). A very familiar, imitative reed stop with long resonators either flaring or in the form of an inverted cone, of metal or wood, found in most organ types since c1500 and taking various forms. (Organs without a Trumpet were the classical Italian organ of c1600, the English pre-Restoration organ and the mature Habsburg organ of the 18th century.) The resonators should be about two-thirds long (6′ for 8′ C). German and English Trumpets in 1650–1950 varied from builder to builder; 17th-century German Trumpets were often short, especially if the flaring was marked and the pipes placed vertically in the case front. 18th-century French Trumpets developed great power and attack, especially in the bass, often using higher pressures, wider tongues and bigger resonators. Spanish Trumpets also followed certain conventions: the Trompeta real was a full-sized vertical reed within the organ; the Trompeta bastarda had shorter resonators, often *en chamade*; the Trompeta magna, Trompeta de batalla and Trompeta imperial were horizontal Trumpets, often of suboctave pitches (16′, even 32′, in the treble). During the late 19th century, exceptional organs in any city of Europe might have had highly imitative Trumpet stops, with higher pressures, perhaps brass resonators, arranged as a fan or *en chamade*.

APPENDIX TWO

Trompes (Fr.). The large, open bass pipes placed apart from, and on either side of, the *Grand orgue* of many large French and Netherlands organs of the later 15th century. A set of ten was fairly common. Other names (e.g. *turres* at Angers Cathedral in 1416) were sometimes found; 'trompe' may signify the 'pendentive', or carved, wooden, semicircular console on which the pipes were placed.

Trumpet. *See* TROMMET.

Tuba. Except in the Latinate contracts of *c*1800, 'Tuba' as a stop name is found almost entirely in the 19th and 20th centuries, and denotes a louder and smoother reed stop than the usual Trumpet, taking whatever form the builder found useful for increasing volume.

Tubal. *See* JUBAL.

Twelfth. The rank of $2\frac{2}{3}'$ open metal pipes forming part of the Diapason chorus. Some early Twelfths, however, were more Nasard-like, especially in England *c*1725.

Twenty-second. A Principal stop of 1' pitch.

Uccelli (It.). *See* VOGELGESANG.

Unda maris (Lat.). A term applied in south Germany during the 18th century – and hence through Walcker (*c*1830) to most major builders of the 19th century – to denote a rank of narrow, open 8' metal pipes, tuned slightly sharp or flat (either to a second rank standing with it or to the organ as a whole) and so producing an undulating effect. The effect was known more widely than the name, being mentioned by Mersenne (1636–7), found in the classical Italian organ as Piffaro and impressing the many 18th- and early 19th-century builders looking for colourful Flute and String stop varieties.

Untersatz (Ger.). The term for pipes placed on a chest below (and at the back of) the main chest of organs in north and central Germany *c*1575–1825, i.e. pipes of the larger pedal stops. In practice the term thus denotes various 16' or 32' pedal stops, particularly stopped wood 32' ranks.

Viejas (Sp.). The 'old women's voice', or thin Vox humana of Spanish organs *c*1750, often *en chamade*. Other fanciful names for particularly thin Vox humana stops were Viejos (Spain, *c*1750), Jungfernregal (Germany, *c*1625) and Vox pueri/tauri (Italy, *c*1600).

Viola da gamba. The name for a large number of stop-types whose only common characteristic is their claiming to imitate the string instrument. (1) In *c*1620, often a Tolkaan.

   (2) During the 17th century in central Europe as a whole, many narrow, cylindrical stops bore the name Viola da gamba or Viol d'amour as well as Salicional, Dulciana etc.

   (3) Many Gamba stops contained conical pipes, like narrow Spitzflöten – Saxony *c*1725, England and south Germany *c*1850, northern Italy *c*1880.

   (4) Many Gamba stops of the 18th century are either very flute-like (south

Germany) or soft, discreet stops of sweet, breathy Diapason tone (as those of G. Silbermann).

(5) In Italy and Spain from c1750, 'Viola' often denoted a regal stop of one or other kind.

Viola pomposa. A broad and fairly strong string-toned stop, developed by G. D. Harrison in the 1930s, and used since in large American organs.

Viole d'orchestre. A very narrow-scaled, keen-sounding string stop, found mostly in organs built in the first half of the 20th century.

Violetta (It.; Sp. *violeta*). (1) Regal stops, with very small, open, conical resonators of 4' or 2', made in the late 18th century.

(2) Miscellaneous string-toned flue stops, 8', 4' or 2', on various of the later 19th-century organ types.

Violina. A medium-scaled 4' stop of string tone, frequently found in the Swell division of 19th-century English and American organs.

Violón (Sp.; Ger. *Violon*). (1) In Spain, an important term for the Stopped Diapason on the Baroque organ, manual or pedal. Thus 'Flautado violón' was the Bourdon.

(2) A common, German, open pedal stop of medium volume and non-descript tone, found during the 18th and 19th centuries. Often a substitute for the Prinzipal 16'.

Violoncello (It.). (1) A Venetian regal stop at 8', with small, rectangular, cross-section resonators of boxwood or pine, placed vertically in front of the case pipes, and in use from c1750 onwards.

(2) Narrow flue stops of various periods and areas in Germany (c1700–1900).

(3) An 8' pedal stop frequently found in 19th- and 20th-century English and American organs.

Vogelgesang, Kuckuck, Nachtigall, rosignolo [rusignolo], **rossignol, uccelli.** National names for the bird-imitating toy stops popular from at least 1450 to 1800 and again in theatre organs c1925. Each builder had his own way of planning such quasi-automata: if the tiny pipes were suspended in water, the twittering was thought to resemble a nightingale; if two were involved and stood a 3rd apart, a cuckoo resulted; if air supply allowed it (and often so much air was taken that no other stops could be drawn), moving statuary might complete the picture; and so on. An important example was the 'Vogelgesang durchs ganze pedal' (Praetorius), which was not a toy stop so much as either a tiny, high Mixture of indeterminate pitch adding a soft glitter, or a regular, high Flute stop.

Voix céleste (Fr.). A term apparently dating from the 1840s to denote a long-familiar effect achieved in the same way as by Unda maris and Piffaro. The narrow-scaled pipes usual for such stops (c1840–1940) gave a sharp heterodyne effect, less voice-like than that intended by classic Italian builders of c1600.

Vox angelica (Lat.). (1) Small reed stops of 2′ found in the organs of some German builders *c*1750 (Stumm).

(2) Soft, small-scaled flue stops on various 19th-century organ-types, including Italian ones.

(3) A free-reed stop used by Walcker and other 19th-century German builders.

Vox humana (Lat.; Fr. *voix humaine*; It. *voce umana*; Sp. *voz humana*). The name of numerous stops whose common characteristic is the claim to imitate the human voice, particularly its thin, undulating quality, and always at 8′. (1) The Renaissance Voce umana was the same as the Piffaro.

(2) Some 16th-century builders used the term for a registration (e.g. Regal + Nasard + Larigot) or for the Regal 'helping to make the Vox humana effect'.

(3) Many Regal types during the 17th and 18th centuries were invented for the purpose, with resonators open or closed; of brass or hardwood; short, half-stopped, cylindrical, capped and pierced, in the form of a double cone or bulbous; etc. Some had their own Schwebung (*see* TREMULANT).

(4) During the late 19th century and the early 20th, some builders (e.g. Willis) made Vox humanas in the traditional manner of Regals; this was often the only timbre in the whole organ that could be regarded as traditional.

Waldflöte (Ger.). A 'forest flute' stop. (1) A wide-scaled, conical, metal Flute of 2′ (sometimes 2⅔′ or 1⅓′) in 17th-century German organs. Praetorius referred to open pipes, though instruments in the Habsburg countries have stopped ones; most were wide-scaled.

(2) Open Flutes of 8′ or 4′ pitch in English, German and American organs of the 19th century, sometimes of metal but usually of wood.

Zimbel (Ger.; Eng. *Cimball, Cymbal*; Fr. *cymbale*; It., Cz. *cembalo*; Sp. *cimbala, zimbala*; Port. *resimbala*). The important, high chorus Mixture separated from the basic Mixture as the *Blockwerk* became divided; in many cases the same as Scharf. (1) Some early Zimbeln contained a Tierce (Terzzimbel), *c*1450–1550 or later, Praetorius recommending such high Mixtures (15.17.19).

(2) The classical French Cymbale was a high Mixture of octaves and 5ths, the ranks breaking twice per octave (cymbalisée).

(3) The 'repeating Zimbel' was a single-rank or compound stop repeating at every octave, *c*1600–1750 in Germany, perhaps in reference to the medieval cymbala, or small, tuned bells.

Zimbelstern (Ger.). A very common toy stop, found mostly in northern Europe *c*1490–1790 but occasionally elsewhere, and consisting of a revolving star placed towards the top of an organ case to whose wind-blown driving-wheel behind the case is attached a set of bells, tuned or (before *c*1700) untuned. Mattheson (1713) thought the effect good for feast days.

Zink (Ger.). Like Cornet, Zink denotes an imitative stop achieving a cornett-like tone either with reed pipes or as a compound flue stop. (1) A Tierce Mixture of the latter type in some early 16th-century contracts.

ORGAN

(2) A reed or Regal stop in others of the same period; later, 'Zinken oder Cornett' was normally a reed stop of the Schalmei kind, particularly a pedal 2′ reed stop useful for cantus firmus melodies in Lutheran Germany.

APPENDIX THREE

Glossary of Terms

Cross references within this appendix are distinguished by the use of small capitals, with a large capital for the initial letter of the entry referred to, for example:
See KEYBOARD.
Teclado (Sp.). KEYBOARD.

Abrégé [table d'abrégé] (Fr.). ROLLERBOARD.

Abstrakte (Ger.). TRACKER.

Abzug (from Ger. *abziehen*: 'to draw off', 'to divert'). A term occasionally used to refer to a rank of pipes forming part of a compound stop that can be detached and used as an independent stop.

Accord (Fr.). TUNING.

Accouplement (Fr.). COUPLER.

Action (Dutch *regeerwerk, traktuur*; Fr. *mécanique*; Ger. *Mechanik, Mechanismus, Traktur*; It. *meccanica*). (1) The mechanism by means of which organ pipes are sounded when a key is depressed or stops are activated.

(2) (Ger. *Spielart*). The way in which an instrument 'speaks'. In this context, 'action' signifies the 'touch' (*see* TOUCH).

Aliquotstimmen (Ger.). *See* MUTATION STOP.

Anche battante (Fr.). BEATING REED.

Anche libre (Fr.). FREE REED.

Anches [jeux d'anches] (Fr.). REED-WORK.

Ancillary [floating] **divisions.** In electric-action organs, divisions which have no 'home' manual; they can be played from any manual to which they are switched by the organist.

Anemometer. A water-manometer; *see* WIND GAUGE.

Angehangte Traktur [hängende Traktur] (Ger.). SUSPENDED ACTION.

Anima (It.). WIND; *see also* FLUE. The term may also denote the block or the windway in a wooden flue pipe.

Antiphonal organ. A division found in some 20th-century electric-action organs; it is located in a part of the room remote from the main organ.

Apollonicon. A large chamber organ including both keyboards and barrels. Proposed by the English organ builders Flight & Robson in 1812 and completed in 1817, the Apollonicon was an attempt to reproduce mechanically the entire orchestra. A similar but smaller instrument built for Viscount Kirkwall is described at length and illustrated in Abraham Rees: *The Cyclopaedia* (London, 1819), xxv: article 'Organ'. See also Ord-Hume: *Barrel Organ* (1978).

Appel (Fr.). A fixed combination pedal found in French organs.

Aufschnitt (Ger.). CUT-UP.

Backfall (Fr. *bascule*; Ger. *Wippe*). In tracker action, a horizontal bar supported by or resting on a fulcrum, to transfer the key action from 'push' to 'pull'.

Bague (Fr.). The upper block in a French double-block reed pipe.

Balancier (Fr.). A 'helper' pneumatic attached to large pallets to lighten the touch in some mechanical-action organs.

Balg (Ger.). BELLOWS.

Bancone (It.). *See* PANCONE.

Band organ. American term for the fairground organ; see Chapter Eight, §4.

Barker lever (Fr. *machine Barker*; Ger. *Barker-Hebel*). A device to lighten key action invented by Charles Spackman Barker in Paris in 1839 and first used by Cavaillé-Coll in his organ for the abbey of St Denis (1841). Its use spread quickly to other countries, and by the end of the 1850s it was in general use in large organs in England, Germany and the USA, as well as in France. It consists of pneumatic assisting motors ('book pneumatics') interposed between the keys and the pallet pull-down wires in an otherwise ordinary mechanical action, the purpose of which is to lighten the finger pressure required to open large pallets and to cancel out the extra resistance caused by coupling manuals. See also Chapter One, §2 (xi) and fig. 14a, and Chapter Five, §2.

Bars. A term for the GRID.

Bascule (Fr.). BACKFALL.

Beard (Ger. *Bart, Kastenbart, Rollbart, Rollerbart*). A device for stabilizing the tone of narrow-scaled (string) flue pipes which came into use in the 19th century. The commonest forms comprise a round or half-round dowel placed between the ears of the pipe, or a metal bar connecting the lower ends of the ears (box beard). In 1876 Anselme Gavioli patented the *frein harmonique* ('harmonic bridge'), an adjustable metal beard attached below the pipe mouth. Originally used only in barrel organs, it later entered the mainstream of organ building, particularly in connection with string stops of narrow scale.

Bearer (Ger. *Damm*). The shim (slightly thicker than the sliders) on which the toe-board rests in a slider-chest.

Beating reed. The commonest type of reed used in organ pipes, in which the tongue beats against the flat surface of the shallot.

Becher (Ger.; Dutch *beker*). RESONATOR.

Bellows (Fr. *soufflerie, soufflet*; Ger. *Balg*; It. *mantice, manticeria*). A term most often used to denote the apparatus by which air is collected and from which it is distributed to the pipes of an organ. An early reference was John de Trevisa's definition of organum (translation of St Augustine, 1398) as an instrument blown 'wyth bellowes'. Direct bellows include the ribless cuneiform 'forge bellows' of the 14th century from which air was pumped by the weight of the body of the bellows-blower, the resulting pressure fluctuated. Indirect bellows of around 1500 had metal or stone weights placed on the top board of the bellows, which were raised by hand and fell by gravity; the multifold or *Spaenbaelge* (a term used rather loosely) seems to be the older, the singlefold or *Faltenbalg* being known only from around 1620, perhaps earlier in some areas (southern Flanders). All such bellows delivered wind directly through trunks to the chests; only towards the end of the 18th century were receivers or reservoirs for collecting wind from the bellows known (Snetzler, c1745; J. H. Zang: *Der vollkommene Orgelmacher*, 1804). Lantern-shaped bellows were known early in the 17th century (M. Mersenne: *Harmonie universelle*, 1636–7), box-bellows at some time in the 18th. Most new organs do not now have bellows but rotary fans supplying air to the reservoir; such systems gradually evolved in the later 19th century and now enable organists to draw many more stops than any composer before about 1850 would have done. *See also* CONCUSSION BELLOWS.

Biseau (Fr.). A term for the LANGUID; it may also denote the BLOCK in a flue pipe.

Block (1) (Dutch *kop*; Fr. *noyau*; Ger. *Kopf, Nuss*; It. *blocco, noce*). The solid piece of lead or wood that holds the shallot and tongue, and on which the resonator rests in reed pipes (see fig. 19).

   (2) (Ger. *Kern*). In a wooden flue pipe, the block of wood that forms the flue, between the foot of the pipe and the mouth (see fig. 17b).

Blockwerk (Ger.; Dutch *Blokwerk*). The undivided chest of the medieval organ (see Chapter Three) based upon a 'double Principal' (open and stopped 8′ etc) without other 'stops' separated off. The term itself may be 18th-century (Utrecht organ documents, 1731), though according to Joachim Hess (*Over de vereischten in eenen organist*, 1807) used by 'old builders'. Accounts are vague. At Rheims (1487) it is known only that the organ had 2000 pipes, at Amiens (1422) that the four-octave keyboard began at 19 ranks and ended at 91, at Dijon (c1350) that those ranks were made up of Principals, Octaves, Super-octaves and Twelfths. As well as 8′, the *Blockwerk* could be based on open 4′ (Louvain, 1445), open 16′ (Delft, 1458) or deeper. The 1480 *Blockwerk* now in Middelburg, Netherlands, had a probable disposition of:

F	16. 8. 4. $2\frac{2}{3}$. 2. 2. $1\frac{1}{3}$. $1\frac{1}{3}$
d′	16. 8. 4. 4. $2\frac{2}{3}$. $2\frac{2}{3}$. 2. 2. 2. $1\frac{1}{3}$. $1\frac{1}{3}$
f′	16. 8. $5\frac{1}{3}$. 4. 4. $2\frac{2}{3}$. $2\frac{2}{3}$. 2. 2. 2. $1\frac{1}{3}$. $1\frac{1}{3}$
f#′	16. 8. $5\frac{1}{3}$. 4. 4. $2\frac{2}{3}$. $2\frac{2}{3}$. $2\frac{2}{3}$. 2. 2. 2. $1\frac{1}{3}$. $1\frac{1}{3}$
g′	16. 8. 8. $5\frac{1}{3}$. 4. 4. $2\frac{2}{3}$. $2\frac{2}{3}$. $2\frac{2}{3}$. 2. 2. 2. $1\frac{1}{3}$. $1\frac{1}{3}$
c#″	16. 8. 8. 8. $5\frac{1}{3}$. 4. 4. 4. $2\frac{2}{3}$. $2\frac{2}{3}$. $2\frac{2}{3}$. 2. 2. 2. $1\frac{1}{3}$. $1\frac{1}{3}$
e″	16. 8. 8. 8. $5\frac{1}{3}$. $5\frac{1}{3}$. 4. 4. 4. $2\frac{2}{3}$. $2\frac{2}{3}$. $2\frac{2}{3}$. 2. 2. 2. $1\frac{1}{3}$. $1\frac{1}{3}$
a″	16. 8. 8. 8. $5\frac{1}{3}$. $5\frac{1}{3}$. 4. 4. 4. $2\frac{2}{3}$. $2\frac{2}{3}$. $2\frac{2}{3}$. 2. 2. 2. $1\frac{1}{3}$. $1\frac{1}{3}$

The most useful description of the sound of a *Blockwerk* is Praetorius's (*Syntagma musicum*, ii, 2/1619) of that at Halberstadt (1357–61):

The large Praestants and the low manual compass, which does not rise high enough for lightness of sound, caused together a deep coarse rumbling as of a dreadful distant thunder, while the many-rank Mixture gave an exceeding shrillness, strong, loud and powerful.

The *Blockwerk* belonged essentially to (*a*) the fixed church organ (as distinct from positives etc) and (*b*) northern Europe. Organs in Bordeaux, Lombardy and Tuscany for the most part already had single ranks by 1450–1500 (S Giustina, Padua, 1493, organ of $16.8.5\frac{1}{3}.4.2\frac{2}{3}.2.1\frac{1}{3}.1$).

Blower. (1) A machine that supplies wind to the reservoir(s). Early versions employed water, gas or electricity to operate the bellows feeders mechanically; these were superseded by the electrically-driven rotary fan blower now in common use.

(2) (Fr. *souffleur*; Ger. *Calcant*, *Kalkant*; It. *calcante*). The person(s) who operates the bellows.

Blowing pedals. A term for the two large pedals which the player depresses alternately to supply wind or suction in reed organs and in some small single-manual pipe organs.

Body (Ger. *Körper*). The resonator of a flue pipe, the part above the mouth and foot.

Bombarde. A reed division found in some French organs.

Book. The hinged, punched cards that operate the playing mechanism of street or fairground organs.

Book pneumatics. Pneumatic motors that are hinged at one end, with the other end free to move to operate pull-down wires, sliders etc.

Boot (Dutch *stevel*; Fr. *pied*; Ger. *Fuss*, *Stiefel*). The lower part of a reed pipe, into which the block fits; see fig. 19.

Bore [wind hole]. A term for the TOE-HOLE.

Borrowing. A term used by Audsley to denote a principle of 'extension'; *see* EXTENSION ORGAN.

Borstwerk (Dutch). BRUSTWERK.

Boursette (Fr.). PURSE.

Box-bellows (Ger. *Kastenbalg*). A type of bellows developed in Germany in the 19th century in which a piston mechanism consisting of two close-fitting boxes was substituted for the feeders.

Broken octave. A term used to designate a variation of the SHORT OCTAVE.

Brustwerk (Ger.: 'breast department'; Dutch *Borstwerk*). A small organ-chest, usually with its own manual, encased compactly above the keyboards and below the *Hauptwerk*, 'in the breast' of the organ. Many early examples contained a regal or two only, and even later the department usually kept its character as a regals or chamber organ. Such subsidiary chests were numerous in the 17th century, the pedal keyboard often communicating with a so-called *Brustpedal* chest. The term *Brustwerk* belongs only to 18th-century theorists like Agricola who standardized terminology; previous names had been 'positive forn an die brust' (A. Schlick: *Spiegel der Orgelmacher und Organisten*, 1511), 'voer yn dye borst' (Amsterdam Oude Kerk, 1539), *Brustpositiff* (M. Praetorius: *Syntagma musicum*, ii, 2/1619; A Schnitger, 1682), 'in der Brust zum Manual' (Praetorius; G. Silbermann, 1710). Some builders of around 1710–30 in central Germany referred to the *Oberwerk* as *Brustpositiv* or *Brustwerk*. If the *Brustwerk* regal rank (placed near the organist for convenient tuning) were played by the main manual's keyboard, as sometimes happened in Italy, Spain and Austria, there might be no written indication that an organ contained such a department. In modern German organs, the *Brustwerk* is often given the shutters of a Swell organ, a compromise producing the true character of neither.

Buffet (Fr.). CASE.

Cabinet organ. (1) (Fr. *cabinet d'orgue*). An alternative term for the chamber organ; see Chapter Four, §10.

(2) A term sometimes used in the USA to refer to the reed organ.

Cadereta [cadireta] (Sp.). A division in Spanish organs analogous to the Chair; it can be located on the gallery rail (*cadereta exterior*) or in the lower part of the organ case (*cadereta interior*).

Calcant (Ger.; It. *calcante*). A bellows-blower. *See* BLOWER (2).

Cammer-Ton (Ger.: 'chamber pitch'). The pitch at which chamber music and, increasingly, church music was performed in Germany in the 18th century. It has been suggested that a pitch level recommended by Praetorius (*Syntagma musicum*, ii, 2/1619) approximates $a' = 425$ Hz. However, Baroque woodwind instruments developed in Paris in the third quarter of the 17th century and imitated in Germany were built to a lower (French) pitch of about $a' = 410$ Hz. Often *Cammer-Ton* was one tone lower than 18th-century *Chor-Ton* (as at Leipzig), but sometimes it was treated as a minor 3rd lower (as at Weimar). To avoid the necessity of transposing the organ part for an organ at *Chor-Ton*, a few such instruments had one or two accompanimental stops tuned to *Cammer-Ton* (e.g. those at the castle at Merseburg, and at the Jakobikirche, Hamburg, 1688–93). The Gottfried Silbermann organ at the Frauenkirche, Dresden (1732–6), was built at *Cammer-Ton*. Another possibility was to have a transposing keyboard, as in the Merseburg Stadtkirche. Where some form of transposition was used a tuning close to equal temperament was necessary.

Caminetto (It.). CHIMNEY.

Canal (Fr.; It. *canaletto*). SHALLOT.

Canale (It.). WIND-TRUNK.

Canna (It.; Sp. *caño*). PIPE.

Case (Fr. *buffet*; Ger. *Gehäuse*). The decorated wooden housing or structural

ORGAN

shell of the classical organ; it incorporates the console and contains the pipes and action. In 20th-century organs located in chambers the term is often incorrectly used to refer to the decorative non-functional façade that covers the chamber opening.

Catenacciatura [riduzione, tavola della catenacciatura] (It.). ROLLERBOARD.

Cavallo (It.: 'horse'). The heavy timber framework that supports classical Italian organs.

Chair [Choir] **organ** (Dutch *rugpositief*; Fr. *positif de dos*; Ger. *Rückpositiv*; It. *positivo tergale*). The keyboard and chest secondary to the Great organ are correctly called Chair organ if the chest has its own case, separate from the main organ and placed behind the organist's back or chair. In England, all known second manuals were of this kind until 1631, when the Chirk Castle organ had both chests placed within the one case. Most later secondary chests were also like this, their sound discreet enough for choral accompaniment; hence the term 'Choir organ'. John Hawkins (*A General History of the Science and Practice of Music*, 1776) thus had it wrong when he said the manual was called 'Choir and by corruption the Chair Organ'. The term 'chaire', 'chayre', 'cheire' etc is known only from the 17th century (King's College, Cambridge, 1605–6) although the manuals themselves were known much earlier. Whether such terms as 'lytell organis' (Sandwich, 1496) indicated a Chair organ is unknown.

Continental terms show much variety before *le positif* and *das Rückpositiv* were adopted as the name for the Chair organ: *positieff an die Stoel* (Delft, Oude Kerk, 1461), *positif de devant* (Rouen, 1524), *au doxal* (Hesdin, 1623), *positiff en rück* (A. Schlick: *Spiegel der Orgelmacher und Organisten*, 1511) etc. *In den stoel* seems to have been widely used (Antwerp, 1505; Herkenrode, 1522; Amsterdam, Oude Kerk, 1539) and often *chaière* (Argentan, 1463) or *la cheyere* (Valenciennes, 1515). Such manuals or departments were known at the end of the 14th century from Rouen to Utrecht, and in the 15th from Spain to Silesia; southern Flemish usage of the term *cheyere* probably led English builders to call it Chair organ. (*See also* RÜCKPOSITIV and Chapter Three §7.)

Channels [grooves, note-channels] (Fr. *gravures*; Ger. *Kanzellen*). (1) The open spaces between the bars of the grid in a slider-chest; they convey wind to the pipes of a given note.

(2) Covered grooves cut into the toe-board or into a block to convey wind to offset pipes.

Cheminée (Fr.). CHIMNEY.

Chest. A term for the WIND-CHEST.

Chiff (Ger. *Vorsprache*). A term used in voicing for the initial fleeting 'consonant' that precedes the steady state of a speaking flue pipe.

Chimney (Fr. *cheminée*; Ger. *Rohr*; It. *caminetto*). The short, narrow, open tube that protrudes upwards from the top of the cap of certain 'half-stopped' flute pipes.

APPENDIX THREE

Choir organ (1) (Fr. *orgue de choeur*; Ger. *Chororgel*). A small supplementary liturgical organ located in the chancel of a church.

(2) A common term for the Chair organ, especially when it is not located in the traditional position on the gallery rail.

Chor-Ton (Ger.: 'choir pitch'). The pitch associated with church organs in 18th-century Germany, sometimes called 'Cornett-Ton' after the Renaissance instrument of that name. Although it has been suggested that Praetorius (*Syntagma musicum*, ii, 2/1619) recommended a pitch level of approximately half a semitone lower than modern pitch (i.e. lower than $a' = 440$ Hz), most organs in Germany in the first half of the 18th century were tuned between three-quarters and a whole semitone higher than modern pitch.

Ciphering [cyphering] (Fr. *cornement*; Ger. *Heulen*). The sounding of an organ pipe without a key being depressed, due to mechanical fault or damage. The word is of unknown origin: 'Sypher' was used in the Leckingfield Proverbs around 1520; 'cipher' was used by Burney with reference to the Haarlem organ in 1773 (*The Present State of Music in Germany, the Netherlands and the United Provinces*) when, like Joachim Hess (*Luister van het orgel*, 1772), he noted that the extra mechanism enabling the organist to block wind from a chest was useful 'in case of a cipher'. Ciphering should not be confused with 'running', i.e. the leaking of wind from one groove or channel to another, audible only when a neighbouring key is depressed. Common reasons for ciphering will be found in a faulty pallet (dust preventing full closure, a pallet being dislodged, warped, damp or catching on guide pins), pallet spring (out of position, too weak, broken), action (tight or entangling tracker, damaged backfall, jammed, bent or rusty pull-down), slider (loose, warped), or key (warped, stuck) and, in non-mechanical actions, failures at various critical points (contacts, relays, key springs, inert pneumatics etc).

Clavier (Fr.). KEYBOARD.

Claviorganum. Claviorgan; see Chapter Eight, §2.

Coin (Fr.). WEDGE.

Combination action (Fr. *appel, pédale de combinaison*; Ger. *freie Kombination*). A term used to denote a device that allows the player to put a group of stops into operation at once. Such actions may be either fixed (unalterable) or adjustable by the player, and are found in organs with every type of key action: mechanical, pneumatic or electric. Early mechanical types of combination action were generally foot-operated, but in electric-action organs thumb-buttons between the manuals are common. *See also* COMPOSITION PEDAL, MACHINE STOP, PISTON, TIRATUTTI.

Compass. The number and extent of the keys in a keyboard or pedalboard.

Composition pedal. The name given in about 1810, probably first by Bishop, to the foot-operated lever of an organ that takes off or brings on predetermined stops, usually by operating on the drawstop itself. It replaced the earlier 'shifting movement' known by Dallam and Smith from about

1675, which comprised a foot-lever operating directly on the ends of the sliders in such a way that on depression the stop was taken off, and on release a spring returned the slider to the playing position. According to the builder Jordan's trade-card of about 1720, its purpose was to put stops 'off and on by the feet, simply or together, at the master's discretion, and as quick as thought, without taking the hands off the keys'. Hopkins (in Hopkins and Rimbault: *The Organ*, 1855), used the term 'single-action' to describe the composition pedal that 'either draws out or thrusts in a given number of sliders' or draw-stops, and 'double-action' for the pedal that did both. Such accessories were as popular in large numbers by about 1825 (John Abbey's small organ for the Paris Exhibition of 1827 had seven), as their pneumatic, electro-pneumatic and electric equivalents have been ever since.

Compound stop. A generic term for a Mixture stop.

Concussion bellows [winker]. A bellows-like pneumatic, or membrane, usually spring-loaded, which is attached to a wind-trunk or pallet box to help smooth out surges in the wind. It is believed to have been invented by an American, William M. Goodrich, in the 1820s.

Conductor. A term for the Conveyance.

Cone-chest (Ger. *Kegellade*). A type of ventil wind-chest with cone-shaped valves found in German organs of the 19th century; see Chapter One, §2 (xii) and fig. 14b.

Conflatorium (from Lat.; *flatus*: 'a blowing', 'blast'). An early medieval term for the unit in which the channels from the various bellows come together to form a single central duct or Wind-trunk. (See fig. 5.)

Console [keydesk] (Ger. *Spielschrank, Spieltisch*; It. *consolle*). The desk from which an organ is played, comprising keyboards, pedal, stop-knobs, switches, etc. The word is almost certainly French, introduced into England at the end of the 19th century and replacing earlier terms (Burney's 'keys' or 'box of keys', Hopkins's 'claviers' etc). It probably ought to refer to detached keyboards, particularly the quadrant-shaped keyboards (not unlike console tables) made by Cavaillé-Coll after the model of E. F. Walcker (1840), and illustrated by theorists from about 1880 onwards (Töpfer, Audsley). Despite similarities in the work of many individual organ builders (G. Silbermann, G. Callido, A. Cavaillé-Coll) and various regulations as to octave width, key length etc laid down by national organists' associations, there has never been much uniformity in console design, even at any one moment in any single country.

Contacts. Wires or plates of silver or bronze that are activated by keys, stops, pistons or pneumatics to convey current to key and stop actions in electric-action organs.

Conveyance [conductor] (Fr. *porte-vent, transmission*; Ger. *Kondukt*; It. *condotto, portavento*). A term for any tubing or wooden duct that conveys wind from the bellows to the wind-chest, or from the wind-chest to the offset pipes.

APPENDIX THREE

Cornement (Fr.). CIPHERING.

Cornett-Ton (Ger.). A term for CHOR-TON.

Coulisse d'accord (Fr.). TUNING-SLIDE.

Counterface (Fr. *saillie*; Ger. *Gegenphase*). A minute chamfering or blunting of the languid edge, found in virtually all organs until the late 19th century.

Coupler (Fr. *accouplement, tirasse*; Ger. *Koppel*). The mechanism whereby pipes of one department or manual are made to sound on the keys of another. The most common system until the early 19th century was the *Schiebekoppel*, or push coupler: one set of keys was pushed in (or sometimes pulled out) to enable some kind of wooden protuberance along the key-shafts (dogs, lugs, small vertical battens etc) to connect in one way or another with a second set of keys and so cause them to be depressed likewise. By 1830 there were mechanisms that would make such connections in one of two ways: (*a*) when a separated row of battens placed between the back shafts of two keyboards was brought into play by a levered mechanism (thus making it unnecessary to remove both hands from the keys when coupling), or (*b*) when the inner action-levers of one manual could be directly linked with those of another (thus in most cases leaving the newly connected keys undepressed). An important organ system was that of 'communication', whereby the pipes of one department were placed on a chest with two pallets per groove, one to each keyboard concerned. Various kinds of electric and pneumatic couplers have been perfected, including those that enable a rank of pipes to be played at 16′, 8′, 4′ and mutation pitches in the so-called 'Extension organ'.

Couplers were probably known in the 15th century. At the Oude Kerk, Delft in 1458, it was specified that the Chair organ might be joined to the Great organ when the organist desired. Henri Arnaut de Zwolle (*c*1450) described a coupler based on lugs that could be brought into play. Pedal-to-*Blockwerk* couplers, perhaps pulling down the manual keys, were also known in Netherlands organs during the following century; but as in the case of other accessories like Tremulants, the builder's contract did not always specify a coupler. The communication system was well developed in Germany by 1600; some later pedal departments, such as Gottfried Silbermann's (1715–40), permanently communicated with the Great organ. Octave couplers, requiring a set of diagonal backfalls reaching across the others to pull down the pallets of notes an octave above, were known by 1800. The Venetian type was called *terzo mano* ('third hand'), and already by 1820 Marcussen in Denmark had made mechanical Extension organs on the same principle, as, it is said, did an Innsbruck builder in the 17th century. In organ music, *organo pleno* often implied coupled manuals, especially in France.

Crescendo pedal (Ger. *Walze, Crescendowalze*). A foot-operated device, usually pneumatic or electrical, which brings on gradually all the stops of the organ from soft to loud; it was developed in the late 19th century. The commonest type is operated by a balanced hinged pedal in the manner of a modern Swell pedal, but an early German version (Rollschweller), favoured by composers such as Max Reger, was operated by a foot-rotated drum.

Crivello (It.). RACKBOARD.

Cube bass. A cube-shaped pipe of 32′ pitch which, by means of a system of valves, can produce several different notes. Invented by John Compton (1876–1957), it is rarely found and is no longer in use.

Cut-up (Ger. *Aufschnitt*). A term used in voicing for the height of the mouth of a flue pipe in relation to its width. Higher cut-ups encourage the development of fundamental, while lower cut-ups encourage more harmonic development.

Cyphering. *See* CIPHERING.

Damm (Ger.). BEARER.

Deckung [Spund] (Ger.). STOPPER.

Denti (It.). NICKING.

Diapason. (1) In organ terminology, the name given to foundation stops (see Appendix Two).

(2) (Fr.). SCALING.

Direct-electric action. A type of action in which electromagnets open the pipe-valves; it was first developed by the firm of Wicks.

Double-expression. An accessory stop found in Mustel harmoniums, invented by Victor Mustel in 1853. It allows the treble and bass halves of the keyboard to make a crescendo or diminuendo independently.

Double organ. The word 'organ' was frequently put in the plural in late medieval sources, though left singular by Chaucer. A 'payre of orgonys' was mentioned at Sandwich in 1444, indicating a single-manual organ; by 1650–70 (Evelyn, Pepys) a 'pair of organs' sometimes indicated two or more manuals. 'Double' occurred in the 16th century not to indicate two rows of pipes, much less two manuals, but perhaps to indicate a keyboard compass longer than the common *F–a″*. In most instances there is no means of knowing what the writer meant. But by 1613 the new two-manual organ of Worcester Cathedral was called 'Double Organs', and it is this kind of instrument which was normally meant both in 17th-century contracts (e.g. Durham, Wells and Canterbury, all 1662) and in the voluntaries for Double organ popular from around 1640. The Canterbury agreement is explicit: 'A Double Organ, viz a great Organ and a Chaire Organ'. In some voluntaries, 'double' is the registration term for Great organ, 'single' for the Chair organ – an interpretation of the phrase even more odd when composers became more specific (cf Blow's 'Vers for the Cornett and Single Organ').

Double touch. A type of key action in which a key depressed past its normal contact point engages a second electric contact that brings on additional stops or couplers. It is used mainly in cinema organs.

Drawstop [stop-knob] (Fr. *tirant, tirant de registre*; Ger. *Registerknopf, Register-*

zug; It. *tiro*). The knob or lever on the console that operates the stop mechanism.

Drehorgel (Ger.) Barrel organ; see Chapter Eight, §3.

Druckschalter [Druckknopf] (Ger.). PISTON.

Duplexing. A term for 'extension'; *see* EXTENSION ORGAN.

Durchschlagende Zunge [Durchschlagzunge] (Ger.). FREE REED.

Durchstecher (Ger.). A condition in a wind-chest in which wind 'runs' from a note being played to one not being played. *See* RUN.

Ears (Ger. *Seitenbärte*). Projecting pieces of metal at the sides of the mouths of some organ flue pipes (particularly in the lower registers) which stabilize the tone. Certain capped metal pipes are also tuned by means of oversized 'ears'. (See Chapter Two, §1.)

Echo organ. A subsidiary chest encased within the main organ, usually with its own keyboard; whatever the kind of organ concerned, the Echo is the department lowest in priority and the one given to the softest tone-colours. Organ music with echo effects (Kotter, Sweelinck, Kindermann, J. S. Bach, Franck etc) rarely requires an Echo department as such, although much organ music around 1900 was written specifically for the far-distant altar or apse organs made feasible by the new electric actions.

Each country had its own kind of Echo organ: a little half-compass manual with Cornet and reed stop behind the music desk (France, 1630), higher up at the back of the organ, with its box-front movable to give swell effects (England, 1710), to the left of the keyboards on the floor (Spain, by 1700) or with swell shutters (Venice, 1775), a large department placed at the back of the organ (south Germany, 1730) or a small chest at the very top of the case with or without swell-lid (larger churches throughout Spain and Germany).

Eight foot. A term used in reference to organ stops, and by extension to other instruments, to indicate that they are pitched at unison or 'normal' pitch (now based on $c' = 256$ Hz), as distinct from Four foot (octave higher) or Sixteen foot (octave lower). Eight foot is only an approximation, since the length of open organ pipe required to sound c will depend on (*a*) the kind or standard of foot, (*b*) the standard of pitch and (*c*) the scale or width, wind pressure and flue size of the pipe concerned. As J. van Heurn observed (*De orgelmaaker*, 1804–5), exact length can be established only when the pipe is voiced. Praetorius (*Syntagma musicum*, ii, 2/1619, p.17) wrote that 'if the customary present-day Cammer-Ton is given to an organ, the lowest C in the Principal is 8′ long', but it must be remembered that he had in mind the slightly shorter Brunswick foot, and that he was merely conforming to an organ-builders' convention and did not intend an exact description.

Before the 16′, 8′, 4′ terminology had become conventional (e.g. Chartres Cathedral, 1542), documents often attempted to be exact, though of course without specifying foot standard. Thus at Valenciennes in 1515 the Principal was '5 piez', probably from G high pitch, perhaps equal to the 'jeu de six piés en ton de chapelle' at St Eloi, Bordeaux, in 1529. Schlick's $6\frac{1}{2}$ Rhine foot F of 1511 was probably much the same as the 'seven voet en effaut' at Zwolle in 1447. The 'werk van 16 voetten' at Delft in 1458 seems to indicate both a sub-octave chorus and low pitch, since the compass began at F.

Electro-pneumatic action. A type of action in which an electrical impulse from the key contact activates a small electromagnet, which in turn activates the pipe-valve or pull-down pneumatic (by opening a pressure or exhaust port). Although such actions were experimented with as early as the mid-19th century, they only came into practical use shortly before 1900.

En chamade (from Fr. *battre la chamade*: 'to sound a parley'). A term indicating a rank of pipes (usually reeds or regals) placed horizontally in the case front of an organ, e.g. 'trompette en chamade'. (See Appendix Two, 'Clarín', 'Dulzian', 'Orlos', 'Trommet'.) Although before the end of the 18th century only Iberian organs had such reeds and regals, the phrase was used neither by Spanish nor Portuguese builders. It first appears in Isnard's contract of 1772 at St-Maximin-en-Var, Provence, for horizontal reeds imitating military trumpet-calls, like the vertical Feldtrompeten (sometimes placed in the case front) and Claríns de mar of 17th-century organs in Germany and Spain. The phrase was popularized in the 19th century by Cavaillé-Coll to describe the reeds he heard as a boy in the southern borderlands and which he imitated in his formative organ of St Sulpice, Paris. 20th-century reeds *en chamade* in England, Germany, and the Netherlands rarely have the particular élan of the 17th-century Spanish models, replacing resonance with power; also, on Spanish organs, external horizontal reeds and regals were always supplementary to interior vertical reeds and regals. The advantages of such stops *en chamade* are their clear, penetrating sound (cf the common direction 'Schalltrichter auf!' for orchestral trumpets); their easy access for tuning; their sheer contrast with the soft, singing flue stops of Spanish organs; their safety from dust; a convincing imitation of (or replacement for) real trumpets in cathedral music from about 1650; and an extravagant appearance. (See figs. 43–5.)

Enharmonic organ [euharmonic organ]. An instrument that has extra keys or pipes, so that pure intervals can be played in all or most keys. Much experimentation was done with enharmonic pipe and reed organs in the mid- and late 19th century by Alley, Poole, Perronet Thompson, Bosanquet, Collin and others.

Equerre (Fr.). SQUARE.

Exhauster. A term sometimes used for the bellows in a suction-type reed organ.

Expression. A stop found on European reed organs that inactivates the reservoir and allows the player to regulate loudness with the blowing pedals.

Expressionsorgel (Ger.). ORGUE EXPRESSIF.

Extension organ. 20th-century term for an organ in which the principle of 'extension' (making one row of pipes available at different octave or overtone pitches) is applied to a major degree. Praetorius (*Syntagma musicum*, ii, 2/1619 drew a table-positive in which the chest of a single row of pipes was so grooved and palleted that it could supply each key with three tones (2′, 1⅓′ and 1′); a few larger examples are known to have been made over the next two centuries or so, but clearly the non-mechanical actions of the late 19th century gave greater opportunities for the system, since they made it easier for key-action and chest-construction to be designed for this purpose. Audsley (*The Art of Organ-building*, 1905) used the terms 'borrowing' for a rank extended beyond the keyboard compass in order to make it available at another octave (e.g. 116 pipes could provide stops at 32′, 16′, 8′, 4′, 2′ and 1′, each to a compass of 56 notes) and 'duplicating' for using a rank of pipes on two or more keyboards, manual or pedal, called 'communication' by English builders from about 1650 to 1800. Marcussen's organ at Siseby (Schleswig, 1819) used both systems; the electric 'unit organ' of 1930 took it a step further by giving each pipe its own chest playable by any key desired. The principle is quite different from that of the coupler, which unites whole keyboards.

Fachada [tubos de fachada] (Sp.). FRONT PIPES.

Faltenbalg. A type of BELLOWS.

Feeder (Fr. *pompe*; Ger. *Schöpfbalg*). The small hand- or machine-operated wedge-bellows that feed wind into the main reservoir in a reservoir-type wind system.

Finestra e riccia (It.). TUNING ROLL.

Fistula (Lat.: 'pipe'). In medieval and Renaissance sources the term is found in various contexts, including organ pipe (*fistula organica*) and wind-trunk (*fistula maxima*). Various organ stops are described as *fistula* with some modifier.

Flautados (Sp.). FLUE-WORK.

Flip-flop (Ger. *Wechselventil*). A term used in mechanical borrowing (extension) to denote a small valve that will admit wind from either of two different sources to a single pipe.

Flue [windway] (Fr. *lumière*, *saillie*; Ger. *Kernspalte*; It. *anima*). The slit in a flue pipe between the edge of the languid (or block) and the lower lip, through which the wind issues to produce sound (see fig. 17). Adjustments to the flue by the voicer help to determine both timbre and loudness. *See also* WINDWAY.

Flue-work (Fr. *flûtes*, *jeux de tuyaux à bouche*; Ger. *Labialpfeifen*, *Labialwerk*; It. *canne ad anima*; Sp. *flautados*). The flue-stops of an organ collectively (as distinct from reed-work), i.e. those in which sound is produced on the duct or flue principle whereby wind is directed through a narrow windway to strike against a lip or edge above. The term refers to the open or stopped Diapasons or Principals, the Flutes, the narrow-scaled, conical, compound and all varieties of metal or wooden stops other than those of the reed-work. The term appears only late in English writings, being absent from such authors as Talbot, Hawkins, Burney and Blewitt, who used only the phrase 'reed stops' to distinguish the non-flues. Hopkins and Rimbault (*The Organ*, 1855) gave alternatives: 'lip, mouth or flue pipes – for they are called by all these names', although Hopkins himself preferred 'flue'. For reasons unclear to other writers, many American authors today prefer the terms 'labial' (flue) and 'lingual' (reed). (See also Chapter Two, §1, and figs. 17 and 18.)

Fonds d'orgue (Fr.: 'organ foundations'). Phrase denoting an organ registration of Principal and Flute ranks at 16′, 8′ and 4′ pitches in a French organ. The 'Fonds d'orgues' was to Gigault (*Livre de musique pour l'orgue*, 1685) a fuller version of the registration 'Concert de Flutes', i.e. a combination of all available flue ranks at those pitches on both Grand Orgue and Positif coupled, without Tremulant and suitable for slow or fairly slow pieces of thick texture. To Bédos de Celles (*L'art du facteur d'orgues*, 1766–78) it meant much the same thing – all the Montres, Bourdons, Flutes, open 8′ ranks and Prestants 4′ – except that a French organ of 1766 had more such ranks than one of 1685, and its bellows enabled more to be drawn. To César Franck 'Jeux de fond' meant a comparable registration of flue foundation stops as opposed to the 'Jeux d'anches' or reeds, which such contemporary builders as Cavaillé-Coll separated off by another wind-ventil. Later composers, such as Messiaen, use the term 'fonds' in the same way.

Foot (Fr. *pied*; Ger. *Fuss*, *Pfeifenfuss*). The part of a flue pipe below the mouth; it supports the pipe and conveys wind from the toe-hole to the flue.

Foundation stops (Fr. *fonds d'orgue*; Ger. *Grundstimmen*). Term for the unison- and octave-sounding ranks of pipes. The French term *fonds d'orgue* is used more specifically to denote Principal and Flute ranks.

Four foot. A term used in reference to organ stops, and by extension also to other instruments, to indicate that they are pitched an octave above the Eight foot, or 'normal', pitch now based on $c' = 256$ Hz. A pipe of average Diapason scale and four feet (1.2m) in length would in fact speak somewhat lower than $c = 128$ Hz, but the foot too has changed in length since this terminology was first used in the 15th century (Delft, Oude Kerk, 1458). In the classic Werkprinzip organ design, the Chair organ is of four foot, the Great of eight, the Pedal of sixteen.

Fourniture (Fr.). The name for the collected ranks of the *Blockwerk* when the principals and flutes had been separated off; see Appendix Two, 'Fourniture'.

Free reed (Fr. *anche libre*; Ger. *durchschlagende Zunge*, *Durchschlagzunge*). A type of reed voice in which the tongue vibrates through an aperture rather than against it (as in a beating reed). Free reeds with qualifying resonators are occasionally found in pipe organs built in the latter half of the 19th century, but the free reed, usually without a resonator, is the basis of the reed organ and related instruments. See Chapter Two, §3 and fig. 21.

Freie Kombination (Ger.). A type of COMBINATION ACTION

Frein harmonique (Fr.). A type of BEARD patented by Anselme Gavioli in 1876.

APPENDIX THREE

Front pipes (Fr. *montres*; Ger. *Prospektpfeifen*; Sp. *fachada, tubos de fachada*). The pipes of the lowest-pitched Principal (Diapason) stop in the organ; they are displayed in the front of the case. With minor exceptions (*see* ORGANETTI MORTI) they were traditionally speaking pipes, although in the 20th century dummy pipes have been frequently used in decorative screens in front of organ chambers. Alternative names given to the Principals (Dutch *praestant*, Fr. *prestant*, Ger. *Prestant*, from Lat. *praestare*: 'to stand in front', and Fr. *montre*) reflect this function.

Full organ. A term for an organ registration (*see also* ORGANO PLENO; the French terms *grand jeu* and *plein jeu* are occasionally used loosely to denote 'full organ'). Each organ school has its own kind of full organ, some having more than one, depending on the kind of music concerned. In England the phrase seems first to appear about 1700, especially to indicate the registration drawn for a new type of homophonic organ prelude, as distinct from the verses and voluntaries for Single, Great and Double organ by Locke, Blow, Purcell and others; it probably denotes all the stops of a Great organ, i.e. Diapason chorus, Tierce mixtures and reeds. By the later 18th century, theorists such as Hawkins (*History*, 1776) and Jonas Blewitt (*A Complete Treatise on the Organ*, *c*1795) used the phrase more or less synonymously with 'chorus', i.e. in reference to the sound produced by all the Great organ stops other than Cornets, Dulcianas, Flutes etc. By the early 19th century, especially when J. S. Bach's bigger preludes and fugues became available in England, the term included couplers and 16' ranks. Today Full organ is interpreted at the organist's discretion, like César Franck's *fff*.

Fundamentalbrett [Fundamentaltafel] (Ger.). TABLE.

Fuss (Ger.). FOOT.

Fussdrücker (Ger.). Toe-piston. *See* PISTON.

Gehäuse (Ger.). CASE.

Genouillère (Fr.). KNEE-LEVER.

Grand Choeur (Fr.). The Great chorus of a French organ. While *grand jeu* and *plein jeu* denote the two kinds of major choruses on the Classical French organ (*c*1600–1800), Grand Choeur suggests rather the group of stops added to the *fonds d'orgue* (16', 8' and 4' ranks) to make Full organ in music of the post-classical period. It is not a registration as such, nor is it normally used by composers. The term significantly appeared in the stop-lists of Cavaillé-Coll's formative organ at St Sulpice, Paris (completed 1862), to denote the 13 reed and mixture stops played from the Grand Orgue manual but placed on a separate chest from the Diapason chorus ranks of the Grand Orgue proper.

Grand jeu (Fr.: 'great registration'). (1) A term found in French organ music (though seldom used by modern composers), denoting one of two registrations: (*a*) the early Diapason chorus, without Flute mutations or reeds, corresponding in smaller organs to the old undivided, stop-less *Blockwerk* (St Etienne, Toulouse, 1531) but as a term soon to be replaced by the better *plein* *jeu* (Chartres Cathedral, 1542); and (*b*) a characteristic combination of Bour-dons, mutations, Cornet and reeds much used by the composers of the French school around 1670–1770. Nivers (*Livre d'orgue*, 1665) still included most manual stops in his *grand jeu*, but Lebègue (*Les pièces d'orgue*, 1676) gave the classical combination of Bourdon 8', Prestant 4', Cornet and Trompette. As such, the *grand jeu* was both used for certain interludes in the Mass (the exuberant finales to the Kyrie, Gloria, Agnus and offertory) and associated with a particular musical style, often contrapuntal or even fugal, sometimes with one hand in a colourful solo against the other on a quieter manual. By 1740, and probably earlier, pedal reeds also took part in the *grand jeu*, like other reeds, Cornets, Tierces and even Tremulants.

(2) In French reed organs, a knob that draws all the other knobs simul-taneously.

Gravures (Fr.). CHANNELS.

Great octave. A term still used by some organ builders and once by organ theorists (Hopkins, in Hopkins and Rimbault: *The Organ*, 1855; Audsley, 1905) to refer to the (pipes of the) octave *C–c*, in distinction to *C'–C* (the 'contra-octave'), *c–c'* (the 'small octave') etc. The term seems to be a transla-tion of *Grossoktave* rather than a reference to the completed short octave of former periods, as has sometimes been thought.

Great organ. Term used in two related but different ways; (i) to denote a large organ as distinct from a smaller chamber organ, in church accounts (York, 1469; Sandwich, 1496; St Andrew's, Holborn, 1553), inventories (1515) and general literature; and (ii) to denote the larger or main manual of a two-manual or double organ of the 17th century (King's College, Cam-bridge, accounts, 1606), as distinct from the Chair organ. Earlier, it is not always clear which is meant. The contents and function of the Great organ correspond to those of the Grand Orgue, Organo Primo, *Hauptwerk* (or *Oberwerk*), *Hoofdwerk* etc., except that the English main manual has not an unbroken tradition for massive Diapason choruses. Those of the 16th and 17th centuries were usually little more than large-scale chamber organs, often in a place traditionally kept for small organs in the Netherlands, Italy etc (e.g. on the screen). Larger Great organs were built from around 1820, particularly under the influence of Dutch organs (especially those of Haarlem) and German composers (especially J. S. Bach). Following Cavaillé-Coll's example, some English builders gave their Great organ keyboards several chests, including major reed departments often on high wind-pressure. But since the Organ Reform Movement of the 1920s, the Great organ has been recognized as essentially a Diapason chorus, not far removed from the *Blockwerk* in concep-tion, and in larger examples containing stops along the lines of $16.16.8.8.5\frac{1}{3}.4.2\frac{2}{3}.2.II.V–X.III.16.8$.

Grid [bars] (Sp. *secreto*). The part of a slider-chest containing the note-chan-nels.

Grooves. A term for CHANNELS.

APPENDIX THREE

Gruccia (It.). The tuning wire in a reed pipe; see REED WIRE.

Grundstimmen (Ger.). FOUNDATION STOPS.

Halving ratio. An aspect of SCALING: whereas the length of a pipe reduces by half for a pitch rise of an octave, a reduction by half of its diameter occurs at a greater rise in pitch, commonly a major 10th (for principal-toned, or diapason, pipes) or a major 13th (for flute-toned pipes).

Hammered metal. From the Gothic period and throughout the Baroque, pipe metal, either lead or tin, was often hammered; this gave it greater strength and density, and probably better uniformity as well. Bédos de Celles describes the process in *L'art du facteur d'orgues* (1766–78).

Hand organ. A colloquial term for the barrel organ; see Chapter Eight, §3.

Hängende Traktur (Ger.). SUSPENDED ACTION.

Haskell bass. A bass pipe invented by William E. Haskell for use where space for bass pipes is limited. A cylinder or canister of smaller diameter is hung inside a short pipe of normal scale, thus lowering the pitch. It is tuned by means of a tuning slide on the cylinder.

Hauptwerk (Ger.: 'chief department'; Dutch *Hoofdwerk*). Like Great organ, Grand Orgue and Organo Primo in some of their usages, *Hauptwerk* today denotes the main manual of an organ. *Werk* itself is an equivalent to *opus* used in church documents (Utrecht, *c*1400) or theoretical manuscripts (Arnaut de Zwolle, MS, Bibliothèque Nationale, Paris, lat. 7295; *c*1450), and was first used to refer to the organ in general (Schlick: *Spiegel der Orgelmacher und Organisten*, 1511). It soon meant by implication the main manual, i.e. the first to be planned, that with the main chorus – as distinct from (*a*) the Chair organ, (*b*) the positive below or above the main chest and (*c*) the pedals (*see* PEDAL). Praetorius (*Syntagma musicum*, ii, 2/1619) still used *Oberwerk* to refer to this main manual, since it was placed above the player; other terms found in church archives and contemporary treatises had been *Principael* (referring to its purpose of supplying the *Blockwerk*), *Werk* (Gorinchem St Jan, 1518), *Manual* (Schlick, 1511), *der vulle Orgel* (Hamburg, Petrikirche, 1548), *Prinzipall-Lade* (Münster Cathedral, 1610). Terminology became stable early in the 17th century, but it was some time before *Hauptwerck* (Würzburg Cathedral, 1614) became the most usually accepted term. The contents of the *Hauptwerk* and its relationship to the other departments are the history of the organ itself.

Hausorgel (Ger.; Dutch *huisorgel*). Chamber organ; see Chapter Four, §10.

Heulen (Ger.). CIPHERING.

Hintersatz (Ger.). The ranks of pipes placed behind the case pipes in the late medieval organ; see Appendix Two, 'Hintersatz'.

Hoofdwerk (Dutch). HAUPTWERK.

Hornwerk. A name given to certain 16th- and 17th-century tower organs of central Germany and Austria. At first such outdoor organs could play only a few chords, and were used for signalling in the same manner as bells. Later they were enlarged and fitted with a self-playing mechanism of the pinned barrel type, enabling them to play melodies in the manner of a carillon. Two examples still exist in operable condition in Austria. One, dating from 1502, is known as the 'Salzburg Stier', and is in the tower of the bishop's castle in Salzburg. It plays three times daily; most of the tunes presently pinned on its barrels are by 18th-century composers, including Haydn and Mozart. Its popular name (Ger. *Stier*: 'bull') is apparently derived from the fact that at the end of each tune all the pipes sound at once. The other extant Hornwerk is in Heilbrunn. (See Quoika, 1959.)

Hydraulic organ. A water organ; see Chapter Eight, §1.

Intonierung (Ger.). VOICING.

Jalousieschweller (Ger.). A Venetian Swell.

Jeu d'orage (Fr.). *See* ORAGE.

Jeux. (1) The standard French registrations of the Renaissance and the Baroque.

(2) A term sometimes applied to free reeds, as in a harmonium.

Jeux de combinaison (Fr.). A MUTATION STOP.

Kalkant [Calcant] (Ger.). A bellows-blower (*see* BLOWER (2)); also the name of the stop-knob which gave a signal to the blower.

Kammerorgel (Ger.). Chamber organ; see Chapter Four, §10.

Kanzellen (Ger.). CHANNELS.

Kanzellendecke (Ger.). TABLE.

Kastenbalg (Ger.). BOX-BELLOWS.

Kastenbart (Ger.). A box-type BEARD.

Keel (Dutch). SHALLOT.

Kegellade (Ger.). CONE-CHEST.

Kehle (Ger.). SHALLOT.

Keil (Ger.). WEDGE.

Keilbalg (Ger.). WEDGE-BELLOWS.

Kern (Ger.). LANGUID or BLOCK in a flue pipe.

Kernspalte (Ger.). FLUE; WINDWAY.

Kernstiche (Ger.). NICKING.

Key (Fr. *touche*; Ger. *Taste*; It. *tasto*). A lever balanced at either its centre or far end. When depressed by a finger or a foot, it operates the mechanism that admits wind into a pipe.

Keyboard (Fr. *clavier*; Ger. *Klaviatur, Tastatur*; It. *tastatura, tastiera*; Sp. *teclado*). A set of levers (keys) actuating the mechanism of a musical instrument. The organ was the first instrument to be played from a keyboard; the hydraulis of the Greeks had primitive keys, which were simply sliders that were pulled out to admit air to the pipes. The earliest European keyboards were simple contrivances, played with the hands rather than the fingers. Praetorius (2/1619) and others after him stated that some primitive organs were played with the fists, the wrists or even the knees, but there is little confirmation of this in medieval documents. The spacing between the organ keys remained that which separated the pipes, sometimes over 10 cm, until an abridgment mechanism was invented. Up to the 13th century the keyboards were usually diatonic except for the inclusion of B♭. They often showed a C as the first key. By the beginning of the 14th century, however, the development of polyphony had caused a widening of keyboard compass and the progressive addition of chromatic keys. Jehan des Murs (first half of the 14th century) mentioned keys for f♯ and g♯, and Jacques de Liège (c1330) wrote that on the organ 'the tone is almost everywhere divided into two semitones'. The late 14th-century organ of Norrlanda in the National Historical Museum in Stockholm still possesses its manual keyboard covering one octave and a 6th, from c to a', fully chromatic, and a pedal keyboard of eight keys, probably from C to B with B♭. The chromatic keys are placed at a higher level, except for the b♭ and B♭, which are ranged among the diatonic ones.

Before the second half of the 15th century the lowest part of keyboard compositions was often based on plainsong, or written in plainsong style. Owing to the limited number of transpositions then performed, there was no need for chromatic degrees other than the B♭ in the bass of the keyboard. This explains why pedal or bass manual keyboards remained diatonic up to a late date. As late as the 17th century, even manual keyboards sometimes lacked the first chromatic degrees when they were provided with a short octave. In the first half of the 15th century keyboards often began at F or B. The B keyboard was only a slight extension of the medieval c one. The significance of the F keyboard is more complex. The following hypothesis provides a possible explanation: the apparent c key had sometimes been used to play the *Gamma ut*; when solmization names were given to the keys, it may have seemed more convenient to call *Gamma ut* the c key (this was feasible at a time when the pattern of raised keys was not yet complete). One note, *F fa ut*, was then added below the *Gamma ut*. The F keyboard would thus have been, in effect, a variant of the B one, producing virtually the same pitches. Later in the 15th century, however, some B keyboards were enlarged down to F, so that two types of F keyboards may then have been in existence, about a 4th apart in pitch. This difference of pitch, the origin of which could be traced in the medieval practice of transposition, survived for almost two centuries. The most common keyboard compass in the second half of the 15th century and the first half of the 16th century was from F to a'', often without F♯ or G♯. In Italy, upper limits of c''' or even f''' were common. The instruments reaching f''' were perhaps made at a lower pitch standard. The low limit was extended to C, often with short octave, in the second half of the 16th century.

By the 17th century organ keys, like the keys of stringed keyboard instruments, had become fairly standardized at something close to modern key width, although in general they were shorter in length. Many different materials have been used for key covers up to the present time, including ivory, bone, boxwood, ebony and occasionally materials such as rare hardwoods, tortoise-shell and mother-of-pearl, but normally a colour contrast between the natural and sharp keys is observed. Manual keyboard compasses average from 45 to 51 keys in the 17th century to 52 to 58 keys in the 18th and 19th centuries; pedal keyboards varied widely, from as few as 8 notes in Italy to 27 notes in Germany, although the latter compass became fairly standardized in all but the smallest organs by the end of the 19th century. A 61-note manual compass (along with a 32-note pedal compass) was adopted by most builders around the beginning of the 20th century, but many present-day builders use a slightly shorter manual compass of 54 or 56 notes and a 30-note pedal compass. For several centuries organ keyboards have normally begun with a C key, although in 18th- and early 19th-century England and America compasses beginning below C, on G′ (and occasionally F′), were commonly employed. *See also* SHORT OCTAVE.

Keydesk. CONSOLE.

Klaviatur (Ger.). KEYBOARD.

Knee-lever (Fr. *genouillère*; Ger. *Kniehebel*). Any of a variety of devices moving either horizontally or vertically, operated by the knee, and used for the production of expressive effects on a number of different types of keyboard instruments. Knee-levers were often provided on reed organs to permit control of loudness, since the feet were already occupied with the pedal-operated bellows. They are found on pipe organs only in the Iberian peninsula and South America.

Kopf (Ger.; Dutch *kop*). BLOCK.

Koppel (Ger.). COUPLER.

Körper (Ger.). BODY.

Korte oktaaf (Dutch). SHORT OCTAVE.

Kurze Oktave (Ger.). SHORT OCTAVE.

Labial pipe. A flue pipe; *see* FLUE-WORK.

Labium (Eng. and Ger.). LIP.

Lade [Windlade] (Ger.). WIND-CHEST.

Languette (Fr.). REED-TONGUE.

Languid [languet] (Fr. *biseau*; Ger. *Kern, Pfeifenkern*). In a flue pipe, an adjustable metal plate fixed inside the pipe-foot; see Chapter Two, §1, and fig. 17a.

Laye (Fr.). WIND-CHEST; *see also* PAN.

Lengüetería (Sp.). REED-WORK.

Lepel (Dutch). SHALLOT.

Lèvre (Fr.). LIP.

Lingual pipe. A reed pipe. *See* REED-WORK.

APPENDIX THREE

Linguetta (It.). REED-TONGUE.

Lip [labium] (Fr. *lèvre*; Ger. *Labium*). The upper or lower edge of the mouth opening in a flue pipe.

Lumière [saillie] (Fr.). FLUE.

Machine Barker (Fr.). BARKER LEVER.

Machine stop. A device applied to chamber organs, sometimes called a 'shifting movement'. An extra slider cancels out the higher-pitched stops when a pedal is depressed, even though their knobs remain drawn. The machine stop was quite common on English chamber organs from the mid-18th century onwards, and was used in echo passages and in pieces having short soft sections or interludes.

Magazinbalg (Ger.). RESERVOIR.

Mantice [manticeria] (It.). BELLOWS.

Manual. A keyboard played by the hands, in contrast to one played by the feet.

Manual coupler. A device whereby one manual may be linked to (and played from) another; *see* COUPLER.

Manualiter. A quasi-Latin term derived from *manualis* ('hand keyboard') to indicate that a piece of organ music so labelled is played on manuals only, as distinct from *pedaliter*. As a term it may be older than *pedaliter* (Schlick: *Spiegel der Orgelmacher und Organisten*, 1511), but it was chiefly used by German composers (and copyists) in the 17th and 18th centuries to help organists, otherwise accustomed to playing pedals, where the musical notation was ambiguous; for example, where it was written on two staves (as in most organ music except strict trios until the 1730s) or in tablature (as in the sources of Buxtehude's music etc). Scheidt (*Tabulatura nova*, 1624), however, implied that in organ chorales the pedal could be used to bring out the theme whether or not it was specified, much as some organists today play with a pedal cantus firmus the indicated *manualiter* preludes in the third section of Bach's *Clavier-Übung*.

Mécanique (Fr.; Ger. *Mechanik, Mechanismus*; It. *meccanica*). ACTION.

Mechanical action. A key and stop action that is operated by purely mechanical means, without pneumatic or electric assistance; it is often referred to as tracker action.

Medio registro. Divided keyboards found in classical Iberian organs from the 17th century onwards. The upper and lower halves of one keyboard often have different stop-lists; depending on the date and the geographical area, keyboards may be divided between *b* and *c′* or *c′* and *c♯′*. Much music was written for such keyboards by Spanish and Portuguese composers of the Renaissance and Baroque periods.

Melodeon. A term extensively used in the USA during the first half of the 19th century to designate a small reed organ with a single keyboard and one or two sets of reeds. The 'rocking melodeon' (also known as the lap or elbow organ) is an instrument of this type played on the lap or on a table; its bellows are activated by a rocking motion of the elbow or the heel of the hand. (See Chapter Nine.)

Mensur (Ger.). SCALING.

Métaphone. An accessory stop on French reed organs, patented by Charles Mustel in 1878. It mutes the tone of the instrument by partly closing the reed cell apertures with a strip of soft leather. See also Chapter Nine, §2.

Mixture stop. A stop composed of several ranks of pipes at various pitches, most often octaves and 5ths. The term is both generic, referring to compound stops in general, and specific, in that Mixture (*Mixtur, mixtuur, mixtura*) is also the name used in some areas and periods for the chief mixture of the Diapason chorus or *pleno* (*lleno, plein jeu, ripieno*). The history of mixture stops is the history of the organ itself, from the big *pleno* at Winchester (10th century) through the medieval *Blockwerke* and Renaissance Mixtura (Barcelona, 1480), Locatio (Schlick, 1511), Hintersatz, Zimbel and Fourniture to the 19th-century Compensation mixture, Progressio Harmonica etc. The chief Baroque additions to the chorus mixtures are the wider-scaled solo or colour mixtures, often with a Tierce rank included, such as Cornet, Hörnli, Sesquialtera, Terzian and Carillon-mixtur. Some mixtures, such as Rauschpfeife, were chorus stops at one period, solo at another. The term 'mixture' appeared late in England (Father Smith's Temple organ, 1688); James Talbot in his MS of around 1695 (Christ Church, Oxford, Music 1187) used it to include solo mixtures. The contents, planning, voicing and scaling of the various mixture stops distinguish national organ schools and test the skill of both ancient and modern builders more than any solo reed or Principal stop.

Mutation stop. In modern organ usage, mutations are those single-rank stops, usually of wide or fairly wide-scaled pipes with a high lead content, pitched at the 5th, 3rd, 7th, 9th etc of an upper octave; hence their other names: 'overtone stops', *Aliquotstimmen* etc. Common examples are the Nasard, Larigot and Tierce; sometimes the stop has two ranks (e.g. Terzian), in which case it really belongs to the mixtures; sometimes the stop is scaled, voiced and constructed of a metal suitable for a Principal rank (e.g. Twelfth), in which case it is not a Flute mutation. Historically, the picture is not simple. *Mutationen* could mean any stops, a synonym for *Stimmen* (J. B. Samber: *Continuatio ad manuductionem organicam*, 1707); in late medieval contracts, *mutaciones* denoted much the same as *jeux* or *jochs*, i.e. registrations or, simply, different sounds (Minorites' church, Barcelona, 1480); in classical French usage, mutation stops include any rank (such as 2' flutes or even solo reeds) which are of wide scale or drawn outside the *plein jeu* chorus (Paris, 1647). The term does not refer to the 'changing' of the fundamental tone to an overtone, as often stated in English sources, but to the varieties of tone or *mutaciones* such stops afford.

APPENDIX THREE

Nicking (Ger. *Kernstiche*; It. *denti*). Small indentations made in the languid edge by the voicer to control excessive chiff or undesirable sizzling.

Noce (It.). BLOCK.

Normal Mensur (Ger.). A system of SCALING.

Note-channels. *See* CHANNELS.

Noyau (Fr.). BLOCK.

Nuss (Ger.). BLOCK.

Oberwerk (Ger.: 'upper department'). The upper chest and manual of a German organ, often (since around 1840) provided with Swell shutters, able by its position to take larger pipes than the *Brustwerk* and other minor chests of a *Werkprinzip* organ. In many sources (e.g. the autograph registrations in Bach's Concerto BWV596) *Oberwerk* denotes *Hauptwerk*, i.e. the main chest above the player, as opposed to the Chair organ.

Praetorius (*Syntagma musicum*, ii, 2/1619) used other phrases such as 'Oben in der Brust' or 'oberste Positiff' if he wished to refer to the *Oberwerk*. Schlick (1511) disparagingly mentioned small subsidiary chests placed within the main case, but the *Oberwerk* found on such organs as that at Kampen (1523) was a major department. That called *boven int werck* at Amsterdam Oude Kerk in 1543 had two chests and took all the colour stops away from the *Hauptwerk*, which was thereby kept to a size convenient for builder and bellows-blower. Such a department was very useful when it had its own keyboard and became highly developed, those in the big four-manual organs of Schnitger (*c*1690) still full of flutes, full-length reeds and other colours giving variety. The *Unterwerke, Seitenwerke, Echowerke* and *Kronwerke* ('under, side, echo, crowning departments') found in later Baroque and Romantic organs are of much less musical significance.

Octave courte (Fr.). SHORT OCTAVE.

Orage [jeu d'orage] (Fr.). A pedal on French organs of the Romantic period built by Cavaillé-Coll and others from around 1856 onwards. It played several of the lowest pedal pipes at once, producing an effect like thunder.

Orchestrion. (1) The name given by Georg Joseph Vogler to a large and, for its time, somewhat revolutionary organ with which he toured England and the Continent in 1789 and 1790. The organ, embodying the principles of his simplification system, had four manuals, pedals and 63 stops, all fitted into a case 9' square. Many of the stops in this organ were free reeds, and these were under variable wind pressure. This, combined with the fact that the entire instrument was enclosed in a swell-box, gave the organ an unusually wide range of expression, possibly its most notable feature.

(2) A term, originally of German origin, widely used in the 19th and 20th centuries to denote a complex mechanical instrument played by pinned barrels or perforated cards or paper rolls. Orchestrions are differentiated from the related street and fairground organs by the fact that they were intended only

315

for indoor use, and for the performance of classical music and dances from the orchestral repertory. They were thus more sophisticated in their voicing, capabilities and design than their outdoor counterparts, and required lower wind pressures. See also Chapter Eight.

Organetti morti. The small, non-speaking decorative pipes often found in the upper part of a classical Italian organ case.

Organetto (It.). (1) A term for a small organ, notably the 14th- and 15th-century instrument generally known as the portative (see Chapter Three, §7).

(2) A term occasionally applied to a street organ or a street piano. An *organetto a manovella* (It.) is a barrel organ.

Organina. A name applied to various types of automatic reed organ. In the late 19th century it was adopted as a trade name for related instruments by the Massachusetts Organ Co. and the Automatic Organ Co. of Boston. The French maker Jérôme Thibouville, best known for his brass and woodwind instruments, used the name for a small automatic reed organ he made in 1905.

Organino (It.). A term for a small organ, notably the 14th and 15th-century instrument generally known as the portative.

Organochordium [organochordon]. A type of claviorgan built in 1782–9 by the Danish organ builder Kirschnigk and developed by Georg Joseph Vogler, with Rackwitz of Stockholm. (See also Chapter Eight.)

Organophone. A harmonium invented by Debain, in which the reeds or vibrators were raised within instead of being beneath the channels.

Organo-piano. A combination of a piano and an *orgue expressif* with two manuals, built by Achille Müller and shown at the Paris Exposition of 1834, where it was awarded the bronze medal.

Organo pleno [pieno] (It.: 'full organ'; Fr. *plein jeu*; Ger. *volles Werk*; It. *ripieno*). A term for an organ registration using the major choruses of the instrument. It has rarely, if ever, denoted that the composer has required the organist to draw every stop; since around 1850 most composers other than French ones have left it to the organist's discretion and the organ-bellows' capacity.

Before that, both the term itself and the registration it indicated varied according to period and area. The 15th-century *Blockwerk* was itself the *plenum* of larger organs, from Spain to the Baltic, from Italy to the North Sea; if it were referred to in a document such as a contract, it would be called 'Principal'. When or where this Diapason chorus was separated into several single or multiple ranks, a term such as *grand jeu* would indicate the total or full organ (St Michel, Bordeaux, 1510), perhaps without flutes, like the 'compimento de l'organo' at S Martino, Bologna (1556).

Plenum and the German terms *volles Werk* and *zumgantzen Werck* are chiefly 17th-century terms, referring to the Diapason chorus codified in many 16th-century sources; the last phrase, however, often means that a stop runs 'through the whole compass', not that it joins 'the total chorus'. In Italy *ripieno* was based on single ranks excluding Flutes (Antegnati, 1608), but later examples are known to have included a Tierce rank (Trent Cathedral, 1687), as sometimes happened with the *plein jeu* in France (*c*1620). In Spain, *plé* (16th century) indicated the chorus in general, *lleno* (17th century) the main Mixture.

From *das Werck* at Hagenau in 1491, which was the total chorus Mixture excluding Diapason and Zimbel, to Mattheson's treatises of 1721, the German organ progressed towards heavier and thicker *plena*, including all stops except reeds, and used not so much for particular colour, like the French *grands* and *pleins jeux*, as for massive effects in preludes, toccatas etc. Some writers, like Praetorius and Werckmeister, insisted that 'families' of stops should not be mixed. It is unlikely that J. S. Bach had a specific combination in mind when he asked for *organum plenum*, whether in 1715 or 1745; however, a contemporary organ builder, Gottfried Silbermann, directed organists to use the manual coupler but no manual reeds or Tierces in the *plenum* (Fraureuth, 1739).

Organo tedesco (It.). Barrel organ; see Chapter Eight, §3.

Organum hydraulicum (Lat.). Water organ; see Chapter Eight, §1.

Orgelbewegung (Ger.). A term sometimes used to refer to the organ revival of the early 20th century; see Chapter Six.

Orgelklavier (Ger.). Claviorgan; see Chapter Eight, §2.

Orgue à manivelle [de Barbarie] (Fr.). Barrel organ; see Chapter Eight, §3.

Orgue de chambre [orgue de salon] (Fr.). Chamber organ; see Chapter Four, §10.

Orgue de choeur (Fr.). CHOIR ORGAN.

Orgue expressif (Fr.; Ger. *Expressionsorgel*). An organ containing free-reed pipes with resonators, a precursor of the reed organ. It was exhibited in Paris by Gabriel-Joseph Grenié in 1810. Its double bellows and reservoir system permitted dynamic variation through control of wind pressure by the player's feet on blowing treadles (see Chapter Nine). The term 'orgue expressif' was later applied to any French harmonium having this kind of expression capability.

Orgue hydraulique (Fr.). Water organ; see Chapter Eight, §1.

Orguinette. Trade name of a small automatic reed organ made by the Mechanical Orguinette Co. of New York (founded in 1878 and later absorbed by the Aeolian Co.).

Pallet [ventil] (Fr. *palette*, *soupape*; Ger. *Spielventil*; It. *ventilabro*). In the windchest of an organ, the valve which, when brought into play by pulling or pushing away from the mortise it otherwise closes, admits wind to the channel or groove of a particular key and hence, if the stop mechanism allows it, to the foot-hole of the pipe(s) of that stop. James Talbot (MS, Christ Church, Oxford, Music 1187, *c*1695), probably influenced by French sources, used the word (usually spelt 'palat') to mean any of the several kinds of valve found in an organ (bellows pallet, key pallet etc).

ORGAN

Pallet box (Ger. *Windkammer*). The substructure of the wind-chest, in which the row of pallets, one for each key in the compass, is housed.

Pan (Fr. *laye*). The upper part of the wind-chest of a reed organ, containing the reed cells and pallet holes.

Pancone [bancone, somiere] (It.). WIND-CHEST.

Pandereta (Sp.). RACK-BOARD.

Panharmonicon. A mechanical instrument, essentially a glorified barrel organ. It was invented by Johann Nepomuk Maelzel and first exhibited by him in Vienna in 1804. The instrument was designed to play orchestral music, and various accounts describe it as capable of imitating the sounds of the french horn, clarinet, trumpet, oboe, bassoon, German flute, flageolet, drum, cymbal and triangle. The sounds were actually produced by various flue, reed and free-reed organ pipes, as well as air-driven percussion devices. See also Chapter Eight.

Pavillon (Fr.). RESONATOR.

Pedal (Fr. *pédale*; Ger. *Pedal*; It. *pedale*). Any of several types of lever, operated by the foot and used for a variety of purposes:

(1) To operate the bellows of a chamber organ or reed organ.

(2) To alter the volume on both pipe and electronic organs (Swell pedals).

(3) The term is used most widely for a series of pedals forming a keyboard played by the feet rather than by the hands.

(4) Levers operating accessory devices such as couplers, tremulants, 'toy' stops etc, or to change stops (composition pedals).

The term 'pedal' is a direct equivalent of certain Latin phrases (for example, the keys 'pro tastandi cum pedibus' at S Maria Novella, Florence, 1379), although early vernacular usages are not at all clear (for example, the *pedalen* at Delft in 1483); the word does not seem to occur in England before about 1525. Like 'organum' itself, *pes* (*pedes*) is a word belonging as much to medieval music as to medieval instruments.

Pedal-board (Fr. *pédalier*; Ger. *Pedalklavier*). The keyboard played by the feet and connected either to its own pipes or to those of the manual(s). There are many types: short sticks protruding from the lower case-front either as simple strips of wood (Halberstadt, *c*1361) or as proto-keys (Norrlanda, *c*1370); small rectangular frames with short straight keys (16th-century Flanders and Italy); the same with longer keys but still for toe-pedalling (16th-century Netherlands and Germany); round studs into which the toe or ball of the foot presses (Iberian organs, 17th–18th centuries); flat, shallow, rectangular boxes through the upper board of which pass short separated pedal keys (France and Belgium, 18th century). What form some pedals took is now uncertain (France in the 17th century, early English pull-downs of the 18th). Some firms (e.g. Walcker, *c*1830) have made double pedal-boards, the upper or shorter keys placed on a slope of about 45°. The concave, radiating 'Willis Pedal Clavier' of the late 19th century has never been popular outside Britain and the USA.

Pedal coupler. A mechanical device which permits any or all of the manual divisions to be played from the pedal keys.

Pédale de combinaison (Fr.). COMBINATION ACTION.

Pedaliter. A quasi-Latin term derived from *pedalis* (a part 'for the feet') to indicate that a piece of organ music so labelled is played by both hands and feet. The word appears to have arisen as an antithesis to *manualiter* and was so used by Schlick (1511). Although it does not indicate a piece played by pedals alone, it does in practice imply one with a developed pedal part. Sometimes composers used it to suggest a large-scale work in several 'voices' (e.g. Scheidt's '*Benedicamus* à 6 voc. pleno organo pedaliter', 1624). However, in the third section of his *Clavier-Übung* Bach seems to have contrasted *manualiter* with a phrase such as 'canto fermo in basso'; but *pedaliter* itself also appeared in music from his circle, chiefly outside the context of organ chorales and pedal melodies, as for example in the autograph MS of BWV535a, and in Buxtehude's C major Praeludium in the 'Andreas Bach' Book.

Pedal keys. Key levers operated by the feet. The early history of the pedal suggests that key levers for the feet could serve many musical purposes. Despite traditional stories, there seems to be no reason to think them a German invention. The protruding sticks for the feet at Halberstadt Cathedral (*c*1361) played a type of large *Blockwerk* while the little positive organ at Norrlanda, Sweden (*c*1370), had them to play the bass pipes. Many 15th-century organs (e.g. those at Troyes, Haarlem, 's-Hertogenbosch and Utrecht) had a group of large open Bourdon pipes (usually ten) placed on a separate chest on the wall to the side of the organ supported by a pendentive or *trompe* (hence their name, *trompes*) and played in most instances by pedal keys which probably worked by admitting wind along conduits running to the pipes. The Ileborgh Tablature of 1448 (ed. in CEKM, i) refers to 'pedale seu manuale'; and the Buxheim Organbook of about 1470 (ed. in DM, 2nd ser., i) to playing the 'tenore inferius in pedali', probably at written pitch. From 1450 to 1550 pedals were of several types: pull-downs to manual keys or pallets with or without a rank or more of chorus or solo pipes (8' Trumpet and 2' Flute were common in the Netherlands by about 1540); pedal-boards playing transmitted stops from a manual; or a pedal organ with independent stops, often including reeds. The compass was ideally up to *c'* and down to the lowest note of the main manual (*F* to *c'* according to Schlick, 1511). By 1600 pedals in some areas had immense versatility, for example, the 26 stops on four chests at Grüningen Schlosskirche.

During the 17th century instruments like those at Grüningen and in the big Hanseatic town churches encouraged the development of alternate right-left toe-pedalling (as evidenced in the works of Heinrich Scheidemann and others), and the writing of both bass and solo lines for the pedal. Praetorius (*Syntagma musicum*, ii, 2/1619) noted that pedals were rare in England and Italy; but composers in northern France, the Netherlands and Germany developed the idea of pedals taking cantus firmus or solo lines, generally *en taille*, that is, with accompaniment above and below. Moreover many of Schlick's recommendations of 1511 are still valid: the pedal should have separate stops, a compass to *c'*, a tolerable length of key (*c*30 cm for naturals and 6 cm for sharps), a bench high enough to allow quick passage-work and keys narrower than the space between them to make two- and even four-part playing easy.

While the 17th and 18th centuries saw variety in the shape, size and playing technique of the pedal-board, nothing new could be added to the musical use of the department. French organists continued to emphasize *en taille* textures; Italian organists kept pedals for 'organ points'; in England pull-downs were rare from 1600 to 1790; and in the Iberian peninsula pedals were largely reserved for pedal points in certain tonalities (C, D, E and F).

In the fully-fledged *Werkprinzip* organ of Hamburg (*c*1690), the pedal was very important and versatile, both aurally and visually; ideally it sounded an octave below the *Hauptwerk* Prinzipal, itself an octave below the *Rückpositiv*. 'German' pedals, that is, straight pedal-boards with independent stops and a compass of *C* to *c'*, became the norm from about 1820 in northern Europe, not least because J. S. Bach's organ works were then becoming increasingly available. On the grounds that organists' hands needed more than one keyboard for quick changes of sound, E. F. Walcker and others sometimes made double pedal-boards, more admired by such theorists as Töpfer (*Lehrbuch der Orgelbaukunst*, 1855) than by players. Composers continued to exploit the traditional alternate-toe technique even in chromatic music, long after such travelling virtuosos as J. G. Vogler had introduced toe-and-heel pedalling.

Pedal organ. Strictly the chest, towers, chamber etc given to the pipes of the pedal department, as distinct from the pedal keys or pedal-board which play them or which, in instruments without a Pedal organ, play the stops of the manual(s). Since the late 14th century the largest organs had some kind of Pedal organ though this may not have included the largest pipes or have been more than an extension of the manual, itself playing a *Blockwerk*. By 1600 in central Germany, the Pedal organ often contained three distinct chests, themselves often divided, and including as well as the biggest bass pipes some of the highest flute and reed solo stops. The preponderance and eventual monopoly of bass stops in the 18th- and 19th-century Pedal organ meant that the department became less versatile than it had traditionally been.

Percussion. (1) A term for any stop in a pipe organ that activates a striking mechanism. Percussion stops are most commonly found in cinema organs, although bell or chime stops (Carillon, Glockenspiel) were not uncommon in the Renaissance and Baroque periods.

(2) A device found in some French reed organs that modifies the sound by causing the reed tongues to be struck by small hammers.

Pfeife (Ger.). PIPE.

Pfeifenbank (Ger.). RACK-BOARD.

Pfeifenfuss (Ger.). The FOOT of a flue pipe.

APPENDIX THREE

Pfeifenkern (Ger.). Languid.

Pfeifenstock (Ger.). Toe-board.

Pied (Fr.). Foot. *See also* Boot.

Pierement. A term used since about 1912 in the Low Countries to designate the street organs with Book playing mechanisms that were common to that area. The origin of the word is unknown. See Chapter Eight, §4.

Pilote (Fr.). (1) Sticker.
 (2) In reed organs, a part of the key action.

Pipe (Dutch *pijpe*; Fr. *tuyau*; Ger. *Pfeife*; It. *canna*; Sp. *caño*). Generic term for a tube, open or stopped, of wood, metal, or other material. Organ pipes are of wood or metal and have two basic constructions: flue pipes, which produce their sound in the same manner as a recorder or tin whistle; and reed pipes, which produce their sound in a manner similar to a clarinet or oboe. They range in size from 64 ft. to less than an inch in speaking length. Flue pipes fall into three general categories, according to their scale and tone colour: Principal, flute, and string. Reed pipes are usually divided into two categories: full-length and fractional-length (regals). *See* Flue-work and Reed-work, and Appendix Two.

Piston (Ger. *Druckknopf*, *Druckschalter*). A button placed above or below the manuals or above the pedal-board, controlling pre-set combinations of stops. The mechanism facilitates rapid changes in registration.

Pitman chest. A type of individual note-valve electro-pneumatic wind-chest developed by Ernest M. Skinner early in the 20th century and still used by some American builders.

Plein jeu (Fr.: 'full registration'). Possibly a corruption of *plain jeu*, 'integrated registration'. While modern composers often use the phrase loosely to denote 'full organ' at the player's discretion, *plein jeu* has two particular meanings in the history of the organ. The phrase itself seems to have arisen some time in the 16th century to describe the combination of stops that gave the same Principal chorus as the old undivided, stop-less *Blockwerk*, i.e. Principals 16', 8', 4' (etc), Fourniture and Cymbale, perhaps with Bourdons. At Notre Dame, Alençon (1537–40), the term *principal du corps* is still used, corresponding to the Dutch, German and probably English term 'principal', i.e. not a single rank but the Diapason chorus as a whole. At Chartres in 1542, the contract refers to the *plain jeu* as an even bigger Diapason chorus, complete with the eight 32' pedal pipes and the doubled and tripled ranks at 8' and 4' pitch. For Mersenne (*Harmonie universelle*, 1636–7), *plain jeu* included a Tierce but not the highest Cymbale mixture. The second purpose of the term was to denote one of two distinct choruses in the great corpus of Classical French organ music from 1670 to 1770, namely the Diapason chorus or *plein jeu* as distinct from the Flute, Cornet, mutation and reed combination of *grand jeu*. Like the other regular and systematic registrations of the Classical French organ, the *plein jeu* became associated with (*a*) particular interludes in the Mass

321

(*plein jeu* for the opening Kyrie, *grand jeu* for the closing etc), and (*b*) a particular musical style, usually sustained, with constant and slowly resolving suspensions, in four or five parts, massive in texture rather than strictly contrapuntal. (*See also* ORGANO PLENO.)

Pneumatic. (1) A small round or wedge-shaped leathered pouch that acts either as a valve (to open a pipe-hole) or as a motor (to operate a stop action, player action, etc).

   (2) The term can also refer to anything operated by or conveying air under pressure.

Pneumatic-lever action. A device to lighten key action; *See* BARKER LEVER.

Pnigeus. In a hydraulis, the hemispherical chamber containing and surrounded by water through which air is forced. (See Chapter One, §2(i), Chapter Three, §1, and fig. 3*a*.)

Poïkilorgue (Fr.). A portable free-reed keyboard instrument, a precursor of the French harmonium. It was invented in Toulouse about 1830 by Aristide Cavaillé-Coll; see Chapter Nine, §1.

Pompe (Fr.). FEEDER. The French term applies to both pipe and reed organs.

Portavento [condotto] (It.). CONVEYANCE.

Porte-vent [transmission] (Fr.). CONVEYANCE; WIND-TRUNK.

Positif de dos (Fr.). CHAIR ORGAN.

Positivo tergale (It.). CHAIR ORGAN.

Pression [pression du vent] (Fr.). WIND-PRESSURE.

Prolongement (Fr.). An accessory stop on French reed organs that allowed selected notes to be held; see Chapter Nine, §2.

Pull-down (Ger. *Zugrute*). The portion of a tracker action system which passes through the bottom of the pallet box via a bushed hole or leather purse and is attached directly to the pallet.

Purse (Fr. *boursette*; Ger. *Pulpete*). A flexible leather pouch in the bottom of the pallet box, tied around the pull-down wire or dowel to prevent wind leakage.

Push coupler. A term for SHOVE COUPLER.

Quint. An organ pipe that is sometimes used to produce, when sounded with another pipe tuned at the 5th below, a difference tone imitating – economically though not elegantly – the sound of a pipe an octave below the lower one. See also Appendix Two, 'Quint'.

Rack-board (Ger. *Pfeifenbank, Rasterbrett*; It. *crivello*; Sp. *pandereta*). A perforated wooden rack that stands on rack-pins above the toe-board, to hold the pipes in place. In most organs it comes just below the pipe-mouths, but in older Italian and Spanish organs it is often located above the pipe-mouths, and is usually made of stiff leather instead of wood.

Radiating pedal-board. A pedal-board with keys in a radiating (rather than straight) pattern, thought to be more convenient for the player. First devised in the 1850s by Henry Willis and S. S. Wesley, it became the virtual standard in England and North America by the beginning of the 20th century, having by then acquired a concave shape, but it has never been fully accepted on the Continent.

Rank. In modern organ terminology, a complete set or row of pipes, usually of the same type, controlled by one stop-knob. Many kinds of stop have more than one rank, notably the compound or Mixture stop, but so have some non-compound stops, such as the several undulating Piffaro or Celeste stops of the 18th and 19th centuries, or the Principal/Diapason stops frequently doubled in the treble during the 15th–17th centuries. In English sources, the term 'ranks' was usually applied to the rows or pipes in a compound stop such as Sesquialtera or Cornet (e.g. the Talbot MS, Christ Church, Oxford, Music 1187, c1695; E. J. Hopkins, in Hopkins and Rimbault: *The Organ*, 1855). 'Stoppes or setts of pipes' (York Minster, 1632) and similar phrases were more usual for 'ranks' in a general sense.

Rasette (Fr.). REED WIRE.

Rasterbrett (Ger.). RACK-BOARD.

Ravalement (Fr.). The enlargement of the keyboard towards the bass; see SHORT OCTAVE.

Récit (Fr.). In the French classical organ, a short-compass division usually played from the top manual and containing solo stops (reeds, cornet mixture). In the 19th century this division was expanded and enclosed to become the *récit expressif*, or Swell.

Reed pipe (Fr. *anche, tuyau à anche*; Ger. *Zungenpfeife, Zungenstimme*; It. *ancia, canna ad ancia*). An organ pipe in which the sound is produced by a vibrating metal tongue modified by a resonator, as distinct from a flue pipe.

Reed puller. A tool with a hooked end, used to remove reeds from reed organs for cleaning or tuning.

Reed-tongue (Fr. *languette*; Ger. *Zunge*; It. *linguetta*). The thin strip of metal (usually half-hard or soft brass) which in beating-reed pipes vibrates against the shallot when the pipe is blown. In free reed instruments it vibrates back and forth through a narrow aperture when blown. Both beating and free reed-tongues are given a curvature, by the voicer, that determines some of their tonal character and such characteristics as quickness of speech.

Reed wire [tuning spring, tuning wire] (Fr. *rasette*; Ger. *Stimmkrücke*; It. *gruccia*). The wire that projects upwards from the boot of a reed pipe. The lower part of it presses the tongue against the shallot, and tuning is accomplished by raising or lowering it. (See fig. 19.)

Reed-work (Dutch *tongwerk*; Fr. *anches, jeux d'anches*; Ger. *Rohrstimmen, Zungenstimmen*; It. *canne ad ancia, registri ad ancia*; Sp. *lengüetería*). The reed stops of an organ collectively (as distinct from flue-work), i.e. those in which sound is produced in each pipe by the wind exciting an elastic metal blade or tongue. The small metal tube cut away longitudinally against which the tongue 'beats' is properly called the reed. Reed-work refers to the Trumpet family of flaring pipes, the Krummhorn family of cylindrical pipes, others of short, fanciful, stopped and half-stopped pipes and all varieties of metal and wooden stops other than those of the flue-work. The term also encompasses the many types of regal and 'free reed' or harmonium stops (see Chapter Two, §3).

In England the term 'reed' seems to have been systematically used first by James Talbot (MS treatise, Christ Church, Oxford, Music 1187, c1695), sometimes in the phrase 'regals or reed' but referring to all reed stops known by him. Occasionally 'reed pipe' (*ryetpijpen*) was used in the Netherlands (Michaelskerk, Zwolle, 1505) and hence, probably, in England; certainly 'rede' was used in a sense of 'reed instrument' by Chaucer (*House of Fame*, 1380) and John Gower (*Confessio amantis*, c1390). It is older than the term 'flue stop' by about two centuries. Burney (*The Present State of Music in Germany, the Netherlands and the United Provinces*, 1773) used the phrase 'reed-work' of the organ in Ulm Cathedral.

Regals. In large organs regal ranks served to give varieties of tone-colour, especially in the manual and pedal *Brustwerk* departments. The latter were in many instances before about 1650 nothing more than a kind of regal instrument incorporated in a church organ. To James Talbot (MS, Christ Church, Oxford, Music 1187, c1695) the name 'regals' was puzzling. He applied it both to full-length reed stops in general and to a little 4' Vox humana stop, but not to a self-contained keyboard instrument. (See Chapter Four, §5.)

Regeerwerk (Dutch). ACTION.

Register. (1) The slider in a slider-chest.

(2) An organ STOP.

(3) The term may also refer to an area of pitch within a stop (i.e., upper, middle, or lower register).

Registerkanzellenlade (Ger.). VENTIL-CHEST.

Registre (Fr.). SLIDER; STOP.

Reproducing organ. A type of self-playing organ, perfected in the early 20th century, that automatically plays music recorded by means of a perforated paper roll. As well as the notes, it reproduces all actions (swell operation, stop changes etc) of the player who made the roll.

Reservoir (Ger. *Magazinbalg*). A bellows-like receiver for wind generated by feeders or a blower. Wind pressure in the reservoir is regulated by springs or weights on the top.

Resonator (Dutch *beker*; Fr. *pavillon*; Ger. *Becher, Resonanzkörper*). The upper body of a reed pipe, the shape and length of which largely determine the timbre of the stop. Resonators may be conical (Trumpet, Oboe), cylindrical (Clarinet, Bassoon) or complex in shape (various regal stops), and may be of varying lengths from double (harmonic) to fractional.

Reversible. A pedal or toe-piston that can put on and take off either a combination of stops (*sforzando*) or a coupler.

Riduzione (It.). ROLLERBOARD.

Ripieno (It.). A term for the principal stops of all pitches in an Italian organ. *See also* ORGANO PLENO.

Rohr (Ger.). CHIMNEY.

Rohrstimmen [Rohrwerk] (Ger.). REED-WORK.

Rollbart [Rollerbart] (Ger.). A type of BEARD.

Rollerboard (Fr. *abrégé, table d'abrégé*; Ger. *Wellenbrett*; It. *catenacciatura, riduzione, tavola della catenacciatura*). The part of a tracker action that transfers motion sideways, usually from the key scale to the wider, chest scale.

Roller organ. A name often applied to a small, self-playing reed organ. Many of these were manufactured in the late 19th and early 20th centuries in the USA and Germany under such names as Ariston, Manopan and Orguinette. They were operated by a hand crank which worked the bellows and fed a card or paper roll through the player mechanism. The repertory of such instruments consisted generally of hymns and popular songs. Some early roller organs played from small pinned barrels (see fig. 63).

Rollschweller (Ger.). A type of CRESCENDO PEDAL.

Rückpositiv (Ger.: 'back positive'). The little organ placed at the organist's back, in the front of the gallery; the second main manual of all major organs from 1400 to 1700. In the smaller organs of most countries it was replaced by the *Brustwerk*, the Choir organ or the Swell, while in Italy there was only ever a handful of examples. The name has varied widely: Chair organ, le Positif, Cadireta, Rugwerk since about 1600; earlier terms include *organum parvum* (Rouen Cathedral, 1387), *positivum tergale* (Arnaut de Zwolle, MS, Bibliothèque Nationale, Paris, lat. 7295, *c*1450), *clavier met positieff* (Oude Kerk, Delft, 1455–61), *orgue a la cadira* (St Mathieu, Perpignan, 1516), *positiff zu rück* (Schlick: *Spiegel der Orgelmacher*, 1511) and *achter den rug* (Oude Kerk, Amsterdam, 1539–42). It is by no means certain when any so-called 'little organ' was a *Rückpositiv* and when it was simply a small organ in another part of the church concerned. *Den stoel* or *im Stuhl* was very common, though this too may not always have denoted *Rückpositiv*, since *im Stuhl* could mean 'in the foot of the main case'. Such writers as Praetorius and builders as Schnitger used the term *Rückpositiff*, but in areas where it was unfamiliar more prolix phrases were invented: 'unum parvum organum retro magistri ipsorum tangentis' (St Sauveur, Aix-en-Provence, 1489; Barcelona Cathedral, 1459–63) or 'un organetto da concerti dietro le spalle dell'Organista' (Banchieri: *Conclusioni del suono dell'organo*, 1609). Tonally, the department was always a contrast to the *Hauptwerk*, firstly by having the Mixture of its *Blockwerk* the sooner separated off (Oude Kerk, Delft, 1458), then by having more single ranks on a slider chest, later still by having more delicate voicing and scaling (Werckmeister: *Erweiterte und verbesserte Orgel-Probe*, 2/1698); but the last characteristic had long been known, judging by Arnaut's reference to its 'sweetness' (*dulcedo*). In some areas of the Netherlands and Denmark it continued to be built until the 1870s, but early in the 18th century central German builders dispensed with it, giving its solo, accompanimental, continuo, colouristic and contrasting functions to the *Oberwerk*. It is still the most important secondary manual for all classical organ repertories.

Run (Ger. *Durchstecher*). A condition in a wind-chest, often caused by excessive dryness, in which glued, shimmed, or gasketed parts have separated sufficiently to allow wind to 'run' from a note being played to one not being played.

Saillie (Fr.). FLUE. The term may also denote the COUNTERFACE.

Scaling (Fr. *diapason*; Ger. *Mensur*). The relationship between the diameter of a pipe and its length. Wide-scaled pipes produce a stronger fundamental; narrow-scaled pipes have a higher harmonic development, at the expense of fundamental. In the early 19th century the theoretician J. G. Töpfer attempted to set a standard for the scaling of principal pipes which he called *Normal Mensur*. This is still used by many builders as a yardstick, although many present-day builders (and, indeed, most of the pre-19th-century builders) use principal scales varying significantly from it. An important element in pipe scaling is the halving ratio. Principal-tone pipes do not halve their diameter at the octave (the 12th pipe) but, more usually, on the 17th pipe, although variable halving ratios are often used. Flute-tone pipes usually halve at an even slower rate, often halving their diameter on the 22nd pipe. In Renaissance and Baroque instruments it is not unusual to find all of the principal ranks, regardless of pitch, to be of the same scale (i.e. all notes of the same pitch will be of the same diameter). In the 19th century many builders made their 8′ principals to a larger scale than those of higher pitch, and many present-day builders also vary scales somewhat in their principal choruses. The size of the building, and the size of the organ itself, are factors in the general scaling pattern.

Schiebekoppel (Ger.). SHOVE COUPLER.

Schleife (Ger.). SLIDER.

Schleifendichtung (Ger.). SLIDER SEAL.

Schleiflade (Ger.). SLIDER-CHEST.

Schöpfbalg (Ger.). FEEDER.

Schweller (Ger.). Swell. A *Schwellkasten* is a swell box; a *Jalousieschweller* a Venetian Swell; and *Schwellwerk* a swell organ.

Schwimmer [Schwimmer-Balg]. A type of wind regulator found in some modern organs. Used primarily to conserve space in small instruments, it consists of a diaphragm and a spring-loaded plate, usually affixed to the bottom of the pallet box. It should not be confused with the concussion bellows, which is simply a shock absorber.

Secreto (Sp.). WIND-CHEST. The term may also denote the GRID.

APPENDIX THREE

Seitenbärte (Ger.). EARS.

Septave. A rare term, occasionally used by organ builders to denote seven diatonic notes of an octave counted upwards from but excluding the tonic. It probably arose at the end of the 19th century as a practical term (perhaps devised by musically illiterate craftsmen) to denote the seven keys on the keyboard itself; it may well derive from English usage, but has no theoretical sanction, nor is it found in even the most practical books on the organ.

Seraphine. A small free-reed keyboard instrument. It was made by John Green of London about 1830. The name was later used in the USA and England to refer to any small reed organ. See Chapter Nine, §1.

Shaking stop. An early English term for the TREMULANT.

Shallot (Dutch *keel, lepel*; Fr. *canal*; Ger. *Kehle*; It. *canaletto*). In reed pipes, a tube with one flattened side and an aperture, against which the reed tongue vibrates. It may be of metal (usually brass) or, in large pipes, of wood, and is fitted into the block.

Shifting movement. *See* MACHINE STOP.

Short octave (Dutch *korte oktaaf*; Fr. *octave courte*; Ger. *kurze Oktave*). A term to denote the tuning of some of the lowest notes of keyboard instruments to pitches below their apparent ones, a practice employed from the 16th century to the early 19th to extend the keyboard compass downwards without increasing the overall dimensions of the instrument.

The short octave was not described in theoretical writings before the 1550s; the alleged description of it in Ramos's *Musica practica* (1482) results from a misinterpretation. However, the system originated earlier in stringed keyboard instruments. It was basically a variable tuning adapted to the requirements of individual pieces, comparable to the scordatura of string instruments. It was first applied to keyboards showing *F* as the lowest key; the *F♯* and *G♯* keys, if present, were tuned to sound lower notes, usually *C, D* or *E*. By the middle of the 16th century, an apparent *E* was added as the lowest key, but it was often tuned to a lower pitch. This soon resulted in the standard tuning known today as the '*C/E* short octave', but keyboard music sometimes called for other tunings, including some chromatic notes. The system was applied to the organ only at the end of the 16th century, since retunings were impractical and the pedal often provided the required low notes. At the beginning of the 17th century, some composers applied scordatura to the chromatic keyboard beginning with *C*, the *C♯* key being retuned to *A'*. This led to the standard '*G'/B'* short octave'.

The short octave developed because the bass part of the keyboard repertory was usually diatonic. From the 17th century onwards, however, composers often demanded a chromatic compass and so keyboards were enlarged, a process known as *ravalement* (literally 'enlargement towards the bass'); or else the two lowest upper keys were split into two parts, the front tuned to the short octave note, and the back to its proper note, a system known as broken octave.

Shove coupler [push coupler] (Ger. *Schiebekoppel*). A type of manual coupler found in many old European organs; it usually serves to couple the lowest manual to the one above. When the lower keyboard is pushed in a short distance it can be played by the keyboard above. *See also* COUPLER.

Simplification system. A method of constructing organ-chests whereby pipes are placed chromatically as near as possible to their notes on the keyboard and the number of pipes is reduced by applying the principle of difference and addition tones. The system is associated with Georg Joseph Vogler (1749–1814), who travelled through Europe 'simplifying' organs in Salzburg, Munich, Berlin and elsewhere by replacing their bulky reeds with free reeds and their costly Mixtures and 32' stops with low Mutations. Most ranks were halved. None of these ideas was new, of course, but Vogler's personal magnetism, though smacking of charlatanry to the enlightened, was effective. Both the contemporary interest in the theory of overtones etc (which noted that $16' + 10\frac{2}{3}'$ ranks gave a soft 32' tone), and the popular need for economy in organs helped his schemes, but his influence on the new big firms of central Europe – Walcker, Moser, Sauer – should not be overestimated.

Sixteen foot. A term used in reference to organ stops, and by extension also to other instruments, to indicate that they are pitched an octave below the Eight foot, or 'normal', pitch now based on $c' = 256$ Hz. At Delft Oude Kerk in 1458, the *16 voeten Blockwerk* ran from F, not C, so the pitch must either have been about a 4th below $c' = 256$ Hz or the *voet* shorter than $1' = 0\cdot3048$ m. Either way, a Great organ of Sixteen foot, i.e. based on an open Diapason of 16' or sub-octave tone, became the ideal in the newly developing church organ, even when the Pedal had its own department.

Sleeplade (Dutch). SLIDER-CHEST.

Slider (Fr. *registre*; Ger. *Schleife*; It. *stecca*, *stecca scorrevole*). In the wind-chest of an organ, the perforated strip of wood placed between one hole admitting wind from the channel below and a second under the foot-hole of the pipe(s) above; when pulled or pushed from the stop-knobs at the console the slider admits wind to that foot-hole when a pallet is opened. The vast majority of all organs built between 1500 and 1850 had slider-chests, at first for the Chair organ only, since multiple or spring-chests were thought preferable for the bigger departments; it has since been revived as the system truest to the perfected classical organ. The term itself has an uncertain history: 'register' is used in some French and English sources (cf the harpsichord register, similarly a perforated strip of wood moving lengthwise), but J. A. Hamilton (*Catechism of the Organ* 1842) used 'slider' as the accepted term. (See also Chapter One, §2.)

Slider-chest (Dutch *sleeplade*; Ger. *Schleiflade*; It. *somiere a tiro*). One of the oldest forms of wind-chest, still used extensively today. The name comes from the use of perforated sliders for the stop action.

Slider seal (Ger. *Schleifendichtung*). A device placed between the slider and the table or toe-board which helps to prevent leakage and running between notes. The commonest types are rings of compressible felt or foam, or spring-loaded plastic 'telescopes', one for each pipe.

Solo organ. Specifically the manual of an organ, usually its fourth, given to strong solo stops (flutes, strings and reeds) which are not normally intended to blend into any traditional manual chorus. Many 16th-century *Brustwerke*, containing only a regal or two, could be considered a kind of Solo organ, as could the new *Récit de cornet* manuals of the 17th (St Séverin, Paris, 1610). While French builders went on to develop their *Récits* (i.e. short-compass melodic manuals), some began to separate off the larger reeds, putting them on their own chest for purposes of steady wind-supply rather than specific music (Notre Dame, Paris, 1733); at the same period, some German builders gave their organs *Solowerke* with more stops than the usual *Petite écho* manuals (*Solowerk* of 16.8.8.8.8.8.8.8.8.4.4.4.4 at Ochsenhausen, 1729). The orchestral idea of organs encouraged by such writers as Vogler and J. H. Knecht (*Vollständige Orgelschule*, 1795) led to the secular organs of the mid-19th century that very often contained extravagant manuals devoted to solo stops. These were sometimes the third manual (Cyclorama organ, Colosseum, Regent's Park, London) but more often the fourth (Panopticon organ, Leicester Square, 1853, for a while in St Paul's Cathedral). The new high-pressure reeds of Hill, Cavaillé-Coll, Walcker etc were useful, especially in town hall organs were the instrument often did duty for an orchestra. The term 'solo organ' also belongs to this period, i.e. around 1845.

Solo stop. As organ builders began separating off the medieval *Blockwerk* ranks, the fashion grew for new instrumental or other musical effects to be included. At Notre-Dame in Antwerp, for instance, van der Distelen's organ of 1505 was said to contain Trumpet, Waldhorn, Schalmei, Zinck, Quintadena, high Flute and Hohlpfeife. By the time Praetorius was writing (*Syntagma musicum*, ii, 2/1619), the range of flue, reed and regal stops was immense, including overblowing flue stops and horizontal regals. All these would be in some sense 'solo stops'. But the prime example, in the sense of a solo stop being *(a)* drawn alone in one hand and *(b)* accompanied by soft stops in the other, was the Cornet. This was known as a colourful stop in many guises before it was given its own half-compass keyboard. Music incorporating melodies for solo stops reached its peak around 1750 in France and England, and the new solo stops of the 19th century (especially high-pressure reeds and large-scale flutes) only continued a tradition long influencing builders and composers alike.

Somiere (It.; Fr. *sommier*). WIND-CHEST.

Somiere a tiro (It.). SLIDER-CHEST.

Somiere a vento (It.). SPRING-CHEST.

Soufflet [soufflerie] (Fr.). BELLOWS.

Souffleur (Fr.). A bellows-blower; *see* BLOWER (2).

Soundboard. The WIND-CHEST, or its upper part.

Soupape [palette] (Fr.). PALLET.

Sourdine (Fr.). A device found in reed organs that reduces the amount of wind reaching the reeds, thus softening the tone.

Speaking stops. In modern organ terminology speaking stops are those that produce a sound when brought into play, as distinct from those stop-knobs, stop-levers etc that operate couplers, wind valves, registration aids and other 'accessories'. The term 'speaking pipes' was used in the 1728 advertisement for the organ in St Mary Redcliffe, Bristol; Hopkins's distinction (Hopkins and Rimbault: *The Organ*, 1855) was between 'sounding stops' and 'accessory stops', while Audsley's term (*The Art of Organ-building*, 1905) was 'speaking stops'. The distinction is not always justified, as some auxiliary or accessory stops also make a sound (e.g. the Zimbelstern and toy stops).

Specification. Term used by organ theorists to denote a list of the speaking stops, accessories and compass of an organ. To a builder, however, 'specification' would include technical information on the bellows, action, pressure, chests, case, façade, placement etc, as well as the pipes and stops. The term was used by Hopkins (Hopkins and Rimbault: *The Organ*, 1855) as an occasional alternative to such phrases as 'a list of the contents' or 'the distribution of stops'. Previous English writers used only such phrases: 'List of stops' (J. A. Hamilton: *Catechism of the Organ*, 1842), 'Catalogue of the Stops' (Burney), 'Schedule' (Father Smith at the Temple Church, 1688) and 'The Name and number of the stoppes' (Dallam's contract at York, 1632).

Sperrventil (Ger.; Fr. *ventil*). The 'blocking valve' on an organ for preventing wind reaching a chest, saving it for other chests or keeping it from sounding a ciphering note. It is useful to the player as a registration aid, as it allows the fast addition of manual reeds or heavy pedal stops while playing.

Spielart (Ger.). TOUCH.

Spiele (Ger.). (1) A term applied to a rank of free reeds, as in a reed organ.

(2) In central Germany it also refers to a combination of stops. Gottfried Silbermann used this term in his registration lists for the organs in Fraureuth (1739–42) and Grosshartmannsdorf (1738–41).

Spieltisch [Spielschrank] (Ger.). CONSOLE.

Spring-chest (Ger. *Springlade*; It. *somiere a vento*). A type of wind-chest used extensively in the Renaissance period, and built in Italy into the 19th century. It is a note-channel-and-pallet chest in which the stop action consists of additional small pallets under the pipe-holes, held closed by springs until pushed open by the stop-lever bar. (See Chapter One, §2(v) and fig. 5c.)

Spund [Deckung] (Ger.). STOPPER.

Square (Fr. *équerre*; Ger. *Winkel*). An angle of wood or metal used in the key or stop action of a tracker action mechanism to transfer motion from horizontal to vertical, or around corners.

APPENDIX THREE

Stecca [stecca scorrevole] (It.). SLIDER.

Stevel (Dutch). BOOT.

Sticker (Fr. *pilote*; Ger. *Stecher*). A rigid rod, usually of wood, exerting a pushing action in organ and piano mechanisms. The principle of the sticker is applied to several parts of the organ: *(a)* chiefly, as a shorter or longer rod pushed down or up when a key is depressed and so transmitting that motion directly or indirectly to the appropriate wind-chest pallet; *(b)* as a short rod opening such valves as the pipe-pallets of each stop in a spring-chest, the sprung valve of a tremulant etc. The term has an uncertain history, being used by builders long before theorists; J. Talbot (MS treatise, Christ Church, Oxford, Music 1187, *c*1695) made somewhat ambiguous use of it, and in 18th-century England it was sometimes replaced by 'strikers' (W. Tans'ur: *The Elements of Music Display'd*, 1772).

Stimme (Ger.: 'voice', 'part'). STOP.

Stimmhorn (Ger.). TUNING CONE.

Stimmkrücke (Ger.). Tuning wire; *see* REED WIRE.

Stimmring [Stimmzug] (Ger.). TUNING-SLIDE.

Stimmrolle (Ger.). TUNING ROLL.

Stimmung (Ger.). TUNING.

Stop (Fr. *registre*; Ger. *Register, Stimme*; It. *registro*). A general term denoting a specific rank of pipes, or group of ranks (compound stop). There are two possible explanations for the term, which itself suggests a blocking of organ sound, not an opening: *(a)* that it refers to the slider whose protruding end was often worked directly by the organist and which, when extracted, is seen as a strip of wood pierced regularly with holes, and *(b)* that it refers to the mechanisms (sliders or otherwise) that cut off or stop certain ranks from the *Blockwerk* Mixture. Thus the 'fewe stops as may be convenient' dividing the *Blockwerk* at All Hallows, London, in 1519 may refer not to stop-knobs, etc, or even to sliders, but to Dutch-style spring-chests and double chests that allowed some ranks to be stopped off by means of a secondary valve. This would correspond with the German term *Sperrventil*, i.e. 'stopping' valve. By 1540 terminology was stabilized and Henry VIII's inventories refer even to 'halfe stoppes' and 'one [w]hole stoppe' in a modern way. Other languages use clearer terms: *tirant* (15th-century Spain: small organs with 'drawing' sliders), *registre* (Fougères, 1474), *registri* (Cattaro, 1488), *Registern* (A. Schlick: *Spiegel der Orgelmacher*, 1511), *regestres sive tirans* (Avignon, 1539).

Stop-jamb. The portion of the console from which the drawstops project.

Stop-key. *See* STOP-TABLET.

Stop-knob. *See* DRAWSTOP.

Stopped pipe. A flue pipe in which the upper end is sealed by a movable stopper, movable cap, or soldered-on cap. Caps and stoppers are used for tuning, but pipes with fixed caps are tuned by means of large ears that shade the mouth. A stopped pipe will produce a note of approximately the same pitch as an open pipe twice its length, because of the doubling back of the standing wave.

Stopper (Fr. *tompion*; Ger. *Deckung*, *Spund*). A gasketed, tight-fitting plug in the top of a stopped wooden pipe; it is raised and lowered by means of a handle for tuning purposes. Some 19th- and 20th-century English builders also used stoppers in zinc stopped pipes.

Stop-tablet [stop-key]. A device used in some electric-action organs instead of a stop-knob; it rocks on a fulcrum to make an electrical contact, activating the stop action.

Street organ. A barrel organ; see Chapter Eight, §3. *See also* ORGANETTO.

String (Ger. *Streicher*, *streichende Stimme*). A species of narrow-scaled flue pipes voiced to produce an overtone series similar to that of a bowed string. One of the earliest string stops, the Gamba, appeared in the 18th century; in the 20th century attempts at close imitation of actual instruments produced stops such as the Viole d'orchestre. String stops are often accompanied by a second rank, tuned slightly sharp (Celeste) to produce an undulating effect.

Superoctave (Ger. *Superoktave*). (1) An organ stop. The name denotes the Principal-scaled rank an octave above the so-called Octave (*Oktave*). The latter was itself an octave above the basic Principal rank of the department concerned. Thus if the *Prinzipal* is 16' and the *Oktave* 8', the *Superoktave* is 4'; or respectively 8', 4' and 2'. Not until German influences became strong in the mid-19th century was the term ever used on English organs in preference to 'Fifteenth'. In Germany itself, *Superoktave* as a rank in large organs emerged out of the Mixture only from around 1550, previous 2' ranks being scaled as flutes of various types.

(2) As the name of an organ coupler, Superoctave is normally a misnomer, the coupler concerned being an Octave coupler playing notes an octave above, not an octave above the octave.

Suspended action (Fr. *traction suspendu*; Ger. *angehangte Traktur*, *hängende Traktur*; It. *transmissione sospesa*). An early but still-used form of mechanical action in which all motion is pulling motion. In its best examples it is extremely sensitive to the player's touch.

Swell-box (Ger. *Schwellkasten*). An enclosure with movable shutters controlled from the console to vary the loudness of the pipework within. Usually the Swell organ is the only division so enclosed, but in the early 20th century it was not uncommon to find Choir organs, Solo organs, portions of the Great organ, and sometimes an entire organ so enclosed.

Swell organ (Fr. *récit expressif*; Ger. *Schwellwerk*). The manual department of an organ whose pipes are enclosed on all sides by a box, one side of which incorporates a device (lid, flap, shutters, sashed panel etc) that can be opened and closed by connection with a foot-lever or pedal. Thus enclosed may be a stop or half-stop, or several departments (Choir organ, Solo organ) or even the whole organ (examples by S. Green, *c*1780). The connection from foot-

APPENDIX THREE

lever to swelling device can be mechanical, pneumatic, electrical etc and may be so made that fine gradations in the degree of closure are possible.

The first Swells of significance are the enclosed Echo boxes of Spanish and later English organs provided with liftable lids or, also later, sliding front panels like sash windows. In Spain (Alcalá, *c*1680) the Swell box was often put round a stop or two on the main manual chest; only later did it enclose a whole department, usually either on the floor of the organ or tucked away at the top. Single stops were always those for treble solos of an expressive nature (Corneta, Trompeta, Flute); they were so in England until about 1780. French and English organs had their Echo stops on their own treble keyboard, the chest placed in the breast of the organ. Abraham Jordan's advertisement in the *Spectator* (8 February 1712) for his new Swell in St Magnus, London Bridge ('never . . . in any organ before'), refers to an organ with four sets of keys; thus the Swell was probably an extra Echo department. By 1740 (though not earlier) a Swell organ was regarded as indispensable; it took a larger chest, was moved into a position above the great chest and by around 1800 had ousted the Choir organ as the chief second manual.

Despite Burney's failure to find them, Swell organs were not uncommon in Europe: large departments low in the organ case, with vertical or horizontal shutters (Venice, *c*1770), little Echo boxes with a solo stop or two (Berlin, 1727; Rostock, 1770), the whole organ in a box (Abbé Vogler, 1784), perhaps with a 'balanced' Swell pedal-lever (Frankfurt, 1827) not requiring to be notched into place like the 'nag's head swell'. Swelling of the sound could also be obtained by double or triple touch and by playing free reeds on a higher wind pressure (Wilke and Kaufmann, 1823). Even in the 1850s English and French builders like Hill and Cavaillé-Coll made noticeably more discreet Swell organs in their ecclesiastical than in their secular organs. Refinement in the making of Swell organs has since concerned the size and variety of chests, their positioning, the accuracy of the pedal and the characteristic flue-and-reed battery that inspired most organ composers from 1840 to 1940. The device has since been recognized as essentially irrelevant to the nature of the true organ and thus without a place in the modern classical designs despite attempts in Germany and elsewhere to compromise by enclosing traditional *Oberwerk* and *Brustwerk* chests.

Table (Ger. *Fundamentalbrett, Kanzellendecke*). The upper surface of the grid of a slider wind-chest, on which the sliders run.

Tastatur (Ger.; It. *tastatura, tastiera*). KEYBOARD.

Taste (Ger.; It. *tasto*). KEY.

Tavola della catenacciatura (It.). ROLLERBOARD.

Teclado (Sp.). KEYBOARD.

Temblores [trémolo] (Sp.). TREMULANT.

Temperaments. Tunings of the scale in which some or all of the concords (i.e. 3rds and 5ths) are made slightly impure in order that few or none will be left distastefully so. Equal temperament, in which all the semitones are equal, is used in most modern organs, but there is much interest in historical systems. Mean-tone, in which a number of pure or nearly pure major 3rds are divided into two equal whole tones, and which favoured the common keys (up to three sharps or flats), was used on the Continent until the early 18th century and in England and North America until the middle of the 19th. 'Compromise' (or 'circulating') temperaments, such as those devised in the 18th century by Werckmeister, Vallotti, Kirnberger, Chaumont, Young etc, allowed the use of a wider range of keys and chromaticism; they have had a considerable revival since the 1970s because of the colour they give to music written before the 19th century.

Terza mano (It.: 'third hand'). A term that usually denotes the SUPEROCTAVE manual coupler. See also Appendix Two, 'Terza mano'.

Theatre organ. American term for the cinema organ; see Chapter Five, §5.

Thunder pedal. A pedal found mainly on French organs of the Romantic period. *See* ORAGE.

Tirant [tirant de registre] (Fr.). DRAWSTOP.

Tirante (It.). TRACKER.

Tirasse (Fr.). COUPLER, especially a pedal coupler. *Tirasse du Positif* (*Tir. P.*) means 'choir to pedal'; *Tirasse du Récit* (*Tir. R.*) 'swell to pedal'; *Tirasse du Grand Orgue* (*Tir. G. O.*) 'great to pedal'; and *Tirasse G. P. R.* that all three couplers are to be engaged.

Tiratutti. A device found in Italian organs from at least the early 18th century; it enabled the player to draw all the ranks of the Ripieno simultaneously by drawing a single knob.

Toe-board (Ger. *Pfeifenstock*). The board or boards on the top of the windchest, bored with chamfered holes, on which the pipes stand.

Toe-hole [bore, wind hole]. The opening in the foot of a pipe that admits wind from the wind-chest; it can be adjusted by the voicer to vary the volume.

Tompion (Fr.). STOPPER.

Tongue. *See* REED-TONGUE.

Tongwerk (Dutch). REED-WORK.

Touch (Ger. *Spielart*). A term used to describe either the amount of force required to depress a key or the distance that a key may be depressed. Thus an organ may be said to have a heavy or a light touch, as well as a deep or a shallow touch. The weight and the depth of the touch of organs are far less standardized than those of pianos and depend in part on whether the action is electric or mechanical.

Touch-box. The part of a TUBULAR-PNEUMATIC ACTION, above the keys, that contains air under pressure. See fig. 15*a*.

Touche (Fr.). KEY.

Toy stop. A colloquial term used to refer to the various 'sound effect' stops on cinema organs (e.g. sleigh bells, Chinese block, snare drum, klaxon, marimba, etc.). More recently the term has also been applied to the accessory stops of Renaissance and Baroque organs, such as birdcalls, drums, cymbel-stern, glockenspiel, etc.

Tracker (Fr. *vergette*; Ger. *Abstrakte*; It. *tirante*). A flexible strip, usually of wood, exerting a pulling action (cf Dutch *trekken*, from Lat. *trahere*: 'to draw', 'to drag') and transmitting motion from one plane to another; as such it is part of the mechanism or action connecting the key of an organ with its pallet, or valve. In many organs a horizontal tracker connects the key shank (often via a square) to a roller and rollerboard (which transmit the motion transversely) while a vertical tracker connects the roller (or key shank directly) to the pallet. All things being equal, the nearer to the midpoint of the key shank that the tracker directly pulling the pallet is connected, the lighter the action. The term itself has an uncertain history, being no doubt used by builders long before theorists; James Talbot (MS treatise, Christ Church, Oxford, Music 1187, *c*1695) used 'trigger' and 'ribs', but 'tracker' became common from at least the 1840s.

'Tracker organ' is a relatively recent term used loosely to denote the organ with mechanical rather than electric or pneumatic action. (See figs. 8–10.)

Tracker action. MECHANICAL ACTION.

Tracker bar. The perforated bar over which the music roll runs to activate the playing mechanism in self-playing organs with electro-pneumatic action.

Traction suspendu (Fr.). SUSPENDED ACTION.

Traktur (Ger.; Dutch *traktuur*). ACTION.

Transmissione sospesa (It.). SUSPENDED ACTION.

Traps. Percussion stops in cinema organs.

Treadles. BLOWING PEDALS.

Tremulant [tremolo] (Fr. *tremblant*; Sp. *temblores*, *trémolo*). A mechanical device, dating from the 16th century, which causes an undulating effect in the sound by disturbing the wind. The external type (*tremblant à vent perdu*, *tremblant fort*; *Bocktremulant*) accomplishes this by allowing intermittent puffs of wind to escape; the internal type (*tremblant doux*) by means of a hinged flap that floats up and down inside the wind-trunk. In early English organs the tremulant was known as the 'shaking stop'.

Trundle. A rotating rod with arms which transfers motion from the stop-knob rod to the slider in a mechanical stop action.

Tubular-pneumatic action. A type of action in which air under pressure, admitted to a lead or copper tube by the key, operates a pneumatic which admits wind to the pipe. It was developed in the late 19th century and used extensively in England and the USA, but fell into disuse after the first decade of the 20th century.

Tuning (Fr. *accord*; Ger. *Stimmung*). The adjustment of the intervals or the overall pitch level of an instrument. In organs, flue pipes are commonly tuned by slightly lengthening (flattening) or shortening (sharpening) the pipe body. Open pipes are tuned by means of flaring the top out or coning it in with a tuning cone, or by raising or lowering the tuning-slide or roll. Stopped pipes are tuned by raising or lowering stoppers or fitted caps. Sharply tapered open pipes or stopped pipes with fixed caps are tuned by shading the mouth with large ears. Reed pipes are normally tuned by raising or lowering the tuning wire, thus lengthening or shortening the vibrating length of the reed-tongue. Slots or tuning-slides at the top of reed pipes are normally used only for the regulation of loudness.

Tuning cone [tuning horn] (Ger. *Stimmhorn*). A double-ended tool with one depressed and one pointed cone; it is used for bending in (flattening) or out (sharpening) the tops of open flue pipes.

Tuning roll [tuning scroll] (Ger. *Stimmrolle*; It. *finestra e riccio*). A slot cut near the top of an open metal pipe or reed resonator, the centre part of which is rolled up or down to change the length of the slot. As tuning rolls can affect the timbre of flue pipes they are used mostly in string stops, where their effect is desirable.

Tuning-slide [tuning-collar] (Fr. *coulisse d'accord*; Ger. *Stimmring*, *Stimmzug*). A collar with overlapping edges, made of a springy material such as aluminium or tin-plated steel. It fits snugly around the top of an open metal pipe and is moved up or down for tuning. A 20th-century innovation, it is currently in common use.

Tuning spring [tuning wire]. Alternative terms for REED WIRE.

Tuyau (Fr.). PIPE.

Tuyauterie (Fr.). Pipework.

Two foot. A term used in reference to organ stops, and by extension also to other instruments, to indicate that they are pitched two octaves above the Eight foot, or 'normal', pitch now based on $c' = 256$ Hz. A 'two-foot organ' is one whose biggest open Principal pipe is or would be 2′ (60 cm) long at C, irrespective of any larger stopped pipes; nor does the terminology imply that the compass extends to C, since it could apply to a stop or department of any compass. The *Brustwerk* department of the ideal *Werkprinzip* organ was a two-foot positive organ incorporated in the main organ case.

Unit orchestra. The name originally given by Robert Hope-Jones to the type of organ he designed to substitute for instrumental players in theatres. It later became better known as the cinema organ (in the USA, the theatre organ). See Chapter Five, §§4 and 5.

Unit organ. A type of EXTENSION ORGAN.

Universal air chest. A type of individual-valve wind-chest in which all pipes stand over a large chamber filled with wind, instead of receiving wind from a pallet box or ventil channel, as in more traditional wind-chests. It was invented by John T. Austin in the 1890s and is still used by the Austin firm.

Untersatz (Ger.). The term for pipes placed on a chest below (and at the back of) the main chest of organs in north and central Germany from around 1575 to 1825.

Valve. A term generally used to refer to the round pipe-valves in wind-chests with electric or pneumatic action; it may also occasionally refer to pallets or ventils.

Vent (Fr.). WIND.

Ventil. (1) Any large valve which admits wind to a chest or stop. In 19th-century French organs the reed stops sometimes had a separate pallet box and could be brought on with dramatic effect by use of a ventil pedal.

(2) PALLET.

Ventilabro (It.). PALLET.

Ventil-chest (Ger. *Registerkanzellenlade*). A type of individual-valve chest developed in 19th-century Germany in which each stop had its own wind supply, which could be put in or shut off by the stop action.

Vergette (Fr.). TRACKER.

Verstimmt (Ger.). Out of tune.

Vocalion. A type of reed organ. The instrument was developed by James Baillie-Hamilton of England, originally in an attempt to combine the sounds of free reeds and strings. A modified instrument in which wires were attached to heavy reed-tongues was demonstrated before the Royal Musical Association in 1883, but the wires were deleted from the three-manual vocalion shown at the International Inventions Exhibition of 1885 in London. In the same year Baillie-Hamilton exhibited the vocalion in the USA and began its manufacture in Worcester, Massachusetts, in 1886. Ranging in size from foot-operated single-manual models to ones with two (or occasionally three) manuals and pedal, the vocalion is basically a reed organ on the pressure principle, but with unusually wide reed-tongues. It is therefore somewhat bulkier than the average reed organ, but produces a smoother, more powerful sound. This characteristic made the vocalion, often decorated with a façade of dummy organ pipes, popular for use in small churches in the late 19th and early 20th centuries.

Voicing (Ger. *Intonierung*). The means by which the timbre, loudness etc of organ pipes are given their desired quality and uniformity. Without 'voicing', it is unlikely that a newly made organ pipe, however accurately formed, will speak at all (save possibly with a rough and irregular sound). A voicer has therefore to make a number of fine manipulations and adjustments to each pipe. In flue pipes, a basic adjustment concerns the amount of wind which is allowed to issue from the flue or windway. This may be controlled either by increasing or decreasing the size of the toe-hole (a method common since the mid-18th century) or by leaving the toe-hole open and widening or narrowing the flue itself. Both methods are still used, occasionally in combination. Also of importance is the cut-up of the mouth. A high cut-up yields a smoother, more fundamental tone, while a lower one encourages harmonic development but at a loss of fundamental. Thus flutes are usually cut up on the high side, while strings and quintadenas are on the low side, principals (diapasons) being somewhere in between. Wind pressure is a factor in determining the best cut-up, because the cut-ups must be correspondingly higher or lower for a similar sound to be produced from identical pipes on higher or lower wind pressures.

It is essential that the plane of the upper lip be parallel to that of the lower lip. If the languid is too low or the upper lip pulled out too far, the pipe is said to be 'quick' and in extreme cases will overblow; if the languid is too high or the upper lip pressed into too much, the pipe will be 'slow' and in extreme cases will cease speaking. Flutes are generally voiced on the quick side, strings on the slow side and principals just barely quick enough to overblow or flutter when forced beyond their normal wind pressure. In wooden pipes the block (corresponding to the languid) is immovable, and the adjustments made by the voicer will consist in modifying the height of the upper lip, the position of the cap, the angle and width of the flue and sometimes the angle of the upper lip. Some fine adjustments that affect the tone-colour of flue pipes include arching or 'skiving' of the upper lip, changes to the height and bevel of the languid face and 'nicking' of the languid edge. Until the end of the 18th century it was customary to blunt or 'counterface' the languid edge, which tended to discourage the 'sizzle' in the pipe sound. This practice continued in many instances into the 19th century and has been revived by some 20th-century builders. A knife-edged languid requires shallow, widely-spaced nicking to achieve the same purpose; a small amount is usually necessary to fine regulation, and does not adversely affect articulation or 'chiff'. Deep, close nicking, however, particularly when done on the lower lip as well as the languid, destroys both chiff and harmonic development; this was extensively practised in the early 20th century and is still necessary for modern string-toned pipes. Many larger flue pipes have projections ('ears') at the sides of their mouths which help to focus the sound and sometimes need adjustment by the voicer. Beards below the ears or 'rollers' between them were developed in the 19th century to stabilize the speech of narrow-scaled pipes and are also adjusted by the voicer.

In reed pipes the thickness and curvature of the reed-tongue are the major factors determined by the voicer. The tongues are usually of 'half-hard' brass (although some tone-colours require soft brass or harder phosphor bronze) and are cut to size by the voicer. Both the width of the tongue and the opening in the shallot affect tone somewhat, but the most critical operation in reed voicing is the curving of the tongue, done with a burnisher on a wood or metal block. Too little curvature will produce weakness or silence; too much will make the attack slow. Pipes of the trumpet type usually speak best when the tongue has a slight extra curvature at its tip. Until the late 19th century it was common to file reed-tongues slightly thinner at the end, to improve attack at low wind pressures. High pressures used in the early 20th century necessitated thicker tongues, often weighted (by an amount adjusted by the voicer) at their tip in the lowest two or three octaves. Such tongues produced a smoother, more fundamental tone. The loudness of reed pipes is regulated not on the toe, which is usually fully open, but by adjusting the length of the resonator in conjunction with the vibrating length of the reed-tongue. Very fine adjustments are sometimes made to the length by which the shallot projects from the block.

Organ pipes are usually pre-voiced in the builder's workshop by means of a small organ called a 'voicing jack'. This device has interchangeable racks to accommodate pipes of various sizes, so that the pipes are within easy reach of the keyboard, with the voicer's tool shelf above. Racked at the back of the voicing jack is a permanent set of pipes to which the set being voiced can be tuned. Voiced pipes are placed in the organ while it is set up in the workshop, and further adjustments are made. Final voicing, called 'finishing', can take several months for large instruments and is done after the organ is installed.

Volles Werk (Ger.). A 17th-century term for the diapason chorus; *see* ORGANO PLENO.

Vorsprache (Ger.). CHIFF.

Walze [Crescendowalze] (Ger.). CRESCENDO PEDAL.

Walzenorgel (Ger.). Barrel organ; see Chapter Eight, §3.

Wasserorgel (Ger.). Water organ; see Chapter Eight, §1.

Water gauge. *See* WIND GAUGE.

Wechselventil (Ger.). A type of valve; *see* FLIP-FLOP.

Wedge (Fr. *coin*; Ger. *Keil*). A tapered piece of hardwood or metal that holds the reed-tongue and the shallot in the block of a reed pipe (see fig. 19).

Wedge-bellows (Ger. *Keilbalg*). The traditional form of bellows, hinged at one end; the upper leaf is raised to fill the bellows with wind.

Wellenbrett (Ger.). ROLLERBOARD.

Werkprinzip (Ger.: 'department principle'). A term coined probably by the *Orgelbewegung* of the 1920s to describe the system for building organs in which each 'department' or *Werk* (i.e. a keyboard with its chest or chests) has its own separate structure. For convenience the keyboards (manual or pedal) are brought together at one console, but the earliest examples of the Chair organ (Utrecht Cathedral, *c*1390) may also have had their keyboard separate, behind the organist (*see* CHAIR ORGAN and RÜCKPOSITIV). Depending on requirements an organ may be built of several *Werke*, each of which is structurally separate but which together are acoustically an entity. A likely order of size is:

Hw
Hw + dep. pedal
Hw + Bw + dep. pedal
Hw + Rp + dep. pedal
Hw + Rp + independent pedal
Hw + Bw + pedal towers

Hw + Rp + pedal towers
Hw + Bw + Rp + dep. pedal
Hw + Bw + Rp + pedal towers
Hw + Ow + Bw + Rp + pedal towers

(Hw = Hauptwerk; dep. pedal = pedal pull-downs; Bw = Brustwerk; Rp = Rückpositiv; Ow = Oberwerk; pedal towers = 1 or 2 chests in tall boxes to right and left.)

Usually, each department is built up on a Diapason rank (16' pedal, 8' Hw etc), hence the wrong explanation of the term as denoting '*Werke* based on a *Prinzipal*'. Almost all northern European organs before around 1700 were built according to one or other of the plans; exceptions were those French, Spanish and English organs in which the subsidiary chest was placed within the main case (echo, solo Cornet etc). The system's reputed advantages are that separate cases ensure maximum resonance and dispersal, departments can be added (at Lüdingworth, Hw/Bw of 1598, Rp/towers 1682) and such departments have different function and sound; but non-*Werkprinzip* organs also allow these, and the strongest reason for building such organs today is that most of the organ music of 1500–1720 was written for them.

Wind (Fr. *vent*; Ger. *Wind*; It. *anima*). Air under pressure; it is raised by a bellows or blower, stored in part of the wind-chest, and admitted to the pipes by the key action.

Wind canal. *See* WIND-TRUNK.

Wind-chest [chest, soundboard] (Fr. *laye, sommier*; Ger. *Lade, Windlade*; It. *pancone, somiere*; Sp. *secreto*). In the classical organ, the wind-chest is a long, broad but rather shallow wooden case, holding (in a closed-off substructure, the pallet box) wind from the bellows under pressure. It receives the wind when the pallet is opened, and then distributes it to the pipes placed on the soundboard above; the chest is partitioned latitudinally into as many channels or grooves as there are notes in the keyboard compass. Other kinds of chest have been devised, but the classic chest is itself also open to a variety of detail in its distribution of wind to the pipes. Before around 1420 all organs had only one sound per manual or pedal chest; in the course of the following 100 years three important inventions allowed builders to give separate sounds: the multiple chest (where a key would connect to two chests), the spring-chest (where a 'stop' had its own row of secondary pallets admitting wind individually to its pipes) and the slider-chest. The 18th-century English term 'wind-chest' has an uncertain history; James Talbot's word in his MS treatise of around 1695 (Christ Church, Oxford, Music 1187) is 'wind-box'; like *Lade* (Oude Kerk, Delft, 1458) it is closer to the medieval *cista* (box, chest, kist) than was the French *sommier* (Notre Dame, Rouen, 1382).

Winddruck (Ger.). WIND PRESSURE.

Wind gauge [water gauge] (Ger. *Windwaage*). A device for measuring wind pressure at the pipe chest, in the trunks etc. According to German authors

(Werckmeister, Adlung, Töpfer) a gauge was first invented by Christian Förner in 1667, but he may only have been publicizing a perfected example. The device had a single column of water which was raised a measurable extent when placed above any air vent (e.g. a pipe-hole in the chest). Töpfer (*Die Orgelbaukunst*, 1833) improved its reliability by giving it a double column. The water-manometer (E. J. Hopkins's 'anemometer') has an S-shaped transparent tube placed on its side; in a bend of this the water rests until moved by the pressurized air admitted at one end of the tube. The pressure of air is measured as the difference between the lower and upper surfaces of water in the bent tube. Thus '$2\frac{1}{2}''$ wind' (i.e. about 6 cm) indicates that the surface pushed by the air fell $1\frac{1}{4}''$ (3 cm), the other surface beyond the bend raised $1\frac{1}{4}''$.

Wind hole. *See* TOE-HOLE.

Windkammer (Ger.). PALLET BOX.

Windkanal (Ger.). WIND-TRUNK.

Wind pressure (Fr. *pression, pression du vent*; Ger. *Winddruck*). Wind pressures in organs are normally quite low, and are measured in inches on a water gauge. Until the 20th century organs generally spoke on pressures of from two to five inches, but in the first half of the 20th century pressures as high as 100 inches were used on rare occasions for special stops by builders such as Hope-Jones. Pressures above ten inches are uncommon, however, and most builders now work with pressures under five inches.

Wind stabilizer. A device which gives the player the choice of flexibility or stability in the wind system, usually by activating or deactivating a concussion bellows. It has been in use since the 1970s, mainly by American builders.

Wind-trunk [wind canal] (Fr. *porte-vent*; Ger, *Windkanal*; It. *canale*). A large wooden or metal tube for conveying the wind of an organ from the bellows to the wind-chest. In medieval organs the main wind-trunk was called *fistula maxima*.

Windwaage (Ger.). WIND GAUGE.

Windway (Fr. *lumière*; Ger. *Kernspalte*). In a wooden flue pipe the windway is the passage between the opening of the pipe foot and the flue, which is the slot between the face of the block and the inner side of the cap or lower lip (see fig. 17b). The form of the windway determines the size and shape of the air jet impinging on the upper lip, which through the formation of edge-tones energizes the air column. The throat is that part of the windway hollowed out of the block; its conformation influences the timbre of the pipe. In metal pipes the flue is formed between the edge of the languid and the lower lip derived from the wall of the pipe foot (fig. 17a). *See also* FLUE.

Winkel (Ger.). SQUARE.

Winker. A term for CONCUSSION BELLOWS.

Wippe (Ger.). BACKFALL.

ORGAN

Zug (Ger.). A word meaning organ stop or, more generally, the stops on any keyboard instrument. *See also* DRAWSTOP.

Zugrute (Ger.). PULL-DOWN.

Zunge (Ger.). REED-TONGUE.

Zungenstimmen (Ger.). REED-WORK.

APPENDIX FOUR

Index of Organ Builders

Cross-references within this appendix are distinguished by the use of small capitals, with a large capital for the initial letter of the entry referred to, for example: See CASSON, THOMAS; or, in running prose, THOMAS CASSON.

Abbey, John (York) (1785–1859). English builder. In 1827 he moved to Paris, where he built several cathedral organs, initiated the use of 'orgues du choeur' and introduced such innovations as free reed stops. His sons and grandson continued to operate the firm, considered at one time second only to Cavaillé-Coll; it ceased operations in 1935.

Abbott & Smith. English firm. It was formed in Leeds in 1869 by Isaac Abbott, who had completed his training with William Hill, and continued until 1964. The firm built a large number of instruments, including around 250 organs in Yorkshire, many in Methodist churches and town halls.

Abbrederis, Matthäus (1652–after 1725). Austrian builder. He was a leading builder in the upper Rhine valley around 1700; his work was in a conservative, early Baroque style.

Aeolian-Skinner. American firm. It was formed by the merger of E. M. Skinner Co. with the organ division of the Aeolian Co. in 1931 as the Aeolian-Skinner Organ Co. Under the leadership of G. Donald Harrison it introduced the 'American classic' tonal concept in the 1950s and built organs for many leading universities and urban churches. The firm began to decline after the death of Harrison in 1956 and ended its operations in 1973.

Agati. Italian family of organ builders. Pietro Agati was apprenticed to Tronci and began building in Pistoia in 1760. His sons Nicomede (1796–1885) and Gisoué, active in Tuscany in the 19th century, built many organs in the classical style.

Ahrend, Jürgen (*b* 1930). German builder. He was in partnership with Gerhard Brunzema in Leer (East Friesland) in 1954–72. The style of his later organs is strongly influenced by historic north German instruments, several of which have been restored by his firm.

Aigner, Josef (1809–87). Tyrolean builder, also an organist. Active from about 1837 in and around Schwaz, he was one of the first builders in the Tyrol to abandon the 'short octave'.

343

ORGAN

Åkerman, Per (1826–76). Swedish builder. He studied in Brussels and Paris and was the first to introduce French Romantic practices to Swedish organ building. C. J. Lund became his partner in 1860; under the name of Åkerman & Lund the firm began in the 1970s to build tracker-action organs with a French tonal bias and continued to operate into the late 1980s.

Alberdi Recalde, Lope (1869–1948). Spanish builder. He was apprenticed to Aquilino Amezúa in Barcelona, becoming the director of the firm in 1895. A prolific builder, he was one of the first in Spain to use electric action.

Albiez, Winfried (*b* 1938). German builder. Trained by Walcker, he formed Albiez-Orgelbau in Lindau, Switzerland, in 1969; the firm builds tracker-action organs.

Alexandre. French firm of reed organ makers. It was formed in 1829 in Paris by Jacob Alexandre (1804–76) to make accordions; after patents were acquired in 1841–5 from Alexandre Martin of Provins, the firm also manufactured the 'orgue-mélodium'. Jacob's son Edouard later joined the firm, which by the 1860s operated a large factory in Ivry-sur-Seine that made harmoniums of all sizes.

Alley, Joseph (1804–80). American builder. He was active in Newburyport (Mass.) from 1826. With Henry W. Poole he built two 'euharmonic' organs (1849–51); these could play in pure intonation in the most common keys by using added pipes.

Amezua y Noriega. *See* GONZÁLEZ DE AMEZUA Y NORIEGA, RAMÓN.

Andersen, Poul-Gerhard (1904–80). Danish builder. A pioneer of the Danish Organ Reform Movement, he was apprenticed to Marcussen and later managed its division in Copenhagen. He wrote *Orgelbogen* (1956), an important book on organ building, and in 1963 opened a workshop in Copenhagen.

Andersson, Gustaf (1797–1872). Swedish builder. He was trained in Germany and opened his own workshop in 1824; his son Frans became his partner in 1850 and ran the firm from 1859.

Andover. American firm. It was formed as the Andover Organ Co. in 1955 and in 1961 became C. B. Fisk, Inc. (*see* CHARLES BRENTON FISK); in the same year a new firm was formed under the original name by Leo Constantineau and Robert J. Reich. This is now a multiple partnership, comprising two departments that specialize in building new organs and restoring old ones.

Andrews, George Norton (1832–1904). American builder. He trained with his father, Alvinza, and worked in Utica (NY) until around 1885. His son George moved to California in 1886 to set up a new shop there.

Andueza, Juan de (*c*1650–1686). Spanish organ builder. He is regarded as an innovator and a leading representative of the late 17th-century Madrid school; he built organs for several important Spanish churches after 1675.

Antegnati. Italian family of builders and musicians. They were active from the late 15th century to the mid-17th in Brescia, and are credited with more than 250 organs. The most distinguished members of the family were Gian

Giacomo (*b* 1501), and Graziadio (*b* 1525) and his son Costanzo (1549–1624), author of *L'arte organica* (1608). The typical Antegnati organ employed spring-chests, low wind pressures and mean-tone tuning.

Appleton, Thomas (1785–1872). American builder. He was apprenticed to William Goodrich and was his associate in 1810–20. He opened his own workshop in 1821 in Boston, where he became one of the leading builders during the next 30 years. His work is characterized by meticulous craftsmanship, a refined tone and handsome 'Greek revival' casework.

Audsley, George Ashdown (1838–1925). American designer of Scottish birth. He emigrated to the USA in 1892 and was briefly involved in the Art Organ Co. around 1900. He later wrote several influential books, including *The Art of Organ-building* (1905).

Austin, John Turnell (1869–1948). American builder of English birth. In 1899 he opened a factory in Hartford (Conn.) to build instruments with his unique 'universal air chest' design. An inventive, talented builder, he also produced the first all-electric console, a player mechanism and many machines still used in the factory. In 1937 his nephew Frederic B. Austin became president of the firm, which was reorganized as Austin Organs, Inc.; Frederic's son Donald succeeded him in 1973.

Avery, John (1738–1808). English builder. He was active in London in the late 18th century; his work was highly regarded, and ranged from cathedral organs to chamber organs.

Bader. German family of builders. Daniel Bader (?*c*1560-1636) may have been a pupil of Arnold Lampeler and worked in Antwerp and Liège. His son Hans Heinrich (*d* 1681) was, with his own four sons and a grandson, active and influential in Westphalia. Their organs followed the Lampeler pattern and used spring-chests well into the 18th century.

Baillie-Hamilton, James. Founder of the VOCALION Organ Co.

Balbiani. Italian family of builders. Lorenzo Balbiani (1798–1876) was active in and around Milan; as was his son Natale (1836–1912). Lorenzo's grandson Celestino married into the Vegezzi-Bossi family of organ builders; his descendants still own the firm under the name of Balbiani–Vegezzi-Bossi.

Ballesteros. Spanish family of builders. José Ballesteros y Lafuente (*c*1710–after 1763) was active in Valladolid; builders who may have been his descendants worked in the area until the mid-19th century.

Banci, Giovanni (1803–74). Italian builder. He was apprenticed to Agati, and later worked in Castiglion Fiorentino. He built organs that were often small but unusually versatile, and characterized by handsome cabinet work.

Barckhoff, Carl (1849–1919). American builder of German birth. Trained in Germany, he emigrated to the USA in 1865 with his father Felix (*d* 1878) and brother Lorenz and formed a firm in Philadelphia. The firm changed its location frequently from 1878, settling in Virginia in 1913. At the time of

Carl's death the firm had built more than 3000 organs; Carl's work was continued by his son, H. C. Barckhoff.

Barker, Charles Spackman (1804–79). English builder and inventor. He invented a pneumatic organ action that was ultimately adopted by Cavaillé-Coll and other European builders. He moved to Paris in 1837 and later worked for Cavaillé-Coll, then Daublaine & Callinet. In the 1860s he collaborated with Albert Peschard on experiments with electric organ actions.

Bärmig, Johann Gotthilf (1815–99). German builder. He was active in Saxony from 1846. His organs were considered excellent but tonally conservative, favouring 18th-century scaling. He also built harmoniums.

Bartola. American firm. It was formed as the Bartola Musical Instrument Co. around 1910 in Oshkosh (Wisc.) by Daniel W. Barton (1884–1974) to manufacture percussion attachments for theatre pianos. Later, it built many cinema organs in Chicago. The firm was known as the Maxcy-Barton Organ Co. from 1929 until it ceased operations in 1935.

Bates. English firm. It was established around 1812 in London by Theodore Charles Bates. G. Longman was a partner in around 1824–33; the firm later became Bates & Son. and remained in business until 1864. A large portion of its output consisted of chamber and barrel organs.

Bätz. Netherlands family of builders. Johann Hendrik Hartmann Bätz (1709–70), a Thuringian by birth, was apprenticed to Christian Müller. His work was continued by his sons and grandsons, of whom Jonathan was responsible for much distinguished 19th-century work. C. G. F. Witte joined the firm around 1850 and eventually took over the business.

Bautzen. German firm formed in 1872 by the EULE family.

Baumann, Johann Carl (1714–94). German builder. He may have been trained by the Stumm brothers, and he built small but colourful organs; he also made pianos, one of which was owned by Mozart. His work was continued by his sons Konrad Isaac and Matthias Christian.

Bazzani, Giacomo (d 1856). Italian builder. He was active in and around Venice. In 1821 he acquired the firm of Callido with his sons Alessandro (d 1872) and Pietro (d 1880). His nephews Giacomo and Pietro, with their sons Alessandro and Lorenzo, continued to operate the firm into the 1960s.

Beatty, Daniel F. American firm of reed organ makers. It was formed around 1868 in Washington (NJ) and specialized in mass production. It ceased operations in the 1880s.

Beck. German family of builders. They were active and influential in and around Halle during the 16th century. The most noteworthy members of the family were Esaias (d 1587) and David (fl 1587–1601), who are given credit for developing the style of the central German Baroque organ.

Beckerath, Rudolf von (1907–76). German builder. He studied with Victor Gonzalez in Paris and Theodor Frobenius in Denmark. During the 1930s he worked as a consultant in Hamburg, where in 1949 he opened a workshop to restore historic organs and build new tracker-action instruments based on historic principles. Although his work was soon acclaimed worldwide, Beckerath resisted enlarging his firm so as to retain full artistic control over all its work.

Bedient, Gene R. (*b* 1944). American builder. After studying at the University of Nebraska he was apprenticed to Charles McManis. In 1969 he opened a workshop in Lincoln, Nebraska; his organs are strongly influenced by historic principles.

Bédos de Celles, Dom François (1709–79). French builder. A Benedictine monk, he built several organs in the mid-18th century, but is best known for his *L'art du facteur d'orgues* (1766–78), one of the most important organ-building treatises of the period.

Bernat-Verí, Jorge Bosch. *See* BOSCH BERNAT-VERÍ, JORGE.

Bert, Pierre (*fl* 1517–44). French builder. He was active in northern France, notably in Rouen, Angers and Le Mans.

Beuchet-Debierre, Joseph (1904–70). French builder. A grandson of Louis Debierre, he became director of Cavaillé-Coll's workshop in Paris before taking over the large firm of Debierre in Nantes in 1947.

Bevington. English firm. It was formed in 1794 by Henry Bevington, who had been apprenticed to Ohrmann & Nutt. With his sons Henry and Martin he built more than 2000 organs of excellent quality and conservative tonal design during the 19th century; many were exported.

Bewsher & Fleetwood. English firm. It was formed in Liverpool around 1820 and from 1845 was known by the name of William Bewsher. It was sold to Gray & Davison in 1857.

Binns, James Jepson (*d* 1929). English builder. He was the head voicer for Abbott & Smith from 1875 and formed his own firm in 1880 in Leeds; tonally his organs were influenced by the work of Edmund Schulze. He patented a thumb-piston combination action that could be changed while playing.

Bishop. English firm. It was formed in 1807 by James C. Bishop (1783–1854), who originated the Clarabella stop and built somewhat advanced pedal divisions. After his death various partners were involved in the operation of the firm, in particular Starr and Richardson. Edward H. Suggate took charge of the firm, now known as Bishop & Son, in 1880; his family still controls it.

Blancart [Blanckard]. Flemish family of builders. Among its notable members were Charles, who was active around 1570 in Ghent, and Jasper, active around 1578 in England.

Blangz, Hans. Name by which Hans Suys was sometimes known; *see* SUISSE.

Blasi, Luca (*fl* 1585–1605). Italian builder. He was active in Rome and the surrounding area, where he built organs for several important churches. The success of his water organ in the Quirinale gardens (*c*1597) led Clement VIII to grant him exclusive rights for the building of similar instruments.

ORGAN

Bommer, Johann Jakob (*fl c*1720–67). Swiss builder. He is regarded as one of the most important builders in eastern Switzerland of the early 18th century; his organs have close stylistic links with those of Swabia and south Germany.

Boody, John H. Partner in the firm of Taylor & boody.

Booth, Joseph (*c*1769–1832). English builder and inventor. He was active in Wakefield from 1824 and invented an early pneumatic key action, first used in an organ in 1827. His son Francis (*d* 1874) continued the business after his death; later it was run by Alfred Kirkland, who moved the firm to London and merged it with that of Bryceson.

Bosch Bernat-Verí [de Bernat-Verí], **Jorge** (1737–1800). Spanish builder. Considered the most famous builder in Spain in the late 18th century, he built important organs in Palma de Mallorca, Madrid and Seville.

Bossard [Bossart, Bosshart]. Swiss family of builders. Active in the 17th and 18th centuries, its most notable members were Josef (1665–1748) and Viktor Ferdinand (1699–1772). The style of their instruments was south German, with some French and Italian influences; a treble undulating Suavial stop was a typical feature. Early 19th-century organs by Franz Josef Remigius Bossard (1777–1853) were criticized for their stylistic conservatism.

Botzen. Danish family of builders and organists. Peter Karstensen Botzen was a builder whose sons Johan Petersen (*c*1641–1719) and Peter Petersen (*c*1661–1711) built several large organs in and around Copenhagen.

Bozeman, George (*b* 1936). American builder. He was apprenticed to Otto Hofmann, Robert L. Sipe and Fritz Noack before forming his own firm in 1971 in Massachusetts. In 1972 he moved to Deerfield (NH) with David V. Gibson, his partner until 1982. His firm builds eclectic instruments of all sizes as well as the 'Cortez', a stock design.

Brandenstein, Johann Konrad (*c*1695–1757). German builder. He was presumably a son of Johann Adam Brandenstein, an organ builder of Kitzingen. From 1725 he built a number of imposing instruments in Bavaria. His work was continued by his sons-in-law Johann I. P. Hillebrand and Johann Michael Herberger.

Brebos. Flemish family of builders. Gillis Brebos (*d* 1584) and his sons Gaspar (*d* 1588), Michiel (*d* 1590) and Jan (*d* 1609) did considerable work in Antwerp and Madrid; Hans (*d* 1603), who may have been Gillis's brother, worked in Copenhagen.

Breisiger [Briesger, Bryssiger], **Peter** (*fl* 1516–42). German builder. Active in the upper Rhine region and the Netherlands, he made technical innovations and introduced 'new' stops (Cornet, full-length reeds, narrow-scaled flues). He also wrote an important treatise on organ registration.

Bridge [Bridges], **Richard** (*d* 1758). English builder. Active in London, he also made spinets and harpsichords. Although his organs, built for cathedrals and many churches in London, had unusually handsome casework, Bridge is

348

not known to have made a Chair division. His business was continued by George England (*see* ENGLAND). Handel was one of his supporters.

Brindley & Foster. English firm. It was formed in 1854 in Sheffield by Charles Brindley (*d* 1893), whose son Charles Frederick joined the firm in 1876 after studying with Schulze. A. Healey Foster became a partner in 1884, after which there was much experimentation in pneumatic actions and orchestral voicing. The firm was acquired by Willis in 1939.

Brombaugh, John (*b* 1937). American builder. He was apprenticed to Fisk, Noack and Beckerath before opening his own shop in Ohio in 1968. In 1976 he moved to Eugene (Oregon), where he now builds tracker-action organs based on 17th- and 18th-century north European practices.

Brown & Sons, F. H. English firm. Formed in 1871 in Canterbury, it built many small and medium-sized organs in southern England.

Brunzema, Gerhard (*b* 1927). German builder. He was the partner of Jürgen Ahrend in Germany (1954–72) and the tonal director of Casavant Frères in Quebec (1972–9). In 1979 he formed his own firm in Fergus, Ontario.

Bryceson. English firm. It was formed in 1796 in London by Henry Bryceson to make chamber organs, barrel organs and pianos; later it was known as Bryceson Bros. In 1868 the firm purchased the rights to Barker's electric mechanisms. Taken over by Alfred Kirkland after 1874, it was later acquired by Hill, Norman & Beard.

Buchholz. German family of builders. Active in Berlin, its members included Johann Simon (1758–1825), his son Carl August (1796–1884) and his grandson Karl Friedrich (1821–85), who studied in France and became the firm's director in 1868.

Burdett. American firm of reed organ makers. It was formed as the Burdett Organ Co. by Riley Burdett in 1866 in Chicago and later operated in Erie (Penn.); in 1909 it became the Burdett Piano Co.

Busch. German family of builders. Johann Dietrich Busch (1700–53) was apprenticed in Scandinavia and from 1720 worked for Lambert Daniel Kastens, whose work he continued. His son Johann Daniel (1735–87) ran the firm from 1853. Their organs were conservative and in the tradition of those of Schnitger.

Byfield, John (*c*1694–1751). English builder. He was in partnership with his brother-in-law John Harris until around 1740. He built instruments in the same style as Harris and, was known for his excellent reed stops and many fine organs in London. His work was continued by his son John (*d* 1767), his grandson John (*d c*1799) in partnership with Samuel Green, and his great-grandson John (1766–1806).

Cahman. Swedish family of builders of north German origin. Among its notable members were Hans Heinrich Cahman (*c*1640–99), who was a pupil of Hans Christoph Fritzsche, his brother Johan Herman (*d* 1702) and his son Johan Niclas (*c*1675–1737), who trained many Swedish builders. The family's organs differed from those of north Germany: their mixture stops included a tierce rank, and the instruments usually had fewer reed stops.

Callido, Gaetano (1727–1813). Italian builder. Active in Venice, he worked with Pietro Nacchini, whose work he later continued. His organs show an increased use of divided stops, reeds and narrow-scaled flues. His sons Agostino (*d* 1826) and Antonio (1762–1841) assumed control of his firm before selling it to Giacomo Bazzani in 1821.

Callinet, Louis. Alsatian organ builder; *see* DAUBLAINE & CALLINET.

Carhart & Needham. American firm of reed organ makers. It was formed around 1846 in New York by Jeremiah Carhart, who had completed his training with George A. Prince & Co., and Elias Parkman Needham. The firm patented many improvements including an early version of the suction bellows; it built more than 1500 instruments by 1866 and ceased operations in the 1870s.

Carlen. Swiss family of builders. Matthäus Carlen (1691–1749) was the first builder in the family, which was active in the Valais well into the 20th century. The family's instruments combined south German, French and Italian traits, particularly in the scaling and voicing of the Principals. Among those members of the family who worked in the business later in its history were Felix (*b* 1734), Franz Josef (1779–1845), Gregor (1819–69), Johann Josef Conrad (1849–1926) and Heinrich (1885–1957).

Carlier, Crespin (*d* before 1640). French builder. He worked in the south Netherlands (notably in Lille) until 1600, returning to France at the invitation of Jehan Titelouze to remodel the organ at Rouen Cathedral. He was regarded as the leading organ builder in France in his day, and with the Langheduls is given credit for introducing to France the well-developed Flemish style of organ building.

Carlini, Orestes [Oreste] (*d c*1945). Italian builder. He built and restored organs in Chile in the early 20th century.

Carpenter. American firm of reed organ makers. It was formed by Edwin P. Carpenter (1819–91) in 1850 in Brattleboro (Vermont). Carpenter later worked for Estey and established a new firm in Illinois in the 1860s.

Casavant Frères. Canadian firm. It was formed in 1845 by Joseph Casavant (1807–74) in St Hyacinthe, Quebec, and was later run by his sons Claver (1855–1933) and Samuel (1859–1929), who on their father's death went to study with Abbey in France, where they remained until 1879. In the late 19th century and the early 20th century the firm was a pioneer in the development of electro-pneumatic mechanisms, and in the 1960s was one of the first large north American firms to revive the practice of building tracker-action organs.

Casparini [Caspari]. Family of builders. The family was active in Italy, Austria, Silesia, Poland and east Prussia in the 17th and 18th centuries. Eugen Casparini [Johann Caspar] (1623–1706) and his son Adam Horacy (1676–1745) built many large, important organs in a unique style that successfully blended such German and Italian elements as Cornets, undulating stops, high-pitched mutations and reeds.

Casson, Thomas (1842–1910). English builder and author of several pamphlets on organ construction. He advocated more adequate Pedal divisions and better stop control and formed the Positive Organ Company in London, which built hundreds of small divided-manual organs.

Cavaillé-Coll, Aristide (1811–99). French builder. A member of an established family of organ builders in southern France, he invented early in his career (c1830) the *poïkilorgue*, which became the basis for Mustel's harmoniums. In 1833 he moved to Paris with his father Dominique (1771–1862) to build a large organ for the abbey of St Denis, and later formed his own business. Because of his advanced ideas on wind supply, tonal design (high-pressure reeds, harmonic flutes, gambas) and action (he was the first to employ the Barker lever), he broke with the French classical tradition and is regarded as the father of the French Romantic organ. Cavaillé-Coll built about 500 instruments; after his death the firm's operations were continued by his pupil Charles Mutin.

Cera, Diego [Mosen Cañas] (1762–1832). Spanish builder. He was a friar and missionary working from 1792 in the Philippines, where he built a piano and two organs, one of them the famous 'bamboo' organ at S José de Las Piñas.

Cerveira, António Machado (Xavier) e (1756–1828). Portuguese builder. He was trained by his father, Manuel Machado Teixeira, and was active in the diocese of Coimbra, where he built over 100 organs in the neo-classical style.

Chase. American firm of reed organ makers. It was formed in 1876 by Alvin B. Chase (*d* 1877), whose work was continued by Calvin Whitney (1846–1909); from 1885 Whitney made pianos as well as reed organs.

Chiappa, Giuseppe. Builder of fairground organs. He was trained by GAVIOLI.

Chrismann [Crisman, Chrismanni, Križman, Krismann]**, Franz Xaver** [Frančisek Ksaver] (1726–95). Austrian builder. Ordained as a priest and a student of Nacchini, he was active from around 1764. He extended the 18th-century Venetian style of organ to develop the individual Austrian type known to Mozart and Bruckner.

Church. English firm. Formed by Nigel Church in Stamfordham in 1971, it builds tracker-action organs.

Clarke, William Horatio (1840–1913). American builder and writer on organ building. He had a brief career as a builder in Indianapolis in the 1870s, later moving to Reading (Mass.), where he edited organ music and wrote treatises on organ construction.

Clicquot. French family of builders. Robert Clicquot (c1645–1719) was apprenticed to his brother-in-law Etienne Enocq and later became the partner of Alexandre Thierry. His sons Jean Baptiste (1678–1746) and Louis-Alexandre (c1684–1760) were also builders, as was his grandson Francois-Henri

(1732–90), whose instruments represent the culmination of French classical organ-building. François-Henri built organs for many churches in Paris and elsewhere, and from 1770 to his death was acknowledged as the leading French builder; his work was continued by his son Claude François (1762–1801).

Colin. French family of builders. Among the more notable members of the family, which was active in Nancy, were Jean-Baptiste (*d* after 1699) and his son Dominique (*fl* 1706–20).

Collins. English firm. It was formed in Hertfordshire in the 1960s by Peter Collins, who had been apprenticed to the firms of Bishop and Rieger. His tracker-action organs are noted for their compactness of design.

Compenius. German family of builders. The family was associated with the family Beck and continued its traditions. Timotheus Compenius was active in Würzburg in the late 16th century; his brother Heinrich (*d* 1611) was based in Nordhausen. Heinrich's two sons had important careers: Esaias (*d* 1617) assisted Praetorius in writing his *Organographia*, and Heinrich the younger, of Halle (*d* 1631), was the builder to the Archbishop-Elector of Magdeburg. Other members of the family were Adolph (*d* 1650) and Ludwig (*d* 1671); Jakob Compenius (*d* 1602) may also have been a relative.

Compton, John Haywood (1876–1957). English builder. He worked with Brindley & Foster from 1898 and formed his own firm in Nottingham in 1912. He built electric-action organs characterized by considerable use of extension: many were for cinemas; he later made electrones. The firm's organ department was sold to Rushworth & Dreaper in 1964; Makin took over the electrone division in 1970.

Conacher. English firm. Formed in Huddersfield in 1854, it now operates under the name of Peter Conacher & Co. Ltd.

Conceição, Manoel Lourenço da [Lourenço de Souza] (*fl* 1719–26 and earlier). Portuguese builder and priest. He was active in and around Coimbra and Oporto.

Córdoba, de. Spanish family of builders. Active in Saragossa throughout the 16th century, its members included Juan (*fl* 1504–11), Gonzalvo (*d* after 1550), Martín (*d* 1541), and Hernando (*d* 1577) and his son Hernando Alonso Hernández (1539–1609).

Corrie, Henry John [James Henry] (1786–1859). American builder. He was trained by Elliot in London, worked for Appleton in Boston (1824–8) and later formed his own business in Philadelphia with his sons George J. (*b* 1816) and William A. Corrie (*d* 1896). John Huber was his partner in 1831–7 and William A. Corrie ran the firm in partnership with John Wright in 1859–61; some of Henry John's grandsons became pipemakers for Samuel Pierce.

Crang & Hancock. English firm. Formed in London by John Crang (*d* 1774), John Hancock (*d* 1792) and James Hancock (*fl* 1772–1820), it built a number of church and chamber organs in the late 18th century.

Cumming, Alexander (1733–1814). Scottish designer. A watchmaker by profession, he assisted various London builders in designing barrel organ mechanisms and made improvements on bellows design.

Daalen, Jan van (*b* 1938). American builder. He was trained in the Netherlands and Germany and later worked in Canada. In 1969 he formed his own firm in Minneapolis (Minn.).

Dahm, Johann Jacob (*d* 1727). German builder. He was active in Mainz and became an important figure in the organ-building tradition there; he was made a freeman in 1698. His style was influenced by that of the Schleich family of Frankfurt am Main.

Dallam [Dalham, Dallom, Dallow]. English family of builders. Thomas Dallam (*c*1575–after 1629) built many notable Elizabethan organs as well as a mechanical organ given by Elizabeth I to the sultan of Turkey. His son Robert (1602–1665) worked in Brittany during the Commonwealth, returning to England around 1660 with his sons Ralph (*d* 1673) and George (*d* 1685); another of Robert's sons, Thomas (*c*1635–after 1720), remained in Brittany and built organs with his own sons Toussaint (*b* 1659) and Marc-Antoine (1673–1730), both of whom later went to England. Robert's daughter Katherine married into the HARRIS family.

Dallery. French family of builders. Its members included Charles (1702–70), his nephew Pierre (1735–1801), who was the partner of François-Henri Clicquot from 1767 to around 1778, Pierre's son Pierre-François (1764–1833) and his grandson Louis-Paul (1797–1870). They worked largely in Paris and the surrounding region.

Dargillières. French family of builders and organists. Active in Paris in the 16th century and the early 17th, the family was influential in the development of the French Renaissance organ; among its notable members were Gabriel (*fl* 1559–81), Antoine (*c*1518–72), Antoine's son Roch (*b* 1559) and Jehan, who also made harpsichords.

Daublaine & Callinet. French firm. Formed in 1838 in Paris as Daublaine & Cie, it purchased the Alsatian firm of Louis Callinet (*b* 1797) in 1839. Charles Spackman Barker ran the business from 1842, and Callinet left in 1844 to work for Cavaillé-Coll. The firm then reorganized as Girard & Cie and after 1845 was known as Ducroquet & Cie; it was later acquired by Merklin of Brussels. In 1899 it became the Société Guttschenritter & Decoq.

Dauphin. German family of builders. Johann Eberhard Dauphin (*c*1670–1731) built many well-crafted but tonally conservative organs in east Hesse; his brother Johann Christian (1682–1730) studied under Johann Friedrich Wender and was active in the earldom of Erbach. Johann Christian's son and grandsons continued to operate the business until 1810.

Davis, James (1762–1827). English builder. He formed a business in Lancashire around 1780 with his brother David (1768–1822). After they moved to London around 1790 David went to work for Clementi, selling organs manufactured by James, most of which were for domestic use.

Davison, Frederick. Partner in the firm of GRAY & DAVISON.

Debain, Alexandre François (1809–77). French reed organ maker. He formed a business in 1834 and patented the harmonium, or *orgue expressif*, in 1842; this patent prevented other makers from using the term 'harmonium' for many years.

Debierre, Louis (1842–1920). French builder. He studied in Paris (1859–62) and established a workshop in 1863 in Nantes. By 1912 he had built 195 large organs and 277 portatives. His grandson Joseph Beuchet-Debierre took over the firm in 1947.

Degens & Rippin. English firm, known from 1963 as GRANT, DEGENS & BRADBEER.

De Héman [Hémen, Le Hémen]. French family of builders. Valéran De Héman (1584–1641) a pupil and son-in-law of Crespin Carlier, was a leading builder in the early 17th century; he trained many later builders, including his nephews François (1608–52), Jean (1603–60) and Louis (1601–44), who worked together.

Delhaye [De La Haye]. Flemish family of builders. The earliest known member is Louis Delhaye (*fl* Antwerp, *c*1724). His son and grandson continued his work on a small scale; his great-grandson Jean-Joseph (*b* 1786), with his own son Jean-Corneille-Charles (*b* 1809), brought the family's name to prominence, building significant organs until around 1848.

Derrick & Felgemaker. American firm formed in 1865 by ABRAHAM B. FELGEMAKER and Silas L. Derrick.

Dieffenbach. American family of builders. The family was active in eastern Pennsylvania in the 18th and 19th centuries. John Jacob Dieffenbach (1744–1803) began building in 1776; his work was continued by his son Christian (1769–1829), his grandson David (1798–1872) and his great-grandson Thomas (1821–1900). The family's instruments were small and were designed and voiced in the 18th-century German tradition.

Dinstlinger [Distlinger, Tischlinger]**, Burkhard** [Burckhardt] (*fl* 1474–1507). German builder. He was active in Nuremberg, Innsbruck, Passau, Breslau, Görlitz, Vienna, Freiberg and elsewhere. His organs were built in the late Gothic tradition, with few non-principal stops and only short-length reeds.

Dixon, George (1870–1950). English designer and writer on organs. He was associated in the early 20th century with the firm of HARRISON & HARRISON.

Dobson, Lynn (*b* 1949). American builder. He was apprenticed to Charles Hendrickson and in 1975 formed his own firm in Lake City, Iowa, to build tracker-action organs.

Dodd. Australian firm. It was formed in 1894 in Adelaide by Josiah Eustace Dodd (1856–1952) and his brother Ebenezer, both former employees of Fincham & Sons. It was amalgamated with Gunstar Organ Works around 1940. The firm's organs are based on symphonic concepts.

APPENDIX FOUR

Donati [Donat]. German family of builders. It was active in and around Leipzig. Christoph Donati the elder (1625–1706) also made clavichords; his son Johannes Jacobus (baptized 1663) was a builder at the courts of Gotha and Altenburg, and his work was continued by his son Johann Jacob (baptized 1715). Johann Christoph Gottlob (baptized 1694; *d* 1756), a cousin of Johann Jacob, worked in Glauchau; his sons Christian Gottlob (baptized 1732; *d* 1795) and Gotthold Heinrich (baptized 1734; *d* 1799) continued his business, and became in turn builders to the prince of Saxony; Christian Gottlob's son, August Friedrich Wilhelm (1773–1842), became a builder at the court of Altenburg. The organs of Christoph Donati were north German in style, while those of his descendants were more in the style of Gottfried Silbermann.

Dos Santos. Portuguese family of builders. Luiz António dos Santos, his son Peres António Jozé and his grandson Artur Alexandre were active in Mangualde during the 19th century.

Douwes, Claas (*c*1650–*c*1725). Netherlands builder, organist and writer on music. He was the author of *Grondig ondersoek* (1699), an important historical source of information on the construction of keyboard instruments.

Dressel [Dressler, Drechsler]. German family of builders. Tobias Dressel (1635–1717) worked for the Bavarian builder Matthias Tretzscher; his nephew Christoph made harpsichords and organs, and his twin sons Johann Tobias (1687–1758) and Johann Christian (*b* 1687) are believed to have been apprenticed to Gottfried Silbermann.

Ducroquet. The name under which DAUBLAINE & CALLINET was known after 1845.

Dupont Nicolas (1714–after 1779). French builder. He was active in Nancy from around 1740, building several large organs. His work was continued by his son Joseph (*b* 1747).

Ebert, Jörg (*d* before 1582). German builder. He was active in Rothenburg ober der Tauber by 1531 and worked in Ravensburg in 1542–78. Although he made conservative use of the new, imitative 'concertato' stops of the Renaissance, the Trumpet and Hörndl appear in all his known stop-lists.

Echevarría [Chavarri, Chavarría, Echavaría]. Spanish family of builders of Basque origin. It was active in the 17th and 18th centuries. Several members of the family were monks, including José de Eizaga (*fl* 1659–65), José (*d c*1691) and Domingo (*fl* 1686). Two others, José and Pedro, were active in the mid-18th century in Madrid, where they built several cathedral organs.

Egedacher. German family of builders. It was active in Bavaria and Austria. Johann Christoph Egedacher (1664–1747) travelled to Trent to study the work of other builders; Johann Ignaz (1675–1744), his brother and his nephew continued the work of the firm of Freundt in Passau. Many of the family's instruments were large, containing undulating stops, tierce mixtures and many reed stops.

Eglseder, Georg (*b* 1930). Partner of WILLI PETER.

Ekengren, Jonas (1736–93). Swedish builder. Apparently self-taught, he became a leading builder in Sweden in the late 18th century.

Elliot, Thomas (*c*1759–1832). English builder. He was active in London from 1791. Although his organs were essentially conservative in style, he was one of the first English builders to employ pedal-pipes (*c*1810). He left unfinished his largest instrument, for York Minster; this later was completed by William Hill, Elliot's partner from 1825.

England. English family of builders. The family was active in London. George England (*d* 1773) was Bridge's son-in-law, and appears to have continued his work from 1758; his work was in turn continued by John England (*fl* 1764–90), who may have had Hugh Russell as a partner. John's son George Pike (?1765–1816) worked for his father and took over his business in 1790; he built many good organs in the tradition of Harris and Bridge.

Engler. German family of builders. It was active in Breslau. Michael Engler (ii) (1688–1760), the best known member of the family, was the son of Michael Engler (i) (*c*1650–*c*1720); he built organs with a wide range of foundation stops but few reeds. His work was continued by his son Gottlieb Benjamin (1734–93)

Erben, Henry (1800–84). American builder. He was apprenticed to his brother-in-law Thomas Hall and was his partner from 1824 to 1827. The leading builder in New York until his death, he trained several other builders and built organs for many large churches.

Estey. American firm. It was founded in 1846 for the manufacture of reed organs in Brattleboro, Vermont, by the melodeon maker H. P. Green, and was purchased in 1848 by Jacob Estey (1814–90). Jacob's son Julius (1845–1902) and Levi K. Fuller (1841–96) later joined the firm, which became one of largest in the country, adding pianos (1885), pipe organs (1901) and electronic organs (*c*1950) to its output before ceasing operations in 1956.

Eule. German family of builders. Hermann August Eule (1846–1929), the son of a piano maker, opened a workshop in Bautzen in 1872. His son Georg (*d* 1918) worked for him; his work was later continued by his daughter Johanna, who was in turn followed by Hans (*d* 1971) in 1957. In 1972 the firm became known as VEB Orgelbau Bautzen. Having begun by building romantically voiced organs with cone-chests and, later, purse-chests, the firm in 1953 changed to slider-chests and a more neo-Baroque style of voicing.

Evans, Wardle Eastland (*d* 1884). English reed organ maker. Active in the mid-19th century, he made several types of harmonium including a two-manual model that was popular as a practice instrument for organists.

Evers, Edo (*fl* 1616–30). German builder. He built several significant organs in and around Jever and Emden.

Fachetti [Facchetti, Facchinetti, Brixiensis], **Giovanni Battista** (*fl* 1515–52). Italian builder. He was active in Brescia, where he built organs for several important churches. With the Antegnatis, he helped to make Brescia the most influential Italian centre of organ building in the 16th century.

APPENDIX FOUR

Farrand & Votey. Firm formed in 1883 by William R. Farrand and EDWIN SCOTT VOTEY.

Felgemaker, Abraham B. (1836–1905). American builder. He formed a partnership with Silas L. Derrick in 1865 in Buffalo (NY). The business moved to Erie (Penn.) in 1876 under the name of A. B. Felgemaker Organ Co.; it remained in business until 1918.

Feligiotti. Italian family of builders. Active in Urbania, its notable members included Arcangelo (1729–96) and his son Andrea (1760–1835), both of whom built a number of organs in Tuscany.

Feller. Bohemian family of builders. Franz Feller (1787–1843) began building in 1817; his sons Franz and Anton later went into partnership. Another son, Josef, worked independently.

Fernández, Francisco (c1760–after 1802). Spanish builder. He was active in the region of Valladolid.

Fernández Dávila, Leonardo (d 1771). Spanish builder. He built several important organs in Granada and Madrid in collaboration with Bosch Bernat-Verí.

Ferris, Richard Montgomery (1818–58). American builder. He was apprenticed to Henry Erben and opened his own workshop in 1840 in New York. He was in partnership with William Henry Davis (1816–88) from 1845 to 1849; his half-brother Levi Underwood Stuart (1827–1904) became his partner in 1857 and continued the firm, in which Stuart's father and five brothers were also involved. Ferris's work was of a high quality, and he was the only serious competitor with Erben in the mid-19th century.

Fincham & Sons. Australian firm of English origin. It was formed in 1862 in Melbourne by George Fincham (1828–1910), who had worked for Bevington and other English builders. The firm built over 200 instruments and had branches in Adelaide, Victoria, Perth, Brisbane and Sydney, some of which were managed by Arthur Hobday under the name of Fincham & Hobday.

Fischer, Lukas (b 1934). German builder. He was trained with, among others, Hintz and Walcker, and formed a business in Ruit in 1967 that built tracker-action organs. His workshop was moved to Rommerskirchen in 1970.

Fischer & Krämer. German firm. Formed in 1970 by Friedrich Wilhelm Fischer (b 1933) and Johann Krämer (b 1943), both of whom had been apprenticed to Späth and others. The firm is based in Endingen and builds tracker-action organs in the tonal tradition of Andreas Silbermann.

Fisk, Charles Brenton (1925–83). American builder. He was trained with Walter Holtkamp sr and in 1955 became a joint owner of the Andover Organ Co.; he bought the firm in 1958 and after moving to Gloucester (Mass.) in 1961 changed its name to C.B. Fisk Inc. A pioneer in the building of tracker-action organs in the USA, he based his tonal concepts on his study of the work of historic French, north and south German, Netherlands and American builders, particularly the Silbermann brothers. Except for certain intentionally specialized instruments, his larger organs are eclectic in their design.

Flentrop, Dirk Andries (*b* 1910). Dutch builder. His father, Hendrick (Wichert) Flentrop (1866–1950), formed a firm in Zaandam in 1903; Dirk assumed its direction in 1940 and concentrated on restoring historic instruments and building new tracker-action organs based on historical Dutch tonal principles. The influence of his work has been strong both in the Netherlands and the USA, where a number of his instruments are situated. On Flentrop's retirement Hans Steketee became the director of Flentrop Orgelbouw.

Flight, Benjamin (*c*1767–1847). English builder. He was trained with his father, and opened his own workshop around 1806 in partnership with Joseph Robson; after 1832 his firm was known as Flight & Son. His inventions included an improved form of bellows and an early orchestrion called the Apollonicon.

Fontanes, Simão (*fl* 1737–8). Portuguese builder. A Gallican friar, he built the two organs in Braga Cathedral.

Forceville, Johannes Baptista (*d* 1739). South Netherlands builder. He worked in and around Brussels from about 1680. His instruments display a synthesis of the French and Flemish styles. His work was continued by his son Johannes Thomas (1696–1750).

Formentelli. Italian firm. Formed by Valerio and Bartolomeo Formentelli, it specializes in restorations and new organs in the classical Italian style.

Förner, Christian (1610–78). German builder. The son of a builder from Wettin, he was trained by his brother-in-law J.W. Stegmann (*d* 1637). He studied physics and attempted to apply his scientific knowledge to organ building. Förner invented the water gauge, which was used for measuring wind pressure, and may have been the teacher of 'Father' Smith.

Forster & Andrews. English firm. It was formed by two former employees of Bishop, James Alderson Forster (*c*1818–86) and Joseph King Andrews (*c*1820–96), in 1843. Its early organs were conservative, but the instruments built between 1870 and 1900 were influenced by the work of German and Belgian voicers and are regarded as comparable to Willis's. The firm was sold in 1924 and ceased operations in 1956.

Fourneaux, J.B. Napoléon (1808–46). French reed organ maker. He took over Chameroy's business in Paris in 1836 and was the originator of the percussion action in harmoniums.

Freundt. Bavarian family of builders. Its most important member was Johann Georg (*c*1590–1667) of Passau. His work was continued by Johann (before 1615–78) and Leopold (*c*1640–1727), after whose death the business was taken over by the EGEDACHER family.

Freytag, Hermann Henry. Successor to ALBERTUS ANTHONI HINTZ.

Friederici [Friedrichs]. German family of builders. Active in Saxony, it also made other keyboard instruments. Christian Ernst Friederici (1709–80) may have worked at one time with Gottfried Silbermann.

Fritz, Barthold (1697–1766). German builder. Active in Brunswick, he also made positives and various stringed keyboard instruments.

Fritzsche, Gottfried (1578–1638). German builder. He was regarded, with Hans Scherer and the Compenius brothers, as one of the foremost Renaissance builders in Germany, and is thought to have studied with Johann Lange near Dresden. He was one of the first to provide all three manuals and pedal with an independent principal chorus, and introduced this feature in Hamburg after taking over Scherer's operations there in 1629. With this and other innovations he created the prototype of the Hanseatic Baroque organ, laying the foundation for the work of Arp Schnitger. Fritzsche trained many important builders, including his son Hans Christoph (d c1673) and Friedrich STELL-WAGEN.

Frobenius. Danish firm. It was formed in 1909 in Copenhagen by Theodor Frobenius (1885–1972) and moved to Lyngby in 1925. After Theodor's sons Walther and Erik joined the firm in 1944 it built tracker-action organs with a neo-Baroque tonal design, becoming a leader in this field.

Fuchs. Tyrolean family of builders. Joseph Fuchs (1678–1750) and his son Anton (1711–94) built a modest number of organs. Anton's son Johann Anton (1737–96) was the most important member of the family; he built noteworthy organs with his nephews and Joseph Reinisch.

Führer, Alfred (1905–74). German builder. He was apprenticed to and later worked for Furtwängler & Hammer; he formed his own firm in 1933 in Wilhelmshaven.

Fulgenzi [Fulgentio] **Fiammingo, Vincenzo Beltramo** (fl 1578–1600). South Netherlands builder. He was active in Italy, where he introduced additional manuals, reed stops and other innovations.

Furtwängler, Philipp. German builder. He formed the firm that eventually became HAMMER-ORGELBAU.

Gabler, Joseph (1700–71). German builder. He studied with, among others, G. and J. P. Geissel of Mainz, and opened his own workshop there around 1726. He built several large, complex organs, including those for the abbeys at Weingarten and Ochsenhausen. His organs, with ornate casework, have ample foundation stops and principal choruses in every division, but few reeds or mutations. Gabler introduced the detached console to Upper Swabia and invented the *Kronpositiv*.

Garcimartín, Leandro (1779–1842). Spanish builder. He completed the restoration work of his uncle, Tomás Ginés Ortega, in 1804–5 and later moved to Madrid, where he became a builder to the royal chapel in 1834.

Garrelts, Rudolph (1675–1750). German builder. He was apprenticed to Arp Schnitger and worked in Norden from around 1706.

ORGAN

Gartner. Bohemian family of builders. Its notable members included Anton (1721–?71) and his great-nephew Josef (1796–1863); Josef wrote *Kurze Belehrung über die innere Einrichtung der Orgeln* (1832).

Gavioli. French firm of mechanical instrument makers. The Gavioli family moved to Paris from Italy in 1845 and gained a reputation for the manufacture of barrel organs. In 1892 Anselme Gavioli (*d* 1902) developed a new mechanism for playing fairground organs that enabled the instruments to play longer and more complex music. The firm continued to develop a number of ambitious mechanical instruments before it was bought out by Limonaire Frères in 1910. Several important makers of fairground organs were trained by Gavioli, including Giuseppe Chiappa and Charles Marenghi.

Geib. German family of builders. Johann Georg Geib (i) (1739–1818), who may have studied with the Stumm brothers, formed his own business around 1760 near Saarbrücken. Of his sons, Johann Georg (ii) (1772–1849) continued his work and Johann (John) (1744–1818) emigrated to London (before 1786) and in 1797 moved to New York, where with his twin sons John (1780–1821) and Adam (1780–1849) he made organs and pianos. Adam and his son William continued the firm but made only pianos.

Gerhard. German family of builders. Justinus Ehrenfried Gerhard (?1710–86), who may have been a pupil of Tröbs, was active from around 1739 in Lindig; his organs are compared favourably to those of Silbermann. His son Christian August (1745–1817) and two grandsons continued his work; the firm is now known by the name of Kühn.

Gill Rodríguez, Isidro (*c*1745–after 1790). Spanish builder. He was active in the region of Medina del Campo from 1766. Nicolás Gill Rodríguez, who was probably his son, continued his work.

Girard. French firm allied to DAUBLAINE & CALLINET.

Glatter-Götz, Josef Edler von. Director of RIEGER from 1920.

Gloton, Georges (1876–1955). French builder. He worked for the firm of Cavaillé-Coll–Mutin, and was the director of Debierre until 1947.

Głowiński, Jan (*c*1645–*c*1712). Polish builder. He was active in Kraków and south-eastern Poland, where he built some sizeable instruments from around 1679.

Gomes, Manoel de São Bento [Gomes de Herrara, Manoel Benito] (*b* 1747). Portuguese builder. He was presumably a Benedictine monk, and was active in Coimbra and the surrounding region from around 1719.

Gonzalez. French firm. Formed near Paris in 1921 by Victor Gonzalez (1877–1956) and Victor Ephrème, it was later run by Victor and Fernand Gonzalez and by Victor's grandson Georges Danion.

González de Amezua y Noriega, Ramón (*b* 1921). Spanish builder. He completed his training with Victor Gonzalez and formed his 'Organeria Española' in 1941; he has built or restored more than 400 organs.

APPENDIX FOUR

González Roldán, Gregorio (*c*1685–after 1721). Spanish builder. He was based in Valladolid and is considered an outstanding master of the early 18th-century Castilian school.

Goodrich, William Marcellus (1777–1833). American builder. He is regarded as the founder of the Boston school. Largely self-taught, he worked with various partners from 1804 to 1820, when he opened his own workshop in East Cambridge. He built organs for several major churches on the East Coast, and is said to have invented the concussion bellows for steadying wind. He was one of the first to begin developing an indigenous American style and trained many builders of the succeeding generation. His brother Ebenezer (1782–1841) later became a leading maker of chamber organs.

Granbom, Berndt. German builder who worked with Johann Graurock (*see* GRAUROCK).

Grant, Degens & Bradbeer. English firm. It was formed in 1959 in Hammersmith, London, as Degens & Rippin by E. V. Rippin, John Degens and Eric Atkins in association with Maurice Forsyth-Grant; by 1963 it was known as Grant, Degens & Rippin. Encouraged by Forsyth-Grant the partners studied continental organs and developed a neo-classical style of building. The firm later moved to Northampton; Frank Bradbeer, an architect, became a partner in 1966.

Graurock [Grauwrock, Grorockh, Graerock]. German family of builders. Johann Graurock (i) (*d* by 1558) and his brother-in-law Berndt Granbom (*d* in or after 1519) worked in Emmerich; they belonged to the group of builders in the Lower Rhine area who separated the *Hauptwerk* into two departments, creating the Renaissance *Oberwerk*. Johann's sons Johann (ii) and Wilhelm continued his work; they were followed in turn by Wilhelm's sons Johann (iii) and Bernhard; the last-known work by Johann (iii) dates from 1632.

Gray & Davison. English firm. It was formed in London in 1774 or earlier by Robert Gray (*d* 1796); by 1787 he had been joined by William Gray (*d c*1820), who later entered into a partnership with his son John (*d* 1849). In 1838 Frederick Davison (1814 or 1815–89), who had worked with Hill, married John Gray's daughter and became his partner. The firm's early work was highly regarded; it introduced the Keraulophon stop around 1843, and in the 1850s it introduced many French innovations, but towards the end of the century its organs were regarded as conservative. The firm continued until 1970 under the direction of Charles Davison and his son Jess.

Green, John (*fl c*1815–48). English reed organ maker. A music dealer by profession, he invented the 'Royal Seraphine' around 1831, which he manufactured with Bevington's help in the 1830s.

Green, Samuel (1740–96). English builder. He became the partner of John Byfield (*d* 1799) in 1768 and formed his own business around 1772. In 1780 he succeeded Snetzler as the builder to George III. His business was continued after his death by his widow, Sarah, and his foreman, Benjamin Blyth. His instruments, which ranged from cathedral organs to chamber organs, are regarded as some of the most characteristic of the period.

Gren, Jonas (1715–65). Swedish builder. He was trained in the tradition of Cahman by Daniel Stråhle and entered into a partnership with Peter Stråhle (1720–65), Daniel's nephew, in 1748. The two men, of whom Gren was the theorist and Stråhle the technician, were regarded as the leaders in their craft in Sweden; several builders were trained in their workshop in Stockholm.

Grenié, Gabriel-Joseph (1757–1837). French reed organ maker. In 1810 he exhibited a pressure reed organ in Paris that was capable of dynamic variation; named the *orgue expressif*, it was the precursor of the harmonium.

Griffin, Thomas (*d c*1771). English builder or supplier. Active in London, he provided organs for several of the City's churches.

Grimont, Florentin (*d* after 1807). French builder. A Carmelite friar, he worked chiefly in Brittany from around 1775 to 1789, when he moved to Spain.

Grönlund. Swedish family of builders. Johan William Grönlund (1879–1963) opened a business in 1903 in Kåge; his sons Olof (1910–56) and Gustaf (*b* 1913), who ran the firm from 1940 to 1973, moved the workshop to Gammelstad in 1950. Jan-Olof Grönlund (*b* 1937) took over the firm on Gustaf's retirement in 1973. Its work consists largely of tracker-action instruments.

Grotian, Valentin Ulrich (1663–1741). German builder. He worked in the region around Aurich from about 1688.

Gullbergson, Pehr Olof (1780–1864). Swedish builder. A self-taught builder, he began working around 1830 and became highly regarded in Uppsala province for the high quality of his instruments.

Gunstar. Australian firm that was amalgamated with DODD.

Haas, Friedrich (1811–86). Swiss builder of German birth. He completed his training with the Schaxel family of Baden and E. F. Walcker, and worked in Switzerland from 1840, settling in Lucerne in 1859. He began making sliderless wind-chests and developing Romantic tone qualities such as the Doppelflöte around 1850; at this time he was Switzerland's leading builder. His business was carried on after 1867 by Friedrich Goll.

Hall, Thomas (1794–1874). American builder of English birth. He was apprenticed to John Lowe and opened his own shop in Philadelphia in 1811. He moved to New York around 1816, and was in partnership with his brother-in-law Henry Erben from 1824 to 1827 and with John Labagh (1810–92) from 1846. James L. Kemp became a partner in 1868; after Hall's retirement (1872) the firm continued under the name of Labagh & Kemp until 1891.

Hamel, Marie-Pierre (1786–1879). French builder and writer on organ building. An advocate of the classical French organ, he wrote the *Nouveau manuel complet du facteur d'orgues* (1849).

APPENDIX FOUR

Hamill, Samuel S. (1830–1904). American builder. He completed his training with Henry Erben and opened his own shop in East Cambridge (Mass.) in 1859.

Hammarberg. Swedish family of builders. The family was active for five generations in Göteborg. Adolf Fredrik Pettersson (1811–72) and his son Gustaf Adolf (1840–98) were the first builders in the family. Gustav Adolf's son Olof Pettersson Hammarberg (1871–1942) trained with his father and with Marcussen before organizing the firm under his own name in 1898. Olof's son Nils Olof (*b* 1913) took control of the firm in 1935 and began working in a more classical style; his son Bo Gunnar (*b* 1945) became a partner in 1972.

Hammer-Orgelbau. German firm. It originated with Philipp Furtwängler (1800–67), who began building in 1830 and whose sons Wilhelm (1829–83) and Pius (1841–1910) later entered the firm. Adolf Hammer (1854–1921) became a partner 1883; in the same year the firm moved to Hanover and changed its name to P. Furtwängler & Hammer; it began producing instruments with pneumatic actions in 1893. Hammer's nephew Emil (1878–1958) became the director in 1921; his grandson Christian Eickhoff succeeded him in 1961. The firm again built tracker-action organs from 1931.

Harris. English family of builders. Thomas Harris (*d* *c*1684) married Katherine Dallam and lived in Brittany with the Dallam family (1642–*c*1662); he built organs there and was later active in England. His son Renatus (René) (*c*1652–1724) continued his work and became the only serious rival of Bernard Smith in Restoration England by building imaginative organs with a distinctly French tonal bias. His work was continued by his son John (after 1677–1743), whose sister married John's partner John Byfield (*c*1694–1751); Byfield continued the family business after John's death.

Harris, Murray M. (*d* 1922). American builder. In 1895 he founded the first firm of organ builders in Los Angeles. He soon produced organs of significant size, including a huge instrument for the Louisiana Purchase Exposition (1904) that was later enlarged and moved to the Wanamaker Store, Philadelphia. From around that time the firm was known as the Los Angeles Art Organ Co. Harris left in 1912 and the firm ceased business in 1932 after many reorganizations.

Harrison, G. Donald (1889–1956). English builder. He completed his training with Willis in England and emigrated to the USA in 1927, becoming the technical director of the Aeolian-Skinner Organ Co. in 1931. He was among the first to advocate a return to classical tonal ideals and was the originator of the 'American classic' style of organ.

Harrison & Harrison. English firm. It was formed in 1861 by Thomas Hugh Harrison (1839–1912) after his apprenticeship with Willis. The firm moved in 1870 to Durham and in 1872 was joined by Thomas's brother James. Thomas's sons Arthur and Henry Shaw Harrison entered the business in the 1890s, taking control after 1912. The designer George Dixon was an important influence on the firm in the early 20th century; Cuthbert T. L. Harrison, Henry's son, became the firm's director in 1945.

Hartung. German family of builders of Thuringian origin. Augustinus Hartung (1677–1739) formed a firm that his son, Johann Michael (1703–63), brought to prominence by building solid south German organs in handsome cases. Johann Michael's work was continued by his son Johann Philipp Hartung (1750–1806) in partnership with Johann Peter Kampff.

Haskell, Charles S. (1840–1903). American builder. Trained by Roosevelt, he opened his own shop in Philadelphia in 1893. His son Charles E. Haskell (1878–c1928) continued the business with his own son William (1865–1927). The Haskells are given credit for many inventions: Charles S. Haskell patented several chest and action designs, and William, who later worked for Estey, developed such tonal innovations as labial reeds and the 'Haskell bass', which involved the insertion of a canister-like length of open tubing inside a pipe, so causing it to behave like a much longer pipe.

Hastings, Frank. Partner in the firm of HOOK & HASTINGS.

Haxby, Thomas (1729–96). English builder. He was active in York from 1756, where he made church and chamber organs; he also built spinets, harpsichords, pianos, citterns and violins.

Hayl [Hail, Heyl]. German family of builders. Of Swabian origin, they worked in the Tyrol (c1590–1640). Among the family's active members were Abraham, Daniel, Daniel the younger (c1590–after 1640), who moved to Salzburg, and Simon (c1590–after 1642), who went to Upper Bavaria.

Hedgeland, Frederic W. American builder of English birth. He worked for the firm of KIMBALL.

Hedlund, Olof (d 1749). Swedish builder. He was a pupil in Stockholm of J. N. Cahman, of whose workshop he assumed control around 1737.

Hémen. See De HÉMAN family.

Hencke [Henke], **Johann** (1697–1766). Austrian builder. He was trained in Westphalia and formed his own business in 1725 in Vienna. Hencke is regarded as the leading Viennese builder of his day; he was also associated with Andreas Silbermann.

Hendrickson, Charles (b 1935). American builder. He formed his business in 1964 in Mankato (Minn.) and moved to St Peter (Minn.) in 1967; he specializes in tracker-action instruments.

Hermans, Willem [Guglielmo] (1601–83). Netherlands builder. A Jesuit, he began building organs in Mechelen around 1632. In 1648 he moved to Genoa, where he built organs in a style that blended Flemish and Italian elements.

Herz, Daniel (1618–78). Tyrolean builder. He became the builder at the court at Innsbruck in 1656. His work was widely known, and he became the most important builder in the Tyrol in the 17th century; his tradition was carried on by Jacob Köck (1630–73) and Johann Hackhofer (1645–88).

APPENDIX FOUR

Hildebrandt, Zacharias (1688–1757). German builder. He worked in Saxony, with Gottfried Silbermann (1713–22) and became the builder at the court of the Prince of Saxe-Weissenfels in 1730. While his organs are technically similar to those of Silbermann, they differ tonally in their higher-pitched mixtures, short reeds and string-toned stops. From 1754 Hildebrandt was assisted by his son Johann Gottfried (?1724–75), who continued his work.

Hill. English family of builders. William Hill (1789–1870) worked for Elliot in London from 1815 and was his partner from 1825 to 1832. He was in partnership with Frederick Davison in 1837–8 and with his son Thomas (?1822–93) from around 1855. With the encouragement of Henry Gauntlett he introduced such innovations as large Pedal divisions, high-pressure solo reeds and German tonal concepts from the 1830s and 1840s. Later he adopted the Barker lever and used other mechanical innovations in his large organs, and Thomas introduced pneumatic action and overhanging keys. Thomas's son Arthur George (1857–1923) became a senior partner in 1893; a fine draughtsman, he is best known for his case designs and his two-volume work *The Organ-cases and Organs of the Middle Ages and Renaissance* (1883–91). The firm was amalgamated with that of Norman & Beard in 1916.

Hill, Norman & Beard. English firm. It was formed in 1916 by the merger of Hill & Son with Norman & Beard of Norwich. It was directed by A. G. Hill and G. W. Beard until 1923, when John Christie assumed its direction; from this time a number of cinema organs were built. From 1930 the firm was led by Herbert la French Norman; he was succeeded by his son Herbert John la French in 1960. In 1974 Francis Norman Fowler became the managing director.

Hinners. American firm. It was formed in Pekin (Ill.) in 1879 by John L. Hinners (1846–1906) to make reed and pipe organs. U. J. Albertsen became his partner in 1886, and in 1902 the firm became the Hinners Organ Co. The firm built conservative organs for smaller churches and continued to employ tracker action well into the 20th century. Pipe organ production continued until 1936; reed organs were made until the firm ceased operations in 1942.

Hintz [Hinsch, Hinsz, Hinz], **Albertus Anthoni** (1700–85). German builder. He worked for Franz Caspar Schnitger, whose widow he married, and moved to Groningen, where he built a number of organs with his stepson, Franz Caspar Schnitger the younger, and Hermann Henry Freytag; after Hintz's death his work was carried on by Freytag.

Hobday, Arthur. Manager of branches of FINCHAM & SONS.

Hocquel [Hocqueltz, Hocquet]. Flemish family of builders. They were active in Lorraine in the early 17th century. The family's notable members include Nicolas and his two sons, François (*b* 1617) and Nicolas-François (*b* 1622).

Hodsdon, (Wilfred) Alec (*b* 1900). English maker of harpsichords and clavichords. He restored several kinds of early instrument, including regals and positives.

Hoffmann, Johann (*c*1660–1725). German builder. He was active in Würz-burg from around *c*1695. His teacher was probably Johann Jost Schleich (*c*1645–*c*1707), who introduced the south-east European style to Franconia; Hoffmann's instruments exemplified this tradition.

Holbeck, Severin (*c*1647–1700). German builder of Danish birth. He was active in the Hanseatic area, and from 1690 was the builder at the court of Gotha-Altenburg. Some of his later instruments were for churches in south Germany; Holbeck's work was continued by his son-in-law Johannes Jacobus Donati.

Holbrook, Edwin Lafayette (1824–1904). American builder. The son of the bellfounder and builder George Handel Holbrook (1798–1875), he wor-ked in Millis (Mass.) from 1850 until the 1890s.

Holdich, George Maydwell (1816–96). English builder. He was active from around 1837 in London, where he was noted as a builder of distinguished small church organs; his work was continued from 1894 by Eustace Ingram.

Hollister. Irish family of builders, also harpsichord and piano makers. They were descendants of Robert (*fl* 1688–1715) and Thomas Hollister (*fl* 1695–1720), who were organists in Dublin. Philip (*d* 1760) built instruments in Dublin from around 1732. William Castels (Castles) Hollister (*d* 1802) worked there in the late 18th century; his work was continued by his son Frederick (*b* 1761), a piano maker.

Holt, John W. (1849–1932). English reed organ maker. In 1876 he formed a firm in Birmingham that became a leading maker of large pedal harmoniums, including one of four manuals. His work was continued by his son, also named John W. Holt (*d* 1946); another son, Walter G. Holt, developed the 'Apollo' model for Rushworth & Dreaper.

Holtkamp. American firm. It was formed in 1855 in Cleveland, Ohio, by Gottlieb Ferdinand Votteler (1817–94), and later led by his son, Henry B. Votteler (*b* 1849), who eventually entered into a partnership with J. H. Hettche. Henry H. Holtkamp (1858–1931) joined the firm in 1900, becoming its president in 1905. When Allen G. Sparling became a partner in 1914 the firm became the Votteler–Holtkamp–Sparling Co. Henry's son Walter Henry (1894–1962) assumed leadership of the firm in 1931, bringing the company to prominence with his advocacy of open placement, *Rückpositivs* and classical tonal schemes. Walter H. Holtkamp jr (*b* 1929) became president on his father's death and began building both electric and tracker-action organs.

Holy, Gerhard von (1686–1736). German builder. He completed his train-ing with Arp Schnitger in Hamburg and worked in and around Aurich. In 1711 he received the royal privilege for building in Harlingerland, where he made a number of handsome instruments in the tradition of Schnitger.

Holzhay, Johann Nepomuk (1741–1809). German builder. He worked for his uncle Alexander and later for Karl Josef Riepp before settling in

Ottobeuren. The style of his organs was influenced by the instruments of Riepp and Gabler; with those men Holzhay ranks as one of the leading Swabian builders of the 18th century.

Hooghuys. Belgian family of builders. Active in Bruges, its most important member was Louis Hooghuys (1822–85), son of Simon-Gerardus. The family firm made street organs from 1880; this branch continued into the 1920s under R. Charles Hooghuys, a son of Louis.

Hook & Hastings. American firm. It was formed in Salem (Mass.) in 1827 by the brothers Elias (1805–81) and George Greenleaf Hook (1807–80), former apprentices of William Goodrich. In 1831 it moved to Boston, transferring in 1854 to a large, modern factory, where some of the most notable American church and concert hall organs of the 19th century were built. Francis (Frank) H. Hastings (1836–1916) joined the firm in 1855, becoming a partner in 1871; he introduced advanced Romantic tonal ideas, the Barker lever and small 'stock' organs. Arthur L. Coburn (*d* 1931) became president on Hastings's death, after which the firm declined; it ceased operations in 1936.

Hope-Jones, Robert (1859–1914). English builder. He was trained as an engineer and after 1887 used his skills to develop electric organ actions. He founded his own firm in 1894, forming a partnership with Eustace Ingram of London and Hereford in 1901. In 1903 he emigrated to the USA, where he worked briefly with Austin, Skinner and L. C. Harrison. He formed the Hope-Jones Electric Organ Co. in 1907 in Elmira (NY) but sold his interests in 1910 to the Rudolph Wurlitzer Manufacturing Co.; this firm brought to the cinema organ of the 1920s the radical tonal ideas of his 'Unit Orchestra', as well as its innovations (notably the principle of unification and high wind pressures).

Howard, Emmons (1845–1931). American builder. He was trained with William A. Johnson and later worked for the firm of Steere; he was active in Westfield and Springfield (Mass.) from 1883 to 1929.

Howe. English family of builders. It was prominent in and around London (*c*1485–*c*1670). Its most important members were 'Father' John Howe (i) (*d* 1519) and his son John (ii) (*d* 1571); they built organs for many notable churches and are mentioned in nearly all extant London church records of the period.

Hradetzky. Austrian family of builders. In 1912 Gregor Hradetzky (i) formed a firm, which was re-formed in 1948 by Gregor (ii) (*b* 1909), whose son Gerhard G(regor) (*b* 1944) was trained by his father and Beckerath before he formed a separate firm in 1974 in Oberbergern; there he now builds small organs based on historical principles.

Hutchings, George Sherburn (1835–1913). American builder. He was trained with Hook from 1857 and formed his own firm in 1869 with Mark Plaisted, G.V. Nordstrom, C.H. Preston and J.H. Willcox, under Willcox's name. In 1883 he became the sole owner of the business, which was re-organized as Hutchings–Votey in 1901. His firm built Romantic instruments

ORGAN

of a high quality, and was the chief competitor of Hook & Hastings from the 1870s.

Hüttenrauch, Karl August (1794–1848). German builder. He was apprenticed to Johann Christian Günther in Lichtenwalde and studied mechanics and mathematics in Pest. After 1823 he worked in Glauchau, where he also made pianos.

Ibach. German firm. Formed by Johannes Adolph Ibach (1766–1848), it also made pianos. Johannes Adolph's son Richard (1813–89) took over the direction of the firm's organ building operations in 1869.

Iben, Ibe Peters (1738–1808). German builder. He produced a number of excellent church and domestic organs, conservative in style, in Emden.

Isnard. French family of builders. Jean-Esprit Isnard (baptized 1707; buried 1781) was a major figure in the 18th century, building several large, important organs. His nephew and pupil Jean-Baptiste (1726–1800) worked in Orléans with his brother Joseph (1740–1828), who later settled in Bordeaux, where he repaired organs that had been damaged in the Revolution.

Jahnn, Hans Henny (1894–1959). German writer on organ building. He was an organ consultant to the city of Hamburg in the 1930s and an adviser to the Danish firm of Frobenius (1934–45). His work and writings were influential in the development of the *Orgelbewegung*.

Jann, Georg (*b* 1934). German builder. He worked with Alexander Schuke and the firms of Rieger and Sandtner before taking over the firm of Hirnschrodt in Regensburg in 1974. In 1977 he moved the business to Allkofen under his own name.

Jardine. Family of builders. George (1801–83) was apprenticed to Flight & Robson of London before moving to New York in 1837 with his nephew, Frederick Wincott Jardine (1822–1907), who had been apprenticed to Bishop. Frederick returned to London in 1842 and in 1848 became the manager of Samuel Renn's firm in Manchester, of which he assumed control in 1850 (in partnership with James Kirtland until 1867). Frederick retired in 1874 but his firm continued to operate until 1976. George Jardine remained in New York, where he became a leading builder. His son Edward G. Jardine (*d* 1896), who joined the firm in 1860, studied French organ building and introduced to the USA many continental innovations. Another son, Dudley, built independently under the name of William Smith.

Jehmlich. German family of builders. The brothers Gotthelf Friedrich (1775–1827), Johann Gotthold (1781–1862) and Carl Gottlieb Jehmlich (1786–1867) were trained in the tradition of Silbermann and worked in Dresden. Of Carl Gottlieb's four sons, Carl Eduard (1824–89), a voicer, was the most important; Carl Eduard's sons Emil (1854–1940) and Bruno (1856–1940) built cone-chest organs with pneumatic or electric action. Emil's sons Otto (1903–80) and Rudolf (1908–70) took over the firm in 1936, reverting to slider-chest organs in 1955. The firm is now publicly owned under the direction of Horst Jehmlich.

APPENDIX FOUR

Johannsen [Brouckmann], **Jasper.** Associate of Heinrich Niehoff (*see* NIEHOFF).

Johnson, William Allen (1816–1901). American builder. He built small organs in Westfield (Mass.) from 1844, and soon became a major builder whose organs were found throughout the country. His son William H. Johnson joined the firm in 1871, becoming a partner in 1875 when the name of the firm was changed to Johnson & Son. William Allen retired in 1890; his son ended the company's operations in 1896, possibly because of his unwillingness to convert to pneumatic or electric action.

Johnston, Thomas (1708–67). American builder, also an engraver and musician. He was the first professional builder in Boston, and may have been the first native-born builder in America.

Jordan, Abraham (*d* 1755 or 1756). English builder. He was taught by his father, Abraham (*d c*1716), a distiller who began making organs around 1700. Abraham the younger built up an important business, and introduced the Swell box (1712) to English organs. He may have worked in collaboration with Richard Bridge and John Byfield (1694–1751) in the 1730s.

Joyeuse, Jean de (*c*1635–98). French builder. He was trained in Paris but worked largely in southern France, where he introduced Parisian innovations such as the Grosse Tierce and a new type of bellows.

Karn. Canadian firm of reed organ makers. It was formed in 1867 in Ontario by Dennis W. Karn and John M. Miller and was also known as the Woodstock Organ Co. Later it made pianos and acquired S.R. Warren's organ building firm (*see* WARREN).

Kaschendorff [Caschindorff, Castendorfer, Kastendörffer], **Stephan.** (*c*1425–after 4 February 1499). German builder. He was active from around 1460 in Saxony, where he was considered one of the leading builders. He built organs with independent divisions and used the *Rückpositiv* as early as 1465.

Kastens, Lambert Daniel (*d* 1744). Danish builder of German birth. A pupil of Arp Schnitger, he was the leading builder in Denmark during the high Baroque period. After Schnitger's death Kastens took over his licence in Schleswig, Holstein, Oldenburg and Delmenhorst. In 1724 he opened a workshop in Copenhagen, where he built many new organs for the city's churches after a great fire in 1728.

Kavelens [van Covelen], **Johann** [Jan]. Teacher of Heinrich Niehoff (*see* NIEHOFF).

Kemper. German firm. It was formed by Adolf Kemper (1811–80) and his son Emanuel (1844–1933), who took over the firm of Theodor Voigt in 1868. Emanuel's son Karl Reinhold (1880–1957), a collaborator of H.H. Jahnn in the *Orgelbewegung*, became its director in 1910; Karl's son Emanuel Magnus entered the firm in 1944, expanding its scope to include stringed keyboard instruments. In 1974 Emanuel Reinhold (*b* 1947) became its director, renaming the firm Orgelbau Lübeck in 1981.

Kilgen. American firm. It was formed in 1851 in New York by George Kilgen (d 1902), a German-born builder who had been apprenticed to Voigt, and in 1873 was moved to St. Louis, Missouri. George's son Charles Christian (1859–1932) became a partner in 1886; some of the firm's most notable organs were built during his presidency. After Charles Kilgen's death the firm was reorganized as the Kilgen Organ Co.; after a period of decline it ceased operations in 1960.

Kimball. American firm. It was formed in Chicago in 1857 by William Wallace Kimball (1828–1904) and initially sold only pianos. In 1880 the firm opened a factory to manufacture reed organs, and patented many improvements in the instrument's design; the reed organ department had produced 403,390 instruments by the time it closed in 1922. The organ department opened in 1890 under the direction of Frederic W. Hedgeland, who had been trained in England; this branch closed in 1942, having built more than 7000 organs. The company manufactured electronic instruments from the 1960s.

Kirkland, Alfred. Builder who acquired the firm of Joseph Booth (*see* BOOTH).

Kirtland, James. Nephew of Samuel Renn who continued Renn's work (*see* RENN).

Klais. German firm. It was formed in Bonn in 1882 by Johannes Klais (1852–1925), whose son Hans (1890–1965) and grandson Hans Gerd (*b* 1930) later succeeded to its presidency. From 1948 the firm's work involved building and restoring tracker-action organs; many instruments have been exported.

Klemm [Clemm, Clem], **Johann Gottlob** (1690–1762). American builder of German birth. He was trained in Dresden and emigrated to America in 1733 with a group of Moravians. He built several organs and harpsichords in New York and Bethlehem (Penn.).

Kney, Gabriel (*b* 1929). Canadian builder of German birth. He was apprenticed to Paul Sattel in Speyer and moved to Ontario in 1951. In 1955 he formed his own business with John Bright; this partnership lasted until 1963. The firm now specializes in tracker-action organs.

Koch. German family of organists and builders. Paul the elder (*d* 1546) worked in Zwickau from 1543 with his son Paul the younger (*d* 1580); Stephan (*d* 1590) carried on their work. Georg Koch and his son Georg worked in Glauchau and Zwickau from around 1580 to around 1602.

Koenig. French firm. It was formed in 1896 in Caen by Joseph Koenig (1846–1926), who was a pupil of Mutin; his son Paul-Marie (1887–1977) moved the firm to Paris in 1929. The firm's work balanced elements of the French classical style with that of Cavaillé-Coll.

König. German family of builders. It was active in the Eifel region. Balthasar König (*c*1685–*c*1760) moved to Cologne in 1735; he trained his son Christian Ludwig (1717–89); who later studied with Christian Müller; Christian Ludwig's brothers Johann Kaspar Joseph (1726–63) and Johann Nicolaus

APPENDIX FOUR

(1729–75) worked both independently and for the family. Other members of the family included Carl Philipp Joseph (1750–95) and Adolph Daniel (*b* 1768); these builders continued the family's tradition until around 1803, after which the 'König type' remained a standard model in the German Rhineland until the mid-19th century.

Krebs [Krebser, Kress], **Friedrich** (*d* 1493). German builder. Active in Franconia from 1471, he built several large organs and made significant contributions to the development of the Gothic organ. His work was continued by his nephew Michael Dürr.

Kreutzbach. Danish–German family of instrument makers. Urban Kreutzbach (1796–1868) and his son Richard (1839–1903) built good, conservative organs based on the tradition of Silbermann.

Kuhn. Swiss firm. It was formed in Männedorf by Johann Nepomuk Kuhn (1827–88), whose work was continued by his son Carl Theodor (*d* 1925). The firm developed its own tubular pneumatic action in 1891, and from 1937 was a leader in the *Orgelbewegung*, building neo-Baroque organs with tracker action, many of which were large instruments.

Labagh & Kemp. Firm formed on the retirement of THOMAS HALL.

Ladegast, Friedrich (1818–1905). German builder. He completed his training with Urban Kreutzbach, Mende, Zuberbier and his brother Christlieb Ladegast; he also had contact with the Silbermanns and Cavaillé-Coll. In 1846 he set up his own business in Weissenfels, and was one of the first to adopt the cone-valve chest around 1875. Tonally his instruments were excellent examples of the German Romantic style; they were familiar to Liszt.

Lang [Lange], **Johann** [Hans, Hanss] (1543–1616). German builder. He may have been trained by one of the Scherers of Hamburg. He worked in Leipzig and after 1578 in Kamenz, and was assisted by his son Johann.

Langhedul. Flemish family of builders. The family came from Ieper and was active and influential throughout Europe (*c*1475–1635). Victor (*d* ?1513) was a leading builder in his day; his work was continued by his son-in-law Matthijs de Wulf (*fl* 1515–22) and his son Michiel the elder, who worked in England around 1530. Michiel the elder's son Jan (*d* 1592) worked in France (1583–90) and later in Ghent with Guillaumes (*fl* 1590–95), who was probably his son. Jan's son Matthijs (*d* 1635–6) was perhaps the most important member of the family; he worked in Spain (1592–99) and Paris (1599–1605). Jan and Matthijs, with Crespin Carlier, may be said to have laid the foundation for the French classical organ. Michiel the younger, son of Michiel the elder, was active in Hazebrouck around 1610; Caspar Langhestesel, who worked in the Piedmont region of Italy around 1629, may also have been a member of this remarkable family.

Leavitt, Josiah (1744–1804). American builder, also a physician and organist. He was associated with Thomas Johnston and from around 1791 built church and chamber organs in Boston.

Lefèvre [Lefebvre, Fêvre, Lefeure, Lefébure]. Name of at least 23 French builders. Active from the 16th century to the 19th, most were members of the same family. Antoine (*fl* Paris, 1524–51) and his son Guillaume (*fl* Rouen, 1572–81) were among the earliest builders of this name. Clément (*c*1630–1709) built several large organs in Rouen with his son Germain. The most famous Lefèvre was Jean-Baptiste Nicolas (baptized 1705; *d* 1784), who was active from the 1730s in Rouen; he is regarded as being of comparable importance to F.-H. Clicquot and K.J. Riepp in his influence on the French organ of the 18th century.

Le Hémen. *See* DE HÉMAN family.

Le Picard. Northern French and Flemish family of builders. Philippe (i) (*d* 1702) was active in Amiens from 1667; his work was continued by his sons Antoine, Joseph and Philippe (ii) (*d c*1730). Jean-Baptiste (baptized 1706; *d* 1760), a priest and a son of Philippe (ii), built fine organs in the French style in Liège.

L'Epine [Lépine, Lespine]. French family of builders. Adrian L'Epine worked in Bordeaux (*c*1711–31); his brother Jean-François (i) (*c*1682–1762) was active in Toulouse from 1725. Jean-François (ii) (1732–1817) was a colleague of Bédos de Celles and worked for one of the Isnards and Dominique Cavaillé-Coll; his brother Adrien (*d* 1735) married F.-H. Clicquot's sister.

Lesselier, Guillaume [Leslie, William] (*fl c*1637–41). Scottish builder. Originally from Aberdeen, he built sizeable organs in Rouen (*c*1637–41).

Lewis, Thomas Christopher (*fl c*1861–*c*1900). English builder, also a bell-founder, writer and architect. He worked in London and took his inspiration for organ building from Heinrich Edmund Schulze and Aristide Cavaillé-Coll; he built his largest organ for Southwark Cathedral in 1896.

Lincoln, Henry Cephas (?1789–?1864). English builder. Trained by his father, John, and possibly by Flight & Robson, he held the royal warrant from around 1819 and built a number of good chamber, barrel and church organs; his best work is believed to date from the 1820s.

Lindegrens Orgelbyggeri. Swedish firm. It was formed in 1812 in Göteberg by Mårten Bernhard Söderling (1786–1836), whose sons took over its direction around 1830 and built more than 150 organs. Their pupil Salomon Molander (1833–1905) was the head of the firm with E. G. Eriksson in 1874–7, then continued on his own until 1903, when he was succeeded by Eskil Ragnar Lundén (1881–1945). Harald Lindegren (1887–1956) led the firm from 1918; he was succeeded by his son Tore (*b* 1927).

Lobo, Heitor (*fl* 1537–62). Portuguese builder. He was responsible for some large cathedral organs; the style of those that survive suggests an Italian influence.

Loosemore, John (*b* 1613 or 1614; *d* 1681). English builder. The son of the builder Samuel Loosemore, he was active in Devon from around 1635. His most important organ was built around 1665 for Exeter Cathedral; he also made virginals.

APPENDIX FOUR

Lorentz, Johann [Johan] (*c*1580–1650). Danish builder of German birth. He studied with Nikolaus Maass in Stralsund before opening a workshop in 1608 in Flensburg. He was brought to Copenhagen by Christian IV around 1616 and received a royal privilege in 1639.

Los Angeles Art Organ Co. American firm founded by MURRAY M. HARRIS.

Lund, Carsten (*b* 1940). Danish builder. He worked with Troels Krohn and Poul-Gerhard Andersen before opening his own workshop in 1966 in Copenhagen. He builds tracker-action organs in a neo-Baroque style.

Lupe, de. Spanish family of builders of French origin. Active in Tarazona, its members included Guillaume de Lupe (*c*1540–1607) and his sons Marco (1566–1617) and Gaudioso (1575–1622).

Maass, Nikolaus (*d* 1615). German builder. He was active from 1584 in central and northern Germany – notably in Stralsund and Grimma – and in 1603 settled in Copenhagen, where he was a builder to the royal court. His organs were typical Renaissance instruments, built in the style of David Beck.

McTammany, John (1845–1915). American reed organ maker. He developed an automatic player mechanism for reed organs in 1868 and formed the McTammany Organette Co. in Worcester (Mass.) in 1876. His invention led directly to the development of the player piano.

Maelzel, Johann Nepomuk (1772–1838). German inventor of mechanical instruments. He was active from 1792 in Vienna, where in 1804 he exhibited his panharmonicon, a complex barrel organ that enjoyed great popularity and was often imitated. Maezel also invented the metronome.

Magnusson. Swedish firm. It was formed in 1888 by Johannes Magnusson (1852–1923), a pupil of Salomon Molander. His son Anders (1882–1956) was his partner from 1910; his grandson Stig (*b* 1920), who became a partner in 1947, has been responsible for several innovations in methods of action.

Magnusson, Johannes (1804–75). Swedish builder. He was active in the Växsjö district, where he built small organs which are noted for their classical sound.

Maillard, Paul (*fl c*1610–36). French builder. He was active in Paris, where he built organs for several churches.

Mander, Noel P(ercy) (*b* 1912). English builder and restorer. He worked with Rest Cartwright and Speechly & Sons before forming his own firm in 1936 in London. His son John Pike Mander, after serving an apprenticeship with Beckerath, became a partner in 1975. Mander's work ranges from large organs to positives and regals, and is influenced by classical English practices.

Mannborg, Theodore (1861–1930). German reed organ maker. Trained in Sweden, he made suction reed organs in Saxony from 1889.

Marcussen. Danish firm. It was formed in 1806 by Jürgen Marcussen (1781–1860) and was known in 1826–48 as Marcussen & Reuter. Johannes Lassen Zachariassen (1864–1922), the founder's great-grandson, was the director of the firm from 1902; he was succeeded first by his son Sybrand (1900–60) from 1922 to 1960, then by his grandson Sybrand Jürgen (*b* 1931). Marcussen, which was one of the first firms to adopt *Orgelbewegung* principles, is based in Åbenrå.

Mare, de [de Maar]. German family of builders of Flemish origin. Andreas de Mare (*fl* 1560–99) settled in Groningen, where he built and rebuilt some important organs before moving to Emden. His sons Marten (*c*1540–*c*1612) and Christoffer and their cousin Antonius (*fl* 1612–47) continued the family's work; another builder named Andreas was active as late as 1678. Their organ cases are classed among the finest of the Renaissance.

Marenghi, Charles (*d* 1919). Builder of fairground organs. He was trained by GAVIOLI.

Marín. Spanish family of builders. Gaspar Marín (*c*1540–after 1600) was active in Rioja; Manuel (*c*1575–after 1630), who was probably his son, worked in Valladolid (1588–1630) and is among the most notable Castilian builders of the period.

Marklove, John Gale (1827–91). American builder of English birth. He emigrated to the USA around 1852 and worked for Alvinza Andrews in Utica (NY), where in 1857 or 1858 he formed his own business. His son Clifford continued the firm in partnership with Clarence E. Morey and Al Barnes (as Morey & Barnes); from 1897 to 1935 it continued under Morey alone.

Marr & Colton. American firm. It was formed in 1915 by David J. Marr (1882–1951) and John J. Colton, both of whom had completed their training with Hope-Jones. The firm made many economical cinema organs until 1931, when it was reorganized as the David Marr Co.; it ceased operations in 1947.

Mason & Hamlin. American firm of reed organ makers. It was formed in 1854 in Boston by Henry Mason (1831–90) and Emmons Hamlin (1821–85), who had completed his training with Prince. The firm became a leading maker of melodeons and cabinet organs and from 1883 made pianos as well. Henry Lowell Mason joined the firm in 1888, becoming its president in 1901.

Mason & Risch. American firm of reed organ makers, manufacturers of the vocalion; *see* VOCALION.

Mauracher. Austrian family of builders. The work of Andreas Mauracher (1758–1824) and his son Karl (1789–1844) was continued by several grandsons and great-grandsons, including Josef (1845–1907), who invented several types of chest and key action. Matthäus (1885–1954) and Anton (1896–1962) worked in Linz as 'Gebrüder Mauracher'. The family's firm ended its operations in 1955.

Maxcy-Barton. American firm, formed as the BARTOLA Musical Instrument Co.

Mayer, Joseph Severin (1823–1909). American builder of German birth. He was trained in Germany and worked for three years in New York before moving in 1856 to California, where he was the first to build organs. He settled in the San Francisco area and built 29 church and parlour organs there.

APPENDIX FOUR

Mendoza, Domingo de (c1670–1734). Spanish builder. A pupil of Juan de Andueza, he worked in Madrid from around 1692.

Merklin, Joseph (1819–1905). German builder. He worked in Brussels from 1843, acquired the firm of Ducroquet of Paris in 1855 and moved its main office to Lyons (1870); in 1894 he sold this firm to Kuhn and it continued as Michel, Merklin & Kuhn. Merklin was a prolific builder, responsible for many large organs, and a strong rival to Cavaillé-Coll.

Metzler Orgelbau. Swiss firm. It was formed in 1890 in Graubünden by Jakob Metzler and in 1930 was moved to Dietikon by Jakob's son Oskar, who with his brother Hansueli assumed the firm's direction in 1968. Metzler has carried out many restorations, and was an early adherent of the *Orgelbewegung*.

Midmer-Losh. American firm. It was formed in Brooklyn (NY) in 1860 by Reuben Midmer (1824–95), an Englishman who had worked for Hall and Ferris. Midmer's work was continued by his son, who moved the firm to Long Island and in the 1920s entered into a partnership with C. Siebert Losh. The firm's most notable instrument is the huge organ in the Atlantic City Convention Hall (1932).

Mockers, Felix. Partner in the firm of STIEHR-MOCKERS.

Mofferriz. Spanish family of builders of Moorish origin. Mahoma (Juan) Mofferriz (i) (d c1545) made organs, harpsichords and the earliest Iberian claviorgans. His sons Mahoma (ii) (d before 1524) and Calema (Miguel) and grandsons, Miguel (d 1545) and Gabriel (d 1573) continued the family's work.

Molero, Fernando. Son-in-law of JULIÁN DE LA ORDEN.

Möller. American firm. It was formed in 1875 by Mathias Peter Möller (1854–1937), a Dane who had emigrated to the USA in 1872 and worked for Derrick & Felgemaker; in 1880 the firm moved to Hagerstown, Maryland. Mathias's work was continued by his son M. P. Möller jr (1902–61) and by his son-in-law W. Riley Daniels, whose son Peter Möller Daniels became the firm's director in the 1980s. Richard Whitelegg, a noted English voicer, was the tonal director in the 1930s. The firm builds electric-action organs of 'American classic' tonal design.

Möller [Müller], **Johann Patroklus** (1697 or 1698–1772). German builder. He was active from 1720 in Lippstadt, where he built several large organs. He used spring-chests and was important in developing the typical, colourful 18th-century Westphalian organ, based in the tradition of Bader.

Mönch & Prachtel. German firm. It was formed in 1875 in Überlingen by Xaver Mönch (d 1907), who was later joined by his sons Otto (d 1954) and Franz; his work was eventually continued by his grandson Karl-Otto. Horst-Friedrich Prachtel (b 1934) became a partner in 1972, and on Karl-Otto's retirement in 1975 was joined by Peter-Otto Mönch (b 1952). The firm now builds slider-chest organs.

Moore, A. David (b 1946). American builder. After graduating from the University of Vermont he was apprenticed to C. B. Fisk. He opened a workshop in 1972 in North Pomfret, Vermont, where he builds tracker-action organs influenced by French classical tonal ideals.

Moors [Mors, Morss, de Moer, de Moor]. Flemish family of organists, builders and instrument makers. Active in Antwerp, its members included Anton (i) (*d* 1539) and his sons Cornelis (*c*1500–57) and Anton (ii) (*c*1500–before August 1562). Anton moved to north Germany, where he introduced many Brabantine tonal innovations.

Mooser, (Jean Pierre Joseph) Aloys (1770–1839). Swiss builder, also a piano maker. The son of the builder Joseph Anton Moser (1731–92) of Fribourg, he became the best-known builder in Switzerland during the first half of the 19th century; his organs combine south German and early Romantic styles. His work was continued by his sons Joseph, Alexander and Moritz.

Moreau, Jacobus Franciscus [Jacob François] (*c*1684–1751). Netherlands builder. He worked in The Hague and Rotterdam, where he built several large organs that combined an individual style of voicing with north German traditions. His work was continued by his son Johannes Jacobus [Jean Jacob] (*d c*1762) and his nephew Louis de la Haye the younger.

Morey & Barnes. American firm formed by JOHN GALE MARKLOVE.

Moucherel. French family of builders. Christophe Moucherel studied in Paris, working from 1717 in Toul, where he built several large organs; his brother Sebastian (i) (*d* 1755) made organs and oboes in Nancy. Another brother, Claude (*d* 1744), also worked in Nancy with his son Sebastian (ii) (*b* 1733).

Müller, Christian [Christiaan] (1690–1763). German builder. He was active in Holland and West Friesland and is best known for the large organ (built 1735–8) in the Grote Kerk (St Bavo) in Haarlem. His work was continued by his pupil J. H. H. Bätz.

Mustel, Victor (1815–90). French reed organ maker. He formed the firm of Mustel in Paris in 1853, and in 1855 exhibited a harmonium with 'Double expression' and a new stop (Harpe éolienne). The firm's later inventions, which included the Métaphone and Typophone (a percussion device), helped Mustel's instruments gain popularity. Victor's son Alphonse (*d* 1936), who continued his work, invented the celesta (1886).

Mutin, Charles. Builder who continued the work of ARISTIDE CAVAILLÉ-COLL.

Nacchini [Nachini, Nanchini, Nakić], **Pietro** [Petar] (baptized 1694; *d* 1765). Italian builder of Dalmatian birth. A Franciscan monk, he worked with Pierantoni and Pescetti in 1729 and independently in Venice from around 1733. He built about 500 organs and developed the 18th-century Italian style, introducing such innovations as the *tiratutti*. His pupil Gaetano Callido is believed to have continued his work.

Nassarre, José (*fl* 1730–36). Spanish builder. He was active from around 1730 in Mexico, where he built several large cathedral organs, including those in the Metropolitan Cathedral, Mexico City. He may have been related to the theorist and organist Pablo Nassarre.

Nicholson. English firm. Formed around 1816 in Rochdale, it was later run by Richard Nicholson, whose brothers opened workshops in Walsall, Newcastle upon Tyne and, in 1841, Worcester. The branch in Worcester took over the activities of the branch in Walsall in 1955, and continued to operate into the 1980s.

Niehoff [Nyhoff, Nyeuwenhoff, Nyeuwenhuys, Niegehoff, Neuhoff]. Family of builders. It was active in the Low Countries, the Rhineland, Hessen and Franconia. Heinrich [Hendrik] Niehoff (c1495–1560), who may have been from Münster, served his apprenticeship in Amsterdam with Johann Kavelens (d 1532) whose work he continued in 1533. His brother Hermann (c1495–after 1546) worked with him, as did his son Nikolaus (c1525–c1604), who took over his work. In 1538 Heinrich moved to 's Hertogenbosch, where he studied the work of Breisiger and of Hans Suys, who became his partner; they worked together on several large organs, including that in the Oude Kerk, Amsterdam. After Suys's death (by 1544) Heinrich worked with Jasper Johannsen. He consolidated the innovations of Kavelens (such as wide-scaled chorus stops) and Suys (such as colour stops) in his excellent spring-chest organs, which influenced other Brabantine builders as well as those of the Hamburg school.

Nitrowski. Polish family of builders. Its members were active in and around Danzig. Jerzy Nitrowski (c1605–after 1673) worked from around 1631; his sons Andrzej (c1640–97) and Daniel (c1635–after 1683) built several important organs in the northern Polish style in the second half of the 17th century.

Noack, Fritz (b 1935). American builder of German birth. He was apprenticed to Beckerath before emigrating to the USA in 1959. He worked for Estey and Fisk, opened his own workshop in 1960 in Lawrence (Mass.) and moved to Georgetown in 1970. His tracker-action organs adhere to *Werkprinzip* designs and are tonally influenced by historical and neo-Baroque concepts; they range in size from large church organs to positives, regals and practice instruments.

Nordström, Sven (1801–87). Swedish builder. He built small organs from 1834 in Norra Solberga; his brother Eric worked with him from the 1850s; at the end of the 1870s the business moved to Eksjö.

Norman & Beard. English firm. It was formed by the cabinet maker William Norman of Norwich, who worked for J. W. Walker and T. C. Lewis. William's sons Ernest William (1852–1927) and Herbert John (1861–1936) opened a workshop in 1868 in Diss, Norfolk; the firm later moved to Norwich, and in 1896 John Wells Beard became a partner. The firm built more than 1400 organs before it merged with Hill & Son in 1916; it also made piano pedalboards. The firm continued as Hill, Norman & Beard into the 1980s.

Nutting, William (1815–69). American builder. Largely self-taught, he made organs and reed organs in Randolph and Bellows Falls, Vermont, from the 1840s. In 1848 his brother Rufus patented a reed organ that he called the Aeolodeon.

Odell. American firm. It was formed in 1859 in New York by the brothers John Henry (1830–99) and Caleb Sherwood Odell (1827–93), who had completed their training with R. M. Ferris and William Robjohn. The firm, which patented several action designs in the 1860s and 1870s, was continued on a small scale by the family until the 1970s.

Ohrmann & Nutt. Firm of builders that continued the work of JOHN SNETZLER.

Oldovini, Paschaly Caetanus (*fl* 1758–77). Portuguese builder of Italian origin. He was active in Evora, where he worked on a number of projects at the cathedral.

Orden, Julián de la (*c*1730–94). Spanish builder. His father was the builder Pedro de la Orden; he built several large organs, including those at Cuenca and Malaga cathedrals, from around 1762. His son-in-law Fernando Molero was the official builder at Cuenca Cathedral (1785–9).

Ott, Paul (*b* 1903). German builder. He formed a business in 1932 in Göttingen that after 1945 became an important firm of builders and restorers; it has a large export market.

Packard. American firm of reed organ makers. It was formed in 1839 in Campello, (Mass.) by Isaac T. Packard (*b* 1817), who invented a version of the exhaust (or suction) bellows for reed organs in 1852. The firm moved to Chicago and in 1871 a factory was opened in Fort Wayne (Ind.). Isaac's work was continued by Albert S. Bond, the firm's general manager from 1886.

Paoli. Italian family of builders. The brothers Giacobbe (1796–after 1869) and Michelangelo Paoli (1777–1854) were active in Tuscany; their work was continued by numerous sons and grandsons, of whom Michelangelo's son Raffaelo (1822–after 1893) and grandson Pietro (1844–after 1900) were the most prolific.

Parizot. French family of builders. Claude Parizot (1700–50), a pupil of Christophe Moucherel, was active in Normandy; his nephews Nicolas (1730–92) and Henri (1730–95) worked for him and later opened independent workshops in Le Mans.

Penigk [Pönick, Poenicke], **Johann Peter** (*fl c*1691–*c*1720). German builder. He was a member of a significant group of builders in central Germany. Active in Hof around 1691, he built organs in Saxony, Thuringia and Bavaria.

Pescheur. French family of builders. Pierre (i) (*fl* 1544) and Nicolas (?1555–1616) began the family's tradition. Nicolas did much work in Paris after 1600; his son Pierre (ii) (*b* ?1587; *d* between 1637 and 1640) introduced several innovations, such as the independent Cornet, which marked the transition between the Carlier type of organ and later Parisian styles.

Peter, Willi (1907–78). German builder. Trained by Sauer, he formed his own business in 1945 in Cologne. Georg Eglseder (*b* 1930) and Helmut Klöpping (*b* 1936) became his partners in 1977; their firm has built about 500 organs.

Pfannmüller [Phanmüller, Phanmulner], **Friedrich** (*c*1490–before 1562). German builder. He was active in the upper Palatinate from around 1538 and worked on the organ in St. Vitus's Cathedral, Prague (1553–62). His organs are transitional in that they depart in some respects from the Gothic style; they also show Flemish influences.

Pfeffer, Johann Georg (1823–1910). American builder. Trained in Germany, he emigrated to the USA in 1854 and settled in 1858 in St Louis (Missouri), where from around 1860 he built more than 600 organs, most of which were for Catholic churches. After 1882 four of his sons joined the firm, which was sold to Kilgen in 1910.

Phelps, Lawrence Irving (*b* 1923). American builder. He was trained with the Aeolian Skinner Organ Co. and Walter Holtkamp and was the tonal director of Casavant Frères (1958–72). From 1972 to 1981 he operated his own firm in Erie (Penn.), and he became the tonal director of Allen Organs in 1983. An advocate of *Orgelbewegung* principles, he is also a prolific writer.

Pierce, Samuel (1819–95). American builder. He was trained in the Hook workshop and formed a pipemaking business in 1847 in Reading (Mass.), which supplied pipes to organ builders nationwide. Taken over in 1897 by William A. Dennison, his firm ceased operations in 1970.

Pieterszoon, Adriaan (?*c*1400–80). Netherlands builder. Active in the Low Countries from around 1446, he built several large but conservative organs.

Pilcher. American firm. It was formed in 1833 by Henry Pilcher (1798–1880), who had emigrated to the USA around 1832. The son of the London builder William Pilcher (*fl* 1820–40), he opened his business in Newark (NJ) and New Haven (Conn.) before moving around 1858 to St Louis (Missouri) with his sons Henry jr (1828–90) and William (*b* 1830). In 1872 Henry jr and his three sons moved the firm to Louisville (Ky), where it prospered and built many large organs. It remained under the family's control until it was sold to the firm of Möller in 1944.

Pirchner. German family of builders associated with the firm of REINISCH.

Plum, Peter (*b* 1937). German builder. He was trained in Aachen and Ludwigsburg and later worked with the firm of Walcker. He established a consultancy in 1966 and subsequently built organs to his own designs; he is also known as an author and lecturer.

Positive Organ Co. Firm formed by THOMAS CASSON.

Prachtel, Horst–Friedrich. Partner in the firm of MÖNCH & PRACHTEL.

Prato, Lorenzo da (*fl* 1470–75). Italian builder. Active in Bologna, he was a member of the important 15th-century Tuscan school, to which his father Giacomo also belonged. He is known principally for his work in the Basilica of S Petronio, Bologna.

ORGAN

Prescott, Abraham (1789–1858). American reed organ maker. He began manufacturing small 'lap organs' in 1836 in Concord (NH); by the 1850s his firm had produced many seraphines and melodeons. Prescott also made bass viols.

Prince, George A. (1818–90). American reed organ maker. He formed a firm in Buffalo (NY) around 1840; it was one of the first to attempt large-scale production of melodeons, for which Prince took out several patents in 1846. His work was continued by his brother (Samuel) in partnership with Charles E. Bacon in 1879.

Pröbstl. German family of builders. Its members included Joseph (1789–1866), who began building in 1823 and worked in Füssen from 1826, and his son Balthasar (1830–95), after whose death the family workshop was taken over by Hermann Späth (1867–1917).

Puche [Puig]. Spanish family of builders. Tomás Puche was active in Saragossa around 1550; Cosme, who may have been Tomás's brother, was a builder in Alfajarín. Other members of the family were Juan (*b* c1550), who was active from 1584 to 1587, and Miguel (*d* ?1688), who worked in Toledo (1649–63).

Puget. French family of builders. Théodore Puget (1799–1883) formed a firm in Toulouse in 1834; his work was continued in 1877 by his sons Eugène (1838–92) and Jean-Baptiste (1849–1940), whose son Maurice (1884–1960) later became the head of the firm.

Putz. German family of builders. Active in Lower Austria, it built organs in the south German style. Andreas Putz (*fl* 1613–57), his sons Georg (*d* 1694) and Jakob (*d* 1706) and his grandson Martin (*d* 1700) built several large organs; in 1636 Andreas installed a Hornwerk in the abbey at Lambach.

Pyke, George (*fl* 1765–90). English builder, also a maker of organ clocks. He was the teacher of Samuel Green.

Rabiny. Alsatian family of builders. In 1787 Joseph Rabiny (1732–1813), a nephew and pupil of Riepp, established himself in Rouffach, where he built in the tradition of Riepp, Silbermann and Clicquot; his work was continued by Callinet. His half-brother Gregoire (i) (1740–after 1790) worked at Vicdessos, and his son Gregoire (ii) (1766–after 1812) worked in Rouffach and Epinal.

Reinisch. Tyrolean family of builders. Joseph Reinisch (1776–1848) worked with Franz and Franz Xaver Fuchs; his son Franz (i) (1801–88), grandson Franz (ii) (1840–1921) and great-grandson Karl (1876–1932) continued his work. Karl's brother Franz (1878–1969) was a notable pipemaker who built organs with Johann Pirchner (i) (1900–72) from 1932. Johann Pirchner (ii) (*b* 1928) directed the firm from 1962, when it became Reinisch, Pirchner & Co.

Renn, Samuel (1786–1845). English builder. He worked with his uncle, James Davis, and was in partnership with John Boston in Lancashire (1822–35); his work was continued by his nephew James Kirtland, who was in partnership with Frederick Wincott Jardine from 1850 to 1867. Renn adapted the factory system to his organ building, but this did not result in any loss of quality.

Rensch. German firm. It was formed by Richard Rensch (*b* 1923) in 1956 in Lauffen; Rensch, who had studied with Walcker, in 1965 invented a mechanical combination action. His son Christhard (*b* 1952) was trained with the firm of Rieger in Austria and became his father's partner in 1976. The firm builds tracker-action organs.

Reubke, Adolf (1805–75). German builder. A self-taught builder, he was active in Quedlinburg from 1839. He experimented with pneumatic actions and built Romantic organs equal to those of Walcker and Ladegast; his work was continued by Ernest Röver.

Reuter. American firm. It was formed in 1917 by Adolph C. Reuter (1880–1971), A. G. Sabol and Henry Jost, and moved in 1919 to Lawrence, Kansas, where more than 2000 electro-pneumatic organs have been built. R. Franklin Mitchell, an exponent of the 'American classic' design, became the firm's chairman in 1982, with Alfred Neutel as its president.

Rieger. Austrian firm. It was formed in 1845 in Silesia by Franz Rieger (1812–85), whose sons Otto (i) (1847–1903) and Gustav (1848–1905) took over the firm in 1873; Otto's son Otto (ii) (1880–1920) led the firm from 1904. Josef Edler von Glatter-Götz took control of the business in 1920, in partnership with his sons Egon (1911–40) and Josef Karl Maria (*b* 1914), then moved it to Schwarzach around 1945. The firm builds tracker-action organs that are noted for their imaginative, modern casework.

Riepp, Karl Joseph (1710–75). German builder. Trained in southern Germany, he worked in eastern France with his brother Rupert (*b* 1711; *d* between 1747 and 1750) from 1742. His organs, notably those at Ottobeuren, combine characteristics of both the French and German schools; Riepp's work was continued by his nephew and pupil, Joseph Rabiny.

Ritter, Johann Nikolaus (1702–82). German builder. He was apprenticed to Müller and worked for Schröter, Gottfried Silbermann and Trost before opening his own workshop with Graichen (1701–60) in 1739 in Hof. Ritter was the most important builder in his day in east Franconia; his work was continued by Friedrich Heidenreich (1741–1819) and his son Eberhard Friedrich (*c*1770–1830).

Robson, Thomas Joseph F. (*d* 1876). English builder. He continued the work of his father, Joseph Robson, who had been a partner of Benjamin Flight (*c*1806–32). Thomas built several important organs; he was one of the earliest English builders to use pedal pipes. He was succeeded by his son Charles.

Rodensteen [Rottenstein-Pock]. Netherlands family of builders. Israel Rodensteen was active around 1507; Raphael (*d* between 1552 and 1554) and his son Hermann (*b* *c*1510–20; buried 1583) were the most important and influential members of the family: they built large organs throughout the Netherlands, Germany and Austria. Hermann's brother Gabriel worked independently.

Röder, Johann Michael (*fl* 1713–45). German builder. He was apprenticed to Arp Schnitger and later worked in central Germany, where he built organs in a style closer to that of Michael Engler (ii).

Roethinger. French firm. It was formed in 1895 by Edmond Alexandre Roethinger (1866–1953), whose work was continued by his son Max (*b* 1897) and grandson André (*b* 1928). The firm, which is known for its restoration work, is situated near Strasbourg.

Rohrer, Johann Georg (1686–1765). Alsatian builder. He was trained in Bohemia, settled in Strasbourg in 1709, and studied in Paris in 1722–8. His career was hampered by an unhappy marriage.

Römer. Family name of several Austrian builders. Johann Ulrich Römer (*b* ?after 1650) and his brother Ferdinand Josef (*c*1657–1723) were active from around 1684 in Vienna, where Ferdinand Josef had a court appointment. Andreas Josef Römer (*b* 1704; *d* before 1750) and his son Anton (1724–79) worked in Brno and Graz; Anton also made clavichords.

Roosevelt, Hilborne Lewis (1849–86). American builder. He worked for Hall & Labagh and built his first organ in their shop in 1869; shortly afterwards he opened his own shop in New York with his brother Frank (1862–95). The Roosevelts experimented with electric action and adopted European Romantic tonal concepts, to the point of importing reed stops from Paris.

Ruprecht. German family of builders. Its members, who were active in the Netherlands and Westphalia, included Heironymus Ruprecht (*fl* 1626–61), Johannes (*fl* 1658–75 in Boppard), and Conrad (*fl* 1656–1706).

Rushworth & Dreaper. English firm. It was formed in Liverpool in the early 19th century by William Rushworth; in the early 1900s it merged with the music retail firm of Dreaper. Under the direction of Alastair Rushworth, the firm builds instruments in a neo-Baroque style.

Ryder, George Horatio (1839–1922). American builder. He was apprenticed to Hook before opening a business in 1870 in Boston with Joel Butler (who set up on his own in 1871). In 1883 he moved to Reading (Mass.), where he built small organs of a high quality until his retirement in 1896.

Sá Couto (Lagoncinha), Manoel de (*d* 1846). Portuguese builder. He built a number of good neo-classical organs from 1799 in and around Braga.

Sans, Tiburcio (*b* 1652). Spanish builder. Apprenticed to an uncle in Madrid, he was sent around 1692 with his brother Felix to install and repair organs in Mexico.

Sauer, Wilhelm (1831–1916). German builder. He studied with his father, Ernst (1799–1873), and completed his training in France, England and Switzerland; he worked in particular with the firms of Walcker and Cavaillé-Coll. In 1857 he formed his own company in Frankfurt an der Oder; acquired after his death by Oscar Walcker and managed by Karl Ruther (1867–1955), the firm reopened in 1945 under the direction of Anton Spallek (1895–1970) and his son Gerhard (*b* 1931). The firm's late 19th-century work shows a creative fusion of French and German Romantic characteristics; its later organs are more neo-Baroque.

Sawyer, John William (*d* 1919). English reed organ maker. He founded a business in 1885 in Leeds that made large two- and three-manual instruments for church use.

Schantz [Tschantz]. American firm. It was formed in 1873 in Ohio by Abraham J. Tschantz (1849–1921) to make reed organs; from 1890 it made pipe organs and soon afterwards developed the Zephyr fan blower. After 1900 Abraham's sons Edison (1878–1974), Oliver (1882–1938) and Victor (i) (1885–1973) joined the firm; they were followed by his grandsons John, Paul and Bruce, who later were principals of the company with Victor Schantz (ii) and Jack Sievert. Between 1945 and 1970 the firm built more than 11,000 organs.

Scheibe, Johann (*c*1680–1748). German builder. He was active from 1710 in Leipzig, where he rebuilt church organs; in this he may have been influenced by the tonal ideas of J. S. Bach, especially with regard to reeds.

Schentzer, Johannes [Hans] (*fl* 1508–41). German builder. He was active in the south-west region of Germany, where narrow-scaled flues, tierce mixtures and various short-length reeds were being introduced.

Scherer. German family of builders. Among its members were Jakob Scherer (*d* 1574 or later), who took over the business of Jakob Iversand in 1537, and his son Hans (*fl* *c*1600–31); together they played an important part in the development of the Hamburg tonal and visual style that culminated in the work of Gottfried Fritzsche.

Scherr [Sheer]. Danish family of instrument makers. The organ builder Johan Nicolai Scherr (*d* 1804) and his son Emilius Nicolai (1794–1874) emigrated to the USA in 1822 and settled in Philadelphia, where they made organs and stringed instruments.

Schiedmayer, J. & P. German firm of reed organ makers. It was formed in 1853 in Stuttgart and made both pressure and suction instruments, including a large concert harmonium produced in 1897; in the same year the firm was reorganized as Schiedmayer Pianofabrik.

Schiörlin, Pehr (1736–1815). Swedish builder. He was a pupil of Jonas Wistenius in Linköping and became his partner in 1769. His early work was classical, but in the 1790s he fell under the Romantic influence of Vogler.

Schlag. German family of builders. In 1831 Christian Gottlieb Schlag (1803–89) took over the firm of Kiesewetter in Jauer and with his brother Johann Karl (1808–69) continued the business at Schweidnitz. Christian Gottlieb's sons Theodor (1847–1918) and Oskar (1848–1918) became partners in the firm in 1869 and received an appointment to the royal court in 1900. In

1903 Theodor's sons Reinhold (1874–after 1952) and Bruno (1879–1903) entered the firm, which ended its operations around 1918.

Schleich, Johann Jost. Teacher of JOHANN HOFFMANN.

Schlicker, Herman L(eonhard) (1902–74). American builder of Bavarian birth. He was trained with Steinmeyer and Marcussen, emigrated to the USA in 1925 and after working for the firms of Wurlitzer and Tellers opened his own business in 1932 in Buffalo (NY). An early advocate of the *Orgelbewegung*, he used expansion chambers on electric chests and made tracker-action instruments from 1963. His firm was continued by his widow and son-in-law, then sold in 1981 to Conrad and Theresa Van Viegen.

Schlimbach. German family of instrument makers. Its members were active in Franconia. Johann Caspar Schlimbach (1777–1861) made organs, pianos and harmoniums from 1806; his work was continued by his son Martin (1811–1901). Of his other sons Gustav (1818–94) built organs in Speyer (1845–*c*1889) and Balthasar (1807–96) worked in Würzburg. Balthasar's son Martin Josef (1841–1914) and his grandson Alfred (1875–1952) continued his work.

Schmahl. Swabian family of instrument makers. Its members included a number of organ builders: Johann Michael Schmahl (1654–1725) formed a firm in Heilbron with his sons Johann Friedrich (1693–1737) and Johann Adam (1704–57), a noted builder; another son, Georg Friedrich (1700–73) formed a branch in Ulm; and a third branch was formed at Zittau by Georg Friedrich's son Leonard Balthasar (1729–79).

Schmid, Gerhard (*b* 1925). German builder. He was trained with several builders and opened his own business in 1955 in Kaufbeuren. Schmid has built more than 120 tracker-action organs and undertaken many restorations.

Schmidt, Paul (*b* 1715–16; *d* 1798). German builder. A pupil of Caspar Sperling, he was regarded as the most important builder in Mecklenburg and Schwerin in the second half of the 18th century. He was active from 1745 and built instruments in the east German tradition.

Schneider, Andreas (*b* ?before 1640; buried 1685). German builder. He worked from 1677 in Höxter, where he built spring-chest organs in the tradition of Bader; he was the first to introduce Netherlands stops to Westphalia.

Schnitger. German family of builders. Arp Schnitger (1648–1719) worked with his cousin Berendt Huess (*d* 1676) and continued his work. He built more than 150 organs in northern Germany and the Netherlands in the mature Hamburg style. These are characterized by well-developed chorus work and colourful reeds and mutations; his influence continued into the 20th century. His sons Johann Georg (baptized 1690; *d* after 1733) and Franz Caspar (baptized 1693; *d* 1729) were later active in the Netherlands.

Schoenstein. American firm. It was formed in 1877 by Felix Fridolin Schoenstein (1849–1936), who had been apprenticed to the orchestrion maker

Hubert Blessing in Germany. Schoenstein moved from Baden to San Francisco in 1868, at first working for Mayer. In the early 20th century his sons Louis (*d* 1980), Otto and Erwin joined the firm. In the 1980s the firm was managed by Louis' son Terrence, his nephew Paul, and Jack Bethards.

Schramm, Johann Jacob (1724–1808). German builder. He was active in Mülsen St Niclas. Although he completed his training with Gottfried Silbermann, his organs tend to incorporate more narrow-scaled stops than do Silbermann's organs.

Schrider [Schreider, Schröder, Shrider], **Christopher** [Christoph] (buried 1751). English builder of German birth. He was the son-in-law of Father Smith, whose work he continued in 1708. He built many organs in the style of Smith, and held the royal appointment, which later passed to his son Christopher (*d* 1763).

Schröter, Johann Georg (1683–1750). German builder. He worked in Erfurt, where he built small and medium-sized organs of a high quality.

Schuelke, William [Wilhelm] (1848–1902). American builder of German origin. He was trained in Germany, moved to Ohio in 1864 and formed a business in 1875 in Milwaukee. His son Max (1878–1975) continued his work; another son, William J. Schuelke (1888–1960), worked independently from around 1916.

Schuke. German firm. It was formed in 1894 when Carl Alexander Schuke (1870–1933), who had worked for the firm of Sauer, took control of the firm of Gottlieb Heise (1785–1848) in Potsdam; a branch was opened in Berlin in 1950. Schuke's work was continued by his sons: in 1953 Karl-Ludwig-Alexander (*b* 1906) became the director of the firm in Potsdam (renamed VEB Potsdamer Schuke-Orgelbau in 1972), and in the same year Hans-Joachim (*b* 1908) became the head of the branch in Berlin. The Schukes abandoned electro-pneumatic action for tracker-action in 1933.

Schulze. German family of builders. Johann Andreas (*c*1740–1810) and his son Johann Friedrich (1793–1858) were active in Paulinzelle; Johann Friedrich's sons Heinrich Edmund (1824–78), Herward (*c*1830–1908) and Eduard (1830–80) continued his work in 1858. The family's work was influenced by that of Johann Gottlob Töpfer and was popular and influential in England after 1851.

Schwab, Matthias (1808–64). American builder of German birth. He was trained in Freiburg and was the earliest known builder in Cincinnati, where he worked from 1831 to 1860.

Schwan, Olof (1744–1812). Swedish builder. A pupil of Jonas Gren and Peter Stråhle, he worked for Matthias Swahlberg from 1771; he later operated independently. His work was influenced to a slight degree by the ideas of Vogler.

Schwarbrook, Thomas. *See* SWARBRICK, THOMAS.

Schwarz, Thomas Jakob (1695–1754). Czech builder. A Jesuit lay brother, he was active in Bohemia, Moravia and Silesia; he worked in the style of Michael Engler (ii).

Seifert. German family of builders. Ernst Hubertus Seifert (1855–1928) studied with Jahn and formed a business in 1885 in Cologne. In 1906 he opened a branch of the firm in Kevelaer, and in 1915 entrusted it to his son Romanus (1883–1960), who later continued his work. Romanus's son Ernst (*b* 1910) later took over the firm, abandoning electric action for tracker-action; Helmut Seifert (*b* 1916) took charge of the firm's branches.

Serassi. Italian family of builders. Giuseppe Serassi (i) (1694–1760) and his son Andrea Luigi (1725–99) were active in Bergamo from around 1730. Andrea's son Giuseppe (ii) (1750–1817) was the most important member of the family; he built spring-chest organs in which Romantic stops and special effects were superimposed on the classical Italian scheme. Another son of Andrea and a grandson continued his work into the late 19th century.

Sesma, de. Spanish family of builders. Active in Saragossa; its members included José de Sesma (Infanzón) (*c*1630–99), his son Jorge (*d* 1690) and his son Francisco (*c*1660–after 1717), who built several cathedral organs.

Setterquist. Swedish family of builders. In 1845 Erik A. Setterquist, the adopted son and a pupil of Johan Samuel Strand, formed a business in Hallsberg. His son Gustaf (1842–1906) became a partner in 1874; his work was continued by his own son Gunnar (i) (1879–1936) and his grandson Gunnar (ii). The firm moved to Örebro in 1860; it ceased operations in 1977.

Seuffert. German family of builders. Johann Philipp Seuffert (1693–1780) was apprenticed to Hoffmann and took over the workshop of F. C. Hillenbrand around 1722. He became the court builder at Würzburg in 1731; his son Franz Ignaz succeeded him in 1760. Another son, Johann Ignaz, worked in France and in the Rhenish Palatinate.

Séverin [Severijn], **André** [Andries, Andry] (*c*1605–73). Netherlands builder. He was probably a pupil of Florent Hocquet, and worked in Liège; he is regarded as the most important builder in the Meuse valley in the 17th century.

Sharp, Ronald (William) (*b* 1929). Australian builder. Trained as an engineer, he has built several large organs of unique mechanical and visual design, notably that in the Sydney Opera House (1969–79).

Sieburg, Jodokus [Jost] (*d* 1686). German builder. He may have been of Saxon origin and was active in East Friesland with his brother Johann from around 1642.

Silbermann. German family of builders and instrument makers. Andreas Silbermann (1678–1734), who completed his training with Eugen Casparini and Friedrich Ring, was active in Strasbourg (*c*1699–1704) and worked in Paris for Francois Thierry (1704–6). He settled in Strasbourg, and his work was continued by his sons Johann Andreas (1712–83) and Johann Daniel (1717–66). Gottfried Silbermann (1683–1753) worked for his brother

APPENDIX FOUR

Andreas (*c*1701–10), then was active in Freiberg and in Dresden, where he also made clavichords and pianos, as his nephew Johann Heinrich did later. The manner in which the Silbermanns successfully blended south German and French elements had a lasting influence in Alsatia and Saxony.

Simmons, William Benjamin Dearborn (1823–76). American builder. He was apprenticed to Appleton and was in business with Thomas McIntyre (1845–51); George Fisher became his partner in 1856 and he was in partnership with John Henry Willcox (1827–75), between 1858 and 1860. Simmons was an innovator: he introduced equal temperament, the Barker lever and German tonal ideas to the Boston school.

Skinner, Ernest M(artin) (1886–1961). American builder. He was apprenticed to Ryder and Hutchings and formed his own firm in 1901 in Boston. He lost control of the firm after its merger with the Aeolian Co. (*see* AEOLIAN-SKINNER), and formed a new firm with his son Richmond in Methuen around 1932, this was later continued by Carl Bassett. Skinner invented the pitman chest and was the leading proponent of orchestral voicing in the early 20th century.

Slegel [Schlegel]. Netherlands family of builders. It originated in Zwolle. Jorrien (i) (*d* before 1568) and his sons Cornelis (*d* 1593) and Michiel (*d* *c*1585) built several large organs in northern Germany from around 1545. Michiel's son Jorrien (ii) (*d* after 1615) and his grandson Jan (*d* before 7 Oct 1604) carried on the family's work.

Smith [Schmitt, Schmidt], **'Father' (Bernard)** [Bernhard, Baerend, Baerent] (*c*1630–1708). English builder. He was either of north German or Netherlands origin and may have been trained by Förner. Active in London from 1667, he was the chief rival of Renatus Harris. He built organs for many notable churches, including St Paul's Cathedral (1694–9), and became the King's organ maker in 1681. Smith's work was continued by his son-in-law Christopher Schreider; two of his nephews, Gerard and Christian Smith, opened their own workshops in 1689 and 1690.

Smith American. American firm of reed organ makers. It was formed in 1852 in Boston; by 1885 it had built 112,000 instruments of all sizes and had branch offices in Kansas City and London.

Smits. Netherlands family of builders. The brothers Nicolaas Lambertus (1790–1831) and Franciscus Cornelius (i) (1800–76) were self-taught; they were influenced by treatises by Bédos de Celles and Jan van Heurn. Franciscus restored old organs and built good new ones of a high quality in an eclectic style; his son Franciscus Cornelius (ii) (1834–1918) and grandson Henricus Wilhelmus Josephus (1871–1944) continued his work.

Snell Bros. English firm of reed organ makers. It was formed around 1864 in London by E. and W. Snell and made domestic and church instruments until 1907.

Snetzler, John [Schnetzler, Johannes] (1710–85). English builder of Swiss origin. He studied with his cousin J. C. Speissegger and possibly with J. I. Egedacher before moving to London around 1742, where he built fine church organs and chamber organs in a style that was essentially English. Snetzler, who was the builder to George III, introduced the Dulciana and other narrow-scaled stops to English building. After his death his business was continued by the Swede Jonathan Ohrmannn and W. Nutt (as Ohrmann & Nutt).

Société Guttschenritter & Decoq. French firm affiliated with DAUBLAINE & CALLINET.

Solha, Francisco António (*fl c*1755–after 1794). Portuguese builder. He was of Spanish origin and probably came from Galicia; his workshop was in Guimarães.

Späth (i). German family of builders. Johann Jakob Späth (1672–1760) was active before 1727 in Regensburg; his son Franz Jakob (1714–86) made both pianos and organs.

Späth (ii). German firm. It became active in Ennetach in the late 19th century. Karl Späth (1899–1971) became a partner of the firm in 1928 and was made its director in 1964; he was succeeded by his son Günther.

Späth, Hermann (1867–1917). German builder who took over the workshop of PROBSTL in 1895.

Speissegger, Johann Conrad (1699–1781) Swiss builder. A cousin of John Snetzler, he worked in Schaffhausen. He may have been the father of the organ builder and repairer John Speissegger (Spiceacre), who moved to Charleston, South Carolina, in the 18th century.

Standbridge, John C. B. (1800–71). American builder of English birth. He opened a workshop around 1840 in Philadelphia; his work was continued by his sons John G. and George O. Standbridge.

Stark. Bohemian family of builders. Abraham Stark (1659–1709), who was trained by his father, opened his own workshop before 1695 in Elbogen, where he built in the tradition of the Putz family. His work was continued by his brother Wenzel (1670–1757).

Steere [Steer], **John Wesley** (1824–1900). American builder. He was apprenticed to W. A. Johnson and formed his own firm in 1867 in Westfield (Mass.) with George W. Turner (1829–1908), who had also been associated with Johnson and who remained a partner of Steere until 1892. He moved the firm to Springfield in the 1890s and took his sons John S. Steere (1847–98) and Frank J. Steere as partners; the firm continued until 1920, when it was purchased by E. M. Skinner.

Stein, Adam (1844–1922). American builder of German birth. He worked for Hall & Labagh, Johnson and Roosevelt before opening his own business in 1893 in Roosevelt's former branch factory in Baltimore. His son Edwin (1875–1950) joined the firm and later worked for the Aeolian Co.

Stein, Johann (Georg) Andreas (1728–92). German builder. He worked for his father, Johann Georg Stein, for Johann Andreas Silbermann and for Franz Jacob Späth; from 1750 he lived in Augsburg, where he built a large organ in the Barfüsserkirche. Later he made pianos and became a friend of Mozart.

Steinmann. German firm. It was formed in 1910 in Vlotho by Gustav Steinmann (i) (1885–1953), who had completed his training with Friedrich Ladegast. His son Gustav (ii) (*b* 1913) became the firm's director in 1953 and was succeeded in 1967 by his own son Hans-Heinrich Steinmann-Delius (*b* 1938), who had been apprenticed to Beckerath.

Steinmeyer, G. F. German firm. It was formed in 1847 in Oettingen by Georg Friedrich Steinmeyer (1819–1901), who had been trained by A. Thoma and E. F. Walcker; under his management the firm built and restored several notable organs. His son Friedrich Johannes (1857–1928) became a partner in 1884 and was succeeded by his own son Hans (1889–1970), who had worked in the USA (1913–20). Hans's son Fritz (*b* 1918) became the firm's director in 1967.

Stellwagen. German family of builders. Friedrich Stellwagen (*d* 1659) worked in Hamburg with Gottfried Fritzsche, whose daughter he married. He opened a workshop in 1635 in Lübeck, where he built several important organs. Stellwagen is given credit for introducing the Trichterregal stop, his son Gottfried (*fl* ?1660–65) worked in Güstrow and Holstein.

Stevens, George (1803–94). American builder. He was apprenticed to William Goodrich, whose workshop in Cambridge (Mass.) he took over in 1833 in partnership with William Gayetty (*d* 1839). His brother William (1808–96) worked for him before opening his own workshop with James Jewett around 1855.

Stiehr-Mockers. Alsatian firm. It was formed by Jean-Michel Stiehr (1750–1829), who had completed his training with Stieffel and Josias Silbermann. Jean-Michel was joined around 1860 by his sons Joseph (1813–67), Fernand and Xavier and his nephew Felix Mockers (1818–81); his work was continued by Joseph's son Leon (1840–91) and Joseph and Louis Mockers. The firm built its organs in a conservatively Romantic style.

Stråhle, Peter. Partner of JONAS GREN.

Strand. Swedish family of builders. Pehr Strand (1758–1826) worked from 1791 in Stockholm; his son Pehr Zacharias (1797–1844), who continued his work, was trained in Germany, and became an important builder.

Stuart, Levi Underwood. Partner of RICHARD MONTGOMERY FERRIS.

Stumm. German family of builders. The family was active for six generations. Its most important members were Johann Michael (1683–1747), his sons Johann Philipp (1705–76) and Johann Heinrich (*d* 1788) and Johann Heinrich's sons Franz and Michael. The family built more than 370 organs of a high quality in the region lying within Mannheim, Saarbrücken, Koblenz and Frankfurt am Main.

Sturm, Kaspar (*d* after 1599). German builder. Active from 1568 to 1591 in Regensburg and Ulm, he built in the conservative south German style of the period.

Suisse. Probable root of the names of four Renaissance Netherlands builders, who may have been related. Leibing (Lieven, Levinus) Sweys (Zwits), sometimes given the cognomen 'von Köln', was active around 1438–69; Sebastian Zwysen 'Sebastian van Diest alias Moukens', worked as a builder in Hasselt and Diest (1523–7); Joos Swijssen was active in Antwerp in 1510. Best known was Hans Suys (Suest, Suess, Zuess, Zwits, Blangz) 'von Nürnberg' or 'von Köln' (*fl* 1498–1539), who worked after 1539 with HEINRICH NIEHOFF.

Swarbrick [Schwarbrick, Schwarbrook, Swarsbrick, Swabridge, Swarbutt], **Thomas** (*d* ?*c*1753). English builder. He worked in London for Renatus Harris and possibly for M. A. Dallam; from 1705–6 he worked independently. He moved in 1716 to Warwick, where he built in the style of Harris.

Swart, Peter Janszoon de (1536–97). Netherlands builder. He worked in Utrecht with Cornelis Gerritszoon (*d* 1559) and was later associated with Jan Jacobszoon du Lin. His output was large, but in a conservative style; his son Dirk Peterszoon de Swart continued the family business until around 1620.

Sweys, Liebing [Lieven, Levinus]. Alternative form of the name Leibing Sweys; *see* SUISSE.

Swijssen, Joos. Netherlands builder; *see* SUISSE.

Tafall y Miguel, Mariano (*c*1813–74). Spanish builder, also an organist and composer. Active in Galicia in the 1850s, he wrote *Arte completo del constructor de órganos, o sea guía manual del organero* (1872–6), an important treatise on organ building.

Tamburini. Italian firm. It was formed in 1893 in Crema by Giovanni Tamburini (1857–1942), who had invented the double-compartment windchest while working with Pacifico Inzoli. His work was continued by his sons Anselmi Umberto and Severgnini Luigi and his grandsons Franco and Luciano Anselmi Tamburini. The firm has built and restored many large organs, and makes both slider-chests and spring-chests.

Tannenberg [Tanneberg, Tanneberger], **David** (1728–1804). American builder of German birth. He moved to Pennsylvania with Moravian colonists in 1749 and worked for J. G. Klemm, whose work he continued in 1762. He built organs in the Saxon style and may have been the first full-time organ builder in America; he also made clavichords and virginals. His work was continued by his son-in-law Philip Bachmann (1762–1837).

Taylor & Boody. American firm. It was formed in 1977 in Middletown (Ohio) by George K. Taylor (*b* 1942), who had been apprenticed to Brombaugh, and John H. Boody (*b* 1946), who had been apprenticed to Noack. The firm moved to Staunton (Va) in 1979. It builds mechanical-action organs of traditional design.

Teixeira, Manuel Machado. Father of ANTÓNIO MACHADO E CERVEIRA.

APPENDIX FOUR

Telford, William (*d* 1885). Irish builder. He formed a firm in 1830 in Dublin that was later known as Telford & Telford. He built church and barrel organs, mostly in Ireland.

Thamar, Thomas (*fl* 1665–74). English builder. He worked in and around Cambridge, building organs in a conservative, pre-Restoration style.

Thierry [Thiéry]. French family of builders. Its members were active in Paris. Pierre Thierry (1604–65) was apprenticed to Valeran De Héman and worked with Carlier before opening his own workshop (before 1649). His son Alexandre (1646 or 1647–1699) became one of the leading exponents of the French classical style, working at one time with Robert Clicquot. His work was continued by his son François (1677–1749), who is given credit for making the first *Bombarde* manual (at Notre Dame, Paris, 1730–33).

Thomas. Canadian firm of reed organ makers. Formed as the Thomas Organ Co. in 1832 in Woodstock (Ontario) by Edward G. Thomas, it made many instruments that had elaborate case designs and melody solo stops. In 1895 James Dunlop became the owner of the firm which continued until the 1920s as the Thomas Piano & Organ Co.

Thümmler, David Gotthilf (1801–47). German builder. He worked for the firm of Walcker before settling in Zwickau in 1833. His organs, which were highly regarded, were built in the tradition of Silbermann.

Titz [Tetz]. German family of builders and reed organ makers. Active in the lower Rhine region, its members included Heinrich (*d* 1759), Wilhelm (*d* 1775) and Wilhelm's son Johannes Henricus (1745–1826).

Trampeli [Trampel]. German family of builders. Its members included Johann Paul Trampeli (1708–64), who continued the work of Adam Heinrich Gruber around 1734, his sons Johann Gottlob (1742–1812) and Christian Wilhelm (1748–1803) and Christian Wilhelm's son Friedrich Wilhelm (1790–1832). Johann Gottlob was the most important member of the family; he built more than 100 organs in the style of Gottfried Silbermann.

Traxdorf [Drassdorf, Drossdorf], **Heinrich** (*fl c*1440–44). German builder. One of the first to break away from the Gothic style, he built some significant organs in Mainz and Nuremberg.

Treat, James Elbert (1837–1915). American builder. He was a distant relative of Barzillai Treat (1780–1845), who was active in Bristol (Conn.); he worked for William A. Johnson, Henry Erben, Hutchings, Plaisted & Co. and the reed organ maker George Woods. As the head of the Methuen Organ Co. from 1886 he built several distinguished instruments; he became the partner of James Cole in 1907 and later worked for E. M. Skinner.

Trebs [Tröbs, Trebes], **Heinrich Nikolaus** (1678–1748). German builder. He studied around 1698 with Christian Rothe in Salzungen, becoming the court builder at Weimar in 1712. He collaborated on some organs with J. S. Bach, who was the godfather to his son Johann Gottfried (baptized 1713).

Tretzscher, Matthias (1626–86). German builder. He worked with his stepfather Jakob Schedlich and his step-brother Andreas Schedlich from 1641 and became the court organ builder at Kulmbach in 1653.

Tronci. Italian family of builders. Its members worked in Pistoia from the 18th century to the 20th. Antonio and Filippo Tronci studied with Domenico Cacioli in Lucca and were active around 1745–85; Luigi and Cesare were active in the 1860s.

Trost, Tobias Heinrich Gottfried (1673–1759). German builder. He studied with his father, Johann Tobias Gottfried (*d c*1719), who was probably a pupil of Förner, and with whom he worked from around 1701. In 1718 he moved to Altenburg, where he was appointed the court builder in 1723.

Tsuji, Hiroshi (*b* 1933). Japanese builder and organist. He was apprenticed to the firms of Schlicker in the USA and Flentrop in the Netherlands and opened his own workshop in 1964 near Tokyo. He later moved to Shirakawa and began a study of historic European organs in 1971; his instruments have tracker action and classical voicing; several are in the north German or Italian style.

Tugi [Tugy, Tughin, Tügi, Dügy, Stucki], **Hans** [Johannes; Hans von Basel] (*c*1460–1519). Swiss builder. He worked in Basle from around 1487; by 1500 he was regarded as one of the most important builders in the region.

Van Dinter. Netherlands family of builders. Baron Ludovicus Van Dinter (1782–1835) built small organs in Tegelen; seven of his sons became builders, including Mathius [Mathiu] (1822–90), who married the daughter of Lambertus Vermeulen and worked in Weert. His son Louis (1851–1932) emigrated to the USA and in 1874 opened a business in Detroit; the firm moved to Mishawaka (Ind.) in 1888.

Van Peteghem. Flemish family of builders. Pieter Van Peteghem (1708–87) of Ghent was apprenticed to Guillaume David. His work was continued by his sons Lambertus Benoit (1742–1807) and Egidius Franciscus and his grandson Pieter Karl.

Van Vulpen. Dutch firm. It was formed in 1940 in Utrecht by the brothers Rijk (*b* 1921) and Adrianus Van Vulpen (*b* 1922). The style of its new organs and restoration work is rooted in the Netherlands classical tradition.

Vater, Christian (baptized 1679; *d* 1756). German builder and harpsichord maker. He studied with his father, Martin, and Arp Schnitger and set up his own business in 1702 in Hanover. His son Johannes succeeded him as a court builder; his brother Anton made harpsichords and clavichords in Paris.

Vegezzi-Bossi. Italian family of builders, affiliated with the firm of BALBIANI.

Verdalonga, José (*fl* 1797–early 19th century). Spanish builder. He built or rebuilt several important organs; his work was continued by his son Valentin and his son-in-law Leandro Garcimartín.

Vermeulen. Netherlands firm. It was formed in 1730 in Alkmaar by Johannes Vermeulen (*c*1680–1751) with his son Theodorus (1719–1797) and continued by his grandson Joannes (1770–1826) and his great-grandsons Lambertus (1794–1875) and Henricus (1801–78); from the late 18th century the firm was located in Weert. Among those members of the family who later ran the firm were Peter Jan (1830–1910), Joseph (1876–1946) and Frans (1880–1914); in the 1980s the firm was led by Ernest, Frans, Jan and Joost Vermeulen.

Visser-Rowland. American firm. It was formed in 1973 in Houston, Texas, by Pieter Visser (*b* 1940), who had been apprenticed to Verscheuren, and Jan Rowland (*b* 1944), who completed his training with Walcker.

Vocalion. American firm of reed organ builders. It was formed in 1886 as the Vocalion Organ Co. to manufacture vocalions in Worcester (Mass.) by James Baillie-Hamilton (*b* 1837), a Scotsman who had developed the instrument. The vocalion was later produced by the New York Church Organ Co., and after 1890 by Mason & Risch in Worcester (Mass.).

Vogler, Georg Joseph [Abbé Vogler] (1749–1814). German organist, also a theorist and composer. His 'Simplification System', and the Orchestrion he built to demonstrate it, encouraged a number of builders to experiment with free reeds and to suppress mixtures.

Votey, Edwin Scott (1856–1931). American builder. He was trained as a reed organ maker with Estey and formed a partnership in 1883 with William R. Farrand (1854–1930). The firm built organs from 1887 in Detroit and bought out the firm of Roosevelt in 1893; it made several large organs before merging with the Aeolian Co. in 1897. Votey turned his attention in 1895 to the pianola, which he had invented; he sold his organ interests in 1901 to G. S. Hutchings, who reorganized the firm under the name of Hutchings–Votey.

Votteler, Gottlieb Ferdinand. Founder of the firm that later became HOLT-KAMP.

Wagner, Joachim (1690 or 1691–1749). German builder. He was active in Prussia from 1719, where he became the leading builder. He worked in the tradition of Silbermann, incorporating such Silesian features as narrow-scaled flue stops and the Quint 5⅓ in the pedal.

Wagner, Johann Michael (*c*1720–after 1789). German builder. In Laubach he collaborated with J. C. Beck on at least one organ and built a number of instruments with his brother Johann Christoph (*c*1725–after 1770).

Walcker. German firm. It was formed in 1780 in Cannstadt by Johann Eberhard Walcker (1756–1843). His son Eberhard Friedrich (1794–1872) moved the firm to Ludwigsburg, where he built many large organs and in 1842 introduced the *Kegellade*. Eberhard Friedrich's sons Heinrich, Fritz, Paul and Karl continued his work, and Paul took over the firm of Wilhelm Sauer in 1910. Oscar Walcker (1869–1948) replaced Paul in 1916; his grandson Werner Walcker-Meyer (*b* 1923) became the director of the firm in 1948.

Walker. English firm. It was formed in 1827 in London by Joseph W. Walker (1802–70), who had worked with G. P. England from around 1818. Joseph's work was noted for its bright choruses, open wood flutes and early use of the

Barker lever; it was continued by his son James John (1846–1922). After the firm reorganized in 1975 it moved to Brandon, Suffolk, and became an important builder of tracker-action organs in the 1980s.

Walpen. Swiss family of builders. It was related by marriage to the Carlen family. Johannes Martin Walpen (1723–1782 or 1787) worked in Reckingen with his sons Joseph Ignatius (1761–1836), Wendelin (*b* 1774) and Johannes Sylvester (1767–1837), who later worked in Lucerne and whose own son Sylvester (1802–57) was highly regarded in central Switzerland. The family's organs were quite conservative in style.

Warren. American family of builders. The brothers Samuel Russell Warren (1809–82) and Thomas D. Warren (*d* 1862) were apprenticed to Appleton in Boston. In 1837 Samuel moved to Montreal, where he was briefly in partnership with George W. Mead; Thomas D. Warren was Appleton's partner from 1847 to 1850. Samuel's son Charles S. Warren continued and enlarged the business and moved it to Toronto in 1879; Dennis W. Karn became a partner in 1896. The firm of Karn & Warren was later known under Karn's name.

Weber, Franz (1825–1914). Tyrolean builder. The son of the piano and organ maker Mathias Weber (1777–1848), he completed his training with Balthasar Pröbstl and built conservatively styled organs from around 1852; his brother Alois (1813–89) and son Johann (1860–1947) worked with him.

Wegmann. German family of builders. Johann Conrad Wegmann (*d* 1738) was the court builder at Darmstadt from 1732 and was associated with Johann Christian Köhler, who with Wegmann's son Philipp Ernst (1734–78) continued his work. Philipp Ernst's work was in turn continued by his son Johann Benedikt Ernst (1765–1828) and his daughter Maria Anna (1764–1802), whose sons Johann (1790–1860) and George Christoph Ebert (1797–1871) continued the family's tradition.

Weidtman. German family of builders. Peter Weidtmann (i) (1647–1715) formed the family's business around 1675 in Ratingen; this was continued by his son Thomas (1675–1745) and his grandsons Peter (ii) (baptized 1698; *d* 1753) and Johann Wilhelm (1705–60). The family built in the straightforward Baroque style of the lower Rhineland.

Weigle. German firm. It was formed in 1845 in Stuttgart and moved in 1888 to Echterdingen. The firm developed a pneumatic action and 'membrane' chest in the 19th century that became widely copied; it built tracker-action organs from the 1970s.

Wheatstone, Charles (1802–75). English reed organ maker. He was active in London, where he patented the aeolina (1828) and symphonium (1829); he also invented the concertina.

Wicks. American firm. It was formed in 1906 in Highland (Ill.) by the brothers Louis J. (1869–1936), Adolph Aloys (1873–1943) and John Frank (1881–1948) Wick. The brothers' first organs had tracker or pneumatic action; in 1914 they developed a direct-electric action that was used from that time onwards. John Henry (1912–40) and Martin M. Wick (*b* 1919) later assumed management of the firm; Martin became its president in 1948.

Wilcox & White. American firm of reed organ makers. It was formed around 1876 in Meriden (Conn.) by Henry Kirk White and Horace C. Wilcox to make roll-playing Mechanical Orguinettes. Later it built instruments of all sizes, including one resembling an upright piano, before it discontinued its operations in 1921.

Wilhelm, Karl (*b* 1936). Canadian builder of Romanian birth. After completing his training with Laukhuff, Renkewitz and Metzler in Europe he emigrated to Canada in 1960 to work for Casavant Frères. He formed his own firm in 1966 in Mont St Hilaire, Quebec, that makes organs of classical design, all of which have tracker-action.

Wilkinson. English firm. It was formed in 1829 in Kendal by William Wilkinson, an early experimenter in electric organ action. The firm remained in the family until it was acquired by Rushworth & Dreaper in 1968.

Willcox, John Henry (1827–75). Partner of WILLIAM BENJAMIN DEARBORN SIMMONS from 1858 to 1860 and of GEORGE SHERBURN HUTCHINGS from 1869. He was also well known as an organ recitalist.

Willis, Henry (1821–1901). English builder. He was apprenticed to John Gray from 1835 and later worked for W. E. Evans. He formed his own business around 1848 in London, where he built some of the best engineered and most typically English organs of the 19th century; his instruments have well-balanced choruses and powerful reeds. His sons Henry and Vincent became partners in 1878, they were succeeded by Willis's grandson Henry, who revitalized the firm in the 1920s, then by his great-grandson, also named Henry.

Wirsching, Philipp (1858–1926). American builder of German birth. A graduate of Würzburg University, he was trained in Germany and emigrated to the USA in 1886; he formed a firm in 1888 in Salem, Ohio, where he developed a cone-chest in the German style. He worked for Farrand & Votey after 1895; his own firm was reorganized in 1905.

Wistenius, Jonas (1700–77). Swedish builder. He was trained in Königsberg and opened a workshop in 1741 in Linköping, where he built more than 70 small organs. Wistenius began the East Gotland tradition of building.

Woeckherl [Wöckerl, Weckherle], **Johannes** [Hanss] (*d* 1660). Austrian builder. He was active from around 1607 in and around Vienna; his pipework has been favourably compared with that of Kavelens.

Woffington, Robert (*d c*1820). Irish builder. His father and grandfather were prominent organists in Dublin, and he is said to have been a pupil of Ferdinand Weber. He made pianos and organs from around 1785; his son Thomas continued his business until 1835.

Wolff, Helmuth. Canadian builder of Swiss birth. After serving an apprenticeship with Metzler he worked for de Graaf, Rieger, Fisk and Casavant. He

ORGAN

formed his own business in 1968 in Laval, Quebec, building tracker-action organs influenced by the French classical style.

Woodstock. Name by which the firm of KARN was sometimes known.

Wordsworth & Maskell. English firm. Formed in 1866 in Leeds, it was known as Wordsworth & Co. from 1888 and Wood Wordsworth from 1920.

Wotton, William (*fl* 1486–89). English builder. He was active in Oxford, where he built organs for several college chapels.

Wulf, Jan (1735–1807). Polish builder. He was trained in the Netherlands and Germany, and worked in Oliwa from around 1671. He may have been the 'Wulf of Malbork', who worked for Daniel Nitrowski (1674–80).

Wurlitzer. American firm of instrument makers and dealers. It was formed by Rudolph Wurlitzer (1831–1914) who emigrated to the USA from Germany in 1853. His third son Farny Reginald (1883–1972) served apprenticeships in Germany and later took charge of the North Tonawanda branch in 1909. The Hope-Jones Organ Company was purchased in 1910, the year in which the popular Wurlitzer Hope-Jones Unit Orchestra cinema organ, 'the Mighty Wurlitzer' was introduced. Wurlitzer Photoplayers were developed for smaller theatres and the firm became the leading maker of cinema organs. Electronic organs were manufactured from 1947.

Yamaha, Torakusu. Japanese reed organ maker. He began using American models in 1887 in Hamamatsu. After the 1890s, under the name of Nippon Gakki Co. Ltd, his business came to include other instruments, but it continued to make reed organs well into the 20th century.

Yates, Roger (1905–75). English builder. He was trained by Willis and formed his own business in 1927 in Nottingham. He moved to Cornwall in 1935, where he became one of the first English builders to build tracker-action organs with classical voicing.

Zachariassen, Johannes Lassen (1864–1922). Director of MARCUSSEN from 1902 to 1922.

Zuess. Form sometimes given for the surname of Hans Suys; *see* SUISSE.

Zwits [Zwysen]. Form sometimes given for the surname of two Netherlands builders; *see* SUISSE.

Sources of additional material on many builders will be found in the 'History' section of the Bibliography.

Bibliography

BIBLIOGRAPHIES

J. W. Warman: *The Organ: Writings and other Utterances on its Structure, History, Procural, Capabilities, etc.* (London, 1898–?1904)

J. H. Burn: 'Bibliography of the Organ', *Dictionary of Organs and Organists* (London, 1921)

R. Fallou and N. Dufourcq: *Essai d'une bibliographie de l'histoire de l'orgue en France* (Paris, 1929)

G. A. C. de Graaf: *Literature over het orgel* (Amsterdam, 1957)

W. M. Liebenow: *Rank on Rank* (Minneapolis, 1973)

CONSTRUCTION

A. Schlick: *Spiegel der Orgelmacher und Organisten* (Speyer and Mainz, 1511/ *R*1959; facs., incl. Eng. trans., ed. E. B. Barber, Buren, 1980)

S. Virdung: *Musica getutscht* (Basle, 1511; ed. and Eng. trans. C. Meyer, 1980)

C. Antegnati: *L'arte organica* (Brescia, 1608); ed. R. Lunelli (Mainz, 1938, rev. 2/1958)

M. Praetorius: *Syntagma musicum*, ii (Wolfenbüttel, 1618, 2/1619/*R*1958 and 1980)

M. Mersenne: *Harmonie universelle* (Paris, 1636–7/*R*1963; Eng. trans., 1957)

A. Werckmeister: *Orgelprobe* (Frankfurt am Main and Leipzig, 1681, enlarged 2/16981970 as *Erweiterte und verbesserte Orgel-Probe*, 5/1783; Eng. trans., 1976)

J. P. Bendeler: *Organopoeia* (Frankfurt am Main, 1690/*R*1972, 2/1739)

P. M. Vogt: *Conclave thesauri magnae artis musicae* (Prague, 1719)

F. Bédos de Celles: *L'art du facteur d'orgues* (Paris, 1766–78/*R*1963–6; Eng. trans., 1977; ed. C. Mahrenholz, Kassel, 1934–6)

J. Adlung: *Musica mechanica organoedi*, ed. J. L. Albrecht (Berlin, 1768/*R*1961); ed. C. Mahrenholz (Kassel, 1931)

J. S. Halle: *Theoretische und praktische Kunst des Orgelbaues* (Brandenburg, 1770)

F.-H. Clicquot: *Theorie-pratique de la facture de l'orgue* (MS 1789; facs. edn. with appx, Kassel and New York, 1968; Eng. and Ger. trans., 1985)

G. C. F. Schlimmbach: *Ueber die Structur, Erhaltung, Stimmung, Prüfung etc. der Orgel* (Leipzig, 1801/*R*1966)

J. van Heurn: *De orgelmaaker* (Dordrecht, 1804–5)

J. C. Wolfram: *Anleitung der Kenntniss, Beurtheilung und Erhaltung der Orgeln* (Gotha, 1815/R1962)

G. Serassi: *Sugli organi, lettere a G. S. Mayr, P. Bonfichi e C. Bigatti* (Bergamo, 1816; ed. O. Mischiati, Bologna, 1973)

T. Faulkner: *Designs for Organs, or: The Organ Builder's Assistant* (London, 1823, 2/1838)

J. Wilke and F. Kaufmann: 'Über die Crescendo und Diminuendo-Züge an Orgeln', *AMZ*, xxv (1823), 113

J. Done: *A Complete Treatise on the Organ* (London, 1830)

J. G. Töpfer: *Die Orgelbaukunst* (Weimar, 1833)

C. Kutzing: *Theoretisch-praktisches Handbuch der Orgelbaukunst* (Bern, 1836)

J. A. Hamilton: *Catechism of the Organ* (London, 1842, enlarged 3/1865)

J. J. Seidel: *Die Orgel und ihr Bau* (Breslau, 1843/R1962; Eng. trans. 1852/R1982)

M.-P. Hamel: *Nouveau manuel complet de facteur d'orgues* (Paris, 1849)

E. J. Hopkins and E. F. Rimbault: *The Organ: its History and Construction* (London, 1855, enlarged 3/1877/R1972)

J. G. Töpfer: *Lehrbuch der Orgelbaukunst* (Weimar, 1855, rev. 2/1888/R1972 by M. Allihn as *Die Theorie und Praxis des Orgelbaues*, rev. 3/1936 by P. Smets)

A. de Pontécoulant: *Organographie* (Paris, 1861/R1973)

T. C. Lewis: *Lewis's Organ Building* (London, 1871, 3/1883)

M. Tafall y Miguel: *Arte completo del constructor de órganos, o sea guía manual del organero* (Santiago de Compostela, 1872–6)

W. H. Clarke: *An Outline of the Structure of the Pipe Organ* (Boston, 1877)

W. E. Dickson: *Practical Organ Building* (London, 1881, 2/1882)

C. A. Edwards: *Organs and Organ Building* (London, 1881)

J. Merklin: *Notice sur l'électricité appliquée aux grandes orgues* (Paris–Lyon, 1887)

M. Wicks: *Organ Building for Amateurs* (London, 1887, 2/1898/R1970)

F. E. Robertson: *A Practical Treatise on Organ Building* (London, 1897/R1973)

J. W. Hinton: *Organ Construction* (London, 1900, 3/1910)

J. Guédon: *Nouveau manuel complet du facteur d'orgues* (Paris, 1903)

G. A. Audsley: *The Art of Organ-building* (New York, 1905/R1965)

T. Casson: *The Pedal Organ: its History, Design and Control* (London, 1905)

O. C. Faust: *A Treatise on the Construction, Repairing, and Tuning of the Organ* (Boston, 1905, 3/1949)

A. Schweitzer: *Deutsche und französische Orgelbaukunst und Orgelkunst* (Leipzig, 1906, 2/1927)

W. E. Ehrenhofer: *Taschenbuch des Orgelbau-Revisors* (Graz and Vienna, 1909/R1980)

W. Lewis and T. Lewis: *Modern Organ Building* (London, 1911, 2/1922)

J. Broadhouse: *The Organ viewed from Within* (New York, 1914/R1926)

E. M. Skinner: *The Modern Organ* (New York, 1917, 6/1945)

J. Matthews: *The Restoration of Organs* (London, 1918, 2/1920/R1982, 3/1936)

C. F. Lewis: *Improvements in and relating to Pneumatic Organs* (Bristol, 1919)

G. A. Audsley: *The Organ of the 20th Century* (New York, 1920)

BIBLIOGRAPHY

H. F. Milne: *How to Build a Small Two Manual Chamber Pipe Organ* (London, 1925)

W. Gurlitt, ed.: *Freiburger Tagung für Deutsche Orgelkunst: Freiberg 1926* (Augsburg, 1926)

T. Telman: *Het orgel; een hand- en leerboek der orgebouwkunst* (Enschede, 1926, 3/1929)

E. Rupp: *Die Entwicklungsgeschichte der Orgelbaukunst* (Einsiedeln, 1929)

R. Whitworth: *The Electric Organ* (London, 1930, 3/1948)

G. Le Cerf and E.-R. Labande: *Instruments de musique du XVe siècle: les traités d'Henri-Arnaut de Zwolle et de divers anonymes* (Paris, 1932/R1972)

A. P. Oosterhof and A. Bouman: *Orgelbouwkunde* (Amsterdam, 1934, 3/1956)

P. de Bree: *Moderne orgelbouwkunst in Nederland* (Tilburg, 1935)

W. Kaufmann: *Der Orgelprospekt in stilgeschichtlicher Entwicklung* (Mainz, 1935, 3/1949)

W. Ellerhorst: *Handbuch der Orgelkunde* (Einsiedeln, 1936)

A. Rougier: *Initiation à la facture d'orgue* (Lyons, 1946)

N. A. Bonavia-Hunt: *The Modern British Organ* (London, 1947)

H. Klotz: *Das Buch von der Orgel* (Kassel, 1953; Eng. trans., 1969)

M. Lange: *Kleine Orgelkunde: Bau und Funktion der Orgel* (Kassel, 1954)

W. Adelung: *Einführung in den Orgelbau* (Leipzig, 1955)

P. G. Andersen: *Orgelbogen* (Copenhagen, 1956; Eng. trans., 1969)

J. E. Blanton: *The Organ in Church Design* (Albany, Texas, 1957)

K. Bormann: *Orgel- und Spieluhrenbau* (Zurich, 1968)

C. B. Fisk: 'The Organ's Breath of Life: some Thought about Wind Supply', *The Diapason*, lx/10 (1969), 18

L. Aubeux: *L'orgue: sa facture* (Angers, 1971)

A. J. Gierveld: *Inleiding tot de orgelbouw* (Zaandam, 1979)

G. Huybens, ed.: *Complete Theoretical Works of A. Cavaillé-Coll* (Buren, 1979; Ger. trans., 1986) [facs. edn.]

P. V. Picerno: 'Antonio Barcotti's "Regolo e Breve Raccordo": a Translation and Commentary', *Organ Yearbook*, xvi (1985), 47

P. Williams: 'Considerations in the Designing of a House-Organ', *The Organbuilder*, iii (1985), 2

G. Taylor and J. Boody: 'The Classical Organ Case: Considerations in Design and Construction', *Charles Brenton Fisk, Organ Builder* (Easthampton, Mass., 1987)

ORGAN PIPES: SCALING, VOICING AND TUNING

G. A. Sorge: *Anweisung zur Stimmung und Temperatur sowohl der Orgelwerke als auch anderer Instrumente* (Hamburg, 1744)

——: *Die geheim gehaltene Kunst von Mensuration von Orgel-Pfeiffen* (MS, c1760; ed. and Eng. trans. C. O. Bleyle, Buren, 1978)

ORGAN

B. Asioli: *Osservazioni sul temperamento proprio degl'istromenti stabili, dirette agli accordatori di clavicembalo ed organo* (Milan, 1816)

H. Willis: *On the Vowel Sounds and on Reed Organ Pipes* (Cambridge, 1829)

E. Gripon: *Recherches sur les tuyaux d'orgue à cheminée* (Paris, 1864)

R. Gerhardt: *Die Rohrflöte, ein Pfeifenregister der Orgel* (Halle, 1884)

W. Brockmann: *Beobachten an Orgelpfeifen* (Berlin, 1886)

W. C. L. van Schaik: *Ueber die Tonerregung in Labialpfeifen* (Rotterdam, 1891)

T. Elliston: *Organs and Tuning* (London, 1894, 3/1898, 7/1919)

A. Cavaillé-Coll: *Etudes experimentales sur les tuyaux d'orgues* (Paris, 1895)

H. Smith: *Modern Organ Tuning* (London, 1902)

W. H. Boyle: *The Art of Pipe Organ Tuning* (Syracuse, NY, 1916)

H. H. Jahnn: *Die Orgel und die Mixtur ihres Klanges* (Klecken, 1922)

N. A. Bonavia-Hunt: *Modern Studies in Organ Tone* (London, 1933)

C. Mahrenholz: *Die Berechnung der Orgelpfeifenmensuren* (Kassel, 1938/R1968)

N. Frobenius and F. Ingerslev: *Some Measurements of the End-corrections and Acoustic Spectra of Cylindrical Open Flue Organ Pipes* (Copenhagen, 1947)

N. A. Bonavia-Hunt and H. W. Homer: *The Organ Reed* (New York, 1950)

J. Backus and T. C. Hundley: 'Wall Vibrations in Flue Organ Pipes and their Effect on Tone', *Journal of the Acoustical Society of America*, xxxix (1966), 936

W. Lottermoser and J. Meyer: *Orgel-Akustik in Einzeldarstellungen* (Frankfurt am Main, 1966)

K.-J. Sachs: *Mensura fistularum: die Mensurierung der Orgelpfeifen im Mittelalter*, i (Stuttgart, 1970)

J. Mertin: 'Thoughts on determining Cut Up in Flue Pipes', *ISO Information*, no.6 (1971), 395

H. K. H. Lange: 'Gottfried Silbermann's Organ Tuning', *ISO Information*, no.8 (1972), 543; no.9 (1973), 647; no.10 (1973), 721

G. Jann and R. Rensch: 'Experiments with Measurements in Reed Pipes', *ISO Information*, no. 9 (1973), 633

J. Goebel: *Theorie und Praxis des Orgelpfeiffenklanges* (Frankfurt am Main, 1975)

C. B. Fisk: 'Some Thoughts on Pipe Metal', *Music: the AGO & RCCO Magazine*, ii/11 (1978), 21; repr. in *American Organist*, xxi/4 (1987), 73

W. Kluge: 'Die statische Festigkeit von Orgelpfeifen', *Acta organologica*, xiv (1980), 251

M. Lindley: 'Pythagorean Intonation and the Rise of the Triad', *RMARC*, xvi (1980), 4–61

K.-J. Sachs: *Mensura fistularum: die Mensurierung der Orgelpfeifen im Mittelalter*, ii (Murrhardt, 1980)

L. G. Monette and C. Stevens: *Organ Tonal Finishing and Fine Tuning* (Baton Rouge, 1981)

A. Reichling: 'Zink als Material für Orgelpfeifen in Geschichte und Gegenwart', *Beitrag zur Geschichte und Ästhetik der Orgel* (Bonn, 1983), 67

H. Greunke: 'The Structural Stability of Lead-tin Alloys used in Organpipes', *Organ Yearbook*, xv (1984), 108

BIBLIOGRAPHY

B. Owen: 'Pitch and Tuning in 18th- and 19th-century American Organs', *Organ Yearbook*, xv (1984), 54

C. Padgham: *The Well-tempered Organ* (Oxford, 1987)

L. F. Tagliavini: 'Notes on Tuning Methods in 15th-century Italy', *Charles Brenton Fisk, Organ Builder* (Easthampton, Mass., 1987)

H. Vogel: 'Tuning and Temperament in the North German School of the 17th and 18th Centuries', *Charles Brenton Fisk, Organ Builder* (Easthampton, Mass., 1987)

HISTORY

General

A. A. Hülphers: *Historisk afhandling om musik och instrumenter* (Westerås, 1773/ R1969)

J. Hawkins: *A General History of the Science and Practice of Music* (London, 1776, repr. 1853/R1963, 1875/R1969)

E. J. Hopkins and E. F. Rimbault: *The Organ: its History and Construction* (London, 1855, enlarged 3/1877/R1972)

J. Norbury: *The Box of Whistles* (London, 1877)

D. Buck: *The Influence of the Organ in History* (London, 1881)

A. G. Hill: *The Organ-cases and Organs of the Middle Ages and Renaissance* (London, 1883–91/R1966)

C. F. A. Williams: *The Story of the Organ* (London, 1903)

H. Degering: *Die Orgel, ihre Erfindung und ihre Geschichte bis zur Karolingerzeit* (Münster, 1905)

G. C. Bedwell: *The Evolution of the Organ* (London, 1907)

J. I. Wedgwood: *Some Continental Organs and their Makers* (London, 1910)

G. L. Miller: *The Recent Revolution in Organ Building* (New York, 1913)

M. E. Bossi: *Storia del'organo* (Milan, 1919)

L. de Bondt and R. Lyr: *Historie de l'orgue* (Brussels, 1924)

G. Frotscher: *Die Orgel* (Leipzig, 1927)

C. W. Pearce: *The Evolution of the Pedal Organ* (London, 1927)

K. G. Fellerer: *Orgel und Orgelmusik: ihre Geschichte* (Augsburg, 1929)

H. G. Farmer: *The Organ of the Ancients from Eastern Sources* (London, 1931)

R. Foort: *The Cinema Organ* (London, 1932, 2/1970)

R. Whitworth: *The Cinema and Theatre Organ* (London, 1932/R1981)

A. Cellier and H. Bachelin: *L'orgue* (Paris, 1933)

H. Klotz: *Über die Orgelkunst der Gotik, der Renaissance und des Barock* (Kassel, 1934, rev. 2/1975)

H. Hickmann: *Das Portativ* (Kassel, 1936/R1972)

F. W. Galpin: *A Textbook of European Musical Instruments* (London, 1937)

H. Bornefeld: *Das Positiv* (Kassel, 1946)

W. Apel: 'The Early History of the Organ', *Speculum*, xxiii (1948), 191

ORGAN

W. L. Sumner: *The Organ: its Evolution, Principles of Construction and Use* (London, 1952, rev. and enlarged 4/1973)

W. Haacke: *Orgeln* (Königstein, 1953)

H. G. Farmer: 'Hydraulis', *Grove 5*

S. dalla Libera: *L'organo* (Milan, 1956)

J. Perrot: *L'orgue de ses origines hellénistiques à la fin du XIIIe siècle* (Paris, 1965; Eng. trans., abridged, 1971)

P. Hardouin: 'De l'orgue de Pépin à l'orgue médiéval', *RdM*, iii (1966), 21–54

H. Norman and H. J. Norman: *The Organ Today* (London, 1966)

P. Williams: *The European Organ 1450–1850* (London, 1966/R1978)

H. H. Eggebrecht: *Die Orgelbewegung* (Stuttgart, 1967)

G. Frotscher: *Orgeln* (Karlsruhe, 1968)

P. Hardouin, P. Williams and H. Klotz: 'Pour une histoire du plein-jeu', *Renaissance de l'orgue* (1968), no.1, p.21; (1969), no.2, p.6; no.3, p.3; no.4, p.6; (1970), nos.5–6, p.31; no.7, p.9; no.8, p.17; *Connaissance de l'orgue* (1971), no.1, p.4; nos.2–3, p.6; no.4, p.8

Organ Yearbook (1970–)

W. Walcker-Meyer: *Die römische Orgel von Aquincum* (Stuttgart, 1970; Eng. trans., 1972)

L. Elvin: *Organ Blowing: its History and Development* (Lincoln, 1971)

N. Meeùs: *La naissance de l'octave courte et ses différentes formes au 16e siècle* (diss., U. of Louvain, 1971)

R. Menger: *Das Regal* (Tutzing, 1973)

P. Hardouin: 'Twelve Well-known Positive Organs', *Organ Yearbook*, v (1974), 20

M. Kaba: *Die römische Orgel von Aquincum* (Kassel, 1976)

S. Ferre: 'The Development & Use of the Bibelregal', *The Diapason*, xviii/2 (1977), 1

W. Salmen, ed.: *Orgel und Orgelspiel im 16. Jahrhundert* (Innsbruck, 1977)

L. Roizman: *Organ* (Moscow, 1979)

P. Williams: *A New History of the Organ: from the Greeks to the Present Day* (London, 1980)

——: 'How did the Organ become a Church Instrument?', *Visitatio organorum*, ed. A. Dunning (Buren, 1980), 603

F. Brouwer: *Orgelbewegung und Orgelgegenbewegung* (Utrecht, 1981)

Orgel, Orgelmusik und Orgelspiel: Festschrift Michael Schneider (Kassel, 1985)

B. Sonnaillon: *King of Instruments: a History of the Organ* (New York, 1985)

Australia and New Zealand

E. N. Matthews: *Colonial Organs and Organ Builders* (Melbourne, 1969)

G. Cox: *Gazetteer of Queensland Pipe Organs* (Melbourne, 1976)

M. Cox: 'A Heritage in Perspective: a Study of New Zealand's Historic Pipe Organs', *JBIOS*, x (1986), 88

Austria

R. Quoika: *Die Altösterreichische Orgel* (Kassel, 1953)

BIBLIOGRAPHY

O. Eberstaller: *Orgeln und Orgelbauer in Oesterreich* (Graz, 1955)

R. Quoika: *Altösterreichische Hornwerke: ein Beitrag zur Frühgeschichte der Orgelbaukunst* (Berlin, 1959)

K. Schütz: *Der Wiener Orgelbau in der zweiten Hälfte des 18. Jahrhunderts* (Vienna, 1969)

G. Bozeman, Jr.: 'The Haydn Organs of Eisenstadt', *Art of the Organ*, i (1971), no.1, p.39; no.2, p.33; no.3, p.41

H. Haselböck: *Barocker Orgelschatz in Niederösterreich* (Vienna, 1972)

A. Forer: *Orgeln in Österreich* (Vienna and Munich, 1973)

Belgium

J. Kreps: 'De Belgische orgelmakers', *Musica sacra* (1932)

G. Moortgat: *Oude Orgels in Vlaanderen* (Antwerp, 1964–5)

Het Rococo-Orgel in Vlaanderen (Roeselare, 1973) [special issue of *Vlaanderen*]

G. Potvlieghe: *Het historisch Orgel in Vlaanderen* (Brussels, 1974)

J. Ferrard: *Orgues du Brabant Wallon* (Brussels, 1981)

M. Haine and N. Meeùs: *Dictionnaire des facteurs d'instruments de musique en Wallonie et à Bruxelles du 9ᵉ siècle à nos jours* (Liège, 1986)

K. d' Hooghe: 'Aspecten van het orgel-onderricht in Vlaanderen', *Orgelkunst* (1987), 7

G. Spiessens: 'Antwerpsen documenten over orgelbouwer Jean–Baptiste Forceville', *10 jaar Mededelingen van het Centraal Orgelarchief 1975–1985* (Brussels, 1987)

Canada

C. Chapais: 'La construction des orgues par les Canadiens français', *Congrès de la langue français au Canada*, ii (1937), 547

H. Kallmann: 'From the Archives: Organs and Organ Players in Canada', *Canadian Music Journal*, iii/3 (1959), 41

H. D. McKellar: 'A History of Two Elliot Organs in Québec Cathedrals', *The Tracker*, xxx/3 (1986), 29

Czechoslovakia

V. Němec: *Pražské varhany* [Prague organs] (Prague, 1944)

Denmark

A. Hammerich: *Et historisk orgel paa Frederiksborg Slot* (Copenhagen, 1897/ R1981)

J. Foss: *Kirkorglar i Danmark* (Copenhagen, 1909)

——: *Forslag til Orgel-dispositionen* (Copenhagen, 1910)

J. Wörsching: *Die Compenius-Orgel auf Schloss Frederiksborg* (Mainz, 1946)

N. Friis: *Orgelbygning i Danmark* (Copenhagen, 1949, 2/1971)

——: *Th. Frobenius & Co. 1909–1959* (Kongens Lyngby, 1959)

——: *Helsingør Domkirke: Sct. Olai Kirkes orgel, 1559–1969* (Helsingør, 1969)

M. Kjersgaard: *Renaissance-orglet i Dronning Dorotheas Kapel på Sønderborg Slot* (Valby, 1976)

ORGAN

England

J. Sutton: *A Short Account of Organs built in England* (London, 1847/R1979)

J. Baron: *Scudamore Organs* (London, 1862)

E. F. Rimbault: *The Early English Organ Builders and their Works* (London, 1865/R1978)

E. J. Hopkins: *The English Medieval Church Organ* (Exeter, 1888)

A. P. Purey Cust: *Organs and Organists of York Minster* (York, 1899)

F. W. Galpin: *Old English Instruments of Music* (London, 1910, 3/1932)

C. W. Pearce: *Notes on English Organs of the Period 1800–1810* (London, 1911)

A. Freeman: *English Organ-cases* (London, 1921)

——: 'Records of British Organ-builders, 940–1660', *Dictionary of Organs and Organists* (London, 1921), 7

——: 'Records of British Organ Builders, Second Series', *Musical Opinion*, xlv (1922), 874

——: *Father Smith* (London, 1926; rev. and enlarged by J. Rowntree, Oxford, 2/1977)

——: 'Renatus Harris', *The Organ*, vi (1926–7), 160

R. M. Roberts: 'Charles Spackman Barker', *The Organ*, xiii (1933–4), 186

J. H. Burn: 'Edmund Schulze's English Organs', *Rotunda*, v/3 (1934), 18

A. Freeman: 'John Snetzler and his Organs', *The Organ*, xiv (1934–5), 34, 92, 163

J. Perkins: *The Organs and Bells of Westminster Abbey* (London, 1937)

A. Freeman: 'John Harris and the Byfields', *The Organ*, xxv (1945–6), 112, 145

W. L. Sumner: *Father Henry Willis, Organ Builder* (London, 1955)

S. Mayes: *An Organ for the Sultan* (London, 1956)

H. J. Steele: *English Organs and Organ Music from 1500 to 1650* (diss., U. of Cambridge, 1959)

B. J. Maslen: 'The Earliest English Organ Pedals', *MT*, ci (1960), 578

C. Clutton and A. Niland: *The British Organ* (London, 1963, 2/1982)

P. Williams: *English Organ Music and the English Organ under the First Four Georges* (diss., U. of Cambridge, 1963)

L. Elvin: *Forster and Andrews, Organ Builders* (Lincoln, 1968)

M. E. Wilson: *The English Chamber Organ, 1650–1850* (Oxford, 1968)

C. Eden: *Organs Past and Present in Durham Cathedral* (Durham, 1970)

J. T. Fesperman: *A Snetzler Chamber Organ of 1761* (Washington, DC, 1970)

B. Matthews: *The Organs and Organists of Salisbury Cathedral 1480–1972* (Salisbury, rev. and enlarged 2/1972)

L. Elvin: *The Harrison Story* (Lincoln, 1973)

R. Fanselau: *Die Orgeln im Werk Edward Elgars* (Göttingen and Kassel, 1973)

J. R. Knott: *Brindley & Foster, Organ Builders* (Bognor Regis, 1973, rev. 2/1984)

J. Uhlworm: *Chorgestühl und Orgelprospekt in England* (Berlin, 1973)

J. B. Clark: *Transposition in 17th Century Organ English Accompaniments and the Transposing Organ* (Detroit, 1974)

D. Dawe: 'The Mysterious Pyke, Organ Builder', *MT*, cxv (1974), 68

BIBLIOGRAPHY

J. McKinnon: 'The 10th-century Organ at Winchester', *Organ Yearbook*, v (1974), 20

M. Sayer: *Samuel Renn, English Organ Builder* (London, 1974)

J. Boeringer: 'Bernard Smith: a Tentative New Chronology', *Organ Yearbook*, vi (1975), 4

J. P. Rowntree and J. F. Brennan: *The Classical Organ in Britain* (Oxford, 1975–9)

L. Elvin: *Forster and Andrews: their Barrel, Chamber and Small Church Organs* (Lincoln, 1976)

W. Shaw: *The Organists and Organs of Hereford Cathedral* (Hereford, 1976)

N. Thistlethwaite: *'E pur si muove*: English Organ-building 1820–1851', *Organ Yearbook*, vii (1976), 101

P. R. W. Blewitt and H. C. Thompson: *The Duddyngton Manuscripts at All Hallows-by-the-Tower* (London, 1977)

JBIOS (1977–)

J. Rowntree: 'Bernard Smith (*c*1629–1708) Organist and Organ-builder, his Origins', *JBIOS*, ii (1978), 10

N. Thistlethwaite: 'Organo Pneumatico', *JBIOS*, ii (1978), 31

B. Owen: 'The Evidence for *Trompes* in the 16th-century English Organ', *Visitatio organorum*, ed. A Dunning (Buren, 1980), 489

R. Pacey: *The Organs of Oxford* (Oxford, 1980)

J. Speller: 'Some Notes on Thomas Swarbrick', *The Organ*, lix (1980), 87

N. J. Thistlethwaite: *A Consideration of the Development of the Organ in England between c1820 and 1870* (diss., U. of Cambridge, 1980)

S. Bicknell: 'English Organ-building 1642–1685', *JBIOS*, v (1981), 5

V. Butcher: *The Organs and Music of Worcester Cathedral* (Worcester, 1981)

P. Hardouin: 'Encore Winchester', *Connaissance de l'orgue*, xxxix–xl (1981), 20

M. Sayer: 'New Light on Hope-Jones', *The Organ*, lx (1981), 20

W. Barry: 'The Keyboard Instruments of King Henry VIII', *Organ Yearbook*, xii (1982), 31

M. Cocheril: 'The Dallams in Brittany', *JBIOS*, vi (1982), 63

R. Downes: *Baroque Tricks* (Oxford, 1983)

N. Thistlethwaite: *The Organs of Cambridge* (Oxford, 1983)

J. Boeringer: *Organa Britannica* (Cranbury, NJ, 1983–)

L. Elvin: *Bishop and Son, Organ Builders* (Lincoln, 1984)

M. Gillingham: 'Sources of Form and Decoration in Old English Organ Cases', *The Organbuilder*, ii (1984), 10

B. Matthews: 'The Dallams and the Harrises', *JBIOS*, viii (1984), 58

B. Owen: 'The Henrician Heyday of the Regal', *Continuo*, vii (1984), 2

N. Thistlethwaite: *A History of the Birmingham Town Hall Organ* (Birmingham, 1984)

S. Bicknell: 'The Organ in Britain Before 1600', *JBIOS*, ix (1985), 28

D. Gwynn: 'Organ Pitch in 17th Century England', *JBIOS*, ix (1985), 65

C. Clutton: 'The British School of Organ Building considered in its Historical Context', *The Organ Club Diamond Jubilee* (London, 1986)

ORGAN

L. Elvin: *Family Enterprise: the Story of Some North Country Organ Builders* (Lincoln, 1986)

S. Jeans: 'The English Chaire Organ from its Origins to the Civil War', *The Organ*, lxv (1986), 49

H. Norman: 'The Normans 1860–1920', *JBIOS*, x (1986), 53

B. Owen: 'Towards a Definition of the English Renaissance Organ', *Early Keyboard Studies Newsletter*, iii (1986), 1

A. Barnes: *John Snetzler: his Life and Instruments* (London and Metuchen, NJ, 1987)

M. I. Forsyth-Grant: *21 Years of Organbuilding* (Oxford, 1987)

D. Wickens: *The Instruments of Samuel Green* (London and Metuchen, NJ, 1987)

N. M. Plumley: *The Organs of the City of London* (in preparation)

Estonia

L. I. Royzman: *Organnaya kul'tura Estonii* (Moscow, 1960)

France

J. B. Labat: *Les orgues monumentales de la facture ancienne et de la facture moderne* (Bordeaux, 1877)

L. Bony: *Une excursion dans l'orgue* (Paris, 1892)

A. Jacquot: *Essai de répertoire des Artistes Lorrains: les facteurs d'orgues et de claveçins Lorrains* (Paris, 1910)

A. Cellier: *L'orgue moderne* (Paris, 1913, 4/1925)

W. Goodrich: *The Organ in France* (Boston, 1917)

A. Gastoué: *L'orgue en France de l'antiquité au début de la période classique* (Paris, 1921)

F. B. Stiven: *In the Organ Lofts of Paris* (Boston, 1923)

F. Raugel: *Recherches sue quelques maîtres de l'ancienne facture d'orgues françaises* (Paris, 1925)

P. de Fleury: *Dictionnaire biographique des facteurs d'orgues nés ou ayant travaillés en France* (Paris, 1926)

F. Raugel: *Les grandes orgues des églises de Paris et du département de la Seine* (Paris, 1927)

——: *Les anciens buffets d'orgues du Département de Seine et Marne* (Paris, 1928)

C. Cavaillé-Coll and E. Cavaillé-Coll: *Aristide Cavaillé-Coll: ses origines, sa vie, ses oeuvres* (Paris, 1929)

P. Brunold: *Le grand orgue de St. Gervais à Paris* (Paris, 1934)

N. Dufourcq: *Documents inédits relatifs à l'orgue français* (Paris, 1934, enlarged 2/1971)

——: *Esquisse d'une histoire de l'orgue en France* (Paris, 1935)

F. X. Mathias: *Les orgues de la cathédrale de Strasbourg* (Strasbourg, 1937)

H. Stubington: 'The Dallams in Brittany', *The Organ*, xix (1939–40), 81, 118

E. Martinot: *Orgues at organistes des églises du diocèse de Troyes* (Troyes, 1941)

J. Wörsching: *Die Orgelbauerfamilie Silbermann in Strassburg im Elsass* (Mainz, 1941, 2/1960)

BIBLIOGRAPHY

N. Dufourcq: *Les Cliquot, facteurs d'orgues du Roy* (Paris, 1942)

P. Hardouin: *Le grand orgue de Saint Gervais à Paris* (Paris, 1949, rev. 3/1975)

W. L. Sumner: 'John Abbey: Organ Builder', *The Organ*, xxix (1949–50), 122

J. Fellot: *L'orque classique français* (Paris, 1962)

P. Meyer-Siat: *Die Callinet-Orgel zu Masevaux* (Mulhouse, 1963)

P. Sicard: *Les orgues du diocèse de Bayonne* (Lyons, 1964)

P. Meyer-Siat: *Les Callinet: facteurs d'orgues à Rouffach* (Paris, 1965)

F. N. Speller: *Aristide Cavaillé-Coll, Organ Builder* (diss., U. of Colorado, 1968)

F. Douglass: *The Language of the Classical French Organ* (New Haven, 1969)

N. Dufourcq: *Le livre de l'orgue français 1589–1789, ii: Le buffet* (Paris, 1969)

J. Martinod: *Répertoire des travaux des facteurs d'orgues* (Paris, 1970–76)

C. Noisette de Crauzat: *L'orgue de la cathédrale de Bayeux* (Caen, 1972) [*Art de Basse-Normandie* special no.]

P. J. Hardouin: *Le grand orgue de Notre-Dame de Paris* (Tours, 1973)

O. Mischiati and L. F. Tagliavini: 'Un anonimo trattato francese d'arte organaria del XVIII secolo', *L'organo*, xi (1973), 3

J. A. Villard: *L'oeuvre de François-Henry Clicquot, facteur d'orgues du Roy* (Poitiers, 1973)

J.-M. Baffert: *Les orgues de Lyon du XVIe au XVIIIe siècle* (Paris, 1974) [special issue, no.11, of *L'orgue*]

J. M. Dieuaide: *Le grand orgue Cavaillé-Coll de la cathédrale de Luçon* (Luçon, 1974)

K. Lueders: 'Amours, délices et grandes orgues', *Music: the AGO & RCCO Magazine*, ix (1975), no.10 p.26, no.12 p.34; x (1976), no.4 p.34, no.5 p.34, no.9 p.42

G. Cantagrel and H. Halbreich: *Le livre d'or de l'orgue français* (Paris, 1976)

J. Happel: *Les orgues en Alsace au XVIe siècle* (Paris, 1976) [special issue, no. 15–16, of *L'orgue*]

C. Noisette de Crauzat: 'Aristide Cavaillé-Coll (1811–1899)', *Acta organologica*, x (1976), 177

L'orgue français (Paris, 1977) [special issue of *ReM*]

L. Souberbielle, ed.: *Le plein-jeu de l'orgue français à l'époque classique (1660–1740)*, i (Montoire-sur-Loire, 1977)

J. Guillou: *L'orgue, souvenir et avenir* (Paris, 1978)

K. Lueders: *L'oeuvre d'Aristide Cavaillé-Coll à Paris* (Paris, 1978) [suppl. to *La flûte harmonique*]

F. Sabatier: 'La palette sonore de Cavaillé-Coll', *Jeunesses et orgue*, x (1979) [special issue]

P. Salies and others, eds.: *L'orgue de l'Insigne Basilique Saint-Sernin Toulouse* (Toulouse, 1979)

P. Hardouin: 'Les grandes orgues de la Basilique de Saint Denis en France', *Connaissance de l'orgue* (1979–80) [special issue]

F. Douglass: *Cavaillé-Coll and the Musicians* (Raleigh, NC, 1980)

Ch.-W. Lindow: *Historic Organs in France* (Delaware, Ohio, 1980) [Eng. trans. by H. D. Blanchard of orig. Fr. MS]

ORGAN

B. Van Wye: 'Ritual use of the Organ in France', *JAMS*, xxxiii (1980), 287–325

P.-Y. Asselin: 'Le temperament en France au 18e siècle', *L'orgue à notre époque* (Montreal, 1981)

M. Cocheril: *Les orgues de Bretagne* (Rennes, 1981)

D. Fuller: 'Zenith and Nadir: the Organ versus its Music in late 18th Century France', *L'orgue à notre époque* (Montreal, 1981)

G. Klein: *Le grand orgue de St. Sulpice* (Paris, 1981) [special issue, no. 20, of *La flûte harmonique*]

S. May: 'St-Michel, Bordeaux Reconsidered', *Organ Yearbook*, xv (1984), 13

P. Vallotton: *Orgues en Champagne* (Saint-Dié, 1984)

J.-L. Bergnes: *Jean-François L'Epine: facteur d'orgues languedocien* (Beziers, 1985)

R. Davy: *Les grandes orgues de l'abbatiale St. Etienne de Caen* (Schwarzach, 1985)

J. Eschbach: 'Aristide Cavaillé-Coll and Internationalism in Organbuilding in 19th-century France', *American Organist*, xix/4 (1985), 51

H. Steinhaus: 'Orgues à Toulouse et dans la Région', *ISO Information*, no.25 (1985), 31–64

P. Vallotton: *Orgues en Normandie* (Saint-Dié, 1985)

C. Noisette de Crauzat: *L'orgue français* (Paris, 1986)

R. Saorgin, R. Sant and S. Sant: *Les orgues historiques du pays niçois* (Briel-sur-Roya, 1986)

P. Vallotton: *Orgues en Franche-Comté* (Saint-Dié, 1986)

J.-A. Villard: 'John Abbey, Organ Builder: his Work in France', *JBIOS*, x (1986), 7

B. Owen: 'The One-manual Anglo-Breton Organ of the 17th Century and its Musical Implications', *Charles Brenton Fisk, Organ Builder* (Easthampton, Mass., 1987)

T. G. Spelle: 'The Organ of Transition in France (1785–1835)', *American Organist*, xxi/4 (1987), 68

Germany

A. Werckmeister: *Organum gruningense redivivum* (Quedlinburg, 1705)

J. H. Biermann: *Organographia hildesiensis specialis* (Hildesheim, 1738)

C. G. Meyer: *Sammlung einiger Nachrichten von berühmten Orgelwerke in Teutschland* (Breslau, 1757)

J. Massmann: *Die Orgelbauten des Gross-Herzogthums Mecklenburg-Schwerin*, i (Wismar, 1875)

G. Bohnert: *Die Ludwigsburger Orgelindustrie in hundertjähriger Entwicklung* (diss., U. of Heidelberg, 1920)

L. Burgemeister: *Der Orgelbau in Schlesien* (Strasbourg, 1925)

E. Flade: *Der Orgelbauer Gottfried Silbermann* (Leipzig, 1926, rev. and enlarged, 2/1953 as *Gottfried Silbermann*)

P. Rubardt: 'Einige Nachrichten über die Orgelbauerfamilie Scherer', *Musik und Kirche*, ii (1930), 111

P. Smets: *Orgeldispositionen: eine Handschrift aus dem XVIII. Jahrhundert* (Kassel, 1931)

BIBLIOGRAPHY

R. Weber: *Die Orgeln von Joseph Gabler und Johannes Nepomuk Holzhay* (Wilheim-Teck, 1931)

W. Haacke: *Die Entwicklungsgeschichte des Orgelbaus im Lande Mecklenburg-Schwerin* (Wolfenbüttel, 1935)

F. Blume: *Michael Praetorius und Esaias Compenius Orgeln Verdingnis* (Wolfenbüttel, 1936)

H. Meyer: *Karl Joseph Riepp, der Orgelbauer von Ottobeuren* (Kassel, 1938)

H. Schweiger: *Abbé G. J. Vogler's Orgellehre* (Vienna, 1938)

G. Frotscher: *Deutsche Orgeldispositionen aus fünf Jahrhunderten* (Wolfenbüttel, 1939)

I. Rücker: *Die deutsche Orgel am Oberrhein um 1500* (Freiburg, 1940)

J. Wörsching: *Der Orgelbauer Karl Riepp* (Mainz, 1940)

W. Supper and H. Meyer: *Barockorgeln in Oberschwaben* (Kassel, 1941)

W. David: *Joh. Seb. Bachs Orgeln* (Berlin, 1951)

W. Supper, ed.: *Der Barock, seine Orgeln und seine Musik in Oberschwaben* (Berlin, 1952)

U. Dähnert: *Die Orgeln Gottfried Silbermanns in Mitteldeutschland* (Leipzig, 1953/R1971)

P. Rubardt: *Die Silbermannorgeln in Rötha* (Leipzig, 1953)

H.-G. Wauer: 'Friedrich Ladegast, ein bedeutender Orgelbauer des 19. Jahrhunderts', *Musik und Kirche*, xxv (1955), 293

T. Peine: *Der Orgelbau in Frankfurt-am-Main* (Frankfurt am Main, 1956)

W. L. Sumner: 'The Organ of Bach', *Eighth Music Book*, ed. M. Hinrichsen (London, 1956), 14–135

F. Bösken: *Die Orgelbauerfamilie Stumm aus Rhaunen-Sulzbach und ihr Werk* (Mainz, 1960)

U. Dähnert: *Der Orgel- und Instrumentenbauer Zacharias Hildebrandt* (Leipzig, 1962)

W. Kaufmann: *Die Orgeln des alten Herzogtums Oldenburg* (Oldenburg, 1962)

W. Metzler: *Romantischer Orgelbau in Deutschland* (Ludwigsburg, 1962)

R. Reuter: *Orgeln in Westfalen* (Kassel, 1965)

K. Bormann: 'Die gotische Orgel von Bartenstein', *Ars organi*, xxix (1966), 989

——: *Die gotische Orgel zu Halberstadt* (Berlin, 1966)

P. Bunjes: *The Praetorius Organ* (St Louis, 1966)

J. Fischer: *Das Orgelbauergeschlecht Walcker in Ludwigsburg* (Kassel, 1966)

R. Quoika: *Der Orgelbau in Böhmen und Mähren* (Mainz, 1966)

F. Bösken: *Quellen und Forschungen zur Orgelgeschichte des Mittelrheins*, i (Mainz, 1967)

K.-L. Schuke: 'Deutsche Orgellandschaft zwischen Elbe, Stralsund, und Görlitz', *Acta organologica*, i (1967), 28

C. H. Edskes, ed.: *De nagelaten geschriften van de orgelmaker Arp Schnitger (1648–1719)* (Sneek, 1968)

W. Kaufmann: *Die Orgeln Ostfrieslands* (Zurich, 1968)

W. Müller: *Auf den Spuren von Gottfried Silbermann* (Berlin, Kassel and Basle, 1968, 6/1982)

ORGAN

A. Hohn: 'Die Orgeln Johann Andreas Silbermann', *Acta organologica*, iv (1970), 11–58

U. Pape: 'Arp Schnitger', *ISO Information*, no.5 (1971), 357

W. Adelung: *Orgeln der Gegenwart* (Kassel, 1972)

E. Schäfer: *Laudatio organi: eine Orgelfahrt* (Leipzig, 1972)

G. Kleeman: 'Die Orgelbauerfamilie Schmahl', *Acta organologica*, vii (1973), 71–106

U. Pape: *Die Orgeln der Stadt Wolfenbüttel* (Berlin, 1973)

O. Schumann: *Orgelbau im Herzogtum Schleswig vor 1800* (Munich, 1973)

G. Fock: *Arp Schnitger und seine Schule* (Kassel, 1974)

U. Pape: 'Philipp Furtwängler (1800–1867)', *ISO Information*, no.11 (1974), 777

G. Beer: *Orgelbau Ibach Barmen (1794–1904)* (Cologne, 1975)

W. Schlepphorst: *Der Orgelbau im westlichen Niedersachsen* (Kassel, 1975)

H.-J. Falkenburg: 'Wilhelm Sauer', *Ars organi*, xxiv (1976), 2071

R. Skupnik: *Der hannoversche Orgelbauer Christian Vater, 1679–1756* (Kassel, 1976)

B. Billeter: 'Albert Schweitzer und sein Orgelbauer', *Acta organologica*, xi (1977), 173–225

P. Meyer-Siat: 'Die Silbermann–Genealogie nach den Strassburger Akten', *Acta organologica*, xi (1977), 137

U. Pape: *Frühromantischer Orgelbau in Niedersachsen* (Berlin, 1977)

H. Winter and C. Edskes: *Orgelstudien*, ii: *Cappel* (Hamburg, 1977); i: *Stade* (Hamburg, 1979)

Die kleine Orgel in St. Jakobi zu Lübeck (Lübeck, 1978)

H. J. Busch: 'Zwischen Tradition und Fortschritt; zu Orgelbau, Orgelspiel und Orgelkomposition in Deutschland im 19. Jahrhundert', *Mundus organorum*, ed. A. Reichling (Berlin, 1978)

C. H. Edskes: 'Der Orgelbau im Ems-Dollart-Gebiet in Gotik und Renaissance', *Ostfriesland*, ii (1978), 29

U. Pape: *Der Orgeln der Kreises Fulda* (Berlin, 1978)

U. Pape and others: *Monographien historischer Orgeln*, i: *Geversdorf/Altenhagen* (Berlin, 1978); iii: *Hohenkirchen* (Berlin, 1980); iv: *Cadenberge* (Berlin, 1984)

U. Dähnert: *Historische Orgeln in Sachsen* (Leipzig, 1980)

J. S. Hettrick: 'The German Organ of the Early Renaissance', *The Diapason*, lxxi/11 (1980), 1

E. Krauss: 'Orgeln der Renaissancezeit in Tirol', *Visitatio organorum*, ed. A. Dunning (Buren, 1980), 399

G. Seggerman and W. Weidenbach: *Denkmalorgeln zwischen Weser und Ems* (Kassel, 1980)

B. Sulzmann: *Historische Orgeln in Baden* (Munich, 1980)

W. Hüttel: 'Zwei Meisterwerke der sächsisch-thuringischen Orgelbaukunst im 18. Jahrhundert', *Acta organologica*, xv (1981), 76

H. Vogel: *Kleine Orgelkunde* (Wilhelmshaven, 1981)

H. Wohnfurter: *Die Orgelbauerfamilie Bader 1600–1742* (Kassel, 1981)

P. K. Reinburg: *Arp Schnitger, Organ Builder* (Bloomington, Ind., 1982)

BIBLIOGRAPHY

W. Müller: *Gottfried Silbermann: Persönlichkeit und Werk* (Frankfurt am Main, 1983)

W. Kalipp: *Die westfälische Orgelbauerfamilie Vorenweg-Kersting (1784–1879)* (Kassel, 1984)

G. K. Ommer: *Neue Orgeln in Ruhrgebiet* (Duisberg, 1984)

W. Renkewitz: *Geschichte der Orgelbaukunst in Ost- und Westpreussen von 1333 bis 1944* (Würzburg, 1984)

H. H. Wickel: *Auswärtige Orgelbauer in Westfalen* (Kassel, 1984)

H. D. Blanchard: *The Bach Organ Book* (Delaware, Ohio, 1985)

S. Jeans: 'August Wilhelm Bach und sein Lehrbuch für Orgel', *Orgel, Orgelmusik, und Orgelspiel: Festschrift Michael Schneider* (Kassel, 1985), 65

P. Schmidt and R. Jaehn: 'Paul Schmidt und Mecklenburgs Orgelbau im 18. Jahrhundert', *Acta organologica*, xviii (1985), 44–265

H. Fischer: *Die Orgeln des Landkreises Bad Kissingen* (Bad Kissingen, 1986)

G. Stauffer and E. May: *J. S. Bach as Organist: his Instruments, Music, and Performance Practice* (Bloomington, Ind., 1986)

H. Völkl: *Orgeln in Württemberg* (Neuhausen-Stuttgart, 1986)

S. Jeans: 'The Organ Builders J. S. and C. A. Buchholz of Berlin', *Organist's Review*, lxxii/3 (1987), 207

K. J. Snyder: 'Buxtehude's Organs', *American Organist*, xxi/5 (1987), 75

Hungary

K. Szigeti: 'Az orgonaépítés története Magyarországon Budavár elestéig, 1541-ig' [The history of organ building in Hungary up to 1541], *Magyar zenetörneti tanulmányok Zoltán Kodály*, ed. F. Bónis (Budapest, 1977), 263

Italy

A. Angelucci: *Notizie sugli organi italiani* (Turin, 1865)

D. Muoni: *Gli Antegnati, organari insigni* (Milan, 1883)

A. Bonuzzi: *Saggio di una storia dell'arte organaria in Italia nei tempi moderni* (Milan, 1889)

D. di Pasquale: *L'organo in Sicilia dal sec. XIII al sec. XX* (Palermo, 1929)

P. Guerrini: *La bottega organaria degli Antegnati* (Brescia, 1930)

R. Lunelli: *Organari stranieri in Italia* (Rome, 1938)

W. Shewring: 'Notes on the Organ in Italy', *The Organ*, xxx (1950–51), 42, 124

L. Salamina: *Organina tradizionale italiana* (Lodi, 1952)

C. Moretti: *L'organo italiano* (Milan, 1955, 2/1973)

W. Shewring: 'Organs in Italy: Brescia and Verona', *The Organ*, xxxv (1955–6), 161

R. Lunelli: *Der Orgelbau in Italien in seinen Meisterwerken* (Mainz, 1956)

——: *Die Orgelwerke von S. Petronio zu Bologna* (Mainz, 1956)

——: *L'arte organaria del rinascimento in Roma* (Florence, 1958)

C. Triani: *Organari bergamaschi* (Bergamo, 1958)

L. F. Tagliavini: 'Mezzo secolo di storia organaria', *L'organo*, i (1960), 70

S. dalla Libera: *L'arte degli organi a Venezia* (Venice, 1962)

ORGAN

——: *L'arte degli organi nel Veneto: la diocesi di Céneda* (Venice, 1966)

E. Girardi: *Gli organi della città di Verona* (Alba, 1968)

O. Mischiati: *L'organo della chiesa del Carmine di Lugo di Romagna* (Bologna, 1968)

M. A. Vente: 'Una polizza d'estimo di Graziadio Antegnati', *L'organo*, vi (1968), 231

F. de Angelis: *Organi e organisti de S. Maria in Aracoeli* (Rome, 1969)

J. Mertin: 'The Old Italian Organ', *ISO Information*, no.2 (1969), 157

G. Radole: *L'arte organaria in Istria* (Bologna, 1969)

L. F. Tagliavini: 'Considerazione sulle vicende storiche del "coriste"', *L'organo*, xii (1974), 119

G. Radole: *L'arte organaria a Trieste* (Bologna, 1975)

U. Pineschi: 'L'organo della pieve di Lizzano pistoiese', *L'organo*, xv (1977), 3–39

E. Selfridge-Field: 'Gabrieli and the Organ', *Organ Yearbook*, viii (1977), 2

P. P. Donati: 'Regesto documentario', *Arte nell'Aretino* (Florence, 1979) [index of terms used in contracts etc]

R. Kremer: 'A Workshop Dedicated to Italian Organ Restoration', *The Diapason*, lxxi/9 (1980), 1

O. Mischiati: *L'organo di Santa Maria di Campagna a Piacenza* (Piacenza, 1980)

M. Bruschi and P. P. Donati: *L'organo della chiesa di Treppio* (Pistoia, 1981)

F. Baggiani: *Gli organi nella cattedrale di Pistoia* (Pisa, 1984)

O. Mischiati: *L'organo Serassi della chiesa di San Liborio a Colorno e il suo restauro* (Parma, 1985)

Japan

L. F. Tagliavini: 'L'organo in Giappone', *L'organo*, xv (1977), 127

B. Owen: 'The Organ in Japan', *The Diapason*, lxviii/9 (1977), 1

J. Kaneko: 'The Dawn of Japanese Organ History 1868–1947', *Organ-Kenkyu*, viii (1980), 61

Mexico

D. W. Hinshaw: 'Four Centuries of Mexican Organs', *Music*, iii (1969)

J. T. Fesperman: 'Two Important Mexican Organs', *The Organ*, xlix (1969–70), 179

J. E. Blanton: 'The Valenciana Organ', *Art of the Organ*, ii (1972), 31

J. T. Fesperman and D. W. Hinshaw: 'New Light on America's Oldest Organs', *Organ Yearbook*, iii (1972), 52

J. Velazco: 'Organos barrocos mexicanos', *Anales del Instituto de Investigaciones Estéticas*, xii (1975), 83

J. Fesperman: *Organs in Mexico* (Raleigh, NC, 1980)

D. A. Flentrop: 'De Orgels in de kathedraal van Mexico-City', *Visitatio organorum*, ed. A. Dunning (Buren, 1980), 189; pubd. separately, Eng. trans. by J. Fesperman (Washington, DC, 1986)

M. Drewes: 'Further Notes on Mexican Organs of the 18th and 19th Centuries', *Organ Yearbook*, xiv (1983), 23

BIBLIOGRAPHY

J. Fesperman: 'The Mexican Legacy of Organs', *MT*, cxxv (1984), 107

S. Tattershall: 'The Organs of Mexico City Cathedral', *The Tracker*, xxi/1 (1987), 4

——: 'A Chronicle of the Restoration of a Mexican Cathedral Organ', *Charles Brenton Fisk, Organ Builder* (Easthampton, Mass., 1987)

Netherlands

Beschryving van het groot en uitmuntend orgel in de St. Jans Kerk te Gouda (Gouda, 1764/R1965)

J. Hess: *Dispositien der merkwaardigste kerk-orgeln welke in de zeven Verëenigde Provincien als med in Duytsland en elders aangehoffen worden* (Gouda, 1774/R1945)

J. Radeker: *Korte beschryving van het beroemde en prachtige Orgel in de Groote of St. Bavoos-kerk te Haarlem* (Haarlem, 1775/R1974)

N. A. Knock: *Dispositien der merckwaardigste kerk-orgeln welke in de Provice Friesland, Groningen en elders aangehoffen worden* (Groningen, 1788/R1971)

J. Hess: *Dispositien van kerk-orgelen . . . in Nederland* (Gouda, 1815)

M. H. van 't Kruijs: *Verzameling van disposities der verschillende orgels in Nederland* (Rotterdam, 1885/R1962)

F. van der Mueren: *Het orgel in de Nederlanden* (Leuven, 1931)

H. Schouten: *Onze oude orgels* (Baarn, 1939)

M. A. Vente: *Bouwstoffen tot de geschiedenis van het Nederlandse orgel in de 16e eeuw* (Amsterdam, 1942)

A. Bouman: *Orgels in Nederland* (Amsterdam, 1943)

H. Schouten: *Nederlandsche orgels en organisten* (The Hague, 1944)

B. Bijtelaar: *De orgels van de Oude Kerk in Amsterdam* (Amsterdam, 1953/R1975)

W. Shewring: 'Historic Organs in Holland', *The Organ*, xxxiv (1954–55), 57

M. A. Vente: *Proeve van een repertorium van de archivalia betrekking hebbende op het Nederlandse orgel* (Brussels, 1956)

——: *Die Brabanter Orgel* (Amsterdam, 1958, 2/1963)

H. L. Oussoren: 'De orgelbouwer Christiaan Müller en zijn werk', *Prospectus van het Haarlemer orgelconcours in 1959, 8 Nederlands Orgelpracht* (Haarlem, 1961)

M. Seijbel: *Orgels in Overijssel* (Sneek, 1965)

M. Hoving: *Het orgel in Nederland* (Amsterdam, 1966)

G. Quaedvlieg: *Maastricht orgelstad* (Maastricht, 1968)

H. A. Edskes and others: *Arp Schnitger en zijn werk in het Groningerland* (Groningen, 1969)

J. Jongepier: *Frieslands orgelpracht* (Sneek, 1970)

F. Peeters and M. A. Vente: *De orgelkunst in de Nederlanden* (Antwerp, 1971; Eng. trans., 1971)

M. A. Vente: *Vijf eeuwen Zwolse orgels 1447–1971* (Amsterdam, 1971)

J. H. Kluiver: *Historische orgels in Zeeland* (Sneek, 1972–6)

M. A. Vente: *Orgels en organisten van de Dom te Utrecht van de 14e eeuw tot heden* (Utrecht, 1975)

ORGAN

A. C. M. Luteijn: *De orgelpijp uit* (Baarn, 1976)

A. J. Gierveld: *Het Nederlandse huisorgel in de 17de en 18de eeuw* (Utrecht, 1977)
Langs Nederlandse orgels (Baarn, 1977–9)

J. Jongepier: *Flentrop orgelbouw 75 Years* (Zaandam, 1978)

J. W. P. Peeters and others: *250 jaar orgelmakers Vermeulen (1730–1980)* (Weert, 1980)

L. van Dijck: ''s-Hertogenbosch, orgelstad in de 16e eeuw', *Visitatio organorum*, ed. A. Dunning (Buren, 1980), 117

P. H. Kriek: *Organum novum redivivum* (Buren, 1981) [rev. edn. of P. H. Kriek and H. S. J. Van Zandt: *Organum novum* (Sneek, 1964)]

J. A. Gierveld: *The Flentrop Collection of Chamber Organs* (Raleigh, NC, 1983)
——: *250 jaar Hinsz-orgel te Leens (1733–1983)* (Leens, 1983)

M. Seijbel: *Orgels rond het Ijsselmeer* (Houten, 1984)

W. J. Dorgelo: *Albertus Anthoni Hinsz, orgelmaker 1704–1785* (Sneek, 1985)

K. Bolt: 'Character and Function of the Dutch Organ in the 17th and 18th Centuries', *Charles Brenton Fisk, Organ Builder* (Easthampton, Mass., 1987)

Philippines

H. G. Klais: 'Philippinische Orgeln aus dem 18. und 19. Jahrhundert', *Acta Organologica*, xiii (1979), 75

Poland

J. Golos: 'Note di storia organaria Polacca', *L'organo*, v (1964–7), 31
——: *Polske organy y muzyka organowa* (Warsaw, 1972)

E. Smulikowska: *Prospekty organowe w Polske jako dziela sztuki* (Warsaw, 1972)

R. Perucki: 'The Organs of the Church of the Virgin Mary, Gdansk, Poland', *The Diapason*, lxxviii/8 (1987), 12

Portugal

M. A. Vente and W. Kok: 'Organs in Spain and Portugal', *The Organ*, xxxiv (1954–5), 193; xxxv (1955–6), 57, 136; xxxvi (1956–7), 155, 203; xxxvii (1957–8), 37

C. de Azevedo: *Baroque Organ-cases of Portugal* (Amsterdam, 1972)

L. A. E. Pereira: 'A organaria portuguesa no secolo XVIII', *Bracara Augusta*, xxviii (1974), 492

W. D. Jordan: 'The Renaissance Organ of Evora Cathedral: New Facts concerning its Origin and Construction', *Organ Yearbook*, xiv (1983), 5
——: 'The Organ in Portugal', *The Organ*, lxv (1986), 163

Slovenia

T. Gergelyi: *Historiské organy na Slovensku* (Prague, 1982)

Spain

A. Merklin: *Aus Spaniens alten Orgelbau* (Mainz, 1939)

J. M. Madurell: 'Documentos para la historia del órgano en España', *Anuario musical*, ii (1947), 203

BIBLIOGRAPHY

M. A. Vente and W. Kok: 'Organs in Spain and Portugal', *The Organ*, xxxiv (1954–5), 193; xxxv (1955–6), 57, 136; xxxvi (1956–7), 155, 203; xxxvii (1957–8), 37

D. Shanks: *The Evolution of the Organ . . . in the major Cathedrals and Collegiate Churches of Spain from the 15th Century to the Present* (diss., U. of Oxford, 1958)

R. Reuter: *Organos españoles* (Madrid, 1963)

R. G. de Amezua y Noriega: *Perspectivas para la historia del órgano español* (Madrid, 1970)

J. Wyly: '17th Century Spanish Trumpets by the Echevarrias', *Art of the Organ*, ii/4 (1972), 7

——: 'Historical Notes on Spanish Façade Trumpets', *Organ Yearbook*, viii (1977), 41

R. G. de Amezua: 'Essai de perspective historique pour la facture d'orgues en Espagne actuellement', *Visitatio organorum*, ed. A. Dunning (Buren, 1980), 1

G. A. C. de Graaf: 'The Gothic Organ in the Chapel of St. Bartholomew in Salamanca', *ISO Information*, no. 22 (1982), 9

A. Howell: '*Organos, Organeros*, and *Organistas* of Spain during the Scarlatti Years', *American Organist*, xix/10 (1985), 91

R. Reuter: *Orgeln in Spanien* (Kassel, 1986)

Sweden

C. F. Hennerberg: *Die swedischen Orgeln des Mittelalters* (Vienna, 1909)

B. Wester: *Gotisk resning i svenska orglar* (Stockholm, 1936)

——: *Kyrkorglar i Sverige* (Stockholm, 1942)

B. Khylberg: 'Orgelbyggarefamiljen Cahman, Hülphers och orgeln i Trefaldighetskyrkan i Kristianstad', *STMf*, xxvii (1945), 61

E. Erici: *Inventarium över bevarade äldre kyrkorglar i Sverige* (Stockholm, 1965)

S. L. Carlsson: *Sveriges kyrkorglar* (Lund, 1973)

M. Kjersgaard and N. F. Beerstahl: *Bjurumsorgeln* (Skara, 1973)

Switzerland

A. Jacques: *Les orgues d'Yverdon* (Yverdon, 1923)

A. Freeman: 'Some Organs in the Valais', *The Organ*, xxvi (1946–7), 145

F. Munger: *Schweizer Orgeln von der Gotik bis zur Gegenwart* (Berne, 1961)

F. Jakob: *Der Orgelbau im Kanton Zürich* (Zurich, 1965)

——: 'Der Hausorgelbau im Toggenburg', *Musik und Gottesdienst*, vi (1967), 1

——: *Der Orgelbau im Kanton Zürich von seine Anfängen bis zur Mitte des 19. Jahrhunderts* (Berne and Stuttgart, 1969–71)

Die Orgeln in der Klosterkirche Muri (Muri, 1970)

F. Jakob: 'Introduction to Swiss Organ-building', *ISO Information*, no. 7 (1971), 463

H. Grugger: *Die bernischen Orgeln* (Berne, 1978)

F. Jakob: 'Der Hausorgel in der Schweiz', *Visitatio organorum*, ed. A. Dunning (Buren, 1980), 368

ORGAN

C. Schweitzer: *Orgeln in der Region Nidwalden und Engelberg* (Lucerne, 1983)
R. Walter: *Die Orgeln des Doms zu Arlesheim* (Arlesheim, 1983)

USA

'Biographical Memoir of William M. Goodrich', *New-England Magazine* (Jan 1834)
'Organ-building in New-England', *New-England Magazine* (March 1834)
The Great Organ of Boston Music Hall (Boston, 1865)
H. K. Oliver: 'An Account of the First Organs in America', *Organist's Quarterly Journal and Review*, ii/1 (1875), 4
G. W. Nichols, ed.: *The Cincinnati Organ* (Cincinnati, 1878)
W. H. Clarke: 'Thomas Appleton', *The Organ*, i/2 (1892), 29
S. H. Hooker: 'Joseph Alley's Enharmonic Organ', *Music*, xi (1897), 677
J. W. Jordan: 'Early Colonial Organ-builders of Pennsylvania', *Pennsylvania Magazine of History and Biography*, xxii (1898), 231
W. H. Clarke: 'American Pioneer Organ Builders', *The Musician*, xi (1906), 92
C. A. Radzinsky: 'Organ Builders of New York, 1800–1909', *New Music Review*, ix/99 (1910), 165
Church Music and Musical Life in Pennsylvania in the 18th Century, ii (Philadelphia, 1927)
W. H. Barnes: *The Contemporary American Organ* (New York, 1930, 5/1952)
E. W. Flint: *The Newberry Memorial Organ at Yale University: a Study in the History of American Organ Building* (New Haven, Conn., 1930)
C. M. Ayars: *Contributions to the Art of Music in America by the Music Industries of Boston, 1640–1936* (New York, 1937/R1969)
C. G. Vardell: *Organs in the Wilderness* (Winston-Salem, 1944)
E. W. Flint: *The Great Organ in the Methuen Memorial Music Hall* (Methuen, 1950)
E. Richards: 'Roosevelt's Place in Organ History', *American Organist*, xxxiii (1950), 415
V. A. Bradley: *Music for the Millions: the Kimball Piano and Organ Story* (Chicago, 1957)
B. Owen: 'The Goodriches and Thomas Appleton', *The Tracker*, iv/1 (1959), 2
T. W. Dean: *The Organ in 18th Century Colonial America* (diss., U. of Southern California, 1960)
R. E. Coleberd, jr: 'Yesterday's Tracker: the Hinners Organ Story', *American Organist*, xliii/9 (1960), 20
J. Fesperman: 'Music and Organs at "The Old North" – Then and Now', *Organ Institute Quarterly*, x/3 (1963), 15
B. Owen: *The Organs and Music of King's Chapel* (Boston, 1965)
R. E. Coleberd, jr: 'John Turnell Austin: Mechanical Genius of the Pipe Organ', *American Organist*, xlix/9 (1966), 14
W. H. Armstrong: *Organs for America* (Philadelphia, 1967)

BIBLIOGRAPHY

V. C. Dieffenbach: *The Dieffenbach Organ Builders* (Elizabethtown, Penn., 1967)

C. O. Bleyle: *Georg Andreas Sorge's influence on David Tannenberg and Organ Building in America during the 18th Century* (diss., U. of Minnesota, 1969)

J. R. Sharp: *Tonal Design of the American Organ: 1910–1969* (diss., Michigan State U., 1970)

W. J. Beasley: *The Organ in America as portrayed in Dwight's Journal of Music* (diss., U. of Southern California, 1971)

W. J. Conner: 'Pipe Scaling in Hook Organs, 1849–1895', *The Diapason*, lxii/10 (1971), 18

S. Hitchings: 'Thomas Johnston', *Boston Prints and Printmakers* (Boston, 1973)

B. Owen: 'A Salem Chamber Organ', *Essex Institute Historical Collections*, cx/2 (1974), 111

J. Fesperman: *Two Essays on Organ Design* (Raleigh, NC, 1975)

O. Ochse: *The History of the Organ in the United States* (Bloomington, Ind., and London, 1975)

A. Robinson, ed.: *The Bicentennial Tracker* (Wilmington, Ohio, 1976)

J. Ogasapian: *Organ Building in New York City: 1700–1900* (Braintree, Mass., 1977)

L. J. Schoenstein: *Memoirs of a San Francisco Organ Builder* (San Francisco, 1977)

V. Brown: 'Carl Barckhoff and the Barckhoff Church Organ Company', *The Tracker*, xxii/4 (1978), 1

U. Pape: *The Tracker Organ Revival in America* (Berlin, 1978)

J. A. Ferguson: *Walter Holtkamp, American Organ Builder* (Kent, Ohio, 1979)

B. Owen: 'Colonial Organs', *JBIOS*, iii (1979), 92

——: *The Organ in New England* (Raleigh, NC, 1979)

D. L. Smith: *Murray M. Harris and Organ Building in Los Angeles 1894–1914* (diss., U. of Rochester, 1979)

J. Ogasapian: *Henry Erben* (Braintree, Mass., 1980)

E. T. Schmitt: 'William Schuelke, Manufacturer of Church and Chapel Organs', *The Tracker*, xxv/1 (1980), 52

J. Fesperman: *Flentrop in America* (Raleigh, NC, 1982)

T. McGeary: 'David Tannenberg and the Clavichord in 18th Century America', *Organ Yearbook*, xiii (1982), 94

U. Pape: *Organs in America* (Berlin, 1982–7)

J. W. Landon: *Behold the Mighty Wurlitzer* (Westport, Conn., 1983)

M. D. Coffey: *Charles Fisk: Organ Builder* (diss., U. of Rochester, 1984)

J. V. V. Elsworth: *The Johnson Organs* (Harrisville, NH, 1984)

M. J. Morris-Keinzle: *The Life & Work of John Brombaugh, Organ Builder* (diss., U. of Cincinnati, 1984)

B. Owen: '18th Century Organs and Organ Building in New England', *Music in Colonial Massachusetts*, ii (Boston, 1985)

——: 'Early Organs and Organ Building in Newburyport', *Essex Institute Historical Collections*, cxxi/3 (1985), 172

ORGAN

D. J. Holden: *The Life and Work of Ernest M. Skinner* (Richmond, Virginia, 1985)

D. L. Junchen: *Encyclopedia of the American Theatre Organ*, i (Pasadena, Calif., 1985)

S. Pinel: 'The Ferrises and the Stuarts', *The Tracker*, xxx/1 (1986), 15

F. Douglass, O. Jander and B. Owen, eds: *Charles Brenton Fisk, Organ Builder* (Easthampton, Mass., 1987)

J. Fesperman: 'Smaller Organs: Evolving American Attitudes since 1933', *Charles Brenton Fisk, Organ Builder* (Easthampton, Mass., 1987)

D. Fuller: 'Commander-in-Chief of the American Revolution in Organ-building: Emerson Richards', *Charles Brenton Fisk, Organ Builder* (Easthampton, Mass., 1987)

B. Owen: 'Joseph Alley and Richard Pike Morss: Early Organbuilders of Newburyport', *The Tracker*, xxxi/1 (1987), 31

BARREL ORGAN AND FAIRGROUND ORGAN

S. de Caus: *Les raisons des forces mouvantes* (Frankfurt am Main, 1615, 2/1624; Ger. trans., 1615)

A. Kircher: *Musurgia universalis* (Rome, 1650/R1970)

C. Schott: *Technica curiosa* (Nuremberg, 1664)

F. Bonanni: *Gabinetto armonico* (Rome, 1722/R1964)

V. Trichter: *Curiöses... Tantz... Exercitien-Lexikon* (Leipzig, 1742)

F. Bédos de Celles: *L'art du facteur d'orgues* (Paris, 1766–78/R1963–6; Eng. trans., 1977; ed. C. Mahrenholz, Kassel, 1934–6)

J. Adlung: *Musica mechanica organoedi*, ed. J. L. Albrecht (Berlin, 1768/R1961); ed. C. Mahrenholz (Kassel, 1931)

M. D. J. Engramelle: *La tonotechnie ou l'art de noter les cylindres ... dans les instruments de concert mechaniques* (Paris, 1775)

H. Mendel: *Musikalisches Conversations-Lexikon* (Berlin, 1878)

H. G. Farmer: *The Organ of the Ancients from Eastern Sources* (London, 1931)

──: *The Sources of Arabian Music* (Glasgow, 1939/R1965)

A. Protz: *Mechanische Musikinstrumente* (Kassel, 1939)

J. E. T. Clark: *Musical Boxes* (Birmingham, 1948, 3/1961) [incl. chapter on barrel organs]

S. Mayes: *An Organ for the Sultan* (London, 1956)

E. Simon: *Mechanische Musikinstrumente früher Zeiten* (Wiesbaden, 1960)

H. Zeraschi: *Drehorgel, Serinette und Barrel-Organ* (diss., U. of Leipzig, 1961)

R. DeWaard: *From Music Boxes to Street Organs* (New York, 1967)

L. G. Langwill and N. Boston: *Church and Chamber Barrel-organs* (Edinburgh, 1967, 2/1970)

A. W. J. G. Ord-Hume: *Collecting Musical Boxes* (London, 1967)

K. Bormann: *Orgel- und Spieluhrenbau* (Zurich, 1968)

M. E. Wilson: *The English Chamber Organ, 1650–1850* (Oxford, 1968) [with biographical notes on makers, incl. many barrel organ makers]

E. V. Cockayne: *The Fairground Organ: its Music, Mechanism and History* (Newton Abbot, 1970)

A. W. J. G. Ord-Hume: *Player-piano: the History of the Mechanical Piano and how to Repair it* (London, 1970)

H. Zeraschi: *Das Buch von der Drehorgel* (Zurich, 1971)

Q. D. Bowers: *Encyclopedia of Automatic Musical Instruments* (New York, 1972)

A. W. J. G. Ord-Hume: *Clockwork Music* (New York, 1973)

H. Zeraschi: *Die Drehorgel in der Kirche* (Zurich, 1973)

L. Elvin: *Forster and Andrews: their Barrel, Chamber and Small Church Organs* (Lincoln, 1976)

A. W. J. G. Ord-Hume: *Barrel Organ: the Story of the Mechanical Organ and its Repair* (London, 1978)

A. A. Reblitz and Q. D. Bowers: *Treasures of Mechanical Music* (New York, 1981)

W. Malloch: 'The Earl of Bute's Machine Organ: a Touchstone of Taste', *Early Music*, xi (1983), 172

WATER ORGAN

T. Nash: *The Unfortunate Traveller* (London, 1594)

G. B. Porta: *I tre libri de spiritali* (Naples, 1606)

S. de Caus: *Les raisons des forces mouvantes* (Frankfurt am Main, 1615, 2/1624; Ger. trans., 1615) [basis of part of I. de Caus: *Nouvelle invention de lever de l'eau* (London, 1644; Eng. trans., 1659)]

R. Fludd: *Ultriusque cosmi majoris* (Oppenheim, 1617–24)

S. de Caus: *Hortus palatinus a Friderico Rege Boemiae* (Frankfurt, 1620)

A. Kircher: *Musurgia universalis* (Rome, 1650/R1970)

C. Drebbel: letter to King James I, in G. P. Harstoffer: *Delitiae mathematicae* (Nuremberg, 1651)

G. Schotto: *Magiae universalis naturae et artis* (Würzburg, 1657)

——: *Mechanica hydraulica pneumatica* (Würzburg, 1657)

F. Mortoft: *Francis Mortoft: His Book* (London, 1658–9/R1925)

T. Powell: *Humane Industry or A History of most Manual Arts* (London, 1661), 32ff

J. Evelyn: *Elysium Britannicum* (MS, Christ Church, Oxford)

G. A. Boeckler: *Architectura curiosa nova* (Nuremberg, 1664)

C. F. Milliet de Chales: *Cursus seu mundus mathematicus* (Lyons, 1674, 2/1678)

D. Diderot and J. le R. D'Alembert: 'Haut-forneau', *Encyclopédie* (Paris, 1751–65), pls. 3–4

M. E. de Montaigne: *Journal de voyage en Italie* (Paris, 1774 [written 1580–81])

H. G. Farmer: *The Organ of the Ancients from Eastern Sources* (London, 1931)

——: *The Sources of Arabian Music* (Glasgow, 1939/R1965)

ORGAN

A. G. Drachmann: *Ktesibios, Philon und Heron* (Copenhagen, 1948; Eng. trans., 1963)

S. Jeans and G. Oldham: 'Water-blown Organs in the 17th Century', *The Organ*, xxxviii (1958–9), 153

S. Jeans: 'Water Organs', *Music, Libraries and Instruments* (Hinrichsen's 11th Music Book), ed. U. Sherrington and G. Oldham (London, 1961), 193ff

S. A. Bedini: 'The Role of Automata in the History of Technology', *Technology and Culture*, v (1964), 24

D. J. de Solla Price: 'Automata and the Origin of Mechanism and Mechanistic Philosophy', *Technology and Culture*, v (1964), 9

J. Perrot: *L'orgue de ses origines hellénistiques à la fin du XIIIe siècle* (Paris, 1965; Eng. trans., abridged, 1971)

A. W. J. G. Ord-Hume: 'Hydraulic Automatic Organs: the Self-playing Water Organs of the Italian Gardens', *Music & Automata*, iii/9 (1987), 2

CLAVIORGAN

R. Russell: *The Harpsichord and Clavichord* (London, 1959)

M. Thomas: 'The Claviorganum', *The Consort*, xvi (1959), 29

M. E. Wilson: *The English Chamber Organ, 1650–1850* (Oxford, 1968)

P. Williams: 'The Earl, of Wemyss' Claviorgan and its Context in Eighteenth-Century England', *Keyboard Instruments*, ed. E. M. Ripin (Edinburgh, 1974/R1977)

W. Barry: 'Preliminary Guidelines for a Classification of Claviorgana', *Organ Yearbook*, xv (1984), 98

REED ORGAN AND HARMONIUM

J. Promberger: *Theoretische-praktische Anleitung zur Kenntnis und Behandlung der Physharmonika* (Berlin, 1830)

Historique du procès en contrefaçon des harmoniums-Debain (Paris, 1845)

J. Turgan: *Les grandes usines: l'orgue expressif de MM Alexandre, père et fils* (Paris, 1846)

J.-L. N. Fourneaux: *Petit traité sur l'orgue-expressif* (Paris, 1854)

E. F. Rimbault: *The Harmonium* (London, 1857)

W. Riehm: *Das Harmonium, sein Bau und seine Behandlung* (Berlin, 1868, 3/1897)

M. Allihn: *Wegweiser durch die Harmonium-Musik* (Berlin, 1870/R)

A. Cerfberr de Médelsheim: *The Harmonium or Organ* (Paris, 1875)

J. Hiles: *A Catechism for the Harmonium* (London, 1877)

J. A. Bazin: 'The First Reed Organs', *The Musical & Sewing Machine Gazette* (14 Feb 1880)

BIBLIOGRAPHY

G. Engel: *Das mathematisches Harmonium* (Berlin, 1881)

J. B. Hamilton: 'The Vocalion', *PMA*, ix (1882–3), 60

J. Lederle: *Das Harmonium, seine Geschichte, Construktion . . .* (Freiburg, 1884)

M. Allihn: *Das hausinstrumente Klavier und Harmonium* (Quedlinburg, 1891)

W. Luckhoff, ed.: *Das Harmonium* (Leipzig, 1900)

H. L. Mason: *The History and Development of the American Cabinet Organ* (Boston, 1901)

A. Mustel: *L'orgue-expressif ou harmonium* (Paris, 1903)

R. A. Mile: *Das deutsch-amerikanische Harmonium* (Hamburg, 1905)

O. Bie: *Klavier, Orgel und Harmonium* (Leipzig, 1910, 2/1921)

S. Karg-Elert: *Kunst des Registrierens für Harmonium* (Berlin, 1911–14)

L. Hartmann: *Das Harmonium* (Leipzig, 1913)

E. Mallin: *The Orchestral Organist & the Mustel Organ* (Paris, 1921)

A. Cellier: *L'orgue moderne* (Paris, 1925)

H. F. Milne: *The Reed Organ: its Design and Construction* (London, 1930)

C. Cavaillé-Coll: 'Le poïkilorgue', *Bulletin trimestriel des amis de l'orgue*, vii (1931), 4

E. Guinedot: *L'Harmonium* (Paris, 1931)

A. Bouvilliers: 'The Harmonium: its History, its Literature', *Caecelia*, lx/1–3 (1934)

T. D. S. Bassett: 'Minstrels, Musicians and Melodeons', *New England Quarterly*, xix (1946), 32

A. Douglas: 'The Reed Organ', *The Organ*, xxviii (1948–9), 136

V. A. Bradley: *Music for the Millions: the Kimball Piano and Organ Story* (Chicago, 1957)

M. Nadworny: 'The Perfect Melodeon', *Business History Review*, xxxiii/1 (1959), 43

J. J. Duga: 'A Short History of the Reed Organ', *The Diapason*, lix/8 (1968), 24

N. E. Michel: *Michel's Organ Atlas* (Pico Rivera, Calif., 1969)

R. B. Whiting: 'A Reed Organ Bibliography', *The Tracker*, xiii/3 (1969), 9

R. F. Gellerman: *The American Reed Organ* (Vestal, NY, 1973)

R. E. Schulz: *The Reed Organ in Nineteenth-century America* (diss., U. of Texas, 1974)

J. H. Richards: 'The Vocalion', *The Diapason*, lxvi/9 (1975), 5

H. Presley: *Restoring and Collecting Antique Reed Organs* (Summit, Penn., 1977)

A. Berner: 'Harmonium' *Grove 6* [see also review, J. H. Richards, *JAMIS*, viii (1980), 69]

G. D. and D. A. Williams: 'A Style 20 Vocalion', *The Tracker*, xxiv/2 (1980), 16

R. B. Whiting: *Estey Reed Organs on Parade* (Vestal, NY, 1981)

P. Fluke and P. Fluke: *Victorian Reed Organs and Harmoniums* (Bradford, 1982)

J. Fox: 'The Aeolian Orchestrelle', *Music & Automata*, i/4 (1984), 253

V. H. Neufeld: 'Reed Organ Tremolos', *ROS Bulletin*, iii/2 (1984), 17

P. Fluke and P. Fluke: 'The Reed Organ – J. W. Sawyer: Reed Organ Builder', *Musical Opinion*, cviii (1984–5), 248

ORGAN

——: 'Alexandre François Debain', *ROS Bulletin*, iv/3 (1985), 3

——: 'A William Hill Reed Organ', *The Organ*, lxiv (1985), 24

——: *Victorian Reed Organs and Harmoniums: the Collection of Phil and Pam Fluke* (Keighley, 1985) [catalogue]

R. F. Gellerman: *Gellerman's International Reed Organ Atlas* (Vestal, NY, 1985)

H. A. Jewell: 'A History of the Wilcox & White Organ Company', *ROS Bulletin*, iv/4 (1985), 3

——: 'The A. B. Chase Organ Company', *ROS Bulletin*, iv/1 (1985), 10

R. E. Pickering: 'A History of the Clough & Warren Organ Co.', *ROS Bulletin*, iv/2 (1985), 6

P. Fluke and P. Fluke: 'John Holt Reed Organs', *Musical Opinion*, cix (1986), 101

——: 'Mustel Harmoniums', *The Organ*, lxv (1986), 26

A. Sanders: 'Melodeons', *ROS Bulletin*, v/1 (1986), 6

W. T. Moore: 'Liszt's Piano-harmonium', *American Organist*, xx/7 (1986), 64

A. W. J. G. Ord-Hume: *Harmonium: the History of the Reed Organ and its Makers* (London, 1986)

P. Fluke and P. Fluke: 'Alexandre Père et Fils', *ROS Bulletin*, vi/1 (1987), 19

——: 'Reed Organ News', *Musical Opinion*, cx (1987), 60

REGISTRATION

General

E. Truette: *Organ Registration* (Boston, 1919)

G. B. Nevin: *A Primer of Organ Registration* (Boston, 1920)

G. A. Audsley: *Organ Stops and their Artistic Registration* (New York, 1921)

N. A. Bonavia-Hunt: *Modern Organ Stops* (London, 1923)

C. Koch: *The Organ Student's Gradus ad Parnassum* (Glen Rock, NJ, 1955)

E. H. Geer: *Organ Registration in Theory and Practice* (Glen Rock, NJ, 1957)

T. Schneider: *Die Namen der Orgelregister* (Kassel, 1958)

J. C. Goode: *Pipe Organ Registration* (Nashville and New York, 1964)

P. Williams: *The European Organ 1450–1850* (London, 1966/R1978)

——: *A New History of the Organ* (Bloomington, Ind., and London, 1980)

Spain

H. Anglès, ed.: *J. Cabanilles: Musici organici . . . opera omnia*, PBC, iv, viii, xiii, xvii (1927–56)

F. Baldello: 'Organos y organeros en Barcelona', *AnM*, i (1946), 225

M. A. Vente and W. Kok: 'Organs in Spain and Portugal', *The Organ*, xxxiv (1954–5), 193; xxxv (1955–6), 57, 136; xxxvi (1956–7), 155, 203; xxxvii (1957–8), 37

M. A. Vente: 'Mitteilungen über iberische Registrierkunst unter berenderer Berücksichtigung der Orgelkompositionen des Juan Cabanilles', *AnM*, xvii (1962), 41

BIBLIOGRAPHY

M. A. Vente and F. Chapelet: 'Connaissance de l'orgue espagnol', *Orgues historiques*, x (1965)

M. J. Corry: 'Spanish Baroque, the Organ and the Music', *Music: the AGO & RCCO Magazine*, iii/4 (1969), 44

J. Wyly: 'La registrazione della musica organistica di Francisco Correa de Arauxo', *L'organo*, viii (1970), 3; Eng. trans., in *Art of the Organ*, i/4 (1971), 9

R. Walter: 'A Spanish Registration List of c1170', *Organ Yearbook*, iv (1973), 40

Italy

A. Banchieri: *L'organo suonarino* (Venice, 1605, rev. 3/1622)

C. Antegnati: *L'arte organica* (Brescia, 1608); ed. R. Lunelli (Mainz, 1938, rev. 2/1958)

G. Diruta: *Seconda parte del transilvano* (Venice, 1609/R1978)

C. Gervasoni: *La scuola della musica* (Piacenza, 1800)

P. Gianelli: *Dizionario della musica sacra e profana* (Venice, 1801, 3/1830)

————:*Grammatica ragionata della musica* (Venice, 1801)

G. Serassi: *Descrizione ed osservazioni del nuovo organo nella chiesa posto del SS. Crocifisso dell'Annunziata di Como* (Como, 1808)

C. Gervasoni: *Nuova teoria di musica* (Parma, 1812)

G. P. Calvi: *Istruzioni teorico-prattiche per l'organo e singolamente sul modo di registrarlo* (Milan, 1833/R1970)

R. Lunelli: *Scritti di storia organaria* (Trent, 1925)

Cenni cronistorici intorno agli organi e organisti della Cattedrale de Feltre (Feltre, 1943)

W. Shewring: 'Notes on the Organ in Italy', *The Organ*, xxx (1950–51), 42, 124

F. Germani: *Metodo per organo*, iv (Rome, 1953)

R. Lunelli: 'Un trattatello di Antonio Barcotto colma le lacune dell' "Arte organica"', *CHM*, i (1953), 153

W. Shewring: 'Organs in Italy: Brescia and Verona', *The Organ*, xxxv (1955–6), 161

R. Lunelli: 'Descrizione dell'organo del duomo di Como e l'attività italiana di Guglielmo Hermans', *CHM*, ii (1956), 255

W. Shewring: 'Organs in Italy: Venice, Treviso, Trent', *The Organ*, xxxvi (1956–7), 18

L. F. Tagliavini: 'Il ripieno', *L'organo*, i (1960), 197

S. dalla Libera: *L'arte degli organi a Venezia* (Venice, 1962)

V. Giacobbi and O. Mischiati: 'Gli antichi organi del Cadore', *L'organo*, iii (1962), 3–58

T. Culley: 'Documenti d'archivio – organari fiamminghi a S. Apollinare a Roma', *L'organo*, v (1967), 213

G. Rádole: 'Note sulla registrazione degli organi nel sei e settecento', *Musica sacra*, xci (1967), 92, 159

L. F. Tagliavini: 'Registrazioni organistiche nei "Vespri"', *RIM*, ii (1967), 365

ORGAN

G. Radole: *L'arte organaria in Istria* (Bologna, 1969)

U. Pineschi: 'L'uso dei registri dell' organo pistoiese nei secoli XVIII e XIX', *L'organo*, xiii (1974), 4

G. Radole: *L'arte organaria in Trieste* (Bologna, 1975)

North-western Europe

A. Schlick: *Spiegel der Orgelmacher und Organisten* (Speyer and Mainz, 1511/ R1959; facs., incl. Eng. trans., ed. E. B. Barber, Buren, 1980)

M. Praetorius: *Syntagma musicum*, ii (Wolfenbüttel, 1618, 2/1619/R1958 and 1980)

S. Scheidt: *Tabulatura nova* (Hamburg, 1624/R1954)

A. Werckmeister: *Orgelprobe* (Frankfurt am Main and Leipzig, 1681, enlarged 2/1698/R1970 as *Erweiterte und verbesserte Orgel-Probe*, 5/1783; Eng. trans., 1976)

F. E. Niedt; *Musicalische Handleitung*, iii, ed. J. Mattheson (Hamburg, 1717)

G. F. Kauffmann: *Harmonische Seelenlust* (Leipzig, 1733–6); ed. P. Pidoux (Kassel, 1951)

J. Mattheson: *Der vollkommene Capellmeister* (Hamburg, 1739/R1954)

F. W. Marpurg: *Historisch-kritische Beyträge zur Aufnahme der Musik* (Berlin, 1754–78/R1970)

J. Adlung: *Musica mechanica organoedi*, ed. J. L. Albrecht (Berlin, 1768/R1961); ed. C. Mahrenholz (Kassel, 1931)

J. S. Petri: *Anleitung zur praktischen Musik* (Leipzig, 1782)

D. G. Türk: *Von den wichtigsten Pflichten eines Organisten* (Halle, 1787/R1966, rev. 2/1838 by F. Naue)

J. H. Knecht: *Vollständige Orgelschule* (Leipzig, 1795)

C. Locher: *Erklärung der Orgelregister* (Berne, 1887; 2/1923/R1971, ed. J. Dobler as *Die Orgel-Register und ihre Klangfarben*)

R. Rudolz: *Die Registrierkunst des Orgelspiels in ihren grundlegenden Formen* (Leipzig, 1913)

G. Schünemann: 'Matthäus Hertel's theoretische Schriften', *AMw*, iv (1921–2), 336

E. Flade: *Der Orgelbauer Gottfried Silbermann* (Leipzig, 1926/R1953)

H. Klotz: *Über die Orgelkunst der Gotik, der Renaissance und des Barock* (Kassel, 1934, rev. 2/1975)

G. Frotscher: *Geschichte des Orgel-Spiels und der Orgel-Komposition* (Berlin, 1935–6, enlarged 3/1966)

H. Meyer: *Karl Joseph Riepp, der Orgelbauer von Ottobeuren* (Kassel, 1938)

J. Wörsching: *Der Orgelbauer Karl Riepp* (Mainz, 1940)

P. Smets: *Die Orgelregister, ihr Klang und Gebrauch* (Mainz, 1943)

U. Dähnert: *Die Orgeln Gottfried Silbermanns in Mitteldeutschland* (Leipzig, 1953/R1971)

M. A. Vente: *Die brabanter Orgel* (Amsterdam, 1958, 2/1963)

M. Blindow: 'Die Trierer Orgelakten, ihre Bedeutung für die deutsche Registrierkunst des 16. Jahrhunderts', *Musik und Kirche*, xxxi (1961), 115

H. Fischer; 'Die Registeranweisung von 1568 für die Hauger Stiftskirche 'in

BIBLIOGRAPHY

Würzburg', *Würzburger Diozesangeschichtsblätter*, xxix (1967), 255

P. Williams; 'The Registration of Schnitger's Organs', *The Organ*, xlvii (1967–8), 156

F. Viderø: 'Some Reflections on the Registration Practice in the Time of Bach', *Art of the Organ*, ii/2 (1972), 5

G. Frotscher: 'Zur Registrierkunst des achtzehnten Jahrhunderts', *Bericht über die Frieburger Tagung für Deutsche Orgelkunst vom 27. bis 30. Juli 1926*, ed. W. Gurlitt (*R*1973)

H. Klotz: *Pro organo pleno* (Wiesbaden, 1978)

C. Krigbaum: 'A Description of the Ochsenhausen Manuscript (1735)', *Bachstunden: Festschrift für Helmut Walcha*, ed. W. Dehnhard and G. Ritter (Frankfurt am Main, 1979)

H. Musch: 'Eine Spiel- und Registriermöglichkeit für das Mitteldeutsche Orgeltrio des 18 Jahrhunderts', *Ars organi*, xxix/3 (1981), 177

H. Klotz: *Studien zu Bachs Registrierkunst* (Wiesbaden, 1985)

L. Bastiaens: 'Registratiekunst in Zuidduitse bronnen (1500–1800)', *Orgelkunst*, no.1 (1986)

H. Vogel: 'Zum Klangstil der norddeutschen Orgelkunst: Anmerkungen zum Verhältnis von Satz und Registrierung', *10 jaar Mededelingen van het Centraal Orgelarchief 1975–1985* (Brussels, 1987)

France

M. Mersenne: *Harmonie universelle* (Paris, 1636–7/*R*1963; Eng. trans., 1957)

F. Bédos de Celles: *L'art du facteur d'orgues* (Paris, 1766–78/*R*1963–6; Eng. trans., 1977; ed. C. Mahrenholz, Kassel, 1934–6)

L. Girod: *Connaissance pratique de la facture des grandes orgues* (Namur, 1877)

W. Goodrich: *The Organ in France* (Boston, 1917)

J. Huré: *L'esthétique de l'orgue* (Paris, 1923)

A. Pirro: 'L'art des organistes', *EMDC*, II/ii (1926), 1181–374

A. Cellier: *Traité de la registration d'orgue* (Paris, 1957)

C. Gay: 'Notes pour servir à la registration de la musique française des XVIIe et XVIIIe siècles', *L'organo*, ii/2 (1961), 169

N. Gravet: 'L'orgue et l'art de la registration en France du XVIe au début du XIXe siècle', *L'orgue* (1961), no. 100, p.3

P. Hardouin: 'Essai d'une sémantique des jeux de l'orgue', *AcM*, xxxiv (1962), 29

——: 'Jeux d'orgues au XVIe siècle', *RdM*, lii (1966), 163

F. Douglass: *The Language of the Classical French Organ* (New Haven, 1969)

N. Dufourcq: *Le livre de l'orgue français 1589–1789*, iv (Paris, 1972)

F. Douglass: 'Should Dom Bédos de Celles play Lebègue?', *Organ Yearbook*, iv (1973), 101

H. Klotz: 'Die nordfranzösische Registrierkunst im letzten Drittel des 17. Jahrhunderts und die Orgeldispositionen Gottfried Silbermanns von 1710 für die Leipziger Paulinerkirche', *Visitatio organorum*, ed. A. Dunning (Utrecht, 1980), 387

ORGAN

M. L. Lieberman: 'A Scientist's Account of the French Organ in 1704', *The Diapason*, lxxiii/2 (1982), 16

S. M. May: 'St-Michel Reconsidered', *The Diapason*, lxxiv/1 (1983), 10

England

T. Mace: *Musick's Monument* (Cambridge, 1676)

J. Marsh: *18 Voluntaries for the Organ ... To which is prefix'd an Explanation of the ... Stops etc.* (London, 1791)

J. Blewitt: *A Complete Treatise on the Organ to which is added a set of Explanatory Voluntaries* (London, *c*1795)

E. J. Hopkins and E. F. Rimbault: *The Organ: its History and Construction* (London, 1855, enlarged 3/1877/R1972)

C. Clutton and A. Niland: *The British Organ* (London, 1963, 2/1982)

F. Routh: *Early English Organ Music from the Middle Ages to 1837* (London, 1973)

N. Plumley: 'The Harris/Byfield Connection: some Recent Findings', *JBIOS*, iii (1979), 113

R. A. Leaver: 'Psalm Singing and Organ Regulations in a London Church *c*1700', *The Hymn*, xxxv/l (1984), 29

W. D. Gudger: 'Registration in the Handel Organ Concertos', *American Organist*, xix/2 (1985), 71

P. Sawyer: 'A Neglected Late 18th Century Organ Treatise', *JBIOS*, x (1986), 76

W. D. Gudger: 'Registration in the 18th-century British Organ Voluntary', *The Diapason*, lxxvii (1986), no.11, p.14; no.12, p.14

ORGAN STOPS

C. Locher: *An Explanation of the Organ Stops, with Hints for Effective Combinations* (London, 1888) [Eng. trans. of *Erklärung der Orgelregister* (Berne, 1887)]

J. I. Wedgwood: *A Comprehensive Dictionary of Organ Stops* (London, 1905)

N. A. Bonavia-Hunt: *Modern Organ Stops* (London, 1923)

C. Mahrenholz: *Die Orgelregister: ihre Geschichte und ihr Bau* (Kassel, 1930, enlarged 2/1942/R1968) [incl. further bibliography]

G. A. Audsley: *Organ-stops and their Artistic Registration* (New York, 1949)

W. L. Sumner: *The Organ* (London, 1952, 4/1973) [incl. further bibliography]

T. Schneider: *Die Namen der Orgelregister* (Kassel, 1958)

P. Smets: *Die Orgelregister: ihr Klang und Gebrauch* (Mainz, 1958)

S. Irwin: *Dictionary of Pipe Organ Stops* (New York, 1962)

P. Williams: *The European Organ 1450–1850* (London, 1966/R1978) [incl. further bibliography]

R. Lüttman: *Das Orgelregister und sein instrumentales Vorbild in Frankreich und Spanien vor 1800* (Kassel, 1979)

General Index

GENERAL INDEX

ORGAN

Index of Organs

INDEX OF ORGANS

INDEX OF ORGANS